2/⁰⁹

History
of
North Carolina

Volume 1
The Colonial and Revolutionary Periods
1584–1783

by
R. D. W. Connor

The Reprint Company
Spartanburg, South Carolina

This volume was reproduced from a 1919 edition in the North Carolina Collection, University of North Carolina, Chapel Hill.

Reprinted: 1973
The Reprint Company
Spartanburg, South Carolina

ISBN 0-87152-133-4
Library of Congress Catalog Card Number: 73-1946
Manufactured in the United States of America on long-life paper.

Library of Congress Cataloging in Publication Data

Main entry under title:

History of North Carolina.

  Reprint of v. 1-3 of the work originally published in 1919.
  Includes bibliographies.
  CONTENTS: Connor, R. D. W. The Colonial and Revolutionary periods, 1584–1783.—Boyd, W. K. The Federal period, 1783–1860.—Hamilton, J. G. de R. North Carolina since 1860.
  1. North Carolina—History. I. Connor, Robert Diggs Wimberly, 1878–1950. II. Boyd, William Kenneth, 1879–1938. III. Hamilton, Joseph Grégorie de Roulhac, 1878–1961.
F254.H67   1973   975.6   73-1946
ISBN 0-87152-133-4 (v. 1)

HISTORY

OF

NORTH CAROLINA

VOLUME I

THE COLONIAL AND REVOLUTIONARY PERIODS
1584—1783

By R. D. W. CONNOR
Secretary North Carolina Historical Commission

ILLUSTRATED

PUBLISHERS
THE LEWIS PUBLISHING COMPANY
CHICAGO AND NEW YORK
1919

Sir Walter Raleigh
The Founder of English-speaking America

PREFACE

In the preparation of this volume, I have approached the history of North Carolina somewhat from a different point of view from that adopted by the historians of this period of our history who have preceded me. My purpose has been to bring out more fully than has heretofore been attempted the relations of North Carolina to the British Empire in America of which it was a part. Those incidents, therefore, in our colonial history in which North Carolina participated in Continental affairs have been more fully stressed than has been the custom with our historians, while others of purely local interest and importance which they have set forth in detail have been but briefly told or omitted altogether. The plan adopted made necessary, of course, the rejection of the chronological order in narrating historical incidents and movements.

These volumes are long overdue and my colleagues and I feel that it is but right to say that the publishers are in no way responsible for the delay. Like everybody else during the past two years we have been constantly interrupted and diverted from our work by numerous extra duties incident to the crisis through which our country has been passing, so that it has been impossible to complete these three volumes of narrative history within the time originally set for their publication. To the publishers who have done everything possible to facilitate our work and have displayed the utmost patience at the delay, we are under many obligations.

To Colonel Fred A. Olds I am under obligations for invaluable assistance in securing illustrations for this volume.

Raleigh, North Carolina,   R. D. W. Connor.
May 16th, 1919.

iii

I dedicate this book

to my father

HENRY GROVES CONNOR

because it was he who first aroused my interest in the history of North Carolina; because by his own life, character and public services he has added dignity and honor to the annals of the State; and because in himself he personifies that reverence for the laws and institutions of democracy, that love of justice, and that faith in the common man which I believe to be characteristic of the people of this Commonwealth.

CONTENTS

CHAPTER I

CHAPTER XX

CHAPTER XXI

CHAPTER XXII

CHAPTER XXIII

CHAPTER XXIV

CHAPTER XXV

CHAPTER XXVI

CHAPTER XXVII

History of North Carolina

CHAPTER I

THE BEGINNINGS OF ENGLISH-AMERICA

The first European who is known to have visited, explored and described the coast of North Carolina was Giovanni da Verrazzano, a Florentine navigator in the service of France. Some writers, it is true, suppose that the Cabots preceded Verrazzano to this region by more than a quarter of a century; but the voyages of the Cabots are involved in so much obscurity, and present so many points for controversy, that it is impossible to ascertain with any degree of certainty just what parts of North America they visited. Verrazzano, on the contrary, left a long and detailed account of his voyage. His purpose, like that of the other explorers of his time, was to find a westward route to Cathay [China]. With a crew of fifty men, well provided with "victuals, weapons, and other ship munition" for an eight-months' voyage, he set sail in the ship Dauphine, January 24, 1524, from a "dishabited rocke by the isle of Madera." After a long and stormy voyage, and when in the thirty-fourth parallel of latitude, he reached a low-lying coast, "a newe land," he declared, "never before scene of any man either ancient or moderne."

Verrazzano's landfall was off the coast of what is now North Carolina near Cape Fear. Turning northward, and occasionally sending his men ashore, he skirted the Atlantic coast as far as Newfoundland; thence he set sail for France, and cast anchor in the harbor of Dieppe early in July. At Dieppe on July 8, 1524, he wrote and dispatched to the king, Francis I, "the earliest description known to exist of the shores of the United States." His observations on the people and the country, all the circumstances considered, are remarkably accurate and enlightening. Although his discoveries led to no settlements, nevertheless they form an important link in the chain of evidence that was slowly revealing to Europe the truth about the New World; and as his report was included in Hakluyt's "Divers Voyages," in 1582, it probably was not without influence upon Sir Walter Raleigh in the formulation of his plans for planting English colonies in America.

The marvelous deeds by which Raleigh and his associates—a group of brilliant soldiers, sailors, adventurers, and scholars—laid the foundation of England's vast colonial empire, found their inspiration in loyalty to the Crown and country, love of liberty, and devotion to religion. At various times in English history an attack on any one of these sentiments has been sufficient to call forth the mightiest exertions of the English nation; during the closing years of the sixteenth century all three were attacked at one and the same time by one and the same arrogant power. Philip II of Spain, proclaiming Elizabeth of England an usurper, had laid claim to her throne, and throughout his boundless dominions had levied and equipped mighty fleets and armies for the purpose of establishing the despotism of Castile by overthrowing the liberties of England. The Pope of Rome had commissioned His Most Catholic Majesty to lead a crusade against the national church of England and "to inaugurate on English soil the accursed work of the Inquisition." As one man, without regard to religious convictions or sectarian prejudices, the English people sprang to the defence of the throne, the Constitution, and the Church with an enthusiasm that stirs our blood even to this day.

In this contest with Spain, says an eminent American historian, England was "pitted against the greatest military power that had existed in Europe since the days of Constantine the Great." The source of Spain's power was her colonial possessions whence she drew the treasure that enabled her to fit out and maintain the armaments with which she threatened England's existence as an independent power. "For England the true policy was limited by circumstances. She could send troops across the Channel to help the Dutch in their stubborn resistance [to Spanish rule], but to try to land a force in the Spanish peninsula for aggressive warfare would be sheer madness. The shores of America and the open sea were the proper field of war for England. Her task was to paralyze the giant by cutting off his supplies and in this there was hope of success, for no defensive fleet, however large, could watch all Philip's enormous possessions at once." It was as the storehouse of the enemy's treasure and the source of his supplies that America first excited real interest among the English people.[1]

The man who best understood England's problem was Walter Raleigh. Hawkins, Grenville, Drake, Cavendish, and those other glorious English "sea kings" of the sixteenth century, understood it well enough so far as it involved the ravaging of Spanish coasts and the plundering of Spanish treasure ships. But Raleigh understood that something more permanent was needed to establish the supremacy of England in Europe and America. It was not enough for English statesmanship to destroy the power of Spain; it must at the same time build up the power of England, and as a step toward this end, Raleigh conceived the policy of establishing English colonies in North America. Such colonies would not only off-set the Spanish settlements in the West Indies, Mexico, and South America, and serve as bases of operations against them; they would also develop English commerce and afford an outlet for English manufactures. All this the far-seeing mind of Raleigh perceived in his great design. The work of Hawkins and Drake, of Grenville and Cavendish, and their fellow sea-rovers, though of great importance in the accomplishment of England's destiny, was destructive; Raleigh's work was constructive in the highest degree, and entitles him to first place among those who won North America for English-speaking peoples.

The first steps which Raleigh took toward carrying his great scheme into execution were in conjunction with his half-brother, Sir Humphrey Gilbert. In November, 1577, some one presented Queen Elizabeth with "A discourse how Her Majesty may annoy the Kinge of Spaine by fitting out a fleet of shippes of war under pretence of Letters Patent, to discover and inhabit strange places, with special proviso, for their safeties whom policy requires to have most annoyed— by which means the doing the contrary shall be imputed to the executor's fault; your Highness's letters patent being a manifest show that it was not your Majesty's pleasure so to have it." The writer offered to destroy the great Spanish fleets which went every year to the banks of Newfoundland to catch fish for the Spanish fast days. "If you will let us do this," he continued, "we will next take the West Indies from Spain. You will have the gold and silver mines and the profit of the soil. You will be monarch of the seas and out of danger from every one. I will do it if you will allow me; only you must

---

[1] Fiske: Old Virginia and Her Neighbours, Vol. I, pp. 11 and 22.

resolve and not delay or dally—the wings of man's life are plumed with the feathers of death." There is no signature to this letter, but the same idea is expressed in several places by Sir Humphrey Gilbert, and historians believe this to be his. At any rate within less than a year Gilbert obtained letters patent for planting an English colony in America, with "special proviso" that there should be no robbing "by sea or by land." In the fall of 1578 Gilbert sailed with a fleet of seven ships, one of which was commanded by Walter Raleigh; but a fight with Spaniards compelled the fleet to put back into Plymouth. Five years later Gilbert sailed again, but this time without Raleigh, "for the Queen's mind had been full of forebodings and she had refused to let him go." The unhappy ending of this voyage is one of the most dramatic episodes in American history.

In 1584 Gilbert's patent was renewed in Raleigh's name. By this patent, dated March 25, 1584, Raleigh was given "free liberty & license * * * to discover, search, finde out, and view such remote, heathen and barbarous lands, contreis, and territories, not actually possessed of any Christian prince, nor inhabited by Christian people." Two provisions of Raleigh's charter deserve especial mention. One declarea the colonists "shall and may have all the privileges of free Denizens, and persons native of England, and within our allegiance in such like ample manner and forme, as if they were borne and personally resident within our said Realme of England, any law, customs, or usage to the contrary notwithstanding." The other provision authorized Raleigh, his heirs and assigns to enact such laws as they judged proper for the government of the colony provided only such laws were not inconsistent with the laws of England.

Raleigh was prompt to take advantage of his patent. Within less than a month he had an expedition ready to sail for America under the command of two experienced navigators, Philip Amadas and Arthur Barlow. They sailed from the west coast of England April 27, 1584, "with two barkes well furnished with men and victuals." A voyage of sixty-seven days brought them, July 2, to "shole water, wher," they said, "we smelt so sweet, and so strong a smel, as if we had bene in the midst of some delicate garden abounding with all kinde of odoriferous flowers, by which we were assured, that the land could not be farre distant: and keeping good watch, and bearing but slacke saile, the fourth of the same moneth we arrived upon the coast, which we supposed to be a continent and firme lande, and we sayled along the same a hundred and

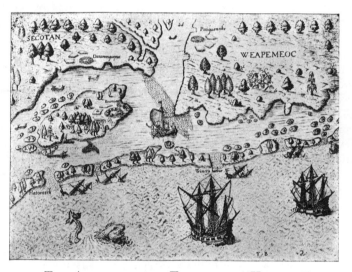

THE ARRIVAL OF THE ENGLISH IN "VIRGINIA"
(ROANOKE ISLAND)
From the De Bry Engravings of the John White Paintings, 1590

twentie English miles before we could finde any entrance, or river issuing into the Sea. The first that appeared to us, we entred, though not without some difficultie, & cast anker about three harquebuz-shot within the havens mouth, on the left hand of the same: and after thankes given to God for our safe arrival thither, we manned our boats, and went to view the land next adjoining, and to take possession of the same, in the right of the Queenes most excellent Majestie, as rightfull Queene, and Princesse of the same, and after delivered the same over to your [Raleigh's] use, according to her Majesties grant, and letters patent, under her Highnesse great seale.'' These important proceedings were performed "according to the ceremonies used in such enterprises.''

The purpose of Amadas and Barlow was to explore the country and fix upon a site for the first settlement. Immediately after the ceremony of taking possession they "viewed the land'' about them, which they found "very sandie and low towards the waters side. * * * We passed from the Sea side towardes the toppes of those hilles next adjoining, being but of meane higth, and from thence wee behelde the Sea on both sides to the North, and to the South, finding no ende any of both wayes.'' A few days later Barlow, with seven of his crew, "went twentie miles'' across the sound, "and the evening following,'' he said, "wee came to an Island which they [the natives] call Roanoak, distant from the Harbour by which we entered, seven leagues: * * * Beyond this Island there is the maine lande. * * * When we first had sight of this countrey, some thought the first land we saw to bee the continent: but after we entered into the Haven, we saw before us another mighty long Sea: for there lyeth along the coast a tracte of Island, two hundreth miles in length, adjoyning to the Ocean sea: * * * when you entred betweene them * * * then there appeareth another great Sea: * * * and in this inclosed Sea there are above an hundreth Islands of divers bignesses, whereof one is sixteene miles long, at which we were, finding it a most pleasant and fertile ground. * * * Besides this Island there are many, as I have sayd, * * * most beautiful and pleasant to behold.''

The visitors seemed to think they had reached a veritable paradise. Their report glowed with enthusiasm for the new country and its people. The "soile'' was "the most plentiful, sweete, fruitfull and wholesome of all the world.'' There were "above fourteene severall sweete smelling timber trees,'' while the "underwoods,'' were mostly of "Bayes and such like.'' They found the same "okes'' as grew in Europe "but farre greater and better.'' In the woods grew "the highest and reddest Cedars of the world.'' The island was "so full of grapes as the very beating and surge of the Sea overflowed them,'' and they were "in such plenty * * * both on the sand and on the greene soile on the hills, as in the plaines, as well as on every little shrubbe, as also climing towardes the tops of high Cedars'' that in "all the world the like abundance'' could not be found. As the men strolled down the coast "such a flock of Cranes (the most part white) arose under'' them "with such a cry redoubled by many ecchoes as if an armie of men had showted all together.'' The island "had many goodly woodes full of Deere, Conies, Hares, and Fowle, * * * in incredible abundance;'' while the waters were alive "with the goodliest and best fish in the world.'' The Indians sent them "divers kindes of fruits, Melons, Walnuts, Cucumbers, Gourdes, Pease, and divers rootes, and fruites very excellent good, and of their Countrey corne, which is very white, faire and well tasted.''

The Englishmen were as much delighted with the natives as with their country. They found them "very handsome and goodly people, and in their behaviour as mannerly and civill as any of Europe.'' The chief of the country, Wingina, who was disabled by a wound received in battle, sent his brother, Granganimeo, to welcome the strangers. Granganimeo "made all signes of joy and welcome, striking on his head and breast and afterwards on ours, to shew wee were all one, smiling and making shewe of the best he could of all love and familiaritie.'' When the Englishmen visited the natives in their villages they "were entertained with all love and kindnesse, and with as much bountie (after their maner) as they could possibly devise.'' Thus the visitors were deceived into the belief that their hosts were "most gentle, loving and faithful, voide of all guile and treason, and such as live after the maner of the golden age.'' Immediately after this bit of rhapsody the report adds: "their warres are very cruell and bloody, by reason whereof, and of their civil dissentions which have happened of late yeares amongst them, the people are marvelously wasted and in some places the countrey left desolate.''

The explorers of course did not neglect the opportunity which the friendliness of the natives gave them for trade. They had brought with them the usual trinkets for which the Indians were always ready to trade furs and skins, gold and silver, pearls and coral. "We fell to trading with them,'' says Barlow, "exchanging some things we had, for Chamoys,

Buffe, and Deere skinnes.'' A bright tin dish especially
pleased Granganimeo and he gave for it ''twentie skinnes,
woorth twentie Crownes''; while for a copper kettle he exchanged ''fiftie skinnes, woorth fiftie Crownes.'' Granganimeo's wife, on her visit to the English ships, wore about
her forehead ''a bande of white Corall''; and ''in her ears
shee had bracelets of pearles hanging downe to her middle
* * * and these were of the bignes of good pease.'' Some
of the women ''of the better sort,'' and ''some of the children
of the kings brother and other noble men'' had copper pen-
dants hanging from their ears. Granganimeo ''himself had
upon his forehead a broade plate of golde, or copper, for
being unpolished we knew not what mettal it should be.'' He
''had great liking of our armour, a sword and divers other
things which we had: and offered to lay a great boxe of pearle
in gage for them, but we refused it for this time, because we
would not make them know, that we esteemed thereof, until
we had understoode in what places of the countrey the pearle
grew.''

Two months were thus spent in exploring the country,
visiting the natives, gathering information, and trading.
''Then,'' says Barlow, ''contenting ourselves with this service at this time, which we hope hereafter to inlarge, as occasion and assistance shal be given, we resolved to leave the
countrey and to apply ourselves to returne to England, which
we did accordingly, and arrived safely in the West of England about the middest of September. * * * We brought
home also two of the savages, being lustie men, whose names
were Wanchese and Manteo.'' The story of this voyage was
heard in England with wonder and delight. Everybody was
charmed with this wonderful new country and its ''gentle,
loving'' people. Elizabeth, delighted that her reign had been
signalized by so great an event, declared that in honor of her
virgin state the new country should be called ''Virginia.''

Raleigh lost no time in preparing a colony for ''Virginia.''
The queen conferred upon him the honor of knighthood as a
reward for his gift of ''Virginia'' to the Crown. He was
wealthy and famous, high in the favor of his sovereign, and
men were anxious to enlist in his service. He found no difficulty, therefore, in securing a colony led by picked men.
For governor he selected Ralph Lane. Lane, who had
already seen considerable service, was then on duty for the
Crown in Ireland, but the queen ordered a substitute to be
appointed in his government of Kerry and Clanmorris, ''in
consideration of his ready undertaking the voyage to Virginia

for Sir Walter Raleigh at Her Majesty's command."[2] Others who were members of Lane's colony were "the wonderful Suffolk boy," Thomas Cavendish, aged twenty-two years, who, before he reached his twenty-ninth year rivaled the exploits of Sir Francis Drake in the Pacific and circumnavigated the globe; Philip Amadas, one of the commanders in the first expedition to Roanoke, and now "admiral" of "Virginia"; John White, the artist of the expedition, sent by Raleigh to make paintings of the country and its people, afterwards governor of the "Lost Colony"; and Thomas Hariot, the historian and scientist of the colony, "a mathematician of great distinction, who materially advanced the science of Algebra, and was honored by Descartes, who imposed some of Hariot's work upon the French as his own."[3] To none who bore a part in the efforts to plant a colony on Roanoke Island, save Raleigh alone, do we owe more than to White and Hariot. The work of "these two earnest and true men" —the splendid pictures of the one and the scholarly narrative of the other—preserve for us the most valuable information that we have of Raleigh's colonial enterprises. Two others who sailed in Lane's expedition were Wanchese and Manteo, the two "lustie" natives who had accompanied Amadas and Barlow to England. The fleet was under the command of the famous Sir Richard Grenville, whose heroic death in the most wonderful sea fight in all history is nobly commemorated by Tennyson in one of the most stirring ballads in our language.

The colony was composed of 108 men. "With marvelous energy, enterprise, and skill Raleigh collected and fitted out in an incredibly short time a fleet of seven ships well stocked and well manned to transport his 'first colonie' into the wilds of America. * * * Never before did a finer fleet leave the shores of England, and never since was one more honestly or hopefully dispatched. There were the 'Tyger,' and the 'Roe Buck,' of 140 tons each, the 'Dorothea,' a small bark, and two pinnaces, hardly big enough to bear distinct names, yet small enough to cross dangerous bars and enter unknown bays and rivers."[4] The fleet sailed from Plymouth April 9, 1585, followed the usual route by way of the Canaries and the West Indies, reached "the maine of Florida" June 20, and

---

[2] William Wirt Henry: Sir Walter Raleigh, in Winsor's *Narrative and Critical History of America*, Vol. III, p. 111.
[3] Ibid.
[4] Stevens: Thomas Hariot and His Associates, p. 50.

three days later narrowly escaped wreck "on a breach called the Cape of Feare." June 26 brought them to Wocokon, part of the North Carolina banks, on the modern map called Ocracoke. The next month was spent in exploring the coast and making the acquaintance of the natives. In the course of these explorations an Indian stole a silver cup from one of the visitors, whereupon the Englishmen "burned and spoiled their corn," and thus sowed seeds of hostility that were soon to ripen into a harvest of blood and slaughter. July 27 the fleet reached Hatteras "and there rested." A month later, lacking two days, Grenville weighed anchor for England, leaving at Roanoke the first English colony that had landed on the shores of America.

Lane's first work was to build a fort and "sundry necessary and decent dwelling houses." From this "new Fort in Virginia," September 3, 1585, he wrote to his friend Richard Hackluyt of London, the first letter, of which we have record, written in the English language from the New World. Lane fairly bubbled over with enthusiasm for the new country, which, he declared, was "the goodliest soyle under the cope of heaven." In fact, he thought "if Virginia had but horses and kine in some reasonable proportion, * * * being inhabited with English, no realme in Christendom were comparable to it." To his exaggerated estimate of the riches of the country, we may trace the failure of Lane's colony. Three things only, he declared, were indispensable to make Virginia desirable for colonization by the English, viz., the finding of a better harbor than that at Roanoke; the discovery of a passage to the South Sea; and gold. Accordingly those energies which he ought to have devoted to the clearing of the forest, the erection of houses, and the tilling of the soil, he exhausted in premature explorations and a vain search for precious metals. In the prosecution of these undertakings the colonists consumed all of their provisions and before the close of their first winter in "Virginia" found themselves reduced to dependence upon the liberality of the savages for food. This, of course, soon proved a precarious and treacherous source of supplies.

During the winter Lane's relations with the Indians seemed to be all that could be desired. Two of the most powerful chiefs sent in their submission and the Indians on Roanoke Island built weirs for the white men and planted enough corn to feed them a year. But appearances were deceiving. Familiarity bred contempt, and the awe with which the red men at first regarded the whites rapidly disappeared

INDIAN WARRIORS OF ROANOKE

From the De Bry Engravings of the John White Paintings

when familiarity proved them to be but common men. No longer to be welcomed as gods, they must be expelled as intruders, and around their council fires painted warriors considered how this object might be most easily accomplished. Their leaders in these plots were Wingina and Wanchese. It was the former's brother Granganimeo, it will be recalled, who had welcomed Amadas and Barlow to the New World; the latter with Manteo had accompanied them on their return to Europe. Granganimeo and Manteo became the fast friends, Wingina and Wanchese the steadfast enemies of the English. Soon after Lane's arrival Granganimeo died, whereupon Wingina, in accordance with some savage custom, changed his name to Pemisapan and began to plot the destruction of the invaders. His plot, which came to a head in the spring of 1586, was shrewdly laid. It embraced all the tribes north of Albemarle Sound, numbering about 1,500 warriors. They agreed to supply no food to the English, and to destroy their. weirs, thus compelling them to scatter in search of food. After setting a day for the general attack, Pemisapan, in order to avoid Lane's daily demand for food, withdrew to Dasamonguepeuk on the mainland.

Pemisapan had planned well. Famine soon threatened the colony and Lane was about to walk into his enemy's cunning trap, when the whole plot was revealed to him. In this emergency he acted with enterprise and courage. Sending word to Pemisapan at Dasamonguepeuk that his fleet had arrived at Croatan from England—"though I in truth," he confesses, "neither heard nor hoped for so good adventure" —he said that on his way to meet it he would stop by Dasamonguepeuk for supplies. Pemisapan was completely deceived. Lane marched upon his camp where he found the savage chief with several of his warriors awaiting him. At the signal agreed upon—the slogan "Christ our victory"— the Englishmen fell upon the savages "and immediately," as Lane reports, "those his chiefe men and himselfe had by the mercy of God for our deliverance, that which they had purposed for us." Pemisapan and several of his warriors were killed, the rest scattered, and the conspiracy fell to pieces. The Englishman adopted the strategy of the savage and beat him at his own game.

A few days after this victory, Sir Francis Drake in command of a fleet of twenty-three sail arrived off the coast. He was a welcome visitor for, says Lane, he made "a most bountiful and honorable offer for the supply of our necessities to the performance of the action wee were entered into;

and that not only of victuals, munitions, and clothing, but also of barks, pinnesses, and boats; they also by him to be victualled, manned and furnished to my contentation." But while preparations were being made to carry these generous measures into execution, "there arose such an unwonted storme, and continued foure dayes that had like to have driven all on shore, if the Lord had not held his holy hand over them." The vessels of Drake's fleet were "in great danger to be driven from their ankoring upon the coast. For we brake many cables and lost many ankors. And some of our fleet which had lost all, (of which number was the ship appointed for Master Lane and his company) was driven to put to sea in great danger, in avoyding the coast, and could never see us againe untill we met in England. Many also of our small pinnaces and boates were lost in this storm." As a result of this experience, Lane, after consultation with Drake, decided to embarke his colony for England. Then Drake, says Lane, "in the name of the Almighty, weying his ankers (having bestowed us among his fleet) for the reliefe of whom hee had in that storme sustained more perill of wrake then [than] in all his former most honourable actions against the Spanyards, with praises unto God for all, set saile the nineteenth of June, 1586, and arrived in Portsmouth the seven and twentieth of July the same yeere."

Lane and his colonists found no precious metals in "Virginia," but they introduced to the English people three articles that have brought more gold and silver into the coffers of English-speaking peoples than the Spaniards took from the mines of Mexico and Peru. These were "uppowoc," "pagatour," and "openauk," articles first described for the English people by Hariot. Though now masquerading under other names we have no difficulty in recognizing in "uppowac" our tobacco, in "pagatour" our Indian corn, and in "openauk" our Irish potato. Everybody knows that the first man of rank to introduce the use of tobacco to the English people was Sir Walter Raleigh. He also introduced the cultivation of the potato into England and Ireland. No greater service was ever rendered the Irish people. So important to their welfare has the potato become that, though not native to the Emerald Isle, it is best known as the Irish potato.

Shortly before Lane's embarkation for England a ship fitted out by Raleigh "at his owne charge" and "fraighted with all maner of things in a most plentifull manner, for the supply and reliefe of his colony then remaining in Virginia," sailed from England for Roanoke Island. This vessel reached Hatteras immediately after the departure of the English colony, "out of this paradise of the world," but finding no settlers, returned to England. Two weeks later Sir Richard Grenville arrived with three ships. After diligent search for Lane's people he too turned his prow homeward; but "unwilling to loose the possession of the countrey which Englishmen had so long held, after good deliberation, he determined to leave some men behinde to reteine possession of the Countrey, whereupon he landed fifteene men in the Isle of Roanoke, furnished plentifully with all maner of provisions for two yeeres, and so departed for England."

Raleigh was not to be deterred from his great work by a single failure. The next year, 1587, "intending to persevere in the planting of his Countrey of Virginia," he sent out a new colony "under the charge of John White, whom hee appointed Governor, and also appointed unto him twelve assistants, unto whom he gave a Charter, and incorporated them by the name of Governor and Assistants of the Citie of Raleigh in Virginia." This colony contained seventeen women and nine children. Ten of the men, it may be inferred from their names, were accompanied by their wives and children. They were, therefore, going to "Virginia" to seek permanent homes. Three vessels, the Admiral, 120 tons, a flyboat, and a pinnace, sailed from Portsmouth April 26, 1587, bearing this little colony to its mysterious fate. Following advice he had received from Lane, Raleigh ordered the fleet only to touch at Roanoke in order to bring off the men left by Grenville, and then to proceed to the Chesapeake Bay where he intended the settlement to be made. This order was not obeyed because the commander of the fleet, Simon Ferdinando, turned out to be a treacherous villain. Upon reaching Hatteras, the governor with forty men embarked in the pinnace for Roanoke Island, and as they left the ship Ferdinando sent an order to the sailors in the pinnace "charging them not to bring any of the planters backe againe," but to leave them in the Island, "except the Governour, & two or three such as he approved, saying that the Summer was farre spent, wherefore hee would land the planters in no other place." From this decision there was no appeal this side of England and White was forced against his will to land his colony on Roanoke Island. This landing occurred "in the place where our fifteene men were left, but we found none of them, nor any signe that they had bene there, saving onely wee found the bones of one of those fifteene, which the Savages had slaine long before." Passing to the north end of the island

they found the houses and the ruins of the fort built by Lane.
The houses were in good condition but the outer rooms "were
overgrown with Melons of divers sorts, and Deere within
them, feeding on those Melons." The work of repairing these
houses and the building of new ones was undertaken without
delay, and thus was begun the second attempt to found an
English colony in America.

Two incidents in the life of this colony will always have a
romantic interest. One was the baptism of Manteo who, in
accordance with Raleigh's instructions, was christened Lord
of Roanoke and Dasamonguepeuk "in reward of his faithful
service." This ceremony occurred on August 13, 1587, and
is the first instance on record of a Christian service by English Protestants within the boundaries of the United States.
A few days later occurred the second such service in connection with the most interesting incident in the life of the little
colony. On the 18th of August, Eleanor Dare, daughter of
Governor White and wife of Ananias Dare, gave birth to a
daughter, who was baptised on the following Sunday, "and
because this child was the first Christian borne in Virginia,
shee was named Virginia." More people perhaps know the
story of Virginia Dare than of any other baby that ever lived
in America, though the last ever heard of her was when she
was but nine days old. The State of North Carolina has commemorated her birth by embracing the very spot whereon
she was born into a county called Dare.

Virginia Dare was but a few days old when occurred the
last recorded event in the life of the settlement. It was necessary for somebody to return to England for supplies. Two
of the governor's assistants were expected to go, but when
the time came they refused to make the trip. Then "the
whole company both of the Assistants and planters came to
the Governour, and with one voice requested him to returne
himselfe into England, for the better and sooner obtaining
of supplies, and other necessaries for them." At first he
would not listen to their entreaties, alleging that many of
the colonists had been induced to come by his persuasion, and
that if he left them he would be accused of deserting the colony. Besides they "intended to remove 50 miles further up
into the maine presently," and he must remain to superintend this removal. But the next day "not onely the Assistants but divers others, as well women as men," renewed their
request and offered to sign a statement "under their hands
and seals" that his return was made at their earnest entreaties. This statement was duly executed and White "being at

the last through their extreme intreating constrayned to returne into England," set sail from Roanoke August 27th. From that day to this the fate of Virginia Dare and the Roanoke settlers has been a mystery.

Upon his arrival in England, White found the whole country astir over the approach of the Spanish Armada called "Invincible." Every English vessel and every English sailor was in demand for the defence of the kingdom. There was no busier man in all England than Sir Walter Raleigh, yet he found time to listen to White's story and to prepare a small expedition for the relief of his colony; but at the very last moment orders came forbidding it to sail. Raleigh's influence, however, was deservedly great, and in April, 1588, he secured permission for two small vessels to go to Roanoke. They set sail but were driven back by Spanish war vessels. It was then too late to give any further attention to the handful of settlers across the Atlantic; the great "Invincible Armada" was bearing down on England's coast and every man's first duty was at his post to defend his home and fireside. Finally the great battle was fought and the Spaniards were driven crushed and shattered from the English Channel. "God blew with his winds and they were scattered."

It was March, 1590, before White finally sailed for Roanoke. Unfortunately he did not command the vessel in which he sailed but embarked as a passenger in a ship engaged in the West Indian trade. He arrived at Hatteras in the afternoon of August 15th. "At our first coming to anker on this shore," he wrote, "we saw a great smoke rise in the Ile Roanoke neere the place where I left our Colony in the yeere 1587, which smoake put us in good hope that some of the Colony were there expecting my returne out of England." The sea was rough and the crew experienced great difficulty in reaching Roanoke Island. On one of the attempts seven men were drowned. The last attempt was made with two boats manned by nineteen men. The experience of this party can best be given in White's own language. Says he: "before we could get to the place, where our planters were left, it was so exceeding darke, that we overshot the place a quarter of a mile; there we espied towards the North end of the Iland ye light of a great fire thorow the woods, to which we presently rowed: when wee came right over against it, we let fall our Grapnel neere the shore, & sounded with a trumpet Call, & afterwards many familiar English tunes of Songs, and called to them friendly; but we had no answer, we therefore landed at day breake, and coming to the fire, we found the grasse &

sundry rotten trees burning about the place. From hence we went thorow the woods to that part of the Island directly over against Dasamonguepeuk, & thence we returned by the water side, round about the North point of the Island, untill we came to the place where I left our Colony in the yeere 1586 [1587]. In all this way we saw in the sand the print of the Savages feet of 2 or 3 sorts troaden ye night, and as we entered up the sandy banke upon a tree, in the very browe thereof were curiously carved three faire Romane letters C R O: which letters presently we knew to signifie the place, where I should find the planters seated, according to a secret token agreed upon between them & me at my last departure from them, which was, that in any wayes they should not fail to write or carve on the trees or posts of the dores the name of the place where they should be seated; for at my coming away they were prepared to remove from Roanoke 50 miles into the maine. Therefore at my departure from them in An. 1587 I willed them, that if they should happen to be distressed in any of those places, that then they should carve over the letters or name, a Crosse X in this forme, but we found no such sign of distresse. And having well considered of this, we passed toward the place where they were left in sundry houses, but we found the houses taken down, and the place very strongly enclosed with a high palisado of great trees, with cortynes and flankers very Fortlike, and one of the chiefe trees or postes at the right side of the entrance had the barke taken off, and 5 foot from the ground in fayre Capitall letters was graven CROATOAN without any crosse or signe of distress; this done, we entered into the palisado, where we found many bares of Iron, two piggies of lead, foure yron fowlers, Iron sacker-shotte, and such like heavie things, throwen here and there, almost over-grown with grasse and weedes. * * * Presently Captaine Cooke and I went to the place, which was in the ende of an olde trench, made two yeeres past by Captain Amadas: where wee found five Chests, that had bene carefully hidden of the Planters, and of the same chests three were my owne, and about the place many of my things spoyled and broken, and my books torne from the covers, the frames of some of my pictures and Mappes rotten and spoyled with rayne, and my armour almost eaten through with rust; * * * but although it much grieved me to see such spoyle of my goods, yet on the other hand I greatly joyed that I had safely found a certaine token of their safe being at Croatoan, which is the place where Manteo was borne, and the Savages of the Iland our friends.''

Preparations were made to proceed to Croatan "with as much speede" as possible, for the sky was threatening and promised a "foule and stormie night." The sailors embarked "with much danger and labour." During the night a fierce storm swept the sound and the next day "the weather grew to be fouler and fouler." The winds lashed the sea into a fury, cables snapt as though made of twine, three anchors were cast away and the vessels escaped wreck on the sand bars by a hair's breadth. Food ran low and fresh water gave out. Captain Cooke now refused to continue the search and determined to go to St. Johns, or some other island to the southward for fresh water and to continue in the West Indies during that winter "with hope to make 2 rich voyages of one." Governor White, much against his wishes, was compelled to acquiesce in this arrangement, but at his "earnest petitions" Captain Cooke agreed to return in the spring and renew the search for the colonists. It is well known that this was not done, for the voyage to the West Indies was unfortunate, the plans of the adventurers went awry, and they were compelled to return to England without going by way of Croatan. Thus was lost the last chance of learning definitely the fate of the "Lost Colony." [5]

---

[5] A discussion of the fate of the "Lost Colony" would be foreign to the purpose of this book. Those who wish to pursue this phase of the subject will find exhaustive treatments of it in "Sir Walter Raleigh's Lost Colony," by Hamilton McMillan, A. M., Advance Presses, Wilson, N. C., 1888; in "The Lost Colony of Roanoke," by Stephen B. Weeks, Ph. D., The Knickerbocker Press, New York, 1891; and in "Virginia Dare," by S. A. Ashe, in the "Biographical History of North Carolina," Vol. IV, pp. 8-18, Charles L. Van Noppen, Publisher, Greensboro, N. C., 1906.

The theory advanced in these interesting discussions is that the colonists despairing of the return of White, moved to Croatan, intermarried with the Croatan Indians, and became the ancestors of the present tribe of Croatans in North Carolina. In support of this theory, appeal is made to White's narrative, above quoted; to John Smith's narrative; to a pamphlet entitled "A True and Sincere Discourse of the Purpose and Ende of the *Plantation* begun in *Virginia*," published in 1610; to Strachey's "History of Travaile in Virginia Britannia," written sometime between 1612 and 1616, but not published until 1849; to John Lawson's "History of Carolina," published in 1709; and finally to the traditions, character, disposition, language and family names of the North Carolina Croatans of the present day.

Doctor Weeks thus summarizes the arguments in support of this theory: "Smith and Strachey heard that the colonists of 1587 were still alive about 1607. They were then living on the peninsula of Dasamonguepeuk, whence they travelled toward the region of the Chowan and Roanoke rivers. From this point they travelled toward the southwest, and settled on the upper waters of the Neuse. John Lederer

The departure of White did not end the search for the colonists. Other expeditions were sent out without success. As late as 1602 such an expedition sailed under the command of Samuel Mace. By the time Mace returned with his repetition of the sad story of failure, Raleigh had been attainted and his proprietorship to "Virginia" had escheated to the Crown. His efforts had cost him a large fortune amounting, it is estimated, to not less than a million dollars of our money. But, though his financial resources were exhausted, his spirit was as determined as ever, and he never despaired of seeing an English colony planted in "Virginia." "I shall yet live to see it an English nation," he wrote just before his fall. To the realization of this prophecy no man contributed more than he. Among those who subscribed funds for the founding of the Jamestown colony were ten of those who constituted the incorporators of the "Citie of Raleigh in Virginia" in 1587. In these men we have the connecting link between the Roanoke settlements and Jamestown. Therefore, although he himself never set foot on "Virginia soil," Raleigh will always be esteemed the true parent of North American colonization. An idea like his has life in it, though the plant may not spring up at once. When it rises above the surface the sower can claim it. Had the particular region of the New World not eventually become a permanent English settlement, he would still have earned the merit of authorship of the English colonizing movement. As Humbolt has said, "without him, and without Cabot, North America might never have grown into a home of the English tongue." [6] This was

---

heard of them in this direction in 1670 and remarked on their beards, which were never worn by full-blooded Indians. Rev. John Blair heard of them in 1704. John Lawson met some of the Croatan Indians about 1709, and was told that their ancestors were white men. White settlers came into the middle section of North Carolina as early as 1715, and found the ancestors of the present tribe of Croatan Indians tilling the soil, holding slaves, and speaking English. The Croatans of today claim descent from the Lost Colony. Their habits, disposition, and mental characteristics show traces both of savage and civilized ancestry. Their language is the English of three hundred years ago, and their names are in many cases the same as those borne by the original colonists. No other theory of their origin has been advanced, and it is confidently believed that the one here proposed is logically and historically the best, supported as it is, both by external and internal evidence. If this theory is rejected, then the critic must explain in some other way the origin of a people which, after the lapse of three hundred years, show the characteristics, speak the language, and possess the family names of the second English colony planted in the western world."—"The Lost Colony of Roanoke," pp. 38-39.

[6] Stebbing: Sir Walter Ralegh, p. 48.

Raleigh's greatest service to England and to the world. "Baffled in his efforts to plant the English race upon this continent, he yet called into existence a spirit of enterprise which first gave Virginia, and then North America, to that race, and which led Great Britain, from this beginning, to dot the map of the world with her colonies." Such are the results that have sprung from the efforts of Raleigh, Lane, and White to plant an English colony on the shores of North Carolina. That judgment, therefore, is correct which declares that, looking back upon the events of the last three centuries, "We can hail the Roanoke settlement as the beginning of English colonization in America." [7]

---

[7] Henry: "Sir Walter Raleigh," in Winsor's *Narrative and Critical History of America*, Vol. III, p. 105.

CHAPTER II

EXPLORATIONS AND SETTLEMENT

Raleigh's efforts to plant a colony on Roanoke Island had failed, but they were not in vain. His work had stimulated the interest of the people of England in America, while his idea of another England beyond the Atlantic aroused in them that spirit of conquest and colonization to which the English race in Europe, in Asia, in Africa, in Australia, in the islands of the sea, and in America owes the world-wide predominance which it today enjoys among the races of mankind. In spite of their losses and disappointments, neither Raleigh nor those associated with him thought for a moment of abandoning their great purpose. They were quick, however, to take advantage of the lessons which their experience had taught them. Their failure had made it clear that the work of colonization was too costly to be successfully borne by any private individual; only the purse of the sovereign, or the combined purses of private persons associated in joint-stock companies were long enough to bear the enormous expenses incident to the settlement of the American wilderness. Out of Raleigh's bitter experience at Roanoke, therefore, came the organization of the great joint-stock company, known as the London Company, which at Jamestown in Virginia planted the first permanent English settlement in America. There is a vital connection between Roanoke and Jamestown. Among the subscribers to the stock of the London Company were ten of the men who had been associated with Raleigh in his efforts to plant a colony at Roanoke; while from the colony into which Jamestown subsequently developed came the first permanent settlers in the region which had been the scene of Raleigh's work.

A glance at the map will show why North Carolina received its first permanent settlers from Virginia. The dangerous character of the Carolina coast and the absence of good harborage made the approach too difficult and uncertain to admit of colonization directly from Europe. This became

apparent from the experience of Raleigh's first colony, and
Raleigh himself, as we have seen, directed John White, in
1587, to seek a site on Chesapeake Bay. His commands,
through no fault of White, were not obeyed and the result,
as White later found to his sorrow, was disastrous. Twenty-
two years later, the London Company, guided by Raleigh's
experience, directed the Jamestown colony toward the Chesapeake. The first settlers, for obvious reasons, sought lands
lying along navigable streams; consequently the water
courses, to a large extent, determined the direction of the
colony's growth. Many of the streams of southeastern Virginia flow toward Currituck and Albemarle sounds in North
Carolina, and the sources of the Roanoke, the Chowan, and
other important rivers of northeastern North Carolina are
in Virginia. Moreover, the soil, the climate, the vegetation,
and the animal life of southeastern Virginia are similar to
those of the Albemarle region. It should be remembered, too,
that until 1663 this region was an organic part of Virginia.
Nothing, therefore, was more natural than that the planters
of Virginia, searching for good bottom lands, should gradually
extend their plantations southward along the shores of Albemarle Sound and the rivers that flow into it.

The Virginians early manifested a lively interest in the
country along the Albemarle Sound. Nansemond County in
Virginia, which adjoins the Albemarle region on the north,
was settled as early as 1609, and during the next few years
many an adventurous explorer, hunter, and trader made himself familiar with the streams that pour into Albemarle and
Currituck sounds. No records remain—perhaps no records
were ever made—of the earliest of these expeditions. The
first report on record of a journey into that region was made
by John Pory, secretary of Virginia, who in 1622 explored
the lands along Chowan River. It is probable that he was
only one of several such explorers, for seven years later
enough was known about that region to induce Sir Robert
Heath, the king's attorney-general, to seek a patent to it
which Charles I readily gave him. Later Heath assigned his
patent to Henry, Lord Maltravers who, about the year 1639,
seems to have made an unsuccessful attempt to plant a settlement within his grant. During the following decade, Sir
William Berkeley, governor of Virginia, sent several expeditions against the Indians along the Albemarle Sound, and
these expeditions resulted in further explorations. One of
these explorers entered Currituck Sound and explored the
country along Albemarle Sound and for some distance up

Chowan River. Four years later, 1650, Edward Bland, a Virginia merchant, led an exploring and trading expedition among the Nottaway, Meherrin, and Tuscarora Indians who dwelt along the Chowan, Meherrin, and Roanoke rivers. During the next two or three years, Roger Green, a clergyman of Nansemond County, also took an active part in exploring and exploiting the region south of Chowan River. In 1654, Francis Yeardley, a son of Governor Yeardley of Virginia, sent an expedition to Roanoke Island which led to other important explorations in what is now Eastern North Carolina; and two years later the Virginia Assembly commissioned Thomas Dew and Thomas Francis to explore the coast between Cape Hatteras and Cape Fear.

Upon their return to Virginia these explorers and traders spread exaggerated accounts of the glories and riches of the regions they had visited. John Pory reported that he found the Albemarle region "a very fruitful and pleasant country, yielding two harvests in a year." Edward Bland declared that it was "a place so easie to be settled in that all inconvenience could be avoyded which commonly attend New Plantations. * * * Tobacco will grow larger and more in quantity than in Virginia. Sugar Canes are supposed naturally to be there, or at least if implanted will undoubtedly flourish: For we brought with us thence extraordinary Canes of twenty-five foot long and six inches round; there is also great store of fish, and the Inhabitants relate that there is a plenty of Salt made to the sunne without art; Tobacco Pipes have beene seene among these Indians tipt with Silver, and they weare Copper Plates about their necks: They have two Crops of Indian Corne yearely, whereas Virginia hath but one." He concludes his description of "that happy Country of New Brittaine" with the positive assurance, that "What I write, is what I have proved." Francis Yeardley, too, who boasted of the "ample discovery of South Virginia or Carolina" by "two Virginians born" did not scruple to magnify their achievement by magnifying the virtues of the country they had explored. It possessed, he declared, "a most fertile, gallant, rich soil, flourishing in all abundance of nature, especially in rich mulberry and vine, a serene air, and temperate clime, and experimentally rich in precious minerals; and lastly, I may say, parallel with any place for rich land, and stately timber of all sorts; a place indeed unacquainted with our Virginia's nipping frost, no winter, or very little cold to be found there."

These explorations and favorable reports were naturally

followed by a southward movement of settlers. Just when this movement began cannot be stated with certainty because, as Ashe has well said, "it was a movement so natural that the particulars are not recorded in the local annals of the time." [1] Enough, however, is known to show that, beginning with Pory's expedition in 1622, the efforts of interested persons to plant settlements within that region, though at times spasmodic, were never entirely abandoned. In 1629 came Heath's grant and his design for establishing a proprietary colony. Ten years later, after Heath had assigned his patent, the king commanded the Virginia authorities to assist Lord Maltravers "in seating Carolina"; and about that time William Hawley appeared in Virginia as "governor of Carolina" and obtained permission from the Virginia Assembly to take into his province a colony of one hundred "freemen, being single and disengaged of debt." His efforts, however, ended in failure. In 1648, Henry Plumpton of Nansemond County, Thomas Tuke of Isle of Wight County, and others who had accompanied the expeditions sent by Governor Berkeley against the Carolina Indians, purchased from the Indians large tracts of land along Chowan River. Two years later, upon his return from "New Brittaine," Edward Bland, for himself and his associates, petitioned the Virginia Assembly for permission to plant a settlement there, and the petition was granted on condition that the promoters "secure themselves in effecting the sayd Designe with a hundred able men sufficiently furnished with Armes and Munition." It is probable that this scheme exhausted itself in the preparation and publication of a pamphlet exploiting the advantages of the country. In 1653, Roger Green, on behalf of himself and other inhabitants of Nansemond County, obtained from the Virginia Assembly a grant of ten thousand acres of land for the first one hundred persons who should settle on Roanoke River south of Chowan and one thousand acres for himself. "In reward of his charge, hazard and trouble of first discoverie, and encouragement of others for seating those southern parts of Virginia," he was permitted as a special favor to lay off his tract "next to those persons who have had a former grant." It is not probable that any settlement resulted from this grant, but the grant itself is historically important because its language leads irresistibly to the conclusion that when it was issued there were already settlers along the waters of Chowan River.

---

[1] History of North Carolina, Vol. I, p. 59.

From that time forward there was no cessation in the slow
but steady flow of settlers into the Albemarle region.   The
early historians of North Carolina saw in these settlers religious refugees fleeing from ecclesiastical oppression in Virginia and New England.   We now know that they were
inspired by no such lofty motives, but that the inducements
for their migration were purely economic.   North Carolina
was founded by men in search of good bottom land.   The
explorers, hunters, and traders who first penetrated the Albemarle wilderness carried back to Virginia, as we have seen,
glowing reports of the mildness of its climate, the fertility
of its soil, and the great variety of its products, while they
pointed out that its broad streams and wide sounds offered
easy means of communication and transportation.   The
opportunities for selecting at will large tracts of fertile lands
were already becoming limited in Virginia, and many a small
planter, recent immigrant, and ambitious servant who had
completed the term of his indenture, heard with keen
interest of the virgin wilderness to the southward where such
land could be had almost for the asking.   That they might
acquire land on easier terms than could be had in Virginia,
attain to the dignity of planters, raise and export tobacco,
and find larger and better ranges for their stock, were the
inducements which led them to abandon Virginia for Albemarle.   All this was well understood by the promoters of the
settlement.   Thomas Woodward, surveyor-general of Albemarle, writing in 1665 to Sir John Colleton, one of the Lords
Proprietors, warned him that the terms offered by the Lords
Proprietors were not well received by the people, and advised
that they be made more liberal for, he declared, it was land
only that settlers came for.   The Lords Proprietors, in recognition of the soundness of this advice, made their terms more
liberal.   It was not, then, religious enthusiasm but the Anglo-
Saxon's keen insatiable passion for land that inspired the
founders of North Carolina.

An occasional record preserves for us the names of some
of those early pioneers.   Thus Robert Lawrence in a deposi-
tion about another matter, made in 1707, declared that in
1661, he "seated a plantation on the southwest side of Chowan
River about three or four miles above the mouth of Marat-
tock where he lived about seven years."   Others whose names
are similarly preserved are Thomas Relfe, Samuel Pricklove,
Caleb Calloway, George Catchmaid, John Jenkins, John Harvey, Thomas Jarvis, and George Durant.   Unfortunately
we know but little about these founders of the Commonwealth.

Lawson tells us that they were "substantial planters" and the meager records of the time attest the accuracy of his statement. Many of them brought into the new settlement retinues of servants and other dependents that would not then have been thought inconsiderable even in the older colonies. As each planter was entitled to fifty acres of land for each person whom he brought into the colony, the number of such persons in his retinue becomes an indication of the planter's wealth and standing in the community. Thus, Robert Peele, who brought seven persons, received a grant for 350 acres of land; John Jenkins, who brought fourteen persons, received 700 acres; John Harvey, who brought seventeen persons, received 850 acres; while Thomas Relfe and George Catchmaid, each of whom was accompanied by thirty persons, received grants of 1,500 acres each.

Their subsequent careers show that they were men of ability and force of character. They quickly became the leaders in the affairs of the colony. Thomas Relfe became provost marshal of the General Court and one of the first vestrymen of the parish of Pasquotank. Samuel Pricklove became a member of the General Assembly. Caleb Calloway served as a representative in the General Assembly, as speaker, and as a justice of the General Court. George Catchmaid was speaker of the General Assembly and exercised great influence over the early legislation of the colony. John Jenkins became the deputy of Lord Craven, one of the Lords Proprietors, and like John Harvey and Thomas Jarvis, subsequently rose to the dignity of chief executive of the province.

Of all the men who assisted in laying the foundations of North Carolina, none was so worthy to stand in the forefront of a people's history as George Durant. In the contracted sphere in which he moved and played his part he displayed qualities of mind and character which would have won for him on a larger and more conspicuous stage a high place among the early patriot leaders of America. He had a faith in democracy far in advance of the age in which he lived, and in many critical events in our early history he showed that he had the courage of his convictions. Enlightened in his views, he was bold in asserting them, resolute in carrying them into execution, and fearless of consequences. Believing the navigation acts unwise, oppressive, and detrimental to the interests of the colony, he led a determined and temporarily successful opposition to their enforcement in Albemarle. In the very presence of the assembled Lords Proprietors, he denounced the man whom they had selected for governor as unfit for the position and threatened resistance to his authority. When an acting governor, exercising authority without legal warrant, sought to secure an Assembly amenable to his will by imposing new and illegal restrictions upon the election of representatives, Durant organized opposition, removed him from office, and set up a government based on popular support. Hating misgovernment and tyranny, he led a popular revolt even against one of the Lords Proprietors who had used his position to plunder and oppress the people, arrested, tried, and condemned him, and drove him out of the province. If in these various crises George Durant seemed to show a greater love for liberty than for order, he at least could plead in justification that it was liberty rather than order that was threatened with destruction; and this plea must be accepted in vindication of his conduct just as a similar plea is accepted in vindication of a subsequent generation of Americans who a century later made a similar choice of alternatives.

The oldest grant for land in North Carolina now extant is the grant to George Durant by Kilcocanen, chief of the Yeopim Indians, dated March 1, 1661 [1662] for a tract lying along Perquimans River and Albemarle Sound which still bears the name of Durant's Neck. There were, however, grants prior to Durant's, for his grant recites a previous one by Kilcocanen to Samuel Pricklove. Indeed, by 1662 such Indian grants had become so common that the Crown ordered them to be disregarded and required the holders to take out new patents under the laws of Virginia. Three years later the surveyor of Albemarle declared that a county "forty miles square will not comprehend the inhabitants there already seated." These settlers, for the most part, came from Virginia, but others came also, and by the close of the first decade of its history the Albemarle colony extended from Chowan River to Currituck Sound.

By 1663, the settlements on the Albemarle had become of sufficient importance to attract attention in England. In them a powerful group of English courtiers saw an opportunity to undertake on a vast scale a colonizing enterprise which promised large returns of wealth and power. Accordingly they sought from the king a grant of all the territory claimed by England south of Virginia, including the Albemarle settlements. In compliance with their request, Charles II issued his famous charter of 1663, by which he erected into a separate and distinct province all the region lying between the thirty-first and thirty-sixth degrees, north latitude, and extending westward from the Atlantic Ocean to the "South Seas." Afterwards it was ascertained that these boundaries did not include the settlements already planted on the Albemarle; a second charter was therefore issued, June 30, 1665, which extended the grant thirty minutes northward and two degrees southward. Since Charles I, in his grant to Sir Robert Heath in 1629, had called this region "Carolana" or "Carolina," Charles II determined to retain the name. He accordingly erected it into the "Province of Carolina" and granted it to eight of his loyal friends and supporters whom he constituted "the true and absolute Lords Proprietors."

The grant to the Lords Proprietors attracted considerable attention and its publication was speedily followed by inquiries for the terms on which settlements within the new province could be made. One of these inquiries purported to come from a group of New England men who were interested in the Cape Fear region. Another proceeded from certain English adventurers who expressed a willingness to embark upon a colonizing enterprise. A third came from "several gentlemen and persons of good quality" in the island of Barbados. Eager to take advantage of all this interest, the Lords Proprietors were preparing replies to these inquiries when an unexpected obstacle arose which threatened to bring all their plans to naught. Claimants under the old Heath charter of 1629 appeared who protested the validity of the title of the new Lords Proprietors to the territory embraced within the province of Carolina; and the Lords Proprietors learned much to their annoyance that many persons who were eager to settle within their grant were deterred from doing so by these conflicting claims. In this dilemma they fell back upon their influence at court and induced the Privy Council, of which two of their number, Clarendon and Albemarle, were members, to declare the Heath patent forfeited on the ground that no settlement had been made within his grant. With the way thus cleared, the Lords Proprietors on August 25, 1663, issued a general "declaration and proposals to all who will plant in Carolina," setting forth a plan of government and stating the terms on which land would be granted. These proposals, however, were for Cape Fear only; for Albemarle, the Lords Proprietors had other plans.

Warned by the fate of the Heath grant, the Lords Proprietors hastened to institute a government in Albemarle in order, as they said, "that the Kinge may see that wee sleepe

not with his grant." The jurisdiction of the first government, established in 1663, was confined to Albemarle County
which embraced a region forty miles square in extent lying to
the northeast of Chowan River. Over this region, in 1664,
William Drummond was commissioned governor. Historians,
unwilling it seems to find any failings in one who afterwards became the victim of the wrath of the detested Berkeley, have agreed in assigning to Drummond a good character
and fair abilities. Their guess at least has the merit that it
cannot be disproved for, in fact, we know nothing about the
man and but little about his administration in Albemarle.
His appointment put into operation the executive branch of
the government; a little later, probably in the early part of
1665, the legislative branch was organized with the freemen
attending in person rather than through their representatives.

Immediately upon its organization, the General Assembly
turned its attention to the consideration of the terms of landholding offered by the Lords Proprietors. These terms were
fifty acres to each settler for himself and a like amount for
every person whom he imported into the colony, for which he
was to pay in specie an annual quit rent of a half-penny per
acre. They were less favorable than the terms which prevailed in Virginia where settlers received larger grants and
were charged an annual quit rent of only a farthing per acre
payable in produce. Accordingly, the first recorded act of
the Albemarle Assembly was a petition to the Lords Proprietors "praying that the inhabitants of the said County
may hold their lands upon the same terms and conditions that
the inhabitants of Virginia hold theirs." This petition was
supported by the Proprietors' surveyor-general, Thomas
Woodward, who pointed out to them that in this matter their
interests were the same as those of the settlers. "The Pro-
portione of Land you have allotted with the Rent, and conditions are by most People not well resented [received]," he
wrote, "and the very Rumor of them discourages many who
had intentions to have removed from Virginia hether.
* * * To thenke that any man will remove from Virginia
upon harder Conditione than they can live there will prove
(I feare) a vaine Imagination, It bein Land only they come
for." Convinced by this reasoning, the Lords Proprietors,
on May 1, 1668, signed and dispatched to Samuel Stephens,
who had recently (1667) succeeded Drummond as governor,
the document which has become famous in our history as the

Great Deed of Grant, in which they granted the Assembly's prayer.[2]

This obstacle to the growth of Albemarle having been thus removed, the Assembly in 1669 adopted a well considered program for the encouragement of immigration. Three acts were passed to prevent speculation in land to the detriment of *bona fide* settlers. The first forbade any person to sell his land rights unless he had resided in the colony for at least two full years; the second threw open to re-entry any partially improved tract that had been abandoned by its owner for as much as six months; and the third forbade any person, except by special permission from the Lords Proprietors, to take up more than 660 acres in any one tract. Another statute passed at the same session protected new settlers for a period of five years after their arrival from suit on any debt contracted, or other cause of action that had arisen outside of the colony. New settlers were also to be exempt from taxation for a period of one year. "Strangers from other parts" were shut out from the lucrative Indian trade under heavy penalties unless they became residents of Albemarle. Finally, as there were no clergymen in the province, it was enacted that a declaration of mutual consent, before the governor or any member of his Council, and in the presence of witnesses, should be deemed a lawful marriage as if the parties "had binn marryed by a minister according to the rites and Customs of England"; that is to say, marriage was recognized as a civil contract.

Some of these measures, especially the stay law and the marriage act, aroused bitter criticism of Albemarle among her neighbors. The Virginians, who doubtless suffered much from the stay law, calmly ignoring the fact that the Albemarle

---

[2] The Great Deed of Grant afterwards became the subject of sharp controversies between the colonial authorities and the representatives of the people. The former regretting the generosity of the Lords Proprietors, sought to break the force of the Great Deed by holding that it was a revokable grant, and that in fact it had been revoked and annulled at various times. The people, who regarded the Great Deed as second in importance only to the charter, vigorously controverted this view. Although it had been officially recorded in Albemarle, the original was preserved with scrupulous care and, sixty-three years after its date, during a controversy about it with Governor Gabriel Johnston. the Assembly ordered that its text be spread upon its journal and the original placed in the personal custody of the speaker. As late as 1856, the Supreme Court of North Carolina in Archibald v. Davis (4 Jones. 133) invoked the Great Deed to sustain the validity of a grant issued in accordance with its provisions by the governor and Council in September, 1716.

act was an exact copy of an act that had been on the statute books of Virginia since 1642, vented their indignation by bestowing upon Albemarle the epithet of "Rogues Harbour." How far this epithet was deserved will be the subject of future inquiry. In the meantime, in spite of her liberal laws, Albemarle grew but slowly, and at the close of the first decade of her history could count a population of scarcely fifteen hundred souls.

CHAPTER III

THE PROPRIETARY GOVERNMENT

The Albemarle settlements were originally within the jurisdiction of Virginia; indeed, there was no design on the part of the settlers to organize another government. This came later after Charles II had erected the region into the province of Carolina. In the list of the Lords Proprietors of Carolina appear some of the greatest names in English history. They were: Edward Hyde, Earl of Clarendon, Lord High Chancellor of England; George Monk, Duke of Albemarle, Master of the King's Horse and Captain-General of all his forces; William Lord Craven; John Lord Berkeley; Anthony Cooper, Lord Ashley, Chancellor of the Exchequer; Sir George Carteret, Vice-Chamberlain of the King's Household; Sir William Berkeley, Governor of Virginia; and Sir John Colleton. To each of these men Charles was under great personal obligations. Clarendon, his constant companion and counsellor during his exile, had been among the foremost in effecting his restoration. His natural abilities had raised him to a position as the greatest of British subjects not of the blood royal; indeed, he was soon to become allied even by blood with the royal family by the marriage to the Duke of York, afterwards James II, of his daughter Anne, through whom Clarendon became the grandfather of two of England's sovereigns, Queen Mary and Queen Anne. To George Monk, more largely than to any other man, Charles owed his crown, for Monk had brought to him the support of the army without which his return to England could not have been effected. Craven had freely spent a considerable fortune in the royal cause. In Lord Berkeley and his brother, Sir William, Charles had two subjects who had adhered loyally to him in good and in ill fortune. The former had followed him into exile; the latter, as governor of Virginia, had kept that colony so loyal to the Crown that it became a land of refuge for unfortunate Loyalists fleeing from the wrath of Cromwell. Anthony Ashley Cooper, afterwards earl of Shaftesbury, a man of winning manners and commanding intellect, had been one of the twelve Parliamentary commissioners who went to Holland to invite Charles to return to England to ascend the throne of his ancestors. Sir George Carteret, while governor of the island of Jersey, had defended his post against the Parliamentary forces in a most gallant manner and had surrendered at last only at the command of Charles himself. The last in the list, Sir John Colleton, had been a valiant soldier for the king in whose service he expended a large fortune. Upon the downfall of the royal cause, he emigrated to Barbados and for a time kept that colony loyal to the Stuarts.

If a monarch was ever justified in using crown lands to reward the services of his friends, Charles II was surely justified in rewarding these men. Not to have done so would have entitled him to first rank among the world's ingrates. To them he owed everything—the assurance of his personal safety, the restoration of his House to its ancient dignity, and the recovery of his throne. If subjects were ever justified in accepting gifts from their sovereign, the Lords Proprietors of Carolina were surely justified in accepting them from Charles Stuart. At great risk to their lives, their fortunes, and their honor, they had rendered him inestimable services. He was an exile, and they restored him to his country; he was a beggar, and they made him a king. What they had done for him was an incomparably greater personal service than any similar service Sir Walter Raleigh ever rendered Queen Elizabeth. Yet among the historians of North Carolina there are those who acclaim Elizabeth's gift of this same region to her ambitious subject, and his acceptance of it, as acts of profound statesmanship and genuine patriotism but who condemn utterly the "careless generosity" of Charles and the "rapacity" of his "parasites." [1] To such an extent do our prejudices often confound our judgment!

The names of the Lords Proprietors, and of the king, are all found today on the map of the Carolinas. In North Carolina are Albemarle Sound and Craven and Carteret counties; in South Carolina, Clarendon and Colleton counties, Berkeley Parish, and the Ashley and Cooper rivers. The name of the two states commemorates the royal grantor. The assertion is often made, it is true, that their name originated in honor of Charles IX of France, but the facts do not sustain this contention. In 1562, Ribaut

---

[1] Hawks: History of North Carolina, Vol. I, pp. 28, 234; Vol. II, p. 74.

founded a Huguenot colony near the present site of Port Royal, South Carolina, which he called Charles-fort. A year later the settlement was abandoned. In 1564, Laudonniere founded another Huguenot colony on St. John's River in Florida and called it Fort Caroline. This colony was destroyed by the Spaniards. Both Charles-fort and Fort Caroline were named in honor of Charles IX, but these names were applied to the forts only; for the region immediately around Fort Caroline, the French used the Spanish name, Florida, while the entire region from the southern extremit, of Florida to the fiftieth degree, north latitude, they called "New France." The name "Carolina" is not found on any of the early French maps. This name was first applied to the whole region in the charter of 1629 to Sir Robert Heath in honor of Charles I, and was retained in the charter of 1663 in honor of Charles II. Writing in 1666, the Lords Proprietors state that "Carolina is a fair and spacious province on the continent of North America, so called in honor of his sacred majesty that now is, Charles the Second, whom God preserve."

In adopting the proprietary form of government for the new colony, Charles followed the precedents set by Elizabeth in her charter to Raleigh and by Charles I in his charter to Heath. The model was the County Palatine of Durham. This interesting experiment dated back to the reign of William the Conqueror. For the better security of his kingdom against his hostile neighbors on the north, William erected along the Scottish border the great County Palatine of Durham over which he placed an executive upon whom he conferred many of the powers and attributes of sovereignty. The palatine exercised the feudal privileges of escheats, forfeitures, and wardship, and had possession of mines, forests, and chases. Within his palatinate, he was supreme in both civil and military affairs. He erected courts and appointed all justices and judges. Writs and indictments ran in his name just as in other counties they ran in the king's name, and offenses were said to be committed against his peace and dignity just as elsewhere they were against the peace and dignity of the king. He exercised admiralty jurisdiction over his coasts and rivers. He could pardon murders, treason, and other felonies. He had his own mint and coined his own money. He raised, equipped, and directed his military forces. He could incorporate towns and cities. Although the amount of revenue to be paid by the palatinate to the Crown was fixed by Parliament, the palatine and his officers determined how it should be raised and collected. Thus while

the Durham Palatinate was a constituent part of the kingdom, in actual administration it had a distinct machinery of
its own. In order that no great feudal family might be
founded to inherit these viceregal powers, William wisely
conferred them upon the Bishop of Durham.

Such was the model to which Charles II turned when he
came to erect the province of Carolina. In his charter, he
declared that the Lords Proprietors should have, exercise,
and enjoy all their "rights, jurisdictions, privileges, prerogatives, royalties, liberties, immunities, and franchises," "as
amply, fully, and in as ample manner as any Bishop of Durham, in our Kingdom of England." The object of the Lords
Proprietors was to plant colonies within their grant from
which of course they anticipated large financial returns;
their motives were declared to be "a laudable and pious zeal
for the propagation of the Christian faith" and the enlarge-
ment of the king's empire. To enable them to carry out
these objects effectively, "full power and authority" was
given them to create and fill offices; to erect counties and
other political divisions for administrative purposes; to incorporate ports of entry, towns and cities; to establish courts
of justice for the punishment of offenses even to the extent
of "member and life"; to commute punishment and pardon
offenses; to collect customs, fees and taxes levied by the General Assembly; to have the advowsons of churches; to grant
titles of honor provided they were not the same as those in
use in England; to raise and maintain a militia, and to commission officers, build forts, put down and punish rebellion,
declare martial law, and wage war against the Indians or
other enemies by land or by sea. While these extensive powers were granted to the Lords Proprietors, great care was
exercised to preserve the rights and privileges of the people.
Laws were to be enacted "by and with the advice, assent and
approbation of the freemen,   *   *   *   or of their delegates
or deputies" who were to be assembled from time to time for
that purpose. All laws were to be "consonant to reason" and
as near as possible in harmony with the laws of England.
The colonists were to be liege subjects of the English Crown
and were to enjoy all "liberties, franchises, and privileges"
of the king's subjects resident within his realm of England.
They were to have the right to carry on trade and commerce,
and no customs were to be laid upon their goods except such
as were "reasonably assessed   *   *   *   by and with the consent of the free people, or the greater part of them." They
could not be compelled to answer to any suit, or tried for any

Reverse

Obverse

Seal of the Lords Proprietors of Carolina

crime in any place beyond the bounds of the province, but they were allowed an appeal to the Crown. Liberty of conscience was guaranteed.

Though the Lords Proprietors derived from their charter ample powers of government, the uncertainty with which they exercised them resulted in weakness and confusion. Plan after plan was promulgated, ordered to be put into execution, and then abandoned for some new scheme. In 1663 they sent to Sir William Berkeley instructions for the establishment of a government in Albemarle, but two years later this plan gave way to a more elaborate scheme called the Concessions of 1665. The Concessions in their turn were supplanted in 1669 by the Fundamental Constitutions drawn by John Locke under the directions of Shaftesbury, but along with the order to put them into effect came instructions modifying their provisions. Adopted and signed by the Lords Proprietors July 21, 1669, and declared to be unalterable and perpetual, the Fundamental Constitutions speedily ran through four revisions and were finally abandoned altogether. The Lords Proprietors continued this sort of tinkering with their government for some years, with the result that "for the first fifty years of the life of the colony," as Doctor Bassett justly remarks, "the inhabitants could not be sure that their government was stable." [2]

The government of Carolina during the proprietary period presents a theoretical as well as a practical side. The former found expression in the Fundamental Constitutions in which the Lords Proprietors embodied their ideal of a colonial government.[3] Their purposes were to secure a stronger government, to establish their own interests with equality and without confusion, to set up a government in harmony with monarchy, and to "avoid erecting a numerous democracy." For the accomplishment of these aims they devised with endless details an elaborate and complicated scheme of government semi-feudal in character, and an arti-

---

[2] Bassett, John Spencer: The Constitutional Beginnings of North Carolina, p. 35 (*Johns Hopkins University Studies*, 12th Series, No. III).

[3] The Fundamental Constitutions have been so often and so fully analysed and discussed that I do not feel it necessary to present such an analysis here. The reader who wishes fuller information is referred to the following: Bassett. J. S.: The Constitutional Beginnings of North Carolina (*J. H. U. Studies*. 12th Series. No. III); Ashe, S. A.: History of North Carolina. Vol. I, Ch. IX; Davis, Junius: Locke's Fundamental Constitutions (*N. C. Booklet*, Vol. VII, No. 1).

ficial arrangement of society based upon an equally artificial division of land. No pains were taken to fit the constitution to the needs or the interests of the people. To say this, however, is not to condemn the Fundamental Constitutions unreservedly for they contain many liberal and enlightened provisions. Among them are the requirements for the registration of births, marriages, and deaths; the registration of land titles; a biennial parliament; the right of trial by jury; and perfect toleration of all forms of Christian worship. Indeed, to quote Doctor Bassett, "Their reactionary features were hardly worse than their generation, and their liberal features were much better than their time." The Lords Proprietors were fully conscious of the impracticability of putting them into full operation at once and contented themselves, therefore, with instructing Governor Carteret "to come as nigh it" as possible.

The practical side of the constitution is found in the government as it really developed. This of course grew out of the actual needs and experience of the people. The first administration was organized in accordance with the plan set forth in the instructions to Governor Berkeley of 1663. "Full power and ample authority" were conferred upon him to appoint a governor and six "fitting persons" as councillors. The governor and his councillors were authorized to appoint all other officials both civil and military, except the secretary and the surveyor whom the Lords Proprietors themselves were to select; and together with the freeholders, or their representatives, were to form the General Assembly with power to make "good and wholesome laws" for the colony. The instructions also contained specific directions concerning the granting of land.

Two years later the instructions of 1663 were superseded by the Concessions of 1665. In this plan the Lords Proprietors reserved to themselves the selection of the governor, the register, the secretary, and the surveyor-general. With the governor was to be associated a Council composed of any even number from six to twelve to be selected by the governor. The legislative branch of the government, the powers of which were limited only by the veto of the Lords Proprietors, was to be composed of the governor and Council and twelve representatives chosen by the freemen; all were to sit together as a single body. Such courts as were necessary were to be provided by the General Assembly but all judicial officials were to be appointed by the governor. Land was to be granted upon terms which, to say the least, were not illiberal. Personal and property rights were secured by ample guarantees; and special provision was made for securing to the people the right of petition to the Lords Proprietors touching any grievance they might have against any colonial official.

Under this plan, the Lords Proprietors contemplated organizing within their grant several separate and distinct governments, or counties. Each was to have its own administration, but all were to be organized on the same basis. Three only of these counties were actually organized. They were: (1) Albemarle, which embraced the territory lying north of Albemarle Sound; (2) Clarendon, which embraced the region about the mouth of Cape Fear River; and (3) Craven, which embraced the territory south of Cape Romaine. Of these counties, Clarendon was soon abandoned and Craven lay wholly

SEAL OF THE GOVERNMENT OF ALBEMARLE

without the region that subsequently became North Carolina; it developed into the province of South Carolina. Albemarle was the parent settlement of North Carolina and alone of the three concerns us.

As the county of Albemarle expanded into the province of North Carolina, so the constitution of North Carolina as a proprietary was an evolution from the plan of government actually established in Albemarle. At its head were the Lords Proprietors each of whom held one of the eight great offices created by the Fundamental Constitutions, viz: palatine, admiral, chamberlain, chancellor, high constable, chief justice, high steward, and treasurer. Corresponding to each of these offices was to be a court, presided over by the official whose name it bore, with supreme jurisdiction of such matters as fell within the sphere of that official's duties. As the Lords Proprietors remained in England, each was represented in Carolina by a deputy. Their first organization under this plan was effected in October, 1669, when the Duke of Albemarle became

the first palatine. Although the other great offices were also
filled and a show was made of keeping them up, they never
exercised their functions and were nothing more than names.
The palatine, however, who was always the eldest of the Lords
Proprietors, really became an active factor in the government.
He presided over the meetings of the Lords Proprietors and
with three others constituted a quorum; his court, consisting
of himself and the other Lords Proprietors, was the only one
of the eight great courts ever organized and exercised many
important functions; while his deputy, sometimes called the
vice-palatine, was governor of the province.

The governor and his Council were the executive authority
within the colony. It is important to remember that throughout the colonial period, the governor was never the representative of the people, but during the proprietary period he represented the Lords Proprietors, during the royal period, the
king. In all important matters his conduct was determined by
instructions from his superiors, and in any conflict between
them and the people it was his duty to promote the interests
of the former rather than of the latter. He was the medium
through which the Lords Proprietors communicated their
wishes and commands, and he was required to keep them fully
informed about colonial affairs. In most of his important
functions he could act only by and with the advice and consent
of his Council, but as the councillors were generally his crea-
tures this limitation on his power was more apparent than
real. He called and presided over the meetings of the Council.
With the advice and consent of the Council, he issued writs for
the election of delegates to the General Assembly, and he convened, prorogued, or dissolved the Assembly at will. No law
could be passed without his concurrence. He could reprieve
persons convicted of crime pending an appeal to the Lords
Proprietors. Acting with the Council, he appointed subordinate judicial and administrative officials; administered to the
higher officials the proper oaths of office and allegiance; issued
and revoked military commissions; and suspended, or otherwise punished public officials, civil, military, or religious, who
violated their trust. Upon order of the Council, he issued warrants for land grants. All business between his government
and other colonies was conducted through him. He was commander-in-chief of the militia and was charged with the duty
of enforcing the laws, preserving order, and protecting the
colony from domestic and foreign enemies. From time to
time, he exercised numerous minor functions such as receiving the probate of wills, granting letters of administration,

taking the census, and the like. The tenure of office, except in the case of William Drummond who was appointed for three years, was during the pleasure of the Lords Proprietors. Besides certain fees the governor received a salary paid by the Lords Proprietors out of funds arising from quit-rents and the sale of land. During a vacancy in the office, the government was administered by the president of the Council.

The course of the development of the province may be traced in the wording of the commissions of the Lords Proprietors to their governors. In 1664 Sir John Yeamans was commissioned "Governor of our county of Clarendon" and William Drummond was appointed to the "Government of the County of Albemarle." Both of these counties, or governments, were within the territorial limits of what is now North Carolina. Although the settlement within Clarendon County was soon abandoned, the Lords Proprietors adhered for several years to their original plan of erecting a number of separate and distinct governments within their province. With the exception of Thomas Eastchurch, the first five successors of Drummond were governors of Albemarle only. The case of Eastchurch is particularly interesting on this point. Two commissions bearing the same date were issued to him, one as "governor and Commander in Cheife of that part of our Province called Albemarle," the other as "Governor and Commander in Cheife of all such settlements as shall be made upon the Rivers of Pamleco and Newse." At that time, 1676, it was the purpose of the Lords Proprietors to erect the region between Albemarle Sound and Cape Fear River into a government separate and distinct from Albemarle. The last "Governor of our County of Albemarle" was Seth Sothel whose commission was issued in 1679. Two years later appears the first indication of a change in the policy of the Lords Proprietors. In 1681 Henry Wilkinson was appointed "Governor of that part of the Province of Carolina that lyes 5 miles south of the River of Pamlico and from thence to Virginia." But Wilkinson never came to North Carolina and the government was administered by Sothel until 1689.[4]

In the meantime it had become customary to refer to that part of the "Province of Carolina" north of Cape Fear River as North Carolina, that to the south, as South Carolina. The effect of this natural division on the policy of the Lords Proprietors is seen in the commission of Phillip Ludwell, 1689, who was "appointed to be Governor of that part of Carolina

---

[4] Andrews, Charles MacLean: "Captain Henry Wilkinson" (*South Atlantic Quarterly*, XV-3).

that lyes North and East of Cape Feare." Two years later
the Lords Proprietors, again changing their policy, determined to have but one administration which should embrace
the whole of Carolina. Accordingly in 1691 they commissioned Ludwell "Governor and Commander in Cheif of Carolina," but fearing that this arrangement might prove impracticable, they authorized him to appoint a "Deputy Governor
of North Carolina." Ludwell's successor, John Archdale,
was commissioned in 1694 "Governor of our whole Province
of Carolina," with authority "to constitute a Deputy or Deputy Governors both in South & North Carolina." The Lords
Proprietors adhered to this policy until 1712, conferring like
authority upon each of their governors during those years.
As the governors resided at Charleston, they chose to administer the affairs of South Carolina in person, and those of
North Carolina through deputies. This fact had important results in the history of North Carolina. It tended to
diminish the dignity and influence of the executive branch of
the proprietary government and correspondingly to increase
the influence and authority of the legislative branch. The result was detrimental to the interests of the Lords Proprietors
and favorable to the development of democratic ideals. Accordingly, in 1710, the Lords Proprietors resolved to abandon
the experiment and to appoint a governor of North Carolina
"independent of the governor of South Carolina" who should
be their immediate representative and responsible immediately to them. This decision was carried into effect in 1712
when Edward Hyde was commissioned "to be Govr Capt Gen^{ll}
Adm^{ll} Command^r in Cheife of that part of ye province of Carolina that lyes N^o & E^t of Cape ffeare Called N^o Carolina."
Hyde's appointment marks the final separation in the government of the two provinces, and thenceforward the governors of North Carolina were again selected by the Lords Proprietors and held office at their pleasure.

The governor was assisted in the administration by a Council. The organization of the Council, and the method of selecting its members, varied with the varying moods of the
Lords Proprietors. In 1663 they directed Governor Berkeley
to select a Council of six. Two years later they fixed its membership at any even number from six to twelve, inclusive, to
be determined by the governor. In 1670, probably with the
idea of making the Council more representative of the varied
colonial interests, they changed the number to ten, five of
whom were to be their own deputies selected by themselves

and five to be selected by the General Assembly. This plan was continued until 1691 when, the Council having become an upper house of the General Assembly, the Lords Proprietors instructed the governor to consider the deputies alone as members. At the same time it was determined that each of the Lords Proprietors should be represented in the province by a deputy. Finally in 1724 the deputies were abolished and the Council was organized with twelve members selected by the Lords Proprietors. The functions of the Council were two-fold, executive and legislative. Together with the governor it composed the executive branch of the government and was charged with many important duties; independently of the governor its executive functions were inconsiderable. Upon the death or absence of the governor, the Council chose a president who administered the government until the vacancy was filled.

The Council also formed part of the legislative branch of the government. Prior to 1691, the legislature, usually called the General Assembly but sometimes referred to as the Grand Assembly, was composed of the governor, the councillors, and the delegates of the people sitting together as one body. After that date the Council became an upper house, and the delegates a lower house called the House of Commons. This development was the result not of design but of custom, and came about in a thoroughly characteristic English way. As acts of the Assembly were not valid until signed by the governor and three deputies, it became the custom of the governor and deputies to meet independently of the Assembly to consider such measures as the Assembly presented for their signatures. Thus the deputies, probably feeling that it was unnecessary for them to pass twice on the same matters, gradually dropped out of the larger body and after a while came to be thought of as a separate and distinct legislative chamber. The Lords Proprietors formally recognized them as such in 1691. At the same time the five councillors elected by the Assembly were dropped from the Council leaving that body composed of the deputies only.

Though not so intended these changes were favorable to the development of democratic institutions. In the first place they removed from the midst of the people's representatives the restraining influence of a body of legislators entirely irresponsible to the people and representing interests distinct from the people's interests and not infrequently hostile to them. But it also brought about a change of even greater importance. The Lords Proprietors had lodged with the governor and Council the power of making laws "by and with the advice and consent" of the people, or their representatives. Thus the representatives of the proprietary interests, not the representatives of the people, enjoyed the right of initiating legislation, and the latter could consider no measures except such as were presented to them by the former. The popular party naturally grew restive under this restriction and early began to demand the "power of proposeing in the parliam[en]t without passing the Grand Councell first." After the withdrawal of the governor and deputies, and the organization of the representatives of the people into a separate and distinct house, it was not possible to deny to the latter one of the most important rights appertaining to a legislative body. Thus the House of Commons became in a real sense a representative democratic institution.

In 1663, the Lords Proprietors instructed Governor Berkeley to organize a government in their province and to give to the "Governor or Governors and Councill or Councillors power by and with the advice and consent of the freeholders or freemen or the Major parte óf them there deputyes or delligates to make good and wholesome laws" for the colony. This was the authority under which met the first law-making body in the history of North Carolina. It seems to have been an example of pure democracy; to it came not the representatives of the people, but the people themselves. Representative government was introduced by the Concessions of 1665 in which the people were instructed to elect representatives to the General Assembly. The number of delegates, who were to be chosen on the first day of January of each year, was fixed at twelve. In 1670, Albemarle County was divided into four precincts—Chowan, Pasquotank, Perquimans, and Currituck— each to be represented in the General Assembly by five delegates. Later as other precincts were erected and given the right to send to the Assembly two delegates each, the number increased until it reached twenty-eight—the highest number reached under the proprietary government. Regular sessions were held biennially, but the governor and Council could convene, prorogue, or dissolve sessions at will. As long as the Assembly sat as a single chamber, the governor, or his deputy, had the right to preside; after the separation into two houses, each house elected its own officers. The speaker of the House of Commons was the highest official in the province in whose selection the people had any voice either directly or indirectly. Usually, therefore, the place was filled by the leader of the popular party. The House of Commons had the right to decide contests involving the election of its members, to expel members, to compel attendance upon its sessions, and to initiate all measures levying a tax or carrying an appropriation. It was fully conscious of its responsibilities and obligations as the popular branch of the colonial government, keenly jealous of its rights and privileges, and quick to resent any encroachment by any other branch of the government. Through a process of evolution the General Assembly, from a position of weakness and subservience to the executive, came to be the chief factor in the government, while the House of Commons, as the only branch of the colonial government in which the people were represented, acquired such an ascendency as to become practically the Assembly.

The judicial system under the proprietary government embraced a general court, precinct courts, a court of chancery, an admiralty court, and in some instances the Council. For several years after the settlement of the colony, the only court was composed of the governor and Council. With the erection of precincts and the creation of precinct courts for local business, the older tribunal became known as the General Court. In addition to its other business it was the appellate court of the colony. In 1685 the Lords Proprietors determined to take the business of this tribunal out of the hands of the governor and Council. They accordingly instructed the governor to appoint "four able, discreet men" as justices who, together with a sheriff, should hold this court. Several years passed, however, before this order was carried into effect; the governor and Council were holding the General Court as late as 1695, but sometime between that date and 1702 the court was organized as the Proprietors had directed. In 1712 another forward step in its organization was taken when a chief justice was appointed who held his commission directly from the Lords Proprietors. He presided over the court which was thereafter composed of a variable number of associates. A curious custom which prevailed during the early years of the court permitted justices temporarily to discard their judicial character and to come down from the bench to represent clients before the court. Subsequently this practice was forbidden by law. The court met three times a year and sat at different times as a court of king's bench, common pleas, and exchequer and as a court of oyer and terminer, and general gaol delivery. Indictments were brought "in the name of our Sovereign Lord the King" who was represented by an attorney-general. The court also exercised certain non-judicial functions such as directing the repair of

roads, the appointment of ferrymen, the regulation of fares
at ferries, and, by direction of the General Assembly, the
apportionment of taxes and the ordering of the payment of
the public indebtedness. Its chief executive officer was the
sheriff or provost marshal. Precinct courts were held by
justices of the peace who were appointed by the governor
and Council. Their jurisdiction extended to civil suits involving less than fifty pounds. They also exercised such non-
judicial duties as caring for the public highways, creating road
districts, appointing constables, granting franchises for mill
sites, and other similar local matters. With their clerks were
recorded, usually in open court, the marks by which settlers
distinguished their cattle, horses, and hogs. The governor
and Council held the chancery court; they also probated wills,
received and examined accounts of administrators and executors, tried public officials for misconduct in office, and heard appeals from the General Court. The Admiralty Court was composed of a judge and subordinate officials who were appointed
by the Admiralty Court in England to whom they were obliged
to report.

CHAPTER IV

WARS AND REBELLIONS

The history of Albemarle as a distinct colony was marked by discontent, tumult, and rebellion. Grievances were real and numerous. The uncertainty as to the terms on which the settlers held their lands; the studied indifference and neglect of the Lords Proprietors; the persistent rumor that Albemarle was to be given over to Sir William Berkeley as sole proprietor; the instability of the proprietary government; the depredations of hostile Indians; the attempts to enforce the navigation acts and to collect the king's customs,—all these things combined to produce dissatisfaction and strife.

Perhaps nothing gave the people more concern than the land question. Ambition to become landowners, as has been stated, was the inducement that had brought most of them to Albemarle. Land was their chief form of wealth and whatever tended to render their holdings insecure produced alarm and unrest. The terms on which they were to hold their lands, the people thought had been determined by the Great Deed of Grant, a document which they held to be "as firm a Grant as the Proprietors own Charter from the Crown." Such was the importance attached to it that the Assembly ordered it to be recorded not only in the office of the secretary of the colony, but also in every precinct in Albemarle, and appointed a special custodian into whose keeping the original itself was committed. This view, however, was not shared by the Lords Proprietors; they held the Great Deed to be a revokable grant which they could annul at will, and from time to time they issued instructions to their governors inconsistent with its provisions. Although the Great Deed fixed quit rents at a farthing per acre, in 1670 the Lords Proprietors instructed Governor Carteret to collect quit rents at the rate of "one halfe penny of lawful English money" per acre; and in 1679, they directed Governor Harvey to fix the amount at a penny. Moreover, the Fundamental Constitutions provided that quit rents for each acre in Carolina should be "as much fine silver" as was in one English penny. It was these frequent changes, doubtless, that gave rise to a rumor, which created widespread apprehension in Albemarle, that the Lords Proprietors "intended to raise the Quitrents to two pence and from two pence to six pence per acre." The people too began to ask whether the Fundamental Constitutions repealed the Great Deed. Apprehension that they might be so interpreted aroused opposition to the Fundamental Constitutions, and some of those who subscribed that document felt it necessary to protest that in so doing they should "not be disanulled" of the rights they enjoyed under the Great Deed. The Lords Proprietors, who could find no record of the Great Deed in their London office, were disposed to deny its existence altogether; but the Albemarle Assembly promptly ordered a certified copy of the original to be sent to them "which convinced the Prop^{rs} that it was a firm Grant and they let the dispute drop." To make matters worse, by still further increasing the feeling of insecurity, as late as 1678 the Albemarle planters had never received from the Lords Proprietors any patents for their holdings. Timothy Biggs writing to them declared that the fact that the "the people have no assurance of their Lands (for that yet never any Patents have been granted under your Lordships to the Inhabitants) is matter of great discouragement for men of Estate to come amongst us because those already seated there have no assurance of their enjoyment."

This strange oversight probably arose from the indifference which the Lords Proprietors felt toward Albemarle. They had been keenly disappointed at the slow growth of the colony. That the settlers had not quickly pushed across Albemarle Sound, cleared plantations on the Pamlico and the Neuse, and opened communications by land with the Ashley River colony, appeared to them to be evidence of a slothfulness of disposition and disregard of their interests that augured ill for the success of the colony, or for its value to them. This, they frankly declared to the Albemarle Assembly, "has bine the Cause that hitherto we have had noe more Reguard for you as lookinge upon you as a people that neither understood your own nor regarded our Interests." Having spent no money on Albemarle, they considered that they lost nothing by leaving that colony to shift for itself while they devoted their attention and resources to the development of the more promising settlement on Ashley River.

To Albemarle, struggling bravely against the forces of nature and the savages of the wilderness, this studied neglect was in itself a grievance, and prominent colonial leaders protested against the injustice of it. Thomas Eastchurch, speaker of the Assembly, informed the Lords Proprietors that enterprising settlers had made several attempts to carry out their wishes, but each time had been frustrated by the Proprietors' own agents who did not want their trade with the Indians disturbed by further settlements among them; and Timothy Biggs, deputy-collector, made bold to tell them that "notwithstanding you have not bene out as yet any thing upon that County in yᵉ Province called Albemarle yet yᵉ Inhabitants have lived and gott Estates under yᵉ Lordᵖˢ there by their owne Industry and brought it to the capacity of a hopefull Settlement and ere these had it had your Lordᵖˢ smiles and assistance but a tenth part of what your Southern parts have had It would have beene a Flourishing Settlement." The Lords Proprietors were convinced of their error and in a frank and generous letter to the Assembly unreservedly confessed the injustice they had done the colony.

At the same time, the Lords Proprietors laid to rest the rumor that they were planning to turn Albemarle over to Sir William Berkeley. Color had evidently been given to this report by their neglect of Albemarle coupled with their great industry in promoting their Ashley River colony. The people of Albemarle would probably have objected to being subjected to any single proprietor; when that proprietor was to be Sir William Berkeley, who was at that very time giving an indication of his true character by his dealings with Bacon's Rebellion, their objection would unquestionably have taken the form of forcible opposition had it become necessary. That they were greatly disturbed by the rumor is certain; the Assembly adopted a remonstrance against the project and dispatched it to England by a special messenger. In this matter, if in no other, the Lords Proprietors were able to give their people complete satisfaction. In the first place, they said, it was their purpose to maintain and preserve the people of their colony in all their "English Rights and Liberties"; in the second place, Albemarle was valuable to them in the development of the rest of their province; for these reasons, they assured the Assembly, "wee neither have nor ever will parte with the County of Albemarle to any person whatsoever But will alwayse maintaine our province of Carolina entire as itt is."

Much of the trouble in Albemarle would never have arisen had the Lords Proprietors been able to establish and maintain a strong, stable government, and to place properly qualified men in charge of it. Their failure to establish such a government has already been discussed. As it was, many of the defects in the system could have been greatly minimized had it been administered by men of prudence, ability, and character. But such men were rare. The Lords Proprietors themselves complained that it was "a very difficult matter to gitt a man of worth and trust" to accept the office of governor, and they were generally unfortunate in the men who represented them in that capacity. Some were weak, others ambitious, covetous, and unscrupulous. Constant strife and tumult marked the administrations of Carteret, Jenkins, Miller, Eastchurch, and Sothel. Carteret growing tired of his thankless task abandoned the colony leaving "yᵉ Governmᵗ there in ill order & worse hands." Jenkins was deposed from office by a dominant faction in the General Assembly. Miller after a brief career of misgovernment and crime was overthrown by armed rebels and forced to flee the country. The same rebels met Eastchurch at the Virginia boundary and although he bore a commission from the Lords Proprietors, forbade his entering Albemarle to assume his office. And Sothel, whose career of crime and tyranny was rivaled only by that of Miller, was like Miller driven from power and banished the province. Some of these uprisings were inspired by the righteous indignation of the people against tyranny and oppression; others had no higher origin than personal animosities and factional rivalries. But whatever their inspiration they were all the results of a political system that was too weak and unstable to command either respect or fear.

From such a government the settlers could expect no protection against hostile Indians. Fortunately there was no powerful tribe to contest the possession of the Albemarle region with the whites. There were, however, small tribes who committed many depredations on the settlements and twice in the history of Albemarle made war on them. In 1666 an outbreak of hostilities imperilled the life of the infant settlement, but peace was restored before any great losses were sustained. Nine years later a more serious war broke out with the Chowanoc Indians. When first known to the whites, in 1584-85, these Indians, then the leading tribe in that region, occupied the territory on both sides of the Meherrin

and Nottoway rivers about where they come together to form
the Chowan. Although their number had greatly dwindled
during the century that followed, they were still formidable
when white men first began to erect their cabins along the
Chowan. At first they offered no opposition to the coming of
the whites, and after the creation of the proprietary entered
into a treaty by which they "submitted themselves to the
Crown of England under the dominion of the Lords Proprietors." This treaty they faithfully observed until 1675. In
the summer of that year the hostile tribes in Virginia, who
were endeavoring to stir up a general Indian war against
the whites, sent emissaries to induce the Chowanocs to go on
the warpath. The Chowanocs were easily persuaded and
without warning struck swiftly and effectively in the usual
Indian fashion. William Edmundson, the Quaker preacher,
writing of his visit to North Carolina in 1676, referring to
the beginning of this Indian outbreak, says: "I was moved of
the Lord to go to Carolina, and it was perillous travelling,
for the Indians were not yet subdued, but did mischief and
murdered several. They haunted much in the wilderness between Virginia and Carolina, so that scarce any durst travel
that way unarmed. Friends endeavored to dissuade me from
going, telling of several who were murdered."

The settlers flew to arms, and for more than a year waged
"open war" upon their enemies. Both sides suffered heavy
losses. In the midst of the struggle the whites received timely
aid from Captain Zachariah Gillam, a well-known New England trader, who arrived in Albemarle from London in his
armed vessel, the Carolina, with a supply of arms and ammunition. Thus strengthened they pushed the war more vigorously than ever and finally, as the Council said, "by Gods assistance though not without the loss of many men," they
"wholly subdued" their formidable foes and drove them from
their lands on the Meherrin which were thereupon "resigned
into the immediate possession of the Lords Proprietors of
Carolina as of their province of Carolina."

Returning from the war against the Indians, the people
under the leadership of George Durant, took advantage of
their being organized and under arms to demand from the
colonial authorities redress of certain grievances growing out
of the enforcement of the navigation acts. This was the beginning of that popular uprising which historians have incor-

rectly called Culpepper's Rebellion. It was occasioned by England's commercial policy. Other causes doubtless accentuated the trouble, but the primary cause was the Navigation Act—"that mischievous statute with which the mother country was busily weaning from itself the affections of its colonies all along the American seaboard." [1] The purpose of the Navigation Act "was to foster the development of national strength by an increase of sea power and commerce." As it affected the colonies, it restricted their carrying trade to vessels of English, Irish, and colonial ownership and forbade the shipment of certain articles, including tobacco, elsewhere than to England, Ireland, or some English colony. Experience soon showed, from the British merchant's point of view, that the statute contained one serious defect. It permitted tobacco, which was subject to a heavy duty when imported into England, to be shipped from one colony to another free of duty. Thus the colonial consumer enjoyed a decided advantage over the British consumer. Moreover—and this is where the rub came—when the colonial merchant, evading the Navigation Act, re-shipped to foreign countries tobacco on which he had paid no duty, he was able to undersell his British competitor who was compelled to add to the price which he charged the foreigner the import tax which he himself had paid to the Crown. The Navigation Act was so imperfectly enforced in the colonies, that this competition became a matter of serious concern to British merchants who finally complained to Parliament about it. In 1673, therefore, Parliament came to their relief by passing an act which levied export duties on certain articles when shipped from one colony to another. On tobacco this duty was fixed at a penny a pound which was to be collected by officials of the Crown.

The passage of this act, which was approved by the Lords Proprietors, alarmed the Albemarle planters. Tobacco was their chief article of export; New England was their principal market. Of their yearly crop, amounting to more than a million pounds, but little found its way, or could find its way directly to England. Poor harbors and shifting sands made the navigation of the Carolina waters too difficult and dangerous for large vessels engaged in trans-Atlantic trade, but the lighter draft coastwise ships of the New England traders were not seriously hindered by these obstacles. The trade of Albemarle accordingly was largely controlled by a few enterprising and not overly scrupulous New England skippers. That

---

[1] Fiske: Old Virginia and Her Neighbours, Vol. II, p. 280.

this was economically bad for Albemarle, the Lords Proprietors understood better than the planters, "itt beinge," they
said, "a certaine Beggery to our people of Albemarle if they
shall buy goods at 2ᵈ hand and soe much dearer than they
may bee supply'd from England and with all sell there Tobacco and other Commodities at a lower rate then they could do
in England." What the Lords Proprietors did not understand was that Nature, not man, had determined the course
of the trade of Albemarle. For instance, in 1676, they directed the governor, "in order to the Incourageinge a Trade
with England," to send them an exact account of the depth
of water in the several inlets and at places where ships could
load and unload "for this has bine soe concealed and uncer-
tainely reported here as if some persons amongst you had
joyn'd with some of New England to engross that poore trade
you have and Keepe you still under hatches." It was, then,
with the expectation that the Navigation Act would destroy
this New England monopoly of the Albemarle trade and build
up a direct trade between Albemarle and the mother country,
that the Lords Proprietors gave it such hearty support. Our
historians generally have condemned their policy because they
have misunderstood the purpose of the Navigation Act. Had
its purpose, and its only result, been "to secure more funds
for the deplenished purse of a needy sovereign," [2] it would
have received scant sympathy from the Lords Proprietors; it
was not to their interest to impoverish their colony for the
benefit of the Crown. But the real purpose of the act was
not to produce a revenue; it was to establish direct trade relations between the colonies and the mother country, and the
Lords Proprietors understood clearly enough the advantages
their colony would derive from such relations. It was the
hope of securing these advantages for their colony, and not
the desire of collecting a revenue for the Crown, that inspired
them to take so much interest in enforcing the act of 1673, as,
on the other hand, it was the fear of this result that moved the
New England traders, and those Albemarle planters who were
associated with them, to offer such a vigorous opposition.

In following the course of this opposition, which finally
broke out in open rebellion, we are led into the obscure mazes
of colonial politics from which it is difficult at times to extricate ourselves with certainty. To a large extent the revolt
against the enforcement of the Navigation Act was but the

---

[2] Ashe: History of North Carolina, Vol. I, p. 113.

continuation of a factional strife that had long been waging
in Albemarle. In 1673, two parties were contending for supremacy. One led by Thomas Eastchurch controlled the lower
house of the General Assembly of which Eastchurch was
speaker. Closely allied with him were Timothy Biggs, deputy of the Earl of Craven, and Thomas Miller whose tyranny
was the occasion for the outbreak. Of the other party, though
John Jenkins, acting governor, was nominally the leader, the
real head and front was George Durant who completely dominated the governor. "Of all the factious persons in the
Country," declared his opponents, "he was the most active
and uncontrollable." Prominent among those who acknowledged his leadership, besides Jenkins, were Valentine Byrd
who, it was said, "drew the first sword" in the revolt, and
John Culpepper, who, declared his enemies (and he had many
of them), was "never in his element but whilst fishing in
troubled waters," and who gave his name to the rebellion of
1677. The contest between these two factions had already
reached a point of great bitterness when it became intensified
by the issues arising out of the efforts to enforce the act of
1673.

In 1675, commissions naming a surveyor and a collector
of customs were sent to Governor Jenkins, accompanied by
instructions that if the men named were not in the colony he
should appoint others in their stead. In these orders the
New England skippers trading in Albemarle read the ruin of
their business and promptly set on foot a report that, if the
duties were collected, they would be compelled to double the
price of their wares; "Upon wch the people were very mutinous and reviled & threatened ye Members of the Councell that
were for setleing ye s^{d} duty." George Durant and his followers, whose interests lay in maintaining commercial relations
with the New England men, supported their cause. As neither
the surveyor nor the collector named in the commissions of
1675 was in the province, it became the duty of Governor Jenkins to fill the vacancies. Accordingly he appointed Timothy
Biggs surveyor and Valentine Byrd collector. The selection
of Biggs was a blind, the selection of Byrd a fraud. The surveyor had nothing to do with the enforcement of the customs
act. Control of that office, therefore, was of less importance
than control of the collectorship, and the Durant party willingly relinquished it to Biggs, a partisan of the Eastchurch
faction, whose selection gave an appearance of good faith
to the whole transaction. The selection of Byrd as collector,

on the other hand, placed the enforcement of the act in the hands of the party that was interested in nullifying it. Byrd fully met the expectation of his friends; he reduced the whole thing to a farce by deliberately closing his eyes to violations of the law, permitting many hogsheads of tobacco to leave the wharves of Albemarle planters marked as ''bait for the New England fishermen.''

In the meantime the affairs of Albemarle were going from bad to worse. Factional feuds grew more and more bitter, and each party when in power carried things with a high hand. Conspiring with John Culpepper, Jenkins attempted to use his official power to destroy their personal enemy, Thomas Miller, whom he had arrested and thrown into prison; while John Willoughby, a justice of the General Court and an adherent of the Durant faction, arrogantly asserting that his ''court was the court of courts and the jury of juries,'' peremptorily denied to Thomas Eastchurch the right of appeal from his decision to the Lords Proprietors. The Assembly party in turn, under the leadership of Eastchurch, were quite as arbitrary. Accusing Jenkins of ''several misdemeanors,'' they deposed him from office, without any pretence of legal right, and threw him into prison. Hastening to justify their action, they drew up a statement of their proceedings and dispatched it, together with a petition for redress of grievances, to the Lords Proprietors by Miller who, at the command of Sir William Berkeley, had been acquitted of the charges against him and released. Miller arrived in England in the summer of 1676 where he met Eastchurch who had gone thither to seek redress of his own grievances.

The Lords Proprietors, greatly perplexed over the situation in their colony, and sincerely desirous of promoting its interests, conferred freely with Eastchurch and Miller. Both impressed them favorably. Eastchurch seemed to be not only ''a gentleman of a very good family,'' but also ''a very discreet and worthy man,'' and much concerned for the ''prosperity and wellfaire'' of Albemarle. As he was speaker of the Assembly, and Miller the bearer of important dispatches from the Assembly, the Lords Proprietors naturally looked upon them as representatives of the people and argued that if anybody could straighten out the tangled affairs of Albemarle, Eastchurch and Miller were the men. Accordingly they appointed Eastchurch governor and procured the appointment of Miller as collector feeling confident that both appointments would be acceptable to the people of Albemarle and taken as evidence of their solicitude for their colony.

Eastchurch and Miller sailed for Carolina in the summer of 1677. Coming by way of the West Indies, their ship touched at the island of Nevis where Eastchurch "lighting upon a woman y^t was a considerable fortune took hold of the oppertunity [and] marryed her," and sent Miller on to Albemarle with a commission as president of the Council to "settle affayres against his coming." Although Eastchurch exceeded his authority in appointing Miller president of the Council, nevertheless Miller was quietly received by the people who submitted without question to his authority both as collector and as acting-governor. As collector he discharged his duties with zeal, demanding an accounting from Byrd, his predecessor, appointing deputies, among them Timothy Biggs, and ma^{k}ing "a very considerable progress" in collecting the king's customs. By his own statement, his collections amounted to "the value of above £8,000 sterling." But as governor, Miller showed himself totally unfit to exercise the power and responsibility with which he had been entrusted. His enemies, omitting "many hainous matters," charged him with corruption, vindictiveness, and tyranny; and the Lords Proprietors were compelled to admit that he "did many extravagant things, making strange limitations for ye choyce of ye Parliam^t gitting pow^r in his hands of laying fynes, wch tis to be feared he neither did nor meant to use moderately sending out strange warrants to bring some of ye most considerable men of ye Country alive or dead before him, setting a sume of money upon their heads." To support his tyranny, he organized and armed a band of his partisans upon pretense of their being for defence against the Indians; and by this "pipeing guard," as it was called, not only kept the people in terror but also imposed a heavy debt on the already bankrupt colony. Consequently, wrote the Lords Proprietors, Miller soon "lost his reputation & interest amongst ye people."

By the beginning of winter the people were in a rebellious frame of mind, and only an overt act and a leader were needed to produce an explosion. Both came soon enough. On December 1, 1677, the Carolina, "a very pretty vessell of some force," Captain Zachariah Gillam in command, arrived from England and cast anchor in Pasquotank River. Gillam had scarcely stepped ashore when Miller arrested him on a charge of having violated the Navigation Act and held him to bail in £1,000 sterling. Here was the overt act; and Gillam shrewdly took advantage of it. He threatened to weigh anchor and carry his cargo out of the country, but the people, aroused to action by the prospect of losing such an opportunity for trade, beset him with entreaties to stay, pledging their support against the governor. The leader too was at hand, for on board the Carolina, returning from London, was George Durant. While in London, Durant had heard with astonishment of the appointment of his enemy, Eastchurch, as governor and had boldly "declared to some of ye Prop^{rs} that Eastchurch should not be Governo^r & threatened to revolt." News of his threat had probably preceded him to Albemarle; at any rate, in his presence Miller scented danger and determined to forestall it. At midnight of the day of Durant's arrival, Miller forced his way into the cabin of the Carolina, armed "with a brace of pistolls," and "presenting one of them cockt to M^r. Geo. Durants breast & wth his other hand arrested him as a Traytour."

The assault on Durant was the signal for revolt. Byrd, Culpepper, and other leaders hastened aboard the Carolina where, in conference with Durant, they planned to overthrow Miller and seize the government. About forty "Pasquotankians," armed by Gillam from the Carolina, rallied to their support and surrounding Miller's house, made him a prisoner, seized the tobacco he had collected on the king's account, and took possession of the public records. They then dispatched armed parties throughout the colony to arrest other officials, among whom was Deputy-Collector Biggs, and issued a "Remonstrance," or an appeal for support to "all the Rest of the County of Albemarle." They had arrested Miller and seized the public records, they declared, "that thereby the Countrey may have a free parlem^t & that from them their aggrievances may be sent home to the Lords"; and they urged the people to choose representatives to an Assembly which should meet at once at Durant's house. To Durant's plantation, therefore, the victorious rebels with their prisoners proceeded by water, and as the little flotilla which bore them to the place of rendezvous dropped down the Pasquotank River, the Carolina, lying at anchor off Crawford's wharf, exultantly flung her flags and pennons to the breeze and fired a triumphant salvo from her great guns.

The appeal of the rebels to the people met with a ready response, and from all parts of Albemarle armed men flocked to Durant's plantation. Among Miller's effects the rebels had found the Great Seal of the province, the use of which gave color of authority to their acts, and while Gillam kept the crowd in a good humor by a free distribution of rum and whiskey which he had brought from the Carolina, Durant and other leaders proceeded to organize a government. First of all, the Assembly consisting of eighteen delegates chosen by the people, met and elected five of their members who, together with Richard Foster, who alone of the Lords Proprietors' deputies had adhered to the rebels, were to form the Council. Before this Council Miller and the other prisoners were brought for trial. In all their proceedings, the rebels scrupulously observed the usual legal forms. Culpepper was appointed clerk, Durant attorney-general, a grand jury was summoned, indictments were presented and true bills returned with due formality. They were proceeding to impanel a petit jury when a bomb was suddenly thrown into their camp. This was nothing less than a message from Eastchurch who, with his bride, had arrived in Virginia and learning of the situation in Albemarle, had sent his proclamation which, as Miller feelingly said, came "at ye very nicke of tyme," commanding the rebels to disperse and abandon their illegal proceedings. This sudden turn of affairs presented a serious question to the rebels. Whatever justification they may have had for revolt against Miller, they could not charge Eastchurch with tyranny and oppression, nor could they deny his legal title and authority as governor, for he bore a commission from the Lords Proprietors. Nevertheless, resolved to carry their revolt through to a successful issue, they hastily "clapt Miller in irons," declared that if Eastchurch attempted to come to Albemarle "they would serve him ye same sauce," and sent an armed force to the Virginia border to prevent his entering the province. Eastchurch appealed to the governor of Virginia for military aid which was readily promised him, but his sudden death before assistance could be given removed all danger to the Albemarle rebels from that quarter.

Now that the rebels had a free hand, prudence characterized their conduct. They dropt the proceedings against Miller and the other deposed officials; convened a free Assembly, organized courts, and conducted the government "by their owne authority & according to their owne modell." To secure funds for the support of the government, the Assembly appointed Culpepper collector and instructed him to take possession of the revenues which Miller had collected. The colony had quieted down and everything was running smoothly when

the escape of Timothy Biggs and his flight to England, brought
sharply to the attention of the rebels the necessity of having
their case properly presented to the Lords Proprietors. The
Assembly, therefore, commissioned Culpepper to go to England to assure the Lords Proprietors of their allegiance, but
at the same time to "insist very highly for right against Miller." They denied the authority neither of the Proprietors
nor of the Crown, and did not regard their conduct as rebellion. The Lords Proprietors, for reasons to be explained,
were willing to accept this view, and Culpepper was on the
point of returning to Albemarle in triumph, when the situation took a sudden and more serious turn.

Miller having escaped from prison had hastened to London and laid his case before the king in Council. Inasmuch
as Miller in his capacity as collector, was a crown official, his
arrest and removal from office, the appointment of Culpepper
in his stead, and the seizure of the customs, were offences
against the royal authority which the crown officials were not
willing to overlook. The Privy Council accordingly ordered
that Culpepper be held without bail in England pending a full
investigation of the affair; and directed the Lords Proprietors to present a complete account of the rebellion in Albemarle together "with an authentick Copy of their Charter."
Apprehensive that this might mean a suit to void their charter for failure to maintain an orderly government in their
colony, the Lords Proprietors were anxious to minimize the
rebellion as much as possible. Accordingly, though compelled
to admit the fact of rebellion, they enlarged upon the crimes
of Miller and his lack of authority to administer the government. They could not, however, gloss over the resistance to
the king's collector, and the seizure of the king's revenues,
for Culpepper acknowledged the facts and threw himself
upon the mercy of the king. But the commissioners of customs urged "that no favor may be shewed him unless he
make or procure satisfaction for the Customs seized and
embeseled by him," and recommended that he be arrested and
brought to trial for embezzlement and treason. Thereupon
the Lords Proprietors came to his rescue on the first charge,
by agreeing "to procure by their authority and influence in
Carolina" a satisfactory settlement of the debt; and Shaftesbury, undoubtedly with the sanction of his associates, successfully defended him against the charge of treason on the
plea that at the time of the rebellion there was no legal government in Albemarle.

On the whole, the Lords Proprietors met this crisis in their affairs wisely. Amid the clamor of contending factions, they found it impossible to discriminate between truth and falsehood, to distinguish the innocent from the guilty, to pronounce judgment with impartial justice; and as they were much more eager to restore peace and the reign of law in their province than they were to punish those who had disturbed its repose, they declined to follow the advice of Biggs and Miller who urged them to employ force in suppressing the rebellion; and they found an excuse if not a justification for the conduct of the rebels not only in the crimes and tyranny of Miller, but also in the fact that he had attempted to act as governor "without any legall authority." Considering the disorders in Albemarle the result of factions, they were desirous of finding a governor who was not a partisan of either side, and who possessed the character and position to command the respect of both. Such a man they thought they had in Seth Sothel who had recently became a Lord Proprietor by the purchase of Clarendon's interest. His associates thought him "a sober, moderate man," "no way concerned in the factions and animosityes" of Albemarle, and possessed of the ability to "settle all things well" in their turbulent colony; and as he was willing to undertake the task, they appointed him governor and at the same time procured his appointment as collector. But on his way to Carolina, Sothel was captured and held to ransom by Algerian pirates.

Pending Sothel's release, the Lords Proprietors commissioned John Harvey governor and the commissioners of the customs appointed Robert Holden collector. Both were satisfactory to the people of Albemarle who "Quyetly and cherefully obeyed" them. After a brief official life, Harvey died in office, and the Council selected John Jenkins as his successor. In this selection the Lords Proprietors acquiesced. It was a clear victory for the Durant party, now completely in the ascendancy. "Although Jenkins had the title [of governor]" the other faction truthfully asserted, "yet in fact Durant governed and used Jenkins but as his property." It was fortunate for the colony that this was so. The Durant party was the only group in the colony strong enough to administer a government successfully and to assure order, and George Durant, its leader, possessed many of the qualities of statesmanship. Under his leadership, order was restored, the laws were enforced, the king's customs were collected "without any disturbance from the people," a tax was levied on the colony to refund the revenues seized and used by the rebels "in the tyme of the disorders"; and the Assembly passed an act of oblivion covering offenses committed during the rebellion. Miller, Biggs, and their followers complained bitterly of the conduct of the government and endeavored to stir up resistance to it, but the people had had enough of strife, and the Lords Proprietors were wearied with factious complaints. They stood squarely behind the constituted authorities in their colony, with the result that in November, 1680, they were able to report that in Albemarle "all things are in quyet and his Maj^tyes Customes quyetly paid by the People."

Unhappily this state of affairs was destined to be of short duration. In 1683, Seth Sothel, who had been released from captivity, arrived in Albemarle bearing a commission as governor. John Fiske is guilty of no exaggeration when he says of Sothel: "In five years of misrule over Albemarle he proved himself one of the dirtiest knaves that ever held office in America." [3] As a Lord Proprietor, he considered himself above the law. He disregarded the instructions of the Lords Proprietors; appointed deputies illegally and "refused to suffer any to act as Deputy who had deputations under the hand and seale of the Prop^rs"; and acted "contrary to all the fundamental Constitutions." He had been in office but a short time when he received a sharp reprimand from his associates, who informed him that no man could "claime any power in Carolina but by virtue of them [Fundamental Constitutions] for no prop^tor single by virture of our patents hath any right to the Governm^t or to exercise any Jurisdiction there unless Impowered by the rest." Complaints soon began to pour in upon them from the people charging Sothel with corruption, robbery, and tyranny. He withheld from subordinate officials and put into his own pocket the perquisites of their offices. He accepted bribes from criminals. He seized without ceremony and appropriated to his own use whatever pleased his fancy, whether a plantation, a negro slave, a cow, or a pewter dish; and if the owner had the effrontery to object he locked him up. He arrested and imprisoned two traders arriving in Albemarle on pretense of their being pirates, although both produced proper clearance papers showing them to be lawful traders, threw them into prison, and seized their goods. One of them died in prison

---

[3] Old Virginia and Her Neighbours, Vol. II, p. 286.

leaving a will naming Thomas Pollock as executor; but Sothel refused to admit the will to probate, and when Pollock threatened to appeal to the Lords Proprietors, he "Imprisoned him without showing him any reason or permitting him to see a copy of his mittimus." George Durant indignantly denounced such unlawful proceedings, whereupon Sothel threw him into prison and confiscated his whole estate "without any process or collor of law and converted the same to yo[r] [his] owne use."

The people of Albemarle endured Sothel's tyranny until 1688. Then doubtless inspired by the Revolution in England they rose against the tyrant, deposed him from office, and prepared to pack him off to England for trial. But Sothel, who feared the wrath of his associates more than the vengeance of the colonists, begged that he might be tried by the General Assembly of Albemarle. He felt sure that the Assembly, though it might remove him from office, would not venture to impose a prison sentence, and in this he calculated correctly. The Assembly found him guilty, banished him from the province for one year, and declared him forever incapable of holding office in Albemarle. The prudence of the Assembly brought its reward. The Lords Proprietors, worn out with the everlasting strife and disorders in their colony, were at first inclined to censure the Assembly, and veto its proceedings, which they declared to be "prejudicial to the prerogative of the Crown and the honor and dignity of us the prop[tors]"; but afterwards, becoming convinced of Sothel's guilt, they removed him from office and wrote to the people of their colony: "Wee were extremely troubled when wee heard of the sufferings of the Inhabitants of North Carolina by the arbitrary proceedings of Mr. Seth Sothel which unjust and Illegal actions wee abhor and have taken the best care wee can to prevent such for the future And that all men may have right done them who have suffered by him."

Seth Sothel was the last governor of Albemarle; his successor, Philip Ludwell, was commissioned "Governor of that part of our Province of Carolina that lyes north and east of Cape feare." In the letter to the Assembly, quoted above, the attentive reader will have observed that the Lords Proprietors referred to the people of that region as the "Inhabitants of North Carolina." The phrase is significant. It indicates not only the growth and expansion of Albemarle, but also points to a change in the policy of the Lords Proprietors. They had abandoned their original plan of erecting several separate and distinct governments in their province; henceforth there were to be but two,—one, of which the Ashley River settlement was the nucleus, was to be the colony of South Carolina; the other, developing out of Albemarle, was to be North Carolina. With the expulsion of Sothel, therefore, the history of Albemarle ends and the history of North Carolina as such begins.

CHAPTER V

GROWTH AND EXPANSION

With the appointment of Philip Ludwell as governor, North Carolina entered upon a brief period of order and progress. Ludwell's instructions reflected the purpose of the Lords Proprietors "to take care of the quiet and safety of the provinces under our [their] Governmᵗ." The first task, therefore, which they imposed upon him was to bring order out of the chaos into which the colony had been plunged by the misgovernment of Seth Sothel. He was to see that their letter to Sothel removing him from office was "carefully delivered to his own hands"; to inquire into the causes of the revolt against him; and to appoint a commission of "three of the honestest and ablest men" in the province not concerned in the revolt to hear and determine "according to Law" all complaints "both Civill and Criminall" growing out of his conduct. If Ludwell found anything in his instructions "deficient or Inconvenient to yᵉ Inhabitants," he was to report it to the Lords Proprietors who promised to "take due care therein." Their readiness to hear and redress the grievances of their people had a good effect, the result of which was seen at the very beginning of Ludwell's administration in the failure of a Captain John Gibbs, a rival claimant to the governorship, to arouse any popular sympathy with his cause.

Under other circumstances, Gibbs' bombastic pronunciamento, now thought of only as a ludicrous and amusing incident, might easily have led to serious results. The grounds upon which "Governor Gibbs" based his claims are not certain; one plausible suggestion is that he had been elected by the Council upon the expulsion of Sothel; another is that he had been appointed by Sothel himself as his deputy. But whatever his grounds, he was not backward in asserting his claims which he set forth in a remarkable proclamation dated "Albemarle, June yᵉ 2ᵈ 1690." He asserted his right to the office of governor, denounced Ludwell as a "Rascal, imposter, & Usurpʳ," and commanded "all Persons to keep the Kings

64

peace, to consult yᵉ ffundamentals, and to render me [him] due obedience, & not presume to act or do by Virtue of any Commission or Power whatsoever derived from yᵉ above sᵈ Ludwell, as they will answer itt, att their utmost perill.'' His claim, he declared, would ''be justified in England and if any of the boldest Heroe living in this or the next County will undertake to Justifie the said Ludwell's illegal Irregular proceeding, let him call upon me wᵗʰ his sword, and I will single out & goe with him into any part of the King's Dominions, & there fight him in this Cause, as long as my Eyelids shall wagg.''

The valiant captain was as good as his word. Four days after issuing his challenge, he led a band of armed followers into Currituck precinct, broke up the precinct court then sitting, made two of the magistrates prisoners, and issued an order forbidding any court ''to sitt or act by any Commission but his.'' But if he expected a popular uprising in his behalf, such as had followed the ''Remonstrance'' of the ''Pasquotankians'' against Miller in 1677, he was doomed to disappointment. The people, conciliated by the attitude of the Lords Proprietors in the Sothel affair, were in no mood for further violence or rebellion; indignant at the outrage perpetrated upon their court, they rallied to the support of lawful government, sprang to arms, and chased ''Governor Gibbs'' and his band out of the province. Gibbs took refuge in Virginia where Governor Nicholson, at Ludwell's request, took a hand in the affair and speedily brought him to terms. Both Ludwell and his bellicose rival thereupon embarked for England to lay their dispute before the Lords Proprietors who promptly repudiated the latter.

Upon his return from England, in 1691, Ludwell brought a new set of instructions based, as the Lords Proprietors privately informed him, not upon the Fundamental Constitutions, but upon their charter from the Crown. This was an important concession to the political sentiment of the people who had never accepted the Fundamental Constitutions, and its practical effect was to relegate that document to its place among the many abortive schemes which well-meaning theorists since the beginning of time have devised for the government of mankind. One of the objects of the new instructions was to strengthen the colonial government, a necessity plainly demonstrated by recent events in both the Carolinas. Greater dignity was to be given the executive authority by placing both North Carolina and South Carolina under a single governor whose hands were to be strengthened by eliminating

GOVERNOR PHILIP LUDWELL
From a portrait in possession of Bennehan Cameron

from the Council the five members chosen by the General Assembly, thus leaving the Council to be composed exclusively of the deputies of the Lords Proprietors. The legislative department was to undergo a similar consolidation. There was to be but one General Assembly for the two colonies to which each of the four counties of Albemarle, Colleton, Berkeley, and Craven was to send five representatives. Such at least was the plan on paper, but it was never carried into effect because upon second thought the Lords Proprietors saw insuperable difficulties in the way. Additional instructions, therefore, were issued providing that, if it was, found "Impracticable for to have the Inhabitants of Albemarle County to send Delegates to the General Assembly held at South Carolina," each colony should continue to hold its own Assembly. At the same time the governor was authorized to appoint a deputy-governor for North Carolina, a provision later extended to South Carolina also. The two governments, therefore, continued separate and independent of each other.

The development of North Carolina had been too slow to keep pace with the plans and expectations of the Lords Proprietors, who sharply reprimanded the Albemarle planters for their failure to open up the wilderness between Albemarle and Charleston. But the Lords Proprietors did not understand the difficulties in the way. Wide sounds, broad rivers, dense forests, almost impenetrable swamps made progress difficult. Shallow inlets and shifting sands barred access to the markets of the world, placed the trade of North Carolina at the mercy of competing Virginia planters and shrewd New England merchants, and retarded the development of agriculture and commerce. Hostile Indians roamed the wilderness, committed many depredations and murders, and twice during the decade from 1665 to 1675 openly went on the warpath. There were, too, as we have seen, numerous causes for discontent which discouraged immigration and deterred the settlers already in Albemarle from undertaking new enterprises. Culpepper's Rebellion completely disorganized the government and for more than two years kept the colony in turmoil. The land question also checked immigration. Since the terms on which land was granted in Albemarle were less favorable than those which prevailed in Virginia, people were naturally slow to abandon the older colony for the new one; and even after the Great Deed partially removed this discrimination, the uncertainty of the titles by which the Albemarle planters held their lands discouraged others from joining them. Still another deterrent to new enterprises was the rumor that the other Lords Proprietors intended to sell their interests in Albemarle to Sir William Berkeley. In spite of all these difficulties, a few adventurers, hardier and bolder, or more restless than their fellows, pushed across Albemarle Sound and attempted to open the way for settlements to the southward; but they were "with great violence and Injustice deprived of any power to proceed any further * * * and were commanded back to your [their] great prejudice and inconvenience" by colonial officials "who had ingrosit ye Indian trade to themselves & feared that it would be intercepted by those who should plant farther amongst them."

A serious obstacle to the growth and prosperity of North Carolina was the hostile conduct of Virginia throughout the proprietary period. From her superior position as a crown colony, Virginia looked down with unconcealed disdain upon all the proprietary colonies around her, but North Carolina was the special object of her aversion. The very existence of that colony was an affront to Virginia. It had been carved out of her ancient domain. It had been populated largely at her expense. It offered keen competition in the staple upon which her prosperity was founded. Its free and democratic society was in sharp contrast to the more aristocratic system that prevailed in the Old Dominion. Whatever checked the growth and development of North Carolina, therefore, Virginians regarded as indirectly promoting the interests of Virginia. This end they sought to accomplish in various ways. They spread abroad evil reports of the people of North Carolina. They attempted to undermine her economic prosperity by hostile legislation forbidding the shipment of North Carolina tobacco through Virginia ports. They encouraged Indians to advance claims to lands which the latter had formally ceded by treaty to the Lords Proprietors, and shielded Indian thieves who preyed upon the horses, cattle and hogs of North Carolina planters. They pretended ignorance of the charter of 1665 and laying claim to the region which that charter had added to the Carolina grant, undertook to close it to North Carolina settlers.

Two laws passed by the Albemarle Assembly in 1669 designed to encourage immigration,—i. e. the stay-law and the law exempting new settlers from taxation for one year—were especially resented by the Virginians, who declared that they were nothing less than open invitations to rogues and vagabonds. Yet the former was an exact copy of the Virginia statute of 1642 which the Virginia Assembly carefully re-enacted in 1663 because it had been inadvertently omitted from a printed collection of the Virginia laws. The Albemarle Assembly even copied the Virginia preamble which set forth as the reason for the statute that many people had "through their engagements in England, forsaken their native country and repaired hither, with resolution to abide here, hoping in time to gain some competency of subsistence by their labors, yet, nevertheless, their creditors, hearing of their abode in the colony, have prosecuted them with their actions to the ruin of said debtors." Unquestionably some scoundrels took advantage of the Albemarle statute, just as others had taken advantage of the Virginia law, but hardly enough of them came to justify Virginia's taunts and reproaches. "Rogues Harbour" was a favorite Virginia epithet for Albemarle. Advertent to the opportunities the statute offered to persons in an adjoining community to defraud their creditors, and attentive to the complaints of their neighbor, the North Carolina Assembly in 1707 exempted settlers from Virginia from the protection of the statute; nevertheless this friendly act did not sooth the ruffled feelings of the Virginians, and the "substantial planters" and industrious servants whom they earnestly tried to keep in Virginia continued to become immediately upon crossing the boundary line into North Carolina "idle debtors," "theeves," "pyrates," and "runaway servants." The people of North Carolina naturally resented these misrepresentations, and finally Governor Walker was goaded by Governor Nicholson's continued "intimations concerning runaways" into sharply repelling the "imputation of evil neighbourhood" which he had cast upon the colony.

Not content with fixing a bad name upon North Carolina, the Virginians undertook to destroy the source of her economic welfare. Tobacco was the staple of both colonies and the Virginia planters early became alarmed at the competition to which the increasing production of Albemarle subjected them. In 1679, the commissioners of the customs wrote that "the quantity of Tobacco that groweth in Carolina is considerable & Increaseth every year but it will not appear by the Customhouse bookes what customes have been received in England for the same for that by reason of the Badness of the Harbours in those parts most of the Tobaccos of the growth of those Countreyes have been and are Carryed from thence in Sloops and small fetches to Virginia & New England & from thence shipped hither. So that the Entries here [London] are as from Virgin^a & New England although the Tobacco be of the growth of Carolina & Albemarle." The

Virginia planters had long sought a way to destroy this competition, and finally in 1679 the Assembly came to their relief by forbidding the importation of tobacco from Carolina into Virginia, or its exportation through Virginia ports. This act was re-enacted in 1705, and again in 1726. It was a hard blow for North Carolina and did not tend to improve her relations with her neighbor.

Another cause for indignation against Virginia was her action in taking under her protection a band of straggling Meherrin Indians who, near the close of the seventeenth century, had moved from "their ancient place of habitation" north of the Meherrin River, and placing themselves at its mouth, had "planted corne and built Cabbins" on the lands which the Chowanocs, after the war of 1675-76, had ceded to the Lords Proprietors of Carolina. Their presence there was a constant menace to the peace of the province. They preyed upon the planters, drove off their hogs and cattle, destroyed their crops, and committed numerous murderous assaults upon their persons, and the planters retaliated with usury. To remove the danger, the North Carolina authorities negotiated a treaty with the Indians which required them "to return to the place of their former habitation," but the Virginia government intervened, assured the Meherrins of its support and protection, and induced them to refuse to carry out their agreement. Col. Thomas Pollock was then sent to remove them by force. With a band of sixty men, he attacked their town, took a large number of prisoners, and threatened "to burn their Cabbins and destroy their Corne if they did not remove from that place." Virginia promptly called upon North Carolina to disavow Pollock's act and demanded his punishment. That colony set up a claim to the lands on which the Meherrins had settled, declared that "the said Indians have their dependence upon and are under the protection of this Government," and denounced the "Clandestine Treaty" between them and the North Carolina government as derogatory to the rights and dignity of Virginia. The Virginia Council dismissed with contempt the statement of facts, as well as the arguments, of the North Carolina government, although as stated by the latter the question involved was "whether near a hundred familys of her Majty's subjects of Carolina should be disseased of their freehold to lett a few vagrant and Insolent Indians rove where they please without any Right and Contrary to their Agreement." Encouraged by Virginia's attitude, the Meherrins continued over a period of years to disregard their treaty, and growing more and more insolent, committed repeated depredations upon the property and assaults upon the persons of the Carolina planters, ''supposing,'' as Governor Hyde complained in a letter to the governor of Virginia, ''they can have protection from you.''

Virginia's concern for these Indians was not inspired by any philanthropic interest in their welfare, but by the fact that in their fate was involved her claim to the region which they had occupied. This claim North Carolina disputed. The dispute arose from the fact that the exact location of the dividing line between the two colonies had never been ascertained and many of the settlers who entered lands along the frontier, ignorant that they were within the Carolina grant, had taken out patents from Virginia. Consequently when the Carolina government, in 1680, claimed jurisdiction over them and demanded payment of quit rents and taxes, Virginia entered a vigorous protest, declaring that those settlers were inhabitants of Virginia and must not ''be in any sort molested disturbed or Griev'd'' by the North Carolina authorities. The controversy thus precipitated was destined to strain the friendly relations of the two colonies for more than half a century. It grew in intensity as time passed and other questions arose to add fuel to the flames. The jurisdiction of the courts became involved, and on one occasion at least, court officials of the two provinces actually came into armed conflict.

The origin of the controversy may be traced to the change which the second charter of the Lords Proprietors made in the northern boundary of Carolina. The charter of 1663 fixed the boundary at the 36th parallel of northern latitude; the charter of 1665 fixed it in a line to be run from ''the north end of Currituck river or inlet, upon a strait westerly line to Wyonoak creek, which lies within or about the degrees of thirty-six and thirty minutes, northern latitude, and so west, in a direct line, as far as the south seas.'' As early as 1681 the Lords Proprietors petitioned the Crown to have the line run as thus described; but Virginia having privately ascertained that such a line would defeat her claims, questioned the existence of the ''p^{r}tended latt^r Grant to the Lords Propryet^{rs} of Carolina.'' On this point, however, she was easily beaten by an inspection of the record. The dispute was thereupon shifted to the location of the natural objects along the line as described in the charter. The chief point at issue was the identity of Weyanoke Creek. Weyanoke Creek was doubtless a well known stream in 1665, but with the passage of years it had lost that name which by 1680 had disappeared from the map. Virginia maintained that it was identical with Wicocon Creek, while North Carolina as stoutly insisted that it was the same as Nottoway River, and both colonies easily secured testimony from early settlers to sustain their contentions. The difference was too considerable to be given up without a contest, since it involved a strip of territory fifteen miles in width.

The chief sufferers in these controversies were the inhabitants of the disputed territory who were of course anxious to have the line fixed. Accordingly in 1699 the Crown ordered that it be run as called for by the charter of 1665. Governor Harvey promptly sent Daniel Akehurst and Henderson Walker to Virginia as commissioners to represent North Carolina; but the Virginia officials alleging that Harvey had not been formally confirmed in his office by the king, refused to recognize his commissioners and informed him that "it is not convenient with us to treat with any person or persons by you appointed." After this experience, North Carolina, suspecting that Virginia's purpose was to resist indefinitely the settlement of the dispute and satisfied that her own claims were well founded, proceeded as if her title to the territory was beyond controversy. Virginia too began to suspect that she could not make good her pretensions. In 1705 the Virginia Council ordered the official surveyor of that province to ascertain "whether the line between this Government and North Carolina if run according to the patent of the Lords Proprietors may cut off any plantations held by titles from this Government," at the same time directing him "to keep secret the intentions of this Government * * * that the people of North Carolina may have no other suspicion than that those Surveyors are only going about laying the Maherin Indians lands."

Nothing more was done until 1709 when both colonies received orders from the queen to settle the dispute. North Carolina accordingly appointed John Lawson and Edward Moseley as her commissioners, while Virginia was represented by Philip Ludwell and Nathaniel Harrison. After several failures to arrange a meeting, the commissioners finally came together at Williamsburg, August 30, 1710. The attitude of the Virginians doomed the enterprise to failure from the first. No good thing could come out of Nazareth. In every act of the Carolina commissioners, the Virginians detected some ulterior, dishonest motive. They accused both Lawson and Moseley of a secret purpose "to obstruct the Settling the Boundarys," charging that they were privately interested in the lands in dispute. The witnesses cited by the North Carolina commissioners were all "very Ignorant persons, & most of them of ill fame & Reputation," while those called by Virginia were "Persons of good Credit." If Moseley raised legal objections to the powers conferred upon the Virginia commissioners, it was "with design to render their conferences ineffectual"; if he questioned the accuracy of their instruments, it was merely one of his "many Shifts & Excuses to disappoint all Conferences with the Commissioners of Virginia"; if his statement of a fact did not correspond with what the Virginians understood it to be, it was set down to his propensity to "prevarication." Such at least the Virginia commissioners, in their efforts to prejudice the Proprietors' case, set down in the report they wrote for the Crown, a report afterwards severely criticised in his "History of the Dividing Line," by Col. William Byrd, one of the Virginia commissioners when the line was finally run in 1728. Colonel Byrd thought that "it had been fairer play" to have furnished Lawson and Moseley a copy of the report thus giving them an opportunity to answer the charges against them; confessed that Moseley "was not much in the wrong to find fault with the Quadrant produced by the Surveyors of Virginia" as it was afterwards shown "that there was an Error of near 30 minutes, either in the instrument or in those who made use of it"; and admitted after careful surveys that the Nottoway River was probably the same as Weyanoke Creek. The spirit with which the Virginia commissioners approached their task in 1710 and their uncompromising attitude made agreement impossible and served only to intensify the ill-feeling between the two colonies.

For a long time the Lords Proprietors did not appreciate the obstacles against which their colony was struggling. They looked upon its inhabitants as a sluggish, unenterprising people who neither understood their own nor regarded the Proprietors' interests; upbraided them for their failure to open communications between the Albemarle colony and the Ashley River settlement, and declared that to be the reason why they had neglected the former in the interest of the latter.

There were not wanting, however, intelligent colonists in North Carolina who labored diligently to present the situation to the Lords Proprietors in its true light. As early as 1665, Thomas Woodward, surveyor-general, wrote them plainly that settlers would not come to Albemarle upon harder conditions than they could secure in Virginia. Thomas Eastchurch presented facts which forced them to acknowledge

that the fault was not with the people but with "those persons
into whose hands wee [they] had committed the Government."
Timothy Biggs bluntly told them that Albemarle owed
nothing to them, and declared that if it had received but a
tenth part of the aid and encouragement which they had given
to the Ashley River settlement it would have been a prosperous colony. The truth gradually dawned upon the Lords Proprietors who tardily took steps to relieve the situation as far
as possible. They granted more liberal terms for land-hold-
ing; instructed their governors to issue patents to landowners; assured the settlers that they had no intention of parting with Albemarle to Governor Berkeley or "to any persons
whatsoever"; and appointed a governor for the region south
of Albemarle Sound whom they instructed to encourage settlements along Pamlico and Neuse rivers. But more important than all of these reforms was the decade and a half of
good government which began with the appointment of Ludwell in 1691.

Ludwell, appointed December 2, 1691, was the first governor of Carolina. His deputies in North Carolina were
Thomas Jarvis (1691-1694) and Thomas Harvey (1694-1699).
In 1693, Thomas Smith succeeded Ludwell, but retired within
less than a year and was succeeded by John Archdale. Both
Smith and Archdale continued Harvey in power as deputy-
governor of North Carolina. Upon the death of Harvey in
1699, Henderson Walker, president of the Council, took over
the administration in North Carolina which he conducted
until the appointment of Col. Robert Daniel in 1703. During the decade and a half in which these men administered
the government, North Carolina enjoyed such a reign of law
and order as she had not known before. Her governors
brought to their task greater abilities, better personal characters, and larger experiences in colonial affairs, than any
of their predecessors. Ludwell had been active for many
years in the public affairs of Virginia where he had won a
reputation for courage, integrity, and devotion to the public
interests. As governor of North Carolina, he showed that
he "understood the character and prejudices of the people
thoroughly; and as he was possessed of good sense and proper
feeling, he had address enough * * * gradually to restore a state of comparative peace." [1] He made himself acceptable to the people by recognizing the validity of the
Great Deed, but by the same act incurred the displeasure of

---

[1] Hawks: History of North Carolina, Vol. II, p. 494.

the Lords Proprietors who, unable to find any record of that document in England, repudiated his action and revoked his commission. John Archdale, the Quaker governor (1694-1697), like Seth Sothel, was a Lord Proprietor, but he was like Sothel in nothing else. He was appointed governor because his predecessor, Governor Smith, advised the Lords Proprietors that it was impossible to settle the disorders which had broken out in South Carolina "except a Proprietor himself was sent over with full power to heal grievances." Archdale's sagacity, prudence, and sound judgment, together with his experience in colonial affairs, pointed him out as the man for the task and he was given extraordinary powers for dealing with the situation. The confidence of his colleagues was justified by the results in both colonies. As a Quaker, Archdale was particularly acceptable in North Carolina where since 1672 the Quakers had grown numerous and influential. He spent the winter of 1696-97 in North Carolina personally directing the government; there his deep religious faith and impeccable personal character tended to encourage religion and morality, while his administration of public affairs was so successful as to elicit from the Assembly the tribute that "his greatest care is to make peace and plenty flow amongst us." Both Jarvis and Harvey, deputies of Ludwell and Archdale, had long been leaders in North Carolina affairs, understood and sympathized with the feelings and ideals of the people, and were men of excellent character and good judgment. Henderson Walker, who succeeded Harvey in 1699, had been in the colony for seventeen years and had served as attorney-general, justice of the General Court, and member of the Council. A man of education, a lawyer of ability, a Churchman of sincere religious convictions, he was deeply interested in the material and the moral and spiritual welfare of the colony, jealous of its good name, and quick to resent the "imputation of evil neighbourhood" which some of its neighbors endeavored to fix upon it. These men gave to North Carolina fifteen years of good government under the stimulus of which the colony grew and prospered.

Settlers pushing across the wide expanse of Albemarle Sound, slowly penetrated the wilderness to the southward. The way was probably opened by English pioneers from Albemarle, but the first settlers south of the Albemarle Sound of whom we have any record were French Protestants. The drastic measures of Louis XIV against the Huguenots, soon to culminate in the revocation of the Edict of Nantes, were al-

ready driving many of these industrious people from France
to seek new homes in England and in English colonies. They
possessed the qualities necessary to make good colonists, and
the Lords Proprietors were eager to induce them to settle in
Carolina. Doubtless with this object in view, in 1683, they had
the Fundamental Constitutions, one clause of which guaranteed religious freedom, translated into French. Large numbers of Huguenots, in their search for religious freedom, as is
well known, settled in South Carolina, while others found their
way to North Carolina. The first Huguenot colonists in
North Carolina came about 1690 from Virginia and settled on
Pamlico River. Their enterprise quickly attracted the attention of the Lords Proprietors who, in 1694, instructed Governor Archdale to erect in that region as many counties as
he thought necessary "for yᵉ better regulating and yᵉ en-
couragemᵗ of yᵉ people." Accordingly the region from Albemarle Sound to Cape Fear was erected into the county of
Archdale although none of the vast wilderness south of Pamlico River was yet inhabited by white men. As the settlement on the Pamlico grew in importance, the colonial authorities thought it advisable to extend to it still further encouragement. In 1696, therefore, the Palatine's Court ordered
that the region extending from Albemarle Sound to Neuse
River be erected into the county of Bath and given the privilege of sending two representatives to the General Assembly.
About this time, too, a pestilence among the Indians decimated
the tribes along the Pamlico and still further opened up that
region to settlers who continued to arrive from Albemarle,
from Virginia, and from Europe.

Among the last were a "great many French Protestants"
who came under the auspices of the king "depending upon
the Royal assurance which was given for their encouraging
the Exercise of the Protestant Religion and the benefit of
the laws of England." In 1704, on a bluff overlooking Pamlico River, they selected a fine site for a town which a
year later they incorporated under the name of Bath. In
1709, when Bath was only five years old, William Gordon, a
missionary, wrote that it "consists of about twelve houses,
being the only town in the whole province. They have a small
collection of books for a library, which were carried over by
the Reverend Doctor Bray, and some land is laid out for a
glebe; * * * in all probability it will be the centre of
trade, as having the advantage of a better inlet for shipping,
and surrounded with most pleasant savannas, very useful for
stocks of cattle." In spite of these fancied advantages, Bath,

though at times the home of wealth and culture, never became anything more than a sleepy little village and derives its chief distinction from the unimportant fact that it was the first town in the province. The settlers on the Pamlico, however, prospered and their good reports induced others to join them. They declared, in 1704, that they had "at vast labour and expense recovered and improved great quantities of land thereabouts"; and this boast was borne out by the Council which, in December 1705, "taking into their serious consideration" the fact that Bath County had "grown populous and [was] daily increasing," divided it into three precincts, and conferred upon each of them the right to send two representatives to the General Assembly. One of these precincts embraced that portion of Bath County south of Pamlico River "including all the Inhabitants of News."

The earliest settlers on the Neuse, like those on the Pamlico, were Huguenots. For the most part, they came from Mannakintown, a French settlement in Virginia a few miles above the falls of the James, founded in 1699 by Claude Phillipe de Richebourg. They had not prospered there "because," as Lawson says, "at their first coming over, they took their Measures of Living, from Europe; which was all wrong; for the small Quantities of ten, fifteen, and twenty Acres to a Family did not hold out according to their way of Reckoning, by Reason they made very little or no Fodder; and the Winter there being much harder than with us, their Cattle failed; chiefly, because the English took up and surveyed all the Land round about them; so that they were hemmed in on all Hands from providing more Land for themselves or their Children."[2] The mildness of the climate in North Carolina, the ease with which lands could be entered there, and the favorable reports of their brethren on the Pamlico lured many of them, including Richebourg himself, away from the James to seek new homes on the Neuse and the Trent. They brought with them the thrift, the industry, and the skill for which their race had been noted in the Old World, and the colony soon felt the effects of their presence. John Lawson, who visited their settlements in 1708, wrote of them: "They are much taken with the Pleasantness of that Country, and, indeed, are a very industrious People. * * * The French are good Neighbours amongst us, and give Examples of Industry, which is much wanted in this Country."[3]

---

[2] History of Carolina (ed. 1718), p. 114.
[3] Ibid., p. 83.

In 1710, the Neuse River settlement was strengthened by the arrival of a colony of German and Swiss immigrants. This colony, in one important respect, differed widely from the other settlements then in North Carolina. All the other settlements were the outcome of individual initiative and enterprise; this one was the result of organized effort. It was composed chiefly of natives of that region along the Rhine known as the Palatinate, whence the name Palatines by which they are generally called. Their story is a tragic one. Protestants in religion, they were under the dominion of an irresponsible Roman Catholic prince who subjected them to many forms of religious persecution. Their country was the battleground of Europe and in the barbarous and sanguinary wars of the seventeenth century was frequently overrun and devastated by hostile armies. To these misfortunes were added the burdens of exorbitant taxes and tolls which swept the greater part of their earnings into the coffers of their rulers. These conditions produced such widespread misery and hopeless poverty, that at the beginning of the eighteenth century many of them determined to seek relief by emigration.

In this determination, they met with encouragement from England. Queen Anne, who looked upon herself as the guardian of the Protestants of Europe, eagerly extended both protection and assistance to all Protestants who sought safety in her dominions. In this policy she received the support of the British nation, and Parliament, in 1709, passed a bill providing for the naturalization of foreign Protestants. Generous as this policy was, it was not altogether free from the taint of selfishness. England needed just such industrious an thrifty people as the German Protestants for the development of her colonial empire. For many years, therefore, those who were interested in colonial enterprises carried on in Germany a widespread propaganda for the purpose of inducing emigration to America. More than fifty books, pamphlets and broadsides relating to Pennsylvania alone were circulated in Germany. Among those whose attention this propaganda attracted was Rev. Joshua Kocherthal, a Lutheran clergyman at Landau in the Palatinate, who, in 1703, went to England, to seek relief for his own congregation. There he seems to have conferred with the Lords Proprietors of Carolina for after his return to Germany he published, in 1706, a glowing account of their province in which he pointed out its advantages as a home for his countrymen. His book aroused such general interest among the Protestants of Germany that by 1709 it had reached its fourth edition. Stimulated by Kocherthal's publication, and secretly encouraged by the British government, the Palatines and other German Protestants in large numbers abandoned their native land to seek new homes in England, or beyond the Atlantic. Following the passage of the naturalization act in 1709, more than 10,000 of them landed in England. They came in such great numbers that the facilities provided for taking care of them proved utterly inadequate. Several months passed before plans could be perfected for their ultimate disposition. Numerous schemes, embracing settlements in England, Ireland, the Canary Islands, and America, were suggested, but of them all, colonization in America seemed the most feasible.

A favorable opportunity for transporting a colony of the Palatines to America was offered by the presence in London of Franz Ludwig Michel and Christopher de Graffenried, representatives of a Swiss syndicate of Bern which had been organized to plant a Swiss colony in America. De Graffenried, who was the scion of a noble German family of Bern, had excellent connections in England through whom he succeeded in interesting English capitalists in his scheme. Even the queen agreed to contribute £4,000 to his enterprise in consideration of his taking 100 families of Palatines to America. In what part of America should he plant his colony? During one of his sojourns in England some years earlier, De Graffenried's interest in America had been aroused by the Duke of Albemarle, one of the Proprietors of Carolina, who had discoursed to him on "the beauty, goodness, and riches of English America," and now that he was about to seek "a more considerable fortune in those far-off countries," his thoughts naturally turned to the province in which the duke had been especially interested. He was confirmed in this determination by information received from John Lawson, surveyor-general of Carolina, who was then in London supervising the publication of his "New Voyage to Carolina." The Lords Proprietors themselves had shown an interest in the Palatines as possible colonists, even proposing to settle all of them between fifteen and forty-five years of age in their province if the queen would defray the expenses of their transportation; and they now offered De Graffenried "very favorable conditions and privileges." De Graffenried, accordingly, determined upon Carolina and purchased in that province 17,500 acres of land to be located south of the Neuse River.

In making his preparations, De Graffenried acted promptly and prudently. From the thousands of Palatines, eager for the enterprise, he chose only "young people, healthy and

laborious and of all kinds of avocations and handicrafts," in
number about 650. Tools, equipment, and ships were all selected with great care. The colony was placed under the
direction of "three persons, notables from Carolina, who
happened then to be in London and who had lived already
several years in Carolina." They were John Lawson, the
surveyor-general, Christopher Gale, the receiver-general, and
another colonial official. Twelve assistants, "both sensible and
able," were appointed from among the colonists themselves.
In all his plans and preparations, De Graffenried had the advice and approval of a royal commission which passed on his
contracts, inspected his transports, and were supposed in
other ways to look after the interests of the Palatines. When
all was ready, the colonists went aboard their ships at Graves-
end and after suitable religious ceremonies weighed anchor
for the New World, leaving De Graffenried in England to
await the arrival of his colony from Bern.

The Palatines sailed in January, 1710. Misfortune dogged
their tracks. The royal commissioners, to whom their interests had been entrusted, had shamefully neglected their duty.
The transports were badly overcrowded. The food supply
was inadequate in quantity and in quality. The cost of transportation had been reduced to the lowest possible amount and
the ship's captain paid in advance for each passenger; the
death of a passenger, therefore, meant a financial gain to the
ship-owners. Even nature seemed to conspire against the welfare of the Palatines. A few days out of port, they were
overtaken by a storm which threatened them with destruction.
Contrary winds tossed them about on the Atlantic for thirteen weeks. Crowded into poorly ventilated quarters, reduced
to a salt diet to which they were not accustomed, attacked
and plundered by a French man-of-war, the wretched Palatines suffered many of the horrors of the middle-passage.
Throughout their long voyage, disease was their constant
companion and death a daily visitor. More than half of them
perished at sea and many others succumbed after landing.
Thus, as De Graffenried says, "that colony was shattered before it had settled."

Sailing up the James River, the survivors of the colony
landed in Virginia, where they were well received, and remained there long enough to recover somewhat from the effects of their voyage. Then, under the guidance of John
Lawson, they set out overland for Carolina. Lawson who
had been entrusted with the task of locating the settlement
chose a point on the tongue of land between the Neuse and

Trent rivers, near the site of the present city of New Bern. No preparations had been made to receive the Palatines. They found themselves in a wilderness, during the hot and unhealthy season, without shelter and with an inadequate supply of food. The experiences of their first summer in America were paralleled only by those of their voyage across the Atlantic. Reduced to the direst poverty, they were compelled, "to sell all their clothes and movables to the neighboring inhabitants in order to sustain their life." When De Graffenried arrived in September, he found them in a wretched condition, "sickness, want and desperation having reached their very climax."

De Graffenried sailed in June with a colony of 100 Switzers, and after "a happy voyage," landed in Virginia on September 10th. Bad news from his Palatines was awaiting him and he pushed on to their relief with as little delay as possible. His hopes, however, of obtaining speedy succour for them were doomed to disappointment. He had expected help from the colonial authorities, in accordance with a promise which the Lords Proprietors had given him, but he found political conditions in North Carolina in such a turmoil that nothing could be obtained from that source. Provisions were scarce in North Carolina and flour that he had ordered from Pennsylvania and Virginia was slow in coming. Consequently, not only was he unable to relieve the distress of his Palatines; he could not even provide for the needs of his Switzers, who, like the Palatines, were soon "obliged to sell their clothes and implements in order to get the necessary victuals from the neighboring inhabitants and keep themselves from starvation." Finally, after a period of intense anxiety and suffering, grain, pork, salt, butter, and vegetables were secured in sufficient quantities for the immediate needs of the colony.

In the meantime De Graffenried had taken steps to bring some order out of the chaos which he had found upon his arrival. He had the land surveyed and the colonists settled on their several tracts. Encouraged by his presence they went to work with a will, cleared the forests, built cabins, erected water-mills for grinding grain, and laid out a town. This town was placed on the point of land between the Neuse and the Trent. It was laid off in the form of a cross with one arm extending from river to river and the other from the extremity of the point back indefinitely. De Graffenried planned to erect a church at each of the four corners. Above the town, he threw across the peninsular a line of fortifications as a protection against the Indians. In honor of his native city, De Graffenried named the town New Bern. Prospects for the future of New Bern seemed so favorable that people in Pennsylvania and Virginia invested in lots there. Indeed, such was the improvement in the situation that De Graffenried boasted that his colonists "within eighteen months [had] managed to build homes and make themselves so comfortable, that they made more progress in that length of time than the English inhabitants in several years." "There was," he adds, "a fine appearance of a happy state of things," when suddenly, without warning, the colony was overwhelmed by the greatest of all its misfortunes. In September, 1711, the most disastrous Indian war in the history of North Carolina broke out and raged with intermittent violence for two years. The losses and suffering fell heaviest upon the settlers along the Neuse. Their cattle were killed or driven off, their crops destroyed, their homes burned; many of the settlers themselves fell victims to the merciless cruelty of the savages. The rest were reduced to such desperation and despair that they determined to abandon the settlement, and De Graffenried went to Virginia to arrange for their removal to a new location on the Potomac. His negotiations failed and the scheme came to naught. De Graffenried himself, broken in fortune and in spirit, now abandoned his efforts and returned to Europe. The Palatines never recovered from the losses they had sustained and soon ceased to exist as a distinct German settlement. Scattered throughout the southeastern section of North Carolina, they were ultimately absorbed in the English population; even their names lost their German forms to conform to the English spelling.

By 1710, settlements extended from the Virginia line on the north to the Neuse River on the south, and up and down the Roanoke, the Pamlico, and the Neuse for twenty and thirty miles inland. The French and Germans were not the only ones who came, for many Virginians were abandoning the older colony for the new, and not a few adventurers were finding their way hither directly from the mother country. For the most part, the Virginians and the English did not follow the French and Germans to the outskirts of the settlements, but entered lands in Albemarle which was rapidly filling up with a sturdy people. While it is impossible to estimate the population of the colony accurately, there is ample evidence of its steady growth. In 1694, for instance, the total number of tithables in the colony as reported to the General Court was 787, which meant a population of about 3,500; eight years later the tithables of Chowan precinct alone were 283, i. e., a total population of about 1,400; and in 1708 the population of Pasquotank was more than 1,300. In 1690, the vanguard of the French colony had just entered the unbroken wilderness along the Pamlico; in 1704, the settlement on the Pamlico had grown so populous that it contained 200 children who had never received the rite of baptism. Further evidence is found in the complaints of the Virginia authorities that North Carolina was draining the Old Dominion of her population. The president of the Virginia Council wrote in 1708, that "many of our poorer sort of Inhabitants daily remove into our neighboring Colonies, especially to North Carolina which is the reason the number of our Inhabitants doth not increase proportionally to what might be expected"; and the Virginia Council explaining this situation said: "the chief cause of this Removal is want of Land to plant and cultivate * * * this has occasioned many families of old Inhabitants whose former plantations are worn out as well as great number of young people & servants just free to seek for settlements in the province of North Carolina where Land is to be had on much easier terms than here, & not a few have obtained grants from that Government of the very same [amount of] land which they would have taken up from this, if liberty had been given for it."

CHAPTER VI

THE CARY REBELLION

The reign of peace and progress which North Carolina enjoyed under Ludwell and Archdale, and their deputies, was of short duration. Henderson Walker, whose administration came to a close in 1703, bequeathed to his successors an issue that for several years divided the people into contending factions, stirred up bitter strife and rebellion, and indirectly brought upon the colony the worst disaster in its history. This issue was the question of an Established Church.

From the creation of their proprietary in 1663, the Lords Proprietors had offered liberal terms, as liberality in religious matters was construed in those days, to all Protestants who should settle in Carolina. In their proposals of August, 1663, to prospective settlers at Cape Fear, they promised "in as ample manner as the undertakers shall desire, freedom and liberty of conscience in all religious or spiritual things, and to be kept inviolably with them, we having power in our charter so to do." A few weeks later, in a letter to Sir William Berkeley, they explained that their reason for authorizing him to appoint two governors in Albemarle was that "some persons that are for liberty of conscience may desire a governor of their own proposing." Moreover, both in the Concessions of 1665 and in the Fundamental Constitutions they provided toleration for all forms of Christian worship in order "that civil peace may be obtained amidst diversity of opinion."

On the other hand, neither the Lords Proprietors nor the settlers understood these promises to be inconsistent with the setting up of an establishment in the colony. Both of the charters of the Lords Proprietors assumed that the Church of England would be the Established Church in Carolina; and in all their plans the Lords Proprietors proceeded upon this assumption. In the Concessions of 1665, in their instructions to their governors, and in the Fundamental Constitutions, their intentions to establish the Church are repeatedly set

84

forth. The Fundamental Constitutions provide that it should be the duty of "parliament to take care for the building of churches and the public maintenance of divines, to be employed in the exercise of religion according to the Church of England; which being the only true and orthodox, and the national religion of all the king's dominions, is so also of Carolina, and therefore it alone shall be allowed to receive public maintenance by grant of parliament."

The Lords Proprietors, therefore, were quite as much committed to the policy of an establishment as they were to that of religious toleration; but as they had allowed nearly two score years to pass without attempting to carry it into effect, the colonists generally had come to think of it as a dead letter. The attempt, therefore, after so many years of neglect to set up an establishment according to these provisions aroused a bitter and determined opposition from all classes of Dissenters. The increase of the Dissenters, especially of Quakers, in numbers and influence, is the most important fact in the early religious development of the colony. This growth was so great as to lead the early North Carolina historians into the error of believing that the colony was settled by religious refugees. As a rule the earliest settlers of North Carolina had been reared within the pale of the Church of England, and had the Church followed them into their new home they would doubtless have remained loyal to her; but forty years passed before a minister of the Established Church found his way into the Carolina wilderness, and in the meantime the field had been occupied and zealously cultivated by others.

The first voice of a Christian preacher heard in North Carolina was the voice of the Quaker, William Edmundson, who came hither in 1672, a worthy bearer of the Christian faith to a new land. In himself he personified the Christian virtues of simplicity, piety, zeal, and charity. Undaunted by the difficulties, discomforts, and dangers of his undertaking, he courageously plunged into the Carolina wilderness to carry his message to the scattered pioneers whom the Church had forgotten, and by his earnestness and eloquence won many of them to his cause. Soon after entering the province he arrived at the house of Henry Phillips who, with his wife "had been convinced of the truth in New England, and came here to live; and not having seen a Friend for seven years before, they wept for joy to see us." Phillips hastily summoned the neighboring planters to a meeting. Because their manners were crude and they violated the proprieties by smoking their pipes during the meeting, Edmundson at first thought they had "little or no religion"; but the readiness with which they "received the testimony" and confessed their faith soon undeceived him. Among the converts at this meeting were a prominent justice of the peace, Francis Toms, and his wife, both of whom "received the truth with gladness." At their urgent request, Edmundson held another meeting at their plantation where they had "a blessed time for several were tendered with a sense of the power of God, received the truth, and abode in it."

The work so successfully begun by Edmundson was taken up by others. In the winter of 1672, George Fox himself, the founder of the Society of Friends, visited the colony where he received an hospitable welcome not only from the Friends but also from the governor and other officials. Passing through Chowan, Pasquotank, and Perquimans precincts, he held several "precious" meetings and made many converts. Then, as he recorded in his journal, "having visited the north part of Carolina and made a little entrance for the truth among the people there, we began to return again towards Virginia, having several meetings on our way, wherein we had good service for the Lord, the people being generally tender and open." Four years later Edmundson returned to Carolina following about the same route that he had taken in 1672. These four years had worked a great change in the colony. Whereas on his first visit, Edmundson had found only two Friends, Henry Phillips and his wife, he now found the Friends quite numerous and well established. "I had several precious meetings in that colony," he says, "and several turned to the Lord. People were tender and loving, and there was no room for the priests, for Friends were firmly settled, and I left things well amongst them." From time to time, during the next quarter of a century, other Quaker missionaries came to Carolina, held "many comfortable meetings," made converts, and organized quarterly meetings. The Carolina Quakers also received accessions to their strength by immigration, especially from Pennsylvania, but the greatest impetus given to their cause was the appointment, in 1694, of John Archdale, a convert of George Fox, as governor. Under Archdale the influence of the Quakers reached its climax. They not only had the governor, but also gained control of the courts, the Council, and the Assembly, for, as Doctor Weeks says, "There was a material reward for being a Quaker, and Churchmen and others who thus found it to their interest deserted their own creeds to enroll themselves among the Friends.'' [1]

Though the Quakers were the most influential religious body in the colony, there were other bodies of Dissenters who were not so well organized. Rev. John Blair, a missionary of the Church, writing in 1704, declared that according to religious preferences, the people of the colony fell into four classes: (1) the Quakers, who ''stand truly to one another in whatsoever may be to their interest''; (2) ''a great many who have no religion, but would be Quakers if by that they were not obliged to lead a more moral life than they are willing to comply to''; (3) a class ''something like Presbyterians,'' whose leaders ''preach and baptize through the country, without any manner of orders from any sect or pretended Church''; and (4) Churchmen, ''who are really zealous for the interest of the Church, [but] are the fewest in number.'' Under the leadership of the Quakers, who, says Blair, ''are the most powerful enemies to Church government,'' the first three classes had united ''in one common cause to prevent any thing that will be chargeable to them, as they allege the Church government will be, if once established by law,'' and against this combination the Church party had been unable to make any headway.

For this situation the Church had only herself to blame. The elaborate organization provided for in the Fundamental Constitutions existed in theory only; no parishes had been laid off, no churches erected, no tithes levied, and no minister had been sent to the colony. Governor Walker wrote to the Bishop of London, within whose ecclesiastical jurisdiction all the American colonies lay, that for fifty years the colony had been ''without priest or altar,'' adding: ''George Fox, some years ago, came into these parts, and, by strange infatuations, did infuse the Quakers' principles into some small number of the people; which did and hath continued to grow ever since very numerous, by reason of their yearly sending in men to encourage and exhort them to their wicked principles; and there was none to dispute nor to oppose them in carrying on their pernicious principles for many years.'' At last, in 1700, the Church in England, aroused to a show of interest in the welfare of her scattered flock in Carolina, sent out a clergyman, Rev. Daniel Brett, to that colony. This sudden interest, however, proved more disastrous than the long neglect

---

[1] The Religious Development in the Province of North Carolina, p. 33. (*J. H. U. Studies,* 10th Series, Nos. V-VI.)

which had preceded it for Brett turned out to be "ye Monster of ye Age." His conduct in North Carolina was so shameful that it wrung from Governor Walker, a zealous Churchman, a bitter cry of protest to the Bishop of London. "It hath been a great trouble and grief to us who have a great veneration for the Church," he wrote, "that the first minister who was sent to us should prove so ill as to give the Dissenters so much occasion to charge us with him."

The Church party needed a leader who could unite and organize its scattered forces. This leader was found in Governor Walker who, upon assuming his duties as governor in 1699, resolved to devote his best energies to the task of securing the necessary legislation for the support of an establishment. Success crowned his efforts in 1701 when the Church party, under his leadership, by "a great deal of care and management," secured control of the Assembly which passed the first vestry act in the history of the colony. This act provided for the organization of vestries, the laying off of parishes, the erection of churches, the maintenance of a clergy, and the levy and collection of a poll tax for these purposes. Elated at their success, the Churchmen of the province began at once to carry the act into execution, and within the next two years erected three churches. The first parish organized in the colony was the Chowan Parish, afterwards known as St. Paul's. Its vestry met for organization December 15, 1701, and has had a continuous existence since that date. "It is not only the oldest organized religious body in the State," observes Bishop Cheshire, "it is the oldest corporation of any kind in North Carolina." [2] The activity of the Churchmen aroused a determined opposition. Those who opposed an establishment on principle allied themselves with those who merely objected to the new taxes to overthrow the Church party and repeal the obnoxious act. "We have an Assembly to sit the 3d November next," wrote Walker to the Bishop of London, in October, 1703, "and there is above one half of the burgesses that are chosen that are Quakers, and have declared their designs of making void the act for establishing the Church." In this, however, they were anticipated by the Lords Proprietors themselves who returned the act with their disapproval because of the inadequacy of the support provided for clergymen.

The ground on which the Lords Proprietors based their

---

[2] "How Our Church Came to North Carolina" in *The Spirit of Missions,* Vol. LXXXIII, No. 5, p. 350.

St. Paul's Church at Edenton

veto indicated that the struggle had just begun and both
parties prepared themselves for it. Two new influences entered
the contest in the Church party's favor. One was a new governor, the other the Society for the Propagation of the Gospel
in Foreign Parts. Lord John Granville, palatine and zealous
Churchman, about this time determined on a more vigorous
policy with regard to the Church in Carolina and issued positive instructions to the governor-general, Sir Nathaniel Johnson, to secure whatever legislation was necessary. Sir Nathaniel undertook to direct personally the fight in South Carolina, while in the summer of 1703 he superseded Walker as
deputy-governor of North Carolina with Col. Robert Daniel
of South Carolina. It was an unfortunate change. While
Walker was a zealous Churchman, he was also a patriotic citi-
zen and was greatly concerned for the welfare of the province;
and although he had earnestly favored the act of 1701, he
had done so in such a way as to arouse as little friction and
strife as possible; compared with what was to follow he had
given to the colony, as the inscription on his tombstone justly
claims, "that tranquillity which it is to be wished it may never
want." Daniel was also a zealous Churchman, but his zeal
ran into bigotry, and he was ruthless and unscrupulous
in his methods. Coincident with his appointment, the Society
for the Propagation of the Gospel in Foreign Parts, recently
organized in England, sent its first missionary, Rev. John
Blair, to North Carolina. The two events were part of the
same scheme for pushing the Establishment. Blair reached
North Carolina in January, 1704, and although he remained
here only a few months his presence was not without influence on the situation. It helped to bring out clearly the
views of every public man in the colony and to array him on
one side or the other; it solidified the Dissenters and their
sympathizers and united and encouraged the Churchmen for
the struggle which all knew was at hand.

Daniel had been instructed to secure the establishment of
the Church in North Carolina, and Blair had come to the colony expecting to find those instructions already enacted into
law. But in the Assembly of November, 1703, the first to meet
after Daniel's arrival, the Quakers as we have seen were in
the majority, and in the March Assembly, 1704, which Blair
expected "would propose a settlement of my [his] maintenance," they still were "the greatest number" and unanimously resolved "to prevent any such law passing." The
only hope of the Church party, therefore, was to find some
means of purging the General Assembly of its Quaker mem-

bers; but this seemed so improbable that Blair gave up in despair and withdrew from his mission. Governor Daniel, however, was determined and fertile in resources; and he soon found a weapon suitable for his purpose. This weapon was the act of Parliament of 1702, which settled the oath of allegiance to Queen Anne who had recently come to the throne. It was nothing more than the usual oath which any good Protestant could take, but as the Quakers would take no oath, their scruples had always been respected in North Carolina. In the new oath, which did not reach North Carolina until the summer of 1704, Daniel saw the weapon he was looking for and resolved to require all officials to take it before entering upon their offices. The Quakers, as he anticipated, declined, and the governor accordingly refused to permit them to take their seats in the courts, the Council, and the Assembly. The expulsion of the Quakers left the Church party in control of the government, and by a majority of "one or two votes" that party put through the Assembly a second vestry act. To make assurance doubly sure, by preventing the return of the Quakers to power, the same Assembly provided an oath of office, without making any exception for Quakers, which all officials and members of the Assembly must take in the future. But the Quakers were not helpless. The other Dissenters rallied to their support; and it seems certain that some influential Churchmen, either because they were opposed to an establishment, or because they resented Daniel's highhanded methods, also came to their assistance. Complaints against Daniel were sent to Sir Nathaniel Johnson, accompanied by a petition for his removal; and Sir Nathaniel, who was involved in a bitter fight over the same question in South Carolina, thought it wise to comply with the North Carolina petition. He removed Daniel and sent Thomas Cary to succeed him.

Cary had long been prominent in the affairs of South Carolina. Although he had been implicated in a rebellion in that province, this offense was more than counter-balanced in the eyes of Governor Johnson by the fact that he was one of the governor's bondsmen. Restless, ambitious, without settled political principles, he knew no rule of action in politics except to support the party which could best advance his own fortunes. Since Cary's chief had so promptly removed Daniel upon complaint of the Quakers, members of that party at once jumped to the conclusion that Cary would espouse their cause, and they accepted his appointment as a signal for a renewal of their political activities. Great was their wrath, therefore, when they found in him a more serious obstacle than Daniel himself had been. Coming into North Carolina with an eye to his own interests, Cary found the Church party strongly entrenched in power and promptly aligned himself with it. He not only repudiated the claims of the Quakers and dismissed them from office upon their refusal to take the oaths, but prevailed upon the Assembly to pass an act imposing a heavy fine upon any person who should presume to perform an official duty without taking the required oaths, or who should promote his own election to any office. Exasperated by this unexpected turn of affairs, the Quakers and their allies determined to carry their case directly to the Lords Proprietors, and in 1706 they sent John Porter to England to seek a redress of their grievances.

Porter was successful in his mission. Through the influence of John Archdale, he obtained from the Lords Proprietors an order suspending the authority of Sir Nathaniel Johnson in North Carolina, removing Cary, naming five new deputies, and authorizing the Council to elect a president who should perform the duties of governor. Returning to North Carolina in October, 1707, armed with this order, Porter found Cary absent and William Glover temporarily administering the government. Since Glover's administration seemed to be giving satisfaction, Porter determined not to disturb it; he, therefore, called together the newly appointed deputies and induced them to elect Glover president of the Council. Though the commission under which he acted required the presence of Cary and the former deputies to make this election legal, Porter concealed this fact from the deputies as well as from Glover; and later when he found that he could not dictate the latter's policy, he pleaded the illegality of Glover's election to justify himself in forcing his removal from office. Porter's apologists have not been able to discern in his conduct anything more than a shrewd political move, but less partial critics will doubtless think it deserving of a severer condemnation.[3] However reprehensible, measured by modern ideals, the policy of the Church party may have been, the actions of its leaders throughout these controversies had been open and above board: on the other hand concealment and dissimulation characterized Porter's conduct in this affair and it cannot be justified by any standard of political ethics that places the public welfare above a partisan tri-

---

[3] Weeks: The Religious Development in the Province of North Carolina, p. 56.

umph. Not only did Porter induce the newly appointed deputies, by concealing from them their lack of legal power to act, to choose Glover as president, he himself later joined such of the former deputies as were retained by the new commission from the Lords Proprietors, including Thomas Cary, in an official proclamation calling upon the people to render to Glover that obedience which was due to him as governor of the province.

Porter, however, soon discovered that he could not control Glover. When the newly appointed Quaker deputies appeared to take their seats in the Council, Glover tendered them the prescribed oaths and upon their declining to take them, refused to admit them to their seats. The old quarrel flared up with renewed bitterness. Fuel was added to the flame by the recent arrival in the colony of two missionaries of the Society for the Propagation of the Gospel and the prospect of a revival of the activities of the Church party increased the alarm of the Dissenters, who now felt justified in resorting to violent measures to protect their interests. Accordingly Porter summoned both the old and the new deputies, informed them of the alleged defect in Glover's title to his office, and over the protest of Glover induced them to declare his election illegal and void. In the meantime the Quaker party had gained a new recruit. When Cary saw how the tide was running, he deserted the Church party and went over, bag and baggage, to its opponents. He and Porter struck a bargain as a result of which Cary was chosen president "by the votes of the very same Councillors who had before chosen Mr. Glover, and all this by virtue of that very same commission which removed him [Cary] from the government." Glover refused to yield; both sides took up arms; blood was shed and the colony reduced to the verge of civil war.

However, better counsels prevailed and the contending factions agreed to submit their claims to an Assembly. At once a new complication arose: by whose writ could an election be legally held? To answer this question was to decide the dispute; accordingly both Glover and Cary issued writs and the election was held amid bitter strife and tumult. When the Assembly met, October 11, 1708, both the Glover set of councillors and the Cary set appeared each claiming the right to be recognized as the upper house of the Assembly. An amusing side-light on this curious situation is found in the action of former Deputy-Governor Daniel. As a landgrave, one of the ranks of nobility under the Fundamental Constitutions, he was entitled to sit in the Council; but unable to decide

which was the true and lawful Council, an 1 fearful of making
a mistake, he sat first with one group and then with the other,
"and," as one historian facetiously remarks, "was equally
uncomfortable with both."[4]　Glover refused to recognize the
newly appointed Quaker deputies because they declined to
take the required oaths. But in the election of assemblymen,
the Cary party had carried the colony, and they proceeded at
once to organize the lower house regardless of Glover's protests.

The Cary party organized the Assembly by the election of
Edward Moseley as speaker. This election was the beginning
of the most remarkable career in our colonial history. For
forty years Moseley's biography is practically the history of
North Carolina, so varied were his activities and so deeply
did he impress his personality on his times. His was that
sort of character toward which men cannot be neutral. Those
who did not hate him adored him. The explanation of this
fact is found not merely in the forcefulness of his personality,
but also in the contradictions of his life and career. An aris-
tocrat by nature, he was a democrat by convictions and in
practice. Often an official of the Lords Proprietors and later
of the Crown, he firmly resisted all encroachments on the
rights of the people. Possessed of vast estates, of many
slaves, and of great wealth, he lived in great simplicity and
was genuinely sympathetic with the poor and the unfortunate.
A devoted Churchman, he steadfastly espoused the cause of the
Dissenters in their fight against an establishment. His enemies while condemning his character could not withhold their
admiration of his abilities. The Virginia boundary-line commissioners in 1710, who could find no terms too strong for
denouncing his motives, at the same time could not refrain
from testifying to "the subtlety [in debate] whereof he is
Master"; and Governor Burrington, his uncompromising foe,
while admitting that Moseley was "a person of sufficient
ability" to be public treasurer, wished that his "integrity
was equal to his ability." The denunciations of his enemies
no less than the eulogies of his friends reveal the dynamics
inherent in the man. He had, as has been well said, the boldness of thought and of action that people admire in their
leaders; the common sense and self-poise on which people
rely in troublous times; and the honesty of purpose which,
regardless of his own interests, made it impossible for him
to wink at the usurpations of authority. An active man of

---

[4] Hill, D. H.: Young People's History of North Carolina, p. 75.

affairs, he was also a student and a lover of learning; his private library, which late in life he gave to the town of Edenton as a foundation for a public library, contained a large collection of books on law, theology, history, and general literature. Looking beneath the surface of the tumult and strife in which his life was largely passed; putting to the acid test of impartial history the hasty and prejudiced judgment of his contemporaries; studying his career in the light of subsequent developments, one is prepared to accept the verdict of the careful historian who says of Edward Moseley: "it was not necessary for him 'to usurp a patriot's all-atoning name,' for he seems to have sincerely loved his adopted colony, and to have served it with the steadfast purpose of making it a home fit for free men." [5]

Such was the man whom the Cary party in the first flush of their triumph elevated to the leadership of the General Assembly. The victors were not disposed to show the vanquished much consideration. They brushed aside the claims of the contesting Glover delegations; passed an act nullifying the test oaths; recognized the Cary councillors as the upper house; and declared Cary president of the Council and ex-officio governor. Against these actions Glover protested. He declared first, that members returned under Cary's writ could not constitute a lawful Assembly because Cary, not being president of the Council, had no authority to issue a writ; and, secondly, that even if legally elected they could not sit as assemblymen until they had taken the oaths required by law, which, of course, the Quaker members had not done. It was, he declared, "a betraying of the trust reposed in the Lords Proprietors by the Crown, to submit the determinations of the Government to any number of men howsoever chosen and delegated, though by the unanimous voice of the whole countrys Except such persons shall first acknowledge their allegiance to the Queen, which both the Common Law and the Statute Law requires to be done by an oath: with which Law the Queen hath not, and the Lords Proprietors can not dispence." This protest was addressed "To the Gentlemen met and pretending themselves to be the House of Burgesses." Glover unquestionably had the better of the legal argument; but Cary had the votes and his Assembly returned Glover's protest to him with the curt statement "that they would not concern themselves in that matter." Glover, seeing that he

---

[5] Hill, D. H.: Edward Moseley: Character Sketch. (*North Carolina Booklet*, Vol. V, No. 3, p. 205.)

COLONIAL CURRENCY

Showing autograph of Edward Moseley

had lost his fight, wisely abandoned the field and beat a strategic retreat into Virginia, leaving Cary in possession of the government and the colony in confusion.

This condition continued for nearly two years before the Lords Proprietors decided to interfere. Finally in 1710 they sent out Edward Hyde, a near kinsman of the queen, as deputy-governor. Hyde arrived in Virginia in August expecting to receive there his commission from Edward Tynte of Charleston, who had succeeded Sir Nathaniel Johnson as governor of Carolina. But before Hyde's arrival Governor Tynte had died without having made out Hyde's commission and although Hyde had in his possession private letters that confirmed his appointment, without a commission he could not legally take over the government. This technical defect in his title, the Gloverites, in their eagerness to dispossess Cary, were willing to overlook, while Cary and his immediate supporters, whatever may have been their personal sentiments, were over-awed by the evident desire of the people for the restoration of peace and harmony and by the "awefull respect" felt for Hyde on account of his family connections. Accordingly all who could pretend to any right to a voice in the matter, including Cary himself, joined in a petition to Hyde to assume the duties of president of the Council until his commission should arrive from the Lords Proprietors, and Hyde promptly complied with their request. In the meantime the Lords Proprietors had decided, December 7, 1710, to appoint a governor of North Carolina "independent of the Governour of South Carolina," and had nominated Hyde for that dignity; but as a recent act of Parliament required the assent of the Crown to appointments of governors of proprietary colonies, a full year passed before all the formalities were finally completed. Hyde's commission as the first governor of North Carolina, therefore, was not issued until January 24, 1712; he opened it and qualified before the Council May 9th. Henceforth the governments of North Carolina and South Carolina were separate and distinct.

In the meantime North Carolina had been passing through one of the stormiest episodes in its stormy career. Hyde's administration had failed to produce the good results so eagerly anticipated. He allowed himself to fall completely under the influence of the Glover faction, insisted that all office-holders must take the prescribed oaths, and in this way purged both the Council and the Assembly of their Quaker members. The other Dissenters, seeing the drift of events, deserted their Quaker colleagues and rode in on the rising tide. Of Hyde's

first Assembly, which met in March, 1711, John Urmstone, a
minister of the Established Church, wrote: "With much difficulty we had the majority * * * The Assembly was
made up of a strange mixture of men of various opinions and
inclinations; a few Churchmen, many Presbyterians, Independents, but most anythingarians—some out of principle,
others out of hopes of power and authority in the government
to the end that they might lord it over their neighbors, all
combined to act answerably to the desire of the president and
Council." The party in control could not resist the opportunity to punish its enemies. Even Governor Spotswood of
Virginia, who detested a Quaker and sympathized with the
principles of the Gloverites, declared that the latter forced
through the Assembly legislation "wherein it must be confessed they showed more their resentment of their ill usage
during Mr. Cary's usurpation (as they call it) than their
prudence to reconcile the distractions of the country." Their
legislation embraced a sedition law for the punishment of
"seditious words or speeches" or "scurrilous libels" against
the existing government; fixed a fine of £100 upon all officials
who refused to qualify "according to the strictness of the laws
in Great Britain now in force"; provided that "all such laws
made for the establishment of the Church" should be still in
force; and declared null and void all court proceedings during
Cary's second administration. They also directed Cary to
account to Hyde for all funds collected during his term of
office; required Edward Moseley to give security for certain
fees which he was accused of illegally collecting; and impeach-
ing Cary and Porter of high crimes and misdemeanors,
ordered them into the custody of the provost-marshal.

Cary determined not to submit tamely to these drastic
measures. Collecting his followers, he withdrew to his plantation on the Pamlico and fortifying his house "with great Guns
and other warlike stores," bade defiance to Hyde. So strongly
was he entrenched that "when the Government had taken a
resolution to apprehend him they found it impracticable to
attempt it." Emboldened by Hyde's irresolution, Cary took
the offensive, and reinforced by "a Brigantine of six Guns,
furnished him by a leading Quaker," and "some other vessels
equipp'd in a warlike manner," he denounced Hyde for attempting to exercise executive authority without a commission, proclaimed himself president of the Council, and
moved to attack Hyde and his Council. Governor Spotswood
of Virginia offered to mediate between the warring factions.
Hyde promptly accepted but Cary "obstinately rejected all

offers of accommodation.'' On June 30, he assailed Hyde's forces which had been gathered at Thomas Pollock's plantation on the Chowan and was severely repulsed leaving his brigantine and her six guns in the hands of the enemy. Cary thereupon fled to the Pamlico where he reassembled his scattered followers and entrenched himself in the house of Captain Richard Roach, who, though an agent of one of the Lords Proprietors, had embraced Cary's cause. Hyde finding himself too weak to attack applied for aid to Spotswood who promptly dispatched to him a company of royal marines. The sight of the queen's uniform so "frighted the Rebellious party" that they threw down their arms and dispersed. Cary and several of his followers fled to Virginia where at Hyde's request they were apprehended and sent to England for trial on charges of sedition and rebellion. No evidence, however, was forwarded to sustain the charges and the prisoners were soon discharged from custody.

CHAPTER VII

INDIAN WARS OF 1711-1715

With the flight of its leader, the Cary Rebellion collapsed, but the fires of factionalism still smoldered and it took a catastrophe of appalling magnitude to quench them. This was the great Indian war that raged in North Carolina from 1711 to 1713. Cary's enemies charged his adherents with inciting the Indians to hostilities, and although the charge rests on too uncertain a basis to be readily credited, yet it cannot be denied that the dissensions among the whites, for which Cary was largely responsible, gave the Indians the opportunity for which they had long been waiting. The causes of the war were not different from the causes of most other Indian wars waged since the white man and the red man first came in contact with each other. The whites, recognizing no right of the Indian to the soil, appropriated it to their own use without scruple, and as they pushed their way to the southward from Albemarle they necessarily drove the Indians before them and seized their hunting grounds. To this injustice they added the greater wrong of kidnapping Indian men, women and children to be sold into slavery. So extensive had this infamous practice become that Pennsylvania in 1705 forbade the further "importation of Indian slaves from Carolina" because it had "been observed to give the Indians of this province some umbrage for suspicion and dissatisfaction." The Meherrins, the Nottoways, the Chowanocs, and other similar tribes, powerless to stay the march of the white man, submitted in sullen anger, but were ever on the watch for a favorable opportunity to strike a blow at their advancing foe. By the opening of the eighteenth century, the power of the Indians had gradually declined until but one tribe remained strong enough to contest the hold of the white man upon the country. The Tuscarora were a warlike nation of northern origin who were near kinsmen of the famous Iroquois of the Long House in Western New York. They possessed towns on the Roanoke and the Pamlico, but their chief towns were on the Neuse and its tributaries, and their hunting-grounds extended as far southward as the Cape Fear. They could muster more than 1,200 warriors.

The immediate cause of the war which the Tuscarora began in 1711, was the recent settlement of the Palatines on the Neuse in 1710; the occasion was Cary's Rebellion which seemed to one watchful chief, whom the whites called Hancock, to offer the very opportunity for attack for which he had been so long waiting. Accordingly during the summer of 1711 he carefully organized a coalition between his own tribe and the Coree, the Pamlico, the Mattamuskeet, and several other smaller tribes. Early in September, under his shrewd leadership, 500 warriors assembled at Cotechney, his principal town on Contentnea Creek, near the present village of Snow Hill, and determined upon September 22d as the date for the attack. So carefully kept was their secret that but a few days before the blow was to fall, Christopher de Graffenreid and John Lawson unwittingly ventured into the very heart of the Tuscarora possessions on an exploring expedition. They were captured and condemned to execution. De Graffenreid, however, by a clever stratagem, saved himself, but Lawson, who, in his "History of Carolina" had eulogized the amiable qualities of these very Indians, was put to a horrible death. No hint of their impending fate was permitted to reach the settlers who continued to receive the Indians into their cabins without suspicion up to the very morning of the attack, and slept peaceably through the preceding night. The war-whoops of the savages, arousing them from sleep at daybreak, were their first intimation of danger. Painted warriors poured out of the woods on all sides and began their horrid work. Within two hours after sunrise, they had butchered 130 settlers on the Pamlico and eighty on the Neuse. Men, women, and children fell indiscriminately beneath their bloody tomahawks, and the dead lay unburied in the hot September sun, food for wolves and vultures. For three days the awful carnage continued with every circumstance of cruelty and horror. Those who were fortunate enough to escape, fled to Bath and other places of refuge leaving the entire region between the Pamlico and the Neuse a scene of ashes, blood, and desolation.

Fortunately, Tom Blunt, chief of the Tuscarora tribe on the Roanoke, had refused to join in the conspiracy against the whites and thus the Albemarle region escaped. Nevertheless the situation in the province was critical in the extreme. The recent dissensions among the people, the refusal of the

Quakers to bear arms, the fears of attack on the western
frontier of Albemarle, the wide-spread destruction of property and the loss of life, and above all the shaken morale of
the people made Governor Hyde's task an extremely difficult
one. He acted with vigor and ability. Calling the General
Assembly in session, he induced it to vote a war credit of
£4,000 and to pass an act drafting for military service the
entire man-power of the colony between sixteen and sixty
years of age. He organized as effectively as possible the
armed forces of the colony; erected forts at strategic points;
and called on Virginia and South Carolina for aid. Governor
Spotswood promptly ordered a force of Virginia militia to
the border near the Tuscarora towns thus assuring their neutrality; but the Virginia government declined to permit troops
to be sent to the aid of North Carolina unless the North
Carolina Assembly would agree to withdraw its claims to
the region in dispute between the two colonies. South Carolina on the other hand, responding promptly and generously,
dispatched to North Carolina a strong force of whites and
Indians under the command of Col. John Barnwell.

Barnwell acted with dispatch and skill. Marching through
300 miles of wilderness, he struck the enemy in two hard-
fought battles near New Bern and forced them to sue for
peace. His first attack resulted in the reduction of Fort Narhantes, about thirty miles from New Bern, January 12, 1712.
Barnwell writes that after his forces had gained an entrance
into the fort, while his white troops were putting the men to
the sword, his Indians got all the slaves and the plunder, adding regretfully "only one girl we gott." Immediately after
this success, he advanced on Cotechney, in which Hancock had gathered a powerful force of Tuscarora and
their allies. Though reinforced by 250 North Carolinians,
Barnwell was less successful here than he had been at
Narhantes. Failing to take the place by storm, he brought
up some cannon which so terrified the Indians that they proposed a truce. To this Barnwell agreed in order to save from
massacre some white women and children whom Hancock
held as prisoners within the fort. A treaty was signed calling for a cessation of hostilities and the delivery of the prisoners in possession of the Indians. The Tuscarora likewise
agreed in the future "to plant only on Neuse River, the creek
the fort is on, quitting all claims to other lands. * * * To
quit all pretensions to planting, fishing, hunting or ranging to
all lands lying between Neuse River and Cape Feare, that entirely to be left to the So. Carolina Indians, and to be treated

as enemies if found in those ranges without breach of peace."

Barnwell naturally expected that his services to North Carolina would be rewarded with great honors and gifts. Instead of these rewards, he found himself subjected to very severe criticism for his failure to press the enemy to a decisive defeat, and disgusted at the ingratitude of the province, and unwilling for his men to return home without some profit, he determined to seek his reward from another source. Under pretence of peace, he lured a large number of Indians to the vicinity of the Coree village near New Bern, permitted his own men to fall upon them unaware, capture many of them and hasten away to South Carolina to sell their victims into slavery. This breach of faith justly incensed the Tuscarora and their allies and destroyed what little confidence they had in the plighted faith of the white men; and before the summer of 1712 was gone they were again on the warpath.

During the summer, yellow fever added its horrors to those of war, and claimed perhaps as many victims. Among them was Governor Hyde. Hyde was succeeded in the administration by Thomas Pollock, president of the Council. Pollock was the rival and antithesis of Moseley. He had come to North Carolina from Scotland in 1683 as the deputy of a Lord Proprietor and throughout his subsequent career was warmly attached to the proprietary interests. Of good Scotch stock, well educated, owner of vast estates and master of a hundred slaves, he was in full sympathy with the ideals and aspirations of the privileged classes. As a devout Churchman, loyal to the interests of the Church, he disliked Dissenters of whatever profession and was particularly hostile to the Quakers whose theology he detested and whose politics he distrusted. In the Glover-Cary contest, therefore, he adhered to Glover whom he accompanied, upon Cary's triumph, into exile in Virginia; later, during the Cary Rebellion, he was Hyde's chief lieutenant. With him the enforcement of laws and the preservation of order were cardinal political principles, and he showed the sincerity of his devotion to them when he suffered imprisonment for resisting Seth Sothel's violations of the law and when he chose exile rather than submit to what he regarded as the perversion of orderly government by Cary's illegal usurpation. To him the call of duty was a command. Upon assuming the duties of governor after Hyde's death, he wrote to the Lords Proprietors: "The real desire to serve his Majesty, your Lordships, and the poor people here, with the impertunity of the council here, have forced me to accept of the administration at this time when the country seemed to labor under insuperable difficulties when in more peaceable times I have refused it.''

Such was the man who had been called to the helm in the darkest hour in the history of North Carolina. The difficulties, as he said, might well have seemed ''insuperable.'' Large sections of the country had been desolated. Along the Neuse, the Trent and the Pamlico, the plantations had been stripped of horses, cattle, and hogs, the crops destroyed, and the cabins reduced to heaps of ashes. The people had no means of recouping their losses as the war had completely wiped out their trade with the outside world ''there being no grain nor little, or no pork this two or three years to send out, so that what few vessels come in can have little or nothing * * * so that many have not wherewith to pay their debts, and but few can supply themselves with clothing necessary for their families.'' To their other burdens, they had been compelled to add an enormous war debt. Constantly threatened by their alert and resourceful enemy the settlers in the stricken region had been compelled to pass the winter and summer huddled together in small forts and stockades thus adding a further drain upon the meager food supply of the Albemarle section. When to all this we add the ''dissention and disobedience as much as ever amongst the people,''. we complete the harrowing picture of the ruin and despair to which the colony had been reduced. Pollock summed up the situation in these words: ''Our enemies strong, and numerous, well provided with armes and ammunition; our people poor, dispirited, undisciplined, timorous, divided, and generally disobedient, and not only [in] a great want of armes and ammunition, but likewise the poor men who have been out in the service of the Country for want of their pay are in want of Clothing, so that they are not well able to hold out in the woods in the cold weather after the Indians.''

Colonel Pollock acted with courage and confidence. In an eloquent plea to the people of the colony he said: ''Our all lies now at stake, our country, our wives, our children, our estates, and all that is dear to us. * * * Let us therefore bear with patience some hardships; let [us] strive against all difficulties. * * * Let us lay aside all animosity, difference, and dissentions amongst ourselves. Let us shun such, as we would shun the plague, that endeavour to raise mutinies, or to sow seeds of dissention amongst us.'' To the regions stricken by war he dispatched food and clothing, arms and munitions, and sent reinforcements of troops. Finding that the northern tribe of Tuscarora were anxious to maintain peace with the whites, he negotiated a treaty of neutrality with their chief, Tom Blunt, who agreed to make an effort to capture Hancock and induce him to make peace. Later a second treaty was made with Blunt in which he agreed to continue his neutrality as to the Tuscarora tribes but to make war with the whites on the Coree, the Pamlico, and other allies of Hancock. Having succeeded in a remarkable degree in uniting the strength of the whites and dividing that of the Indians, Pollock sought and obtained the aid of South Carolina in meeting the new crisis.

That colony a second time came generously to the aid of the hard-pressed North Carolinians. A body of thirty-three white men and about 1,000 Indians was promptly raised, placed under the command of Col. James Moore, and ordered to North Carolina. Co-operating with a force of North Carolinians raised by Pollock, Moore speedily drove the Tuscarora and their allies to the cover of their forts, and on March 20, 1713, attacked Fort Nohoroco. After three days of fierce fighting, he reduced it, inflicting upon the enemy a loss of more than 900 men. Crushed by this blow, the severest ever experienced by the Indians of Eastern Carolina, the remnant of the defeated Tuscarora abandoned North Carolina migrating to New York, where, joining their powerful kinsmen, the Iroquois of the Long House, they changed the celebrated Five Nations into the Six Nations. Hancock's defeat practically closed the war as the only hostiles left to continue the struggle were small tribes which Moore's force quickly reduced. After the close of the war the neutral Tuscarora, with the remnant of the allied tribes remaining in North Carolina were by treaty between the Indians and the provincial government placed under the rule of Tom Blunt. Subsequently at various times small bands of the North Carolina Tuscarora abandoned North Carolina to join their brethren in New York, the last of them moving northward about the year 1802.

Two years after the overthrow of the Tuscarora, North Carolina was able to pay in kind her debt of gratitude to South Carolina. The Yamassee Indians, who had accompanied Colonel Moore on his expedition into North Carolina, having paid off some ancient scores against the Tuscarora in the war of 1711-13, returned to their wigwams in South Carolina to consider their grievances against the English which, it must be confessed, were both numerous and well founded. Instigated by the Spaniards of Florida, who agreed to supply them with arms and ammunition, they formed an

ambitious plan to wipe out of existence the colony of
South Carolina. For this purpose an alliance against the
English was effected between all the tribes in the vast region
from the Cape Fear to the Chattahoochee and beyond the Blue
Ridge. Besides the Yamassee, it embraced the Catawbas, the
Congaree, the Creeks, and the Cherokee, numbering in all more
than 6,000 warriors. It was one of the most formidable Indian
conspiracies in American history. The Yamassee opened the
war with an assault along the southern frontier on Good Friday, 1715, in which they slew more than a hundred settlers,
and threatened the existence of the colony. But the settlers,
after recovering from their surprise, quickly rallied under the
wise and energetic leadership of Governor Craven. Craven
met a large force of Indians who were advancing upon Charleston, and routed them with great slaughter. This victory gave
the colony a respite in which to prepare for hostilities. Appeals to Virginia and North Carolina brought prompt aid from
both, from Virginia upon conditions so stringent that South
Carolina was compelled to ask for their modification, from
North Carolina upon no conditions at all.

Promptly upon receiving intelligence of South Carolina's
danger, Governor Eden recently appointed governor of North
Carolina, called his Council together and upon its advice
ordered the captains who were "command^{rs} in the
Honble ye Governo^{rs} own Regim^t" to call upon their companies
for volunteers to go to the aid of South Carolina under the
command of Colonel Theophilus Hastings; but "in Case of
any Obstinancy and Reluctancy" on the part of the troops to
volunteer, each captain was "to draw out Tenn able men from
Each of ye Companyes provided that they are not those who
have ye most numerous familyes and to see all well provided
with armes and ammunition and to put them under ye said Co^{ll}
Hastings." At the same time, orders were given for the raising of another company consisting of fifty men who were to
be sent to South Carolina under command of Colonel Maurice
Moore. Colonel Moore was a native of South Carolina, but
had accompanied his brother, Colonel James Moore, to North
Carolina during the Tuscarora War, and had decided to cast
in his fortunes with that colony. Hastings and Moore were
both soon ready. The troops under Hastings, numbering
eighty whites and sixty Indians, sailed in the man-of-war
Sussex and arrived at Charleston about the middle of
July; those under Moore marched overland by way of the
Cape Fear. With this aid, and that received from Virginia,
Governor Craven was able to administer a crushing defeat

upon the enemy, whom he drove from the colony and forced to seek refuge among the Spaniards of Florida. Short work was then made of the smaller tribes along the coast, while those in the interior hastened to sue for peace.

In this war, the English came for the first time in hostile contact with the Cherokee, and their first experience with those cunning, warlike mountaineers gave them some indication of the formidable enemies they were to find in them during the next hundred years. After the defeat of the Yamassee, the Lower Cherokee sent a number of their chiefs to Charleston to seek terms of peace. Governor Craven, with the view of impressing these remote tribes with a sense of the greatness and power of the English, determined to send an expedition into their own country to dictate peace in their very midst. This expedition, consisting of Moore's North Carolinians and a company of South Carolinians under Colonel George Chicken, he placed under command of Colonel Maurice Moore. Colonel Moore moved rapidly up the north bank of the Savannah River into the country of the Lower Cherokee, where he made his headquarters. These Indians, laying the blame for their troubles upon the traders, who "had been very abuseful of them of late," reaffirmed their desire for peace, but the Upper Cherokee were still defiant, and Moore found it necessary to send a strong detachment against them. This detachment, under Colonel Chicken, penetrating into the heart of the Cherokee country, met their chiefs at Quoneashee, on the Hiwassee, near the present town of Murphy. These warriors were eager for war with some neighboring tribes, with whom the whites were trying to make peace, and demanded large supplies of guns and ammunition, saying that if they made peace, they would have no means of getting slaves with which to buy ammunition. It was not until after "abundance of persuading" by the officers that they finally "told us they would trust us once again." Peace was then made by the English agreeing to furnish the Cherokee with two hundred guns and a supply of ammunition, and to aid them in hostilities against the tribes with which the English themselves were still at war. Colonel Moore spent the winter among the Cherokee, and in the spring of 1716 returned to Charleston, where he met with a flattering reception. The General Assembly invited him to attend its session to receive "the thanks of this House for his services to this Province, in his coming so cheerfully with the forces brought from North Carolina to our assistance, and for what further services he and they have done since their arrival here."

The Indian wars left North Carolina in a deplorable condition. They had checked immigration, driven many people out of the province, and taken a heavy toll of human life. The destruction of property in the Tuscarora War was widespread. Bath County, the chief scene of conflict, was "totally wasted and ruined." Along the Neuse and the Pamlico all livestock had been driven off or killed, crops had been destroyed, plantations laid waste, and scarcely a cabin had been spared the torch. Conditions in Albemarle, although that county had escaped the ravages of actual fighting, were but little better. Besides supplying its own needs, Albemarle had been compelled for three years to provide for the necessities of Bath County and to support the military forces raised in both the Carolinas against the enemy. Its supply of pork and grain was exhausted, its trade destroyed, and its people, wrote Governor Pollock, reduced to poverty greater than one could well imagine. Throughout both counties want and distress were universal. The poor had been ruined and the rich made poor. With "scarcely corn to last them until wheat time, many not having any at all," without money "wherewith to pay their debts," "having now little or no trade," and therefore unable to "supply themselves with clothing necessary for their families," the people of North Carolina faced the winter of 1713-14 with gloomy apprehensions.

To their private burdens was added the burden of a public debt which Governor Pollock thought was greater than they "will be able to pay this ten or twelve years." In 1712, under the stress of war, the Assembly had unanimously laid "a great duty * * * on all goods exported or imported by land or water," but since these duties could not be collected immediately, it had authorized the emission of bills of credit to the amount of £4,000,—the first issue of paper money in the history of North Carolina—which were to be redeemed by the revenue arising from the duties. The following year another issue of £8,000 was found necessary. North Carolina, therefore, came out of the war heavily in debt and face to face with urgent demands for funds for the work of reconstruction. In 1714, accordingly, in order to redeem the currency already out and to provide for the pressing needs of the province, the Assembly authorized the emission of £24,000 in bills which were made "passable for all debts at rated commodities of the country." By 1722, about one-half of these bills had been retired, and the Assembly of that year issued £12,000 in new bills to redeem the balance, but when the king purchased the province in 1729, £10,000 of the old bills were still outstanding. Accordingly, before the transfer from the Proprietors to the Crown had been completed, in order to retire the £10,000 of outstanding bills and to provide an additional currency of £30,000, the Assembly, "by a pretended Law made in November, 1729," authorized an issue of £40,000.

The Assembly adopted numerous expedients to sustain the value of its currency, but it failed to adhere consistently to the only one, taxation, which could have accomplished that result. Duties were imposed on exports and imports to sustain the issue of 1712, but the duties were not collected. Taxes were also levied to redeem the bills of 1714, and "the Publick Faith was pawn'd" to sustain them; but, as Burrington said, "that Faith was afterwards broke in upon, the Taxes for sinking them were lessened, and afterwards more Bills emitted." As a result, the Assembly was early driven to artificial expedients. In 1715, it found it necessary to declare that all persons who refused to accept the bills for fees or quit rents, or who took them at a discount, were "Guilty of a very Great Breach of the act of the Assembly conserning the currency of these bills." But the most serious blow to their value came from a source over which the Assembly had no control; the Lords Proprietors refused to accept them for any of their fees and rents. A committee of the Assembly was appointed to memorialize the Proprietors on the subject and even to petition them to accept the bills in payment for land in both North Carolina and South Carolina. The Lords Proprietors were reminded that the bills had been issued "to defray the Expence of the Warr to save their Lordships Country from a great danger, and which they had nothing contributed to defend, therefore it was reasonable the Lords should so far partake as to suffer their Rents and Dues to be paid in these Bills." To the Assembly's prayer, however, the Lords Proprietors curtly replied that the clause in the currency act which made the bills receivable for their fees and quit rents was an unreasonable interference "in matters relating only to Us," adding, "We think you have nothing to do with our Lands and therefore you must expect to receive that Clause at least, in that Act of Assembly, repeal'd." At the same time they demanded that all dues to them be paid "in sterling money," or "in produce of the Country equivalent thereto." This demand was a severe blow to the credit of the bankrupt colony, and the result was inevitable. Recognizing the impossibility of preventing depreciation, the Assembly in 1729 accepted the situation and reserved to itself the right to declare annually at what exchange the bills should pass. In the meantime the bills had been sinking lower and lower. As early as 1717 they were passable even in payment of the stipends of missionaries only "at a vast discount." In 1725, they passed at about 5 for 1 of sterling, and in 1733 Burrington declared that he had purchased articles "for which I have pay'd in the Province Bills more than 20s for what cost but one in England."

One beneficial result of the Indian war was assuredly some compensation for its numerous ills. Hancock and his painted warriors destroyed the factionalism that had so long cursed the colony. During the war Cary, released from custody in England, returned to North Carolina, but his arrival excited neither the hopes of his former friends nor the fears of his enemies. Bitter experience had taught both a lesson, and Cary, finding no further opening for the exercise of his talents in North Carolina, departed for the West Indies, where history fortunately loses sight of him. Governor Pollock bore witness to the loyalty with which all factions supported his administration, declaring that the war had extinguished "the fire of difference and division amongst the people." "The Quakers," he said, "though very refractory and ungovernable in Mr. Glover's and Governor Hyde's administration, *   *   *   [I] must needs acknowledge they have been as ready (especially in supplying provision for the forces) as any others in the Government." "Thanks be to God," wrote the missionary, John Urmstone, in the winter of 1713, "we have no disturbance among ourselves, but all peoples hearts unite and every Member of the Government is as happy as the times will admit of under the wise and prudent administration of our good President." When Pollock surrendered the administration to Governor Eden in May, 1714, the colony was enjoying for the first time in a decade a period of "peace and quietness."

CHAPTER VIII

PROBLEMS OF RECONSTRUCTION

The peace which followed the Tuscarora War was not the peace of despair, or of sloth and inaction, nor yet of indifference to the public welfare. The defeat of Cary's revolt against Hyde, the separation of the government of North Carolina from that of South Carolina, and the experiences of the Indian war, all tended to strengthen the government and to discredit the revival of personal factions; the days for such adventurers as Culpepper and Miller, "Governor Gibbs" and Thomas Cary, were gone forever. Never again in its long history, except during the dark days of Reconstruction, was a chief executive of North Carolina to hold his office by a disputed title. The disgraceful quarrels of Everard and Burrington were yet to come, but they involved only the narrow circles of the personal friends of the disputants; the great body of the people stood aloof looking on with amusement or disgust. Issues more important than the ambitions and passions of individual leaders gradually arose, which grew out of conflicting views of the theories and principles of government and formed the basis for logical and healthy political divisions among the people. Although there were no elaborate organizations, or formal declarations of principles and policies, such as characterize modern political parties, nevertheless these divisions were distinct enough in personnel and in opinions for us to think of them as political parties.

First, there was the party which, for lack of a better name, we may call the government party. Its cardinal principle was belief in the necessity for a strong executive. In the administration of the government, it looked for guidance to instructions from the Lords Proprietors—after 1731 from the king—which, however inconsistent they might be with the charter, the Fundamental Constitutions, or even with the principles of the British Constitution itself, it regarded as binding upon all colonial officials. This party found its chief support among members of the Council and other officials who owed their positions to the Lords Proprietors, or to the Crown; among those who hope to promote their financial or social interests through official influence; and among those who sincerely believed that the best interests of the colony would be served by a government as independent of the people as possible. The governor himself was regarded as its leader, although not infrequently some prominent colonist, by reason of his superior abilities or character, as in the case of Thomas Pollock, so overshadowed the governor as to become the real if not the nominal party leader.

Over against this government party was the party which the historians of North Carolina like to call the popular party. This name expresses its political philosophy. Its fundamental principle was that the will of the people should be supreme in the government and that the people's will found expression through their representatives in the General Assembly. "This lawless people," wrote Urmstone in 1717, "will allow of no power or authority in either Church or state save what is derived from them." "The Assembly of this Province," testified Burrington in 1731, "have allways usurped more power than they ought to have." "All the Governours that were ever in this Province," he wrote at another time, "lived in fear of the People * * * and Dreaded their Assemblys. * * * They insist that no Public money can or ought to be paid but by a claim given to and allowed by the House of Burgesses." The people having no voice in the choice of their governor, the highest office within their gift was the speakership of the General Assembly; to that office, therefore, the ambitious politician aspired and to it the leader of the popular party was generally chosen. As the Council was the voice of the government party, so the Assembly was the voice of the popular party, and most of the political history of the colony revolves around the struggles of these two forces for supremacy.

The earliest statement extant of the principles of the two parties is found in the records of the second year of Governor Eden's administration. Its origin is somewhat obscure, but it appears to have grown out of the action of the governor and Council in impressing men and property for military service against the Indians without specific authority from the Assembly. For this action, the Assembly severely criticised the executive department. When this criticism was brought to the attention of the Council, that body unanimously resolved that it "tends very much to yᵉ Infringement of yᵉ Authorityes and powers of yᵉ Government for that it is undoubtedly prerogative to imppress and provide such necessaryes as they shall see fitting on any present Invasion, Insurrection or other pressing Emergencies or unforseen necessaties." Thus the government party, emphasizing the "prerogative" of the executive, in reply to the popular party, which had laid emphasis on the "Authority of Assembly." The views of the latter had been expressed in a resolution, drawn, it is thought, by Edward Moseley, speaker, and for nearly forty years the undisputed leader of the popular party, and unanimously adopted by the Assembly. It declared "that the Impressing the Inhabitants of this Governmᵗ or their Effects under pretence of its being for yᵉ Publick Service without Authority of Assembly is unwarrantable [and] A Great Infringmᵗ of the Liberty of yᵉ Subjects." The popular party thus took its stand in support of the principles upon which the American Revolution was afterwards fought, and from that position it never receded. It is the fact that most of the contests during our colonial history between the executive and the Assembly, i. e., between the government party and the popular party, involved this vital principle that lifts them above the level of petty colonial politics and clothes them with undying interest and significance.

From the bitter experiences through which North Carolina had passed, certain lessons were deducible which were not lost upon the people, and these lessons found expression in the legislation of the time. It was apparent that many of the colony's troubles were traceable to the weakness of government, inefficient and often corrupt administration of public affairs, and the general confusion arising from the uncertainty as to what laws were in force in the province. To remedy these evils, the General Assembly in 1714 determined upon a careful revision of "the ancient standing laws of this Government," and this revision was made by the Assembly in 1715. Its work forms a landmark in the history of North Carolina. When the student of our constitutional development, says Dr. Bassett, comes to this "Revisal of 1715," he experiences a feeling of relief, for here he leaves behind all the confusion and difficulties arising from a dubious system and meager data, and stands at last on solid ground. Doubt gives place to certainty, for now, in well preserved and authentic records, he has before

him a clear outline of the government.[1] He has, indeed, much
more than that, for in these revised statutes, sixty-nine in number, covering nearly a half-century of our history, we find a
picture of the life of the people, a record of their struggles and
achievements, and an expression of their ideals and aspirations.

To strengthen the government, an act "for the more effectual observing of the Queen's Peace, and Establishing a good
and lasting Foundation of Government in North Carolina,"
originally passed in 1711, was brought forward in its entirety.
The preamble is historically interesting. After attributing the
"several Revolutions" that had occurred in the colony, and
the ruin and suffering resulting from them, to "the late unhappy Dissentions" among the people, it asserts that "it has
pleased God in a great Measure to influence us with a deep
Concern for our Calamities, and put into our Hands a Power
and Resolution of removing these threatening Evils and Dangers, and for the future to procure a happy Restoration of
Peace and Tranquility amongst us, by making such good and
wholesome Laws whereby Religion and virtue may flourish,
our Duty to our Prince and Governors be put in practice and
maintained, our Laws, Liberties and Estates preserved and
kept inviolated, and Justice and Trade encouraged." To secure
these results severe punishment "by fine, imprisonment, pillory, or otherwise at the discretion of the court," was provided for persons found guilty of seditious words or conduct,
of spreading "false News" or "scurrilous Libels" against
government, and of participating in conspiracies, riots, or rebellions. As a still further discouragement to future Culpep-
pers, Gibbses, and Carys, the act also declared that any person indulging in such pastimes should be incapable of holding
any office in the province for three years. "And because it has
always happened," continues this interesting statute, "that
upon vacancy of the Government, seditious and Evil-minded
Persons have taken Occasion to dispute the Authority of the
succeeding governor or President, however Elected or Qualified, for want of certain Rules being laid down and approved
of by the Lords Proprietors," the Assembly imposed the duty
of filling such a vacancy upon the Council and specifically directed how it should perform that duty.

Careful attention was also given to problems relating to
the administration of public affairs. Acts were passed pro-

---

[1] The Constitutional Beginnings of North Carolina, p. 60.

viding for the appointment and defining the duties of certain precinct officials; fixing the fees of all officials from the governor down; requiring every officer, unless appointed by the Lords Proprietors, to give bond "for the faithful discharge of his Office"; regulating court proceedings; declaring the methods of probating wills and granting letters of administration; providing for the care of orphans; fixing the age at which a person should be considered a tithable, and directing how lists of tithables should be taken in the several precincts. One important act put into effect that clause of the Fundamental Constitutions guaranteeing biennial sessions of the General Assembly. It fixed the date and places of elections; directed how elections should be held; defined the qualifications for members and for voters; allotted five members each to the precincts of Albemarle County and two each to all other precincts; and declared that "the Quorum of the House of Burgesses for voting & passing of Bills shall not be less than one full half of the House."

This act was a favorite measure of the popular party, but when put to the test it was found to contain defects which nullified its purpose. In September, 1725, in accordance with its provisions, representatives were elected to meet in Assembly in November; but in October, Governor Everard, acting upon the advice of his Council, prorogued the session until April 1, 1726. His action aroused the indignation of the popular party, and in defiance of his proclamation the representatives-elect met at the appointed time and undertook to organize a house. The governor, of course, refused to recognize them as a legal body, and declined to send to them the election returns of members, or to receive their speaker. The representatives thereupon adopted a protest against this "Pretended Prorogation" as "being Contrary to the Laws of this Province, an Infringement of their Liberty & Breach of the Priviledges of the People." Then, having resolved that they would "Proceed to no business until their Lawful Priviledges which they now claim are Confirm'd unto them by the Governor & Council," they adjourned to the date set by the governor's proclamation. However, they were forced to recede from their position because technically they were in the wrong. The act to which they appealed called for biennial sessions, "Provided allways & nevertheless that the Powers granted to the Lords Proprietors from the Crown of Calling, proroguing & dissolving Assemblys are not hereby meant or intended to be invaded, limited or restrained." This provision, of course, placed sessions of the Assembly completely at the mercy of the governors, who did not fail to make full use of it. Another defect in the law was the unequal distribution of representatives among the precincts. This inequality of representation later caused a division in the popular party itself, which their opponents, under the leadership of Governor Johnston, skillfully turned to their advantage. The government party also objected to the provision that fixed upon a majority as a quorum, and to the assumption that the General Assembly had power to erect precincts and grant them representation; these two features gave rise to bitter controversies, and finally, in 1737, led to the repeal of the act by the king in Council.

As there was no printing-press in the colony, the laws were to be had only in manuscript form, copies were scarce and often inaccessible, and public officials in whose custody they were placed were not careful to keep them properly revised. So confused had they become that even officials and attorneys could not say, without long and inconvenient searching of the scattered records, what laws were in force. To clear up this uncertainty the Assembly declared that all laws passed prior to 1715, unless expressly excepted by title, were repealed and that the statutes contained in the revision of 1715 should "be of full force & shall be hence forward deemed, taken & adjudged as the body of the laws of this Government & no other heretofore made." At the same time, inasmuch as North Carolina was "annexed to and declared to be a Member of the Crown of England," and its laws were required by the charter to be in harmony with the laws of England, the Assembly declared that it was manifest "that the Laws of England are the Laws of this Government, as far as they are compatable with our Way of Living and Trade." For the information of the people, court officials were required to see that a copy of the laws be "constantly laid open upon the Court table during the sitting of the Court," and each precinct clerk was to read them aloud once a year, "publickly & in open Court."

Among the laws of England expressly declared to be in force in North Carolina were "all such laws made for the establishment of the Church and the laws made for granting indulgences to Protestant Dissenters." Not only was the legal status of the Church of England thus recognized, it was further declared to be "the only Established Church to have publick encouragement" in North Carolina. A vestry act was therefore passed which divided the province into nine parishes, named vestrymen in each, prescribed their duties, and empow-

ered them "to raise and levy money by the poll" for support
of the Establishment. It was the last vestry act passed under
the proprietary government, and remained in force until
1741.

Ministers were supplied to the colony by the Society for
the Propagation of the Gospel. Its first missionary to North
Carolina was John Blair, who arrived in January, 1704. Blair
found in the colony three small churches. He remained here
only six months, but by travelling "one day with another, Sun-
days only excepted, about thirty miles per diem," and often
sleeping in the woods at night, he succeeded in covering the
parishes of Chowan, Perquimans, and Pasquotank. In them he
organized vestries, instructed them in their duties, preached
twice every Sunday and often on week-days, and baptized
about one hundred children. "There are a great many still to
be baptized," he reported, "whose parents would not conde-
scend to have them baptized with god-fathers and god-moth-
ers." At the end of six months he returned to England to present the needs of the colony to the society.

Four years passed after Blair's departure before the
arrival of William Gordon and James Adams, the next
missionaries of the Church in North Carolina. Gordon
took up his work in Chowan and Perquimans, Adams
in Pasquotank and Currituck. In Chowan, Gordon found
the church badly in need of repair; in Perquimans, he
found a compact little church, "built with more care and
expense, and better contrived than that in Chowan," but still
unfinished. Adams found no church in either of his parishes,
but his presence stimulated the people to resolve "to build a
church and two chapels of ease." Although Gordon remained
in the colony only four months, and Adams but little more than
a year, both of these earnest men made a deep impression
upon the people. Their exemplary characters, their genuine
interest in the welfare of their parishioners, and the sincerity
of their faith and piety did much to silence the enemies and
stimulate the friends of the Establishment.

Following Gordon and Adams came first John Urmstone and then Giles Rainsford. The latter arrived in
June, 1712, and remained about two years. At his first
service he found the people interested, but "perfect
strangers to the Method of the Worship of our Church."
When he preached in "a small Chapel near an Old Indian
Town" a "vast Crowd" came to hear him, but "exprest very
little or rather no devotion in time of the divine Service." On

another occasion the crowd was so great that he was obliged to hold the service out-of-doors "under a large mulberry tree"; here the people were devout and "very ready in their responses as in their method of singing praises to God." Rainsford was a narrow Churchman and immoderate in his arraignment of Quakers and "Quakerism," but he was sincere and upright and displayed intelligent zeal in his labors. The Indians particularly excited his sympathetic interest. He lived five months with the Chowanocs, made himself "almost a Master at their Language," and tried to teach them the principles of Christianity.

In 1717 Ebenezer Taylor came as a missionary to Bath County. He was "aged and very infirm," but neither age nor infirmity could dampen his ardor. For four years he labored zealously and finally, in 1720, met his death from exposure and cold "after having been ten days and nights in an open boat" in the dead of winter. Taylor's successor in Bath was Thomas Bailey, who came about 1725; Bailey's colleague in Albemarle was John Blacknall. Of Bailey and Blacknall, their work and character, it is impossible to speak with certainty. They left no records of their own, and so completely were they involved in the quarrels of Governor Everard and George Burrington that the testimony of their contemporaries is worthless as a basis of judgment. Bailey, whom the vestry of St. Thomas Parish at Bath characterized as "our Pious & Exemplary Minister," was denounced by Governor Everard as "a scandalous drunken man;" while Blacknall, according to the same authority, was "a very good Preacher, a Gent^m perfectly sober, belov'd by all but Mr. Burrington's Party."

Finally, there was the notorious John Urmstone. No difficulty in reaching a correct judgment confronts us here. With his own hand, in numerous letters to the Society for the Propagation of the Gospel, Urmstone revealed his own character both as a man and as a minister, and in neither capacity does he show a single redeeming quality. Quarrelsome, dishonest, self-seeking and avaricious, false in word and faithless in conduct, he was utterly lacking in genuine piety or Christian charity and devoid of the slightest sense of his duty as a minister of the Church. Both the Church and the colony were gainers when, in March, 1721, without notice or explanation, he suddenly deserted his post and sailed for England. His desertion, says Governor Eden, left "nine parishes consisting

ST. THOMAS' CHURCH AT BATH

The Oldest Church in North Carolina

of upwards of 2,500 white souls entirely destitute of any assistance in religious affairs.''

Historians are agreed that the Establishment was a hindrance to the development of religious life in North Carolina, but they attribute this result to different causes. One traces it chiefly to the character of the colonial clergy, another to the insuperable physical difficulties incident to a frontier community. ''The wickedness and carelessness of the people,'' in the opinion of Dr. Weeks, ''was induced in part, no doubt, by the badness of the missionaries. * * * the chief fruit [of their labors] was civil dissension and bloodshed, culminating in foistering on the colony an Establishment which was to be a constant source of annoyance and which is directly responsible for a large share of the backwardness of the State.''[2] Bishop Cheshire, on the other hand, sees in the several vestry acts passed from 1701 to 1715 ''evidence of a reviving interest in religion'' among the people generally. ''In almost all parts of the colony,'' he says, ''the people desired the ministrations of the Church but they were mostly living upon isolated plantations. No missionary could reach and serve a sufficient number of people to form any effective organization. The legal establishment, with its power to levy taxes for the support of the Church, was a real disadvantage, because it provided no adequate support while it took off the sense of obligation from the most zealous members of the Church. Clergymen and missionaries came and labored for a while and then disappeared; some good, some indifferent, others weak and unworthy; and very few of them, even the best, able to deal effectively with the strange conditions of the new and poor settlement.''[3] The historian and the Churchman are both partially right, but neither sees the whole truth. The missionaries, as a rule, were better men than the prejudices of the historian will allow; nevertheless, had they been as zealous as their calling and task demanded, they would have overcome most of the difficulties which the Churchman pleads in extenuation of their failure. During the proprietary period of our history a majority of the people of North Carolina undoubtedly adhered to the teachings and preferred the liturgy of the Church of England, and would have been glad to see that Church strong and flourishing in the colony; but even then many of the ablest Churchmen

---

[2] Church and State in North Carolina, p. 22 (*J. H. U. Studies*, 11th Series, Nos. V-VI).

[3] ''How Our Church Came to North Carolina,'' in *The Spirit of Missions*, Vol. LXXXIII, No. 5, p. 349.

seemed to have had an instinctive feeling that an Established Church was an anomaly in the New World and out of harmony with the spirit of the civilization which they were developing here. Their instinct was right, and that is why the Establishment in North Carolina was a failure.

It cannot be said that the Dissenters were ever reconciled to the Establishment; still, after 1715, they made little or no organized opposition to it. They probably felt that such resistance would be futile and result only in arousing the church party to action. As it was, Churchmen generally displayed but little interest in the Establishment; enforcement of the law was always lax, and its burdens more imaginary than real. But perhaps the chief reason for the lack of organized opposition was the act of 1715, which gave Dissenters a legal status and threw around them the protection of the law. The same act which declared that all laws of England "made for the Establishment of the Church" were the laws of North Carolina also declared to be of equal force in the colony all "laws made for granting indulgences to Protestant Dissenters." The position of Protestant Dissenters in England had been defined in the Toleration Act of 1689, which granted to them the privilege of attending their own places of worship and guaranteed them freedom from disturbance upon condition that they took the oath of allegiance and subscribed the declaration against transubstantiation. In line with this policy, the North Carolina Assembly, immediately after passing the vestry act of 1715, passed "An Act for Liberty of Conscience," which declared "that all Protestant Dissenters within the Government shall have their Meetings for the exercise of their Religion without Molestation." It also granted to Quakers the right to affirm, but forbade them "by virtue of this Act" to serve as jurors, to testify in criminal cases, or to hold office. Although many irritating and unjustifiable restrictions were still imposed upon Dissenters yet this act was recognized as a great step forward, and, as Dr. Weeks says, "From that time the Dissenters, in characteristic English fashion, submitted to the will of the majority and began to fight their battle along legal and technical lines. During the next sixty-two years North Carolina was not without discussion and agitation on ecclesiastical matters, and this dissension, culminating in the Mecklenburg instructions of 1775 and 1776, and crystallizing in the Constitution adopted at Halifax in December, 1776, put North Carolina close to Virginia, the first political organization to solve the problem of a free church in a free state, each independent of the other."[4]

Politics and religion shared the attention of the Assembly of 1715 with immigration and industry. The statutes of 1669 relating to trade, landholding, and foreign debts, which were designed to attract immigration, were re-enacted; while one of the purposes of the act providing for biennial sessions of the Assembly, it was expressly stated, was to secure to the colony through "the frequent sitting of Assembly [which] is a principal safeguard of the People's privileges" such "privileges & immunities" as would attract immigrants and "thereby enlarge the Settlement." Several statutes were passed relating to trade, commerce, and transportation. "For establishing a Certainty in Trade," a legal rating was given to certain commodities at which all persons were required to receive them in payment of debts unless their contracts specifically called for payment in sterling money. To promote facility in trading, as well as to prevent fraud, standards of weights and measures were fixed and entrusted to the care of the vestries, who were required to keep them accessible for testing. Every cooper, for instance, was required to stamp his barrels with his "proper Brand Mark," which must have been previously registered in the office of the precinct clerk, and heavy penalties were imposed for failure to come up to the specifications required by law. Attempts to pass off commodities "not good or Merchantable," or packed in unlawful casks, were punishable by heavy fines. One of the most serious obstacles to the prosperity of the colony had been the absence of grist-mills. Mill sites were scarce and more than fifty years passed after the settlement of North Carolina before a mill was erected in the colony. As late as 1710 De Graffenried states that "there was in the whole province only one wretched water mill." Poor people pounded their grain in wooden mortars, while the wealthy used hand mills, or else imported flour and meal from New England. The Assembly of 1715 sought a remedy for this situation in an act which permitted mill sites to be condemned, but mills erected on such condemned sites were to be "Publick Mills," required by law to grind all grain offered to them at a fixed legal toll. Looking to the improvement of inland transportation and commerce, the Assembly adopted a comprehensive plan for the laying out of roads, the building of bridges, and the establishment of ferries, and for their maintenance; while for the encouragement of inter-colonial

---

[4] Church and State in North Carolina, p. 11.

and foreign commerce it made provision for keeping pilots at Roanoke and Ocracoke inlets who were required "constantly and diligently to make it their business to search & find out the most convenient channels," keep them properly staked out, and to pilot vessels safely over the bars.

Recognizing the importance of towns as centers of trade and commerce, the Assembly for the "Encouragement of the Town of Bath and all other Towns now or hereafter Built within this Government," conferred upon them whenever they should have at least sixty families the privilege of representation in the General Assembly. At this time Bath, Edenton, and New Bern were the only towns in North Carolina. Of Bath, the oldest of these towns, William Gordon wrote in 1709 that it "consists of about twelve houses and is the only town in the province. * * * I must own it is not the unpleasantest part of the country—nay, in all probability it will be the center of a trade, as having the advantage of a better inlet for shipping, and surrounded with the most pleasant of savannahs, very useful for stocks of cattle." The Tuscarora War struck Bath a hard blow from which it never recovered. "We expect to hear," wrote Urmstone in 1714, "that famous city of Bath, consisting of nine houses, or rather cottages, once styled the metropolis and seat of this Government, will be totally deserted." In an effort to revive it the Lords Proprietors in 1716 made Bath a port of entry, but to no purpose; fifteen years later Governor Burrington reported that Bath was "a town where little improvements have been made." A better fortune awaited De Graffenried's "townlet" on the Neuse. The act of 1715 granting representation to towns with sixty families conferred this privilege upon New Bern "altho' there should not be Sixty families Inhabiting in the said Town." In 1723, having recovered somewhat from the disasters of the Indian war, New Bern was incorporated and its boundaries greatly enlarged. It enjoyed an advantageous situation for trade and soon became the largest town, and eventually the capital of the province. For many years New Bern's only rival, as a political and commercial center, was the "Towne on Queen Anne's Creek," which, in 1722, was incorporated under the name of Edenton in honor of Governor Eden whose home was there. From 1720 to 1738, the Assembly held its sessions at Edenton which was accordingly looked upon as the seat of government. Though never counting in colonial times a population of more than four or five hundred, Edenton retained its importance as the political, social and commercial center of the colony until after the Revolution.

CHAPTER IX

THE PASSING OF THE PROPRIETARY

The removal of the constant menace presented by the presence of the Tuscarora, the displacing of personal factions as the mainspring of politics by real political parties, and the strengthening of the authority of government prepared the way for a period of growth and progress in North Carolina for which the legislation of 1715 laid the foundation. Under the stimulus of peace and the resultant feeling of security, the colony was able to repay its debt to South Carolina for her aid in the Tuscarora War; to revive its trade; to free itself from the disgrace of piracy; to increase its population and expand its frontiers; to settle peacefully its long-standing boundary dispute with Virginia; and, finally, to undergo a profound change in its government without a jar.

On May 28, 1714, Charles Eden took the oath of office as governor. He was a man of fair ability and amiable disposition and, except for suspicions of improper dealings with "Blackbeard," the pirate, was generally held in high esteem in the colony. The "peace and quietness" which he found upon his arrival continuing throughout his administration, were favorable to the revival of trade and commerce. Internal trade conditions were improved by a stricter enforcement of the road law. At a single session of the General Court in 1720 three road overseers were indicted and subsequently fined for neglect of their duty in the "making, mending, & Repairing of Roads & Highways." Many new roads were cut through the wilderness. Especially important was the road laid out by Governor Burrington "from Nuse to Cape Fear River about one hundred miles in length," which was a realization in part of the long-cherished plan of the Lords Proprietors to establish a land route between their two provinces. This road not only stimulated trade; it also served as a highway for settlers who were seeking new homes on the Cape Fear. Intercolonial trade which had been practically destroyed by the Cary Rebellion and the Indian wars also showed signs of revival and

New England skippers piloted through the channels of Ocracoke and Roanoke inlets, now marked out in accordance with the pilotage law of 1715, once more cast their anchors at the wharves of the hospitable planters. The erection of a number of saw mills greatly increased the output of lumber as an article of commerce; while during the decade following 1715, tar, pitch and turpentine, commodities for which North Carolina afterwards became so famous, began to appear in the lists of the colony's exports. "Of late," says a report written in 1720, "they [the planters] made ab⁺ 6000 barrells of pitch and tarre which the New England sloops carry first to New England and then to Great Brittain." Efforts were made to keep this reviving trade in legitimate channels by appropriating part of the duty on imports "to Beacon out the Channels from Roanoke to Ocracoke Inlets," and by establishing collection districts at Currituck, at Edenton on the Roanoke, at Bath on the Pamlico, at Beaufort at Topsail Inlet, and later at Brunswick on the Cape Fear; but these measures served chiefly to stimulate smuggling which increased more rapidly than legitimate trade.

Most of this smuggling was done by traders who had purchased their cargoes honestly and became violators of the law only when they evaded the payment of the duties, but much of it was the work of out-and-out pirates. Piracy had long been one of the chief obstacles to the development of the commerce of the Carolinas, the natural dangers that repelled legitimate traders making the Carolina coast a favorite resort for buccaneers. Behind the bars and shifting sands that obstruct the entrances to the Carolina waters scores of pirates rested secure from interference, leisurely repaired damages, and kept a sharp lookout for prey. But nature was not their only ally. The corruption of many of the colonial officials, the weakness of the proprietary government, the willingness of the people to shelter violators of the navigation laws without enquiring too strictly into the nature of their enterprises, all combined with the character of the coast to stimulate smuggling and piracy. The period from 1650 to the close of the first decade of the eighteenth century, John Fiske has aptly called "the golden age of pirates." It was during this period that Carolina was settled and for the reasons just mentioned became a retreat for freebooters. As early as 1683, the Board of Trade complained of the "harbouring and encouraging of Pirates in Carolina and other Governments and Propprietys," but it was not until 1718 that effective measures were taken to destroy the evil.

It would be easy to attach too much significance to these facts and to draw from them conclusions which they do not warrant as to the comparative morality of the people of the Carolinas. In none of the colonies, during the seventeenth century, was there that condemnation of smuggling and that horror of piracy characteristic of more highly organized communities and of more enlightened ages, and the freebooter with a rich cargo for sale knew well enough that neither in Boston nor in New York, in Philadelphia nor in Baltimore, need he fear too close a scrutiny into his title to his property if he were liberal enough with his presents and his rum, and if his prices were satisfactory. Besides, the extent to which piracy flourished in Carolina and in the other proprietary colonies was greatly exaggerated. Most of the reports on the subject came from crown officials, or from officials of crown colonies, who made but little distinction between smugglers and pirates; their reports moreover were part of the propaganda carried on for many years for the purpose of discrediting the proprietary colonies in order to pave the way for their seizure by the Crown.

Nevertheless the evil was serious enough and efforts to induce the colonial authorities to exterminate it proved unavailing. Too many of the officials were hand in glove with the robbers. In South Carolina, Robert Quarry, secretary of the colony, was dismissed from office "for harbouring pirates and other misdemeanors"; his successor, Joseph Morton, was charged with permitting pirates openly to use Charleston harbor for securing their prizes; and John Boone was expelled from the Council for correspondence with the freebooters. In North Carolina, it was charged that Seth Sothel actually issued commissions "to Pyrates for rewards"; that John Archdale sheltered pirates "for which favour he was well paid by them"; that Governor Eden and Tobias Knight, the latter secretary of the colony and acting chief-justice, actually shared the pirates' ill-gotten gains. Perhaps some of these accusations were groundless, but that so many officials fell under suspicion indicates a low state of official morality. Finally, near the close of the seventeenth century, the king, despairing of accomplishing anything through colonial officials, determined to take a hand himself in the matter, and by a judicious mixture of executive clemency and extreme severity soon drove the enemy out of all their strongholds except New Providence and Cape Fear. In 1718, an English fleet captured New Providence. "One of its immediate effects, however," as Fiske observes, "was in turn the whole remnant of the scoundrels over to the North Carolina coast, where they took their final stand."

Among the noted pirates who had made their headquarters at New Providence were Edward Teach, or Thatch, better known as "Blackbeard," and Major Stede Bonnet. The former was merely a pirate,—a swaggering, merciless brute without even that picturesqueness of personality which has clothed so many of his kind with romantic interest and robbed their careers of the horrors which the naked truth would inspire; the latter was a gentleman of birth, wealth and education, who had already won distinction and rank as a soldier when, catching the contagion of the times, in a spirit of adventure, he turned his back upon all and joined "Blackbeard" in his career of crime. After being driven from New Providence, "Blackbeard" made his headquarters at Bath, Bonnet at Cape Fear, and together they harried the coast from Maine to Florida. But the day had passed when it was considered respectable to hold dealings with pirates, and the evil repute which their wild deeds brought upon North Carolina together with the lethargy of the officials in dealing with them, aroused the indignation of such men as Edward Moseley and Maurice Moore. They could effect nothing, however, because, as it was currently believed and afterwards proved, some of the highest officials, including certainly the secretary of the colony, and possibly the governor, were beneficiaries of the pirates, and refused to move against them.

The blows which destroyed piracy in North Carolina waters, therefore, came from South Carolina and Virginia. Governor Robert Johnson of South Carolina had suffered a deep official and personal humiliation at the hands of "Blackbeard" and was eager to wipe out the disgrace. When, therefore, he learned in the summer of 1718, that a pirate was successfully operating off the coast of the Carolinas, he promptly fitted out an expedition under Col. William Rhett, a daring and experienced seaman, and sent him in search of the pirate. Rhett found his enemy lurking behind the bars at the mouth of the Cape Fear River and after a desperate battle of five hours captured him. He proved to be none other than the notorious Bonnet. Carried at once to Charleston, Bonnet was tried, convicted, and hanged. A few weeks later, Governor Spotswood of Virginia receiving information that

Teach was in Carolina waters with a prize, secretly fitted out two sloops manned with crews from British men-of-war then stationed in the James River, placed them in command of Lieut. Robert Maynard of the royal navy, and sent them in search of the freebooter. Maynard found Teach near Ocracoke Inlet and on November 22, 1718, attacked him. The battle long hung in doubt. Fortune finally seemed to favor the pirates when Teach at the head of a strong attacking party boarded Maynard's sloop. Maynard, however, had adopted a stratagem to bring about this very movement, and his men who had been hiding below, now rushed on deck, and in a desperate hand-to-hand conflict killed "Blackbeard" and overpowered his followers. Of "Blackbeard's" crew of eighteen men, one-half had been killed outright; the other half were made prisoners, carried to Virginia, tried and convicted of piracy. The victories over Bonnet and Teach were decisive blows to piracy along the Carolina coast, and after a few more years the black flags of the buccaneers disappeared from our seas.

High public officials had been for some time under suspicion of complicity with the pirates and this suspicion became a certainty when a friendly letter of recent date from Secretary Knight and a memorandum of goods deposited with him by the pirate were found upon the person of the dead "Blackbeard." Knight wrote: "My ffriend, If this finds you yet in harbour I would have you make the best of your way up as soon as possible. * * * I have something more to say to you than at present I can write. * * * I expect the Governor this night or tomorrow who I believe would be likewise glad to see you before you goe. * * * Your real ffriend and Servant, T. Knight." Knight however strenuously denied having received any goods from "Blackbeard," but a search made by Spotswood's officers, accompanied by Edward Moseley and Maurice Moore, revealed the articles concealed in his barn. In spite of this evidence, the governor and Council publicly exonerated Knight, denounced the charges against him as false and malicious, and declared him innocent of wrong-doing; but the evidence was conclusive of Knight's guilt, and the governor's anxiety to prevent his prosecution seemed to many persons to confirm the suspicions attaching to his own relations with the pirate.

These suspicions Moseley and Moore undertook to probe to the bottom. For that purpose they sought to examine the records of Knight's office which, according to the instructions of the Lords Proprietors, were subject to public inspection. Denied this right, with some of their followers they broke into a private house in which the records were deposited, and seized and examined them. For this offense, the governor promptly issued a warrant for their arrest and ordered out a strong armed posse to execute it. Moseley denounced his conduct in vigorous language, declaring that the governor "could easily procure armed men to come and disturb quiet & honest men, but could not (tho' such a Number would have done) raise them to destroy Thack." "It is like the commands of a German Prince!" he exclaimed indignantly. For these and other "seditious words" he was indicted under the statute of 1715 "for the more effectual observing of the King's Peace, and Establishing a good and lasting Foundation of Government in North Carolina," to which his own name, curiously enough, is signed as speaker of the Assembly. The case aroused great public interest. Moseley was the acknowledged leader of the popular party, and his contest with the governor assumed a political importance which lifted it above an ordinary criminal prosecution. Popular sympathy was with Moseley; even the jurors, bound as they were by their oath, seem to have done their best to find a loophole through which they might extricate the popular champion, for while they could not deny that he had uttered the words with which he was charged, they returned as their verdict that "if the Law be for our Sovereign Lord and King, then we find him the s^d Edward Moseley Guilty, but if the Law be for the s^d Moseley then we find him not Guilty." The court decided that the law was against Moseley, imposed upon him a fine of £100, and declared him incapable of holding any office or place of trust in the colony for three years. Thus Eden triumphed, his rival was silenced, and his dealings with the pirates shielded from further investigation, for before Moseley's disabilities were removed, Eden's death had put an end to their controversy.

Eden's successor was George Burrington, a native of that county of Devon, which gave to England so many of those great navigators and adventurers to whom she owed her American empire, the home of Gilbert, Hawkins, Grenville, Drake, and Raleigh. Burrington himself was not without the high spirit and ability which distinguished these men, but he had serious defects of character which rendered it impossible for him to rival their achievements. He had the aggressive spirit and dauntless courage that qualify men for leadership, but he was governed by a violent, uncontrollable temper that invariably drove high-spirited men from the ranks of his followers. He had the restless energy and boundless ambition which inspire men to great enterprises, but he was possessed of an overweening egotism that made him incapable of sinking his personal interests in the interest of a cause. He had the keen insight into current conditions and the resourcefulness of intellect which fit men for the tasks of statesmanship, but he was controlled by a spirit of blind partisanship which destroyed his usefulness for the highest forms of public service.

Burrington was a bundle of contradictions. As governor he was zealous for the good of the province, but he was domineering and tyrannical in his conduct; he was fertile in ideas for its development, but tactless in presenting them to the consideration of others and intolerant of opposition; he was energetic in carrying his plans into execution, but ruthless and unscrupulous in his methods. His zeal for the public welfare was never unmixed with his personal interests for he had staked out for himself vast estates in the province and did not scruple to use his official position to enhance their value. In his relations with other men, he acknowledged no neutrals. There were only friends and enemies. But both his friendships and his enmities were as often dictated by genuine interest in the affairs of the province as by personal feelings; and to advance the one or indulge the other, he was as ready to sacrifice his friends as to crush his enemies, and he did both with equal efficiency. Dissimulation was utterly foreign to his character; he was open and frank in friendship and in enmity, and gave no man cause to doubt where he would stand in any controversy; but with his friends he was selfish and exacting, domineering and, if his interests so dictated, faithless; while with his enemies he was quarrelsome and relentless, vengeful and brutal. His official papers show an intimate knowledge of the country and the measures best adapted to promote its development and considered alone, unconnected with his quarrels, present him as an active, intelligent and efficient official; but they cannot be considered alone, and they reveal him, therefore, as a man of ability, indeed, but utterly disqualified by character for the position he occupied.

Burrington was appointed governor in February, 1723, but he did not arrive in North Carolina until January, 1724. It was characteristic of him that he should align himself with the popular party. Moseley, who was of his Council, received

CHRISTOPHER GALE
First Chief Justice of North Carolina

from him numerous marks of confidence. When about to set
out upon a journey to South Carolina, Burrington designated
Moseley as acting-governor in his absence. He associated himself with Moseley, Moore and other leaders of the popular
party in planting settlements on the Cape Fear. The Assembly, too, found him responsive to its wishes. At its request he
ordered the Carolina land office, which had been closed by
order of the Lords Proprietors, to be re-opened; and although
the Lords Proprietors had forbidden the sale of any land
within twenty miles of Cape Fear, again at the instance of the
Assembly he ordered this instruction to be disregarded. The
government party, which considered the governor as its natural head, keenly resented Burrington's desertion. Chief Justice Gale now became its leader, and early came into hostile
conflict with Burrington who threatened to slit Gale's nose,
crop his ears, "lay him in irons," and blow up his house with
gun-powder. Unable to make headway against the governor
and the Assembly, Gale finally carried his case to the Lords
Proprietors. He charged that Burrington had violently broken
up the sittings of the General Court, thereby rendering the
chief justice incapable of executing his office; that Burrington had made murderous assaults upon him forcing him "in
bodily fear of his life" to flee the province; that Burrington
had been guilty of malpractices in office whereby he had prevented the king's customs officers from performing their duties. These charges, which the Assembly denounced as "malicious," the Lords Proprietors, who were accustomed to such
violent controversies in their province, might have been willing to overlook in view of the material prosperity which the
colony was enjoying under Burrington's energetic administration; but a fourth count against him, hinted at rather than
openly charged, was a more serious matter. It was suggested
that Burrington "intended a Revolution in this Government
as was some years ago in South Carolina." The reference
of course was to the Revolution of 1719 in which the South
Carolinians overthrew the proprietary government and invited the Crown to assume direct control of their affairs. Burrington's efforts to ingratiate himself with the popular party,
his close association with Moseley and with Moore, whose
brother had been a prominent leader in the South Carolina
Revolution, his repudiation of the instructions of the Lords
Proprietors, his zeal in opening the Cape Fear to settlements,
and his visits to South Carolina, all gave color to the suggestion, and alarmed the Lords Proprietors, who in great haste

removed him after he had been but a year in office, and appointed to succeed him Sir Richard Everard, who qualified at Edenton, July 19, 1725.

Neither the Proprietors nor the colony reaped any benefit from the change. It resulted, for the former, in hastening the transfer of their property to the Crown; for the latter, in six years of bad government. Everard had all the vices and none of the virtues of Burrington. His intellect was mean, his character contemptible. As a man he was vain, selfish and cowardly; as governor he practiced nepotism, tyrannized over his colleagues, and accepted bribes. Besides these disqualifications for his place he was strongly suspected of Jacobitism. Upon the death of George I, it is said, he exclaimed with an air of exultation: "Now adieu to the Hanover family; we have done with them!" He had administered the government but a few months before Chief Justice Gale, Thomas Pollock, and other leaders who had hailed his appointment as a great party triumph, were clamoring for his removal. Because of his "great Incapacity and Weakness," they declared, the government had "grown so weak and Feeble" that but for its transfer to the Crown "it could not have subsisted much longer, but must have Dwindled and sunk into the utmost Confusion and Disorder." Everard was the last of the proprietary governors. During his administration the Lords Proprietors surrendered their charter to the Crown,—a step which, though inevitable sooner or later, was doubtless hastened by the utter breakdown of the proprietary government under Everard's direction.

The period covered by the administrations of Eden, Burrington, and Everard, in spite of bad government, was a period of growth and improvement. Immigration increased rapidly, settlements expanded to the west and the south, and four new precincts were erected for the convenience of the new settlers. By 1720 settlements had ceased to hug the coast. Now and then some adventurer, more daring than the rest, with axe in one hand and rifle in the other, had dared to turn his back upon the older communities and plunge into the great unexplored forests to the westward. Along the bank of some stream he would select a fertile spot, clear away the trees, and build his rude cabin. Scores of such cabins were soon scattered throughout the interior. North of Albemarle Sound and Roanoke River, such settlers early pushed across the broad placid waters of Chowan River into the wilderness beyond. In 1722, the Assembly found that "that part of Albemarle County lying on the West side of Chowan River, being part of Chowan Precinct, is now inhabited almost to the utmost of the said County Westward" and that the inhabitants were daily "growing very numerous"; for their convenience, therefore, it erected that region into the precinct of Bertie. Settlers were also pushing southward. The overthrow of the Tuscarora along the Neuse had removed the most serious obstacle to the expansion of the province in that direction, and during the decade from 1713 to 1723, a few scattered adventurers cut their way through the wilderness as far south as White Oak and New rivers in what is now Onslow County. In 1724-25, more than 1,000 families came into the province, most of whom pushed on across the Albemarle Sound into Bath County which filled up so rapidly that before 1730 three new precincts—Tyrrell (1729) at the extreme north end of the county, Carteret (1722) at the extreme east, and New Hanover (1729) embracing the infant settlement on the Cape Fear River, in the extreme south—were found necessary for the accommodation of the people.

About the same time that the opening of the Cape Fear added that fertile region to the province in the South, an important addition was made in the North by the settlement of the long-standing boundary-line dispute with Virginia. Credit for this result was due chiefly to Governor Eden, who in 1716, in a spirit of compromise, reached an agreement with Governor Spotswood of Virginia, which made the settlement possible. It will be remembered that the charter of 1665 called for the line to be run from "the north end of Currituck river or inlet" in a direct westerly direction "to Wyonoak Creek" in 36 degrees, 30 minutes, north latitude. The question in dispute was the location of Weyanoke Creek, Virginia maintaining its identity with Wicocon Creek, North Carolina with Nottoway River. Since this question could never be settled with absolute certainty, the interests of both colonies suggested a compromise. Eden and Spotswood, therefore, agreed upon one of three courses, viz: beginning at the north shore of Currituck Inlet the line should run due west to Chowan River; if it cut the Chowan between the mouths of Nottoway River and Wicocon Creek, it should continue in the same course to the mountains; if it cut the Chowan south of its conjunction with Wicocon Creek, it should run from that point up the river to the creek, thence west; if it cut Blackwater River north of Nottoway River, it should run down the Blackwater to the Nottoway, thence west. This agreement was signed by

both governors and transmitted by Eden to the Lords Proprietors, by Spotswood to the Crown for ratification. Spotswood
urged ratification upon the Crown, saying that the compromise
contained "the only Overture which has been made from ye
beginning, wherein both Governments could be brought to acquiesce"; that while both sides adhered to their original
claims, "it was not easy to foresee an end to this contest,
though the Inconveniencys to both Governments by the continuance of this dispute is very obvious, and likely still to
increase, many people settling themselves in those controverted Lands who own obedience to ye laws of neither Province." Both the king and the Lords Proprietors ratified the
agreement and directed the line to be run accordingly. These
directions were not given, however, until after the death of
Eden and the removal of Spotswood from office.

The line was run in 1728. On the part of North Carolina
the commissioners were Christopher Gale, John Lovick, William Little, and Edward Moseley; on the part of Virginia,
William Byrd, Richard Fitz-Williams, and William Dand-
ridge. The Virginians, desiring to turn their arduous enterprise into a triumphant pageant through the wilderness, made
elaborate preparations in keeping with the dignity of the great
province they represented. That the Carolina commissioners
might come similarly prepared, they took pains to notify them
of their plans. Besides themselves and their retinue of personal servants, they said, their party would embrace a chaplain, scientists and mathematicians, Indian traders, expert
woodsmen, and a company of soldiers. "We shall have with
us a Tent and Marques for the convenience of ourselves and
our Servants. We bring as much wine and rum as will enable
us and our men to drink every night to the good Success of
the following day. And because we understand there are many
Gentiles on the frontier who never had oppertunity of being
Baptized we shall have a Chaplain with us to make them
Christians." The Carolina commissioners, who had not considered any pomp and ceremony as necessary in connection
with their undertaking, were astonished by this announcement
and somewhat perplexed as to the course they should adopt.
Their hard common sense, however, came to their rescue.
"We are at a Loss, Gentlemen," they wrote, "whether to
thank you for the particulars you give us of your Tent Stores
and the manner you design to meet us. Had you been silent
about it we had not wanted an Excuse for not meeting you in
the same manner but now you force us to Expose the naked-

ness of our Country and to tell you we cant possibly meet you in the manner our great respect to you would make us glad to do whom we are not Emulous of outdoing unless in Care & Diligence in the affair we come to meet you about. So all we can answer to that article is that we will Endeavour to provide as well as the Circumstances of things will admit us and what we may want in necessaries we hope will be made up in the Spiritual Comfort we expect from your Chaplain of whom we shall give notice as you desire to all Lovers of Novelty and doubt not of a great many Boundary Christians." "That keen thrust under the guard," comments George Davis, "delivered too with all the glowing courtesy of knighthood, is exquisite. * * * If the Virginians were as familiar with sweet Will as they undoubtedly were with the value of tent stores, they must have had an uncomfortable remembrance of Sir Andrew Aguecheek—'An I thought he had been so cunning in fence, I'd have seen him damned ere I'd have challenged him.' "

The commissioners began their work at Currituck Inlet, March 6, 1728, and having ascertained the exact location of 36 degrees, 30 minutes, north latitude, they drove a cedar post in the seashore at that point to mark the beginning of the line. They then began their westward course. It is not necessary to follow them in their long and difficult task as they cut their way through the tangled wilderness, plunged through noxious swamps, and ferried deep and sluggish rivers. The experience of the surveyors in the Great Dismal Swamp, was full of adventure, hardships and dangers that called for a high degree of intelligence, endurance, and dauntless courage. They were the first white men to pass through that vast wilderness of water and network of trees and vines, through which even the rays of the sun could not penetrate. The survey brought to light many interesting facts and revealed situations full of surprises not only to the commissioners but to the inhabitants along the line. The line, for instance, "cut through William Speight's Plantation, taking the Tobacco House into Carolina and leaving the Dwelling House in Virginia." Several other planters had similar experiences. The intersection of the line with Blackwater River was found to be a half-mile north of the mouth of Nottoway River "which agreed to half a minute with the observation made formerly by Mr. Lawson." Proceeding according to instructions down the Blackwater to the Nottoway, the commissioners ran the line due west from their confluence. Having thus settled the most acute phase of the dispute, the commissioners, on April 5, "considering the great fatigue already undergone, and the danger of Rattle snakes in this advanced season, determined to proceed no further with the Line till the Fall." On September 25th, they resumed their work. Upon reaching the Hycootee River, a tributary of the Roanoke, in what is now Person County, 168 miles from the starting point at Currituck Inlet, the Carolina commissioners resolved to proceed no farther saying that as the line then extended fifty miles beyond the remotest settlement and that many years would elapse before settlers would penetrate so far into the interior, it would involve needless trouble and expense to continue it. The Virginians protested against this step and announced their determination to proceed alone until they should reach the foot of the mountains. This course the Carolina commissioners declared would be "irregular and invalid," contending that a line so run "would be no Boundary." Nevertheless the Virginians, showing more wisdom than their opponents, carried the line farther westward about seventy-two miles into the present county of Stokes. In all they ran it 241 miles from the beginning.

On the whole the settlement was favorable to North Carolina. It vindicated her commissioners of 1709 from the severe strictures cast upon them by their Virginian colleagues, and showed that the Virginia commissioners of that year had been in error 21½ miles. "To the great surprise of all who had read the report of former [Virginia] Commissioners," wrote Lieutenant-Governor William Gooch of Virginia, announcing the result to the Board of Trade, "it is now found that instead of gaining a large Tract of Land from North Carolina, the line comes rather nearer to Virginia than that which Carolina has always allowed to be our bounds." The Carolina commissioners reported that "there was taken by the Line into Carolina a very great Quantity of Lands and Number of Families that before had been under Verginia of which the time would not admit to take an Exact account but computed to be above One hundred Thousand acres and above Three hundred Tythables," i. e., above 1,200 inhabitants. The great gain to both provinces was in the removal of a cause of controversy, the quieting of titles to property, and the establishment of the authority of government over a large number of persons who had taken advantage of the dispute to settle in a strip of territory "where the laws of neither Province could reach them."

The result of the survey was reported not to the Lords Proprietors but to officials of the Crown for when the survey was completed North Carolina had ceased to be a proprietary colony. This result had long been a foregone conclusion. For more than forty years crown officials and agents had carried on a propaganda against the proprietary colonies with the design of bringing them under the direct government of the Crown. The chief reason assigned for this policy was the failure of the proprietary governments to enforce the navigation laws, but other reasons were also given. It was charged that they had failed to accomplish "the chief design" for which they were established; that they enacted statutes "contrary and repugnant to the Laws of England and directly prejudicial to Trade;" that they denied appeals from their courts to the king in Council; that they harbored smugglers and pirates; that they debased their currency and by offering immigrants exemption from taxation, drew people from the crown colonies, thus "undermining the Trade and Welfare of the other Plantations;" that they promoted manufactures which were proper only to England; that they neglected their defenses against attack by Indians and foreign enemies "which is every day more and more to be apprehended, considering how the French power encreases in those parts;" and, finally, that all these evils arose from their misuse of the powers granted in their charters "and the Independency which they pretend to." Accordingly the Board of Trade recommended as the remedy for these evils that "the Charters of the severall Proprietors and others intitling them to absolute Government be reassumed by the Crown and these Colonies be put into the same State and dependency as those of your Majesties other Plantations."

Such a result, however, could not be brought about by summary proceedings; the consent of the Proprietors was necessary, but since the Proprietors did not seem inclined to give their consent voluntarily, the Crown determined upon a line of policy designed to compel compliance. Step by step it proceeded, always in the same direction, to loosen the hold of the Proprietors upon their possessions. As early as 1686 *quo warranto* proceedings were ordered to be instituted against them with the purpose of having their charter forfeited to the Crown. These proceedings failing, the Privy Council, in 1689, recommended action by Parliament to bring the proprietary colonies "under a nearer dependence on the Crown." In line with this recommendation Parliament, in 1696, passed an act requiring that the nominees of the Proprietors for governors of their colonies be approved by the Crown before assuming their duties, and, further, that they give bond to the Crown for the enforcement of the navigation and customs laws. To assure the punishment of violators of these laws, the Crown also proposed to appoint the attorneys-general of the proprietary colonies and to establish in them admiralty courts whose officials were to be appointed by the king. In 1701, upon the recommendation of the Board of Trade, a bill was introduced in Parliament "for remitting to the Crown the Government of several [proprietary] colonies and Plantations in America;" and the surveyor-general of His Majesty's customs, Edmund Randolph, who had been the Crown's most active agent in securing data against the proprietaries, was instructed to appear at the Bar of the House of Lords in support of the measure. But "by reason of the shortness of time and multiplicity of other business" before Parliament, the bill failed of passage; the Board of Trade, however, announced that it would "again come under consideration the next Session of Parliament," and appealed to Governor Nicholson of Virginia for information "relating to the conduct of Proprietary Governours and Governments, * * * more especially in relation to Carolina and the Bahama Islands," which could be used in support of the bill. For some reason not revealed the bill was not pressed. In 1714, it was proposed to require the laws passed by the proprietary governments to be submitted to the Crown for approval, but an inspection of their charters quickly convinced the king's advisers that this could not be done without an act of Parliament. Besides these official attacks, officials and agents of the Crown and of crown colonies poured forth a constantly flowing stream of abuse and misrepresentation of the proprietary colonies, all with the single purpose of wearing out the patience of the Proprietors and inducing them to surrender their charters.

For nearly half a century the Lords Proprietors of Carolina resisted these encroachments of the Crown upon their chartered rights. When *quo warranto* proceedings were begun in 1686, Shaftesbury wrote: "I shall bee as unwilling to dispute his Ma[jes]ties pleasure as any man but this being a Publique Concerne tis not in any perticular man's power to dispose of it." The Lords Proprietors complained that they were given "no oppertunity to rectifie or clear some misinformations" about their colonies laid before the king by Randolph and the Board of Trade, upon which the bills for forfeiting their charter had been based; and they protested against the appointment of the attorney-general and the erection of admiralty courts by the Crown as violations of the terms of their charter. As time passed, however, they realized that they were waging a losing battle. In 1719 came the Revolution in South Carolina, and the ease with which the people overthrew their authority and the eagerness with which the Crown recognized the rebel government revealed the slight hold they had on their provinces. When they considered, too, "the number of the Proprietors, their disunion, the frequency of minorities amongst them, their Inability to procure to themselves Justice from South Carolina with respect to their Quit Rents and their Want of Power to correct the great Abuses committed by the settlement about the Paper Money and other Publick acts to the Prejudice of the British Commerce and an apprehension that in Case of an Invasion the Colony would be lost to the great detriment of the Publick as well as to themselves," they realized the wisdom of yielding to the inevitable. In January, 1728, accordingly, they united in a memorial to the Crown offering to surrender their charter. Negotiations were accordingly opened which resulted in all of the Lords Proprietors agreeing to surrender their political rights, and in seven of them agreeing to sell their property interests for £2,500 each.[1] In addition to the purchase price, the king consented to allow them £5000 for arrears of quit rents due them. The agreement was submitted to Parliament which promptly passed an act embodying the terms of the sale. The conveyance was duly executed on July 25, 1729, the colony passed under the direct authority of the Crown, and the rule of the Lords Proprietors came to an end.

The people of the colony heard the announcement of the transfer with great satisfaction. The Council at once prepared a memorial to the king in which they declared that it

---

[1] The shares were then held as follows: Clarendon's share by James Bertie of Middlesex; Albemarle's by Henry Somerset, Duke of Beaufort, and his minor brother Noell Somerset; Craven's by William Lord Craven; Lord Berkeley's by Joseph Blake of South Carolina; Ashley's by John Cotton, a minor, of the Middle Temple, London; Colleton's by Sir John Colleton of Devonshire; Sir William Berkeley's by Henry Bertie of Buck's County, or Mary Danson of Middlesex, or Elizabeth Moore of London, the title being in litigation; and Carteret's by John Lord Carteret, Baron of Hawes, afterwards Earl of Granville. Carteret though surrendering all his rights of political control, refused to sell his share; accordingly, one-eighth of the original grant was reserved from the purchase and in 1744 was laid off for him wholly within North Carolina.

was "with the greatest Pleasure we Received the Notice of your Majesty's having taken this Government under your Immediate direction." Throughout the colony the change was celebrated with great rejoicings. At Edenton, wrote Governor Everard, "the utmost demonstrations of joy was shewn by all people in generall and the night concluded wth a Compleat illumination and Boon Fires and drinking his Maj^tys health and all the Royall Familys long life."

The people had cause for their joy. Crippled by the commercial policy of their powerful northern neighbor, neglected by the Lords Proprietors, antagonized by the Crown, what those early Carolinians had obtained they got through their own unassisted exertions and without favor from anybody. None of the English colonies had passed through a more desperate struggle for existence. The geographical position of North Carolina was such as placed its commerce at the mercy of Virginia, and there was then, as Saunders observes, no Federal Constitution to prevent unneighborly legislation. The inefficient government of the Proprietors was unable to preserve either order or safety in the province, and was just strong enough to be a source of constant irritation. The Culpepper Rebellion, the Cary Rebellion, the Indian wars and the struggle with piracy severely tested the character and the capabilities of the people. Their situation, for instance, at the close of the Indian wars was almost desperate. Most of the people have "scarcely corn to last them until wheat time, many not having any at all;" "the community miserably reduced by Indian cruelty," and "the inhabitants brought to so low an ebb" that large numbers fled the province; "our intestine broils and contentions, to which all the misfortunes which have since attended us are owing;" "a country preserved which everybody that was but the least acquainted with our circumstances gave over for lost"—these are typical expressions with which the correspondence of the period abounds. That the colony survived these conditions is better evidence of the character and spirit of the people than the sneers and jibes of hostile critics, either contemporary or modern. Had the greater part of the population of North Carolina, or even a considerable minority of it, been composed of "the shiftless people who could not make a place for themselves in Virginia society," as William Byrd and John Fiske would have us believe, all the aristocracy of Virginia and South Carolina combined could not have saved the colony from anarchy and ruin. Yet between the years 1663 and 1728 somebody laid here in North Carolina the foundations of a great state. The foundation upon which great states are built is the character of their people, and the "mean whites" of Virginia are not now, nor were they then, the sort of people who found and build states. No colony composed to any extent of such a people could have rallied from such disasters as those from which North Carolina rallied between 1718 and 1728. Those years were years of growth and expansion. The population increased threefold, the Cape Fear was opened to settlers, new plantations were cleared, better methods of husbandry introduced, mills erected, roads surveyed, ferries established, trade was increased, towns were incorporated, better houses built, better furniture installed, parishes created, churches erected, ministers supplied, the schoolmaster found his way thither, and the colony was fairly started on that course of development which brought it, by the outbreak of the Revolution, to the rank of fourth in population and importance among the thirteen English-speaking colonies in America.

CHAPTER X

ENGLISH AND SCOTCH-HIGHLANDERS ON THE CAPE FEAR

The first three decades of royal rule in North Carolina were decades of growth and expansion. In 1730, the population was confined to the coastal plain and certainly did not exceed 30,000; in 1760, it stretched all the way to the foot of the Blue Ridge Mountains and numbered probably not less than 130,000. Much of this growth was due to natural increase, for large families were characteristic of the people. Not only did the women marry young, but as Brickell takes pains to record they were "very fruitful, most Houses being full of Little Ones, and many Women from other Places who have been long Married and without Children, have removed to Carolina, and become joyful Mothers."[1] But much the greater portion of the increase was from immigration. From South Carolina on the south; from Virginia, Pennsylvania and New Jersey on the north; from England, Scotland and Ireland; from the mountains of Switzerland and from the valleys of the Rhine and the Danube, thousands of hardy, enterprising pioneers poured into North Carolina, filling up the unoccupied places in the older settlements, moving up the banks of the Roanoke, the Neuse, and the Cape Fear, and spreading out over the plains and through the valleys of the Piedmont section.

Explanation of this extraordinary movement is to be found in a variety of causes, all of which acted and reacted upon each other. Land syndicates exploiting the mildness of the climate, the fertility of the soil, and the cheapness of the land, induced many immigrants to come. A spirit of adventure moved others. Hunters and trappers were attracted by the great variety and number of fur-bearing animals in the West. A lofty missionary zeal to preach the

---

[1] Grimes, J. Bryan, (ed.): The Natural History of North Carolina, by John Brickell, M. D. (Dublin, 1737), p. 31.

143

Gospel of Christ to their scattered countrymen and to the savages of the wilderness inspired a choice few. Economic conditions in Scotland; economic and religious conditions in Ireland; economic, religious, and political conditions in Germany drove thousands from those countries to seek new homes on the Carolina frontier. To all these causes should be added the activity of the royal governors, Burrington, Johnston, and Dobbs, who showed a laudable zeal to make known to the people of the Old World the boundless resources of the New World.

During the first decade, 1729-1739, most of the new settlers occupied lands in the section that had been settled during the proprietary period, i. e., the section north and east of Cape Fear River. Into this region immigrants came slowly but steadily. In 1733, Burrington, the first royal governor, wrote: "The Reputation this Government has lately acquired, appears by the number of People that have come from other Places to live in it. Many of them are possessed of good American Estates. I do not exceed in saying a thousand white men have already settled in North Carolina, since my arrival [in 1731], and more are expected." Twenty families had cut their way through the forest to the head of navigation on the Tar River. A hundred families had planted a "thriving" settlement on New River. Others, singly and in groups, had penetrated into the interior as far as the North East River. A small colony of Scotch Highlanders had found homes on the upper Cape Fear. Such was the expansion of settlements, that by 1734 three new precincts were necessary for their convenience. In 1734, the General Assembly finding that New Hanover precinct had "become very populous," erected the New River settlements into a separate precinct called Onslow. Similarly the settlements on Tar and North East rivers were erected into Edgecombe and Bladen precincts. At the close of his administration, Burrington estimated that there had been an increase in the population of more than 5,000 in five years.

None of the new settlements had made such rapid progress as that which Burrington had done so much, when governor for the Lords Proprietors, to plant on the Cape Fear River. The first attempt to plant a settlement on Cape Fear River was made without success by some New England adventurers in 1660. Four years later a party of royalist refugees from Barbados established a colony near the mouth of the river, where, in 1665, they were joined by other Barbadians under

Sir John Yeamans who had been appointed governor. The settlement, which contained a population of about 800 and extended for several miles up the river, was erected into the county of Clarendon. Its prospects were not good and Governor Yeamans soon abandoned it, returned to Barbados, and later joined the colony which the Lords Proprietors had planted on the Ashley and Cooper rivers of which he was appointed governor. The Lords Proprietors, who directed all their energies toward building up the rival settlement to the southward, took but little interest in the Cape Fear colony, and the settlers, after suffering many hardships, abandoned it in 1667.

After the failure of the Clarendon colony, the Cape Fear region fell into disrepute and nearly fifty years passed before a permanent settlement was planted there. Four causes contributing to this delay were the character of the coast at the mouth of the river, the pirates who sought refuge there in large numbers, the hostility of the Cape Fear Indians, and the closing of the Carolina land-office by the Lords Proprietors.

The character of the coast, of course, could not be changed, but those who were interested in the development of the Cape Fear section employed pen and tongue to change the reputation which its very name had forever fastened upon it. "It is by most traders in London believed that the coast of this country is very dangerous," wrote Governor Burrington, "but in reality [it is] not so." The fact remains, however, that this sentence stands as a better testimonial of the governor's zeal than of his regard for truth. A different spirit inspired a later son [2] of the Cape Fear who, with something of an honest pride in the sturdy ruggedness and picturesque bleakness of that famous point, wrote thus eloquently of it: "Looking then to the cape for the idea and reason of its name, we find that it is the southernmost point of Smith's Island, a naked, bleak elbow of sand, jutting far out into the ocean. Immediately in its front are the Frying Pan Shoals pushing out still farther twenty miles to sea. Together they stand for warning and for woe; and together they catch the long majestic roll of the Atlantic as it sweeps through a thousand miles of grandeur and power from the Arctic towards the Gulf. It is the playground of billows and tempests, the kingdom of silence and awe, disturbed by no sound save the seagull's shriek and the breakers'

[2] George Davis.

roar. Its whole aspect is suggestive not of repose and beauty, but of desolation and terror. Imagination cannot adorn it. Romance cannot hallow it. Local pride cannot soften it. There it stands today, bleak and threatening and pitiless, as it stood three hundred years ago, when Grenville and White came near unto death upon its sands. And there it will stand, bleak and threatening and pitiless, until the earth and sea give up their dead. And as its nature, so its name, is now, always has been, and always will be the Cape of Fear.''

But the very dangers that repelled settlers attracted pirates, and the Cape Fear became one of their chief strongholds on our coast. As late as 1717, it was estimated that more than 1,500 pirates made their headquarters at New Providence and Cape Fear. Darting in and out of these harbors of refuge for many years they preyed upon French, Spanish, British and American commerce with the utmost impartiality and with impunity. The capture of Bonnet in 1718 was the beginning of the end. The following day several other pirate vessels were taken off Cape Fear, and as a result of these captures a hundred freebooters were hanged at one time on the wharves of Charleston. When the Cape Fear ceased to be the refuge of crime it became the home of law and industry.

The Cape Fear Indians ''were reckoned the most barbarous of any in the colony.'' Their hostility to the English was implacable. They made war on the Clarendon settlers which was one of the reasons for the failure of that colony. In 1711-13, they joined the Tuscarora; and two years later took an active part in the Yamassee War. Occupying an important strategic position between the two colonies, they made cooperation between them difficult. In the summer of 1715, they cut off a band of friendly Indians whom North Carolina was sending to the aid of South Carolina, but later were in turn defeated by the forces under Col. Maurice Moore. Their power, much weakened by the defeat of the Tuscarora on the north and of the Yamassee on the south, was finally destroyed in 1725, in the battle of Sugar Loaf, opposite the town of Brunswick, by a force under Roger Moore.

But the struggles of the Carolina settlers with the forces of nature, the freebooters of the sea, and the savages of the wilderness would have availed nothing had they yielded obedience to the orders of the Lords Proprietors. In 1712, the Lords Proprietors resolved that no more grants should be issued in North Carolina, but such sales of land only as were made at their office in London were to be good; and two years later, the governor and Council ordered that no surveys should be made within twenty miles of the Cape Fear River. But there were men in North Carolina who were not willing that a group of wealthy landowners beyond the sea should prevent their clearing and settling this inviting region, and about the year 1723 the ring of their axes began to break the long silence of the Cape Fear. They laid off their claims, cleared their fields, and built their cabins with utter disregard of the formalities of law. When Governor Burrington saw that they were determined to take up lands without either acquiring titles or paying rents, he decided that the interests of the Lords Proprietors would be served by his giving the one and receiving the other. At his suggestion, therefore, the Assembly petitioned the governor and Council to reopen the land office in Carolina, and the governor and Council finding officially what they already knew personally that "sundry persons are already seated on the vacant lands for which purchase money has not been paid nor any rents," granted the Assembly's prayer.

Good titles thus assured settlers were not wanting. Conspicuous among the leaders, were Governor Burrington and Col. Maurice Moore. Burrington's claims to this credit were repeatedly asserted by himself and acknowledged by contemporaries who bore him no love. The grand jury of the province, in 1731, bore testimony to the "very great expense and personal trouble" with which he "laid the foundation" of the Cape Fear settlement; while the General Assembly, in an address to the king declared that his "indefatigable industry and the hardships he underwent in carrying on the settlement of the Cape Fear deserve our thankful remembrance." Such testimony to His Sacred Majesty was doubtless very flattering and duly appreciated, but Burrington evidently expected something more substantial, for he complained more than once that the only reward he ever received for his losses and hardships "was the thanks of a House of Burgesses." The first permanent settlement on the Cape Fear was made by Maurice Moore, who, while on his campaign against the Yamassee Indians in 1715, had been attracted by the fertility of the lower Cape Fear region and determined to lead a settlement there. This plan he carried into execution sometime prior to the year 1725, accompanied by his brothers, Nathaniel and Roger Moore. Burrington, in a letter to the Board of Trade in 1732, after he had broken with the popular party, refers to these men in the following passage: "About twenty families are settled at Cape Fear from South Carolina, among them three brothers of a noted family whose name is Moore. They are all of the set known there as the Goose Creek faction. These people were always troublesome in that government, and will, without doubt, be so in this. Already I have been told they will expend a great sum of money to get me turned out." Burrington's reference to their conduct in South Carolina is evidently to the fact that James Moore, their oldest brother, in 1719, led the revolt in South Carolina against the Lords Proprietors and after its success was elected governor. A century and a quarter later, George Davis, himself an eminent son of the Cape Fear, paid the following tribute to Maurice and Roger Moore: "These brothers," said he, "were not cast in the common mould of men. They were 'of the breed of noble bloods.' Of kingly descent,[3] and proud of their name which brave deeds had made illustrious, they dwelt upon their magnificent estates of Rocky Point and Orton, with much of the dignity, and something of the state of the ancient feudal barons, surrounded by their sons and kinsmen, who looked up to them for counsel, and were devoted to their will. Proud and stately, somewhat haughty and overbearing perhaps, but honorable, brave, high-minded and generous, they lived for many years the fathers of the Cape Fear, dispensing a noble hospitality to the worthy, and a terror to the mean and lawless. * * * They possessed the entire respect and confidence of all; and the early books of the register's office of New Hanover County are full of letters of attorney from all sorts of men, giving them an absolute discretion in managing the varied affairs of their many constituents."

Besides the Moores, conspicuous among the early settlers of the Cape Fear were the Moseleys, the Howes, the Porters, the Lillingtons, the Ashes, the Harnetts, and others whose names are closely identified with the history of North Carolina. Of them, Mr. Davis says: "They were no needy adventurers, driven by necessity—no unlettered boors, ill at ease in the haunts of civilization, and seeking their proper sphere amidst the barbarism of the savages. They were gentlemen of birth and education, bred in the refinements of polished society, and bringing with them ample fortunes, gentle manners, and cultivated minds. Most of them united by the ties of blood, and all by those of friendship, they came as one household, sufficient unto themselves, and reared their family altars

---

[3] This is a reference to the tradition that the Moores were descendants of the ancient kings of Leix.

in love and peace." [4] After these leaders had cleared the way, they were joined by numerous other families from the Albemarle, from Barbados, and other islands of the West Indies, from New England, from South Carolina, Pennsylvania, and Maryland, and from Europe.

The oldest grant for land on the Cape Fear now extant, is one to Maurice Moore for 1,500 acres on the west bank of the river, dated June 3, 1725. From this grant Maurice Moore, in 1725, laid off, fourteen miles above the mouth of the river, a tract of 320 acres as a site for a town, and his brother Roger, "to make the said town more regular, added another parcel of land." To encourage the growth of the town, Maurice Moore donated sites for a church and graveyard, a courthouse, a market-house and other public buildings, and a commons "for the use of the inhabitants of the town." The town was laid off into building lots of one-half acre each to be sold only to those who would agree to erect on their lots, substantial houses. Moore then made a bid for royal favor by naming his town Brunswick in honor of the reigning family. But the career of Brunswick did not commend it to the favor of crowned heads or their representatives; it never became more than a frontier village, and in the course of a few years, during which, however, it played an important part in the history of the province, it yielded with no good grace to a younger and more vigorous rival sixteen miles farther up the river, which was named in honor of Spencer Compton, Earl of Wilmington.

The settlement grew rapidly. Writing from the Cape Fear in 1734, Governor Johnston said: "The inhabitants of the southern part of this government, particularly of the two branches of this large river, * * * are a very sober and industrious set of people and have made an amazing progress in their improvement since their first settlement, which was about eight years ago." Large tracts of forest land had been converted into beautiful meadows and cultivated plantations; comfortable, if not elegant, houses dotted the river banks; and two towns had sprung into existence. The forest offered tribute to the lumberman and turpentine distiller; a number of saw mills had been erected while some of the planters were employing their slaves chiefly in "making tar and pitch." A brisk trade in lumber, naval stores, and farm products had been established with the other

---

[4] University Address in 1855.

colonies, the West Indies, and even with the mother country, and before the close of the decade the governor was able to declare that the Cape Fear had become "the place of the greatest trade in the whole province." The collector's books at Brunswick showed that during the year 1734 forty-two vessels cleared from that port. At that time the population of the Cape Fear settlement numbered about 1,200; by 1740 it had increased to 3,000.

Life on the Cape Fear was seen at its best not in the towns but on the estates of the planters scattered along the banks of the river and its branches. In the immediate vicinity of Brunswick the most celebrated were, Orton, the finest colonial residence now standing in North Carolina, where lived and reigned "Old King" Roger Moore, "the chief gentleman in all Cape Fear"; Kendal, the home of "Old King" Roger's son, George, whose wives, "with remarkable fidelity and amazing fortitude, presented him every spring with a new baby, until the number reached twenty-eight;"[5] and Lilliput, adjoining Kendal, first the residence of Chief Justice Eleazer Allen, and later of Sir Thomas Frankland, the great-grandson of Oliver Cromwell. Farther up the river came then and later a succession of celebrated plantations. Forty miles above Brunswick on the east bank of North East River stood Lillington Hall, the home of Alexander Lillington, who led the Cape Fear militia at Moore's Creek Bridge in 1776. On the opposite bank were Stag Park, the Cape Fear estate of Governor Burrington; the Neck and Green Hill, the residences of Governor Samuel Ashe and General John Ashe; Moseley Hall, where lived Sampson Moseley, afterwards a delegate to the famous Halifax convention of 1776; and Rocky Point, the estate of Maurice Moore, described by an English visitor in 1734 as "the finest place in all Cape Fear." Across the river farther down came a series of places, the most historic of which were Castle Haynes, owned by Hugh Waddell, who is buried there, and the Hermitage, owned by John Burgwin, for many years clerk of the Council and private secretary to the governor, which was one of the most celebrated homes in the Cape Fear country for a hundred years. "The great majority of these residences were wooden structures, some of them being large, with wide halls and piazzas, but without any pretence to architectural beauty, and some being one story

---

[5] Sprunt, James: Tales and Traditions of the Lower Cape Fear, p. 58.

ORTON

buildings, spread out over a considerable space. A few were
of brick, but none of stone, as there was no building stone
within a hundred miles; but all, whether of brick or wood,
were comfortable and the seats of unbounded hospitality."[6]

Perhaps the best picture of the Cape Fear settlement at the
close of its first decade is a pamphlet written and published
in London by an English visitor who arrived at Orton in the
afternoon of June 16, 1734. After four pleasant days with
"Old King" Roger, his party set out on their trip up the river
under the guidance of Nathaniel Moore. The first day's trip
carried them past "several pretty plantations on both sides"
of the river, which they found "wonderfully pleasant" and
the following morning brought them "to a beautiful plantation, belonging to Captain Gabriel [Gabourell], who is a great
merchant there, where were two ships, two sloops, and a brigantine, loading with lumber." The night was agreeably
passed at "another plantation belonging to Mr. Roger Moore,
called Blue Banks, where he is going to build another very
large brick house." The visitors were astonished at the fertility of the soil. "I am credibly informed," declared their
chronicler, "they have very commonly four-score bushels of
corn on an acre of their overflowed land. * * * I must confess I saw the finest corn growing there that I ever saw in my
life, as likewise wheat and hemp." That night, they "met
with good entertainment" at the home of Captain Gibbs, whose
plantation adjoined Blue Banks; and the next day dined with
Jehu Davis, whose house was "built after the Dutch fashion,
and made to front both ways, on the river and on the land."
The visitors were delighted with the "beautiful avenue cut
through the woods for above two miles, which is a great addition to the house." They left Davis's house in the afternoon
and the same evening reached Nathaniel Moore's plantation,
which was "a very pleasant place on a bluff upwards of sixty
feet high." Three days after their arrival, "there came a
sloop of one hundred tons, and upwards, from South Carolina, to be laden with corn, which is sixty miles at least from
the bar. * * * There are people settled at least forty
miles higher up," that is, in what is now Cumberland
County. The visitor's last experience in the Cape Fear section was such a one as was calculated to leave with him a
bitter prejudice against the country and its people, but fortunately his mind, recalling the hospitality which he had just

---

[6] Waddell, A. M.: Historic Homes in the Cape Fear Country.
(*North Carolina Booklet*, Vol. II, No. 9, p. 20.)

been enjoying, rose superior to such a feeling. Reaching Brunswick about eight o'clock in the morning of August 11th, on his departure from the colony, he says: "I set out from thence about nine, and about four miles from thence met my landlord of Lockwood Folly, who was in hopes I would stay at his house that night. About two I arrived there with much difficulty, it being a very hot day and myself very faint and weak, when I called for a dram, and to my great sorrow found not one drop of rum, sugar or lime juice in the house (a pretty place to stay all night indeed) * * * which made me re- solve never to trust the country again on a long journey." [7]

Returning to Brunswick from his trip up the river, the English visitor "lay that first night at Newtown, in a small hut." With this slight mention he dismisses the place from his narrative, but had he returned twenty years later he would doubtless have given it as much as a paragraph in a revised edition. Today a visitor describing the Cape Fear section might possibly mention Brunswick for its historic interest, but Newtown, though masquerading under another name, would form the burden of his story. The former, in spite of its name, was not popular with the royal governors who threw their influence to the latter, and the rise of Newtown was fol- lowed by the decline of Brunswick. Newtown was laid off just below the confluence of the two branches of Cape Fear River. It consisted originally of two cross streets called Front and Market, names which they still bear, while the town itself for lack of a better name was called Newtown. From the first Brunswick regarded Newtown as an upstart to be suppressed rather than encouraged. Rivalry originating in commercial competition was soon intensified by a struggle for political supremacy. The chief factor in this struggle was Gabriel Johnston, who, in 1734, succeeded George Burrington as gov- ernor. The new governor became one of the most ardent champions of Newtown and used not only his personal in- fluence but also his official authority to make it the social, commercial and political center of the rapidly growing prov- ince. Encouraged by his favor, Newtown in March, 1735, petitioned the governor and Council for a charter. but the prayer was refused because it required an act of the Assembly to incorporate a town. To the Assembly, therefore, Newtown appealed and as a compliment to the governor asked for incor- poration under the name of Wilmington, in honor of John-

---

[7] Georgia Historical Collections, Vol. II, p. 59.

ston's friend and patron, Spencer Compton, Earl of Wilmington, afterwards prime minister of England. The granting of
this petition meant death to all the hopes of Brunswick. By
it Brunswick would be compelled to surrender to Wilmington
the courthouse and jail, the county court, the offices of the
county officials, the office of the collector of the port, and the
election of assemblymen, vestrymen and other public officials.
Brunswick, therefore, stoutly opposed the pretentions of Wilmington and kept up a bitter struggle against them for four
years. The end came in the Assembly of February of 1739.
Apparently no contest was made in the lower house, for
Brunswick evidently looked to the Council for victory. The
Council was composed of eight members, four of whom were
certainly of the Brunswick party. Accordingly when the Wilmington bill came before the Council four voted for, and four
against it. Then to the consternation of the Brunswickers,
the president declared that as president he had the right to
break the tie which his vote as a member had made, and in
face of violent opposition, cast his vote a second time in the
affirmative. The Brunswick party entered vigorous protests,
but they availed nothing with the governor, who, in the presence of both houses of the Assembly, gave his assent to the
bill.

Brunswick did not accept defeat gracefully, nor did Wilmington bear the honors of victory magnanimously. The feelings aroused by the long struggle and the manner in which
it was finally brought to a close strained their commercial and
political relations and embittered their social and religious
intercourse for many years. This hostility made it necessary
to divide the county into two parishes—St. James, embracing
the territory on the east side of the river, and St. Phillips, embracing that on the west side. But this division did not help
matters much at first, as there was only one minister, and he
does not seem to have had the inexhaustible amount of tact
that was necessary to deal with the situation. Says he: "A
missionary in this river has a most difficult part to act, for by
obliging one of the towns, he must of course disoblige the
other, each of them opposing the other to the utmost of their
power. Notwithstanding the majority of the present vestry at
Wilmington are professed dissenters and endeavored by all
ways and means to provoke me to leave that place, yet they
cannot endure my settlement at Brunswick. While I was
their minister they were offended at my officiating frequently
among them." But Brunswick struggled in vain against the

Wilmington tide. Nature had given to Wilmington a better and safer harbor, and this was an ally which Brunswick could not overcome. Besides far more important matters than the supremacy of one straggling village over another soon claimed their united consideration, and they found that factional quarrels and jealousies would result only in injury to both. After a short time, therefore, when the actors in the early struggle were all dead, when their animosities had been mellowed by time, and when danger from a common enemy threatened the welfare of both, their differences were buried and forgotten, and the two towns stood side by side in the struggle for independence. This union was never broken, for the ties formed during those days of peril proved stronger than ever their differences had been, and Brunswick abandoning the old site united fortunes with Wilmington.

The people whom the English visitor found on the lower Cape Fear in 1734, were mostly of English origin, but had he continued his voyage up the river as far as the head of navigation, he would have found a small settlement lately made by representatives of another race destined to play no small part in the history of North Carolina. These settlers were the vanguard of that army of Scotch Highlanders which began to pour into North Carolina about the middle of the eighteenth century, as the result of political and economic conditions in Scotland. In 1746 occurred the last of those periodical efforts of the Highland clans to restore the Stuarts to the thrones of Scotland and England, which ended in disaster at Culloden. Thereupon, exasperated at these repeated rebellions, the British government determined upon a course of great severity toward the clans. To overthrow the clan system which fostered this rebellious spirit, the government abolished the authority of the chiefs, confiscated their estates, and under heavy penalties forbade the Highlanders to carry arms and to wear the costumes of their clans. The estates of the Highland chiefs were distributed among the British soldiers who, of course, felt none of those natural ties that held chief and clansmen together and cared nothing for the fate of Highland rebels. These new landlords soon introduced a new economic factor in the Highlands. Finding sheep-raising more profitable than farming, they turned thousands of acres which before had been under cultivation into pasture lands, thus depriving large numbers of people of their homesteads. This complete overthrow of their social and economic systems left the people helpless. Rents increased, hundreds of families lost their means of livelihood, and distress became universal.

To enforce these harsh measures, an English army under the Duke of Cumberland, afterwards known in Highland history as "Butcher Cumberland," established headquarters at Inverness, and from that base fell upon the inhabitants and laid waste their country in every direction. Their cattle were driven away or slaughtered; the mansions of the chiefs and the huts of the clansmen were laid in ashes; captured Highland soldiers were put to death with brutal ferocity; women and children, without food, without homes, without husbands and fathers, wandered helplessly among the hills and valleys to die of hunger, cold and want. It became the boast of the English soldiery that neither house nor cottage, man nor beast could be found within fifty miles of Inverness; all was silence, ruin, and desolation.

One ray of light penetrated the darkness. After Culloden, the king offered a pardon to all Highland rebels who would take the oath of allegiance and emigrate to America. Many clansmen hastened to avail themselves of this act of clemency and to the ruined Highlanders America became a haven of refuge. Of all the American colonies North Carolina was perhaps the best known in the Highlands. A few Highlanders had made their way to the upper Cape Fear as early as 1729. Here they found a genial climate, a fertile soil, and a mild and liberal government, and they filled their letters to their friends and relatives in Scotland with praise of the new country. Another influence was introduced in 1734, when Gabriel Johnston, a Scotchman from Dundee, was sent to North Carolina as governor. Johnston is said to have been inordinately fond of his fellow-countrymen, his enemies even charging that he showed favor to Scotch rebels and manifested a woful lack of enthusiasm over the news of "the glorious victory at Culloden." Be that as it may, he certainly took a praiseworthy interest in spreading the fame of North Carolina in the Highlands and was successful in inducing Scotchmen to seek homes in the colony. In the summer of 1739, Neill McNeill, of Kintyre, Scotland, sailed for North Carolina bringing with him a "shipload" of 350 Highlanders who arrived in the Cape Fear River in September of that year. They landed at Wilmington where, it is said, their peculiar costumes and outlandish language so frightened the town officials that they attempted to make the strangers give bond to keep the peace. This indignity McNeill managed to avoid, and taking his countrymen up the river found for them a hearty welcome among the Highlanders there. At the next session of the Assembly, a memorial was presented in behalf of these new settlers, accompanied by a statement, "if proper encouragement be given them, that they'll invite the rest of their friends and acquaintances over." The General Assembly hastened to take advantage of this opportunity, exempting the new settlers from all taxation for ten years. A similar exemption "from payment of any Publick or County tax for Ten years" was offered to all Highlanders who should come to North Carolina in groups of forty or more, and the governor was requested "to use his Interest, in such manner, as he shall think most proper, to obtain an Instruction for giveing encouragement to Protestants from foreign parts, to settle in Townships within this Province." On the heels of this action came the disaster of Culloden, the rise in rents, and the harsh enactments of the British Parliament; and the liberal offers of the North Carolina Assembly, together with the active exertions of the Highlanders already in the colony, produced in Scotland "a Carolina mania which was not broken until the beginning of the Revolution. The flame of enthusiasm passed like wildfire through the Highland glens and Western Isles. It pervaded all classes, from the poorest crofter to the well-to-do farmer, and even men of easy competence, who were according to the appropriate song of the day

'Dol a ah 'iarruidh an fhortain do North Carolina.' " [8]
Shipload after shipload of sturdy Highland settlers sailed for the shores of America, and most of them landing at Charleston and Wilmington found their way to their kinsmen on the Cape Fear. In a few years their settlements were thickly scattered throughout the territory now embraced in the counties of Anson, Bladen, Cumberland, Harnett, Moore, Richmond, Robeson, Sampson, Hoke, and Scotland. With a keen appreciation of its commercial advantages, they selected a point of land at the head of navigation on Cape Fear River where they laid out a town, first called Campbellton, then Cross Creek, and finally Fayetteville.

The Highlanders continued to pour into North Carolina right up to the outbreak of the Revolution, but as no official records of their number were kept it is impossible to say how numerous they were. Perhaps, however, from reports in letters, periodicals, and other contemporaneous documents an

---

[8] "Going to seek a fortune in North Carolina." MacLean, J. P.: The Highlanders in America, p. 108.

estimate may be made with some degree of accuracy. In 1736, Alexander Clark, a native of Jura, one of the Hebrides, sailed for North Carolina with a "shipload" of Highlanders, and settled on Cape Fear River where he found "a good many Scotch." Three years later, as we have seen, McNeill brought over a colony of 350 Highlanders. But the real immigration did not set in until after the battle of Culloden. Seven years after that event, colonial officials estimated that there were in Bladen County alone 1,000 Highlanders capable of bearing arms, from which it is reasonable to infer that the total population was not less than 5,000. The *Scot's Magazine*, in September, 1769, records that the ship Molly had recently sailed from Islay filled with passengers for North Carolina, and that this was the third emigration from that county within six years. The same journal in a later issue tells us that between April and July, 1770, fifty-four vessels sailed from the Western Isles laden with 1,200 Highlanders all bound for North Carolina. In 1771, the *Scot's Magazine* stated that 500 emigrants from Islay and the adjacent islands were preparing to sail for America, and later in the same year Governor Tryon wrote that "several ship loads of Scotch families" had "landed in this province within three years past from the Isles of Arran, Durah, Islay, and Gigah, but chief of them from Argyle Shire and are mostly settled in Cumberland County." Their number he estimated "at 1,600 men, women, and children." A year later the ship Adventure brought a cargo of 200 emigrants from the Highlands to the Cape Fear, and in March of the same year Governor Martin wrote to Lord Hillsborough, secretary of state for the colonies: "Near a thousand people have arrived in Cape Fear River from the Scottish Isles since the month of November with a view to settling in this province whose prosperity and strength will receive great augmentation by the accession of such a number of hardy, laborious and thrifty people." In its issue of April 3, 1773, the *Courant*, another Scottish journal, reports that "the unlucky spirit of emigration" had not diminished, and that many of the inhabitants of Skye, Lewis and other places were arranging to sail for America in the following summer. In subsequent issues, during the same year, that journal records that in June between 700 and 800 emigrants sailed for America from Stornoway; in July, 800 from Skye and 840 from Lewis; in August, another 150 from Lewis; in September, 250 from Sutherlandshire and 425 from Knoydart, Lochabar, Appin, Mamore, and Fort William; and in October, 775 from Moray, Ross, Sutherland, and Caithness.

The Highlanders continued to come even after the Revolution was well under way. In June, 1775, the *Gentleman's Magazine* records that "four vessels, containing about 700 emigrants," had sailed for America from Glasgow and Greenock, "most of them from the north Highlands." In September of the same year, the ship Jupiter, with 200 emigrants on board, "chiefly from Argyleshire" sailed for North Carolina, and as late as October, 1775, Governor Martin notes the arrival at Wilmington of a shipload of 172 Highlanders. From 1769 to 1775, the Scotch journals mention as many as sixteen different emigrations from the Highlands, besides "several others." Not all of these emigrants came to North Carolina. Georgia, New York, Canada, and other colonies received a small share, but "the earliest, largest and most important settlement of Highlanders in America, prior to the Peace of 1783, was in North Carolina along Cape Fear River."[9] In 1775 Governor Martin wrote that he could raise an army of 3,000 Highlanders, from which it is a reasonable conclusion that at that time the Highland population of North Carolina was not less than 20,000. Several of the clans were represented, but at the outbreak of the Revolution the MacDonalds so largely predominated in numbers and in leadership that the campaign of 1776, which ended at Moore's Creek Bridge, was often spoken of at the time as the "insurrection of the Clan MacDonald."

Though unfortunate economic conditions lay behind this Highland emigration, it is not therefore to be supposed that the emigrants belonged to an improvident and thriftless class. They were, in fact, among the most substantial and energetic people of Scotland and they left the land of their nativity because it did not offer them an outlet for their activities. "The late great rise of the rents in the Western Islands of Scotland," said *Scot's Magazine* in 1771, "is said to be the reason of this emigration." "The cause of this emigration," the same journal repeats in 1772, "they [the emigrants] assign to be want of the means of livelihood at home, through the opulent graziers engrossing the farms, and turning them into pastures." Some of the landlords became alarmed and offered better terms to tenants, but the offer came too late to check the movement. Governor Tryon says that many of them were skilled mechanics who "were particularly encouraged to

[9] MacLean: The Highlanders in America, p. 102.

settle here by their countrymen who have been settled many years in this province;" and Governor Martin, in the letter quoted above, describes them as a "hardy, laborious, and thrifty people." Nor should it be supposed that they arrived in Carolina empty-handed. The *Scot's Magazine* in 1771 tells us that a band of five hundred of these emigrants had recently sailed for America "under the conduct of a gentleman of wealth and merit, whose ancestors had resided in Islay for many centuries past." Another colony, according to the same journal, was composed of "the most wealthy and substantial people in Skye" who "intend to make purchases of land in America"; while the *Courant*, in 1773, declared that five hundred emigrants who had just sailed were "the finest set of fellows in the Highlands," and carried with them "at least £6,000 sterling in ready cash." From the single county of Sutherland, in 1772 and 1773, about fifteen hundred emigrants sailed for America, who, according to the *Courant* carried with them an average of £4 sterling to the man. "This," comments that journal, "amounts to £7,500 which exceeds a year's rent of the whole county." It is not easy to arrive at any satisfactory conclusion as to the financial condition of the Highlanders after their arrival in North Carolina. On the whole they were poor when compared with their English neighbors, but their condition was undoubtedly a great improvement over what it had been in Scotland.

From governors and Assembly the Highlanders received numerous evidences of welcome to their adopted country. The governor commissioned several of their leaders justices of the peace. In 1740 the Assembly exempted them from taxation for ten years, and offered a similar exemption to all who should follow them. For the convenience of the new settlers, the region around Campbellton was erected into a county which, with curious irony, was named in honor of "Butcher Cumberland." The first sheriff of the new county was Hector McNeill, but the services of a sheriff seem to have been so little in demand that his fees for the whole year amounted to only ten pounds. Another important event in the development of the Highland settlements, was the passage by the Assembly of an act for the building of a road from the Dan River on the Virginia line through the heart of the province to Cross Creek on the Cape Fear, and another leading to it from Shallow Ford on the Yadkin. These roads threw the trade of all the back country into Cross Creek which soon became one of the chief towns of the province.

The Highlanders desired to reproduce in Carolina the life they had lived in Scotland, but changed conditions, as they soon found, made this impossible. True no law made it illegal for the clans to maintain their tribal organizations, or forbade the chiefs to exercise their hereditary authority, or made it a crime for the clansmen to bear arms or wear tartans. But as the basis of the clan system was military necessity, in the absence of such necessity the system could not flourish. In Scotland the clansmen had obeyed their chief in return for his protection against hostile neighbors; in Carolina there were no hostile neighbors, law reigned supreme, and under its benign sway the humblest clansman was assured of far more effective protection of life and property than the most powerful chief in the Highlands could possibly have given him. As soon as the clan system became unnecessary it became irksome and irritating, and rapidly disappeared. With its passing passed also the meaning, and therefore, the usefulness, of the Highland costume, which was soon laid aside for the less picturesque but more serviceable dress of their English fellow countrymen. Their language was destined to a similar fate. When preaching in English to the Highlanders at Cross Creek in 1756, Hugh McAden found that many of them "scarcely knew one word" he spoke. The Gaelic made a brave struggle against the English, but a vain and useless one. Entrenched in an impregnable stronghold as the language of all legal, social, political and commercial transactions, the English tongue effected an easy conquest, and the Gaelic soon disappeared as a common medium of expression. Under these circumstances the peculiar institutions and customs of the Highlanders gave way before those of their adopted country, and after the second generation had followed their fathers to the grave nothing remained to distinguish their descendants from their English neighbors save only their Highland names.

CHAPTER XI

THE COMING OF THE SCOTCH-IRISH AND GERMANS

While the Highlanders were moving up the Cape Fear River, two other streams of population were flowing into the province and spreading out over the plains and valleys of the Piedmont section. Though flowing side by side, they originated in widely separated sources and throughout their courses kept entirely distinct one from the other. One was composed of immigrants of Scotch-Irish, the other of immigrants of German descent.

The term Scotch-Irish is a misnomer, and does not, as one would naturally suppose, signify a mixed race of Scotch and Irish ancestry. It is a geographical, not a racial term. The so-called Scotch-Irish were in reality Scotch people, or descendants of Scotch people who once resided in Ireland. Into Ireland they came as invaders and lived as conquerors, hated as such by the Irish and feeling for the Irish that contempt which conquerors always feel for subjugated races. From one generation to another the two peoples dwelt side by side, separated by an immense chasm of religious, political, social, and racial hostility, each intent upon preserving its blood pure and uncontaminated by any mixture with the other. Thus the Scotch in Ireland remained Scotch, and the term "Irish" as applied to them is merely a geographical term used to distinguish the Scotch immigrants who came to America from Ireland from those who came hither directly from Scotland. In fact the term "Scotch-Irish" is American in its origin and use, and has never been known in Ireland, where the descendants of the Scotch settlers are distinguished from the Irish proper by the far more significant terms of "Irish Protestants" and "Irish Presbyterians." Another name, "Ulstermen," often applied to them, especially within recent years, is derived from the province in which they are chiefly found.

The ancestors of these people came originally from the

Lowlands of Scotland, and were introduced into Ireland by James I in pursuance of his policy of displacing the native Irish, always so bitterly hostile to the British Crown, with a new people upon whose loyalty the government could depend. For the success of his plan he needed a people whose aversion to the Irish and to their religion would operate as a barrier to any intermingling of the two races. Of all his subjects, the Scotch Presbyterians of the Western Lowlands were best suited for his purpose. Possessed of intense racial pride, they would not intermarry with the Irish. The most uncompromising of Protestants, they would resist to the uttermost the attacks of Catholicism. Tenacious of their property rights which they would owe to the generosity of the king, they would maintain and defend his Crown at all hazards. Accordingly, having confiscated the Irish estates in Ulster, in 1610, James brought from Scotland a colony of Lowlanders whom he settled upon them. This was the beginning of a great migration from Scotland to Ireland. During the decade from 1610 to 1620, 40,000 Scotch Presbyterians were thus settled in Ulster. They were among the most industrious, thrifty and intelligent people in the world. In Ulster they drained the swamps, felled the forests, sowed wheat and flax, raised cattle and sheep, and began the manufacture of linen and woolen cloth which they were soon exporting to England. As Greene says: "In its material result the Plantation of Ulster was undoubtedly a brilliant success. Farms and homesteads, churches and mills, rose fast amid the desolate wilds of Tyrone. * * * The foundations of the economic prosperity which has raised Ulster high above the rest of Ireland in wealth and intelligence were undoubtedly laid in the confiscation of 1610." [1]

From Ireland descendants of these Scotch settlers came to America. Anomalous as it may seem, it is nevertheless true that the immediate causes of this second emigration arose out of the fact that the Scotch settlement in Ireland had succeeded too well. Planted there in 1610 to develop the country industrially and establish a strong Protestant civilization, a century later the success of their industrial enterprises was the envy of their competitors in England, while the tenacity with which they held to their religious convictions gave offense to the bishops and clergy of the Established Church. By the close of the seventeenth century, the linen

---

[1] A Short History of the English People, Revised Edition, p. 458.

and woolen manufactures of Belfast, Londonderry, and other cities of Ulster had grown so prosperous that English manufacturers complained of the competition, and at their solicitation, the British Parliament passed a series of acts that greatly restricted the output of the Irish factories and placed them at the mercy of their English rivals. About the same time, the High Church party in England secured the passage of laws making it illegal for Presbyterians in Ireland to hold office, to practice law, to teach school, and to exercise many of their other civil and religious rights. "All over Ulster there was an outburst of Episcopalian tyranny."

In these two sources, one economic, the other religious, originated the Scotch-Irish emigration to America. During the fifty years preceding the American Revolution thousands of thrifty Protestants left Ireland never to return. In 1718 there was mention of "both ministers and people going off." In 1728, Archbishop Boulter, Primate of Ireland, stated that above 4,200 had sailed within the past three years. In 1740, a famine in Ulster "gave an immense impulse" to emigration, and during the next several years the annual flow to America was estimated at 12,000. During the three years, 1771 to 1773, emigration from Ulster is estimated at 30,000, of whom 10,000 were weavers. This movement, says Froude, "robbed Ireland of the bravest defenders of the English interests, and peopled the American seaboard with fresh flights of Puritans. Twenty thousand left Ulster on the destruction of the woolen trade. Many more were driven away by the first passing of the Test Act. * * * Men of spirit and energy refused to remain in a country where they were held unfit to receive the rights of citizens; and thenceforward, until the spell of tyranny was broken in 1782, annual shiploads of families poured themselves out from Belfast and Londonderry. The resentment which they carried with them continued to burn in their new homes; and, in the War of Independence, England had no fiercer enemies than the grandsons and great-grandsons of the Presbyterians who had held Ulster against Tyrconnell."[2]

Occasional settlers of Lowland Scotch and Scotch-Irish descent were found in North Carolina at a very early date. In 1676, William Edmundson, the Quaker missionary, records his visit to James Hall, who with his family "went from Ireland into Virginia," whence he removed into North

---

[2] The English in Ireland, Vol. 1, p. 392.

Carolina. John Urmstone, the missionary of the Church of England, in 1714, lists among his numerous grievances the fact that three of his vestrymen were "vehement Scotchmen Presbyterians." The Pollock family was of Lowland stock, and while Thomas Pollock himself came to North Carolina, some of his brothers emigrated to the North of Ireland. But one must be careful not to make too much of the presence of these pioneers of the Lowland Scotch and Scotch-Irish in North Carolina. They were simply isolated instances of individuals of an adventurous spirit who broke away from their home ties to seek their fortunes in a new land, and cannot be considered as a part of the great Scotch-Irish immigration of the eighteenth century.

The first of these settlers who came to North Carolina as an organized group were brought into the province by land companies. In 1735 Arthur Dobbs and "some other Gentlemen of Distinction in Ireland," associated with Henry McCulloh, a London merchant, presented a memorial to the Council of North Carolina "representing their intention of sending over to this Province several poor Protestant familys with design of raising Flax and Hemp." For this purpose they sought a grant of 60,000 acres of land on Black River in New Hanover precinct. The grant was made and in the following year the immigrants arrived and were settled in what is now Sampson and Duplin counties where they organized themselves into two congregations called Goshen and the Grove. Others followed, sent hither by Arthur Dobbs, himself a Scotch-Irishman, who in 1753 was appointed governor of North Carolina. In November of that year there arrived at New Bern a brigantine "from Belfast, in Ireland, sent hither by his Excellency Governor Dobbs, with a great Number of Irish Passengers, who are come to settle in this Province." A small colony of Swiss was also settled in the same community. In the meantime, in 1736, McCulloh, in association with Murray Crymble, James Huey and others, among them Arthur Dobbs, had embarked upon a much vaster scheme. Upon their petition, an order in Council was issued, May 19, 1737, under which warrants for 1,200,000 acres were allowed them to be located in the back country chiefly along the Yadkin, the Eno, and the Catawba rivers. Under the terms of his grant, McCulloh, the moving spirit in the enterprise, was to settle within it a large number of "substantial people" who were "to carry on the Pott Ashe Trade" and to raise "hemp and other naval stores." But these

ARTHUR DOBBS

grandiose schemes were never realized.   As late as 1754,
McCulloh had actually settled but 854 people within his grant.
Innumerable difficulties arose, especially in Mecklenburg and
Anson counties, between his agents and the people.   There
were disputes over boundary lines, quit rents, and titles,
which led to frequent riots and bloodshed, and finally in
1767, forced McCulloh and his associates to surrender their
grants to the Crown.

Of the Scotch-Irish immigrants who poured into North
Carolina from 1735 to 1775, a few landed at Charleston and
moved up the banks of the Pee Dee and Catawba rivers into
the hill country of the two Carolinas, but the great majority
landed at Philadelphia whence they moved into Western Virginia and North Carolina.   High prices of land deterred them
from settling in Pennsylvania.   In 1751, Governor Johnston
expressed the opinion that Pennsylvania was already "over-
stocked with people."   In 1752, Bishop Spangenberg, the
Moravian leader, declared that many settlers came into North
Carolina from England, Scotland, and the northern colonies,
"as they wished to own lands and were too poor to buy in
Pennsylvania or New Jersey."   To the same effect wrote
Governor Dobbs who, in 1755, said that as many as 10,000
immigrants from Holland, Britain and Ireland had landed
at Philadelphia in a single season, and consequently many
were "obliged to remove to the southward for want of lands
to take up" in Pennsylvania.   Many of these immigrants
were induced to pass through Virginia into North Carolina
because of the severity of the Virginia laws on religion in
comparison with those of the latter colony.   But there was
still another reason why the Scotch-Irish were attracted to
North Carolina in such large numbers.   During the thirty
years from 1734 to 1765 the chief executives of North Carolina were Gabriel Johnston, a native of Scotland, and Matthew Rowan and Arthur Dobbs, who were both Scotch-Irish-
men from Ulster, and all three exerted themselves personally
and officially to induce Scotch-Irish immigrants to settle
here.   The route which these settlers followed from Pennsylvania into North Carolina is plainly laid down on the maps
of that day as the "Great Road from the Yadkin River
through Virginia to Philadelphia."   It ran from Philadelphia through Lancaster and York in Pennsylvania, to Winchester in Virginia, down the Shenandoah Valley, thence
southward across the Dan River to the Moravian settlements
on the Yadkin.   The distance was 435 miles.   Commenting on

the movement by this route, Saunders says: "Remembering the route General Lee took when he went into Pennsylvania on that memorable Gettysburg campaign, it will be seen that very many of the North Carolina boys, both of German and of Scotch-Irish descent, in following their great leader, visited the homes of their ancestors and went hither by the very route by which they came away. To Lancaster and York counties, in Pennsylvania, North Carolina owes more of her population than to any other known part of the world,[3] and surely there never was a better population than they and their descendants—never better citizens, and certainly never better soldiers."[4]

This great tide of Scotch-Irish immigrants rolled in upon that section of North Carolina drained by the headwaters of the Neuse and the Cape Fear, and by the Yadkin, the Catawba, and their tributaries. As early as 1740 scattered families were living along the Hico, the Eno, and the Haw. In 1746, according to the family records of Alexander Clark, a few families removed from the Cape Fear to the "west of the Yadkin," where they joined others who had already broken into that wilderness. But prior to 1750 immigration into that remote region was slow, after that date, family followed family, group followed group in rapid succession. In 1751, Governor Johnston noted that "Inhabitants flock in here daily, mostly from Pennsylvania and other parts of America, and some directly from Europe. They commonly seat themselves toward the west and have got near the mountains." Bishop Spangenberg, in 1752, declared that "there are many people coming here because they are informed that stock does not require to be fed in the winter season. Numbers of [Scotch-] Irish have therefore moved in." In 1775 Governor Dobbs, writing of seventy-five families who had settled on his lands along Rocky River, a tributary of the Yadkin, said: "They are a colony from Pennsylvania, of what we call Scotch-Irish Presbyterians who with others in the neighboring Tracts had settled together in order to have a teacher [i. e., minister] of their own opinion and choice." This was a typical pioneer Scotch-Irish community, held together on

---

[3] The accuracy of this statement is open to question; most of the Scotch-Irish and German settlers, who came thence into North Carolina, merely passed through Pennsylvania without ever residing there.

[4] Prefatory Notes to *Colonial Records of North Carolina*, Vol. IV, p. xxi.

the frontier by common religious sympathies. A good index to the rapid increase of such communities in North Carolina, from 1750 to 1755, is found in the number of "supplications for ministers" which they sent up to the annual Synod of Philadelphia. In 1751, Rev. John Thomson, whom the Synod had directed to correspond with "many people" of North Carolina who desired to organize congregations, visited the Scotch-Irish settlements along the Catawba. He was the first preacher of any church in all that region, yet when Hugh McAden came through the province four years later, he preached to more than fifty such Scotch-Irish congregations most of which were west of the Yadkin. How rapidly the number of these immigrants increased is shown by a letter from Matthew Rowan, acting-governor, in 1753. He writes: "In the year 1746 I was up in the Country that is now Anson, Orange, and Rowan Countys. There was not then above one hundred fighting men: there is now at least three thousand for the most part Irish Protestants and Germans, and dayley increasing." This means that within six years the population of about 500 had increased to at least 15,000.

Still another indication of the rapid increase of population on the western frontier is the dates of the formation of new counties in that section. One should bear in mind that these counties as they now exist, though still retaining their old names, have not retained their original boundary lines: the frontier county in colonial days had no western boundary, but ran as far westward as white population extended. Accordingly every time a county was formed from the western end of an existing county, we know that white population had moved farther westward. In 1746, Edgecombe, Craven, and Bladen had such far-reaching western extensions. But so fast was population increasing and the colony expanding that in that year Granville was cut off from Edgecombe, Johnston from Craven, and three years later, Anson from Bladen. The boundaries of these new counties extended to the mountains and beyond. In 1752, Orange, still farther westward, was taken from Granville, Johnston and Bladen; and in 1753 Rowan was cut off from Anson. Nine years later another part of Anson, still farther to the westward, was taken to form Mecklenburg, which had become the center of the Scotch-Irish settlements. Thus within sixteen years, as a result of the influx of Scotch-Irish and German immigrants into Piedmont Carolina, six new counties were found necessary for their convenience.[5]

It is difficult to arrive at a just estimate of the character of the Scotch-Irish. There is perhaps no virtue in the whole catalogue of human virtues which has not been ascribed to them; no great principle of human liberty which has not been placed to their credit; no great event in our history in which they are not said to have played the leading part. Eulogy has exhausted the English tongue in their praise. But eulogy is not necessarily history, and history must strive to preserve the true balance between praise and censure. We know that the Scotch-Irishman was domestic in his habits and loved his home and family; but we know also that he was unemotional, seldom gave expression to his affections, and presented to the world the appearance of great reserve, coldness, and austerity. He was loyal to his own kith and kin, but stern and unrelenting with his enemies. He was deeply and earnestly religious, but the very depth and earnestness of his convictions made him narrow-minded and bigotted. He was law-abiding as long as the laws were to his liking, but when they ceased to be he disregarded them, peaceably if possible, forcibly if necessary. Independent and self-reliant, he was opinionated and inclined to lord it over any who would submit to his aggressions. He was brave, and he loved the stir of battle. He came of a fighting race; the blood of the old Covenanters flowed in his veins, and the beat of the drum, the sound of the fife, the call of the bugle aroused his fighting instincts. His whole history shows that he would fight. that he might be crushed but never subdued. In short, in both his admirable and his censurable traits, he possessed just the qualities that were needed on the Carolina frontier in the middle of the eighteenth century, qualities that enabled him to conquer the great wilderness of the Piedmont plateau, to drive back the savages, and to become, as Mr. Roosevelt has said, "the pioneers of our people in their march westward, the vanguard of the army of fighting settlers, who with axe and rifle won their way from the Alleghanies to the Rio Grande and the Pacific."[6]

Moving over the same route as the Scotch-Irish, and also coming from Pennsylvania, flowed the stream of German

---

[5] Hanna estimates the Scotch population in North Carolina in 1775 at about one-third the total population, i. e. 65,000.—*The Scotch-Irish in America*, Vol. I, pp. 82-84.

[6] Winning of the West, Vol. I, p. 134.

immigrants who came into North Carolina from 1745 to 1775.
Various motives prompted their migration. Some came in
search of adventure and good hunting grounds. Others were
looking for good lands and, like the Scotch-Irish, turning
their backs on Pennsylvania because of the high price of
lands in that colony. Still others were inspired by religious
zeal. The first and smallest of these three groups became
hunters and trappers, and in the vast unexplored forests
extending along the foothills of the Alleghanies and covering the mountain sides, they chased the fox and the deer,
hunted the buffalo and the bear, shot the wolf and the
panther, and trapped the otter and the beaver. With the
opening of spring, they would gather up their stores of
furs and skins and seek the settlements, frequently going as
far north as Philadelphia and as far south as Charleston, to
dispose of their winter's harvests. Typical of this class of
immigrants was Daniel Boone, who, though not of German
ancestry, was born in a Pennsylvania-German settlement and
came to North Carolina along with the tide of German immigration. Those who came in search of land found it of course
plentiful, cheap and fertile. The only capital needed on the
Carolina frontier was thrift, energy, and common sense, and
these the Germans possessed in a marked degree. Accordingly many thousands of them, driven from the Fatherland
by unfavorable economic conditions, carved handsome estates
for themselves and their children out of the Carolina wilderness, dotting the banks of the Yadkin and Catawba rivers
with their neat, pleasant farms, and their plain but comfortable cabins. A third class of Germans came to North Carolina in search of religious freedom and fields for missionary
activity. Like their neighbors, the Scotch-Irish, they were
inspired by a fervent religious zeal, but many of them came,
not so much to seek religious freedom for themselves as to
carry the Gospel to the Indians. They represented three
branches of the Protestant church,—the Unitas Fratrum, or
Moravian Church, the Lutheran, and the German Reformed.

The most distinct of the German settlements in North
Carolina was the one made by the Moravians in Wachovia.
In 1752, the Moravians at Bethlehem, Pennsylvania, moved
by a desire to find a home free from all religious interference, by a purpose to carry Christianity to the Indians, and
by a wish to develop a community on their own peculiar principles without outside meddling, determined to plant a settlement on the Carolina frontier. With that thoroughness which

Augustus Gottlieb Spangenberg

was one of their most marked characteristics, they first dispatched an exploring party under the leadership of Bishop Augustus Gottlieb Spangenberg, to view the land and select the site for the colony. Spangenberg's party proceeded first to Edenton, thence crossed almost the entire length of North Carolina, and ascended to the very summit of the Blue Ridge Mountains where they viewed the headwaters of streams that rise in North Carolina and flow into the Mississippi River. A journal in which the good bishop recorded the minutest details of their expedition tells us in simple and impressive language the story of the dangers and hardships which the members of his party encountered. Sickness, cold and hunger were among the least of their sufferings. After a thorough and painstaking survey the party selected a tract of land in what is now Forsyth County containing about 100,-000 acres. "As regards this land," wrote the bishop, "I regard it as a corner which the Lord has reserved for the Brethren. * * * The situation of this land is quite peculiar. It has countless springs and many creeks; so that as many mills can be built as may be desirable. These streams make many and fine meadow lands. * * * The most of this land is level and plain; the air fresh and healthy, and the water is good, especially the springs, which are said not to fail in summer. * * * In the beginning a good forester and hunter will be indispensable. The wolves and bears must be extirpated as soon as possible, or stock raising will be pursued under difficulties. The game in this region may also be very useful to the Brethren in the first years of the colony."

It was Bishop Spangenberg who called the settlement Wachovia. The word is derived from two German words, "wach" a meadow, and "aue" a stream. Wachovia lay within the possessions of Lord Granville and from him the Moravian Brethren purchased it in August, 1753. Two months later their plans were all completed, and on October 8, 1753, twelve unmarried men set out from the Moravian settlement at Bethlehem, Pennsylvania, to break ground for the settlement in North Carolina. No better evidence is needed of the shrewd, common sense of those German settlers than the simple fact that this small band, whose mission was to lay the foundation of civilization in the wilderness, consisted of a minister of the Gospel, a warden, a physician, a tailor, a baker, a shoemaker and tanner, a gardener, three farmers, and two carpenters. In the community which they went out to establish there was to be no place for drones. It is also interesting to note that they were fully conscious of the significance of their undertaking. Looking far into the future they foresaw the growth and development of their community and the intense interest with which posterity would inquire into its beginnings. Accordingly from the very beginning they recorded their daily doings to the minutest and most trivial details.

The little band of Moravian Brethren made their journey from Pennsylvania to Carolina in a large covered wagon drawn by six horses. Nearly six weeks were required for the trip. When they left Pennsylvania they were oppressed with heat; when they reached North Carolina the ground was covered with snow. At 3 o'clock Saturday afternoon, November 17th, they reached the spot where now stands the town of Bethabara, better known in its immediate neighborhood as "Old Town." There they found shelter in a log cabin which had been built but afterwards deserted by a German trapper named Hans Wagoner. It was an humble abode, without a floor and with a roof full of cracks and holes, but in it the Brethren held their first divine service and had their first "love feast." Sunday was observed as a day of real rest, but was followed by weeks of earnest, manly toil. One of their first cares was to enlarge their cabin and to lay in a supply of provisions for the winter. Their rifles supplied them with game in abundance. Salt was procured from Virginia, flour and corn from the Scotch-Irish settlements on the Yadkin, and beef from those on the Dan. In December they sowed their first wheat. A few days later came the Christmas season, and on Christmas Eve they gathered around the great open fire in their log cabin to hear again the wonderful story of Bethlehem. "We had a little love feast," says their faithful journal, "then near the Christ Child we had our first Christmas Eve in North Carolina, and rested in peace in this hope and faith. * * * All this while the wolves and panthers howled and screamed in the forests near by."

Throughout their first year the Moravian Brethren kept steadily at their tasks, and before the year had gone they had in operation a carpenter shop, a tailoring establishment, a pottery, a blacksmith shop, a shoe shop, a tannery and a cooper shop; had harvested wheat, corn, tobacco, flax, millet, barley, oats, buckwheat, turnips, cotton, garden vegetables; had cleared and cultivated fields, cut roads through the forests, built a mill an 1 erected several cabins. They made long journeys to Philadelphia and to Wilmington. The physician, Doctor Lash, made trips twenty, fifty and even a hundred miles through the forests to visit the sick and relieve the suffering. The Brethren had many visitors who came long distances to consult the physician or to secure the services of the shoemaker or the tailor. Within three months, during the year 1754, 103 visitors came to Wachovia. The next year the number was 426. Visitors were so numerous that the Brethren decided to build a "strangers' house.". This was the second building in Wachovia. Four days after it was finished it was occupied by a man and his invalid wife who came to consult the physician. Travel between Wachovia and Pennsylvania was frequent and the little colony continued to grow. More unmarried men and later a few married couples came from Pennsylvania, and by 1756 the Bethabara colony numbered sixty-five souls. Until the outbreak of the French and Indian War, the Moravians were on friendly terms with the Indians. Indeed, one of their purposes in coming to North Carolina was to preach the Gospel to the Indians who soon began to speak of the settlement at Bethabara as "the Dutch fort, where there are good people and much bread." But with the breaking out of the war the savages became hostile, and their enmity gave the Moravian Brethren much trouble. The Brethren were compelled to build forts, to arm every man in the colony, and to place sentinels around the settlement. The Moravians were frequently called upon to go to the defense of their white neighbors. From thirty to forty miles around families sought refuge at Bethabara where all learned to love and respect the Moravian Brethren, and not a few applied for membership in the Moravian Church.

After the close of the war the settlement grew more rapidly. Two towns, Bethabara and Bethania, were founded before 1760, but from the first the Brethren intended that the chief town should be in the center of Wachovia, and they thought the closing of the Indian war and the re-establishment of peace a favorable time to begin it. The first act in the founding of this new town, which received the name of Salem, took place January 6, 1766. During the singing of a hymn, work was begun by clearing a site for the first house, and on February 19th eight young men moved into it. Other houses were then erected in quick succession, and during the next years many of the Bethabara community moved to

Salem, where they were joined by more Brethren from Beth lehem, and by a goodly number directly from Germany. Salem soon became the principal settlement of the Moravians in North Carolina. In 1773, an Englishman who visited Salem, left an interesting description of the town and its people as they appeared just upon the eve of the Revolution. "This society, sect or fraternity of the Moravians," he wrote, "have everything in common, and are possessed of a very large and extensive property. * * * From their infancy they are instructed in every branch of useful and common literature, as well as in mechanical knowledge and labour. * * * The Moravians have many excellent and very valuable farms, on which they make large quantities of butter, flour and provisions, for exportation. They also possess a number of useful and lucrative manufactures, particularly a very extensive one of earthenware, which they have brought to great perfection, and supply the whole country with it for some hundred miles around. In short, * * * they certainly are valuable subjects, and by their unremitting industry and labour have brought a large extent of wild, rugged country into a high state of population and improvement." [7]

As a rule the Germans came into North Carolina as organized bodies. The Moravians, as has been seen, kept their organization intact and distinct from all others, but Reformed and Lutheran congregations frequently united to build churches and support ministers. Two such congregations, desiring to build a church in common, drew up an agreement in which they stated as their reason for uniting that "Since we are both united in the principal doctrines of Christianity, we find no difference between us except in name." Prior to the Revolution many such union churches were built throughout the present counties of Guilford, Alamance, Orange, Randolph, Davidson, Davie, Iredell, Cabarrus, Stanly, Union, Mecklenburg, Lincoln, Catawba, and Burke. The first of these settlements was made about 1745. In that year Lutheran congregations were organized on Haw River. In the same year Henry Weidner, a Pennsylvania-German, entered what is now Catawba County as a hunter and trapper; before 1760 he had been joined by other German settlers in number sufficient to form a congregation. The first Germans in Rowan County appeared about 1750. Three years later, Matthew

---

[7] Smyth, J. F. D.: A Tour in the United States of America, Vol. I, pp. 214-17.

Rowan, acting-governor, wrote that "our three fruntire County's are Anson, Orange, and Rowan. They are for the most part settled with Irish Protestants and Germans, brave, Industrius people. Their Militia amounts to upwards of three thousand Men and Increasing fast." We are not without evidence of how fast this increase was. A correspondent of the *South Carolina and American General Gazette,* writing from Williamsburg, Virginia, in 1768, says: "There is scarce any history either ancient or modern, which affords an account of such a rapid and sudden increase of inhabitants in a back frontier country, as that of North Carolina. To justify the truth of this observation, we need only to assure you that twenty years ago there were not twenty taxable people within the limits of the county of Orange; in which there are now four thousand taxable. The increase of Inhabitants, and the flourishing state of the other adjoining back counties, are no less surprising and astonishing." Four thousand taxables means about 16,000 people. Most of these, of course, were Scotch-Irish, but the Germans formed a large percentage of the total. In 1771, the vestry of St. Luke's Parish, Salisbury, stated that in Rowan, Orange, Mecklenburg, and Tryon counties there "are already settled near three thousand German protestant families, and being very fruitful in that healthy climate, are besides vastly increasing by numbers of German protestants almost weekly arriving from Pennsylvania and other provinces of America." According to Governor Dobbs, the frontier families generally embraced from five to ten members each; on this basis, therefore, allowing for probable exaggeration, the total German population of Rowan, Orange, Mecklenburg and Tryon counties in 1771 must have been not less than 15,000.[8]

Like the Scotch Highlanders, the Germans in North Carolina endeavored to preserve their language and customs. In 1773, an English traveller who had lost his way in the vicinity of Hillsboro, records in his journal: "It was unlucky for me that the greater number of the inhabitants on the plantations where I called to inquire my way, being Germans, neither understood my questions nor could make themselves intelligible to me." It was not until years after the Revolution that English became the common language in the German settlements. The first English school among them was

---

[8] Faust estimates the German population in North Carolina in 1775 at 8,000.—manifestly an under-estimate.—*The German Element in the United States,* Vol. I, pp. 284-85.

opened in Cabarrus County in 1798. English made its way
slowly against the opposition of the older people who clung
tenaciously to the language of their cradles, and finally won
only because their children, wiser than their parents, were
unwilling to go through life under the handicap of being
ignorant of the very language in which they had to transact
their daily affairs. In one respect the fate of the Germans
was harder even than that of the Scotch Highlanders,—the
former lost not only their language, but their names also,
for as time passed, most of the German names became Angli-
cized. Thus Kuhn became Coon, Behringer became Bar-
ringer, Scheaffer became Shepherd, Albrecht became Al-
bright, Zimmerman became Carpenter, so that many families
in North Carolina today whose names indicate an English
ancestry are really of German descent.

Estimates of the population of North Carolina prior to
the census of 1790 vary widely, and when attempts are made
to go still further and estimate the proportion of the various
racial elements in that population the divergences are greater
still. Nevertheless, taking all these estimates into consideration, and adopting a very conservative course, one can
scarcely resist the conclusion that, placing the total population in 1760 at 130,000 is certainly not open to the criticism
of exaggeration. The same data on which this estimate is
based lead to the conclusion that the number of negro slaves
in the colony at that time was about one-fourth of the total
population. Doubling Faust's estimate of the German population, which the data seem to justify, accepting Hanna's estimate of the Scotch as one-third of the total, and rejecting
all other elements, i. e., French, Swiss and Welsh, as too
small to be taken into account, and the Indians, who were not
included in any of the estimates, we arrive at the following
analysis of the population of North Carolina in 1760:

English	45,000
Scotch	40,000
German	15,000
Negroes	30,000
Total	130,000

The English and Scotch were born subjects of the British
Crown, and the Germans, therefore, were the only important
foreign element in the white population. To place them, and

those who claimed titles to property derived from them, upon an equality with the English and Scotch, the Assembly, in 1764, enacted ''that all Foreign Protestants heretofore inhabiting within this Province, and dying seized of any Lands, Tenements, or Hereditaments, shall, forever hereafter, be deemed, taken, and esteemed to have been naturalized, and intituled to all the Rights, Privileges, and Advantages of natural Born Subjects.''

CHAPTER XII

SOCIETY, RELIGION AND EDUCATION

It is obviously impossible in the brief space of a single chapter to give an adequate account of the social, religious and educational ideals and practices of any large and complex community through a century of its history. All that will be attempted here, therefore, will be a very brief statement of some of the more important of these ideals and practices in colonial North Carolina to which nothing more than mere reference can be made in the general narrative which makes up this volume.

In colonial times, class distinctions were sharply drawn. The highest social group was that which was composed of the large planters, professional men, and public officials. Many of them were connected by family ties with the gentry of England, Scotland, and Ireland and they sought to maintain in America the social distinctions which characterized their class in the Old World. Speaking broadly they were men and women of education, culture, refinement and character. Evidence of their social rank is found in the application to them of such terms as "gentleman," "esquire," "planter," all of which had a technical significance when used, as they commonly were, in such official documents as wills, deeds, and court records. The general use of such insignia as family crests and coats-of-arms was also indicative of the social rank of the planters. Says a scholarly Virginia historian: "There is no reason to think that armorial bearings were as freely and loosely assumed in those early times as they are so often now, under republican institutions; such bearings were then a right of property, as clearly defined as any other, and continue to be in modern England, what they were in colonial Virginia. In the seventeenth century, when so large a proportion of the persons occupying the highest position in the society of the colony were natives of England, the unwarranted assumption of a coat-of-arms would probably have been as soon noticed, and perhaps as quickly resented, as in England itself. The prominent families in Virginia were as well acquainted with the social antecedents of each other in the mother country as families of the same rank in England were with the social antecedents of the leading families in the surrounding shires; they were, therefore, thoroughly competent to pass upon a claim of this nature; and the fact that they were, must have had a distinct influence in preventing a false claim from being put forward. In a general way, it may be said it was quite as natural for Virginians of those times to be as slow and careful as contemporary Englishmen in advancing a claim of this kind without a legal right on which to base it, and, therefore, when they did advance it, that it was likely to stand the test of examination by the numerous persons in the colony who must have been familiar with English coats-of-arms, in general. * * * The possession of coats-of-arms by the leading Virginian families in the seventeenth century is disclosed in various incidental ways. Insignia of this kind are frequently included among the personal property appraised in inventories. And they were also stampt on pieces of fine silver-plate." [1] A more frequent use was to stamp impressions on seals of letters and valuable papers. That what Mr. Bruce says of the use and significance of such insignia in Virginia is equally true of North Carolina, is shown by an examination of the wills and other valuable papers of colonial families, many of which are sealed with crests and arms which show close relationship between their signers and the gentry of the mother country.

Just below the planters in social rank was the largest single social group in the colony which was composed chiefly of small farmers, who tilled the land with their own hands. Their life was crude. They enjoyed few luxuries and fewer refinements. They worked hard, played hard, lived hard. Brickell declares that some of them "equalize with the Negroes in hard Labour." On holidays, or between working seasons, they indulged in such sports as horse-racing, cock-fighting, wrestling, and on these occasions generally drank hard and deep of strong liquor. "I have frequently seen them," wrote Brickell, "come to the Towns, and there remain Drinking Rum, Punch, and other Liquors for Eight or Ten Days successively, and after they have committed this Excess,

---

[1] Bruce: Social Life of Virginia in the Seventeenth Century, pp. 105-108.

will not drink any Spirituous Liquor, 'till such time as they take the next Frolick, as they call it, which is generally in two or three Months.'' Despite crudities and excesses, due chiefly to the hard, circumscribed life of a frontier community, they possessed the sterling qualities characteristic of English yeomen. They, too, had a keen class consciousness and took as much pride in being able to write after their names, as their wills and other records testify, such terms as ''farmer,'' ''husbandman,'' ''yeoman,'' as the planters did in using terms similarly descriptive of their social rank. ''I, Thomas West, of Bertie County and Province of North Carolina, Yeoman,'' thus Thomas West begins his will. A strong, fearless, independent race, simple in tastes, crude in manners, provincial in outlook, democratic in social relations, tenacious of their rights, sensitive to encroachments on their personal liberties, and, when interested in religion at all, earnest, narrow and dogmatic, such were the people who chiefly determined the character of the civilization of North Carolina.

Next in the social order were the indentured white servants among whom were represented many classes and conditions. Some—fortunately a negligible number—were convicts sold into bondage as a punishment for crime. Another class entered in the official records as criminals were guilty only of political offenses. Many of the followers of the Duke of Monmouth after his defeat at Sedgemore in 1685 were deported to the colonies under sentences of servitude. An even more unfortunate class were the women and children who had been kidnapped in London and other large cities and sent to the colonies to supply the increasing demands for labor. But the largest number of indentured servants were those who had voluntarily taken upon themselves the obligations of service in order to pay for their passage across the Atlantic. Some of this class were of low moral and intellectual development, but most of them were energetic, industrious and thrifty persons who had simply taken the only means open to them to leave the Old World for the greater opportunities of the New World. At the expiration of their terms of service their masters were required by law to fit them out decently with food and clothes; in the case of a man-servant, the master must also furnish ''a good well-fixed Gun.'' An indentured servant, at the expiration of his term, was also entitled to take up fifty acres of land. Thus many of this class entered the ranks of the small farmer group and by industry and frugality became good, substantial citizens.

The lowest social group was, of course, composed of negro slaves. From the beginning of the colony the soil of North Carolina was dedicated to slavery. It was recognized in the Concessions of 1665 and in the Fundamental Constitutions. The Lords Proprietors encouraged it by granting fifty acres for each slave above fourteen years of age brought into the colony. At a court held in February, 1694, several persons appeared and proved their rights to land by the importation of negroes. Besides negroes the whites early adopted the custom of reducing to slavery Indians captured in battle.

Necessity made the slave code harsh and cruel. Stringent restrictions were thrown around the movements of slaves. They were not to be permitted to leave their masters' plantations without proper tickets of identification stating the place from which, and the place to which they were going; and similar restraints, under severe penalties, were placed on their right to hunt, to bear arms, and to assemble together or communicate with one another at night. The Fundamental Constitutions gave masters "absolute power and authority over negro slaves," but the king, after purchasing the colony, sought to mitigate this law by securing to the slave his right to life. It was not, however, until 1754 that the Assembly considered making the wilful killing of a slave punishable by death, and even then the Council rejected the bill. In 1773 a similar measure introduced by William Hooper passed both houses and was rejected by the governor. The following year such an act was passed by both houses, and was the last law, but one, that was signed by a royal governor of North Carolina. Barbarous punishments were inflicted upon slaves convicted of crimes. Brickell records that he had frequently seen negroes whipped until large pieces of skin were hanging down their backs, "yet," he added, "I never observed one of them shed a tear." A negro, mulatto, or Indian convicted of perjury was punished by being compelled to stand for one hour with his ear nailed to pillory, after which he was released by having his ear cut off; then a similar proceeding was followed with the other ear; and the punishment was completed by the infliction of thirty-nine lashes on his bare back, well laid on. Negroes guilty of rape were often castrated. There are on record instances of negroes, who had been convicted of murder, being burned at the stake by order of the court. It would be easy, however, to make too much of the severity of these punishments, and to draw unwarranted conclusions from them, for it ought not to be forgotten that they were inflicted at a time when the criminal codes of all nations were disgraced by cruel and barbarous practices.

The earliest slaves in the colony were undoubtedly pagans, and their masters as a rule were willing enough for them to remain so. This attitude was due less to indifference than to a widespread belief that it was illegal to hold a Christian in bondage. In 1709, Rev. James Adams reported that there were 211 negroes in Pasquotank Precinct, "some few of which are instructed in the principles of the Christian religion, but their masters will by no means permit them to be baptized, having a false notion that a Christian slave is, by law, free." This belief, however, was not universal and some masters permitted their slaves to be baptized. Gradually it died out altogether and the baptism of slaves who professed Christianity became general.

The hold which the institution of slavery secured on the colony is indicated by its rapid growth. Careful estimates, some of which are official, show the population of negroes at various times as follows: 1712, 800; 1717, 1,100; 1730, 6,000; 1754, 15,000; 1756, 19,000; 1765, 30,000; 1767, 39,000. The increase was due chiefly to births. In 1754, only nineteen negroes were entered in the customs-house at Bath; and during the preceding seven years the average number annually brought in at Beaufort was only seventeen. The stronghold of slavery was in the East where, as early as 1767, the negroes out-numbered the whites.

Historians do not agree in their delineation of the character of the settlers of North Carolina. There are those, of whom perhaps George Davis, the historian of the Cape Fear, was the most eminent, who would have us believe that they "were no needy adventurers, driven by necessity— no unlettered boors, ill at ease in the haunts of civilization, and seeking their proper sphere amidst the barbarism of the savage," but that "they were gentlemen of birth and education, bred in the refinement of polished society, and bringing with them ample fortunes, gentle manners, and cultivated minds." [2]   On the other hand there are others who, like John Fiske, could see in colonial North Carolina nothing more than "a kind of back-woods for Virginia," "an Alsatia for insolvent debtors," "mean white trash," and "outlaws," from the northern colony. Fiske divides the early settlers of North Carolina into two classes: First, the thriftless, im-

[2] University Address, 1855.

provident white servant class who could not maintain a respectable existence for themselves in Virginia; second, the "outlaws who fled [from Virginia] into North Carolina to escape the hangman." [3] Neither picture is true, for if Davis insists that the shield is all gold, none the less does Fiske insist that it is all of a baser metal. The truth lies between. Undoubtedly there were enough well-born, educated leaders among the population to give a cultured tone to the best society in the colony; and undoubtedly there were enough escaped outlaws to stimulate the vigilance of the officers of the criminal law. But both together constituted no larger percentage of the population of North Carolina than of the other colonies and in none of them were they ever more than a very small minority. Between the two extremes, constituting them as now the bone and sinew of the population, were those sturdy, enterprising, law-abiding, and liberty-loving middle class Englishmen who have always from Crecy and Agincourt to Yorktown, Gettysburg, and Mons formed the strength and character of English-speaking peoples. After the middle of the eighteenth century came that great tide of Scotch peoples who renewed and strengthened but did not essentially alter these characteristics of the great mass of the population of colonial North Carolina.

The best contemporary account of the social and industrial life of the colony during the first seventy-five years of its existence is that found in Brickell's "Natural History of North Carolina," published in 1737. The author was a physician and scientist of ability whose residence for several years in the colony gave him ample opportunity for observation. Says he: "The Europians, or Christians of North-Carolina, are a streight, tall, well-limbed and active People. * * * The Men who frequent the Woods, and labour out of Doors, or use the Waters, the vicinity of the Sun makes Impressions on them; but as for the Women who do not expose themselves to the Weather, they are often very fair, and well-featured, as you shall meet with any where, and have very Brisk and Charming Eyes; and as well and finely shaped, as any Women in the world. * * * They marry generally very young, some at Thirteen or Fourteen; and she that continues unmarried, until Twenty, is reckoned a stale maid, which is a very indifferent Character in that Country. * * * The Children * * * are very Docile and apt to learn any thing, as any

---

[3] Old Virginia and Her Neighbours, Vol. II, p. 316.

Children in Europe; and those that have the advantage to be
Educated, Write good Hands, and prove good Accountants.
* * * The young Men are generally of a bashful, sober
Behaviour, few proving Prodigals, to spend what the Parents
with Care and Industry have left them, but commonly Improve it. * * * The Girls are not only bred to the Needle
and Spinning, but to the Dairy and domestic Affairs, which
many of them manage with a great deal of prudence and conduct, though they are very young. * * * The Women are
most Industrious in these Parts, and many of them by their
good Housewifery make a great deal of Cloath of their Cotton,
Wool, and Flax, and some of them weave their own Cloath
with which they decently Apparel their whole Family though
large. Others are so Ingenious that they make up all the
wearing apparel both for Husband, Sons and Daughters.
Others are very ready to help and assist their Husbands in
any Servile Work, as planting when the Season of the Year
requires expedition: Pride seldom banishing Housewifery.
* * * The Men are very ingenious in several Handycraft
Businesses, and in building their Canoes and Houses * * *
Their Furniture, as with us, consists of Pewter, Brass, Tables,
Chairs, which are imported here commonly from England:
The better sort have tolerable Quantities of Plate, with other
convenient, ornamental and valuable Furniture. There are
throughout this settlement as good bricks as any I ever met
with in Europe. All sorts of handicrafts, such as carpenters,
coopers, bricklayers, plasterers, shoemakers, tanners, tailors,
weavers, and most other sorts of tradesmen, may with small
beginnings, and good industry, soon thrive well in this place
and provide good estates and all manner of necessaries for
their families.''

Land and slaves were then, as they continued to be
throughout the South until 1865, the chief form of wealth in
Eastern North Carolina. Consequently the growth of towns
was very slow and life in the colony was seen at its best on the
great estates of the planters scattered along the banks of the
rivers and their tributaries. Many of these planters counted
from 5,000 to 10,000 acres in their estates, while not a few
were lords of princely domains embracing from 30,000 to
50,000 acres, and were masters of as many as 250 slaves. In
1732 Thomas Pollock of Bertie County devised 22,000 acres
of land, besides 10 other plantations, and 75 slaves; Edward
Moseley, in 1749, mentioned in his will tracts embracing 30,-
000 acres, besides three other plantations, and 88 slaves;

Thomas Pollock of Chowan County, in 1753, left 40,000 acres and 16 other plantations, and 75 slaves; Governor Gabriel Johnston's estate included more than 25,000 acres and 103 slaves; Cullen Pollock mentioned in his will 150 negroes; while Roger Moore of New Hanover County in 1750 mentioned 250 slaves. The prices of negroes of course varied according to time and the individual negro. In 1694 James Phillpotts of Albemarle County left 6,000 pounds of pork for the purchase of a negro. In 1680 the estate of Valentine Bird included 12 negroes valued at £310 sterling; in 1695 a negro man and his wife belonging to Seth Sothel's estate sold for £40; in 1745 an old negro woman belonging to James Winwright of Carteret County sold for £100, a negro boy for £150, a negro man for £200, and another for £250, these prices probably being reckoned in proclamation money.

The river courses afforded the best sites for plantations not only because of the greater fertility of the bottom lands, but also because of the greater ease of transportation. Brickell tells us that "Both Sexes are very dexterous in paddling and managing their Canoes, both Men, Women, Boys, and Girls, being bred to it from Infancy." At the planter's wharf sloops, schooners, and brigantines were loaded with cargoes of skins, salt pork and beef, tallow, staves, naval stores, lumber, tobacco, corn, rice, and other products of the plantation to be carried away to the West Indies and exchanged for rum, molasses, sugar, and coffee, or to Boston where the proceeds were invested in clothing, household goods, books, and negroes. In 1734, Edward Salter of Bath, in his will, directs his executors to load his brigantine with tar and send it to Boston to be exchanged for young negroes. In 1753 the exports from North Carolina plantations were 61,528 barrels of tar; 12,052 barrels of pitch; 10,429 barrels of turpentine; 762,000 staves; 61,580 bushels of corn; 100 hogsheads of tobacco, and 30,000 deer skins, besides lumber and other commodities.

On an elevated site overlooking some river and generally approached through a long avenue of oaks, cedars, or poplars, stood the "Manor House," or as the negroes called it the "Big House." Brickell says that in their houses "the most substantial Planters generally use Brick, and Lime, which is made of Oyster-shells; * * * the meaner Sort erect with Timber, the outside with Clap-boards, the Roofs of both sorts of Houses are made with Shingles, and they generally have Sash Windows, and affect large and decent Rooms with good Closets, as they do a most beautiful Prospect by some noble

River or Creek.'' These residences were often characterized by the huge white columns, broad verandas, wide halls, large and spacious rooms, which have become famous as the ''colonial'' style. Whether of wood or brick all were the seats of unbounded hospitality. John Lawson tells us that ''the planters [are] hospitable to all that come to visit them; there being very few housekeepers but what live very nobly and give away more provisions to coasters and guests who come to see them than they expend among their own families.'' Hospitality to strangers and travellers was regarded as a social duty which the wealthy planters, owing to the absence of inns and comfortable taverns, felt impelled to exercise for the honor of the province. Indeed, upon a lonely plantation, a garrulous traveller or a genial sea-captain who brought news of the outside world, was ever an honored and a welcome guest, for whom the housekeeper brought out her finest silver and china ware, her best linen and her most tempting morsels, while the planter regaled him with the choicest liquid refreshments which his cellar afforded, for as Brickell assures us, ''the better Sort, or those of good Œconomy'' kept ''plenty of Wine, Rum, and other Liquors at their own Houses, which they generally make use of amongst their Friends and Acquaintance, after a most decent and discreet Manner.''

Every great plantation was almost a complete community in itself. Each had its own shops, mills, distillery, tannery, spinning wheels and looms, and among the slaves were to be found excellent blacksmiths, carpenters, millers, shoemakers, spinners, and weavers, and other artisans. ''The Cloathings used by the Men,'' Brickell tells us, ''are English Cloaths, Druggets, Durois, Green Linen, etc. The Women have their Silks, Calicoes, Stamp-Linen, Calimanchoes, and all kinds of Stuffs, some whereof are Manufactured in the Province. They make few Hats, though they have the best Furrs in plenty, but with this Article, they are commonly supplied from New-England, and sometimes from Europe.'' In their homes the planters were supplied not only with all the necessities of a pioneer community, but enjoyed many of the comforts and luxuries usually found only in a long established society. An examination of their wills, inventories, and other documents shows among their household furniture an ample supply of those fine old mahogany tables, sideboards, bedsteads, couches, chairs, and desks which excite the envy of modern housekeepers and deplete the purses of modern husbands. That the Carolina housekeeper was prepared to play the hospitable hostess to the most particular guest or the most pompous colonial potentate who might chance to honor her board, is well attested by the excellent silver, china, and glassware which adorned her sideboard. The diamond rings, earrings, necklaces, and other jewelry which the colonial dame passed down as heirlooms to her children and grandchildren show clearly enough from whom the twentieth century dame inherited her love of finery and personal ornaments; while a goodly sprinkling of silver and gold kneebuckles, shoebuckles, and other such trinkets betrays the vanity with which the colonial planter displayed his silk-stockinged calf and shapely foot.

Much of what has been written above applies only to the older communities in Eastern Carolina; some modifications are necessary in describing conditions in the back country. There farms were smaller, agriculture was less dependent upon slave labor, and the land, therefore, was better tilled. Industrial enterprises were more important. With the Scotch-Irish and German settlers industries which the eastern planters usually left to negro slaves were conducted by skilled laborers. Among the most prosperous settlers in those communities were the weavers, joiners, coopers, wheelwrights, wagon-makers, tailors, blacksmiths, hatters, rope-makers, and fullers. The Germans in Wachovia early set up "a number of useful and lucrative manufactures, particularly a very extensive one of earthenware, which they have brought to a great perfection, and supply the whole country with it for some hundred miles around." [4] What Doctor McKelway says of the Scotch-Irish applies also to the Germans in Carolina. Their chief wealth was "in their own capacity to manufacture what they needed. When the goods brought with them began to wear out, the blacksmith built his forge, the weaver set up his loom, and the tailor brought out his goose. A tannery was built on the nearest stream and mills for grinding the wheat and corn were erected on the swift water courses. Saw mills were set up, and logs were turned into plank. The women not only made their own dresses but the material as well, spinning the wool and afterwards the cotton into lindsey and checks and dying it according to the individual taste. * * * In other words the people were an industrial as well as an industrious people." [5]

---

[4] Smyth: A Tour in the United States of America, Vol. I, p. 214.
[5] The Scotch-Irish in North Carolina. (*N. C. Booklet*, Vol. IV, No. 11, pp. 15-16.)

They were all farmers who owned few slaves and as a rule tilled the soil themselves. A traveller who had traversed the entire length of the State from Edenton to Wachovia makes this interesting observation: "The moment I touched the boundary of the Moravians, I noticed a marked and most favorable change in the appearance of buildings and farms; and even the cattle seemed larger, and in better condition. Here, in combined and well-directed effort, all put shoulders to the wheel, which apparently moves on oily springs. We passed in our ride New Garden, a settlement of Quakers from Nantucket. They, too, were exemplary and industrious. The generality of the planters in this State depend upon negro labor and live scantily in a region of affluence. In the possessions of the Moravians and Quakers all labor is performed by the whites. Every farm looks neat and cheerful; the dwellings are tidy and well furnished, abounding in plenty." [6]

As a rule the English planters of the East called themselves Churchmen. In 1765 Tryon wrote, "Every sect of religion abounds here except the Roman Catholic, * * * though the Church of England I reckon at present to have the majority of all other sects." Its numerical superiority, however, was not the measure of its influence. The Church in North Carolina paid the penalty of all organizations which enjoy the legal support and patronage of government. Besides those who were Churchmen from religious convictions, the rolls of the Church included others, perhaps even more numerous, who called themselves Churchmen from political, business, or social reasons. Nominally members of the Establishment, they were without serious religious convictions of any sort, and contributed nothing to the real welfare of the Church, to which their membership was rather a hindrance than an aid. On the other hand, those who became members of the dissenting denominations did so from genuine religious convictions and were fired with fervor and zeal in the propagation of their faith. Consequently the religious history of North Carolina in colonial times is of interest and significance less on account of the Established Church than for the growth and contributions of the dissenting denominations.

The royal authorities were even more determined upon a legal establishment than the proprietary authorities had been. It was, indeed, difficult for statesmen of the eighteenth century to think of a monarchy without an established church; the

---

[6] Watson, Elkanah: Men and Times of the Revolution, p. 293.

epigram of James I, "No bishop, no king," seemed to them to express the true relation between the Church and the State. Consequently we find that under the royal administration emphatic instructions were issued to each governor commanding him to secure the necessary legislation for the support of the Church. Burrington failed in his efforts, not because of the influence of the dissenting interests, which were small at that time, but because of his utter inability to act harmoniously on any public matter with the representatives of the people. His successor, Johnston, was more successful. In 1739, Johnston reported that there were but two places in the province at which divine services were regularly held, and as a zealous Churchman he lamented "the deplorable and almost total want of divine worship throughout the province," which he thought was "really scandalous" and a reproach which the Assembly "ought to remove without loss of time." The Assembly in 1741, therefore, passed a vestry act which proved, however, to be ineffective. In 1748 Governor Johnston wrote that "a Multitude of children are unbaptized" along the Cape Fear for "the want of a Minister [which] is very sensibly felt in that large District;" while about the same time Rev. James Moir declared that many people were becoming Baptists for lack of clergymen of the Church of England to minister to their religious needs.

In 1754 Governor Dobbs secured a more satisfactory act, but the Crown repealed it by proclamation because it conferred the right of presentation upon the vestries. "This was the beginning," says Doctor Weeks, "of a triangular fight between Dissenters, democratic Churchmen, and supporters of the rights of the Crown. The ecclesiastical history of the next ten years is of interest chiefly because of the stubborn resistance to the enforcement of church laws by the Dissenters, the stubborn determination of the Churchmen to have an establishment with the right of presentation, and the steady opposition of the Crown to both parties." [7] The Crown repealed vestry acts passed in 1758, 1760, 1761 and 1762 on the ground that the right of presentation by vestries was "incompatible with the rights of the Crown and the ecclesiastical jurisdiction." These quarrels were of course injurious to the real interest of the Church. They left the clergy without support, and their number began to decrease. In 1764 Dobbs stated that there were only six orthodox clergymen in the

---

[7] Church and State in North Carolina, pp. 32-33.

colony, "four of which," he added, "are pious and perform
their duty." Under Tryon and Martin the situation showed
a marked improvement. The number of clergymen increased
to eighteen; the vestry act passed in 1764 for five years was
renewed in 1768 for another five, and in 1774 for ten years,
"the longest existence that ever was allowed to any vestry act
in this province." Commenting on this renewal, Rev. James
Reed, the missionary of the Society for the Propagation of
the Gospel at New Bern, said: "I sincerely wish the period
had been shorter, or indefinite for there is the greatest probability that in ten years the dissenting interest will be strong
enough to carry everything in the Assembly, and that the
Vestry Act will then receive its quietus." But the vestry act,
and with it the Established Church, was not to receive its
"quietus" from the dissenting interests in the Assembly.
Both went down along with other monarchical institutions,
before the revolutionary movement of 1776, for when the convention of that year came to adopt a constitution for the
newly independent State, Churchmen joined with Dissenters
in inserting a section prohibiting the "Establishment of any
one religious Church or Denomination in this State in Preference to any other."

In 1760, Rev. James Reed lamented the fact that a "great
number of Dissenters of all denominations" had settled in
North Carolina, mentioning especially Quakers, Presbyterians, Baptists and Methodists. First in point of time were
the Quakers. Since the visits of Edmundson and Fox to North
Carolina, the Quakers had grown rapidly in numbers. Prior
to 1700 their efforts were directed chiefly to securing a foothold; their growth came after that date. In the eastern section of the colony it was the result of expansion among the
native population, in the back country it was due to immigration. In 1729 Governor Everard attributed the growth of
Quakerism to the absence of clergymen of the Established
Church. Four years later, Governor Burrington gave another
reason,—"the regularity of their lives, hospitality to
strangers, and kind offices to new settlers," he wrote, "inducing many to be of their persuasion." To these causes may be
added the zeal of their missionaries who in 1729, wrote
Everard, were "very busy making Proselytes and holding
meetings daily in every Part of this Government." Doctor
Weeks records the visits to North Carolina between 1700 and
1729 of seventeen missionaries, three of whom were women.
In 1700 the Society was confined largely to Perquimans and

Pasquotank precincts. It began to cross the Albemarle Sound about 1703 and by the middle of the century had planted itself in many of the precincts of Bath County. When the colony was transferred to the Crown, the Quakers were "considerable for their numbers and substance." Under the royal government the Society continued to grow in Eastern Carolina, but not very rapidly. Missionaries came in, held meetings wherever they could secure a group of people, and organized several monthly meetings. Monthly meetings were established in Carteret in 1733, in Dobbs in 1748, and in Northampton in 1760. In Northampton and other counties bordering on Virginia the growth was due chiefly to the overflow from Virginia, but in the other counties it was the natural expansion of the native element. "For as this country was at first settled in a great measure by Baptists and Quakers," wrote William Orr, a missionary of the Society for the Propagation of the Gospel, in 1742, "so their descendants (though they come to church now and then) yet they still retain, and are more or less under the influence of their Fathers' Principles."

The planting and growth of Quakerism in the back country was due not to expansion from within but to immigration from without. Quaker immigrants, chiefly from Pennsylvania, began to come about 1740 and soon spread over the territory now embraced in Alamance, Chatham, Guilford, Randolph, and Surry counties. They were a strong and healthy race and their presence added to the population of the colony a stable element characterized by thrift, industry and energy. In 1751 the Cane Creek Monthly Meeting was organized in what is now Alamance County. Three years later the famous New Garden Monthly Meeting, the mother of many others, was organized. From New Garden most of the meetings in that section of the State took their rise. Although the Quakers increased in numbers after the transfer of the colony to the Crown, comparatively they lost ground. Says their leading historian, Doctor Weeks: "The promise of an aggressive and rapid growth in the youth of Quakerism was not fulfilled in its maturer years. This promise was particularly clear in North Carolina. During the seventeenth century the records show that the Society in that colony was quietly but steadily extending its outposts and was being strengthened by immigration and conversion. To such an extent was this true, that in 1716 Rev. Giles Rainsford writes to the Society for the Propagation of the Gospel that the 'poor colony of North Carolina will soon be overrun with Quakerism and infidelity if not timely prevented by your sending over able and sober missionaries as well as schoolmasters to reside among them.' But this almost phenomenal growth of the native element ceased soon after the Established Church became well organized. Quakers never played in North Carolina under royal government the part they had played under the government of the Proprietors. * * * The Revolution, like the Civil War, was a time of suffering to the Quakers. Many left their ranks and were disowned to take part in the struggle for liberty, and the Society was much depleted.'' [8]

"The Presbyterians," wrote Tryon in 1765, "are settled mostly in the back or westward counties," that is to say in the sections of the colony settled by the Scotch-Irish and Scotch-Highlanders. Presbyterianism as an organized religion was introduced into North Carolina by the Scotch and a brief account of its introduction has been given elsewhere in this volume. The earliest Presbyterian settlements in North Carolina were those made in 1736 on the McCulloh grants in Duplin and New Hanover counties. More than twenty years passed before a Presbyterian clergyman was regularly settled in the colony, but Presbyterian missionaries began to make periodical visits as early as 1742, and in 1744 supplications were sent from North Carolina to the Synod of Philadelphia. In 1755 came Hugh McAden, a truly great missionary, who did more, perhaps, than any other person to establish Presbyterianism on a firm foundation in North Carolina. Traversing almost the entire length and breadth of the province, from the Catawba on the west to the Neuse and the Pamlico on the east, from the Roanoke on the north to the Cape Fear on the south, he visited places on the extreme frontier where not only "never any of our missionaries have been," but where the voice of a Christian minister had never before been heard, and preached in private houses, in courthouses, in churches and chapels, under the trees of the forest, wherever, indeed, he could gather two or three together. Scotch, Germans and English, Presbyterians, Lutherans, Quakers and Churchmen, and "irregular" people who knew "but little about the principles of any religion," all flocked eagerly to hear him. He began his great missionary tour in North Carolina on April 3, 1755 and brought it to a close on

---

[8] Southern Quakers and Slavery, pp. 124-25.

May 6, 1756, and all along his route left Presbyterian communities firmly established.

As a result of McAden's labors many supplications went up from North Carolina to the Synod of Philadelphia. In 1757 came Rev. James Campbell, the first Presbyterian minister to serve a regular pastorate in North Carolina. He settled on the Cape Fear, a few miles above Cross Creek, where for a decade or more he served three churches. In 1758, Rev. Alexander Craighead, the first Presbyterian minister in Western North Carolina, accepted a call to Sugar Creek Church in what is now Mecklenburg County, and from 1758 to 1766, was the only minister in all the region between the Yadkin and the Catawba. Following McAden, Campbell and Craighead, came Henry Patillo, who in 1765 accepted a call to Hawfields, Eno, and Little River churches in Orange County; David Caldwell, more famous as a teacher than as a preacher, who in 1765 became pastor of Alamance and Buffalo churches in Guilford County; and others scarcely less distinguished in the religious history of North Carolina. In 1776 the Presbyterian churches of the Carolinas had been organized into the Orange Presbytery, with eight members in North Carolina and four in South Carolina. Foote records the names of eight ministers who were then regular pastors of Presbyterian congregations in North Carolina.

Perhaps the most aggressive of the colonial missionaries were those of the Baptist faith. Individual Baptists were found in North Carolina as early as 1695, but whence they came, or in what numbers is not known. The first Baptist congregation organized in the colony was at Shiloh in what is now Camden County. It was organized by Paul Palmer in 1727. Governor Everard writing in 1729, says: "Quakers and Baptists flourish amongst the No. Carolinians   *   *   *   owing to the want of Clergymen amongst us.   *   *   *   Both Quakers and Baptists in this vacancy are very busy making Proselytes and holding meetings daily in every Part of this Government.   *   *   *   when I first came here, there was no Dissenters but Quakers in the Government and now by the means of one Paul Palmer the Baptist Teacher, he has gained hundreds." By this time too Joseph and William Parker had organized the Meherrin Church. Fired with missionary zeal and finding a fertile field for their work, the Baptists pushed it with vigor and success. In 1742 William Sojourner organized the Kehukee Association in Halifax County, and from this center radiated influences which were quickly extended into all the counties along the Roanoke from Bertie and Hertford on the east to Granville on the west, and as far south as Bladen County. In 1775 came Shubal Stearn of Boston, who erected a meeting-house on Sandy Creek in Guilford County. Under Stearn's pastorship the congregation flourished, great crowds coming for many miles and from all directions to hear him preach. Within less than three years the membership of his congregation had grown to more than nine hundred. By 1776 the Baptists had become a power in the colony, having established at least one church in every county. It is estimated that they then had forty congregations with many branches which afterwards developed into independent churches.

The introduction of the German Reformed, the Lutheran, and the Moravian churches into North Carolina was coincident with the coming of German settlers. It is strange that, except the Moravians, none of these German immigrants, although of a deeply religious nature, brought regular pastors with them, and that many years passed before congregations were regularly organized and pastors installed. The Reformed and Lutheran churches were closely allied and many of their early churches were union churches. Missionaries of course came and went, but it was not until 1768 that a regular German Reformed pastor came and not until 1773 that the Lutherans had a regular pastor. In 1768, Rev. Samuel Suther, a Reformed preacher, settled in Mecklenburg County. He was an indefatigable worker and to him is chiefly due the organization of most of the Reformed congregations prior to 1776. The mother churches of the North Carolina Lutherans are St. John's, established in 1768 at Salisbury, Zion, commonly called "Organ Church," on Second Creek in Rowan County, and St. John's, founded in 1771, on Buffalo Creek in what is now Cabarrus County. "The pioneer minister of the Lutheran Church in the province of North Carolina" was Adolphus Nussman, who came thither from Germany in 1773. Nussman was accompanied by J. Gottlieb Arndt who came as a schoolmaster, but on August 22, 1775, at "Organ Church," was ordained to the ministry. He was "the first Lutheran minister ever ordained in North Carolina." Suther, Nussman and Arndt worked in practically the same territory, from Mecklenburg and Rowan on the west to Orange on the east, ministering to Reformed and Lutherans alike. Unlike the other German settlers the Moravians brought ministers with them. First in the list of the twelve brethren who came in

1753 to lay the foundations of the colony was Rev. Bernhard Adam Grube. The great obstacle of language, added to their position on the extreme frontier surrounded by the more aggressive Scotch-Irish Presbyterians, prevented the German churches from making any progress in North Carolina beyond the German settlements, so that they never became the force in the province to which their numbers and the character and intelligence of their membership might be thought to entitle them.

The last of the great Protestant denominations to seek a foothold in North Carolina, prior to the Revolution, was the Methodist Church. "The Methodist preacher came not to represent and build up a denomination, because at that time he belonged only to a society in the Church of England, but his mission was to preach the gospel to a lost and dying race." [9] The most eminent of this type of the early preachers of Methodism to visit North Carolina was Rev. George Whitfield who came to the colony as early as 1739. Writing from Bath in 1739 he said, "I am here, hunting in the woods, these ungospelized wilds, for sinners." Whitfield made several visits to North Carolina meeting always with a cordial reception from people, clergy and officials. When he preached at New Bern, in 1765, according to Rev. James Reed, who wrote eulogistically of his sermon, people "came a great many miles to hear him;" while Governor Tryon declared that his sermon at Wilmington "would have done him honour had he delivered it at St. James' allowing some little alteration of circumstances between a discourse adapted for the Royal Chapel and the Court House at Wilmington." Whitfield, however, was still a communicant of the Church of England, and made no effort to establish a new organization. As early as 1760 there were people in the colony calling themselves Methodists, to whom the missionaries of the Established Church always refer with great bitterness; but Whitfield, during his visit in 1764, declared that they were improperly so called as they were followers neither of himself nor of John Wesley, and none except their followers were properly called Methodists. This view seems to be accepted by the best authorities on the history of Methodism.

The first Methodist preacher to come to North Carolina was Rev. Joseph Pilmoor who had been sent to America by John Wesley. Pilmoor came in 1772 and at Currituck Court-

[9] Grissom: History of Methodism in North Carolina, Vol. I, p. 24.

House, September 28, 1772, had "the honor of preaching the first Methodist sermon in the colony." On his tour through North Carolina he frequently preached in the chapels of the Established Church; and at Brunswick in January, 1773, he preached in St. Philip's Church to "a fine congregation." Pilmoor was followed by Rev. John Williams who, in 1773, organized the first Methodist Society in North Carolina. The following year he organized societies in "a six weeks circuit which extended from Petersburg (Va.) to the south over Roanoke River some distance into North Carolina." The early Methodist pioneers in North Carolina met with remarkable success. In 1775 as a result of their preaching a great revival swept over the northern section of the colony from Bute County eastward. A participant, writing about it, says: "My pen cannot describe the one-half of what I saw, heard, and felt. I might fill a volume on this subject, and then leave the greater part untold." As a result of this revival 683 new members in North Carolina were reported to the Fourth Conference which was held at Baltimore, May 21, 1776, and a North Carolina circuit was established with Edward Dromgoole, Francis Poythress, and Isham Tatum as preachers. As their field of labor was unlimited, they penetrated great portions of the colony, and laid firmly the foundations of Methodism in North Carolina.

By 1775 Churchmen were outnumbered by Dissenters who were a unit in opposition to the Establishment. Besides the principle of the Establishment itself, there were three features which accompanied it in North Carolina that were especially offensive to the dissenting denominations. They were the application of the principles of the Schism Act to North Carolina, the militia laws as they affected ministers of the Gospel, and the marriage law. Although the Schism Act had been repealed in England in 1719, Burrington was instructed to enforce it in North Carolina, and similar instructions were sent to his successors under the royal administration. The governor was to allow no person to come from England "to keep school" in North Carolina "without the license of the Lord Bishop of London," and to see that "no person now there or that shall come from other parts shall be admitted to keep school in North Carolina without your license first obtained." The militia laws exempted clergymen of the Established Church from militia duty, but not the ministers of any of the dissenting denominations until 1764 when exemption was extended to Presbyterian clergymen who were "regularly called to any congregation." Both the Schism Act and the exemption features of the militia laws were offensive to Dissenters rather in what they implied than in their actual application. Only three instances are on record of efforts to enforce the former and while these are three too many, it should not be forgotten in estimating the importance of the Schism Act in our educational history that they were the exceptions and not the rules. The militia laws, too, were too feebly enforced generally to work any hardship in practice on the dissenting clergy.

The case of the marriage law, however, was different. It was a real grievance against which the dissenting clergy justly protested. By an act of 1666 magistrates were permitted to perform the marriage ceremony. The vestry act of 1715 continued this authority to magistrates in parishes where there were no ministers. In 1741 a special marriage law was passed which confined the right to perform the marriage ceremony to clergy of the Established Church, and where no such clergymen were accessible to magistrates. This act chiefly affected the Presbyterians. It appears that in colonial times it was not the practice of Baptist ministers to perform the marriage ceremony. Quakers followed their own customs. The Methodists came too late to be much affected by the act. The Presbyterian clergy protested against the injustice of it, refused to obey it, and performed the marriage ceremony without license or publication of the banns. By 1766 they had grown strong enough to secure a modification of the law. A new act was passed which legalized all marriages performed by Presbyterian clergymen and permitting those who were "regularly called to any congregation" to perform the ceremony. But even this act fell far short of justice, for it required that all fees should be paid to the minister of the Established Church in the parish in which the marriage occurred unless he had refused to act. Bitter protests arose from all dissenting denominations and petitions especially from the Presbyterian congregations, poured in upon the Assembly. In 1770, therefore, the Assembly passed an act granting relief to the Presbyterian clergy only, but the king disallowed it. Relief finally came from the people themselves. One of the ordinances adopted by the Convention of 1776 provided "That all regular ministers of the Gospel of every Denomination having the Cure of Souls shall be empowered to celebrate Matrimony according to the rites and ceremonies of their respective churches."

The history of education is really a part of the history of

religion in colonial North Carolina. Among Churchmen and Dissenters alike education was considered one of the functions of the church and most of the early teachers were either preachers or candidates for the ministry. The first attempts to establish schools in North Carolina were made under the patronage of the Society for the Propagation of the Gospel; its missionaries "brought with them the first parish or public libraries and its lay readers were the first teachers." Brickell whose work was published in 1737 says that the lack of orthodox clergymen in the colony was "generally supply'd by some School-masters, who read the Lithurgy, and then a Sermon out of Doctor Tillitson, or some good practical Divine, every Sunday. These are the most numerous, and are dispersed through the whole Province." After the purchase of the proprietary interests by the Crown an effort was made, as has already been pointed out, to confine the privilege of teaching to communicants of the Established Church, but fortunately without success. The most recent of the historians of education in North Carolina holds the opinion that in spite of the attempts to apply the Schism Act, "the intellectual and educational life of the colony was somewhat encouraged and assisted" by the establishment of the Church, and there is ample evidence to sustain his view.[10] The clergy of the Society for the Propagation of the Gospel were the first missionaries of education to North Carolina, and their letters to the Society are filled with earnest and persistent appeals for teachers as well as for preachers.

There were probably schoolmasters in North Carolina prior to 1700, but the first professional teacher here of whom we have any record was Charles Griffin, a lay reader of the Established Church, who came from the West Indies in 1705 and opened a school in Pasquotank County. In 1708 his school was transferred to Rev. James Adams and Griffin removed to Chowan County where he opened a school. Governor William Glover bore testimony to Griffin's "industry" and "unblemished life." Even the Quakers patronized his school; indeed, his association with them was so intimate that he became "tainted" with their principles and finally joined their Society. For this reason, probably, he lost his school in Chowan County; at any rate Rev. William Gordon reported that in 1709 he "settled a schoolmaster [in Chowan], and gave some books for the use of the scholars, which the church-wardens

---

10 Knight: Public School Education in North Carolina, p. 5.

were to see left for that use, in case the master should remove." Another of the early colonial teachers whose name has come down to us was "one Mr. Mashburn who," wrote Rev. Giles Rainsford in 1712, "keeps a school at Sarum on the frontiers of Virginia between the two Governments. * * * What children he has under his care can both write and read very distinctly and gave before me an account of the grounds and principles of the Christian religion that strangely surprised me to hear it." We have abundant evidence that there were other schoolmasters in North Carolina contemporaneously with Griffin and Mashburn but unfortunately their names are unknown.

Although teachers were scarce it would be an error to infer from that fact that the planters were either ignorant or illiterate themselves, or indifferent to the education of their children. In 1716 Governor Eden was of the opinion that if the Society for the Propagation of the Gospel would furnish the teachers "the Inhabitants would willingly pay them the greatest part of their salaries." Evidence in support of his opinion is found in the provisions made by the planters in their wills for the education of their children. "I will," declared Alexander Lillington, in 1697, "that my Executors carry on my Son, John, in his learnings as I have begun, and that All my Children be brought up in Learning, as conveniently can bee." Thomas Bell, in 1733, desired that the profits from his estate be devoted to the education of a niece and nephew, "in as handsome and good a matter as may be." It was Edward Salter's wish, in 1734, that his son should "have a thorough education to make him a compleat merchant, let the expense be what it will."

In infancy children were taught at home, or in the elementary schools in North Carolina, but for their higher education they were sent to Virginia, New England, and to the English and Scotch Universities. In 1730 George Durant directed that his son "should have as good Learing [learning] as can be had in this Government." Edward Moseley, in 1745, provided for the higher education of his children when it should become time for them to have "Other Education than is to be had from the Common Masters in this Province" adding, "for I would have my Children well Educated." Stephen Lee directed that his son be educated either in Philadelphia or Boston, while John Skinner provided for the education of his son in North Carolina, "or other parts." John Pfifer of Mecklenburg County wished his children "to have a reasonable Education and in particular my said son Paul to be put through a liberal Education and Colleged.'' When Governor Gabriel Johnston died, in 1752, he left a legacy to a nephew ''now at school in Newhaven in the Colony of Connecticut.''

In 1721 John Hecklefield desired that his son be educated ''after the best thought manner this country will admit.'' There is ample evidence to show what was ''the best thought manner'' of education of that day. One of its outstanding features was religious instruction; boys and girls were trained in the teachings of Christianity. On the secular side emphasis was laid on practical or vocational education. William Standid desired his son to be taught ''to read, rite, and cifer as far as the rule of three.'' Joshua Porter directed his executor to ''see y^t my Son and Daughter may be Carefully learnt to read and write and Cypher, and y^t they may be duly Educated.'' Specific directions were often given for the education of boys in the professions, commerce, and the trades, and girls in household duties. Thus John Baptista Ashe, in 1734, says: ''I will that my Slaves be kept at work on my lands, and that my Estate may be managed to the best advantage, so as my sons may have as liberal an Education as the profits thereof will afford; and in their Education I pray my Executors to observe this method: Let them be taught to read and write, and be introduced into the practical part of Arithmetick, not too hastily hurrying them to Latin or Grammar, but after they are pretty well versed in these let them be taught Latin and Greek. I propose this may be done in Virginia; After which let them learn French, perhaps Some French man at Santee will undertake this; when they are arrived to years of discretion Let them study the Mathematicks. To my Sons when they arrive at age I recommend the pursuit and study of Some profession or business (I could wish one to ye Law, the other to Merchandize,) in which Let them follow their own inclinations. I will that my daughter be taught to write and read and some feminine accomplishments which may render her agreable; And that she be not kept ignorant of what appertains to a good house wife in the management of household affairs.''

There were, of course, no free public schools, but the education of the poor, and especially of orphans was provided for in the apprenticeship system which the colonies inherited from England. Masters and guardians were required to give their wards the ''rudiments of learning,'' and to teach them a trade or occupation. In 1695 the General Court of Albemarle County bound an orphan, "being left destitute," to Thomas Harvey, "the said Thomas Harvey to teach him to read;" and in 1698 another orphan was bound to Harvey and his heirs "they Ingagen to Learn him to Reed." The minutes of the court are full of such entries. The guardian, or master, was required to enter into bond for the faithful performance of his duty. There are also instances of legacies being left for the education of the poor. In 1710 John Bennett of Currituck directed "that forty Shillings be taken out of my whole Estate before any devesion be made to pay for ye Schooling of two poor Children for one whole year;" and that if he should fail of heirs, his estate "to remaine and bee for ye use and bennefitt of poor Children to pay for their Schooling and to remaine unto ye world's End." Since, however, there was no failure of heirs, the legacy never became available for educational purposes. Two more famous legacies to education were those of James Winwright of Carteret County, 1744, and James Innes of New Hanover, 1754. Winwright left the "yearly Rents and profits of all the Town land and Houses in Beaufort Town," after the death of his wife, to be used "for the encouragement of a Sober discreet Quallifyed Man to teach a School at least Reading Writing Vulgar and Decimal Arithmetick" in the town of Beaufort, and set aside £50 sterling "to be applyed for the Building and finishing of a Creditable House for a School and Dwelling house for the Master." Unfortunately so far as known no school was ever established on the Winwright foundation. Better use was made of the Innes legacy. Colonel Innes left his plantation called Pleasant Point, "Two negero Young Woomen, One Negero Young Man and there Increase," a large number of hogs, cattle and horses, his books, and £100 sterling "For the Use of a Free School for the benefite of the Youth of North Carolina." The legacy did not become available for educational purposes until after the Revolution. In 1783 the Assembly chartered the Innes Academy in Wilmington.

A marked impulse was given to education by the coming of the Scotch-Irish and Germans. In every community where they settled a church and a schoolhouse sprang up almost simultaneously with the settlement. The German schools were taught by teachers who came from Germany and in the German language. Among the Scotch-Irish the influence of Princeton College was strong. Many of their religious leaders, and such lay leaders as Alexander Martin, Waightstill Avery, Samuel Spencer, Ephraim Brevard, Adlai Osborne, and William R. Davie, were Princeton graduates. To the Scotch North Carolina owes the establishment of her first classical schools, the development of which was so marked a feature of the educational history of the State during the first half of the nineteenth century. In 1760, Rev. James Tate, a Presbyterian clergyman, opened at Wilmington Tate's Academy, the first classical school in North Carolina. During the same year, Crowfield Academy, said to have been the beginning of Davidson College, was founded in Mecklenburg County. The most noted of this class of schools was Rev. David Caldwell's school, founded near the present site of Greensboro in 1767. For many years, this famous "log college," with an average annual enrollment of between fifty and sixty students, was the most important institution of learning in North Carolina, serving, as has been said, "as an academy, a college, and a theological seminary."

It was in connection with the establishment of an institution of higher learning, under the auspices of the Presbyterians, that occurred the most notable of the efforts to enforce the Schism Act in North Carolina. In January, 1771, the Assembly, acting upon the recommendation of Governor Tryon, incorporated at Charlotte a school for higher learning called Queen's College. It was designed to enable such of the youth of the colony who had "acquired at a Grammar School a competent knowledge of the Greek, Hebrew, and Latin Languages, to imbibe the principles of Science and virtue, and to obtain under learned, pious and exemplary teachers in a collegiate or academic mode of instruction a regular or finished education in order to qualify them for the service of their friends and Country." The college was authorized to confer degrees. For its endowment a tax was levied on all spirituous liquors sold in Mecklenburg County for ten years. Since its patronage and support would come chiefly from Presbyterians, all of the incorporators, except two, were of that faith, but to forestall anticipated opposition in England, the president was required to be a member of the Church of England. In return for the timely aid he had received from the Presbyterian clergy and laity alike in the War of the Regulation, Tryon earnestly urged the king's approval of the act; but the Board of Trade, while commending the principle of religious toleration, questioned whether the king ought "to add Incouragement to toleration by giving the Royal Assent to an Establishment, which in its consequences, promises great and permanent Advantages to a sect of Dissenters from the Established Church who have already extended themselves over that Province in very considerable numbers." The Board, therefore, advised that the act be disallowed, and the king vetoed it April 22, 1772. A year passed, however, before his action was certified to the governor, Josiah Martin, who had succeeded Tryon, and in the meantime Queen's College had opened its doors to students. In spite of the royal disallowance, it continued its work without a charter until the king's approval to acts of the North Carolina legislature was no longer necessary. In 1777 the General Assembly granted another charter in which the institution's name was changed from Queen's College to Liberty Hall.

Almost without exception these efforts to promote education were made by the church. Except its efforts through the Established Church, the colonial government did practically nothing for education. Governor Gabriel Johnston and Governor Arthur Dobbs both urged upon the Assembly the importance and duty of making "provision for the education of youth," but the Assembly did nothing until 1745 when it passed an act for the erection of a schoolhouse at Edenton which, however, was never built. Bills for the establishment of free schools introduced in 1749 and in 1752 failed of passage. Finally in 1754 the Assembly appropriated £6,000 for the purpose of building a school, but afterwards used the money for the support of the French and Indian War. In 1759, and again in 1764, Governor Dobbs petitioned the Board of Trade to permit an issue of paper money to replace this fund, and the Assembly, in 1759, requested that some of the money appropriated by Parliament to reimburse the colony for its expenditures in the war might be used for establishing free schools, but both requests were refused. The only legislation that bore any practical results were acts passed in 1766 incorporating an academy at New Bern and in 1770 incorporating an academy at Edenton. However, the agitation of these years in behalf of education had good results. Its fruit is seen in Section XLI of the Constitution of 1776, the foundation of our public school system of today, which provides: "That a school or schools be established by the Legislature, for the convenient Instruction of youth, with such Salaries to the Masters, paid by the Public as may enable them to instruct at low prices; and all useful Learning shall be duly encouraged and promoted in one or more Universities."

Two other indications of the intellectual standards of the

people were the extent and character of their libraries and the position of the press among them. The first libraries were brought to the colony by the missionaries of the Society for the Propagation of the Gospel. They consisted chiefly of religious and doctrinal books, intended primarily for the instruction of the people in the orthodox faith. About 1705, Rev. Thomas Bray established a free public library at Bath. The books were so carelessly kept that in 1715 the Assembly passed an act "for the more effectual preservation of the same." In 1728 Edward Moseley offered the Society for the Propagation of the Gospel a free public library for Edenton, but no evidence exists that his offer was accepted, and the books probably remained in his private library. James Innes left his library to the free school which he had endowed under his will. In the home of nearly every planter were to be found small libraries of good books. Their wills and inventories from early times show the existence of many such libraries numbering from 25 and 50 volumes to more than 500. Edward Moseley's library inventoried 400 volumes, Jeremiah Vail's 230, Dr. John Eustace's 292, Rev. James Reed's 266, James Milner's 621. There were many others similar to these. The library begun by Governor Gabriel Johnston and continued by his nephew Samuel Johnston at "Hayes" was probably the largest and most important library in the colony, containing more than 1,000 volumes. Most of the books in these libraries were treatises on theology, moral philosophy, law, history, and medicine and were in Greek, Latin, Hebrew, German and French, as well as in English. In them were Xenophon, Homer, Ovid, Horace, Virgil, Sallust, Juvenal, Caesar, Puffendorf, Grotius, Coke, Blackstone, Montesquieu, Shakespeare, Milton, Pope, Dryden, Gray, Voltaire, Bacon, Swift, Steele, Addison, Bunyan, Plutarch's "Lives," "The Complete Angler," Locke "On the Human Understanding," "Antidote Against Popery," "Tristram Shandy," "Tom Jones," "Letters of Abilard," Raleigh's "History of the World," *The Spectator, The Tatler, The Annual Register,* and many other similar works, all testifying to "a degree of culture not often believed to have existed in North Carolina in the eighteenth century." [11]

The press was late in coming to North Carolina and until long after the Revolution its influence was negligible; indeed, except Georgia, North Carolina was the last of the thirteen

---

[11] Knight: Public School Education in North Carolina, p. 11.

colonies to receive the printing press. The absence of towns, the diffusion of the population over a vast territory, the lack of a regular post and means of communication, and, finally, the small demand for book$ and periodicals among the people generally made the maintenance of a press too precarious to invite capital. There was no popular demand for newspapers and except for the public printing there was not enough business in the colony to support a printing establishment. The first press in the colony, therefore, was set up and sustained by the patronage of the General Assembly. In 1749, in order to secure the printing of a revision of the laws, the Assembly chose James Davis public printer at an annual salary of £160 proclamation money, and gave him a copyright on all government publications. Accordingly Davis set up his press at New Bern and began work June 24, 1749. In 1751 he issued Swann's Revisal, so called because Samuel Swann was chairman of the commission which prepared it, the first book published in North Carolina. Because of the yellowish hue of the parchment in which it was bound it became popularly known as "The Yellow Jacket." During his career as public printer, which extended over a period of thirty-three years, Davis issued several other revisions of the laws. In 1753 he published Clement Hall's "Collection of Christian Experiences," which is "the first book or pamphlet so far as known to be compiled by a native of North Carolina." [12]

Davis was also the father of journalism in North Carolina. There was, of course, no popular demand for newspapers in the colony. Among the planters along the Cape Fear, *The South Carolina Gazette,* which had a correspondent at Brunswick, had a small circulation, while *The Virginia Gazette* served those along the Roanoke. In 1755 appeared the first issue of *The North Carolina Gazette.* It was published on Thursdays and bore the imprint: "Newbern: Printed by James Davis, at the Printing-Office in Front-street; where all persons may be supplied with this paper at Sixteen shillings per Annum: And where Advertisements of moderate length are inserted for Three Shillings the first week, and Two shillings for every week after. And where also Book-binding is done reasonably." *The Gazette* was published for six years when it was suspended. In 1764 Davis began to issue the *North Carolina Magazine, or Universal Intelligencer.* How long this new

[12] Weeks: The Pre-Revolutionary Printers of North Carolina (*N. C. Booklet,* Vol. XV, No. 2, p. 112).

venture continued is not known. In 1768 *The Gazette* was revived and continued for a decade. It was again suspended
in 1778 because the printer's son, who was his chief reliance
in the business, had been drafted into the army.

The right of appointment of a public printer was one of the
political issues in dispute between the governor and the
Assembly. In 1764, on account of charges of neglect of duty
brought by Dobbs against Davis, the Assembly appointed a
committee to secure another public printer, and this committee induced Andrew Steuart of Philadelphia to come to
North Carolina. But the bill to appoint a public printer was
defeated in the Council, whereupon Governor Dobbs appointed Steuart "his Majesty's printer." The House of Commons took umbrage at this exercise of prerogative, declared
that it knew of "no such office as his Majesty's printer," and
denounced the appointment of Steuart as an act "of a new and
unusual nature unknown to our laws" and "a violent stretch
of power." It accordingly voted £100 to Steuart as compensation for his trouble and expense in coming to North Carolina and re-appointed Davis public printer. Steuart, who was
the second printer in the province, settled at Wilmington
where in September, 1764, he began the publication of *The
North Carolina Gazette and Weekly Post Boy.* It had but a
brief existence being suspended in 1767. The chief incident of
interest in its history occurred during the resistance to the
Stamp Act on the Cape Fear when the Cape Fear patriots
compelled Steuart to issue his paper without the stamps required by the law, a skull and bones appearing in the margin
with the legend, "This is the Place to affix the Stamp."

In 1769 Steuart was drowned in the Cape Fear River and
his press was purchased by Adam Boyd. This "third and last
of the pre-Revolutionary printers," says Doctor Weeks, "was
not a printer at all. He was what we should call in this day
a publisher." [13] In 1769 Boyd began the publication of *The
Cape Fear Mercury* which he continued to issue until well
into the year 1775. *The Mercury* is perhaps the most famous
of the pre-Revolutionary papers of North Carolina because of
its connection with the famous Mecklenburg Declaration controversy. On August 8, 1775, Governor Josiah Martin declared in his "Fiery Proclamation" that he had "seen a most
infamous publication in *The Cape Fear Mercury* importing to

---

[13] Pre-Revolutionary Printers of North Carolina (*N. C. Booklet*,
Vol. XV, No. 2, p. 116).

be resolves of a set of people stiling themselves a Committee for the County of Mecklenburg most traiterously declaring the entire dissolution of the Laws Government and Constitution of this country,'' and it was long thought that if a copy of this issue of *The Mercury* could be found it would settle the controversy by proving the authenticity of the Declaration of May 20th; but when a copy was finally discovered it was found to contain the Resolves of May 31st. *The Mercury* suspended publication soon after this issue.

CHAPTER XIII

POLITICAL AND CONSTITUTIONAL CONTRO-
VERSIES

The transfer of Carolina from the Lords Proprietors to the Crown worked no important changes in the outward form of the machinery of government. Governor, Council, and Assembly, as well as the systems for the administration of land, finance, defense, and justice, remained as they were. The Crown merely took the place of the Lords Proprietors as the immediate source of power. This meant that a single executive, capable of a sustained policy, had succeeded a many-headed executive, of constantly varying personnel and ever-changing policy; that a tried and proven plan of administration had displaced an experiment which had failed. The change made possible a stability of purpose, promptness of action, and vigor of administration of which the proprietary government was incapable. But while there was no change in the outward form of government, there was a marked change in its purpose and spirit. The interests of the Lords Proprietors centered in dividends, those of the Crown in the development of the British Empire. Financial returns, therefore, inspired the spirit of the one, imperial interests that of the other. Imperial interests required the subordination of local interests; the Crown, accordingly, as the source of the former, acted upon the theory that its authority in colonial affairs rested solely upon the royal prerogative, and undertook to conduct the colonial government through instructions which it held to be binding upon both governor and Assembly. Such, however, was not the view of the colonists. They held that the purchase by the Crown carried with it only such powers as the Lords Proprietors had enjoyed; that these powers were defined and limited by the charter of 1665 which guaranteed to the people certain rights and privileges of which they could not be legally deprived; and that the Crown was bound to administer the affairs of the colony in accordance with those guarantees.

Seal of the Province of North Carolina, 1739-1767

These conflicting theories, together with conflicting imperial and local interests, made harmony impossible. The
Crown, on the one hand, intent upon the larger affairs of the
Empire, was too prone to ignore the rights and interests of
the colony; the colony, on the other hand, with its own affairs uppermost in its consideration, never really sought to
understand and sympathize with the policy of the Crown.
The result was inevitable. Controversies between the executive department, which upheld the prerogative of the Crown,
and the legislative department, which championed the rights
and privileges of the people, characterize the political history
of North Carolina as a crown colony. Was it the prerogative of the Crown, or the right of the Assembly to determine
how quit rents should be paid? To fix the fees of public officials? To control the expenditures of public funds? To
erect precincts with the privilege of representation? To ascertain the quorum of the House of Commons? To determine
the jurisdiction of the courts? Many of the controversies
growing out of these questions were trivial in themselves,
but behind them all lay the vital issue whether the colonial
Assembly was to be a real legislative body, representative of
the people, with the power of independent judgment and
action, or whether it was to be reduced to a mere vehicle
for registering the royal will, expressed through instructions
to the governor, and unless these controversies are studied
with this fundamental fact in view they lose most of their
interest and all of their significance.

The Crown purchased Carolina in July, 1729, but sent out
no governor until February, 1731. During this year and a
half, Sir Richard Everard continued to hold office by authority of his commission from the Lords Proprietors. But a
commission from the Lords Proprietors had lost most of its
virtue in North Carolina and Sir Richard himself no longer
commanded that personal respect which might have proved a
substitute for it. Consequently during that period a condition bordering upon anarchy prevailed in the colony. The
governor was utterly discredited. The Assembly held but
one session and the Crown afterwards declared that to be
illegal. The Council was suspended. The General Court
was suppressed. Many of the precinct courts ceased to function. The Admiralty Court—a crown court—having no re-
straint on its actions, took advantage of the situation "to
draw all manner of Business" to it, proceeding "in such an
Extraordinary Manner as occasioned a General Discontent

and Ferment among the People." Laws were unenforced. The public revenues were not collected. Corruption was rife in official circles. The governor, who had no other notions of government, it was said, than as it gave him power to act as he pleased, openly declared his contempt for the laws of the colony, enforced his will by arbitrary arrests and imprisonments, demanded and took exorbitant fees, and accepted from the Assembly "a present" of £500 for signing a bill emitting £40,000 of paper currency contrary to his instructions. Nobody paid quit rents. Blank patents covering thousands of acres were issued and located for which no purchase money was paid. In a word, "the Province [was] in the greatest Confusion, [and] the Government had sunk so low that neither Peace nor Order subsisted." The Lords Proprietors complained of the Crown's delay in setting up an efficient government, declaring that not only their own personal affairs, but also those of the people "greatly suffer from the present unsettled conditions," and begged that either the transfer be expedited or else they themselves be restored to "the full and free exercise of all the powers granted" them by King Charles II. The people, too, grew impatient; they urged the recall of Governor Everard and the prompt settlement of the government upon a firmer basis.

In seeking the removal of Governor Everard the people of North Carolina enacted the fable of the frogs who prayed for a king. They exchanged Sir Richard Everard for George Burrington. Burrington, it will be recalled, lost his place under the Lords Proprietors in 1725 because the Proprietors were persuaded that he contemplated stirring up a revolution to compel them to transfer their property to the king. Where then should he be, when the transfer was actually made, but in London pressing upon the crown officials his claims to consideration. Success crowned his efforts. In January, 1730, he was notified of his appointment as first royal governor of North Carolina and a few days later received his commission. His commission was signed January 25, 1730, but Burrington remained in England awaiting his instructions which were not completed until December 30th. In January, 1731, he sailed for North Carolina, arrived at Edenton February 25th, summoned such of his councillors as were within reach, and in their presence took the oath of office.

Members of the popular party, with whom he had cooperated during his former administration, hastened to welcome him. Some of them, notably John Baptista Ashe and Edmund Porter, he had selected as councillors. The Grand Jury "for the whole Province of North Carolina" declared that they accepted his appointment as "a very great instance" of the king's favor to the colony, and the General Assembly, in an address to the king, echoed the sentiment, declaring that they were in duty bound to acknowledge Burrington's appointment "as a particular mark" of the king's indulgence. Burrington announced to the Assembly that in him they had a governor "that is entirely your Friend and Wellwisher;" and the Assembly expressing their "great pleasure" at his appointment felt "fully assured that we shall not want your best Endeavours to promote the lasting happiness of the People of the Province." But the leaders of the popular party soon found that the Burrington who needed their support in executing his designs against the Lords Proprietors was a different person from the Burrington who seeing his hopes fully realized was enjoying the fruits of his labors; and the echoes of their exchange of courtesies were almost immediately drowned in an explosion produced by irreconcilable differences.

The match to the powder was the governor's 19th instruction, in which the Crown offered, upon two conditions, to remit to the people the back rents for which in the purchase of Carolina it had allowed the Lords Proprietors £5,000. These conditions were, first, that the Assembly pass an act requiring the registration of all landholdings in the colony, thus providing an accurate rent roll for the Crown; second, that all quit rents and officers' fees, which had previously been paid in "rated commodities," or in provincial currency, be paid in proclamation money.[1] The importance of this proposal will be appreciated when it is remembered that the people did not hold their lands in fee but as tenants of the Crown paying annual quit rents for their holdings. Assuming the Assembly's prompt and unquestioning obedience, Burrington had had prepared a bill carrying out the Crown's instructions as to quit rents, and with the advice of his Council, had already fixed the fees of colonial officials in proclamation money and put them into effect by executive order. But the Assembly proved unexpectedly independent. It asserted

---

[1] "Current specie of foreign coinage the value of which was ascertained and fixed in sterling money by proclamation of the Crown."—Ashe, History of North Carolina, Vol. I, p. 229. At a later date provincial currency was also so called.

that the arrears of quit rents in North Carolina were too small to be a matter of any importance; resolved that, since there was not enough specie in the province with which to pay quit rents and fees, "all such payments be made in some valuable commoditys, or in the Bills now currant in this Province at proper Rates;" and declared that the regulation of officers' fees was a matter for the legislative, and not the executive power. "For nearly twenty years," it said, "the Officers' fees have been paid in Paper Currancy at the Rates mentioned in the Acts of Assembly." But Burrington insisted that the king's instructions gave "the Governour and Council Power to regulate and Settle Fees" in proclamation money, thereby "repealing all Laws that declare Fees shall be received otherways." This direct blow at the legislative power alarmed the House which resolved that by the charter of Charles II, the people of North Carolina were to "have, possess [and] enjoy all Libertys, Franchises, and Privileges" enjoyed by the people of England, among which was the guarantee "that they shall not be taxed or made lyable to pay any sum or sums of money or Fees other than such as are by Law established;" it therefore requested the governor to forbid the payment of fees in proclamation money "until such time as the Officers' Fees shall be regulated by Authority of Assembly." This resolution was as a red flag to a bull. The Council condemned it as "a great invasion of his Majesties Prerogative;" Burrington declared it an "unreasonable complaint," and denounced its author as "a Thief that hides himself in a house to rob it and fearing to be discovered, fires the house to make his escape in the smoak."

Burrington attributed the opposition to his course to Edward Moseley, who was not only speaker of the House but also public treasurer, and determined to destroy him. For this purpose, he brought out two more instructions, one forbidding the paying out of any public money except upon warrant of the governor, thus depriving the Assembly of all control over the public funds, except the privilege of being "permitted from time to time to view and examine all accounts of money" disposed of "by virtue of laws made by them;" the other directing that all commissions issued by the Lords Proprietors be withdrawn and no public office be held except by a commission from the king. Burrington laid these instructions before the Assembly accompanied by a declaration of his purpose to appoint "a fitt person" as public treasurer. The Assembly resented this fresh encroachment upon its rights and privileges, declared that no public money ought to be disbursed except as directed by the General Assembly, i. e., the governor, Council, and House of Commons, and asserted that in fiscal affairs the Commons, "in Conjunction with the Governor and Council, hath a larger right than only to view and Examine Publick Accounts." Furthermore, it expressed the opinion that the other instruction "doth not extend to officers appointed by Act of Assembly," as was the public treasurer, but only to those who held commissions from the Lords Proprietors; the governor, therefore, need not trouble himself to appoint a public treasurer because that office was already filled by a person with whose "ability and integrity" the House was "very well satisfied," one, moreover, "who was appointed to that office in an Act of Assembly by the Governor, Council and Assembly and such an officer so appointed is not to be removed but by the like Power." To this open defiance of the king's instructions the governor and his supporters in the Council could think of no better answer than to charge the House with trying "to create animositys and ferment divisions;" nor could they resist the temptation to take a fling at Moseley. They admitted that Moseley was "a person of sufficient ability" to be treasurer, and "heartily wished his integrity was equal to it." This insult to its leader drew a sharp reply from the House, which stood loyally by him, and Burrington's attack resulted merely in widening the breach between the two branches of the government.

After his first Assembly, the governor determined not to hold another session until he could secure from his superiors in England confirmation of his instructions on the questions at issue. By successive prorogations, therefore, he prevented a session until July, 1733, when he was able to announce that the Crown adhered to its original instructions, and especially forbade his accepting quit rents and fees "in any other specie but in proclamation money." The Assembly countered with the rejoinder that they too had consulted their "principals" who had "recommended nothing more earnestly to us than that we should not consent to burthen them with such payments." So the quarrel flared up anew. The Assembly, in support of their contentions, having appealed to the Great Deed of Grant, were greatly perturbed to find its validity denied by the crown officials. But this merely added fuel to the flames. Neither side would yield. The representatives of the people would not obey the king's instructions; the representative of the Crown would not assent to anything short of complete submission. Round and round the circle both sides pursued the old arguments with wearisome iteration and reiteration, but with no results.

In the "several hot debates and messages" which passed between the Assembly and the governor, the Assembly was firm, but always calm and respectful. Burrington on the other hand was insolent, dictatorial, and abusive. "If the Kings Instructions are contrary to some Laws of this Province," he said, "the Governor must act in Obedience to the Kings Commands, therefore you must not be Surprized that whatever Your Law directs contrary to my Instructions is not taken Notice of [by] Me." The violence of the language in which he commanded a like obedience from the Assembly, and denounced all who opposed him, passed all bounds of reason and decency. Quit rents and fees, control of the public purse, the selection of a treasurer, the character of the present incumbent, and all other causes of controversy, dwindled into issues of secondary importance; the rights, the privileges and the dignity of the Assembly as a representative body were at stake and the House resolved to maintain them at all costs. When the governor denounced the author of its resolution against the payment of fees in proclamation money as a thief, the House replied that the resolution "was the Unanimous Voice of the whole House, no one member dissenting thereto," and resolved that the governor's message was a "great indignity and contempt put on the whole House, a Breach of Privilege, and tended to the deterring the members from doing their Duty."

At the very beginning of the controversy, the popular party gained a point by creating a division in the Council. "I endeavoured all I could to prevent this madness," wrote Burrington, "but I cannot answer for the Follys and Passions of Men." John Baptista Ashe led the way, and by "false reasoning and fallacious arguments," won over Edmund Porter and William Smith, the chief justice. About the same time two other councillors, Nathaniel Rice and Joseph Jenoure, were called out of the province. Only Cornelius Harnett [1] and Robert Halton were left upon whom the governor could depend. "By this," Burrington complained, "Ashe, Smith and Porter gained their end for then my own vote made but an equality in the Council which obliged me to put an end to the session." This division in the Council was never cemented; indeed, it grew wider for Harnett, too,

---

[1] Father of the Revolutionary patriot of the same name.

soon joined the governor's enemies. From that time until his recall, Burrington poured upon the heads of Ashe, Porter, Harnett and Smith such a flood of abuse and billingsgate as probably never before or since disgraced the official dispatches of a public officer. Ashe was an "ungrateful" villain, "altogether bent on mischief;" Porter "a man of most infamous character;" Harnett "a disgrace to the Council;" and "Baby" Smith, "a silly, rash boy, a busy fool and egregious sot, to which," continued the irate governor, "I must add that I know him to be an ungrateful perfidious scoundrel." Smith resigned from the Council; Porter was suspended; Harnett was driven out by the governor's abuse; and Burrington, in clear violation of his instructions, replaced them with two new councillors, John Lovick and Edmund Gale, whose votes were at his command.

Burrington's enemies refused to remain quiet under his attacks. They poured complaints in rapid succession upon the Board of Trade. They even raised funds to send Chief Justice Smith to England to prefer charges against the governor. But neither written complaints nor personal appeals contributed so much to Burrington's downfall as his own dispatches, which revealed but too plainly his unfitness for his office. The Board of Trade in replying to them, began with advice and ended with censure. They demanded that he explain the opprobrious epithet which he had applied to Chief Justice Smith. They declared that while they would not venture to pass judgment between him and Porter, they could not but observe that Porter had been "acquitted by the old Councillors and only condemned by those whom you have nominated for new ones." They disapproved his appointment of the new councillors; condemned his practice of voting on bills pending before the upper house, and censured his domineering attitude toward the Assembly. Smarting under their strictures, Burrington flung policy to the winds, and gave full vent to his temper. More and more bitter grew his quarrels, more outrageous his conduct. Public business halted in the face of his private feuds. Three times he convened the Assembly, and three times prorogued it without securing the passage of a single act. Finally, in the summer of 1734, the Board of Trade determined to bear with him no longer, order his recall, and sent Gabriel Johnston to succeed him.

Johnston took the oath of office at Brunswick, November 2, 1734. He was a Scotchman of good birth and education.

He had studied at the University of St. Andrews in which he had afterwards lectured as professor of oriental languages. Early in life, abandoning literature for politics, he went to London to seek his fortunes as a political writer. There he attracted the attention of Spencer Compton, Earl of Wilmington, and Lord President of the Privy Council, who extended his patronage to him. It was through Compton's influence that Johnston was appointed governor of North Carolina. In learning, culture and character, he was superior to any of his predecessors. His learning, however, as Chalmers observes, "degenerated a little into cunning." No breath of scandal attaches to his personal conduct. He had not the itching palm like Everard, nor was he given to profanity, violence and drunkenness like Burrington. Indeed, so little did he seek to advance his own personal fortune that at his death his salary was thirteen years in arrears. But as governor, "he was exceedingly arbitrary, not to say unscrupulous, in his methods," and the ethics of some of his official acts were not above criticism. His experiences in British politics seem to have given him a predilection for sharp practices, or, as he termed it, "management," in political affairs. To secure the passage through the Assembly of a bill in which he was interested, for instance, he "prevailed" upon some of the "most troublesome" members to absent themselves; and at another time, with a similar object in view, he purposely convened the General Assembly when and where he knew his opponents could not attend. On the whole, he showed less consideration for the Assembly and a greater regard for the king's prerogative than Burrington, and was even bolder and more determined in carrying out his instructions.

Johnston not only maintained all the positions taken by Burrington in the quit rents controversy, but also insisted that the king had a right to fix upon the places at which the rents must be paid. The Assembly, on the contrary, held that rents were payable on the land, and in support of their position appealed to "the Ancient Laws and usage" of the province. The governor's reply to their appeal injected into the controversy a new and startling issue. While in England seeking the removal of Burrington, Chief Justice Smith had discovered the order of the Lords Proprietors requiring that all acts of the General Assembly be submitted to them for confirmation; otherwise they should expire at the end of two years. His investigations also revealed the fact that so little had this order been heeded, that of all the laws then in force in North Carolina, six only, and those of minor importance, had been thus confirmed. Bristling with importance at his discovery, he hastened to submit to the legal advisers of the Crown the question whether all the unconfirmed laws were not null and void. These officials had not rendered their decision when Smith returned to North Carolina, but he felt so certain that they would confirm his opinion, that he persuaded Governor Johnston and the majority of the Council to adopt it. Accordingly, when the Assembly appealed to the "Ancient Laws" of the province, Johnston and his Council replied that they could not pay "any regard" to them because having never been confirmed by the Lords Proprietors, they were all null and void. This reply brought forth a storm of angry protests. Passions ran high. In the heat of debate, Moseley and Chief Justice Smith came to blows. But the stanch old Scotch governor was undaunted by the tempest which raged about him. He boldly told the Assembly that the king was not dependent upon their consent for power to collect his rents, and "in order to convince the people that his Majesties just revenue did not depend upon any Acts of their Assembly," he issued a proclamation directing that quit rents be paid at specified places, and "in gold and silver," or in bills current at a rate of exchange for sterling to be fixed by the Council. To show his determination to carry out his policy, he erected a court of exchequer to collect rents by distress if necessary, appointed Eleazer Allen receiver-general for North Carolina, although that office for both Carolinas was already held by John Hammerton of South Carolina, and put the militia under the command of officers upon whose obedience and loyalty to him he could rely. At first the very boldness of his course resulted in "a general submission" to his orders, and he was able to report that in the autumn of 1735, the collections amounted to £1,200 sterling, at the same time predicting that the spring collections would be double that amount.

But Johnston's optimistic predictions failed to be realized. "General murmurs" of opposition soon began to be heard. John Hammerton, indignant at the governor's action, hastened into North Carolina, publicly denounced the appointment of Eleazer Allen as illegal, and "had the impudence" to issue a proclamation forbidding the payment of rents to him. Still more potent was the influence of Edward Moseley, who not only refused to pay his own quit rents, but urged the people to follow his example. To him Eleazer Allen attributed "all the difficultys and obstructions which had attended the several collections of the quit rents." The murmurs quickly grew into loud protests and threats of violence. At a report, fortunately false, that a man had been imprisoned at Edenton for refusing to pay his rents, 500 men in Bertie and Edgecombe rose in arms and set out to rescue him by force, "cursing his Majesty and uttering a great many rebellious speeches." Complaints poured into the General Assembly that the collectors were exacting payments in currency at rates of seven and eight for one of sterling, to which, when resorting to distress, they added "extravagant charges." Against these "illegal proceedings," the Assembly protested, but in vain. Thereupon, catching something of the governor's spirit, they answered his bold challenge with a challenge even more daring,—they ordered the collectors of the king's revenue into the custody of their officers!

It was in just such an emergency that Johnston revealed his superiority to Burrington in statecraft. Burrington would have met it with bluster accompanied by a volley of oaths and a torrent of curses; Johnston, on the contrary, resorted to what he euphemistically called "management." One of the questions on which he had taken issue with the Assembly was the validity of blank patents, i. e., patents for land in which the date, the name of the patentee, the location of the land, the number of acres, and the amount of the purchase money were all or in part left blank. Many such patents had been issued after the Lords Proprietors had closed their Carolina land office, and as Johnston said, were "hawked about the country" in large numbers, the purchasers locating their lands and filling in the blanks as they pleased. Johnston held such patents invalid and as thousands of acres, estimated at nearly half a million, were held under them, his contention aroused intense opposition. Finding himself checkmated in his efforts to collect quit rents, he proposed to yield his position on blank patents if the Assembly would recede from their position on quit rents. A bargain was promptly struck. The governor agreed to confirm titles held under blank patents; the Assembly consented to prepare a rent roll and to limit the number of places at which quit rents should be payable. Both sides yielded somewhat on the medium in which rents should be paid, the governor consenting to accept certain rated commodities, or their value in provincial currency, the Assembly consenting that the value of provincial currency should be fixed by a commission consisting of the governor and representatives from the Council and the House of Commons. In 1739, a bill embodying these provisions passed both houses of Assembly, was promptly signed by the governor, and both governor and Assembly congratulated themselves and each other that the long dispute was at an end.

But their congratulations were premature. The Crown vetoed the act on the ground that vesting the power to regulate the value of money ''in any person whatsoever, might be of dangerous consequence, and highly prejudicial to the trade of the nation.'' At the same time Johnston suffered another defeat for the law officers of the Crown decided against him in all of his contentions relative to the Great Deed, how and where quit rents were payable, and the validity of the provincial laws which had not been confirmed by the Lords Proprietors. With his position greatly weakened by these defeats, he again took up the controversy with the Assembly. In 1741 he called the session, as he wrote, ''in the most southern part of the Province on purpose to keep at home the northern members who were the most numerous and from whom the greatest opposition was expected,'' but to no purpose. Similar failures met him in 1744, 1745, and 1746. Finally, in 1748, he secured the passage of an act which satisfied him.

By this time questions concerning the king's quit rents had lost much of their interest and importance by the creation of the Granville District which transferred half the land in the province and more than half the revenues arising from the land, from the king to a private proprietor. It will be remembered that when the Lords Proprietors surrendered their charter to the king in 1728, John Lord Carteret, afterwards Earl of Granville, decided to retain his interest in the soil. No steps however were taken to lay off his share until 1742. Acting then upon the advice of the Board of Trade the king decided that Granville was entitled to one-eighth of the original grant which embraced nearly all the region between the northern boundary of North Carolina and the southern boundary of Georgia as far west as the South Sea. In 1742, therefore, he directed that five commissioners representing the Crown and five representing Granville be appointed with full authority to locate and set out Granville's claim.

In their work the commissioners seemed to consider Lord Granville's interests paramount to those of either king or colony. It was manifestly fair that the burdens incident to the creation of this immense private estate should be shared on some just basis by all of the three colonies, North Carolina, South Carolina, and Georgia, which had been erected out of the original proprietary; nevertheless in order that Lord Granville might enjoy the advantages of having his estate in a solid tract the commissioners decided to cut the whole of it out of North Carolina. An important consideration with them in making this decision was the fact that by adopting the North Carolina-Virginia boundary line as the northern line of the Granville District, they would have to run the southern line only. Beginning, therefore, on Hatteras Island at 35° 34′ north latitude, they carried the line in 1744 as far west as Bath. In 1746 it was carried to Haw River, thence twenty years later to Rocky River, and finally, in 1774, to the Blue Ridge Mountains. It ran through the site of the present town of Snow Hill, followed what is now the southern boundary of Chatham, Randolph, Davidson, Rowan, and Iredell counties, and fell just below the southern line of Catawba and Burke counties. Between it and Virginia lay an immense region, sixty miles in width, embracing about 26,000 square miles of territory, one-half the present state of North Carolina, and containing in 1744 more than two-thirds of the inhabitants and an even larger percentage of the wealth of the province.

Throughout this vast region, Lord Granville, though possessing no political authority, was virtually the irresponsible ruler over the property rights of the people for the territorial system which he set up was beyond the control of either Crown or Assembly. For the administration of his estate he maintained a land office at Edenton with a large organization including agents, surveyors, entry takers, and numerous subordinate officials. The inefficiency and corruption of these officials, unrestrained by any watchful authority, soon became a public scandal. Granville himself was a victim of their frauds and abuses, but the chief victims were his tenants. They suffered from the exaction of excessive fees, the collection of illegal quit rents, and the issuance of fraudulent grants. In 1755 the Assembly's committee on propositions and grievances reported such practices of Granville's agents as grievances which "do retard the Settlement of that part of the Government of which his Lordship is proprietor." During the next few years the abuses grew with such rapidity that in 1758 Granville's tenants petitioned the Assembly for relief. The Assembly appointed a committee to investigate the charges and this committee after a thorough investigation made a report which attests not only the dishonesty but also the resourcefulness of the agents in devising schemes to defraud the settlers. Some of their practices were the issuing of grants for the same tract by the same agent to more than one person; the issuing of grants for the same tract by different agents to different persons; the bribing of officials to change the names of grantees in the entry-book and to issue to other parties deeds for land for which the original grantee had already paid the entry fees; the issuing of grants improperly signed, and therefore void, so that later they might issue the same grants to other persons, of course collecting fees from all of them; and, finally, the collection of excessive fees and quit rents. The fees in the Granville District, according to Governor Dobbs, were double, and sometimes treble, the fees of the Crown in the rest of the province, and while the king's fees were paid in paper currency, Granville's agents would accept no payments except in gold and silver. In spite of these undoubted frauds and abuses the Assembly was powerless to grant the relief sought and could do nothing more than send a remonstrance to Lord Granville.

It must not be supposed that Granville was privy to these practices or indifferent to the complaints of his tenants. In 1756 he wrote to his agent, Francis Corbin: "Great and frequent complaints are transmitted to me of those persons you employ to receive entries and make surveys in the back counties. It is their extortions and not the regular fees of office which is the cause of clamor from my tenants. Insinuations are made, too, as if those extortions were connived at by my agents; for otherwise, it is said they could not be committed so repeatedly or so barefacedly." Of course none of the excess fees found their way into his coffers; indeed, he would have been fortunate if he had received those to which he was legally entitled. It was said that one of his agents on going out of office advised his successor to remember the proverb of the new broom, and not to remit too much to the earl at first as equal remittances would be expected in the future; besides, what was more to the point, such a mistaken policy might lead to investigations that would prove awkward to former agents. The trouble was not with Lord Granville; it was with the system which enabled a private individual to exercise so much control over the fortunes and happiness of people with whom he had no sort of sympathetic connection.

Finding the Assembly powerless and despairing of relief from Lord Granville, the people finally took matters in their

own hands. One result of their complaints had been an order
from Granville to Corbin to publish his table of fees which revealed abundant evidence of systematic abuses and frauds and
led to demands upon the agents to disgorge their illegal gains.
In the winter of 1759 an armed mob surrounded Corbin's house
in Edenton, aroused him in the dead of night, compelled him
to go with them to Enfield, seventy miles distant, and there
exacted of him a bond in the sum of £8,000 that he would within
three weeks' time exhibit his books for inspection and refund
all excess fees. But after his release, instead of complying
with his agreement Corbin inspired prosecutions against four
of his assailants and upon their refusing to give bail had
them thrown into prison at Enfield. This act was the signal
for an explosion. From all the surrounding country armed
settlers rode into Enfield, broke open the jail, overpowered the
jailer, released the prisoners, and inaugurated a reign of lawlessness throughout a large part of the Granville District.
Corbin abandoning his prosecutions fled in terror. Some of
the sheriffs were openly in sympathy with the mob and the
attorney-general, Robin Jones, was so thoroughly intimidated
that he refused to prosecute the rioters and appealed to the
governor to take action. The Assembly urgently supported
his appeal, but the governor refused to move and in his turn
became a target for the Assembly's denunciation. In defending himself to the Board of Trade against the strictures of
the Assembly, Dobbs denounced the dishonesty of Granville's
agents, expressed his sympathy with the people, and declared
that their conduct had been grossly misrepresented and exaggerated. The riot, therefore, was never suppressed by legal
procedure, the rioters went scot free, and conditions in the
Granville District continued volcanic until the proprietorship
was abolished.

Throughout its history the Granville District was a source
of discord, weakness and division in the colony. For many
of the most important affairs of its inhabitants, it was almost
a province within the province. Its existence was the cause of
numerous controversies over the location and boundaries of
the grants of other large landowners, and even of grants issued
by the Crown. With that indifference to former grants so
characteristic of colonial officials, the commissioners had included within the Granville District nearly 500,000 acres of
the McCulloh grant, and while Granville and McCulloh themselves had little difficulty in adjusting their conflicting claims,
their agreement did not prevent constant friction between

their agents and surveyors. There were clashes too between the agents of Granville and those of the Crown. The former charged Governor Dobbs with issuing grants for land within the Granville District while Dobbs retorted that Granville's line encroached for a depth of at least nine miles upon the king's land. These disputes and conflicts kept the frontier in a state of continual disorder and tended to discourage the immigration of substantial settlers. Many less desirable immigrants, taking advantage of the situation, squatted on lands along the border between the king's district and that of Lord Granville without taking out grants and without paying quit rents. Under such conditions it was impossible to instill into them that respect for law which is the foundation of free government. The colony also suffered from the utter indifference of the second Lord Granville, who succeeded to the title in 1763, to his Carolina estate. He allowed his land office at Edenton to remain closed for several years, thus depriving North Carolina of many excellent settlers who would have taken out grants within his district.

Financially, too, the Granville District was a great drawback to the colony. Quit rents derived from the land in this immense region went not into the public treasury but into the pockets of a private individual, or of his corrupt agents. Thus a large part of the revenues from the richest and most populous half of the colony were used for other purposes than support of the government. Consequently the burden fell so much more heavily upon the poorer half. This fact had no little to do with the stubbornness of the Assembly in holding out against the king's instructions relative to a permanent civil list.

The dual territorial and fiscal system made necessary by the existence of the Granville District was a source of division and weakness in North Carolina. The province was neither an economic nor a political unit. A northern and a southern treasurer were necessary. There was a northern and a southern party. To these divisions of interests primarily may be traced the controversy over representation which wrecked Governor Johnston's administration. These different interests continued throughout the colonial period. As late as 1773, on the very eve of the Revolution, Governor Martin complained that the Granville District created a division in the colony which for many years had "fatally embarrassed its Politics." Considering the whole history of the Granville District, therefore, Martin was fully justified in declaring that it was "not only profitless to the Proprietor, but a nuisance to this Colony."

Governors, Assembly, and people were all agreed not only as to its baneful effects, but also as to the proper remedy for its evils. The remedy was purchase by the Crown. In 1767 Governor Tryon declared that its purchase by the Crown "would more than treble the value of the quit rents:" that it was "an object so extremely coveted, to a man, by the inhabitants settled there" that it would no doubt result in the passage of "any law his Majesty would propose for the better and more easy collecting his quit rents." "If it could be purchased for sixty thousand pounds sterling," he added, "it would be cheap; it is certainly the most rising interest on the continent of America." To like effect wrote Governor Martin who in 1771 said, "It seems here an universally acknowledged principle that this Country will never enjoy perfect peace until that proprietary which erects a kind of separate interest in its bowels is vested in the Crown." The Assembly too was of the same mind. In 1773 the House of Commons appointed a committee, composed of its strongest leaders, "to take into consideration Lord Granville's Territory in this Province, with respect to the settlement of the same, and to propose some plan to quiet the Inhabitants in their possession." The plan proposed and agreed to by the Assembly was to request the king to "be graciously pleased to purchase the same, that the said Lands may be held of him as other Lands are held of his Majesty in his District in this Colony." But nothing came of these suggestions; the Revolution came on, independence was declared, and Lord Granville being then an alien enemy, the Assembly in 1782 solved the problem of the Granville District by the short and effective method of confiscation.

The creation of the Granville District in 1744 was an important element in enabling Governor Johnston to secure the passage of the quit rent law of 1748, but a more important element still was the representation quarrel inaugurated by the Assembly of November, 1746, which threw the quit rent controversy completely in the shade. The most determined opposition to the governor in the quit rents controversy had come from the inhabitants of the old county of Albemarle who claimed to hold their land under the Great Deed of Grant. The Great Deed gave them better terms than the Crown was disposed to allow and they were determined not to surrender their advantage. Another advantage which they enjoyed enabled them to sustain their position. This was the right which each precinct in Albemarle had of sending to the General Assembly five representatives, whereas the other precincts sent but two each. This privilege originated early in the proprietary period when Albemarle was the only county in Carolina, and was not extended to the precincts which were subsequently erected in Bath County.

As these new precincts grew in wealth and population they came to look upon this inequality as a discrimination against them, while the expansion of the colony southward toward the Cape Fear gave rise to sectional interests different from the interests of Albemarle, which served to emphasize it. The commercial interests of the Cape Fear settlers, who enjoyed the advantage of direct trade with the mother country, often conflicted with those of Albemarle, whose trade necessarily went through Virginia and the other colonies, and legislation in the interests of one section was frequently considered ruinous by the other. Personal ambitions and sectional rivalries also increased the dissatisfaction of the southern precincts. New Bern was ambitious to displace Edenton as the seat of government, and her pretensions were supported by the precincts south of Albemarle Sound. The people in the southern precincts, especially those along the Cape Fear, complained that it was a hardship to compel them to go to Edenton, in the extreme northeastern corner of the province, across two wide sounds, in order to consult the public records in the secretary's office, to transact business in the General Court, and to attend sessions of the General Assembly. But all their efforts to move the capital to a more central place were defeated because the counties north of Albemarle Sound had a majority in the Assembly. The controversy came to a head in June, 1746, when the proposal to make New Bern the capital was again defeated, and the session closed with a sectional quarrel that split the popular party in two. In this division, the shrewd politician at the head of the government saw his opportunity and hastened to make the most of it.

Making common cause with the southern members, Johnston prorogued the Assembly to meet in November at Wilmington, expecting that so many northern members would refuse to attend at that season and at such a distance, that the southern members would control the House. In fact, the former had openly declared that, because of the inclemency of the season and the difficulties of travel, they would not attend a winter session at Wilmington. Since they composed a majority of the House, they of course expected that no session could be held without them. But in this they reckoned without their host, for they could not foresee that Samuel Swann, John Starkey, and other southern leaders, for the sake of a petty sectional advantage and at the behest of a royal governor, would surrender one of the most cherished principles of the popular party, namely, that no number less than a majority should be considered a quorum of the House of Commons. Yet this is just what they did. With only fifteen members in attendance, out of a total membership of fifty-four, Speaker Swann declared a quorum present and notified the governor that the House was ready for business. The business of the session was cut and dried. But two bills were considered, one making New Bern the capital and regulating circuit courts, the other reducing the representation of the Albemarle counties [2] from five to two members each. Johnston hastened to dispatch the two acts to England for approval, saying: "I have got a law passed for fixing the seat of Government at Newbern, and a tax laid for Public Buildings. There was only one other law passed then, viz., an Act for ascertaining the number of representatives for each County, the inequality of which has been one great source of the Disorders of this Colony." Not a word about the revolutionary method by which the two bills were passed through the Assembly!

But the northern counties were not so reticent. They protested loudly against the trick of which they were the victims, denounced the whole proceedings as a fraud, and solemnly agreed that they would not recognize the validity of the pretended acts of the rump Assembly. Accordingly, when the governor issued writs for a new Assembly to meet in February, 1747, and directed the northern counties to return but two members each, the people refused obedience and in each county chose five as usual. The House, of course, promptly declared the elections null and void, threw out the returns, and directed that new elections be held. Thereupon the northern counties appealed to the king. A long and bitter controversy followed. Three issues were presented, viz.: the right of the northern counties to five members each; the number of representatives necessary to constitute a quorum of the House; and the validity of the act complained of. The governor, assisted by certain of his councillors, presented the case

---

[2] In March, 1739, Albemarle and Bath counties were abolished and their subdivisions, theretofore known as precincts, became counties.

for the southern counties; Wyriott Ormond and Thomas
Barker, prominent attorneys, represented the northern counties. Both sides argued their contentions with skill and ability. The governor contended that the only basis for the claims
of the northern counties was the Biennial Act of 1715 which
the king had repealed in 1737. The northern counties, on the
other hand, traced their claim back to the Fundamental Constitutions and the unbroken practice of the colony under the
Lords Proprietors. By careful searching of the records, by
numerous depositions as to what practice had been followed,
and by hearing long and tedious arguments, the crown officials sought diligently and impartially to arrive at a correct
decision. The main point, i. e., the right of the northern counties to five members each, they decided in favor of the northern counties; they thought, however, that a majority was not
necessary for a quorum, saying that "such a constitution is
very extraordinary and liable to great inconvenience"; nevertheless, as the act in question had been "passed by management, precipitation and surprise," they advised the king to
veto it.

Eight years passed between the appeal and the decision,
years of confusion, rebellion and almost of anarchy throughout the northern half of the province. The first election held
under the act of 1746 had given the governor an Assembly
amenable to his will and he determined to hold it together as
long as possible. Elected in 1747, it held thirteen sessions,
and was not dissolved until 1754, after Johnston's death.
During these years the northern counties refused to send representatives to the Assembly. They denied the constitutional
authority of an Assembly in which they were not allowed
their full representation. They held its acts to be null and
void. They would not use the currency emitted by its authority. They refused to pay taxes. They declined to serve as
jurors in the General Court organized under the act of 1746,
or to submit to its judgments. In a word, as Bishop Spangenberg wrote in 1752, throughout the northern counties there
existed "a perfect anarchy. As a result, crimes are of frequent occurrence, such as murder [and] robbery. But the
criminals cannot be brought to justice. The citizens do not
appear as jurors, and if court is held to decide such criminal
matters no one is present. If any one is imprisoned the prison
is broken open and no justice administered. In short, most
matters are decided by blows. Still the county courts are
held regularly and what belongs to their jurisdiction receives

customary attention.'' The last statement throws a flood of light on this curious situation. The people would not submit to the jurisdiction of the General Court because it was held under authority of an act passed by the rump Assembly of November, 1746, nevertheless they maintained their county courts in full vigor and cheerfully submitted to their decrees because they were held under the long established laws of the province.

Governor Johnston, dying in 1752, did not live to see the end of the controversy which his ''management'' had fastened on the province. After a brief interval, during which first Nathaniel Rice and then Matthew Rowan, as presidents of the Council, administered the government, Arthur Dobbs was appointed governor. Dobbs was the head of an ancient family in Carrickfergus, Ireland. He had had a varied and not undistinguished career, having served as high sheriff of County Antrim, as representative of Carrickfergus in Parliament, and as surveyor-general of Ireland. But he was best known for his interest in Arctic explorations; he had even made an attempt to discover the Northwest Passage, and had written treatises on the subject. His interest in North Carolina began with 'the purchase of the colony by the Crown. As early as 1733 he was a member of a syndicate which purchased 60,000 acres in New Hanover precinct upon which the company settled a colony of Irish Protestants. He also had other landed interests in North Carolina. It was doubtless this connection with the colony that suggested his appointment as governor.

It was an unfortunate selection. Without the energy and ability of Burrington, lacking Johnston's force of character and political shrewdness, Dobbs entertained more exaggerated ideas of the prerogative of the Crown and less tolerance for the constitutional claims of the Assembly than either. At sixty-five years of age, he was too old to adapt himself to the strange conditions of a new country and too infirm to grapple successfully with the difficult problems of colonial administration. During the decade covered by his administration, these difficulties increased as year by year his capacity to cope with them diminished. Says Saunders in his admirable analysis of Dobbs' character, ''his mental faculties, probably never very great, weakened and finally gave way under the strain * * * and in December, 1762, a stroke of palsy, that deprived him of the use of his lower limbs, all the winter, put an end to all hope, for the time, at least, of his future usefulness.

He rallied, however, and if he did, indeed, escape the drivel-
ling imbecility of old age, he committed its supreme folly by
marrying a very young girl. Complimented in 1755 for his
vigor and intelligence, in 1762 he was told by the lords of
the Board of Trade that his dispatches were so very incorrect,
vague and incoherent that it was almost impossible to discover his meaning, and that as far as they could be understood, they contained little more than repetitions of propositions he had made to them before, and upon which he had
received their sentiments fully and clearly expressed."[3] To
which it must be added that as his mental faculties decreased,
his irritability, his dictatorialness, and his egotism increased,
rendering co-operation with him impossible. Such was the
man which the British colonial system of the eighteenth
century selected to administer the public affairs of a sensitive
and highly excitable people at a time when the fate of the
British Empire hung upon the vigor, intelligence and harmony
with which all its parts co-operated in its defense.

Dobbs arrived at a conjuncture favorable for a successful
administration. The people were tired of internal strife. The
French and Indian War was then in progress and imperial
interests for the first time in the history of the colony absorbed the attention of the people. Dobbs, too, was the bearer
of the decisions of the Crown in the issues raised by Governor
Johnston and these decisions were on the whole favorable to
the colony. Furthermore he brought instructions to dissolve
the old rump Assembly elected in 1747, which half the colony
regarded as illegal, and to call a new Assembly in which representation should be distributed as it had been prior to 1746.
This Assembly met in New Bern, December 12, 1754. It was
the first Assembly since June, 1746, in which all the counties
were represented. Evidence of the seriousness of the division
in the popular party was seen in the contest for the speakership. For the first time in fourteen years a candidate for the
speakership appeared against Samuel Swann, who had long
been the leader of the popular party and was now the leader
of the southern faction. After a sharp contest, he was defeated by John Campbell, leader of the northern faction.
The morning after the election, Dobbs wrote to the Board of
Trade, "Although there may be some little sparring betwixt
the parties, yet both have assured me it shall have no effect
upon public affairs or make my administration uneasy."

---

[3] Prefatory Notes to *Colonial Records of North Carolina*, Vol.
V, p. viii.

In spite of his sanguine anticipations, Dobbs soon found himself involved in controversies with the Assembly over a greater variety of issues than any of his predecessors. Some of the less important of these concerned the right of the Assembly to elect the public treasurer, to name an agent to represent the colony before the various boards in England, to appoint a public printer, and to fix the fees of provincial officials. On these issues the Board of Trade generally sustained the Assembly even to the point of rebuking the governor for the persistence of his opposition. When Dobbs, for instance, rejected an aid bill because it contained a clause naming an agent in England, in whose choice he claimed a right to be consulted, the Board of Trade wrote to him that it was none of his business "either in point of Right or Propriety to interfere in the nomination of an Agent so far as regards the Choice of the person" for "in this respect the Representatives of the people are and ought to be free to chuse whom they think proper to act," and that while the method of appointment in this particular case was irregular, "yet when we consider the necessity there was of some supply to answer the exigency of the Service in the present calamitous State of his Majesty's Southern Provinces, we cannot but think it was too trivial an Objection to have been admitted as a reason for rejecting that Supply." But on the more important issues, such as the number of members necessary to constitute a quorum of the House of Commons, the right of the Assembly to determine the qualifications and tenure of judges, and its right to control the expenditure of public funds, the Board of Trade fully sustained the governor.

The quorum controversy Dobbs inherited from the Johnston administration. The popular party, contending for the principle of the Biennial Act of 1715, that "the quorum of the House of Burgesses for voting and passing of Bills shall not be less than one full half of the House," based its contention upon "the Constitution and constant usage and practice" of the colony. Such a constitution, on the other hand, the crown officials, calling to mind the practice of the British Parliament in which 40 members out of a total of 556 were a quorum, considered "very extraordinary and liable to great inconvenience," so they instructed Dobbs to consider fifteen members a quorum of the Assembly. This instruction the Assembly resolutely refused to obey. In October, 1760, in April, 1762, in December, 1763, and in February, 1764, the members declined to obey the governor's commands that they form a House with less than a majority, "denying His Majesty's right of constituting fifteen to be a quorum." The governor blustered and scolded and the Board of Trade denounced the Assembly's course as "an indecent opposition to the just authority of the Crown," but to no purpose; the Assembly refused to yield and the issue remained to vex the administration of Dobbs' latest successor under the Crown. It was not finally settled until the people took the government into their own hands in 1776.

In the quorum controversy the Assembly held a stronger legal position than it did in the controversy over the qualifications and tenure of judges, though perhaps not a more just one. It was conceded that the appointment of a chief justice, with a tenure during the king's pleasure, was a prerogative of the Crown. For this great office attorneys were usually sent out from England whose personal character and legal learning did not always measure up to the dignity and responsibility of their position. Owing their appointment and their tenure to the will of the governor they were perhaps too often amenable to executive influence. To curtail this influence as much as possible, as well as to provide for the increasing needs of the growing colony, the Assembly passed an act which provided for associate, or assistant justices upon whom, in the absence or disability of the chief justice, it conferred full jurisdiction, at the same time so arranging the circuits that the chief justice could not possibly attend more than half the courts. These associate justices were to be appointed by the governor, but the Assembly was careful to limit his choice by fixing such qualifications as practically to exclude all non-resident attorneys, and to secure their independence by giving them a tenure during good behavior.

These "new and unprecedented" features, crown officials considered violations of the king's prerogative, and upon their advice the king vetoed the act and instructed Dobbs not to consent to any such provisions in the future. Thus again did Prerogative challenge Privilege, undo what the Assembly had declared to be necessary for the "ease" of the people and the "due and regular administration of justice," and ride roughshod over the personal ambitions of numerous aspiring attorneys. Here then were all the elements for a pretty quarrel. It flared up at once bringing with it as Dobbs said, "a stagnation of Justice." The controversy reached its crisis in 1760. Called into special session to vote an aid to the king for war purposes, the Assembly obstinately refused even to consider an aid bill unless the governor would consent to its court bill. The contest raged with great bitterness. The governor lashed the members fiercely and the Assembly retorted by holding a secret session in which it brought an arraignment against Dobbs "without an equal until that brought against King George at Philadelphia by the United Colonies on the 4th of July, 1776." [4] It declared that "by the injudicious and partial appointment of Justices not qualified for such trust and the abrupt removal of Others whose Characters have been liable to no objection, Magistracy has fallen into Contempt and Courts have lost their Influence and dignity." These explosions, however, cleared the atmosphere and led the way to a compromise. In return for a supply, the governor agreed to sign the court bill provided a clause was inserted limiting its duration to two years unless approved by the king. Needless to say this approval was never given, and the only reward Dobbs received for his pains was a stinging rebuke from his official superiors. The Assembly fared better for the incident showed it a way to accomplish its purpose by adopting the simple expedient of passing court laws containing the desired provisions and limited in their operation for two years. This practice was followed for more than a decade.

Most of the controversies which have been discussed, especially those over the election of the public treasurer, the appointment of the colonial agent, and the qualifications and tenure of judges, were involved in the great controversy over finances, and were, in fact, subsidiary to it; that is to say, the Assembly used its power over the public purse to force from the executive concessions on these other questions. The French and Indian War which continued through most of Dobbs' administration brought unprecedented demands for money and gave to financial affairs greater importance than they had ever had before. No man was more British in his enmity to the French, or more Protestant in his hostility to their religion, than Dobbs, and he made the wringing of money out of the province for the prosecution of the war the paramount object of his administration. The Assembly met his demands as liberally as it thought the circumstances of the colony justified, but it could not satisfy the governor. Greater demands urged in impolitic language brought on numerous

---

[4] Saunders: Prefatory Notes to *Colonial Records of North Carolina*, Vol. VI, p. xxi.

sharp controversies over the prerogatives of the Crown and the privileges of the Assembly in fiscal affairs.

These controversies involved two classes of funds. First, there was North Carolina's share of the appropriation made by the British Parliament to reimburse the colonies for their large expenditures in prosecuting the war; and, second, money appropriated directly by the General Assembly. Dobbs claimed the right to dispose of the first by executive order, and at times drew upon it for the equipment and pay of troops. His right to do this the Assembly disputed, and its position was sustained by the Board of Trade. Much more significant was the controversy over appropriations. The governor complained of the habit of the Assembly of tacking onto supply bills extraneous matters, such as the appointment of a colonial agent, and of using its control over such bills to force concessions in other matters, as it did in the court law controversy. But these phases of the dispute involved no principle; the chief issue was the claim of the Assembly to the sole right to frame supply bills. In 1754, the Council having proposed an amendment to an appropriation bill, the Assembly promptly rejected it and unanimously resolved "that the Councill in taking upon them to make several material Alterations to the said Bill whereby the manner of raising as well as Application of the Aid thereby granted to his Majesty is directed in a different Manner than by that said Bill proposed have acted contrary to Custom and Usage of Parliament and that the same tends to Infringe the Right and Liberties of the Assembly who have always enjoyed uninterrupted the Privilege of Framing and modelling all Bills by Virtue of which Money has been Levied on the Subject for an Aid for his Majesty." Having made good this principle, the Assembly voted money for support of the war with a liberality which even Dobbs acknowledged. After 1758, however, the governor made a total failure in his efforts to direct the Assembly. More zealous than judicious, he allowed himself to become involved in a silly quarrel over what the Board of Trade called a "trivial" matter, in which he imagined the king's prerogative was affected, and rather than yield a little where resistance could do no good, he foolishly threw away the supplies which a burdened people reluctantly offered. Quarrel followed quarrel; the sessions were consumed with quarrels. The Assembly refused to frame supply bills at the governor's dictation, and in an outburst of wrath, he wrote to the Board of Trade that the members were "as obstinate as mules" and appealed to the king to strengthen his authority for "supporting his Majesty's prerogative" in the colony.

In these controversies with Dobbs, one's sympathies are naturally with the Assembly. Nevertheless when one considers the threat which the vast designs of France held out against the very existence of the British Empire in America, the danger which hung over the colonists themselves from the hostility of the savage and relentless allies of the French, and the urgent necessity for unity and harmony in all the English-speaking colonies, one cannot altogether escape the feeling that the Board of Trade was justified in rebuking the Assembly for its "unfortunate and ill-timed disputes * * * at a time when the united efforts of all his Majesty's subjects are so essentially necessary to their own security and to the promoting the general interest of the Community."

The Assembly's justification must be sought in its conviction that it was fighting the battles of constitutional and representative government. Its appeal was constantly to the "Constitution" and the "usage and practice" of the colony. By "Constitution" it meant the Carolina charter and the practices which had grown up under it. Among its provisions was a guarantee that the people of Carolina should "freely and quietly have, possess and enjoy" as fully as if they were residents of England, "all liberties, franchises, and privileges, of this our kingdom, * * * without the molestation, vexation, trouble, or grievance, of us, our heirs, and successors; any act, statute, ordinance, or provision, to the contrary notwithstanding." Furthermore, the charter contained certain provisions which, though not among those "liberties, franchises and privileges" which the people enjoyed as Englishmen, were yet equally as binding upon both ruler and subject. In the quorum controversy, for instance, the Assembly based its contention on that clause of the charter which provided for the making of laws by and with the advice and consent of the freemen, "or the greater part of them, or their delegates or deputies," and asserted that "the King had no right to lessen the Quorum by his Instructions." These chartered rights, the Assembly held, had not been affected by the transfer of the colony to the Crown, and could be neither abridged nor abrogated without the consent of the people. As late as 1761, Dobbs wrote that the Assembly contended that the charter "still subsisted" and that it bound the king as well as the people. The Assembly felt, therefore, that it was fighting the battles of representative government, which the royal governors had set themselves to destroy.   Dobbs summed up the situation when he wrote, "The Assembly think themselves entitled to all the Privileges of a British House of Commons and therefore ought not to submit to His Majesty's honorable Privy Council further than the Commons do in England, or submit to His Majesty's instructions to His Governor and Council here," and appealed to the king to strengthen his hands that he might more effectually "oppose and suppress a republican spirit of Independency rising in this Colony."

CHAPTER XIV

INTER-COLONIAL AND IMPERIAL RELATIONS

The change from a proprietary to a crown colony swept North Carolina more fully than ever into the current of inter-colonial and imperial affairs. Its administration now passed under the immediate supervision of a committee of the Privy Council officially entitled the Lords Commissioners for Trade and Plantations, but better known as the Board of Trade. To enable this board, to which was committed the general supervision of colonial affairs, to carry out its task, power was given it to recommend to the king in Council suitable persons for governor, councillors, judges and other colonial officials; to draft instructions to governors, and to correspond with them; to examine laws passed by colonial assemblies and to recommend to the king in Council those which ought to be approved and those which ought to be vetoed; to hear complaints of oppression and mal-administration in the colonies and to report its findings to the king in Council; to require accountings of public funds voted by colonial assemblies; to "execute and perform all other things necessary or proper for answering our royal intentions in the premises;" and, finally, in order to make its power effective, to send for persons and papers, and to examine persons under oath. Although it had no executive power of its own, nevertheless its advice was sought and generally adopted by the Privy Council which had ultimate authority in colonial affairs. The Board of Trade, writes Andrews, "developed fairly definite ideas as to what the British policy towards the colonies should be; it maintained in the Plantation Office a permanent staff of secretaries and clerks who became the guardians of the traditions of the office; and upheld, during periods of political manipulation and frequent change, a more or less fixed colonial program." [1]

The Board of Trade displayed remarkable consistency in

---

[1] Andrews, Charles McLean: The Colonial Period, p. 136.

its colonial program and held tenaciously to certain principles of imperial government. It sought to make the governments of the colonies, as far as possible, conform to a single administrative type and by retaining control of the executive and judiciary to preserve and strengthen their dependence upon the home government. North Carolina felt the influence of these policies even before the purchase by the Crown. We have already seen how the Board of Trade sought to bring North Carolina under its administrative control, first through action by Parliament, then through *quo warranto* proceedings; and how, when both of these methods failed, through gradual encroachments upon the chartered rights and privileges of the Lords Proprietors, it finally forced them to surrender their charter. Similar proceedings, at times even more arbitrary ones, were taken with other proprietary colonies. Closely allied with this policy were the efforts of the board to strengthen its authority over the colonies through undivided control over their executive and judiciary officers. Even in the proprietary governments, an act of Parliament required nominees of the Proprietors for governor to be approved by the king before they could qualify. In the royal colonies the board undertook to establish permanent civil lists in order that the governors, judges and other officials might be independent of the assemblies for their salaries and hence be free to carry out imperial policies unhampered by local interests. With the same object in view it required judges to be commissioned during the king's pleasure only.

These policies met with intense opposition in the colonies. In North Carolina Burrington and Johnston, in obedience to their instructions, called upon the Assembly to provide permanently "a competent salary" for the governor, but the Assembly replied that if the king wished the governor's salary to be so fixed, he could pay it out of his quit rents. The Board of Trade accordingly adopted the suggestion, but the collection of quit rents depended upon legislation by the Assembly, and the Assembly, as we have seen, refused to obey instructions relating to them. Quit rents, therefore, were so seldom collected in North Carolina that Burrington's salary was never paid, while Johnston's, at the time of his death, was thirteen years in arrears. In its instructions to Dobbs, the Board of Trade introduced an additional clause, common to its instructions to governors of other colonies, that the Assembly should fix a civil list "without limitation in point of time." But the Assembly steadfastly refused. "I can see no prospect of getting a fixed salary to the Governor or his successors,'' wrote Dobbs to the Board of Trade. '' * * * There seems to be an established maxim fixed in the several Assemblies of the colonies to keep the Governors and Government as much in their power as they can.'' Like his predecessors, Dobbs was compelled to look elsewhere for his compensation.

Control of the judiciary in the imperial interests turned less upon the question of salary than upon the tenure of the judges. The colonies insisted that judges be commissioned during good behavior, but the Board of Trade instructed the governors to issue no commissions except during the king's pleasure. In 1754 Governor Dobbs was compelled to break through his instructions on this point and consent to an act which provided for judges during good behavior, but the king, upon the advice of the Board of Trade, promptly repudiated his action. In 1761 the Board of Trade assumed an inflexible attitude on this point. It removed the governor of New Jersey from office for failure to enforce this policy. In the same year it reported adversely upon two judiciary acts of the North Carolina Assembly largely because they provided for judges during good behavior, for it confessed that in other respects, the acts were ''not only regular and uniform'' in themselves, but were also ''consonant to the principles and Constitution of the Mother Country'' and ''properly adapted to the situation and circumstances'' of the colony. Thus in one colony after another the judiciary was brought under the control of the Crown and after 1762 all judges held office during pleasure only. The colonies never became reconciled to this policy and when they came in 1776 to declare their independence of the mother country, they listed it among those things which justified their action.

The Board of Trade kept constantly in view not only the relations of the colonies to the empire, but their relations to each other and to the savage nations with which they came in contact. Many of its most important activities concerned inter-colonial relations and Indian affairs. Under its supervision came such problems as boundary line controversies, inter-colonial trade policies, and the relations of the several Indian nations to each other as well as to the whites.

Prior to 1700 few of the colonies had such well defined boundaries as to be free from boundary disputes which always involved questions that could not be settled by those directly interested in them. In those between crown colonies and proprietary colonies, as illustrated in the North Carolina-Virginia boundary dispute, both king and proprietors had interests to be considered. The colonies themselves were deeply concerned as the controversies frequently involved the enforcement of criminal laws, the execution of judicial processes, the collection of taxes, service in the militia, Indian affairs, and other governmental problems. Private interests too were numerous and complicated. Titles to land along the contested lines rested upon the right of the government under which they were claimed to issue the grants, and conflicting claims often led to disorders, riots, and bloodshed.

No better illustration of conditions growing out of a disputed boundary can be found than those which arose along the North Carolina-South Carolina border from 1753 to 1764. As early as 1735 commissioners representing the two provinces had agreed upon the thirty-fifth parallel of latitude as the boundary but many years passed before it was located by survey. In 1753 complaint was made to the North Carolina Council that South Carolina surveyors had entered the Waxhaw settlement north of the thirty-fifth parallel and were surveying under grants from South Carolina tracts of land which were "the property of several persons * * * within in this Province to the great Disturbance of their Peace and Quiet." The Council thereupon advised the governor to issue orders to both the civil and military authorities to arrest all such surveyors and bring them to trial. Two years later Governor Dobbs charged that Governor Glen of South Carolina had "spirited up some of the settlers" on his lands, which had been patented under the laws of North Carolina in 1746, "to take out warrants of survey from him and he would support them," adding, "When Mr. Glen would begin with me, it may be presumed no private person could escape him." But the chief sufferer in these disputes was Henry McCulloh whose grants lay along the border. In 1756 it was charged that Governor Glen was "daily granting warrants of survey" within McCulloh's tract. Conflicts between rival surveyors, and between those claiming under their surveys, were often attended with fatal results. Anarchy and lawlessness prevailed in many border communities for the region in dispute became "a kind of sanctuary to Criminals and Vagabonds by their pretending as it served their purpose that they belonged to either Province."

But there were other actions of the South Carolina authorities which were even more irritating to North Carolina officials than the surveys. The governor of South Carolina, for in-

stance, required settlers north of the thirty-fifth parallel to
attend his militia musters and undertook to impose fines
upon those who refused to obey his summons, commissioned
justices of the peace north of that line, encouraged settlers
there to refuse to pay taxes to the North Carolina government, and warned Governor Dobbs himself "not to molest
them." Encouraged by his support, a band of settlers in Anson County fell upon the sheriff while he was collecting taxes
and imprisoned him, and Dobbs, "to prevent further confusion, was obliged to overlook it." At times officials of
the two provinces actually came into armed conflict. In 1755,
in a letter to Dobbs, Glen denounced "several outrages" by
citizens of North Carolina upon inhabitants of South Carolina,
"which," he added, "having been committed under the colour
of authority by persons pretending to be officers of your
Government, the offense was the more intolerable." To which
Dobbs replied that the North Carolina officials had "only repelled an invasive force" sent from South Carolina to survey land, collect taxes, and impose fines within the jurisdiction of North Carolina.

These charges and counter-charges finally led to an open
breach between the two governors. They were in truth too
much alike to get along together harmoniously. What Dobbs
said of Glen applies with equal truth to himself, that he was
"too opinionated and self-sufficient to have any dealings with
him." Glen's air of superiority and condescension ruffled
his adversary's sense of dignity. Your letter, wrote Dobbs,
in reply to a letter just received from Glen, was written "in
a very extraordinary style, I may say dictatorial, not as one
Governor to another having equal powers from his Majesty,
and independent of each other, but as if I was dependent
upon you, and obliged to give you an account of my behaviour
in transacting affairs of this Government." Throwing aside
all pretense of diplomacy Dobbs wrote to the Board of Trade
that he would have no further dealings with Glen, and in this
position the board seems to have sustained him for, greatly
to Dobbs' satisfaction, it removed Glen from office.

Such incidents showed the necessity for an impartial tribunal with power to settle controversies between colonies. This
tribunal was found in the Board of Trade. One of its first
problems concerning the Carolinas after their transfer to the
Crown was the settlement of their boundary. At the time the
transfer was completed both George Burrington and Robert
Johnson, the newly appointed royal governors, were in Lon-

don awaiting their instructions, and since both had been officials under the Lords Proprietors and were supposed to be familiar with colonial conditions, the Board of Trade directed them to agree on a boundary line between their provinces. After a conference, in which they were joined by "some other gentlemen belonging to those provinces," they reached an agreement which the Board of Trade approved. Accordingly it issued instructions directing the two governors to appoint commissioners to run a line to begin at the sea thirty miles southwest of the mouth of Cape Fear River, and keeping that distance from the river, to run parallel with it to its source, thence due west as far as the South Sea. Afterwards at the suggestion of Governor Johnson, and without consulting Burrington, the board added as an alternative, that if the Waccamaw River lay within thirty miles of Cape Fear River, then it should be the line from the sea to its source; from which the line should continue parallel with the Cape Fear River at a distance of thirty miles to its source, thence due west to the South Sea.

Disputes of course arose over the meaning of these instructions. The source of the Waccamaw was found to be within thirty miles of the Cape Fear and this fact gave Burrington basis for claiming the Waccamaw as the boundary; its mouth, on the contrary, was at least ninety miles from Cape Fear, and Johnson insisted that the word "mouth" should be read into the instructions as its omission "was only a Mistake in the wording of it." Burrington in a public proclamation warned all persons against taking out warrants from the South Carolina authorities for land north of Waccamaw River, and Johnson in a similar proclamation replied to him. The two governors could not agree and were compelled to call in the Board of Trade to decide between them. Governor Johnson declared that Burrington's interpretation "would bring his boundary into the bowels of our present settlements," and urged a "speedy running" of the line according to the claims of South Carolina. But North Carolina was not satisfied with the Cape Fear River as her western boundary, as such a line would cut her off from any westward development. Burrington, therefore, urged upon the board reasons for changing the line from the Cape Fear River to the Pee Dee River, saying that the former line was "intricate and difficult," and that the expense of running it would be £2,000 sterling, while the Pee Dee was a natural boundary open to neither of these objections. If the whole region between the Cape Fear and the

Pee Dee were sold, he added, probably with a sardonic grin, "it would not prove sufficient to pay commissioners, chains, carriers, and labourers," necessary to run the Cape Fear line. The North Carolina Council endorsed Burrington's suggestion and advised him not to appoint commissioners until the Board of Trade had passed upon it. But the board promptly rejected it, saying that it would not think of altering its instruction "upon hearing one party only" and directed Burrington to "put that instruction in execution." But George Burrington was determined that the line should not be so run and he never lacked expedients for carrying his purposes into effect. By prolonging the debate on the advantages of the Pee Dee line, and when defeated in that, by referring to the Board of Trade the problem of paying for the survey, he managed to postpone the running of the line for three years, so that when he was recalled in 1734, nothing had been done. Whatever one may think of the ethics of his tactics, their success is not open to criticism for they saved to North Carolina that vast region west of Cape Fear River and between the thirty-fifth and thirty-sixth parallels of north latitude, now the richest section of the commonwealth.

In 1734 Gabriel Johnston succeeded Burrington. Upon his arrival at Cape Fear, he was asked by Governor Johnson whether he "had not brought over a more plain instruction about the dividing line," to which he replied in the negative, at the same time stating his intention of carrying the old instruction into execution. Further interchange of views led to an agreement to appoint commissioners to adjust the differences between the two governments. In 1735, therefore, Governor Johnson appointed Alexander Skene, James Abercrombie, and William Walters to represent South Carolina, and Governor Johnston appointed Robert Halton, Eleazer Allen, Matthew Rowan, Edward Moseley, and Roger Moore to represent North Carolina. The commissioners met at Lilliput, the home of Eleazer Allen on the Cape Fear, in March, 1735, and remained in session six weeks. A spirit of compromise pervaded their deliberations. The South Carolina commissioners, wrote Governor Johnston, "desired that without adhering with too much rigour to the words of the instruction, which favoured our pretensions very much, we would agree to such reasonable propositions as they designed to make us, and then join our endeavours to get this agreement ratified at home." The North Carolina commissioners met this suggestion in the spirit in which it was offered, the governor himself setting the example. "After many conferences held during the space of six weeks," wrote the South Carolina commissioners, "by the kindly interposition of Gabriel Johnston * * * [we] had the happiness to remove a difference which had long subsisted between the two provinces and finally to settle and adjust the limits to the mutual satisfaction of both."

The line agreed upon was to begin at the sea, thirty miles southwest of the mouth of Cape Fear River, to run thence in a northwest course to the thirty-fifth parallel of north latitude, thence due west to the South Sea; if before reaching the thirty-fifth parallel, it came within five miles of the Pee Dee River, it should then run parallel with the Pee Dee at a distance of five miles to the thirty-fifth degree, thence due west to the South Sea; provided that at no point should it approach nearer than thirty miles to the Cape Fear River; and provided, further, that when it reached the reservation of the Catawba Indians, it should be so run as to throw those Indians into South Carolina. This agreement, which the South Carolinians "consented to with great joy," was signed by all the commissioners, April 23, 1735, and later was approved by the Board of Trade which wrote, "We shall always have a proper regard to so solemn a determination agreed to by persons properly empowered by each of the Provinces." The commissioners hastened to carry their agreement into effect. They began their survey May 1, 1735, and during the summer and fall ran the line something over 100 miles from the coast. A deputy surveyor afterwards took the latitude of Pee Dee River at the thirty-fifth parallel and set up a marker there which for several years was considered to be the boundary at that place. In their work, the commissioners "endured vast fatigue." Most of the line ran through uninhabited woods in many places impassable until they had cleared the way. There were, too, several large and rapid rivers which were crossed only with great danger and difficulty. In spite of these hardships and difficulties, testified Governor Johnston, they "performed their business with great diligence and exactness." Although their work did not put an end to the controversies between the two provinces, it fixed the line from which no substantial deviations were afterwards made. Surveys in 1737, in 1764, and in 1772 carried it as far west as Tryon Mountain where it stopped until after North Carolina and South Carolina had ceased to be British colonies.

The boundary dispute between the two provinces was intimately connected with their trade relations. For commercial reasons the settlers along the upper waters of the Pee Dee and Catawba rivers wanted the line to be so run as either to throw them into South Carolina, or to leave the Pee Dee River wholly in North Carolina. The explanation of their wishes is found in the fact that Charleston was their chief market. An inhabitant of Mecklenburg County, writing in 1768 about the building of a palace for the governor at New Bern, declared that "not one man in twenty of the four most populous counties will ever see this famous house when built, as their connections and trade do, and ever will, more naturally centre in South Carolina." It was much easier for them to float their produce down the Pee Dee and Catawba rivers to Charleston than to carry them overland to Wilmington and New Bern.

Instead of encouraging this trade, South Carolina in the supposed interest of her own merchants, laid heavy duties on products imported from North Carolina. In 1762 the Council petitioned the king to order the southern boundary of the province to be carried farther south to Winyaw where the Pee Dee River enters the Atlantic Ocean "as by our having one side of Winyaw we should have a free navigation to the Sea and enjoy the Benefit of the inland Navigation of the Yadkin, Rocky, Great and Little Pee Dee Rivers, which though they all run through the Heart of this province enter the Sea at Winyaw, and as there are heavy Dutys laid in South Carolina upon the produce of this province we [they] are from that reason rendered totally useless to both provinces as the Boundary now stands." Thus the North Carolina settlers were caught between the devil of geographical obstacles to trade on the one side and the deep blue sea of artificial restrictions on the other. The Board of Trade to which they appealed, admitted that South Carolina's policy "must in its consequence destruct the Commerce of His Majesty's subjects in North Carolina," and promised relief. But nothing came of this promise, and North Carolina began to seek measures of retaliation and relief on her own account. In 1751 the Assembly levied heavy duties on spirituous liquors imported into Anson County from South Carolina, and later forbade the ranging of South Carolina cattle within the bounds of North Carolina.

But retaliatory measures and vain petitions to the Crown were less effective than the constructive measures which accompanied them. Such a measure was the act, passed in 1762, for the incorporation of a market town called Campbellton at the head of navigation of the Cape Fear River. One of the reasons cited for the passage of this act was the hope that "the trade of the counties of Anson and Rowan which at present centers in Charlestown, South Carolina, to the great prejudice of this Province, will be drawn down to the said town." To promote this result acts were also passed for the building of roads from the Dan River on the Virginia line and from Shallow Ford on the Yadkin to Campbellton. These wise measures ultimately turned much of the trade of the back country from Charleston to Campbellton, thence down the Cape Fear to Wilmington, brought the West into closer relations with the East, and checked the tendency of the western counties of North Carolina to become mere outlying districts of South Carolina.

Between the Albemarle section of North Carolina and Virginia existed trade relations similar to those between the back country and South Carolina. Those relations and Virginia's hostile policy based on them have already been discussed. But while North Carolina remained a proprietary colony no tribunal existed sufficiently interested in its welfare with power to grant relief. Its transfer to the Crown, however, placed it in a much more favorable position with respect to its more powerful northern neighbor. The Albemarle planters were quick to understand their new status, and in 1731 sought relief by appealing to the Board of Trade to repeal the Virginia statute of 1726, originally passed in 1679, which prohibited the shipment of North Carolina tobacco through Virginia ports. The petitioners declared that tobacco was the chief product by which they "subsisted and provided their families with all kinds of European goods," that they could not export it through their own ports because of the shallow inlets along the North Carolina coast, and that unless the relief they sought was granted they would either be reduced to poverty or be compelled to "fall upon such usefull Manufactorys" as would render unnecessary the importation of European goods "and consequently be prejudicial to the Trade of Great Britain." Suggestions that the colonies might establish manufacturing enterprises always frightened British statesmen, and the hint of the Albemarle planters had the desired effect. The Board of Trade adopted their view of the Virginia statute, and upon its recommendation the king repealed the obnoxious act, November 25, 1731.

The repeal of this statute and the settlement of their boundary line removed the chief causes of controversy between the two colonies. Another source of ill feeling was removed when North Carolina assumed the dignity of a crown colony, a change which made necessary the adoption by the Virginia government of a more respectful official attitude toward the younger colony. But perhaps the most important element in drawing the two colonies together was the influence of the German and Scotch-Irish settlers who, after 1735, poured into the back country of both provinces. Coming in search of good land, these settlers cared little whether they found it on the headwaters of the James or on the headwaters of the Yadkin. They brought with them none of the ancient prejudices that existed in the older communities of both provinces. Members of the same family setting out together from Philadelphia would often separate, some finding the object of their search in Virginia, others passing on into North Carolina. Their church organizations, too, Presbyterian, Lutheran, German Reformed, and Moravian, existing independently of vestry laws, took no account of provincial boundary lines. Finally, the presence on their frontier of powerful savage nations which struggled desperately to stay their advance, was an ever-present common danger which drew them into the bonds of a common defence. Under the stimulus of these influences ancient prejudices and feelings of hostility between the two colonies gradually gave way to sentiments of genuine respect and mutual good will.

The presence of powerful Indian tribes on their western frontier gave the governments of Virginia, North Carolina, South Carolina and Georgia many common problems which drew them into closer relations with each other. Unfortunately these relations were not always of a friendly character. Speaking broadly, and with respect only to their relations to the English colonies, there were two classes of Indian nations. First there were those who had been reduced to the position of tributaries to the whites; secondly, those whose territory had not yet been violated by the feet of white settlers and who were still sufficiently numerous and powerful to maintain their independence. Each of the colonies had taken certain of the former class under its protection, was keenly jealous of its authority over them, eager to engross their trade, and quick to resent any encroachments upon their rights and interests. Indian affairs in general, however, came within the activities of the Board of Trade which exercised a general supervision over them and determined the broad lines of policy to be followed.

In 1730 the board instructed Burrington to make a report

on the several tribes in North Carolina and their numbers. In Eastern North Carolina he found representatives of six nations. One of these had formerly been tributary to Virginia but had recently, by the running of the Carolina-Virginia boundary line, been brought within the jurisdiction of North Carolina. The other tribes were the Hatteras, the Mattamuskeets, the Pottasketes, the Chowanocs, and the Tuscarora. None of them, except the Tuscarora, exceeded twenty families. They were indeed but miserable remnants of the once powerful tribes of the ancient lords of the forest. The greater part of the Tuscarora had been driven out of the province as a result of the wars of 1711-1713, and that nation, formerly so formidable and warlike, whose power had been all but sufficient to destroy the English colony, was now reduced to about 200 fighting men who had been preserved only through the timid and treacherous policy of their chief, Tom Blunt. In 1730 these nations all lived within the English settlements on reservations set apart for them by the provincial government. After the Tuscarora War the Assembly, in 1715, passed an "Act for Restraining the Indyans from molesting or Injureing the Inhabitants of this Government and for Secureing to the Indyans the right and property of their lands." Commenting on this act after fifteen years of trial, Burrington said, "This Law has proved very convenient to prevent any irregularities and misunderstandings with the Tributary Indians that live among us who have ever since behaved peaceably and are now excepting the Tuscaroras decayed and grown very inconsiderable."

Over the affairs of these tributary nations, in their relations with the whites and with each other, the provincial government exercised complete control. The Indians could sell no land without the approval of the governor in Council; they were forbidden to hunt beyond the bounds of their reservations without special license; their commercial dealings with white traders were subjected to rigid supervision. These restrictions were imposed upon them less to restrain their freedom than to protect them against injustice from their white neighbors. In 1741 the Council took the precaution to have the bounds of the Tuscarora reservation surveyed and recorded in the secretary's office "to prevent any Incroachments or disputes with the white people who live round about them." If a tribe wanted to sell any of its land, its chiefs were called into the presence of the governor and Council, the deed was read and explained to them, and upon their acknowledgment that they had received the money and were satisfied, the governor approved the sale. To protect them from the machinations of unscrupulous traders, the Council in 1731 appointed five commissioners of Indian affairs to supervise their commercial dealings with the whites. An illustration of the care with which the Council guarded these commercial transactions occurred at its session on October 14, 1736, when a petition was presented on behalf of Susanna Everard, executrix of Sir Richard Everard, "setting forth that the Tuskarrora Indians are indebted to the said Susanna £203 in Drest Deer Skins and praying that they may be compelled to discharge the same." The Council refused to act on the petition but referred it to the commissioners for Indian affairs and to prevent frauds from being practiced upon the Indians passed an order that "for the future the Indians Traders do not presume to trust or give any credit to the Indians and that the aforesaid Commissioners take care to see this Order observed." How complete was the government's authority over these tributary tribes appears from the act of the Tuscarora in 1739 in petitioning the governor for permission to choose a "king." The governor granted the petition, fixed the time and place of election, and directed that the Indians "present to his Excellency for his approbation such Person as they shall agree upon and make choice for their King."

The government's control over the Indians' inter-tribal relations was necessary to the preservation of peace in the settlements, for while these tributary tribes were subdued by the whites they still nourished their hereditary enmities among themselves which might at any time involve the whites as well as the red men. The Tuscarora were particularly hard to hold in the leash. They could not forget that in the days of their power they had domineered over the surrounding tribes, nor altogether forego that pleasure in the days of their decline. In 1730 they fell upon "the Saponies and other petty Nations associated with them," in Virginia, and drove them to seek refuge among the Catawba. For the Catawba they cherished a consuming hatred. In their life-and-death struggle against European civilization in 1711-1713, Catawba warriors had gone to the aid of their enemies, and half a century later, when Bishop Spangenberg passed through their reservation on his way to the Catawba country they sent by him a message of defiance to their enemies asking him to tell them "that there were enough young men among them who knew the way to the Catawba Town." In 1732 Burrington wrote that "there happens small acts of Hostility now and then in hunting on the upper parts of Cape Fear River between our Indians and the Cataubes of South Carolina, which we look to be for our advantage, thinking Indians love and will be doing a little mischief, therefore had rather they should act it upon their own tawny race than the English."

But Burrington overlooked the danger of this policy to the whites, arising from the jealousy with which each colony guarded the interests of its tributary tribes. In 1730 the Virginia government protested vigorously to the North Carolina government against the attacks of the Tuscarora on the Saponies and trouble between the two colonies was averted only by Burrington's prompt action in demanding redress from the Carolina Indians. The mutual hostility between the Tuscarora and the Catawba continually stirred up ill feeling between the two Carolinas. The Catawba dwelt along the waters of the Catawba River and were well known to the Carolinians as allies in the Tuscarora War and as enemies in the Yamassee War. When John Lawson passed through their country in 1701 he found them a "powerful nation." They then numbered perhaps 7,000 people, were able to call 1,500 warriors to battle, and dwelt in numerous towns scattered over an extensive territory. Thirty years later continuous warfare with the more powerful Tuscarora and Cherokee nations, smallpox, and various forms of debauchery introduced by white traders had decreased their number to less than 500 warriors, reduced their towns to six miserable villages, and contracted their territory to a narrow strip along the Catawba River not more than twenty miles in length. Except in 1715, when they joined the Yamassee conspiracy, they had been constant and loyal friends of the English. South Carolina asserted jurisdiction over them and, as we have seen, in her boundary line agreement with North Carolina, stipulated that the line should be so run as to throw their reservation wholly within her territory.

The Catawba were hereditary enemies of the Tuscarora, who constantly raided their possessions in South Carolina. Unfortunately in these raids they were often joined by warriors from the Five Nations who seized or destroyed horses, cattle, slaves, and other property without inquiring whether they belonged to their enemies or to the whites. These raids finally became so numerous and so destructive that in 1730 the settlers complained to Governor Johnson and Johnson sent William Wattis as his agent to the

Tuscarora to demand satisfaction for their past conduct and guarantees for the future. At his request Burrington summoned the Tuscarora chiefs to a conference with himself and the Council and in their presence Wattis presented South Carolina's complaints and demands. He sought to frighten the Tuscarora chiefs into compliance by telling them that if they refused "our Governor would look on them as Enemys and send the Cherokees and Catawbos to cut them off." His charges they met with denial of guilt, and his threat they received with scorn. The only interest they showed in it was to ask whether any "white men would come with the Catawbos to war," and to demand "why could we not let them that were Indians alone make war against Indians without meddling with it."

South Carolina's threat alarmed Burrington much more than it did the Tuscarora. The latter, having received assurances of support from the Five Nations, told Burrington that while they desired to keep the peace with the whites, yet if South Carolina sent white men against them "it may bring on a Warr with the English in General, and may be a matter of consequence to the Country." Burrington knew this was no idle threat but was unable to impress the seriousness of the situation on Governor Johnson. He therefore turned to the Board of Trade to which he wrote: "We expect our Indians will be attackt by those of South Carolina. The Northern Indians called the Five Nations are in Alliance and Amity with ours and have promised to assist them with a Thousand men part of which are already come into this Province." The Board of Trade fully appreciated the gravity of the matter and wrote at once to both Burrington and Johnson to hold their Indians in check and directed Governor William Cosby of New York "to interpose his authority with the five Indian Nations" to keep them quiet. It thought the situation so grave that it appealed to the queen, then acting as regent in the absence of the king, to use her personal authority with the governors of the Carolinas to prevent a war that would certainly "be of the most fatal Consequences to both these Colonies."

South Carolina therefore did not carry out her threat, but the situation strained her relations with North Carolina for a long time. Although the Catawba were allies of the English, and tributaries to a sister colony, they offered every obstacle in their power to the settlement of the region in North Carolina along the upper Pee Dee and Catawba rivers which the governors of South Carolina, particularly Governor Glen, insisted ought to be given to that colony. About 300,000 acres of the McCulloh grant were within this region and were "claimed by the Catauboe Indians and which they will by no means permit any white Settlers thereon." Again, in 1749, "several wicked and evil disposed Persons in Anson County * * * had the boldness and Insolence to declare that the present Settlers in that County had no right to the Lands by them possessed and that even his Majesty had no right to those Lands. Which declaration was made to and in presence of the Catawba Indians to the apparent disturbance of the said settlement of Anson County and tending to breed and foment a misunderstanding between his Majesty's said subjects and the said Catawba Indians." The North Carolinians believed—and during the administration of Governor Glen, 1743-1756, had grounds for their belief—that these activities were instigated and supported by officials of the South Carolina government.

To the west of the Catawba dwelt their powerful and inveterate enemies, the Cherokee. With the exception of the Five Nations, the Cherokee were historically the most important Indian nation in American history. They were, as already stated, "the mountaineers of the South, holding the entire Allegheny region from the interlocking headstreams of the Kanawha and Tennessee southward almost to the site of Atlanta, and from the Blue Ridge on the east to the Cumberland Range on the west, a territory embracing an area of about 40,000 square miles, now included in the states of Virginia, Tennessee, North Carolina, South Carolina, Georgia, and Alabama."[2] Those who dwelt in the Keowee Valley in South Carolina were known as the Lower Cherokee, those on the Little Tennessee as the Middle Cherokee, and those on the Holston as the Upper Cherokee. According to the best authorities they had in 1735 "sixty-four towns and villages, populous and full of children," with a total population of not less than 17,000 of whom 6,000 were fighting men. Four years later an epidemic of small-pox, brought to Carolina in a slave ship, swept away nearly half their number. The awful mortality was due largely to their ignorance of this new and strange disease. Knowing no proper remedy for it, the poor savages sought relief in the Indian's universal panacea for

---

[2] Mooney, James: Myths of the Cherokee. (Nineteenth Annual Report of American Bureau of Ethnology, Part I, p. 14.)

all "strong" sickness, viz., cold plunge baths in the running streams. No worse treatment could have been devised. The pestilence swept unchecked from town to town. Despair fell upon the nation. The priests, losing faith in their ancient ordinances, threw away their sacred paraphernalia. Hundreds of warriors on beholding their frightful disfigurement committed suicide. In spite of these losses, however, the Cherokee remained strong in numbers and in geographical position. Before 1730 they treated with the white man on terms of equality and had never bowed to his yoke; while both French and English eagerly sought alliance with them in their struggle for the mastery in North America.

The French, after planting their first permanent settlement in the South at Biloxi Bay, in 1699, had made rapid advances upon the back country of the Carolinas. By 1714 they had reached the Coosa River on which, a few miles above the site of Montgomery, they had built Fort Toulouse, known to the English as "the fort at the Albamas." They were so much more successful in their dealings with the Indians than the English that by 1730 most of the tribes between the settlements of the European rivals were either in active alliance with them or strongly disposed in their favor. In 1721 the Board of Trade in a report to the king described the situation as follows: "The Indian Nations lying between Carolina and the French settlements on the Mississippi are about 9,200 fighting men of which number 3,400 whom we formerly Traded with are entirely debauched to the French Interest by their new settlement and Fort at the Albamas. About 2,000 more * * * Trade at present indifferently with both, but it is to be feared that these likewise will be debauched by the French unless proper means be used to keep them in your Majesty's Interest. The remaining 3,800 Indians are the Cherokees, a Warlike Nation Inhabiting the Apalatche Mountains, these being still at enmity with the French might with less difficulty be secured, and it certainly is of the highest consequence that they should be engaged in your Majestys Interest, for should they once take another part not only Carolina but Virginia likewise would be exposed to their Excursions."

Recognizing the wisdom of this advice, the royal government immediately after the transfer of the Carolinas to the Crown, dispatched Sir Alexander Cumming on a secret mission to the Cherokee. The king's envoy met the Cherokee chiefs and warriors at their ancient town of Nequassee, the present Franklin, North Carolina, in April, 1730. His bold bearing so impressed the red men that they conceded all of his demands and agreed to an alliance with the English. In order to cement this alliance, Cumming persuaded them to send a delegation of seven chiefs to England. At Whitehall these grim savages of the New World were received by the king with great solemnity, and there in the name of their people, did homage to him by laying at his feet the "crown" of their nation which consisted of four scalps of enemies and five eagle tails, the "feathers of peace." On September 9, 1730, they concluded with the Board of Trade a treaty in which they stipulated: To live together with the English "as the children of one Family whereof the Great King is a kind and loving Father;" to be "always ready at the Governor's command to fight against any Nation whether they be white men or Indians who shall dare to molest or hurt the English;" to "take care to keep the trading path clean and that there be no blood in the path where the English white men tread;" not "to trade with the white men of any other Nation but the English nor permit white men of any other Nation to build any Forts, Cabins, or plant corn amongst them;" to apprehend and deliver "any Negro slaves [who] shall run away into the woods from their English masters;" to leave to punishment by due process of English law any Indian who should kill an Englishman, and any Englishman who should kill an Indian. This treaty was confirmed with solemn ceremony by both the contracting parties. The English as a token of friendship gave the red men a substantial supply of guns, ammunition, and red paint, while Chief Scalilasken Ketaugusta, in behalf of his colleagues, concluded an eloquent harangue by "laying down his Feathers upon the table," and saying, "This is our way of talking which is the same to us as your letters in the Book are to you, and to you Beloved Men we deliver these feathers in confirmation of all we have said and of our Agreement to your Articles." Soon after this ceremony the chiefs took ship for Carolina where they arrived, wrote Governor Johnson, "in good health and mightily well satisfied with His Majesty's bounty to them."

The relations of the colonies with the great Indian nations, such as the Iroquois, the Cherokee, and the Creeks, grew in importance as the rivalry between the French and the English grew in intensity. These tribes occupied such vast stretches of territory which touched upon so many colonies, that it soon became apparent that questions growing out of their relations could not be considered merely as provincial questions. In 1757, the North Carolina Assembly declared that the "many flagrant Frauds and Abuses" committed by white traders in their commercial relations with the Indians, "cannot but tend to alienate their Affections, and give the French the greater opportunity of insinuating themselves and carrying on their destructive Schemes against the British Colonies." Both the mother country and the colonies, therefore, came to see that all such Indian affairs were really imperial questions, and the king acting upon the advice of the Board of Trade decided to take them under the immediate supervision of the Crown. In 1757, therefore, Virginia, North Carolina, South Carolina, and Georgia were erected into a southern department for Indian affairs and Edmund Atkins was commissioned by the Crown "Agent for and Superintendent of the Affairs of the several Nations or Tribes of Indians inhabiting the Frontiers of [those provinces] and their Confederates." The object aimed at, as Governor Dobbs said, was "to connect all our Indian Allies in one Interest in Conjunction with the other provinces in which the Indians reside." Its success of course depended upon the sympathetic co-operation of the several colonies. In December, 1757, therefore, the North Carolina Assembly passed an act which placed trade with the Catawba, Cherokee and other "Western Indians within the limits of this Province" completely under the supervision of Atkins and his successors, and clothed them with ample power to enforce their authority. In 1763 Atkins was succeeded by Captain John Stuart who continued in office until after the Revolution had removed the British government as a factor in Indian affairs.

CHAPTER XV

COLONIAL WARS

In their political and commercial affairs the colonies felt their connection with the mother country chiefly in its burdens and restrictions, but they found some compensation in the protection which their connection with the British Empire assured them. Their peace and safety were constantly threatened from three allied sources. First there were enemy Indians whose presence was an ever threatening danger. Then the southern colonies in particular were never free from the menace of the Spaniards in Florida for, as Fiske graphically puts it, Carolina was "the border region where English and Spanish America marched upon each other." But greater than the danger from either Indians or Spaniards was the danger from the French. In 1608, one year after the founding of Jamestown, Champlain founded Quebec and secured for France the region drained by the St. Lawrence; in 1682 La Salle, inspired by dreams of a great continental empire, seized the mouth of the Mississippi and established the supremacy of France over all the region drained by the Father of Waters. Between these two distant heads, stretched the vast empire of New France. The interests of New France clashed with those of New England everywhere along their far-flung frontiers, and these clashing interests brought the two colonial empires into a century-long life-and-death struggle for supremacy in North America. The several stages of this contest were marked by four wars known in American history as King William's War (1689-1697), Queen Anne's War (1702-1713), King George's War (1744-1748), and the French and Indian War (1754-1763).

For North Carolina and South Carolina, the proximity of the Spanish and French settlements held a three-fold danger. There were, first, the danger of a direct attack upon their unprotected coast towns; second, the danger of an indirect attack through the Indians; and, third, the danger of being cut off entirely from farther westward expansion. The two colonies were fully alive to the seriousness of their situation and as we have seen freely assisted each other in meeting it. But they also realized that the menace was not to them alone, but to the whole of British-America and they long sought in vain to impress the home government with this view. St. Augustine afforded the enemy an excellent base for operations against the Carolinas both by land and by sea. In 1686 a Spanish force from St. Augustine invaded South Carolina and destroyed the colony at Port Royal. In 1702, upon the outbreak of Queen Anne's War, South Carolina sent an expedition against St. Augustine, but it ended in disaster. Four years later a combined French and Spanish squadron attacked Charleston, but was beaten off with heavy losses. During these wars, according to Governor Burrington, parties from French and Spanish privateers and men-of-war "frequently landed and plundered" the coast of North Carolina, and the colony was put to "great expenses" in "establishing a force to repell them." Two of the Lords Proprietors declared, "That in 1707 when Carolina was attacked by the French it cost the Province twenty thousand pounds and that neither His Majesty nor any of his predecessors had been at any charge from the first grant to defend the said Province against the French or other enemies."

It was, however, by their indirect attacks through the Indians that the Spaniards and the French inflicted the greatest losses upon the Carolinas. In 1715 they organized the great Indian conspiracy that resulted in the Yamassee War. These rival and generally hostile tribes, said a group of South Carolina merchants in a petition to the king for aid, "never yet had policy enough to form themselves into Alliances, and would not in all Probability have proceeded so far at this time had they not been incouraged, directed and supplied by the Spaniards at St. Augustine and the French at Moville [Mobile] and their other Neighbouring Settlements." In a letter to Lord Townsend, the king's principle secretary of state, Governor Craven declared that if South Carolina were destroyed, as at one time seemed not improbable, "the French from Moville, or from Canada, or from old France" would take possession and "threaten the whole British Settlements." The Carolina officials could not make the home government understand that the attack was not merely a local Indian outbreak, aimed at South Carolina alone, but that it was a phase of the general policy of the French in their struggle for supremacy in America and was aimed at all the British American dominions.

Even more serious than these wars, because if successful more permanent in their results, were the French plans in the Mississippi Valley. In a memorial to the Board of Trade, in 1716, Richard Beresford, of South Carolina, called attention to the fact that the French along the Mississippi River had already encroached "very far within the bounds of the Charter of Carolina" and had "settled themselves on the back of the improved part of that Province." If permitted to remain there they would become a permanent obstacle to the westward march of English settlements, confining them to the narrow region between the Atlantic and the Alleghanies. Yet all efforts to arouse the home authorities to a realization of the danger were vain. The Lords Proprietors could not, and as long as the Carolinas remained proprietary colonies, the Crown would not lift a hand in their defence. It was not until after South Carolina, in 1719, had thrown off the rule of the Lords Proprietors, largely because of their inability to aid in the defence of the colony, that the Board of Trade manifested any interest in the situation. In 1720 it advised the king that considering that the people of South Carolina "have lately shaken off the Proprietors Government, as incapable of affording them protection, [and] that the Inhabitants are exposed to incursions of the Barbarous Indians, [and] to the encroachments of their European neighbours," he should forthwith send a force for the defence of that colony. But this advice, like the repeated appeals of the colonies, went unheeded and the Carolinas were left to their own resources.

The home government, however, finally awaked to a realization of the stakes at issue and in the third of the series of wars for supremacy in America undertook to co-operate with the colonies on a large scale. The war really began in 1739 when England declared war on Spain, though France did not formally enter the struggle until five years later. In attacking Spain, England's purpose was to break down the Spanish colonial system and open Spanish-American ports to English commerce. The government accordingly planned to strike a blow at some vital point in Spain's American colonies with a combined force of British and American troops. In the summer of 1740, therefore, the king called upon the colonies for their contingents of men and money. This was the first call ever made upon them as a whole for co-operation in an imperial enterprise, and the colonies responded with enthusiasm. Throughout the summer preparations were actively pushed forward both in England and in America, and in October a fleet of thirty ships of the line and ninety transports, carrying 15,000 sailors and 12,000 soldiers sailed from Spithead, England, for Jamaica, where they were joined by American troops from all the colonies except New Hampshire, Delaware, South Carolina, and Georgia. Delaware's contingent was probably counted in that of Pennsylvania, while those from South Carolina and Georgia were probably kept at home to protect their frontiers from attack by the Spaniards of Florida. The other nine colonies sent thirty-six companies of 100 men each. Of these Massachusetts contributed six, Rhode Island two, Connecticut two, New York five, New Jersey two, Pennsylvania eight, Maryland three, Virginia four, and North Carolina four.

In July, 1740, Governor Gabriel Johnston received instructions from the king directing him to convene the Assembly and inform it of the government's plans. The king declared that he "had not thought fit to fix any particular quota" for the colony as he did not want to place any limitation on its zeal, but he expected it to exert itself in the common cause as much as its circumstances would allow. In reply to the governor's message, the Assembly promised to "contribute to the utmost" of its power and assured him that "no Colony hath with more chearfullness contributed than we shall to forward the intended descent upon some of the Spanish Colonies." This promise was promptly made good. The Assembly passed an act levying a tax of three shillings on each poll in the colony, payable, owing to the scarcity of money among the people, in "commodities of the country" at fixed rates, provided adequate machinery for its prompt collection, and directed that warehouses be erected for storing the proceeds. The governor expressed the "highest satisfaction" at the Assembly's action, saying: "You have now given evident proof of your unfeigned zeal for his Majesty's service and considering the circumstances of the country contributed as liberally as any of our neighbouring colonies." He estimated the levy authorized by the Assembly at £1,200 sterling, which was sufficient to equip and subsist four companies of 100 men each until they could join the army at Jamaica when they would be put on the payroll of the Crown.

The governor's call for recruits brought a prompt response. Four companies containing a total of 400 men, a force in proportion to population equivalent to 25,000 at the present time, were quickly enrolled. "I have good reason to believe," wrote the governor to the Duke of Newcastle, "that we could easily have raised 200 more if it had been possible to negotiate the bills of exchange in this part of the continent; but as that was impracticable, we were obliged to rest satisfyed with four companies." Three of these companies were recruited in the Albemarle section, the other at Cape Fear. The Albemarle companies were under command of Captains Halton, Coletrain, and Pratt, the Cape Fear company under Captain James Innes. The former embarked at Edenton early in November, 1740, and sailed for Wilmington where they were joined by Captain Innes' company. Says the Wilmington correspondent of the *South Carolina Gazette,* November 24, 1740: "The 15th Inst. Capt. James Innes, with his compleat Company of Men, went on board the Transport to proceed for the General Rendezvous. They were in general brisk and hearty, and long for Nothing so much as a favorable Wind, that they may be among the first in Action. Capt. Innes has taken out Letters of Marque and Reprisal, and if any Spanish Ship is to be met with, he doubts not of giving a proper account of them. * * * The Governor and Assembly of this Province proceeded with great Spirit on this Occasion, the lower House chearfully granted an Aid to his Majesty of £1500 Sterling, to assist in Victualling and Transporting their Quota of Troops. When so poor a Province gives such Testimony of their Zeal and Spirit against our haughty Enemy, it is to be hoped the Ministry at Home will be convinced that it is the Voice of all his Majesty's Subjects, both at home and abroad, Humble the proud Spaniard, bring down his haughty Looks."

From Wilmington the North Carolina companies sailed directly for Jamaica where they joined the united British and colonial forces. The squadron was under the command of Admiral Edward Vernon; the army was first under Lord Cathcart, and after his death under General Wentworth. Sir William Gooch, then governor of Virginia, was in immediate command of the "American Regiments." In February, 1741, the fleet sailed to attack Cartagena on the coast of Venezuela. From the first the expedition was doomed to failure. Ill-feeling and rivalry between the land forces and the naval forces thwarted every movement. The only successful effort made throughout the campaign was the assault on Boca-Chica (little mouth), the entrance to the harbor of Cartagena. North Carolina troops participated in this attack. The forts were carried, the fleet entered the harbor, and troops were landed to attack the forts defending the town. This attack on the forts was repulsed with severe losses, heavy rains set in, an epidemic of fever broke out among the troops, and within less than two days half of them were dead or otherwise incapacitated for service. Nothing was left but acknowledgment of defeat, re-embarkation and return to Jamaica. The lives of 20,000 men had been sacrificed to the incompetency and jealousy of the commanding officers. Of the North Carolina contingent but few survived. The Cape Fear company, originally 100 strong, reached Wilmington in January, 1743, reduced to 25 men.

North Carolina's losses on this expedition, however, were not comparable to those she suffered at home. For eight years Spanish and French privateers infested her waters, captured her ships, ravaged her coasts, plundered her towns, and levied tribute upon her inhabitants almost with impunity. In May, 1741, they captured two merchantmen out of Edenton "before they had been half an hour at sea," while the owner of one of them "had the Mortification to see his Vessel and Cargo taken before his face as he stood on the shore." Within the next ten days, four other ships fell victims to the same privateers. On May 12th, a sloop bound from North Carolina to Hull, England, was captured off Cape Fear. In July another merchantman was taken "within the Bar of Ocracoke;" the owner estimated his loss at £700 sterling. The same privateer had already taken six other prizes. In August reports from Wilmington mentioned the capture of a schooner and a sloop besides "many other vessels" bound for that port. The Indian Queen, North Carolina to Bristol, was taken in October. Similar reports run through the succeeding years. In June, 1747, it was reported "that there are now no less than 9 Spanish Privateers cruizing on this coast." The Molly, from Cape Fear to Barbados; the Rebecca, from Charleston to Cape Fear; the John and Mary, from Cape Fear to Bristol, "with a Cargo of Pitch, Tar and Turpentine;" and an unnamed vessel from London to Cape Fear, were but a few of their prizes. In July, 1748, three ships were "cut out of Ocracoke Inlet" by Spanish privateers. Of the great majority of captures no reports are now available, but some idea of the havoc wrought in colonial commerce may be gathered from the shipping reports of the *South Carolina Gazette*. That periodical reported as clearing between Charleston and North Carolina ports during the five years before the declaration of war, 1735-1739, inclusive, eighty vessels; during the five years, 1744 to 1748 inclusive, the same paper reported as clearing between the same ports only twenty-one vessels.

It is not without interest to note that as the privateersmen revived memories of the deeds of "Blackbeard," so also they made skillful use of the same inlets and harbors that had so often sheltered the famous pirate. "The Spaniards," it was reported, in 1741, "have built themselves Tents on Ocracoke Island; Two of the Sloops lie in Teache's Hole," where they found shelter from the British men-of-war. After cruising about Chesapeake Bay and ravaging the Virginia coast, says a report in July, 1741, they sought safety from the Hector, a 40-gun man-of-war, "in Teache's Hole in North Carolina where they landed, killed as many Cattle as they wanted, and tallowed their Vessels' Bottoms." Another favorite rendezvous was Lookout harbor "where they wood, water, kill Cattle, and carry their Prizes till they are ready to go (with them) to their respective Homes." Men-of-war were afraid to seek them in Lookout harbor because of their "Want of Knowledge of it."

Resistance to the Spaniards was feeble and spasmodic. The Assembly made appropriations for the erection of forts at Ocracoke, Core Sound, Bear Inlet, and Cape Fear, but none of them proved of any service. Fort Johnston, named in honor of the governor, afterwards played an important part in the history of the Cape Fear region, but during the Spanish War was ineffective as a defence against the enemy. In June, 1739, before the declaration of war and in anticipation of it, the king authorized Governor Johnston to issue letters of marque and reprisal against Spanish shipping, and a few privateers were fitted out at Wilmington, but the results of their work were negligible. For instance, in July, 1741, Wilmington merchants fitted out two privateers, one of twenty-four guns, Captain George Walker, the other a small sloop, Captain Daniel Dunbibin, "to go in quest of the Spanish Privateers which infest this Coast," but as late as September no news had been received of them. British men-of-war also patrolled the coast. There were the Hector, forty guns, Captain Sir Yelverton Peyton, the Tartar, Captain George Townsend, the Swift, Captain Bladwell, the Cruizer, and another, name not mentioned, under command of Captain Peacock. But the merchants found grounds for complaining of the lack of vigilance even among the men-of-war, and it was openly charged that "the Spaniards were so encouraged by the Indolence, if not the C——ce [cowardice] of Sir Y——n" [Yelverton], that they ravaged the coast with impunity. Other British commanders, however, were more active. In July, 1741, Captain Peacock compelled the Spaniards to abandon their shelter at Ocracoke and to burn "the Tents they had built on Ocracoke Island." May 26, 1742, the Swift after an all day chase overtook a privateer off Ocracoke Inlet and engaged her in battle. The privateer, however, got the best of the fight, shot away the mainstays and forestays of the Swift, compelling her to put back into Wilmington for repairs, and then escaped in the darkness. A few months later the Swift had better luck, capturing a large Spanish sloop which she brought into Wilmington and converted into a British privateer.

Emboldened by their successes, the Spaniards became ambitious. In 1747 they attacked and captured the town of Beaufort which they held for several days and plundered before being driven out. The next year their audacity reached its climax in an attack on Brunswick. September 3, 1748, three Spanish privateers, the Fortune, a sloop of 130 tons, carrying ten 6-pounders and fourteen swivels, Captain Vincent Lopez, the Loretta, carrying four 4-pounders, four 6-pounders, and twelve swivels, Captain Joseph Leon Munroe, and a converted merchantman, appeared off the Cape Fear bar. Two days later they dropped anchor off Brunswick and opened fire upon the shipping there. At the same time a force which they had landed below the town attacked from the land side. Taken by surprise, the inhabitants fled in confusion. The enemy thereupon seized five ships "and several small craft" that were in the harbor, captured the collector of the port and several other men, and "plundered and destroyed everything without fear of being disturbed."

But the inhabitants quickly recovering from their surprise organized a force of eighty men, under command of Captain William Dry, and returned to the attack. They in turn surprised their enemy in the midst of their plundering, killed or captured many of them, drove the others to the shelter of their ships, and were vigorously "pursuing their good fortunes till they were saluted with a very hot fire from the commodore sloop's great guns, which, * * * however, did not prevent their killing or taking all the stragglers." The Fortune continued the bombardment till suddenly "to our great amazement and (it may be believed) joy, she blew up." Most of her crew, including her commander and all of his officers, perished in the explosion or were drowned. Thereupon, the Loretta, which had gone up the river in pursuit of a prize, "hoisted bloody colours," dropped down the river again, and opened fire "pretty smartly" on the town. But this turned out to be mere bluster. Soon lowering her "bloody colours," she "hoisted white in her shroud" and sent a flag of truce ashore "desiring to have liberty to go off with all the vessels, and promising on that condition to do no further damage." But Captain Dry boldly replied "that they might think themselves well off to get away with their own vessel, that he could not consent to their carrying away any other, and would take care they should do no more damage; but he proposed to let them go without interruption if they would deliver up all the English prisoners they had, with everything belonging to the place." The Spaniard's only answer to this defiance was to abandon all of his prizes except the Nancy, which he had armed and manned with a Spanish crew, and to slip quietly down the river under a white flag. He anchored off Bald-Head and let it be known that he was ready to negotiate for an exchange of prisoners. This was soon effected through a commission sent by Major John Swann who had arrived from Wilmington with 130 men and taken command. The Spaniard then put to sea and disappeared.

In this attack, the Carolinians escaped without the loss of a man. They had two slightly wounded, none killed. Their property losses, however, were heavy for what the Spaniards "did not carry away they broke or cut to pieces." Nevertheless the Carolinians won a great triumph, for as they justly boasted, "notwithstanding our ignorance in military affairs, our want of arms and ammunition (having but 3 charges per man when we attacked them), the delay of our friends in coming to our assistance, and the small number [we] were composed of (many of which were negroes)," they had beaten off a much superior enemy consisting of 220 men and three armed ships, compelling them to abandon their prizes, and causing them a loss of 140 men, more than one-half of their force, including their commanding officer.

The attack on Brunswick was made more than two months after peace had been declared. On June 17, 1748, the Board of Trade wrote Governor Johnston, "Preliminaries for a Peace have been signed at Aix-la-Chapelle by the Ministers of all the Powers engaged in the war." This treaty, however, settled none of the questions at issue between the rivals in America; it merely afforded them a breathing spell in which to prepare for a greater struggle yet to come. The French, much more alive to the situation than their rivals, began at once to take advantage of this lull in the contest. Realizing that something more than mere assertion of title was necessary to secure to them the territory along the Ohio and the Mississippi, which formed so large a part of New France, they built a series of strong forts to connect the two distant heads of their empire. By the middle of the eighteenth century, therefore, the long frontier between Montreal and New Orleans was defended by more than sixty forts. Many of these forts stood on land claimed by New York, Pennsylvania, Virginia, and the Carolinas, yet in these colonies, only a few people clearly appreciated the significance of the French movements, or understood how to check them. The most significant of the English counter-movements was the organization in London and Virginia of the Ohio Land Company for planting English settlements on the east bank of the Ohio River. But this region was also claimed by the French and it was here that the first clash came. In 1753 Governor Robert Dinwiddie of Virginia learning that the French were encroaching upon this territory sent Major George Washington on his famous mission to demand their withdrawal. Upon their refusal, Dinwiddie ordered Washington to seize and fortify the point where the Alleghany and Monongahela rivers unite to form the Ohio. But Washington had scarcely begun his work when a superior force of Frenchmen appeared, drove him away and erected on the site he had chosen a strong fortress which they called Fort Duquesne. Thus began the great war which was to decide the mastery of North America.

In this contest the English had the advantage of numerical strength and interior lines, but these advantages were fully offset by the unity of command and purpose which prevailed with the French. From Quebec to New Orleans, all New France moved in obedience to a single autocratic will. The English on the other hand were divided into thirteen separate governments, politically independent of each other, and largely self-governing. Not a soldier could be enrolled, not a shilling levied in any English colony until a popular assembly had been persuaded of its wisdom; and no concerted movement could be undertaken until many different executives had been consulted and many different legislative bodies, jealous of their authority and hostile to every suggestion that conflicted with their local interests, had given consent. The French of course were aware of this situation and counted it as one of the strong elements in their favor. "The French," observed Governor Dinwiddie, in 1754, "too justly observe this want of connection in the Colonies, and from thence conclude (as they declare without reserve) that although we are vastly superior to them in Numbers, yet they can take and secure the Country before we can agree to hinder them." He thought that an act of Parliament might be necessary to cure the evil. The necessity for co-operation was clearly understood in England and the government urged it upon the colonies in almost every dispatch that crossed the Atlantic. In July, 1754, President Rowan of North Carolina received a rebuke from the government because of his "total Silence upon that part of His Majesty's orders which relate to a concert with the other Colonies." But except among a few far-sighted leaders no sentiment existed in any of the English colonies in favor of a closer union. In 1754, at the beginning of the great war, the colonies rejected with scant ceremony the Albany Plan of Union which, especially as a war measure, had many excellent features to recommend it.

The attitude of North Carolina toward the Albany Plan was typical of the attitude of the other colonies. Governor Dobbs laid it before the Assembly at its December session in 1754 and asked for its consideration saying that the king had instructed him "to promóte a happy union among the provinces for their General Union and Defence." But the Assembly was not interested in it. It merely ordered the plan to be printed and distributed among its members "for their Mature Consideration," but postponed discussion to the next session and then forgot it. Other colonies gave it even less consideration. The colonies had to drink deep of the cup of bitter experience, of suffering and disaster, before they were ready for a real union.

In another respect, too, the French had an advantage over the English. The French settlements were little more than military outposts, garrisoned by trained soldiers, fully equipped with the best arms, and commanded by experienced officers. The English colonies on the other hand were industrial and agricultural communities, thoroughly non-militaristic and almost wholly unprepared for war. Here again the situation in North Carolina was typical. Although that colony had just gone through the Spanish War in which its troops had been defeated, its coasts ravaged and its towns plundered, the lessons of that experience had been lost upon both governor and people. Not a fort protected its long frontier, and the money appropriated for defences along the coast had been largely unspent. No fortifications had been erected at Ocracoke, Lookout, or Topsail Inlet. At Cape Fear, Fort Johnston was still unfinished and almost totally unmanned. Though the plan called for sixteen 9-pounders and thirty swivels, the fort contained only five 6-pounders and four 2-pounders, and had no regular garrison.

Preparations for offense were no better. On paper the militia numbered more than 15,000 infantry and 400 cavalry, but long neglect had destroyed its organization. President Rowan complained in 1753, that from the indolence of Governor Johnston, the militia had fallen into decay. One of the first acts of Governor Dobbs upon assuming the administration in 1754 was to call for a militia return. The result was alarming. There were twenty-two counties each of which was supposed to have a fully organized regiment. The returns showed that in most of them there were organizations in name only, and in many not even that. Beaufort had no colonel. In Bertie County eight companies were "without officers." Five of Edgecombe's fourteen companies reported their captains "removed, laid down, or dead." Every one of Granville's eight companies was without a captain. In New Hanover the major had "thrown up" his commission. In Orange the colonel had resigned, five captains had left the county or refused to serve, fourteen lieutenancies and ensigncies were vacant. Tyrrell reported: "The Coll. dead, the Lieut. Coll. and Major have neglected to act." Four counties made no returns.

The disorganization was bad, the equipment worse. Governor Dobbs stated that the militia were "not half armed" and that such arms as they had were "very bad." Great was his alarm upon finding "that there is not one pound of [public] gunpowder or shot in store in the Province, nor any arms;" nor were there "twelve barrels of gunpowder in the Province in Traders hands." He felt compelled to appeal to the king for ammunition because "at present we have no credit and must pay double price if any is imported by merchants." He afterwards learned that Beaufort County had on hand fifty pounds of public gunpowder. Beaufort also reported 150 pounds of large shot, but "no arms in the publick store." Chowan had 400 pounds of bullets and swan shot, but no powder and no arms. The militia of Johnston County were "indifferently armed," and without ammunition. Bladen, Carteret, Duplin, Edgecombe, Granville, New Hanover, Northampton, Onslow, Pasquotank, Perquimans, Tyrrell, all reported "no arms," or "no arms or ammunition." Six counties made no report on arms and ammunition, probably because they had none. In Granville County the men were drilled with wooden clubs! The situation was somewhat relieved by a gift from the king, in 1754, of 1,000 stand of arms which were distributed to the exposed counties on the western frontier, to the counties on the coast, and to the companies raised for service in Virginia. But even this relief was largely nul-

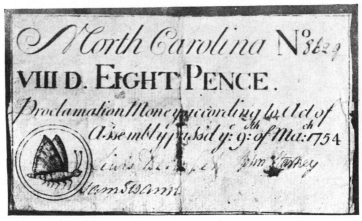

CURRENCY ISSUED DURING FRENCH AND INDIAN WAR

lified by the conduct of the troops in Virginia, who, after Braddock's defeat, "deserted in great numbers," taking their arms and equipment away with them.

Anticipating hostilities with the French, the king in August, 1753, instructed the governors of all the English colonies "in case of Invasion" to co-operate with each other to the fullest extent. Immediately after the attack on Washington, therefore, Governor Dinwiddie hastened to call upon the governors of Pennsylvania, New York, Maryland, New Jersey, Massachusetts, South Carolina, and North Carolina for assistance in driving the French from Fort Duquesne. President Rowan, then acting-governor of North Carolina, met his Assembly February 19, 1754, and laid the situation before it. He felt sure, he said, that the people of North Carolina would not "sitt still and tamely see a formidable forreign Power" dispossess the English of their western territory, and he asked the Assembly to exert itself "to the utmost in the common cause" by voting at once "a good and seasonable supply" for the support of a military force to assist in the expulsion of the French and their allies. His appeal found a ready response. The Assembly declared that the action of the French "must fire the Breast of every true Lover of his Country with the warmest Resentments" and "certainly Calls for a speedy Remedy." It promised "to furnish as many forces as we can conveniently spare towards this so necessary an Expedition" and "to consider of such ways and means Immediately to supply the Treasury as the Circumstances of our Constituants will admitt" for their maintenance.

The Assembly acted promptly and liberally. Without a dissenting vote it appropriated £12,000 "for raising and providing for a regiment of 750 effective Men to be sent to the Assistance of Virginia." President Rowan did not expect the maintenance of these men to fall upon North Carolina after their arrival in Virginia, so when he ascertained later that each province must maintain its own soldiers, he realized that the £12,000 would be insufficient to support 750 men. Accordingly he was compelled to reduce the force to 450 men. But even this number was 150 more than Virginia raised for the same expedition although it was for the defence of her own soil. The regiment was placed under command of Colonel James Innes who had commanded the Cape Fear company in the Cartagena expedition. Governor Dinwiddie hailed his appointment with great satisfaction, saying to President Rowan, "I am glad Your Regiment comes under the Command of Colo. Innes, whose Capacity, Judgment and cool Conduct, I have great Regard for." He testified to the sincerity of his sentiments by appointing Innes commander-in-chief of the expedition. Colonel Innes hastened at once to the front, leaving his regiment to follow. He arrived at Winchester, Virginia, July 5th, two days after the defeat of Washington's Virginians at Great Meadows; thence he hurried on to Wills Creek, where he afterwards built Fort Cumberland, 140 miles from Fort Duquesne, and there took formal command of the colonial forces.

North Carolina's response to Virginia's appeal for aid was liberal, but her liberality was nullified by extravagance and bad management. President Rowan fixed the pay of privates at three shillings a day and that of officers in proportion, an

extravagance of which Dinwiddie very justly complained because of its effect on the Virginia troops who received only
eight pence a day. Rowan also invested large sums in pork
and beef to be sent to Virginia and sold for Virginia currency
with which to pay the troops after their arrival in that colony, and on most of these transactions he lost heavily. The
organization of the regiment proceeded slowly and this delay
too added to the expense. Consequently the £12,000 appropriated by the Assembly was entirely expended before the
troops ever reached the front, and when they arrived at Winchester, the place of rendezvous, they found that no provisions
and no ammunition had been collected there for them. Their
pay, too, was in arrears. Colonel Innes appealed to Governor
Dinwiddie for advances, but Dinwiddie had no funds which
he could use for this purpose. "I can give no orders for en-
tertaining your regiment," he replied, "as this Dominion will
maintain none but their own forces." Consequently the North
Carolina regiment had scarcely reached Winchester before it
was disbanded and sent home without having struck a blow at
the enemy.

That the struggle had opened so unfavorably for the English was due primarily to their lack of preparation and co-
operation. In October, 1754, therefore, Governor Dinwiddie,
Governor Horatio Sharpe of Maryland, and Governor Dobbs
held a conference at Williamsburg to formulate plans for a
joint attack on Fort Duquesne. Dobbs laid these plans before
his Assembly in December and asked for men and money to
carry them into execution. The Assembly responded by authorizing a company of 100 men for service in Virginia and
another of fifty men for service on the North Carolina frontier, and by voting £8,000 for their subsistence. The company
destined for Virginia was placed under the command of the
governor's son, Captain Edward Brice Dobbs, formerly a
lieutenant in the English army. But before the plans of the
Williamsburg conference could be carried out, they were superseded by others on a much larger scale, arranged in April,
1755, at a conference held at Alexandria, Virginia, between
several of the colonial governors and General Edward Braddock, who had been sent from England to take command of the
forces in Virginia for the reduction of Fort Duquesne. These
new plans called for simultaneous campaigns against the
French on the Ohio, on the Niagara, and on Lake Champlain.
Although North Carolina was not represented at this meet-

ing, both governor and Assembly entered heartily into the arrangements. Captain Dobbs was ordered to move his company at once to Alexandria where Braddock was assembling a force for the expedition against Fort Duquesne. Three months later all British America was thrown into consternation by the disastrous ending of this expedition. Dobbs' North Carolinians, being absent at the time from the main army on a scouting expedition, escaped destruction, but many of them, sharing the general demoralization of the British forces, deserted and made their way back home. With what remained Captain Dobbs joined Colonel Innes at Fort Cumberland, where he continued for nearly a year helping to guard the Virginia frontier.

Immediately after Braddock's defeat, Governor Dobbs convened the Assembly in special session and in a sensible, well-written address pointed out the seriousness of the situation and suggested that "a proper sum cheerfully granted at once will accomplish what a very great sum may not do hereafter." The Assembly promptly voted a supply of £10,000 and authorized the governor to raise three new companies "to protect the Frontier of this Province and to assist the other Colonies in Defence of his Majesty's Territories." To command these companies, the governor commissioned Caleb Grainger, Thomas Arbuthnot, and Thomas McManus captains and sent them to New York to aid in the operations against the French at Niagara and Crown Point. At the same time he ordered Captain Dobbs to withdraw his company from Fort Cumberland and join the other North Carolina companies in New York. Captain Dobbs, promoted to the rank of major, was appointed to command the battalion. The governor declared that he took this action because he found that if Captain Dobbs' company remained in Virginia it would only do guard duty on the frontier, without making any attempt against Fort Duquesne, since the English there had no officers competent to make a plan of operations, nor any artillery; nor was there any likelihood of any assistance from either Maryland or Pennsylvania, "as they don't seem Zealous for the Common Cause of the Colonies." The North Carolina troops arrived at New York May 31st, and shared in the disasters which resulted in the loss of Oswego and the failure to wrest Crown Point from the French. Since the capture of Oswego threw open to the enemy the entire English frontier from New York to Georgia, problems of home defence so strained the resources of the colony that North Carolina was unable to continue to support her troops in New York; the governor accordingly directed their officers to try to induce the men to enlist either in the Loyal American Regiment, or in the regulars. Those who took neither course were allowed to return to North Carolina.

After the loss of Oswego, the Earl of Loudoun, commander-in-chief of the British forces in America, notified the southern governors to prepare for the defence of their frontiers since the French then had free access by the Great Lakes to send troops to the Ohio, and also to attack them through their Indian allies. The situation was so serious that he called a conference at Philadelphia, March 15, 1757, of Dobbs, Dinwiddie, Sharpe, and Denny of Pennsylvania, that he might "concert in Conjunction with them a Plan for the Defence of the Southern Provinces." He informed the governors that since the greater part of the British troops in America would be needed in the northern campaign, he could give the southern colonies only 1,200 regulars, for the rest they would have to shift for themselves. It was agreed, therefore, that they should raise 3,800 men, distributed as follows: Pennsylvania 1,400, Maryland 500, Virginia 1,000, North Carolina 400, and South Carolina 500, making with the regulars, 5,000 men. Of these, 2,000 were to be used in defence of South Carolina and Georgia which were threatened with attack by sea as well as by land. Returning from this conference, Dobbs immediately convened the Assembly, and in a brief and pointed message explained the agreement he had made for the province and asked for the means to carry it out. The Assembly promised, in spite of the large debt already contracted in the common cause, to vote the necessary supplies. An act was accordingly passed appropriating £5,300 and providing for 200 men "to be imployed for the service of South Carolina or at home in case not demanded or wanted there." These troops were speedily raised and ordered to South Carolina under command of Colonel Henry Bouquet, the British officer assigned to command in the southern colonies. At the same time, Governor Dobbs ordered the militia in the counties along the South Carolina border to be ready to join Colonel Bouquet at his command without waiting for further orders from him. However, they were never called upon for active service.

The summer of 1757 was one of the gloomiest in the annals

of the British Empire. Success everywhere crowned the arms of France. In Europe disasters followed each other so rapidly, and some of them were so disgraceful, that Lord Chesterfield exclaimed in despair, "We are no longer a nation!" In America, Braddock's army had been destroyed; Oswego had fallen; the Crown Point expedition had failed; Fort William Henry had been captured. New France "stretched without a break over the vast territory from Louisiana to the St. Lawrence," [1] and not an English fort or an English hamlet remained in the basin of the St. Lawrence, or in all the valley of th• Ohio. In the wigwams of the red men the prestige of the British arms had been so utterly destroyed that the Indians called Montcalm, "the famous man who tramples the English under his feet." [2] But a change was at hand. In July, a new force came into the contest which was destined in a few brief months to wrest from France every foot of her American empire and assure to men of the English-speaking race complete supremacy on the continent of North America. This force was the genius of William Pitt, "the greatest war minister and organizer of victory that the world has seen." [3] Under his leadership the year 1758 was as glorious as that of 1757 had been gloomy. In every quarter of the globe the arms of England were victorious. In Europe and in Asia victory followed victory with dazzling rapidity. In America Louisburg fell, Fort Frontenac surrendered, and Fort Duquesne was captured. "We are forced to ask every morning," wrote Horace Walpole, "what new victory there is, for fear of missing one."

The Assembly of North Carolina had quarreled with Dobbs, but the words and spirit of Pitt inspired it, "notwithstanding the indigency of the country," to renewed efforts in support of the war. On December 30, 1757, Pitt called upon the province, together with other southern colonies, for a force to reduce Fort Duquesne. He appealed to their pride and patriotism by declaring that he would not "limit the Zeal and Ardor of any of His Majesty's Provinces" by suggesting the number of troops for it to raise, but asked each for "as large a Body of Men * * * as the Number of its Inhabitants may

---

[1] Green: Short History of the English People. Revised edition, p. 748.
[2] Parkman: Montcalm and Wolfe, Vol. I, p. 489.
[3] Fiske: New France and New England, p. 315.

allow.'' The North Carolina Assembly, pleading as its excuse for not doing more that the colony's debts incurred in defence not of itself alone, but also of Virginia, New York, and South Carolina, amounted "to above forty Shillings each Taxable," which was "more than the Currency at present circulating among us," voted an aid of £7,000 and 300 men. It requested that these troops be sent to General John Forbes, whom Pitt had sent to Virginia to command the expedition, "without loss of time." Governor Dobbs placed this battalion under the command of Major Hugh Waddell, a young officer whose services on the North Carolina frontier had already attracted wide attention. Waddell raised, organized, and equipped his battalion with dispatch, and marched them to join the forces of General Forbes.

Very different was Forbes' course from that of Braddock. No foolish boastings of the superior prowess of British regulars, no equally foolish contempt for the prowess of his foe, no scorn of his provincial troops and their officers, no neglect of the principles of frontier warfare, betrayed him to his ruin. Among his colonial troops Hugh Waddell and his Carolinians stood high in his esteem. Waddell, wrote Governor Dobbs, "had great honour done him being employed in all reconnoitering parties; and dressed and acted as an Indian; and his Sergeant Rogers took the only Indian prisoner who gave Mr. Forbes certain intelligence of the Forces in Fort Duquesne upon which they resolved to proceed." The reference to Sergeant Rogers is to the following incident. Winter had set in and the British general, with his army in a mountainous region, ill prepared to pass the winter in such a wilderness, or to lay a winter seige to a strongly fortified fort, and without accurate information of his enemy's force, was in a dilemma whether to retire to a more favorable position for the winter, or to push on. He therefore offered a reward of £50 to any one who would capture an Indian from whom information as to the enemy's situation could be obtained. Sergeant John Rogers, of Waddell's command, won this reward by bringing in an Indian who told Forbes that if he would push resolutely on, the French would evacuate Fort Duquesne. The British commander followed the red man's advice. Upon his approach, the French garrison fled, and Fort Duquesne, dismantled and partially destroyed, fell without a blow into the hands of the English general who immediately renamed it Fort Pitt, because as he said in a letter to Pitt, "it was in some measure the being actuated by your spirit that now makes me master of the place."

The victories of 1758, together with the fall of Quebec in 1759, removed the French as a serious factor in the war and brought peace with them in sight. But the war was not at an end for the colonies still had to reckon with the Indians. In the North the confederated tribes under Pontiac continued to make war on the English, while in the South the Cherokee warriors who had acted as allies of the British against Fort Duquesne returned from that expedition to arouse their tribe to hostilities. In 1755 they could call to arms more than 2,500 warriors. Besides the Cherokee, the two Carolinas had also to reckon with the Catawba who had, in 1755, about 250 warriors. Both Cherokee and Catawba were nominally friends of the English, but for several years the French had been undermining the English influence with such success that at the outbreak of the French and Indian War the preference of the Indians for the French was but thinly veiled and nothing but policy prevented their joining forces with their new friends. The English were fully aware of this situation and took immediate steps to hold both nations to their allegiance.

The outbreak of war on the Ohio was accompanied by manifestations of hostility by the Carolina Indians. In December, 1754, therefore, the Assembly provided for a company of rangers for the protection of the frontier. Governor Dobbs entrusted this work to Hugh Waddell, a young Irishman, not yet twenty-one years of age, and but recently arrived in the province, who was, wrote Dobbs, "in his person and character every way qualified for such a command, as he was young, active, and resolute." The governor's choice was fully justified by the results. The young officer acted with energy in raising and organizing his company, and was soon scouting on the frontier where his presence tended to keep the Indians quiet. It soon became evident, however, that a larger force and some permanent forts would be necessary. In the summer of 1755, therefore, Governor Dobbs visited the western settlements to study the situation. He was on this tour when he received information of Braddock's defeat. Hastening to New Bern, he convened the Assembly, September 25, and in a forceful address set forth the defenceless condition of the province, the growing influence of the French over the Cherokee Indians, and the necessity for prompt action to defeat their schemes. Besides sending aid to New York this Assembly ordered that a fort be erected on the North Carolina frontier. The execution of this work was entrusted to Captain Waddell who, selecting a site "beautifully situated in the fork of Fourth Creek, a Branch of the Yadkin River about twenty miles west of Salisbury," erected there a fort which he named in honor of the governor. In 1756 a committee of the Assembly, of which Richard Caswell was a member, after an inspection reported that the fort was "a good and substantial Building" and that its garrison of forty-six men appeared to be well and in good spirits.

Besides his military duties, Captain Waddell was charged with diplomatic duties. In February, 1756, as the representative of North Carolina he was associated with Peyton Randolph and William Byrd, representatives of Virginia, in negotiating an offensive and defensive alliance with the Cherokee and Catawba nations. The noted chief, King Haiglar, represented the Catawba and Ata-kullakulla the Cherokee. Atakullakulla was one of the most remarkable Indians of whom we have any record. Bartram, the eminent botanist and traveller, described him as a man of small stature, slender build and delicate frame, but of superior abilities. Noted as an orator and a statesman, he was "esteemed to be the wisest man of the nation and the most steady friend of the English." The treaties signed by these representatives stipulated that the English should build three forts within the Indian reservations to protect them against the French while the Cherokee were to furnish 400 warriors to aid the English in the North. Accordingly South Carolina built Fort Prince George at Keowee on the headwaters of the Savannah and Virginia built Fort Loudoun on the Little Tennessee at the mouth of the Tellico. It fell to North Carolina to build a fort for the protection of the Catawba, but Captain Waddell had scarcely begun work on it, on the site of the present town of Old Fort, when he was ordered to stop as the Catawba had repented of their agreement and desired that no fort be built among them. The Cherokee also became alarmed when a garrison of 200 men was sent to Fort Loudoun, which Major Andrew Lewis of Virginia was building, and their great council at Echota ordered the work stopped and the garrison withdrawn,

HUGH WADDELL

saying plainly that they did not want so many armed white
men among them. Even Ata-kullakulla was now in opposition
to the English. Despite the treaties, therefore, the situation
was highly unsatisfactory and there were strong grounds for
believing that several murders along the Catawba and Broad
rivers in North Carolina were the joint work of "French
Indians" and Cherokee.

Nevertheless, the Cherokee, in accordance with their agreement, sent a considerable body of warriors to aid the English
against Fort Duquesne. This policy of calling in the aid of
Indians in military affairs was to say the least always of
doubtful wisdom; in this case it was disastrous. The trouble
began in the spring of 1756 with an expedition which Major
Andrew Lewis undertook against the hostile Shawano on the
Ohio, with 200 white troops and 100 Cherokee. The expedition
ended in disaster. Some of the Cherokee returning home having lost their own horses, captured some horses which they
found running loose and appropriated them to their own use.
Thereupon the Virginia frontiersmen fell upon them, killing
sixteen of their number. At this outrage the hot blood of the
young warriors, who were none too friendly to the English at
the best, flared up in a passion for immediate revenge. The
chiefs, however, counseled moderation until reparation could
be demanded of the colonial governments in accordance with
their treaties. But Virginia, North Carolina, and South Carolina all refused to take any action in the matter. While the
women in the wigwams of the slain warriors were wailing
night and day for their unavenged kindred, and the Creeks,
who were in alliance with the French, were taunting the Cherokee warriors with cowardice for submitting so tamely to their
wrongs, came news of the fall of Oswego and other English
disasters in the North. The Cherokee thirst for revenge was
now mingled with contempt for English arms, and the young
men could no longer be restrained. They fell upon the back
settlements and spread terror far and wide until Governor
Dobbs sent sufficient reinforcements to Captain Waddell to
enable him to check the ravages of the enemy.

Thus the situation remained throughout 1757 and 1758.
Murders by the Indians followed by prompt reprisals by the
whites kept both in a state of constant suspicion. While they
were in this inflammable state of mind, 150 Cherokee warriors
were sent to join the English in defence of the Virginia

frontier. They were unruly and dangerous allies, being, as Governor Dinwiddie said, "a dissatisfied set of People." The capture of Fort Duquesne, November 25, 1758, merely accentuated the danger, for the French driven from the Ohio immediately concentrated their intrigues upon the tribes on the Tennessee and the Catawba. Depredations on the back settlements by "French Indians" became more and more frequent, and their influence over the Cherokee became daily more apparent. In May, 1759, both the Carolinas were alarmed by reports of "many horrid murders" committed by the Lower Cherokee along the Yadkin and the Catawba. In July came another report of murders in the vicinity of Fort Dobbs by bands of Middle Cherokee. The white settlers, in great alarm, were abandoning their homes and "enforting themselves," some in Fort Dobbs, others among the Moravians at Bethabara. Governor Dobbs hastily withdrew sixty men from Fort Granville at Ocracoke and Fort Johnston and sent them with some small cannon to the defence of the West with orders to cooperate with the militia of Orange, Anson and Rowan counties. Hugh Waddell, promoted to the rank of colonel, was again sent to Fort Dobbs to take command on the frontier. He had scarcely reached his post when he received orders to hasten to the aid of Governor Lyttleton of South Carolina who was conducting an expedition against the Lower Cherokee, but while on the march with his rangers and 500 militia, he was halted by an express from Governor Lyttleton who had made peace with the enemy.

This peace, however, was of short duration. No sooner had Lyttleton withdrawn his forces from Fort Prince George than Oconostota, the young war chief, who had suffered personal injuries at the hands of Governor Lyttleton, attacked the fort after treacherously murdering its commanding officer. War immediately broke out along the whole frontier. On the night of February 27, 1760, the dogs at Fort Dobbs by "an uncommon noise" warned Colonel Waddell that something unusual was going on outside. Investigation showed that the fort was surrounded by Cherokee warriors. After a hot fight Waddell beat them off with serious losses. Another band preparing for a night assault on Bethabara was frightened away by the ringing of the church bells. Still others laid waste the settlement at Walnut Cove. Across the mountains, Oconostota laid seige to Fort Loudoun. In June, 1760, a relief expedition under Colonel Archibald Montgomery, consisting of 1,600 Scotch Highlanders and Americans, penetrated the Cherokee country as far as Echoee, near the present town of Franklin, where in a desperate engagement with the Cherokee, June 27, 1760, Montgomery was defeated and compelled to retreat to Fort Prince George. His retreat sealed the fate of Fort Loudoun. The garrison after being reduced to the necessity of eating their horses and dogs capitulated on condition that they be allowed to retire unmolested with their arms and sufficient ammunition for the march, leaving to the enemy their remaining warlike stores. Unfortunately the commanding officer, Captain Demeré, failed to carry out these terms in good faith and the Indians discovering his breach of the treaty fell upon the retreating soldiers, killed Demeré and twenty-nine others and took the rest prisoners.

Harrowing reports of atrocities and butcheries, which continued to spread throughout Virginia, North Carolina, and South Carolina, aroused those colonies to a grim determination to put an end to the power of their ruthless foes. A campaign was accordingly planned in which the three colonies were to have the assistance of Colonel James Grant and his regiments of Scotch Highlanders. In June, 1761, Grant assembled at Fort Prince George an army consisting of regulars, colonial troops, a few Chickasaw Indians and almost every remaining warrior of the Catawba, numbering 2,600 men. Refusing Ata-kullakulla's request for a friendly accommodation, Grant pushed rapidly forward into the Cherokee country along the trail followed the previous year by Montgomery, until he came within two miles of Montgomery's battlefield. There on June 10th he encountered the Cherokee upon whom he inflicted a decisive defeat. He drove them into the recesses of the mountains, destroyed their towns, burned their granaries, laid waste their fields, and "pushed the frontier seventy miles farther to the west." The Cherokee, compelled to sue for peace, sent Ata-kullakulla to Charleston where he signed a treaty that brought the war to an end. In the meantime, Virginia troops had invaded the country of the Upper Cherokee and on November 19th at the Great Island of the Holston, now Kingsport, Tennessee, forced them to sign a treaty independently of the middle and lower towns. These blows broke the power of the Cherokee, who were never again strong enough to stay the westward march of the white race.

Although the fall of Quebec definitely decided the contest as between France and England, peace between the two powers was not signed until 1763. By this treaty France and Spain ceded to England all their North American possessions east of the Mississippi River. The probable effect on the Indians of the removal of their French and Spanish allies from this region was a problem which gave the British government serious concern; and to allay any possible suspicion and alarm which it might occasion among the southern tribes, the king instructed the governors of Virginia, North Carolina, South Carolina, and Georgia to hold a conference with them at Augusta, Georgia, and explain to them "in the most prudent and delicate Manner," the changes about to take place. This congress met November 5, 1763. Present were Lieutenant-Governor Francis Fauquier of Virginia, Governor Arthur Dobbs of North Carolina, Governor Thomas Boone of South Carolina, Governor James Wright of Georgia, John Stuart, Indian agent for the Southern Department, twenty-five chiefs and 700 warriors of the Chickasaw, Choctaw, Creek, Catawba, and Cherokee nations. Six days of oratory and feasting resulted in a treaty of "Perfect and Perpetual Peace and Friendship" between the Indians and the English, which provided for mutual oblivion of past offenses and injuries, the establishment of satisfactory trade relations, the punishment by each party of offenders of its own race for crimes against members of the other race, and the fixing of the boundaries of the Indian reservations. On November 10th the four governors and the Indian agent, on part of the king, and the twenty-five chiefs, on part of their tribes, signed the treaty. The event was celebrated by the bombing of the guns of Fort Augusta and the distribution among the Indians of £5,000 worth of presents sent them by King George.

While these events were transpiring on the frontier, French privateers were busy along the coast. Immediately after the declaration of war, using French and Spanish ports in the West Indies as bases, they began to appear off the Carolina coast and to reenact the scenes of the Spanish War. The defenseless state of the coast gave them ample opportunity for carrying on their work. On one occasion, "for want of a Fort to defend the entrance and Channel" of the Cape Fear, "the Privateers seeing the masts of the Ships at anchor in the road within the Harbour, over the sandy Islands, went in and

cut out the ships and carried them to Sea.'' Such coast fortifications as had been constructed were ''Incapable of Defence
for want of Artillery,'' which both governor and Assembly
vainly begged the home government to supply, but some protection to shipping was afforded by American privateers. A
few, sailing under letters of marque and reprisal issued by
Governor Dobbs, were fitted out at Wilmington and Brunswick. In the spring of 1757 the brigantine Hawk, armed with
16 carriage guns and 20 swivels, manned with 120 men,
Thomas Wright captain, and the sloop Franklin, armed with
6 carriage guns and 10 swivels, manned with 50 men, Robert
Ellis captain, sailed out of Cape Fear River. Some months
later came a report that the Hawk sailing into ''a French port
in Hispaniola'' had taken there ''a pretended Danish Vessel
with 135 Hogsheads of Sugar [and] 30 Barrels of Coffee.''
Occasionally, too, a British man-of-war cruising off the coast,
would look in at Cape Fear and other North Carolina ports.
But they were not as assiduous as they might have been in the
performance of their duty. On March 22, 1757, Governor
Dobbs declared that H. M. S. Baltimore, which was supposed
to be stationed at Cape Fear, had not been at her station three
weeks all told since his arrival in North Carolina; and at
another time he charged that her captain spent the winter
months at Charleston because there were ''no balls or entertainments'' at Cape Fear. It is not surprising, therefore, that
merchants complained that ''notwithstanding our great
superiority in the West Indies,'' French privateers had captured seventy-eight English and American vessels, some of
which were owned by North Carolina merchants, and carried
them as prizes to Martinique. But after 1757 the navy like
the army coming under the spell of Pitt's genius, began to
display greater zeal and activity in running down the enemy.
Captain Hutchins, H. M. S. Tartar, reported in June, 1759,
that during a cruise of three days off Ocracoke he had neither
seen nor head of a French privateer. Three months later,
Wolfe's triumph at Quebec put an end to privateering in
American waters.

News of the fall of Quebec reached Brunswick October
24th. ''Our Governour upon this occasion,'' wrote the Brunswick correspondent of the South Carolina Gazette, ''ordered a
tripple discharge of all the cannon at this town and Fort Johnston, all the Shipping displayed their colours and fired 3

rounds; and yester evening was spent in an entertainment at his excellency's in illuminations, bonfires and all kinds of acclamations and demonstrations of joy. Today's rejoicings are repeated at Wilmington.''

The war had borne heavily on North Carolina both in men and money. It is impossible to say how many soldiers the colony raised as no accurate returns exist, indeed, none were ever made. At various times, however, the Assembly authorized the recruiting of more than 2,000 men and there is no reason to suppose that they were not enrolled; there were indeed probably more for many a settler took down his musket and went forth to war on the frontier whose name was never entered on any muster roll. Nor does this number include the militia who were called into active service but of whose service no records exist. More than half of the 2,000 provisionals authorized by the Assembly were sent into service in other colonies. Of North Carolina's financial contributions, more accurate information is available. On November 24, 1764, Treasurer John Starkey reported to the Assembly that since 1754 the colony had issued £72,000 of proclamation money, current as legal tender at the rate of four for three of sterling. Of this amount, £68,000 were still in circulation in 1764. The Assembly also issued for war purposes treasury notes bearing interest at 6 per cent to the amount of £30,776, of which in 1764 £7,000 were still out. The war, therefore, had cost North Carolina £102,776, of which £27,776 had been paid, leaving a debt of £75,000. Reckoning the population at 130,-000, the public debt contracted in support of the war amounted to upwards of 15s per capita. For the redemption of this war debt the Assembly levied a tax of 4s on the poll and a duty of 4d a gallon on spirituous liquors. During the war Parliament appropriated £200,000 to reimburse all the colonies for their expenditures, and an additional £50,000 for Virginia, North Carolina, and South Carolina. A quarrel between the governor and the Assembly over the control of this fund resulted in North Carolina's receiving only £7,789 from both funds which certainly was much less than her just share.

Over against the colony's losses and expenditures, however, may be placed the benefits resulting from the expulsion of the French from her western territory and the removal of the Cherokee from the path of her westward expansion. To these material results must be added the even greater moral benefits, viz., the breaking down of many of the barriers of local prejudices due to her former isolation and the germination of a sense of her common interest and common destiny with the rest of British America which, like the other colonies, she brought out of her experiences in this first continental event in American history.

CHAPTER XVI

WESTWARD EXPANSION

In 1764 Governor Dobbs, who had grown peevish with age, was given permission to surrender the cares of his office to a lieutenant-governor and return to England. While he was busily packing for his trip "his physician had no other means to prevent his fatiguing himself than by telling him that he had better prepare himself for a much longer voyage." He set sail on this "longer voyage" March 28, 1765.

Dobbs was succeeded by William Tryon who took the oath of office at Wilmington April 3, 1765. It was Tryon's misfortune to administer the government of North Carolina in times of domestic violence and civil strife and so to have his name associated with events which cannot even now be discussed with that calmness and impartiality which alone gives value to the judgments of history. However, the load of obloquy which tradition so long heaped upon his name has been largely lifted by the publication within recent years of contemporaneous records which reveal the man and his career in a new and better light. The ablest of the colonial governors of North Carolina, he was distinguished for the energy of his character, the versatility of his talents, and the variety of his interests. His public papers, which are far superior to those of any of his predecessors, reveal him as a man of great executive ability, keen insight, and liberal views. He had the ability to see and understand the view-point of the colonists and he always strove to represent it fairly, even when he heartily disapproved of it. His critics love to dwell on his extravagance and love of display; but perhaps this fault—to which, indeed, he must have pleaded guilty—may be traced less to personal vanity than to his views of public policy. He entertained exaggerated ideas, common to his time, of the proper method of upholding the dignity of exalted official position, and had high notions of authority, which he enforced with a strong hand, but his public conduct was always inspired by a sense of official duty and never, as so many of his critics have charged, by vindictiveness. His tact was unfailing, and his genius for winning the personal friendship of those who most vigorously opposed his public policies was remarkable. Long after he had left the colony, the General Assembly bore testimony to their conviction of his "good intentions to its welfare," and gave a striking expression of "the great affection this Colony bears him, and the entire confidence they repose in him."

One of the important results of the French and Indian War was the opening of the region beyond the Alleghanies to settlement by the English. The English colonies had long been advertent to the importance of this region to their future expansion. In 1748 the Board of Trade reported "that the settlement of the country lying to the westward of the great mountains would be for His Majesty's interest and the advantages and security of Virginia and the neighboring colonies;" and in 1756 Sir Thomas Pownall wrote that "the English settlements as they are at present circumstanced, are absolutely at a standstill; they are settled up to the mountains and in the mountains there is nowhere together land sufficient for a settlement large enough to subsist by itself and to defend itself and preserve a communication with the present settlements." Both England and France claimed this vast region, but in 1763 by the terms of the Treaty of Paris, which brought the French and Indian War to a close, France was compelled to withdraw her claims leaving only the Indians to contest the inevitable advance of the English settlers.

Virginia, North Carolina, and other colonies had long asserted jurisdiction over this western region, but the British government was not disposed to recognize their claims. In 1763, immediately after the signing of the Treaty of Paris, the king issued a proclamation forbidding settlements beyond the mountains and instructing the colonial governments to issue no grants in that region. How long this proclamation would have delayed the colonization of the West had the people obeyed it cannot be said; as it was the hardy pioneers on the frontier calmly disregarded it, took the problem of settlement into their own hands, and within half a decade after the close of the French and Indian War began to cross the mountains and build their cabins along the Watauga, the Holston, and the Cumberland rivers without permission of either king or royal governors.

All of that part of the region beyond the Alleghanies which is now embraced within the State of Tennessee was included in the Carolina grant of 1665 and was therefore nominally within the jurisdiction of North Carolina. From North Carolina it received its first settlers. Although at the time of the Treaty of Paris no attempt had been made to plant white settlements within its limits, the region had long been familiar to English traders and hunters. In 1748, Thomas Walker of Virginia led a band of hunters far into the interior of what is now Middle Tennessee, giving names to the Cumberland Mountains and the Cumberland River. In 1756, as we have already seen, the English built Fort Loudoun on the Tennessee River. Most famous of all the hardy pioneers who explored this region was Daniel Boone who as early as 1760 was hunting along the Watauga River. The following year at the head of a party of hunters Boone penetrated the wilderness to the headwaters of the Holston as far as the site of the present Abingdon, Virginia. From this time forward he was constantly hunting in the Tennessee and Kentucky country. Boone and his fellow hunters brought back to the settlements in Virginia and North Carolina glowing reports of the richness and beauty of the land beyond the mountains and thus paved the way for the pioneers of more settled habits whose purpose was to carve out of the wilderness homes for themselves and their children.

A study of this westward movement reveals no feature that has not already appeared in the movements which resulted in the settlement of the older communities. Like the original settlement on the Albemarle, it was not the result of organized effort but of spontaneous, individual enterprise, a perfectly natural overflow of population from the parent colony. First a few hardy, adventurous individuals broke their way into the wilderness; soon they were followed by an occasional family, and, finally, as the movement gathered momentum, by groups of families. The same motives, too, which inspired the settlers in the older communities, reappear as the inspiration of those in the new. We find in both the same restless spirit of adventure, the same desire for new and cheap land, and the same discontent with political, economic and social conditions in the parent country. Such discontent was wide-spread throughout the back country of Virginia, North Carolina, and South Carolina. In North Carolina it culminated in the organization of the Regulators and their disastrous attempts to secure reforms in the colonial administra-

Daniel Boone

tion. In contrast with the ills at home were the freedom, the unlimited opportunities, and the charms of adventure in a new land; and the choice of the new was made by hundreds who after 1768 joined in that migration across the Alleghanies which resulted in the founding of the states of Kentucky and Tennessee.

The earliest settlements beyond the Alleghanies were made **in that broad and beautiful valley** between the Great Smoky and Unaka ranges on the east and the Cumberland Mountains on the west, through which the Holston, the Watauga, the Nolichucky, the Clinch and the French Broad rivers flow to form the Tennessee. In 1768 a few Virginians settled at Wolf Hills on the Holston River, the present Abingdon, whence settlements gradually expanded southward until they reached the Watauga where some North Carolinians built homes in the winter of 1768-69. Most of the settlers on the Watauga came from the back counties of Virginia and North Carolina, and were of Scotch-Irish stock. Among them of course, as in all frontier communities, were to be found some of the outcasts of civilization, but they were not the dominant element in the settlement, nor did they determine its character. The great majority of the settlers "were men of sterling worth; fit to be the pioneer fathers of a mighty and beautiful state. They possessed the courage that enabled them to defy outside foes, together with the rough, practical commonsense that allowed them to establish a simple but effective form of government, so as to preserve order among themselves."[1] Since their political and social ideals were genuinely democratic, it is not strange that out of their experience should have come the first government springing from the people ever organized by native-born Americans.

The most important figure in the history of the Watauga settlement is that of James Robertson. Born in Virginia, Robertson was carried to North Carolina in his eighth year and grew to manhood in what is now Wake County. Like a later and more famous native of Wake County who also moved to Tennessee, Andrew Johnson, Robertson was taught to read and write by his wife. Although never attaining more than a "rudimentary education," Robertson was, says Roosevelt, "a man of remarkable natural powers; * * * his somewhat sombre face had in it a look of self-contained strength that made it impressive; and his taciturn, quiet, masterful way of

---

[1] Roosevelt: Winning of the West, Vol. I, p. 219.

dealing with men and affairs, together with his singular mixture of cool caution and most adventurous daring, gave him an immediate hold even upon such lawless spirits as those of the border. He was a mighty hunter; but, unlike Boone, hunting and exploration were to him secondary affairs, and he came to examine the lands with the eye of a pioneer settler.'' [2] Such was the man who, in 1770, discontented with the conditions then prevailing in the back counties of North Carolina, set out from his Wake County home to cross the Alleghanies and become the ''Father of Tennessee.''

Robertson was so delighted with the beauty and fertility of the valley of the Watauga, that he determined to carry his family there. Accordingly he remained just long enough to raise a crop of corn, and then returned to North Carolina for them. Conditions in the back counties had gradually grown worse; discontent was more wide-spread than ever. He had no difficulty therefore, in interesting his friends and neighbors in the new country beyond the mountains and when he set out on his return to Watauga he was accompanied by about a dozen families besides his own. This accession of sturdy settlers assured the permanence of the settlement, yet it was only the vanguard of the army that soon began to pour into that region, as a result of the overthrow of the Regulators at Alamance, May 16, 1771. Morgan Edwards, a Baptist preacher who visited the back counties of North Carolina in 1772, wrote that many of the Regulators ''despaired of seeing better times and therefore quitted the province. It is said that 1,500 families departed since the battle of Alamance and to my knowledge a great many more are only waiting to dispose of their plantations in order to follow them.'' Although this estimate is certainly an exaggeration, yet it is indicative of the extent of the emigration from North Carolina to Watauga and the other western settlements. When Watauga asked to be annexed to North Carolina in 1776, the petition was signed by 111 settlers.

These settlers had come to Watauga believing it to be in Virginia, but in 1771 Anthony Bledsoe, a surveyor, discovered that it was really in North Carolina. His discovery was somewhat disconcerting since most of the people had settled there because of their dissatisfaction with political conditions in North Carolina. They were therefore reluctant to appeal to North Carolina for protection, or to acknowledge the juris-

---

[2] Winning of the West, Vol. I.

diction of the North Carolina government. Accordingly under the leadership of Robertson they determined to set up a government of their own. This determination resulted in the Watauga Association, the first government erected beyond the Alleghanies and the first written constitution by native Americans. At a general meeting, the inhabitants qualified to take part in so important an undertaking chose thirteen representatives, apparently one for each block-house or palisaded village, to represent them in the first frontier legislature. These representatives met at Robertson's station and selected five commissioners, among whom were Robertson and John Sevier, destined to fame surpassing even the fame of Robertson, to administer the government. The commissioners exercised both judicial and executive functions. They recorded wills, issued marriage licenses, made treaties with the Indians, decided cases at law, punished criminals, and supervised the morals of the community. In their judicial capacity they gave their constituents no cause to complain of the law's delay. An instance frequently cited as typical of their exercise of their judicial functions is that of a horse thief who was arrested on Monday, tried on Wednesday, and hanged on Friday. So sure and swift was their execution of the criminal law that some unruly citizens chose to flee to the Indians rather than submit to Watauga justice.

One of the first problems which the Watauga Association as an organized government had to solve was its relations with the Indians. The same year in which the association was formed, 1772, Virginia made a treaty with the Cherokee which fixed the southern boundary of that colony, 36°30′ north latitude, as the dividing line between the whites and the Indians west of the Alleghanies. Thereupon Alexander Cameron, the British agent resident among the Cherokee, demanded that the Watauga settlers withdraw from their lands which, of course, fell within the Indian reservation. The settlers refused and in their refusal were supported by the Cherokee themselves who, reluctant to lose the trade of the whites, requested that they be allowed to remain provided they encroached no farther on the domains of the Indians. Accordingly a treaty was made by which the Indians leased their lands to the settlers for a period of eight years. This treaty established peaceful relations between the two races which continued until the outbreak of the Revolution.

The first result of the Revolution was to bring Watauga into closer relations with the mother colony. At the beginning of the dispute between the king and the colonies, the Watauga settlers, as was to be expected of men of their race, embraced the cause of the colonies, "resolved to adhere strictly to the rules and orders of the Continental Congress," and "acknowledged themselves indebted to the United Colonies their full proportion of the Continental expense." In 1775 they united with the settlers on the Nolichucky River to form Washington District,—the first political division to be honored with the name of Washington,—and the next year petitioned the North Carolina Provincial Council to be annexed to North Carolina and admitted to representation in the Provincial Congress. The petition was granted and on December 3, 1776, John Sevier, the first representative from beyond the Alleghanies, took his seat in the Provincial Congress at Halifax just in time to participate in the formation of the first constitution of the independent State of North Carolina. The next year Washington District became Washington County, a land office was opened, and a system of land grants similar to that of North Carolina was instituted. In spite of war the settlement continued to grow and in 1779 Sullivan County was erected out of Washington. Nevertheless it seems not to have been contemplated that Washington County should remain permanently a part of North Carolina, for the Declaration of Rights, adopted in 1776, expressly provides that the clause which defines the boundaries of the State as extending from sea to sea, "shall not be construed so as to prevent the Establishment of one or more Governments Westward of this State, by the consent of the Legislature."

By this time other settlements had been made even farther west than the Watauga, in which Richard Henderson, an eminent North Carolina jurist, was the moving spirit. Like many of his contemporaries, Henderson had become affected with the fever for western lands and had begun to dream of vast proprietaries beyond the mountains in which he was to play the part of a William Penn or of a Lord Baltimore. He had made the acquaintance of Boone whose good judgment, intelligence and character had so impressed him that in 1763 he sent Boone to explore the region between the Cumberland and Kentucky rivers. During the next decade Boone prosecuted his explorations with great vigor, perseverance and daring, but the story of his romantic career is too well known to need repetition here. In 1774, as a result of his work, Henderson organized at Hillsboro a land company, first called the

Louisa Company, later the Transylvania Company, to promote the settlement of this region. Prominent among the incorporators besides Henderson himself were John Williams of Granville County, one of the first superior court judges of North Carolina under the Constitution of 1776, James Hogg, Nathaniel Hart and Thomas Hart of Orange County. In March, 1775, at Sycamore Shoals on Watauga River, Henderson and his associates negotiated a treaty with the Overhill Cherokee Indians by which the Indians sold to the Transylvania Company all the vast region between the Cumberland and Kentucky rivers, which Henderson named Transylvania.

Even before the treaty was completed, Daniel Boone had been sent forward to open a trail from the settlements on the Holston to the Kentucky River. This trail was the first regular path into the western wilderness and is famous in the history of the frontier as the Wilderness Trail. Leading through the Cumberland Gap, it crossed the Cumberland, Laurel and Rockcastle rivers, and terminated on the Kentucky River. There on April 1, 1780, Boone began to lay the foundations of Boonesborough where he was joined twenty days later by Henderson with a party of forty mounted riflemen. At Boonesborough Henderson opened a land office and proceeded to issue grants and to organize a government for the colony of Transylvania.

These activities, however, were somewhat premature. The Transylvania purchase was in direct controvention of the king's proclamation of 1763, and neither the British nor the colonial authorities would recognize its validity. Since part of the new colony lay within Virginia and part within North Carolina, the governors of both colonies issued proclamations declaring Henderson's treaty with the Indians null and void. Governor Martin of North Carolina denounced it as a "daring unjust and unwarrantable Proceeding," forbade the company "to prosecute so unlawful an Undertaking," and warned all persons that purchases of lands from the Transylvania Company were "illegal, null and void." Henderson and his associates the governor characterized as an "infamous company of Land Pyrates." But in 1775 proclamations of royal governors had lost something of their former effectiveness, and Henderson and his company proceeded with their enterprise in disregard of the two governors' prohibition. Failing to secure recognition from the colonial governments, in September, 1775, the company sent James Hogg to Philadelphia to appeal to the Continental Congress for admission into the ranks of the United Colonies as the fourteenth colony. But both Virginia and North Carolina, whether under royal rule or as independent states, were opposed to such a surrender of their western lands, and they succeeded in securing the rejection of the petition. After this rebuff, Henderson's grandiose scheme collapsed. However in compensation for the "expence, risque and trouble" to which he and his associates had been put, in 1778 Virginia granted them 200,000 acres in that part of Transylvania which lay within her limits, and in 1783 North Carolina made a similar grant within her western territory. That part of Transylvania which fell within the limits of Virginia afterwards became the State of Kentucky; the rest together with Watauga became Tennessee.

In 1779, the indefatigable Henderson opened a land office at French Lick on Cumberland River and invited settlers to purchase grants. Among those who came was James Robertson, who quickly became the leader of the new colony as he had been at Watauga. In 1780 on a high bluff at French Lick, Robertson built a block-house which he named Nashborough in honor of Abner Nash who had just been elected governor of North Carolina. Later it became Nashville. The early history of the Cumberland settlement resembles that of Watauga. In the face of crop failures, Indian attacks and other hardships which threatened it with destruction, it was held together by the genius of Robertson, and on May 1, 1780, representatives· from the several communities met and adopted a temporary plan of government which they called the Cumberland Association modeled after the Watauga Association. It was to be effective only until the settlement could be organized as a county of North Carolina, which was done in 1783 when the Cumberland Association became Davidson County with James Robertson as its first representative in the General Assembly.

The tracing of the development of these western settlements in a continuous story has carried us chronologically somewhat beyond the period of Tryon's administration in which they originated and to which we must now return. Tryon met his first Assembly at New Bern, May 3, 1765. He had already evolved in his own mind a really constructive program for the colony, part of which he laid before the Assembly. It embraced the fixing upon a permanent seat of government, the establishment of a postal system, the promotion of religion, the encouragement of education, and other progressive policies. The Assembly met his suggestions with favor, but before it could carry them into execution, North Carolina became involved in the Stamp Act quarrel, which was scarcely settled before the War of the Regulation broke out. Tryon's administration, therefore, began in storm and strife and closed in war and bloodshed. Yet to its credit, besides other measures which will be discussed elsewhere, must be placed the quieting of a gathering storm among the Cherokee Indians, the fixing upon a seat of government and the erection there of a suitable public building, and the crushing of a dangerous insurrection in the very heart of the province.

In spite of domestic violence and emigration the decade from 1765 to 1775 was a period of growth and improvement. In 1766 Tryon expressed the opinion that North Carolina was "settling faster than any [other colony] on the continent; last autumn and winter," he added, "upwards of one thousand wagons passed thro' Salisbury with families from the northward, to settle in this province chiefly." All the back country, from Salisbury to the foot of the mountains, and beyond, was filling up "with a race of people, sightly, active, and laborious."

This influx of population brought on a troublesome situation with the Cherokee Indians. As the settlers pushed westward they encroached more and more on the Cherokee lands, depriving the Lower Cherokee of their most valuable hunting grounds. Daily contact between the two races produced conflicts and frequent bloodshed. Nor was the trouble confined to the Cherokee. A similar situation existed all along the borders of Virginia, North Carolina, South Carolina, and Georgia. The complaints of the Cherokee, wrote John Stuart, "have been echoed through all the Nations." The Cherokee, the Creeks, and the other Indians of the Southern Department were alarmed and discontented, and ready upon the slightest provocation to take up the hatchet.

Peace could be preserved only by establishing plain and unmistakable boundaries and forbidding each race to encroach upon the territories of the other. John Stuart exerted himself to secure adjustments in all the colonies in his department. In February, 1766, he wrote to Governor Tryon that "the fixing of a boundary Line is a measure necessary and essential to the preservation of peace with the Indian Nations." But Tryon hesitated to move because he had received no instructions bearing on this matter and had no money with which to defray expenses. Happily both these causes for delay were soon removed. The secretary of state for the colonies directed him to apply himself "in the most earnest measure" to remedy the complaints of the Indians and to prevent hostilities, and in November, 1766, the Assembly agreed to meet the expenses of the survey. In April, 1767, the Council unanimously advised Tryon to go in person to meet the Cherokee chiefs, and since this advice fell in with his own wishes, he decided to adopt it.

The commissioners to represent the colony in running the line were John Rutherford, Robert Palmer, and John Frohock. To escort himself and the commissioners Tryon ordered out a detachment of fifty men from the Rowan and Mecklenburg militia which he put under the command of Colonel Hugh Waddell. Although he was going into a hostile country, among a savage and treacherous race, to settle a dispute which was about to bring on war, Tryon has been severely criticised for his action in ordering out these troops. And yet the only criticism of his conduct which can be justified by the facts should be aimed at his fool-hardiness in venturing upon so dangerous an expedition with so weak an escort. At Salisbury he was joined by Alexander Cameron, deputy superintendent of Indian affairs in the Southern Department. The march westward from Salisbury was begun May 21, 1767. On June 1 Tryon met the Cherokee chiefs at "Tyger River camp," where after exchanging "talks" they came to an agreement as to the boundary. The survey was started June 4, which Tryon regarded as an especially auspicious date since it was the king's birthday. Rutherford, Palmer, Frohock, Cameron, and the Cherokee chiefs composed the surveying party. They began the line at a point on Reedy River where the South Carolina-Cherokee line, recently run, terminated and continued it fifty-three miles northward to a mountain which the surveyors named in honor of the governor. Tryon himself had already returned to Brunswick. He had made a favorable impression upon the Indians who named him "The Great Wolf." Upon his return to Brunswick he issued a proclamation setting out the line agreed upon, forbidding any purchases of land from the Indians, and prohibiting the issuance of any grants within one mile of the boundary line. When the Assembly met in December it thanked the governor for "superintending in person" the running of this line and appropriated money for paying the expenses of the survey, which amounted to about £400.

Upon his return from this expedition Tryon turned his attention seriously to the erection of the public building at

New Bern for which the Assembly of November, 1766, following his recommendation, had made an appropriation. Other
governors had repeatedly urged the necessity for such action.
"The Publick Records," wrote Governor Johnston, nearly
twenty years before, "lye in a miserable condition, one part
of them at Edenton near the Virginia Line in a place without
Lock or Key; a great part of them in the Secretary's House
at Cape Fear about Two Hundred Miles Distance from the
other; Some few of 'em at the Clerk of the Council's House at
Newbern, so that in whatever part of the Colony a man happens to be, if he wants to consult any paper or record he must
send some Hundred of Miles before he can come at it." In
1744 he told the Assembly that the unsatisfactory condition of
public affairs and the "shamefull condition" of the laws,
which were "left at the mercy of every ignorant transcriber
and tossed about on loose scraps of paper," were largely due
to "the want of a fixt place for the dispatch of publick business. It is impossible," he continued, "to finish any matter
as it ought to be while we go on in this itinerant way. * * *
We have now tried every Town in the Colony and it is high
time to settle somewhere." The soundness of this advice was
indisputable, yet the Assembly did nothing. The trouble was
the question could never be considered on its own merits. The
act of 1746, fixing the capital at New Bern, was involved in
the representation controversy and vetoed by the king upon
the protest of the northern counties. In 1758, upon the recommendation of Governor Dobbs, the Assembly passed an act
fixing the capital at Tower Hill, on the Neuse River about
fifty miles above New Bern; but the Board of Trade claimed
for the Crown the right to select the site for a capital and
rebuked Dobbs for consenting to the act. Besides, after its
passage it was found that Dobbs himself owned the land on
which the town was to be located, and charges of speculation
and corruption were so freely circulated that the Assembly
itself asked the king to disallow the act.

Here the situation stood when the outburst of loyalty and
good-feeling which followed the repeal of the Stamp Act gave
Tryon a favorable opportunity for asking the Assembly for
funds to erect a suitable public building at New Bern. The
Assembly, in November, 1766, complied with the request, appropriating £5,000 for the purpose. A year later an additional appropriation of £10,000 was made. The work begun
in 1767 was finally completed in 1770. The building, though
called the "Governor's Palace," contained in fact a residence

THE TRYON PALACE

for the governor, a hall for the Assembly, a council chamber, and offices for the provincial officials. Built of brick and trimmed with marble, it was admittedly the handsomest public building in America. Its erection brought much undeserved odium upon Tryon. True it fastened a debt upon the province which it could ill afford at that time; nevertheless it is pertinent to remark that this debt was incurred not by the governor but by representatives of the people. The governor merely expended the money which the Assembly voted. Nor can there be any doubt that the establishment of a permanent capital, the concentration of the public records in a central depository, and the erection of suitable executive offices and legislative halls greatly facilitated and improved the transaction of the public business.

While all this is undoubtedly true, yet it was an unfavorable time for the Assembly to enter upon such an expensive enterprise. The eastern men, who controlled the Assembly and upon whom chiefly the burdens of the Stamp Act would have fallen, in their joy at being relieved of those burdens, forgot that other sections of the province had grievances of their own. The back counties were already deeply agitated over abuses in the administration of their local affairs and the inequalities in the system of taxation, and a wise administration would not have given them an additional cause for dissatisfaction. Their complaints were aimed not so much at the fact of erecting a provincial building as at the method adopted for raising the money. This method was the imposition of a poll tax for three years which fell on rich and poor alike and was particularly burdensome in the back settlements where money was so scarce. They complained that "as the people in the lower counties are few in proportion to those in the back settlements, it [a poll tax] more immediately affects the many, and operates to their prejudice; for * * * a man that is worth £10,000 pays no more than a poor back settler that has nothing but the labour of his hands to depend upon for his daily support." The Regulators of Orange County, at a meeting held on August 2, 1768, told the sheriff, "We are determined not to pay the Tax for the next three years, for the Edifice or Governor's House. We want no such House, nor will we pay for it." Thus the erection of the "Governor's Palace" was closely connected with those two events, the Regulation and the Stamp Act, which hold so large a place in the history of North Carolina during the decade from 1765 to 1775 .

CHAPTER XVII

THE WAR OF THE REGULATION

The War of the Regulation is one of the most sharply controverted events in the history of North Carolina. The controversy, however, does not so much concern the facts, as in the case of the "Mecklenburg Declaration," as it does the conclusions to be drawn from them. One group of historians sees in the Regulators a devoted band of patriots who at Alamance fired the opening gun of the American Revolution; another sees only a mob, hating property and culture, delighting in violence and impatient of all legal restraints, whose success would have resulted not in the establishment of constitutional liberty but in the reign of anarchy. Neither view is correct; the former is based upon a misunderstanding of the American Revolution, the latter upon a misunderstanding of the Regulation.

The Regulation had its origin in the social and economic differences between the tidewater section and the "back country" of North Carolina. These differences were largely the results of racial and geological divergencies. In the East, as has already been pointed out, the people were almost entirely of English ancestry; in the West, Scotch-Irish and Germans predominated. In the East an aristocratic form of society prevailed, based upon large plantations and slave labor; in the West, plantations were small, slaves were few in number, and the forms and ideals of society were democratic. Between the two sections stretched a sparsely settled region of pine forest which formed a natural barrier to intercourse. The East looked to Virginia and the mother country for its social, intellectual, and political standards; for the West, Philadelphia was the principal center for the interchange of ideas, as well as of produce. With slight intercourse between them, the two sections felt but little sympathetic interest in each other. While the East had taken on many of the forms and luxuries of older societies, the West was still in the pioneer stage. Some old Regulators long afterwards declared that at the time of the Regulation there was not among all their acquaintances one who could boast a cabin with a plank floor, or who possessed a feather bed, a riding carriage, or a side saddle.

There was, however, one set of people in the "back country" who aped the manners of the eastern aristocracy, and by their haughty bearings, selfish and mercenary spirit, and disregard of the sentiments if not the rights of the people, drew upon themselves an almost universal detestation and hatred. They were the public officials, who were a sufficiently numerous and compact group to form a distinct class. The people had but little or no voice in the choice of these officials and therefore no control over them. The colonial government was highly centralized. Provincial affairs were administered by officials chosen by the Crown, local affairs by officials chosen by the governor. Upon the recommendation of the assemblymen from each county, the governor in Council appointed the county justices, who administered the local government. The county justices nominated to the governor three freeholders from whom he selected the sheriff. The governor also appointed the registers and the officers of the militia. There was a clerk of the pleas who farmed out the clerkships of the counties. Moreover these local officials controlled the Assembly. No law forbade multiple office-holding, and the assemblymen were also generally clerks, justices, and militia colonels, who formed what in modern political parlance we call "courthouse rings." Where these "rings" were composed of high-minded, patriotic men, as in most of the eastern counties, government was honestly administered; but in the "back country" such officials were rare, local government was usually inefficient, often corrupt, and generally oppressive.

It was this system of centralized office-holding that prevented the Regulators' receiving prompt and effective redress of their grievances. Their grievances were excessive taxes, dishonest officials, and extortionate fees. Taxes were excessive because they were levied only on the poll so that the rich and the poor paid equal amounts. The scarcity of money in the "back country" added to the hardships of the system, for it frequently gave brutal and corrupt sheriffs and their deputies an excuse to proceed by distraint, collect an extra fee for so doing, and sell the unhappy taxpayer's property at less than its real value to some friend of the sheriff. The Regulators charged that the officers and their friends made a regular business of such proceedings. That the officers with rare exceptions were either dishonest or inefficient is indisputable. A large percentage of the taxes collected by them, estimated by Tryon in 1767 at fifty per cent, never found its way into the hands of the public treasurer. In 1770 the sheriffs were in arrears £49,000, some of which extended as far back as 1754. It was reported that at least half of this sum could not be collected from those officials. The arrears of the officers were greatest in Anson, Orange, Johnston, Rowan, Cumberland, and Dobbs counties. While much of it was due to inefficient methods of accounting, there is no question that the greater part of it can be charged to corruption in office. Sheriffs, clerks, registers, and lawyers were all paid in fees fixed by acts of the Assembly. But these fees were frequently unknown to the people, who were compelled to accept the officers' word for the proper amount. Officers too would generally manage to resolve a service for which a fee was attached into two or more services and collect a fee for each. That such practices were not always technically illegal or corrupt, and that popular rumor frequently exaggerated or misrepresented the facts in particular cases, is unquestionably true, but equally true it is that the people had ample ground for complaint which a government properly responsive to popular sentiment would have speedily removed.

But the government was not responsive to popular sentiment, and it only needed somebody to give voice and direction to the general discontent to set the whole countryside aflame. The three names most conspicuously connected with the agitation which led to the organization of the Regulation are Herman Husband, Rednap Howell, and James Hunter. Husband was a native of Maryland, Howell of New Jersey, and Hunter of Virginia. All three had been caught up in the stream of emigration which flowed from the middle colonies into North Carolina during the middle of the eighteenth century, and had settled in Orange County. Husband was a Quaker and seems to have been endowed with those qualities of business shrewdness, industry, and thrift characteristic of adherents of that sect. Better educated than the people generally among whom he lived, he was fond of reading political tracts which he distributed rather extensively among his neighbors. He had some gift of expression which enabled him to set forth in simple and homely fashion the grievances of the people in pamphlets to which he gave a wide circulation. Thus he became pre-eminently the spokesman of the people. Twice they elected him to represent them in the General Assembly. Essentially an agitator, he shrank from violence and when the quarrel which he had done so much to bring on reached the point of appeal to arms, either from cowardice as his enemies charged, or from religious scruples as his apologists would have us believe, he abandoned his followers and rode hurriedly away from the scene of action. Husband had a counterpart in Howell. The former was serious, blunt, bitter; the latter, witty, pointed, and genial. Howell, who was an itinerant school teacher, is known as the bard of the Regulation. Endowed with a talent for versification, he celebrated the personal characteristics of the officers, their public conduct, and their rapid rise at the expense of the people from poverty to affluence. in "ambling epics and jingling ballads" that have not yet lost their lively interest. His keen sarcasm, his well-aimed wit, and his broad humor set the whole back country laughing and singing at the expense of the officers. Of the triumvirate mentioned, James Hunter seems to have been the man of action. He is known as the "general" of the Regulation. Early associating himself with the movement, upon finding petitions to the governor and appeals to the courts alike ineffective, he advocated resort to forcible measures. Asked to take command at Alamance, he gave a reply which in itself is expressive of the Regulators' own conception of their movement. "We are all free men," he said, "and every man must command himself." After Alamance, Husband, Howell, and Hunter were all outlawed and forced to flee from the province. Hunter alone returned. Later, in the contest with the mother country, he joined the Revolutionary party, and rendered good service in the cause of independence.

Except Governor Tryon, the most prominent leader of the opposing forces was Edmund Fanning. A native of New York, after graduating from Yale College in 1757, he studied law and, in 1761, came to Carolina and located at Hillsboro. Although he may not have been as poverty-stricken upon his arrival as Rednap Howell represents, there can be no doubt that he soon "laced his coat with gold." He was the personification of the office-holding class which has already been described, uniting in his own person the offices of assemblyman, register of deeds, judge of the Superior Court, and colonel of the militia. One need not think him deserving of all the infamy that has been heaped upon him to understand the sentiments of the people toward him. That he was a man of culture and more than average ability there can be no dispute. To his equals he was kind, hospitable, considerate; to his inferiors, patronizing, supercilious, overbearing. He despised the "common people," and they cordially reciprocated the sentiment. They believed that he had acquired his wealth, which he displayed with great ostentation, "by his civil robberies." Although on the evidence he may be fairly acquitted of the charge of deliberate and positive dishonesty, he was unquestionably guilty of abusing his official power and influence for the purpose of perpetuating an oppressive system and obstructing all efforts at reform. He was, indeed, the progenitor of the race of carpetbaggers.

The Regulation was not an isolated event. It was in fact but the culmination of a spirit of restlessness and discontent at existing conditions that had long been abroad in the province. Evidence of it was seen in the outbreak of violence occasioned by the collection of taxes in Anson County and in the riots in the Granville District. In 1765 such riots also broke out among the squatters on the George Selwyn lands in Mecklenburg County when attempts by Selwyn's agents to survey these lands so that deeds might be issued and quit rents collected led to armed resistance in which John Frohock, Abraham Alexander, and others were severely beaten by angry settlers and Henry Eustace McCulloh, Selwyn's agent, was threatened with death. Similar conditions prevailed in Granville County. George Sims of Nutbush, Granville County, on June 6, 1765, issued his famous "Nutbush Address," in which he set forth in graphic language, "the most notorious and intolerable abuses" which had crept into the public service in that county. It was not, he said, the "form of Government, nor yet the body of our laws, that we are quarreling with, but with the malpractices of the Officers of our County Courts, and the abuses which we suffer by those empowered to manage our public affairs." Extortionate fees and oppressive methods of collecting fees and taxes formed the burden of his complaint. He called upon the people to meet for a discussion of reform, but the only result of his appeal was a petition to the Assembly for redress of grievances which was stillborn.

The failure of the movement in Granville was probably due to lack of organization. Organized opposition to the inequalities in the law and malpractices in its administration began in Orange County. At the August term, 1766, of the County Court at Hillsboro, a group of Sandy Creek men, inspired by the success of the Sons of Liberty in resisting the

Stamp Act, issued an address calling upon the people to send delegates to a meeting at Maddock's Mill to inquire "whether the free men of this county labor under any abuses of power or not." The address was read in open court and the officers present, acknowledging that it was reasonable, promised to attend the meeting. On October 10, twelve delegates appeared, but no officers. Apparently under the influence of Edmund Fanning, who denounced the meeting as an insurrection, they had repented of their promise and sent a messenger to say that they would not attend because the meeting claimed authority to call them to an account. The delegates, therefore, were compelled to content themselves with a proposal that the people hold such a meeting annually to discuss the qualifications of candidates for the Assembly, to inform their representatives of their wishes, and to investigate the official acts of public officers. But public office-holders in 1766 did not acknowledge their responsibility to the people. Accordingly they threw all of their personal and official influence against the proposal, and the Sandy Creek men, discouraged at the lack of popular interest and support, abandoned their project.

Though the agitation continued, no further organized opposition was attempted until the spring of 1768. Almost simultaneously a report reached Hillsboro that the Assembly had given the governor £15,000 for a "Palace" and the sheriff posted notices that he would receive taxes only at five specified places and if required to go elsewhere he would distrain at a cost of 2s. 8d. for each distress. The coincidence caused wide comment. The people declared they would not pay the tax for the Palace. They denounced the sheriff's purpose as a violation of the law and determined to resist it. Accordingly they organized themselves into an association, which they later called "The Regulation," in which they agreed: (1) to pay no more taxes until satisfied that they were according to law and lawfully applied; (2) to pay no fees greater than provided by law; (3) to attend meetings of the Regulators as often as possible; (4) to contribute, each man according to his ability, to the expenses of the organization; and (5) in all matters to abide by the will of the majority. They sent to the officers a notice in which they demanded a strict accounting and declared that "as the nature of an officer is a servant of the publick, we are determined to have the officers of this county under a better and honester regulation than they have been for some time past." This formidable pronunciamento was received by the officers with an outburst of indignation.

Fanning denounced the people for attempting to arraign the officers before "the bar of their shallow understanding" and charged them with desiring to set themselves up as the "sovereign arbiters of right and wrong."

The officers seem not to have appreciated the gravity of the situation; or else they desired to put the resolution of the Regulators to a test. No other explanation seems possible for their blunder, when the situation was acutest, in seizing a Regulator's horse, saddle, and bridle and selling them for taxes. A storm of popular fury greeted this challenge. The Regulators rode into Hillsboro, overawed the officers, rescued their comrade's property, and as evidence of their temper fired several shots into Fanning's house. When this affair was reported to Fanning, who was absent attending court at Halifax, he promptly ordered the arrest of William Butler, Peter Craven, and Ninian Bell Hamilton, called out seven companies of the Orange militia, and hurried to Hillsboro to take command. Immediately upon his arrival he reported the situation and his own actions to Tryon and asked for authority to call out the militia of other counties if it became necessary. The governor, who quite properly accepted his subordinate's report at its face value, acted with his accustomed vigor. He authorized Fanning to use the Orange militia to suppress the insurrection, ordered the militia of Bute, Halifax, Granville, Rowan, Mecklenburg, Anson, Cumberland, and Johnston counties to be in readiness to respond to Fanning's call, sent a proclamation to be read to the people, and offered to go himself to the scene of action if Fanning desired his presence. The Council, declaring the Regulators guilty of insurrection, approved these actions of the governor.

In the meantime the officers, alarmed at the storm they had raised, offered to meet the Regulators and adjust their differences. To Fanning they explained their offer as a subterfuge to gain time. The Regulators on the contrary accepted it in good faith and immediately made preparations for the meeting. They appointed a committee to collect data relating to the taxes and fees and required its members to take an oath to do justice between the officers and the people to the best of their ability. Fanning was determined to prevent any such meeting. While the Regulators were making their preparations, he collected a band of armed men and swooping down upon Sandy Creek, arrested Butler and Husband on a charge of inciting to rebellion and hurried them off to prison at Hillsboro. At this high-handed act 700 men, many of whom were not Regulators, seized their guns and marched on Hillsboro to rescue the prisoners. It was now the officers' turn to become frightened. They threw open the prison doors, released their captives, and hurried them off to turn back the mob. Along with them went Isaac Edwards, the governor's private secretary, who promised the people in the name of the governor that if they would peaceably disperse, go home quietly, and petition the governor in the proper manner, the governor would see that justice was done them. Since this promise was exactly in line with their own plans, which had been interrupted by the arrest of Husband and Butler, the Regulators accepted it gladly. In spite of Fanning's opposition, they appointed a committee which prepared their case and laid it before the governor. But Tryon repudiated the promise of his secretary, saying Edwards had exceeded his authority, refused to deal with the Regulators as an organization, demanded that they immediately disband, and expressed his hearty approval of Fanning's course. At the same time he stated for the information of the people the amount of poll tax due for the year 1767, promised to issue a proclamation forbidding the officers' taking illegal fees, and ordered the attorney-general to prosecute any officer charged in due form with extortion.

In July, 1768, Tryon went to Hillsboro in the hopes that he might induce the people to submit to the laws. While he was there, the Regulators met to consider his reply to their petition. They told him that his proclamation forbidding the taking of illegal fees had had no effect, and they had decided to petition the Assembly in order to strengthen his hands. Other meetings were held and several communications, both verbal and written, passed between the governor and the Regulators. In one of them he told the Regulators that he was ever ready to do them justice and as evidence of it he had ordered the attorney-general to institute prosecutions against officers charged with extortion, one of whom was Colonel Fanning himself. In a letter written by the governor and approved by the Council, August 13, and sent to a meeting of the Regulators, August 17, appears the key to the explanation of the differences between the governor and the Regulators. The latter, either from distrust of the courts or ignorance of the law, expected the governor to give evidence of his sincerity by summary proceedings against the offending officials; the governor on the contrary knew that he could move only through the courts and that every step must be in due legal form. "By your letter delivered to me the 5th instant

*   *   *'' he wrote, ''I have the mortification to find   *   *   *
the friendly aid I offered to correct the abuses in public offices
(which it was my duty to tender) [is] considered by you insufficient. The force of the proclamation was to caution public
officers against and to prevent as much as possible extortion:
It is the province of the Courts of Law to Judge and punish
the Extortioner.'' At the same time he took them to task for
their unwillingness to wait upon legal process against those
whom they charged with abusing their public trust.

One of Tryon's purposes in going to Hillsboro was to
secure protection for the Superior Court when it met in September to try Husband and Butler. Such protection could be
secured either by obtaining from the leaders of the Regulators
a bond that no attempt at rescue would be made, or other
insult offered the court; or by calling out the militia. Tryon
preferred the first of these alternatives, since it would save
the province a considerable expense, but the Regulators for
very good reasons refused to give it. The governor, therefore,
in the exercise of a wise precaution called out the militia.
Some difficulty was encountered in enrolling a sufficient force
since most of the people of the surrounding counties were
tainted with Regulating principles, but Tryon tactfully won
over the leading preachers of the Lutherans, Presbyterians,
and Baptists and largely through their influence secured 195
men from Rowan, 310 from Mecklenburg, 126 from Granville,
and 699 from Orange. Two small independent companies, an
artillery company, and the general officers brought the force
up to 1,461 men. It was one of the most remarkable organizations in military history. More than one-fifth of the entire
force were commissioned officers. They included six lieuten-
ant-generals, two major-generals, three adjutant-generals,
seven colonels, five lieutenant-colonels, and many majors, captains, aids-de-camp, and minor officers. Characteristically
enough, Edmund Fanning, who was to be tried for extortion
by the court which this imposing array was called out to protect, and Maurice Moore, who was to sit as an associate justice
of the court, were both colonels in active command. Most of
the high officers were councilmen, representatives, justices, or
holders of other political offices. At a council of war held in
Hillsboro, attended by no officer of lower rank than major,
thirty-four members were present, of whom six were members
of the Council, eighteen of the Assembly. ''Thus,'' comments
Dr. Bassett, ''to guard the Superior Court a military force
was called out which embraced, either as high officers or as

gentlemen volunteers, one-fourth of the members of that body [the Assembly] to which the Regulators had decided to appeal. The above contrast indicates how completely the forces of central and local government, both civil and military, were in the hands of a small office-holding class, which was distributed throughout the counties. As we contemplate such a state of affairs we are struck with the fact that nothing short of a popular upheaval could have brought redress to the Regulators."[1]

Tryon's precautions were wisely taken. The Regulators assembled to the number of 3,700, but, overawed by the governor's display of force, made no attempt to interfere with the proceedings of the court. Husband was tried and acquitted; Butler and two other Regulators were convicted and sentenced to fines and imprisonment. None of them, however, was punished, for Tryon, having vindicated the authority of government, adopted a policy of leniency. He released the prisoners and suspended the payment of their fines, and later, upon the advice of the king, pardoned them. Fanning was tried for extortion and found guilty on five counts, but the judges, upon a motion in arrest of judgment, held their judgment in reserve, and so far as the records show no further action was ever taken on the case. Fanning promptly resigned his office as register. The Regulators pointed to the result as justifying their distrust of the courts. In this instance, however, their distrust was not well-founded for from any point of view, Fanning was guilty of nothing worse than a misconstruction of the law. It seems clear that he was not even guilty of that. He was charged with taking 6s. for registering a deed when, it was alleged, he was entitled to only 2s. 8d. Yet before entering upon his office he was advised by the county court that he was entitled to 6s. and odd pence, while the attorney-general of the colony had advised him that he was entitled to 8s. 7d. on any deed. After his conviction the case was referred to the attorney-general of England and to John Morgan of the Inner Temple, London, both of whom were of opinion that not only was Fanning entitled to more than he took, but that under no aspect of the case could he be guilty of extortion, since his action in seeking advice from the county court clearly disproved any intention to commit

---

[1] "The Regulators of North Carolina," p. 178 of the *Annual Report of the American Historical Association*, 1894.

a fraud.[2]   But the Regulators were in no frame of mind to appreciate these fine points; all they could see was that Fanning, although found guilty of extortion, had escaped punishment, and they bitterly resented the outcome.

In the meantime the Regulating spirit had spread to other counties. In some of them it found expression in acts of violence. A band of about thirty men from Edgecombe County attempted unsuccessfully to rescue an insurgent leader who had been imprisoned in the Halifax jail. In Johnston County a mob attacked the county court. In Anson a hundred armed men entered the courthouse, broke up the sitting of the county court, drove the justices off the bench, and then entered into an oath-bound association to assist each other in resisting all efforts of the sheriff to collect taxes. Later, however, apparently upon the advice of the Orange County Regulators, the Anson Regulators abandoned violent methods and sought a redress of their grievances through a petition to the governor, from whom they received the same promise that had been given to the Regulators of Orange. In Rowan County, also, an organization existed which attempted to prosecute the officers for extortion, but failed because the grand jury refused to return true bills.

The courts failing them, the Regulators decided to appeal to the Assembly. In the summer of 1769, the governor dissolved the old Assembly and ordered the election of a new one. In Orange, Anson, Granville, and Halifax counties the Regulators returned their entire delegations while they made their influence felt in Rowan and other counties. When the Assembly met, several petitions were presented setting forth the grievances of the Regulators together with their suggestions for reform. The Assembly certainly was not unsympathetic with their appeal, but because of some resolutions which it

---

[2] The whole trouble lay in the differences between the popular and the legal construction of the law. For registering a deed the law allowed a fee of 2s. 8d. Fanning was accused of extortion because in registering Deed 13 he had charged 6s. Besides the deed itself, there were three endorsements which required to be registered. To the people, deed and endorsements formed a single instrument for which the register could collect one fee; to Fanning they formed four instruments on each of which he was entitled to a fee. Fanning's construction was upheld by the attorney-general of North Carolina, the attorney-general of England, and John Morgan of the Inner Temple. Morgan gave it as his opinion that Fanning was entitled to four fees, viz.: (1) For the deed; (2) for the certificate of the examination of the *feme covert;* (3) for the certificate of the persons examining; (4) for the oath of execution and order to register.

had adopted on the questions at issue between the colonies and the British ministry, it suffered a sudden and unexpected dissolution before it could take up the measures necessary to redress the Regulators' grievances. It showed its attitude toward their petitions, however, by resolving just before dissolution, "that if any public officer shall exact illegal fees, or otherwise under colour of his office unduly oppress the people, such officer so acting shall on conviction thereof receive the highest censure and punishment this House can inflict upon him." The men who composed the Assembly appeared to be so ready to listen to the complaints of the Regulators that James Iredell declared a majority of them were themselves of Regulating principles.

It seems clear that legal remedies would have been provided for their grievances had the Regulators been willing to wait upon the slow process of lawmaking. That the laws needed amendment was not denied, but the Assembly from its very nature as a legislative body could not move with the speed which the impatience of the Regulators demanded. The reformer is naturally a radical, the lawmaker is, or ought to be, a conservative, and when he does not move fast enough for the reformer, the latter frequently becomes impatient and runs into excesses in words or deeds. So it was with the Regulators. Impatience at what they considered the indifference of all branches of the colonial government to their grievances led them into excesses which no government entitled to the name could think of condoning. For, to break into courts of justice, driving the judges from the bench, to "tear down justice from her tribunal," and contemptuously to set up mock courts filling the records with billingsgate and profanity; to drag unoffending attorneys through the streets at the peril of their lives, and wantonly to assault peaceable citizens for refusing to sympathize with lawlessness—these surely are not proper methods of redressing grievances, however oppressive, in a civilized community under a government based upon the will of the people.

Such were the methods which lost the Regulators the sympathy of the Assembly and compelled both the king's governor and the people's representatives to look less to the redress of grievances than to the suppression of anarchy. When the Superior Court, Judge Richard Henderson presiding, met at Hillsboro, in September, 1770, a mob of 150 Regulators, led by Herman Husband, James Hunter, Rednap Howell, and William Butler, armed with sticks and switches, broke into the courthouse, attempted to strike the judge, and compelled him to leave the bench. They next assaulted and severely whipped John Williams, whose only offense was that he was a practicing attorney. William Hooper was "dragged and paraded through the streets, and treated with every mark of contempt and insult." Turning next to Edmund Fanning, the mob pulled him out of the courthouse by his heels, dragged him through the street, and gave him a brutal whipping. Breaking into his house, they burned his papers, destroyed his furniture, and demolished the building. Alexander Martin, Michael Holt, Thomas Hart, "and many others," were whipped. Rioting through the streets of the town, the Regulators amused themselves in typical mob-fashion by smashing the windows of private residences and terrorizing the inhabitants. Unable to enforce order Judge Henderson adjourned court and escaped from the town under cover of darkness. The next day the Regulators assembled in the courtroom, set up a mock court, secured the docket, and entered upon it their own judgments and comments upon the several cases. In McMund vs. Courtney the comment was "Damn'd Rogues;" in Wilson vs. Harris, "All Harris's are Rogues;" in Brumfield vs. Ferrel, "Nonsense let them agree for Ferrell has gone Hellward;" in Brown vs. Lewis, wherein judgment was entered by default, it was "The Man was sick. It tis damned roguery;" in Fanning vs. Smith, "Fanning pays costs but loses nothing;" in Hogan vs. Husbands, "Hogan pays & be damned;" in Richardson vs. York, "Plaintiff pays all and gets his body scourged for Blasphemy;" while in Humphries vs. Jackson the entry is "Judgment by default the money must come to the officers."

These outrages threw the colonial officials into a panic. The Orange County officials loudly demanded a special session of the Assembly. The governor hastily summoned the Council to give their advice as to "the properest measures to be taken in the exigency." The Council urged that the militia be immediately called into active service. The air was full of rumors. First came news of the burning by incendiaries of Judge Henderson's dwelling and stables in Granville County. Hard upon this report, followed rumors that the Regulators were gathering in force for a descent upon New Bern to overawe the Assembly. In the midst of the excitement the Assembly met, December 5th. "Born as it was in terror," says Dr. Bassett, "it is not surprising that it should have passed away in blood." For a time the members kept their heads admirably. In their reply to the governor's message they declared that the conduct of public officers in some parts of the colony had "given just cause of complaint" which was due chiefly to "an inconsistent and oppressive fee Bill," and promised to remedy the evils as far as possible. Acts were accordingly passed relating to the appointment of sheriffs and their duties, ascertaining attorneys' fees, more strictly regulating officers' fees, providing for the more speedy collection of small debts, placing the chief justice on a salary, and erecting the counties of Wake, Guilford, Chatham, and Surry, all lying in the region embraced within the Regulation. All these laws were in line with the demands of the Regulators. But while the House was considering them, a report was received that the Regulators had assembled at Cross Creek preparatory for their march on New Bern. Reformatory measures were hastily side-tracked and punitive measures given the right of way. The Assembly had already in its message to the governor denounced the "daring and insolent attack" of the Regulators on the court at Hillsboro; declared that their "dissolute principles and licentious spirit" rendered them too formidable for the ordinary process of law; and recommended the adoption of "measures at once spirited and decisive." The measure adopted was introduced by Samuel Johnston and is generally known as the "Johnston Act." It provided that the attorney-general might prosecute charges of riot in any Superior Court in the province, declared outlaws all those who avoided the summons of the court for sixty days, allowed such outlaws to be killed with impunity, and authorized the governor to employ the militia to enforce the law. Like most laws passed in passion and fear its very severity largely defeated its purpose. As Haywood truly remarks, it is doubtful if so drastic a measure ever passed another American assembly; but the Assembly felt, as James Iredell expressed it, that "desperate diseases must have desperate remedies."

The Regulators met the Assembly's "desperate remedies" with defiance. Husband having been expelled from the Assembly and imprisoned at New Bern for a libel on Maurice Moore, the Regulators were prevented from releasing him by force only by the grand jury's failure to return a true bill against him. Determined to extend and strengthen their organization, they dispatched emissaries into Bute, Edgecombe, and Northampton to stimulate and organize disaffection in those counties. In Rowan they denounced the Assembly for passing a "riotous act," swore they would pay no fees, resolved that no judge or king's attorney should hold any court in Rowan, threatened death to all clerks and lawyers who came among them, and declared Edmund Fanning an outlaw whom any Regulator might kill on sight. Rednap Howell, writing from Halifax to James Hunter, February 16, 1771, said: "I give out here that the Regulators are determined to whip every one who goes to Law or will not pay his just debts; * * * that they will choose Representatives but not send them to be put in jail; in short to stand in defiance and as to thieves to drive them out of the Country." When Tryon appointed a term of Superior Court to be held at Hillsboro in March, 1771, the judges filed with the Council a formal protest saying that under the conditions existing in that part of the province which were "rather increasing than declining," they could not hold such a court with any hopes of dispatching business or any prospect of personal safety to themselves; and the Council, thinking that the time had come for law to take a stand against anarchy, advised the governor to call out the militia and march against the Regulators "with all expedition." This advice was hailed with relief by the law-abiding people of the colony, who were worn out with the reign of violence, lawlessness, and terrorism which the Regulators had set up.

Tryon lost no time in getting his military preparations under way. He ordered General Hugh Waddell with the Cape Fear militia to proceed at once to Salisbury to overawe the Rowan Regulators, raise the western militia, and march on Hillsboro from the west. Tryon himself in command of the eastern militia was to march from New Bern and unite with Waddell at Hillsboro. On March 19th, he ordered the colonels of the several counties to hold militia musters and secure 2,550 volunteers. In the counties affected by the influence of the Regulators difficulties in raising men arose, and in none of the counties were the quotas secured. Altogether Tryon raised a force of 1,068 men, of whom 151 were commissioned officers, while Waddell raised 284 men, of whom 48 were commissioned officers. Among these officers were Robert Howe, Alexander Lillington, James Moore, John Ashe, Richard Caswell, Francis Nash, and Griffith Rutherford, all of whom subsequently won military distinction in the war of the Revolution, and Abner Nash, John Baptista Ashe, and Willie Jones, who attained high civil positions during and after the Revolution. Tryon reached Hillsboro May 9 without meeting any opposition, but Waddell had been checked by a superior force of Regulators and because his men would not fire on them was compelled to fall back on Salisbury. Consequently he did not join Tryon until after the battle of Alamance.

On May 14, Tryon encamped on Great Alamance Creek, a few miles west of Hillsboro. Two days later he formed his line of battle and marched forward to meet the enemy who had gathered about 2,000 strong. The Regulators were numerically superior to the militia, but the latter enjoyed every other advantage. Neither side really wanted to bring on a battle. Tryon still hoped that the Regulators upon his display of force would submit and disperse, while the Regulators had not lost hope of securing a peaceable adjustment of their quarrel. Accordingly while the two forces lay on their arms facing each other, each reluctant to bring matters to a final test, they sent a petition to the governor requesting to be permitted to lay their grievances before him. To this petition Tryon very properly replied that as long as they remained under arms in "a state of War and Rebellion," he could hold no negotiations with them, and demanded that they disperse and submit to the laws of their country. He gave them one hour to come to a decision. The infatuated people treated his reply with contempt and foolishly declared that a fight was all they wanted. At the expiration of the hour, Tryon sent an officer to receive their reply. The officer told them that unless they dispersed the governor would fire upon them. "Fire and be damned!" was their answer. Thereupon the governor gave the order. His men hesitated. Rising in his stirrups he cried out, "Fire! Fire on them or on me!" The militia obeyed, the Regulators replied, and the action became general. Organization and discipline as usual won the day. After two hours of fighting the undisciplined mob was driven in confusion from the field. Perhaps the most remarkable feature of this remarkable battle was the poor marksmanship on both sides. Tryon's casualties were nine killed, sixty-one wounded, the Regulators' casualties were nine killed and a large unascertained number wounded. Fifteen Regulators were captured, one of whom, James Few, who had previously been outlawed, was summarily executed in compliance with the insistence of the militia, who demanded an example.

After his victory, Tryon's course was marked by good judgment and leniency. He had the wounded Regulators cared for by his own surgeons. The next day he issued a proclamation offering pardon to those, with a few exceptions, who would submit to the government and take the oath of allegiance. Fourteen of the prisoners taken in the battle were tried at a special term of the Superior Court, twelve of whom were convicted of high treason and sentenced to death. Six of the number were hanged, the others at Tryon's request were pardoned by the king.

Alamance was the climax of Tryon's administration in North Carolina. He had already received notice of his appointment as governor of New York, and a few days after his victory he bade his army farewell and set out for his new province. He was soon followed by Edmund Fanning.

The Regulation was at an end. Its leaders were dead, fugitives, or in concealment, its members scattered and disheartened. James Few had been executed on the battlefield. Benjamin Merrill and James Pugh, convicted of treason, had paid the penalty for their crime, Husband, Howell, and Hunter had sought safety in flight. Hamilton, Butler, and others were in hiding. After Tryon's departure some of these leaders, who had been excepted from his offer of general amnesty, applied to his successor, Governor Josiah Martin, for pardon which, however, was not then granted. The Regulators generally availed themselves of Tryon's offer of pardon. Within six weeks after the battle of Alamance, 6,409 had submitted to the government and taken the oath of allegiance. The British government advised the General Assembly to pass a general amnesty act, but the two houses could not agree on its terms and the proposed act failed of passage. The course of events, however, favored the cause of the Regulators. In 1775, when the men who had followed Tryon at Alamance were themselves organizing committees, congresses, and armies for rebellion, the old Regulators manifested such a "favorable disposition" toward the royal government that the king sent to his governor in North Carolina "a Power, under the Great Seal, to pardon all those who were concerned in the Rebellious Insurrections in 1770, Herman Husband only excepted." About the same time the Provincial Congress sitting at Hillsboro and presided over by the author of the Johnston Act, resolved that the former Regulators "ought to be protected from every attempt to punish them by any Means whatever." Thus the despised and feared "banditti" of the back country, courted by king and revolutionists alike, found safety in the quarrels of their former enemies, and had they been asked to express their view of the situation they would probably have quoted the old adage that when thieves fall out, honest men get their dues.

In any discussion of the Regulation the question arises, Did the Regulators begin the Revolution and at Alamance shed the first blood in the cause of independence? Upon the answer to this question must depend our judgment of the historical importance of the Regulation. The Regulators made no such claim for themselves: on the contrary when an opportunity was offered to fight for independence a great majority of them arrayed themselves against it. The oath which Tryon compelled them to take after the battle of Alamance is often urged as a sufficient justification of their course during the Revolution; but every American who pleaded the cause or fought the battles of independence had repeatedly taken a similar oath. There is a fundamental difference, which Dr. Bassett points out, between the Regulation and the Revolution. The Regulators were not contending for a great constitutional principle lying at the very foundation of human government such as inspired the men who fought the Revolution. Every grievance of which the former complained could have been removed by their own representatives in an assembly chosen by the people; the American people sent no representatives to the British Parliament. The former, therefore, resisted oppressive methods of administering laws passed by their own representatives; the latter, it need scarcely be said, revolted against taxation without representation. The one was an insurrection, the other a revolution. The distinction is plain and goes to the root of the whole matter. A revolution involves a change of principles in government and is constitutional in its significance; an insurrection is an uprising of individuals to prevent the execution of laws and aims at a change of agents who administer, or the manner of administering affairs under forms or principles that remain intact. There is of course all the difference in the world between the two. It is this difference, for instance, that raises the resistance to the Stamp Act on the Cape Fear far above the revolt of the Regulators in dignity and significance, and elevates the former but not the latter above the level of a riot. The Americans denied the validity of the Stamp Act because in passing it Parliament, as they believed, assumed to itself an authority which it did not rightfully possess, and thus undermined their constitutional liberties. The Regulators did not dispute the constitutional right of the Assembly to enact the laws of which they complained; they merely objected to the improper execution of those laws. Then, too, there is no continuity between the Regulation and the Revolution. The principles of the revolt against the Stamp Act did not die with the repeal of the act, but became the living issues in the great Revolution. The movement of the Regulators expended itself at Alamance and died out with the removal of the causes and persons which gave rise to it. However just their cause may have been, it did not involve a vital principle of political freedom, and it seems clear that it is a total misconception of the real significance of the American Revolution as well as of the Regulation to call Alamance the first battle in the cause of independence.

CHAPTER XVIII

THE STAMP ACT AND THE CONTINENTAL ASSOCIATION

When Tryon took the oath of office April 3, 1765, the Stamp Act was the chief topic of discussion in the political circles of America. The new governor was a man of much greater force and ability than any of his predecessors. Courtly, versatile, tactful and resourceful, he knew how to win the favor of men and understood the secrets of leadership. If any man could have induced the people of North Carolina to accept the Stamp Act, he was the man. But those with whom he had to contend were men of equal ability and determination and had, moreover, far more at stake than he. Before his arrival they had already made up their minds what course they intended to pursue. At the October session, 1764, the Assembly in their reply to Governor Dobbs' address declared their opposition to the right of Parliament to impose internal taxes in the colonies as being "against what we esteem our Inherent right and Exclusive privilege of imposing our own Taxes," and had united with Massachusetts and the other colonies in protesting against the proposed stamp duty. When Tryon asked John Ashe, speaker of the Assembly, what the attitude of the colony would be toward the Stamp Act, Ashe promptly replied with great confidence: "We will resist it to the death."

In this determination the representatives received loyal support from their constituents. Indeed, from the first, opposition to the Stamp Act in North Carolina was a popular movement, though directed and controlled by a few trusted leaders. At Cross Creek, New Bern, Edenton, and other places in the province, during the summer of 1765, public demonstrations were made against it. But for obvious reasons the Cape Fear, as the center of the colony's trade and the residence of the governor, became the chief scene of the resistance and its course determined the course of the province. At Wilmington large crowds gathered from the surrounding counties, drank "Liberty, Property and no Stamp Duty;" hanged Lord Bute

in effigy; compelled the stamp master, William Houston, to resign his office; and required Andrew Steuart, the printer, to
issue the *North Carolina Gazette* on unstamped paper.
Alarmed at these demonstrations, Tryon called into consultation a number of the leading merchants, assured them if they
would not resist the Stamp Act, that he would urge the ministry to exempt North Carolina from its operation, and offered
"as a further inducement to the reception of the small
stamps" and as a pledge of his good faith, to pay himself the
duties on all instruments whereon he was entitled to any fee.
To this shrewd proposition the merchants replied that every
view of the Stamp Act confirmed them in their opinion that
it was destructive of those liberties which, as British subjects,
they had a right to enjoy in common with their fellow subjects
of Great Britain; that they could not consent to his paying
for the small stamps as "an admission of part would put it
out of our power to refuse with any propriety a submission
to the whole;" that they thought, therefore, it "more consistent as well as securer conduct" to resist the execution of
the act to the utmost of their power.

The issues were thus joined. But no occasion arose to put
the resolution of the people to a test until November 28th, when
the sloop Diligence, Captain Constantine Phipps, with an
assignment of stamps, cast anchor at Brunswick. Quickly
spread the news of her arrival. Up and down the Cape Fear,
and far into the country, men snatched their rifles and hurried
to Brunswick. Under the command of Hugh Waddell and John
Ashe, they presented a resolute front to the king's man-of-
war, and declared their purpose to resist by force if necessary
any attempt to land the king's stamps. Captain Phipps prudently declined to test the sincerity of their threat and made
no attempt to carry the stamps ashore. A month passed, and
Governor Tryon wrote, "the Stamps still remain on board the
said ship;" and after still another month, he added, "where
they still continue." It is impossible now to realize fully
just what such conduct meant, but we may be sure that Ashe
and Waddell, and the men who followed them, knew what they
dared when, with arms in their hands, they thus defied the
king's officers. Treason it was, of course; but while the merchants and planters of the Cape Fear might have felt confident
of escaping the penalties of treason they well knew they could
not, if the situation remained long unchanged, escape the penalties of ruin. Vessels rocked idly at their anchorage and sails
flapped lazily against their masts, for Wilmington and Bruns-

wick were closed ports. Ships bound for the Cape Fear passed by to other ports, and the merchants expected nothing less than the total destruction of their trade. Nevertheless, as Tryon wrote, they were "as assiduous in obstructing the reception of the Stamps as any of the inhabitants. No business," he continued, "is transacted in the Courts of Judicature * * * and all Civil Government is now at a stand. This stagnation of all public business and commerce, under the low circumstances of the inhabitants, must be attended with fatal consequences to this colony if it subsists but for a few months longer." The situation in other parts of the colony was no better. "Tho' the people here," wrote the Rev. James Reed of New Bern, "are peaceable and quiet yet they seem very uneasy, discontented, and dejected. The Courts of Justice are in a great measure shut up and it is expected that in a few weeks there will be a total stagnation of trade."

With the opening of the New Year the struggle reached its climax. Two vessels arrived at Brunswick, the Dobbs from Philadelphia, and the Patience from St. Christopher, neither of which had stamps on her clearance papers. Although each vessel presented to the collector, William Dry, a statement signed by the collectors at Philadelphia and St. Christopher that no stamps were to be had at either place, nevertheless Captain Jacob Lobb, of the cruiser Viper, declared both vessels outlaws and seized them in the name of the king. Later a third vessel, the Ruby, shared a like fate. Captain Lobb delivered their papers to Collector Dry that proceedings might be instituted against them in the Admiralty Court. Thereupon Dry consulted the attorney-general, submitting to him three queries: first, whether failure to obtain clearances on stamped paper justified the seizures; second, whether judgment ought to be given against the vessels "upon proof being made that it was impossible to obtain clearances" on stamped paper; third, whether the proceedings should be instituted in the Admiralty Court at Halifax, Nova Scotia, rather than at Cape Fear.

The passions of the people were profoundly stirred by these proceedings, but while the attorney-general was preparing his answer, they were admirably suppressed. When the answer was finally given, it was an affirmative to each of the collector's questions. Instantly the smothered flames flared into open conflagration. The people generally entered into an association that "We the subscribers * * * mutually and solemnly plight Our Faith and Honour that We Will at any Risque whatever, and whenever called upon, Unite and Truly and Faithfully Assist each other, to the best of Our Power, in preventing entirely the Operation of the Stamp Act.'' Wilmington peremptorily refused the usual provisions to the king's vessels, the angry people seized the boats sent ashore for supplies and threw their crews into the common jail. Forty of the leading men of the Cape Fear section joined in a letter to William Dry warning him against the course advised by the attorney-general. A party of unknown men entered the collector's house, broke open his desk, and seized the ships' papers. The people of the surrounding counties snatched their guns, hurried to Wilmington, organized an armed association composed of ''the principal gentlemen, freeholders and other inhabitants of several counties,'' took an oath to resist the Stamp Act to the death, and marched to Brunswick to rescue the outlawed vessels.

It was late in the afternoon of February 19th, when they entered the little village before which lay the king's cruiser and near which the king's governor dwelt. Hearing at Brunswick that Captain Lobb was concealing himself in the governor's house, the ''inhabitants in arms,'' as Tryon always called them, turned their steps in that direction. Though fully determined to seize Lobb and force him to surrender the vessels, the leaders were equally determined to protect the governor from insult. Accordingly, Cornelius Harnett and George Moore waited on him in advance of their followers and offered him a guard. But they had misjudged their man. Whatever else he may have been, William Tryon was not a coward. He haughtily commanded that no guard be sent to give its protection where it was neither necessary nor desired, and with this rebuff, Moore and Harnett retired. Immediately a band of armed men surrounded the house and demanded the surrender of Captain Lobb. But Tryon stood firm, and peremptorily refused to communicate any information to the ''inhabitants in arms,'' saying that as they had arms in their hands they might break open his locks, force his doors, and search his house if they chose to do so. But the leaders, having no quarrel with Tryon, were not ready for such violent measures; and learning in some other way that Captain Lobb was not there, they detailed a small guard to watch the governor's house and withdrew to Brunswick for the night.

The next morning a delegation from the ''inhabitants in arms'' went aboard the Viper and demanded the release of the Ruby and the Patience. The Dobbs, having given proper security, had already been released. Afraid to refuse and unwilling to comply, Lobb begged a respite till the afternoon. In the meantime he held a conference with the governor and other officials to whom he declared his purpose to release the Ruby, at the same time expressing his unalterable determination to hold fast to the Patience. Half a loaf to the people and half to the government, he thought ought to satisfy both. It did satisfy Tryon who expressed his approval of the division. At the same time he urged Lobb not to consider him, his family or his property as he was only "solicitous for the honor of the government and his Majesty's interest in the present exigency." With this understanding the conference was brought to a close. But the other party was not so easily satisfied. When the delegation from the "inhabitants in arms" returned to the Viper they dissented so vigorously, that Captain Lobb was forced to surrender to them both their half and the government's half also. He based his compliance on the ground that he did not think "it proper to detain the sloop Ruby any longer," and had suddenly discovered there were "perishable commodities on board the sloop Patience." But such transparent excuses could not deceive the governor. Tryon was utterly astonished when he learned that Lobb had surrendered completely to the people, but his astonishment was turned to disgust and contempt upon hearing that Lobb in a fit of fright had directed the commanding officer at Fort Johnston to spike his guns lest they be captured and turned on the king's ships by "the inhabitants in arms." His reprimand was severe and contemptuous. The detention of the Patience, Tryon declared, was "a point that concerned the honor of the government," Lobb's surrender of the vessel he considered a breach of faith for it made his situation "very unpleasant, as most of the people by going up to Wilmington in the sloops would remain satisfied and report through the province they had obtained every point they came to redress," while Lobb's excuses for the order to Captain Dalrymple, commander at Fort Johnston, the governor denounced as "totally contrary to every sentiment I entertained."

But Tryon himself was not to be exempt from similar treatment. It is true the people had obtained every point they came to redress, but their work was not finished until they had made sure no other points would arise that would require redressing. There could be no assurance of this, so long as there remained in the province any royal official with authority to sell stamps and seize vessels who was at liberty to exercise his authority. Accordingly the leaders made up their minds to take the same precaution against this as they had taken in the case of Houston. During the afternoon of February 20th, wrote Tryon, "Mr. Pennington, his Majesty's Comptroller, came to let me know there had been a search after him, and as he guessed they wanted him to do some act that would be inconsistent with the duty of his office, he came to acquaint me with this enquiry and search." The governor offered the comptroller a bed for the night and the protection of his roof, both of which the frightened official gratefully accepted. Early the next morning the "inhabitants in arms" sent Colonel James Moore to demand that they be permitted to speak with Pennington. To this demand Tryon replied: "Mr. Pennington being employed by his Excellency on dispatches for his Majesty's service, any gentleman that has business with him may see him at the Governor's house."

About ten o'clock Tryon observed "a body of men in arms from four to five hundred," moving toward his house. Three hundred yards away they drew up in line and sent a detachment of sixty men down the avenue to the door. The leader and spokesman of this detachment was Cornelius Harnett. Then followed the most dramatic scene of the struggle over the Stamp Act, a brief but intense contest between William Tryon, representative of the king's government, and Cornelius Harnett, representative of the people's will, for possession of one of the king's officers. Two better representatives of their respective causes could not have been found. Each was acute, determined and resourceful, and each sincere in believing his the better cause. Tryon, the ablest of the colonial governors and one of the most forceful Englishmen ever sent in an official capacity to America, "could accomplish more," we are told, "by the forcefulness of his personality and the awe inspired by his mere presence than other rulers could do by edicts and armies."[1] Cornelius Harnett "could be wary and circumspect, or decided and daring as exigency dictated or emergency required."[2] In the interview that followed, Tryon had no forcefulness of personality or awe of presence which he could afford to hold in reserve; and Harnett was compelled to be both wary and decided, both circumspect and daring.

Harnett opened the interview by demanding that Pennington be permitted to accompany him. Tryon replied that the

---

[1] Smith, C. A.: "Our Debt to Cornelius Harnett," *University of North Carolina Magazine*, May, 1907, p. 383.

[2] Hooper, A. M.: "Cornelius Harnett," *University of North Carolina Magazine*, Vol. IX, p. 334-335.

comptroller had come into his house seeking refuge, that he was an officer of the Crown, and as such should receive all the protection the governor's roof and dignity of character could afford him. Harnett insisted. "The people," he said, "are determined to take him out of the house if he is longer detained, an insult," he added quickly, "which they wish to avoid offering to your Excellency." "An insult," retorted Tryon, "that will not tend to any consequences, since they have already offered every insult in their power, by investing my house and making me in effect a prisoner before any grievance or oppression has been first represented to me." During this conversation Pennington "grew very uneasy," and said "he would choose to go with the gentlemen," and the governor again repeated his offer of protection. But Pennington was doubtful of the governor's power to make good his offer, however excellent his intentions might be, and he decided to go with Harnett. To the governor, however, he declared that whatever oaths might be required of him, he would consider as acts of compulsion and not of free will; adding that he would rather resign his office than do anything inconsistent with his duty. "If that is your determination," replied the disgusted governor, "you had better resign before you leave here." Harnett quickly interposed his objection to this course, but Tryon insisted and Pennington agreed with him. Paper and ink were accordingly brought and the resignation was written and accepted. "Now, sir," said Tryon bitterly, "you may go;" and Harnett led the ex-comptroller out of the house to his followers who were waiting outside.

The detachment then rejoined the main body of the "inhabitants in arms," and the whole withdrew to the town. There they drew up in a large circle, placed the comptroller and the customs-house officials in the center, and administered to them all an oath "that they would not, directly or indirectly, by themselves, or any other person employed under them, sign or execute in their several Offices, any stampt Papers, until the Stamp Act should be accepted by the province." The clerk of the court and other public officials, and all the lawyers, were sworn to the same effect; and as each took the pledge the cheers of the crowd bore the news to the enraged and baffled governor as he sat in his room keenly conscious of his defeat. The letter in which he described these events to his superiors in England, it has been truly said, "contained the must humiliating acknowledgment of baffled pride and irredeemable failure that Tryon was ever called upon to pen."[3] Their work finished, the "inhabitants in arms" dispersed quietly and quickly to their homes.

"It is well worthy of observation," as the *North Carolina Gazette* boasted, "that few instances can be produced of such a number of men being together so long and behaving so well; not the least noise or disturbance, nor any person seen disguised with liquor, during the whole of their stay in Brunswick; neither was any injury offered to any person, but the whole affair was conducted with decency and spirit, worthy the imitation of all the Sons of Liberty throughout the continent." This splendid record was due to the high character and lofty purposes of the men who led and who composed that body of men to whom Tryon always refers as "the inhabitants in arms." "The mayor and corporation of Wilmington," he wrote, "and most of the gentlemen and planters of the counties of Brunswick, New Hanover, Duplin, and Bladen, with some masters of vessels, composed this corps."

Throughout the contest Harnett and the other leaders received loyal support from the people. They were in the midst of it upon the day set by the governor's writ for the election of representatives to the Assembly. Wilmington manifested its approval of Harnett's course by electing him without opposition, and New Hanover County unanimously elected John Ashe and James Moore. But the Assembly was not to meet any time soon. Tryon was too prudent a politician to convene a session while the people were in such a rebellious mood. He foresaw that Parliament would likely repeal the Stamp Act and hoped by announcing that fact when the Assembly met to insure the good humor of the lower house. It was not until November, therefore, that he ventured to face the people's representatives. He opened the session with a conciliatory message. But the members, irritated at his delay in calling them together, replied with such asperity and show of temper, that the Council denounced their message as "altogether indecent, without foundation and unmerited." The reply cut the governor to the quick, but he kept his temper and met the strictures of the Assembly with admirable moderation and dignity.

Whatever one may think of Tryon, there can be but one just opinion of his bearing throughout these trying ordeals. He bore himself on every occasion with dignity, courage and

---

[3] Smith: *University of North Carolina Magazine*, May, 1907, p. 384.

fidelity to his trust. His dispatches even when acknowledging defeat are conspicuous for their good temper. We search in vain for the ill-tempered invectives and impassioned superlatives that characterize the dispatches both of Dobbs, his predecessor, and of Martin, his successor. Closing his letter to Secretary Conway, he says: "Thus, sir, I have endeavored to lay before you the first springs of this disturbance as well as the particular conduct of the individual parties concerned in it and I have done this as much as I possibly could without prejudice or passion, favor or affection." The impartial reader will pronounce that in this endeavor he reached a remarkable degree of success. Nor was his courage less marked than his dignity. When shielding Lobb on the evening of February 19 and when standing between Pennington and the "inhabitants in arms" on the morning of the 21st, one feels sure that he would have seen his house go down in ruins or up in smoke before he would have yielded one inch to the besiegers. In this courage straight from his heart originated his unfeigned and unconcealed contempt for the conduct of Captain Lobb. We feel assured that William Tryon would have buried himself, his crew and his enemies in the bottom of the Cape Fear River beneath the wrecks of the Viper, the Diligence, the Dobbs, the Patience, and the Ruby, all, before he would have broken his engagement and embarrassed his superior officer. His sympathies were with the people in their struggle, and the duty imposed upon him a disagreeable one, but he faced it like a man and performed it faithfully. The king had entrusted him with the execution of the laws in North Carolina and that trust he regarded, rightly or wrongly, as superior to any obligations he owed to the people of the province. He was not their governor; he was the king's vicegerent, and his first duty was to obey the commands of his master.

To say this of Tryon is not to depreciate the honor and the glory that belong to his opponents. To Harnett and Ashe and Moore and Waddell and the men who followed them, North Carolinians owe their liberty, and no true American anywhere will deny to them the credit that belongs to those who see the right and fearlessly pursue it. Throughout the contest the "inhabitants in arms" carried every point at issue. But the most remarkable feature of the struggle was its absolute openness and orderliness. No attempt at concealment, no effort at disguise betrayed a doubt in the minds of the people that they were engaged in a righteous cause. The resistance was made by men on terms of familiarity with the governor, under the guns of the king's ships, and in the broad open light of day. Conscious of the rectitude of their purpose, the moral if not the legal right of their conduct, they felt that any attempt at concealment would be an admission, at least, of a doubt in their minds of the propriety of their course, and this they scorned to make.

The Americans of course had not been left to fight their battle alone. They had sympathizers among every class of Englishmen. In Parliament itself an incomparable group of orators and statesmen, led by such men at Pitt, Burke, Barré, and Conway in the Commons, and Camden and Rockingham in the Lords, supported their petitions and remonstrances with an earnestness and ability which could have been born of nothing less than a firm conviction that they were fighting the battle of English as well as American freedom. The king and ministry were finally forced to yield. The Stamp Act was repealed and the news was received throughout America with an outburst of joy and loyalty in which a wise ruler would have read a lesson of warning as well as of encouragment. North Carolina joined heartily in the rejoicing. New Bern celebrated the event with a public banquet and ball. The mayor and "Gentlemen of Wilmington," most of whom had recently been in arms against the governor, joined in a sincere address of congratulations to him. They assured him of their kindly sentiments toward him personally, explained that their recent opposition had been based solely upon their conviction that "Moderation ceases to be a Virtue when the Liberty of British Subjects is in danger," expressed appreciation of the "honor and justice of the British Parliament, whose prudent resolutions have relieved us from the Melancholy Dilemma to which we were almost reduced," and acknowledged the repeal as a mark of the king's "attention to the Distresses of his American Subjects." The colony as a whole had no voice in these rejoicings because Tryon had refused to convene the Assembly, but when the Assembly did meet in November the members complained bitterly of the governor's action which had deprived them of the opportunity "to concur with our Sister Colonies" in expressing their gratitude for "the tender and paternal care of our most Gracious Sovereign, and the wisdom and justice of the British Parliament. * * * But it is the peculiar misfortune of North Carolina," they continued, "to be deprived of those means which the other provinces peaceably enjoy (and to which this has also an unquestionable right) of making known such their dutiful dispositions; and if we are wanting in the general suffrage, we hope the censure will fall on those only whose indiscretions are the cause of it."

During the fight against the Stamp Act the Massachusetts Legislature issued a circular letter inviting all the colonies to send delegates to a congress to be held at New York to concert measures of resistance. Nine colonies responded. In North Carolina Governor Tryon refused to convene the Assembly in time for the election of delegates, and North Carolina, together with New Hampshire, Virginia, and Georgia, was not represented. The sentiment in these colonies, however, was in perfect harmony with the sentiment expressed by the Stamp Act Congress. From the struggle over the Stamp Act, therefore, was born a sentiment for a union of the colonies that contained the germs of nationality, and the development of this sentiment in the contests with the mother country from 1765 to 1775 gives to the events of that decade their chief significance. The Declaratory Act, which accompanied the repeal of the Stamp Act, asserted the right of Parliament to legislate for the colonies "in all cases whatsoever." The Townshend Acts passed in June 1767, attempted to put this assertion into practice. Under a pretense of regulating commerce, Parliament levied duties on certain commodities, principally tea, imported into the colonies, and directed that the revenues derived therefrom be used to pay the salaries of colonial officials, thus rendering them independent of the colonial assemblies. This scheme gave a new impulse to the union sentiment. Massachusetts led the way with the famous circular letter of 1768 inviting the co-operation of the other colonies in concerting measures of resistance in order that their remonstrances and petitions to the king "should harmonize with each other." But unity of action on the part of the colonies was the last thing the king and ministry desired, and they saw in this letter nothing less than an effort "to promote unwarrantable combinations and to excite and encourage an open opposition to and denial of the authority of Parliament." Accordingly they commanded the Assembly of Massachusetts to rescind the letter and the assemblies of the other colonies to treat it with contempt on pains of "an immediate prorogation or dissolution." But Massachusetts refused to rescind, and the other colonies applauded her spirit and imitated her action.

When the Assembly of North Carolina met, Speaker John Harvey laid the Massachusetts letter before the House. Greatly to the disgust of the more aggressive leaders, the House, though it did not treat it with the contempt which the king required, declined to take any formal notice of it and contented itself with merely giving the speaker verbal directions to answer it. It then resolved to send to the king "an humble, dutiful and loyal address," praying a repeal of the several acts of Parliament imposing duties on goods imported into America, appointed a committee consisting of John Harvey, Joseph Montfort, Samuel Johnston, Joseph Hewes, and Edward Vail to prepare it, and instructed the colony's agent, Henry Eustace McCulloh, to present it. Thus the Assembly missed the real significance of the proposal of Massachusetts, viz., unity of action, and by its conduct, according to Lord Hillsborough, secretary of state for the colonies, gave "great satisfaction to the king." Union was the great bugbear of the king and ministry; they did not doubt of their ability to bring the colonies to terms if they could keep them from co-operating with each other, and accordingly fought desperately against every step on the part of the Americans toward union. Samuel Johnston and Joseph Hewes were so disgusted at the "pusillanimity" of the Assembly that they declined to serve on the committee, but the other members, under the leadership of Harvey, acted more wisely. They assumed that the Assembly intended for them to act in concert with the committees of the other colonies, and thus improved on their verbal instructions. Their action saved North Carolina from the odium which a failure to support the common cause would have brought upon the colony and paved the way for the more spirited co-operation of the future.

The committee's address to the king was an able state paper and rang true to the American doctrine of "no taxation without representation." They reminded the king that in the past whenever it had been "found necessary to levy supplies within this Colony requisitions have been made by your Majesty or your Royal Predecessors and conformable to the rights of this people, and by them chearfully and liberally complied with," and while promising a like compliance in the future, maintained that "their Representatives in the Assembly alone can be the proper Judges, not only of what sums they are able to pay, but likewise of the most eligible method of collecting the same. Our Ancestors at their first settling, amidst the horrors of a long and bloody war with the Savages, which nothing could possibly render supportable but the prospects of enjoying here that freedom which Britons can never purchase at so [too] dear a rate, brought with them inherent in their persons, and transmitted down to their posterity, all the rights and liberties of your Majesty's natural born subjects within the parent State, and have ever since enjoyed as Britons the priviledges of an exemption from any Taxation but such as have been imposed on them by themselves or their Representatives, and this Priviledge we esteem so invaluable that we are fully convinced no other can possibly exist without it. It is therefore with the utmost anxiety and concern we observe duties have lately been imposed upon us by Parliament for the sole and express purpose of raising a Revenue. This is a Taxation which we are fully persuaded the acknowledged Principles of the British Constitution ought to protect us from. Free men cannot be legally taxed but by themselves or their Representatives, and that your Majesty's Subjects within this Province are represented in Parliament we cannot allow, and are convinced that from our situation we never can be.''

Along with this address went instructions to McCulloh of whom they required ''a Spirited Co-operation with the Agents of our Sister Colonies and Those who may be disposed to Serve us in Obtaining a Repeal of the Late Act Imposing Internal Taxes on Americans without Their Consent and the Which is Justly Dreaded by Them to be Nothing more than an Introduction to other acts of the same Injurious Tendency and fatal Consequences.'' In the same spirit of unity Harvey declared in his letter to the Massachusetts Assembly that the North Carolina Assembly will ''ever be ready, firmly to unite with their sister colonies, in pursuing every constitutional measure for redress of the grievances so justly complained of. This House is desirous to cultivate the strictest harmony and friendship with the assemblies of the colonies in general, and with your House in particular.'' When this letter was received in Boston the *Boston Evening Post* triumphantly declared: ''The colonies no longer disconnected, form one body; a common sensation possesses the whole; the circulation is complete, and the vital fluid returns from whence it was sent out.''

As a warning to the other colonies the ministry selected Massachusetts for punishment. Persons suspected of encouraging resistance to Parliament were to be arrested and sent to England for trial; town-meetings were to be suppressed; and two regiments were ordered to Boston to overawe that town. The blow was aimed at Massachusetts alone, but the other colonies promptly rallied to her support and raised the cry that Massachusetts was suffering in the common cause. Virginia acted first. Her Assembly denounced the government's action in a series of spirited resolutions, and sent them to the other assemblies ''requesting their concurrence therein.'' In consequence they suffered dissolution, but the burgesses promptly met as a convention, agreed on a "Non-Importation Association," and circulated it throughout the colonies.

On November 2, 1769, John Harvey laid the Virginia resolutions before the North Carolina Assembly. The House, without a dissenting voice, adopted them almost *verbatim,* agreed on a second protest to the king, and instructed their agent, after presenting it to have it printed in the British papers. Convinced that the king was deaf to their prayers, they now began to appeal to their British brethren. They again denied the right of Parliament to levy taxes in America, affirmed the right of the colonies to unite in protests to the throne, and denounced as "highly derogatory to the rights of British Subjects" the carrying of any American to England for trial, "as thereby the inestimable priviledge of being tried by a jury from the Vicinage, as well as the liberty of summoning and producing witnesses on such Tryal, will be taken away from the party accused." "We can not without horror," they declared, "think of the new, unusual, and permit us withall humbly to add, unconstitutional and illegal mode recommended to your Majesty of seizing and carrying beyond sea the Inhabitants of America suspected of any crime, [and] of trying such person in any other manner than by the Ancient and long established course of proceeding." "Truly alarmed at the fatal tendency of these pernicious Councils," [sic], they earnestly prayed the king to interpose his protection against "such dangerous invasions" of their dearest privileges. These proceedings, when reported to the governor, sealed the fate of that Assembly. Sending in haste for the House, he censured them for their action, declared that it "sapped the foundations of confidence and gratitude," and made it his "indispensable duty to put an end to this Session."

This sudden turn of affairs caught the Assembly unprepared for dissolution. Much important business, especially the adoption of the "Non-Importation Association," remained unfinished. Everybody realized that the effectiveness of non-importation as a weapon for fighting the Townshend duties depended entirely upon the extent to which it was adopted, and the fidelity with which it was observed. Any one colony therefore could easily defeat the whole scheme. When the North Carolina Assembly met in October, 1769, the association had been pretty generally adopted by the other colonies; consequently, the action of North Carolina was awaited with some concern. The leaders of the Assembly realized the situation fully, and were by no means ready to go home until they had taken the necessary action to bring the colony in line with the continental movement. Accordingly, immediately upon their dissolution, following the example of Virginia, they called the members together in convention to "take measures for preserving the true and essential interests of the province." Sixty-four of the seventy-seven members immediately repaired to the courthouse and re-organized as a convention independent of the governor. John Harvey was unanimously chosen moderator. After discussing the situation fully through a session of two days, the convention came to a series of resolutions which of course affirmed "invincible attachment and unshaken fidelity" to the king, but protested with great vigor against the acts of Parliament levying internal taxes in the colonies and depriving them of their constitutional right of trial by jury as having a "tendency to disturb the peace and good order of this government, which," the members boldly asserted, "we are willing, at the risque of our lives and fortunes, to maintain and defend." The resolutions set forth a complete non-importation program. They pledged the subscribers to a course of economy, industry, and thrift; to "encourage and promote the use of *North American manufactures* in general, and those of this province in particular;" neither to import themselves, nor to purchase from others, any goods, except paper, "which are or shall hereafter be taxed by act of Parliament for the purpose of raising a revenue in America;" and to look upon "every subscriber who shall not strictly and literally adhere to his agreement, according to the true intent and meaning thereof, * * * with the utmost contempt." This association was signed by sixty-four of "the late representatives of the people * * * being all that were then present," and by them recommended to their constituents in order to show their "readiness to join heartily with the other colonies in every legal method which may most probably tend to procure a redress" of grievances.

When the policy of non-importation was tried in opposition to the Stamp Act it was not successful, and the Loyalists ridiculed the attempt of Virginia to revive it as a weapon against the Townshend Acts. But a new element had now entered into the situation: the union sentiment had developed into a reality, and the opponents of the government, taking advantage of this fact, pushed the movement with vigor and success. Colony after colony joined the movement, and when North Carolina came in, the Whig papers declared with great satisfaction: "This completes the chain of union throughout the continent for the measure of non-importation and economy."

But it was a simpler matter to adopt an association than to
enforce it. The Tories, of course, opposed the whole scheme,
and would gladly have welcomed an opportunity to defeat it.
Their chance seemed to come when in April, 1770, Parliament
repealed all the duties except the one on tea. The Tories hoped
and the Whigs feared that this concession would break up the
non-importation associations. While the former applauded
the magnanimity of Parliament for yielding so much, the latter
denounced the ministry for yielding no more, and regarding the
partial repeal merely as a trap, redoubled their efforts to keep
the association intact.

In North Carolina the merchants of the Cape Fear were the
largest importers of British goods, and everybody recognized
that their action would determine the matter. No non-importation association could be made effective without their co-operation. Fortunately, Cornelius Harnett, one of the chief
merchants of the province, was also chairman of the Sons of
Liberty, and his influence went far toward determining the
course of the Cape Fear merchants. As soon as information
of Parliament's action reached Wilmington, he called a meeting of the Sons of Liberty in the Wilmington District to take
proper action. A large number of "the principal inhabitants"
attended at Wilmington, June 2, and "unanimously agreed to
keep strictly to the non-importation agreement," and to co-
operate with the other colonies "in every legal measure for
obtaining ample redress of the grievances so justly complained
of." In order to make their resolution more effective, they
chose a committee to consult upon such measures as would
best evince their "patriotism and loyalty" to the common
cause, and "manifest their unanimity with the rest of the
colonies." This committee was composed of thirty members
representing all the Cape Fear counties and the towns of Wilmington and Brunswick. Among its members were Cornelius
Harnett, who was chosen chairman, James Moore, Samuel
Ashe, Richard Quince, and Farquard Campbell, the most prominent merchants and planters of the Cape Fear section. They
declared their intention to enforce strictly the non-importation association; denounced the merchants of Rhode Island
"who contrary to their solemn and voluntary contract, have
violated their faith pledged to the other colonies, and thereby
shamefully deserted the common cause of American liberty;"
declared that they would have no dealings with any merchant
who imported goods "contrary to the spirit and intention" of
the non-importation association; and constituted themselves
a special committee to inspect all goods brought into the Cape

Fear and to keep the public informed of any that were imported in violation of the association. They then ordered their resolves to be "immediately transmitted to all the trading towns in this colony;" and in the spirit of co-operation, Cornelius Harnett wrote to the Sons of Liberty of South Carolina to inform them of their action. In this letter he said:

"We beg leave to assure you that the inhabitants of those six counties and we doubt not of every county in this province, are convinced of the necessity of adhering to their former resolutions, and you may depend, they are tenacious of their just rights as any of their brethren on the continent and firmly resolved to stand or fall with them in support of the common cause of American liberty. Worthless men * * * are the production of every country, and we are also unhappy as to have a few among us 'who have not virtue enough to resist the allurement of present gain.' Yet we can venture to assert, that the people in general of this colony, will be spirited and steady in support of their rights as English subjects, and will not tamely submit to the yoke of oppression. 'But if by the iron hand of power,' they are at last crushed; it is however their fixed resolution, either to fall with the same dignity and spirit you so justly mention, or transmit to their posterity entire, the inestimable blessings of our free Constitution. The disinterested and public spirited behaviour of the merchants and other inhabitants of your colony justly merits the applause of every lover of liberty on the continent. The people of any colony who have not virtue enough to follow so glorious examples must be lost to every sense of freedom and consequently deserve to be slaves."

The interchange of such views and opinions among the several colonies greatly strengthened the union sentiment; while the practical operation of the non-importation associations revealed to both the Americans and the ministry the power that lay in a united America.

CHAPTER XIX

DOWNFALL OF THE ROYAL GOVERNMENT

Soon after his victory at Alamance, Tryon left North Carolina for New York. He was succeeded by Josiah Martin who took the oath of office August 12, 1771. Martin, as Saunders observes, was a man ill calculated to conduct an administration successfully even in ordinary times. Stubborn and tactless, obsequious to those in authority and overbearing to those under authority, he found himself suddenly placed in a position that required almost every quality of mind and character that he did not possess. He was, it is true, an honest man, but he was intolerant and knew nothing of the art of diplomacy. Sincerely devoted to the king, whom he thought it no degradation to regard literally as a master, he had no faith in the sincerity of the Americans when in one breath they declared their loyalty to the Crown and in the next demanded from the Crown a recognition of their constitutional rights. "Insufferably tedious and turgid, * * * his dispatches make the tired reader long for the well-constructed, clear-cut sentences and polished impertinences of Tryon," and show that he was utterly incapable of understanding the people whom he had been sent to govern.[1] No worse selection could have been made at that time; the people of North Carolina were in no mood to brook the petty tyranny of a provincial governor, and Martin's personality became one of the chief factors that drove North Carolina headlong into revolution and prepared the colony, first of all the colonies, to take a definite stand for independence.

Their experience with the Stamp Act and the Townshend Acts taught the king and ministry the power that lay in a united America, and henceforth they avoided as far as possible such measures as would give the colonies a common grievance upon which they could unite. Their change of policy embraced

---

[1] Saunders: Prefatory Notes to *Colonial Records of North Carolina*, Vol. IX, p. iv.

two principles both of which the Americans promptly repudiated. One was the principle of the Declaratory Act. The other was the assumption that the king's instructions to the provincial governors were of higher authority than acts of assemblies and were binding on both assemblies and governors alike. For the next three years these instructions "played an important part in American politics. * * * They came under the king's sign manual, with the privy seal annexed. It was said that officials could not refuse to execute them without giving up the rights of the Crown. A set was not framed to apply to all the colonies alike, but special instructions were sent to each colony as local circumstances dictated. Hence the patriots could not create a general issue on them."[2] The Americans at once perceived their danger, and were not to be caught by it; when they came a few years later to adopt a Declaration of Independence, this policy of the king was one of the "facts submitted to a candid world," in justification of their action.

In North Carolina the battle was fought out on a very important local measure involving the jurisdiction of the colonial courts, about which the king issued positive instructions directing the course which the Assembly should pursue. Thus a momentous issue was presented for the consideration of the people's representatives: Should they permit the Assembly to degenerate into a mere machine whose highest function would be to register the will of the Sovereign; or should they maintain it as the Constitution intended it to be, a free, deliberative, law-making body, responsible for its acts only to the people? Upon their answer to this question it is not too much to say hung the fate of their remotest posterity. It should be recorded as one of the chief events in our history that the Assembly had the insight to perceive the issue clearly and the courage to meet it boldly. "Appointed by the people [they declared] to watch over their rights and priviledges, and to guard them from every encroachment of a private and public nature, it becomes our duty and will be our constant endeavour to preserve them secure and inviolate to the present age, and to transmit them unimpaired to posterity. * * * The rules of right and wrong, the limits of the prerogative of the Crown and of priviledges of the people are in the present age well known and ascertained; to exceed either of them is highly unjustifiable."

---

[2] Frothingham: The Rise of the Republic of the United States, p. 252.

The point at issue was the "foreign attachment clause" in
the court law. British merchants who transacted business in
the province through agents without ever being present in person, became in course of time extensive landowners here. The
Tryon court law contained a clause empowering the colonial
courts to attach this property for debts owed by such merchants to North Carolinians. The merchants objected to the
clause, but the king refused to veto the act because by its own
provision it was to expire at the end of five years and he expected, when a new bill was framed, to have the clause omitted
without interfering with the business of the courts. Accordingly he instructed Governor Martin not to approve any bill
containing the attachment clause.

The struggle began in the Assembly of January, 1773, and
during that and the next two sessions was the occasion of one
of the best conducted debates in the history of the colonial
Assembly. Both sides maintained their positions with ability.
The Council acting under instructions declined to pass the Assembly's bill unless it was so amended as to provide that attachment proceedings should be "according to the laws and
statutes of England." But the Assembly reminded the Council that in England such proceedings existed by municipal
custom, not by statute, and were "so essentially local" in their
application "as not to admit of being extended by any analogy
to this province." They contended that "to secure a privilege
so important the mode of obtaining it should be grounded in
certainty, the law positive and express, and nothing left to the
exercise of doubt or discretion." They therefore rejected the
Council's amendment. After much debate a compromise was
effected by the addition of a clause suspending the operation
of the act until the king's pleasure could be learned. The
Assembly thereupon sent it to their agent in London with instructions to leave no stone unturned to secure the royal signature. He was to say to the king that "so important does
this matter appear to this Province that they cannot by any
means think of giving it up, * * * choosing rather the
misfortune of a temporary deprivation of Laws than to form
any system whereby they may be left without remedy on this
great point."

To this appeal the king replied by rejecting the bill and instructing Governor Martin to create courts of oyer and terminer by the exercise of the "ever ready prerogative." In
March, 1773, therefore, the governor appointed Richard Caswell and Maurice Moore judges to sit with Chief Justice
Martin Howard to hold these courts. Thus another element

of discord was injected into the controversy, for when the Assembly met in December, the governor was compelled to inform them of the "royal disallowance" of the court law, and at the same time to ask for money to meet the expenses of his prerogative courts. The Assembly's refusal was sharp and peremptory. They declared that while "one of the greatest calamities to which any political society can be liable," the suspension of the judicial powers of the government, had befallen the province, and no hope of redress through "the interposition of Government" remained, "yet the misery of such a situation vanishes in competition with a mode of redress exercised by courts unconstitutionally framed: it is the blessed distinction of the British Code of Laws that our civil and criminal Jurisdiction have their foundation in the Laws of the Land, and are regulated by principles as fixt as the Constitution. We humbly conceive that the power of issuing Commissions of Oyer and Terminer and General Gaol Delivery, delegated by his Majesty to your Excellency, cannot be legally carried into execution without the aid of the Legislature of this Province, and that we cannot consistent with the Justice due to our Constituents make provisions for defraying the expense attending a measure which we do not approve."

The governor and his Council protested, argued, pleaded, and threatened. The Council predicted that unless courts were speedily established the "Province must soon be deserted by its Inhabitants and an end put to its *name* and *political* existence," and reproached the House for bringing the colony to this distressed situation "for the sake only of a Comparatively small advantage supposed to lie in a mode of proceeding by attachment, a proceeding unknown both to the Common and Statute Law of the Mother Country." This message drew fire from the House. The issue now involved much more than a mere legal procedure; the independence of the Assembly as a legislative body was at stake. "This House," retorted the Assembly, "ever faithful to the discharge of the important trust reposed in them by the Inhabitants of this Province have in the conduct of every Public Measure, * * * had in view the interest and happiness of our constituents, as the grand object that ought to govern all our determinations. * * * Conscious from our late melancholy experience of the unhappy consequences that attend the extinguishment of the Civil and Criminal Jurisdiction in this Province, We dread the continuance of the calamity and submit still to suffer, only to avoid a greater misfortune. * * * This House for themselves and their constituents heartily acknowledge the

necessity for Court Laws, and without anticipating the horrors
of the desertion of the Inhabitants of this Colony and the extinguishment of its name and political existence, they experience in the present unhappy State of this Province sufficient
to induce them to wish a change upon legal constitutional
principles.   *   *   *   Were the attachment Law as formerly
enjoyed by us as small an advantage, compared with that of
having Court Laws as you contend it is, the right we possess to
that is equal to the rights to a more important object; in the
smallest, it [a surrender of the right] is bartering the rights
of a people for a present convenience, in a greater it would be
the same crime aggravated only by its circumstances.   We
observe with surprise that a doctrine maintained by a former
House of Assembly is now adopted by you, and that you dis-
close as your opinion that attachments are not known to the
Common or Statute Law of England; what then did Government tender to this people in lieu of their former mode, when
it proffered to the last Assembly *a mode of attachment agreeable to the laws of England?''*

Finding appeals to loyalty and threats of punishment equally
unavailing, and caught in his inconsistency, the governor determined to send the members home to consult their constituents, and accordingly sent his private secretary to command
the House to attend him at the Palace.   Knowing well enough
what this meant, the House took a parting shot well calculated
to ruffle his spirits.   A committee was appointed to draw an
address to the king, and was instructed ''as the most effectual
means to promote its success,'' to request Governor Tryon,
''who happily for this Country for many years presided over
it, and of whose good intentions to its welfare we feel the
fullest convictions,'' to forward it to his Majesty and support
it ''with his interest and influence.''   He was asked to ''accept
of this important Trust as testimony of the great affection this
Colony bears him, and the entire confidence they repose in
him.''   The members of the committee to prepare this address
were Harvey, Johnston, Howe, Ashe, Hooper, Hewes, Isaac
Edwards and Harnett.   After adopting this insulting resolution as much to show their contempt for Martin as their regard
for Tryon, the members of the House proceeded to the Palace
where they were dismissed.   The governor asked them to represent the facts to the people fairly, saying, ''I am fully persuaded they know too well their own interests to make such a
sacrifice [as the absence of courts entailed], or to approve your
conduct.   That I may give you opportunity to learn their sentiments, I now,   *   *   *   prorogue this Assembly.''

But it was useless for the governor to appeal from the Assembly to the people; it was but an appeal from the teachers to the taught. To send the former back to their constituents was but to send them to gather fresh endorsements and receive renewed support in their contest. When they returned in March, 1774, they told the governor that they had consulted the people, had stated to them candidly the point for which they contended, and had informed them how far the king was disposed to indulge their wishes. "These facts," they declared, "we have represented to them fairly, disdaining any equivocation or reserve that might leave them ignorant of the Conduct we have pursued or the real motives that influenced it. And we have the heartfelt satisfaction to inform your Excellency that they have expressed their warmest approbation of our past proceedings, and have given us positive instructions to persist in our endeavors to obtain the process of Foreign Attachments upon the most liberal and ample footing." To this message the governor replied in one of his few really good papers. He wrote with conflicting feelings for he was compelled to defend an instruction of his master with which he did not entirely sympathize. Passing by the "just exultation" with which the Assembly told him of their constituents' approval of their course, he made an eloquent plea for compromise. But the Assembly stood firm, passed the usual bill with the usual clause, and, declaring that they had pursued every measure to relieve the colony from its distressed condition, sent it to the governor. The governor rejected it. This brought the struggle to an end for the only other Assembly that met in North Carolina under royal rule was in session but four stormy days and did not have time to consider the court law. North Carolina, therefore, remained without courts for the trial of civil causes until after independence was declared. Among the causes recited in the Declaration of Independence to justify that action, was the following: "He [the king] has obstructed the administration of justice, by refusing his assent to laws for establishing judiciary powers."

The situation in North Carolina was indeed serious. In March, 1773, Josiah Quincy, Jr., of Boston, traveling through the province, noted that but five provincial laws were in force, that no courts were open, that no one could recover a debt except for small sums within the jurisdiction of a magistrate's court, and that offenders escaped with impunity. "The people," he declared, "are in great consternation about the matter; what will be the result is problematical." [3] Many were disposed to charge the whole trouble to the governor. They did not believe that he had "properly or judiciously explained to the government at home" the necessity for the protection they sought; and they charged to his "spirit of intolerance and impatience" the failure of the Assembly to pass a county court law, "the jurisdiction of which would have been so limited that it could not possibly have operated to the disfavor of any British merchant," and the want of which subjected the people of the province to innumerable inconveniences. But there was no disposition on the part of the leaders of the popular party to shirk their own responsibility. Fortunately they received loyal support from their constituents, who chose rather to bear all the inconveniences of the situation than to surrender the independence of their judiciary. The royal government was thoroughly beaten because the people made anarchy tolerable.

Throughout the colonies, the Whig leaders, as we may now call them, saw through the policy of the king in trying to avoid a general issue, and held many an anxious conference to devise a working plan for united action. One of the most important, as it was one of the most interesting of these conferences, was held between Josiah Quincy, Jr., of Massachusetts, and Robert Howe and Cornelius Harnett, of North Carolina, at the home of the latter on the Cape Fear. Quincy arrived at Brunswick, March 26, and spent the next five days enjoying the hospitality of the Cape Fear patriots. He found William Hill "warmly attached to the cause of American freedom;" William Dry "seemingly warm against the measures of British and continental administration;" William Hooper "apparently in the Whig interest." The night of March 30th he spent at the home of Cornelius Harnett. Here all doubt of his host's political sentiments vanished. "Spent the night," he records, "at Mr. Harnett's, the Samuel Adams of North Carolina (except in point of fortune). Robert Howe, Esq., Harnett and myself made the social triumvirate of the evening. The plan of continental correspondence highly relished, much wished for, and resolved upon as proper to be pursued." [4]

The "plan of continental correspondence" was, of course, original with neither Quincy nor Harnett. Samuel Adams had already put a system of provincial correspondence into opera-

[3] Memoir of the Life of Josiah Quincy, Jr., p. 117 et seq.
[4] Memoir, p. 120.

tion in Massachusetts; and a few days before Quincy arrived in North Carolina, but too late for the news to have reached Wilmington, the Virginia Assembly had issued a circular letter proposing to the other assemblies the organization of a system of inter-colonial committees to carry on a "continental correspondence." During the summer several of the colonies adopted the plan. The decision of North Carolina had been practically settled at Wilmington in March, but as the Assembly was not to meet until December, no official action was taken until then. On the second day of the session, John Harvey, the speaker, laid the Virginia resolutions, together with the resolutions and endorsements of Massachusetts, Rhode Island, Connecticut and Delaware, before the House; and Howe, Harnett and Johnston were appointed a committee to draw an answer which they were to report to the House. In their report they recommended hearty concurrence in the "spirited resolves" of the Virginia Assembly, particularly "in the measure proposed for appointing Corresponding Committees in every Colony, by which such Harmony and communication will be established among them, that they will at all times be ready to exert their united efforts * * * to preserve their just rights and Liberties * * * which appear of late to be so systematically invaded;" and they nominated as a Standing Committee of Correspondence and Enquiry" for North Carolina John Harvey, Robert Howe, Cornelius Harnett, William Hooper, Richard Caswell, Edward Vail, John Ashe, Joseph Hewes, and Samuel Johnston. It was to be the particular business of this committee "to obtain the most early and authentic intelligence of all such Acts and resolutions of the British Parliament, or proceedings of Administration as may relate to or effect the British Colonies in America and to keep up and maintain a correspondence and communication with our Sister Colonies respecting these important considerations," and to report their proceedings to the Assembly. The work of this committee bore good fruit, for the members brought to their task a truly national spirit in dealing with continental affairs. To use a modern political term, they adopted a platform in which they declared that the inhabitants of North Carolina "ought to consider themselves interested in the cause of the town of Boston as the cause of America in general;" that they would "concur with and co-operate in such measures as may be concerted and agreed on by their Sister Colonies" for resisting the measures of the British ministry, and that in order to promote "conformity and unanimity in the Councils of America," a Continental Congress was "ab-

solutely necessary." The significance of this system of committees was soon apparent. Indeed, as John Fiske declares,
it "was nothing less than the beginning of the American union.
* * * It only remained for the various inter-colonial committees to assemble together, and there would be a congress
speaking in the name of the continent." [5]

In the meantime came the Boston Tea Party, followed
promptly by the four "intolerable acts" which closed the port
of Boston, annulled the charter of Massachusetts, authorized
the transportation beyond sea for trial of persons accused of
crime, and legalized the quartering of troops on the people of
Massachusetts. These acts aroused the whole continent and
led to the call for a Continental Congress. The suggestion for
such a congress found instant favor. It was intended, following the precedent established with the Stamp Act Congress,
that the delegates should be chosen by the assemblies. When
Governor Martin learned of these plans, he determined to prevent North Carolina's being represented by refusing to convene the Assembly until too late for them to elect delegates.
Tryon had successfully adopted this expedient to prevent the
election of delegates to the Stamp Act Congress, but Martin
lacked a good deal of having Tryon's tact and political shrewdness, nor did he enjoy the personal popularity which had enabled Tryon to meet successfully many delicate situations. Besides the popular party was now organized for resistance and
its leaders were not the kind of men to be caught twice in the
same trap. Accordingly when Martin's private secretary
communicated the governor's determination to Speaker Harvey, Harvey flew into a rage, exclaiming, "In that case the
people will hold a convention independent of the governor!"

On April 5, 1774, Samuel Johnston wrote to William Hooper: "Colonel Harvey and myself lodged last night with Colonel
[Edward] Buncombe, and as we sat up very late the conversation turned on Continental and provincial affairs. Colonel
Harvey said during the night, that Mr. Biggleston told him,
that the Governor did not intend to convene another Assembly
until he saw some chance of a better one than the last; and
that he told the Secretary that then the people would convene
one themselves. He was in a very violent mood, and declared
he was for assembling a convention independent of the Governor, and urged upon us to co-operate with him. He says he
will lead the way, and will issue handbills under his own name,
and that the committee of correspondence ought to go to work

---

[5] The American Revolution, Vol. I, p. 81.

at once. As for my own part, I do not know what better can be done. Without Courts to sustain the property and to exercise the talents of the Country, and the people alarmed and dissatisfied, we must do something to save ourselves. Colonel Harvey said he had mentioned the matter only to Willie Jones of Halifax, whom he had met the day before, and that he thought well of it, and promised to exert himself in its favor. I beg your friendly counsel and advice on the subject, and hope you will speak of it to Mr. Harnett and Colonel Ashe, or any other such men.''

Harvey's bold and revolutionary proposition fell upon willing ears. The popular leaders gave it their united support. The Committee of Correspondence declared that if the governor carried out his determination they would ''endeavor in some other manner to collect the Representatives of the people.'' Maturer consideration, however, led to the conclusion that the call for such a convention had better come from the people themselves. Accordingly the movement was launched at Wilmington, July 21, by a great mass meeting attended by men from all the Cape Fear counties. William Hooper was called to the chair. The meeting declared it ''highly expedient'' that a provincial congress independent of the governor be held and invited the several counties of the province to send delegates to it. This call met with a prompt and cordial response. Rowan, Craven, Pitt, Johnston, Granville, Anson, and Chowan counties led the way. In those counties popular meetings were promptly held, patriotic resolutions adopted, and delegates elected to the proposed congress. Through all these resolutions ran the spirit of liberty and union. The Wilmington meeting favored action ''in concert with the other Colonies.'' Anson County thought that North Carolina ought to act ''in union with the rest of the Colonies.'' Rowan County struck the highest note in a resolution declaring it to be ''the Duty and Interest of all the American Colonies, firmly to unite in an indissoluble Union and Association.'' All the meetings endorsed the proposed Continental Congress. Thirty-six counties and towns joined in the movement by choosing delegates to meet in a provincial congress at New Bern, August 25, 1774.

These proceedings produced consternation at the Governor's Palace. Hastily calling his Council in session, the governor represented the situation to them as exceedingly grave and likely ''to draw His Majesty's displeasure on this Province,'' and sought advice as to ''the measures most proper to be taken, to discourage or prevent these Assemblies of the

People.'' The Council after taking a whole day "maturely to consider the Subject,'' could think of nothing better than a proclamation which the governor gravely issued, August 13th. He not only directed that the people should hold no further county meetings, but "more particularly that they do forbear to attend, and do prevent as far in them lies, the meeting of certain Deputies, said to be appointed to be held at New Bern on the 25th Instant.'' One of Josiah Martin's most glaring faults as a ruler was his utter lack of a sense of humor; he took his resounding proclamation in dead earnest and was greatly perturbed to find that nobody else shared this view with him. On August 25th, he again called his Council together, notified them that many of the delegates had come to New Bern for the Congress, and asked their advice whether he could take "any further measures" to prevent their meeting; and was gravely informed that it was the Council's "unanimous opinion that no other steps could be properly taken at this juncture.''

When the Congress met on August 25th, seventy-one delegates answered the roll call. Among its members were John Campbell, John Ashe, and Richard Caswell, former speakers of the Assembly; William Hooper and Joseph Hewes, soon to become immortalized as signers of the Declaration of Independence; Samuel Johnston and Abner Nash who, like Caswell, were destined to become governors of North Carolina; but on none of these eminent men did the Congress fix its choice when it came to select its presiding officer. The thoughts of all centered at once upon one man, John Harvey, father of the Congress, who was its unanimous choice as moderator.

The man thus called to preside over the most revolutionary body that ever met in North Carolina, had been for a decade the undisputed leader of the popular party in the province. Then in his fiftieth year, he had been in public life ever since reaching his majority. In 1746 he entered the Assembly as a representative from Perquimans County, just in time to become involved in the representation controversy that marked the closing years of Governor Johnston's administration. Sympathizing fully with the views of the northern counties, he refused during the next eight years to sit in an Assembly which he believed to be unconstitutionally organized; but when the controversy was ended and the victory won, he again appeared in his seat which he continuously occupied during the remaining twenty-one years of his life. Out of his first experience in public life, Harvey brought an intense hostility to government by prerogative that made him during the rest of his career the colony's most aggressive champion of constitutional representative government. He held that the charter upon which the colonial government was founded was a compact between sovereign and people which neither could rightfully violate. He insisted that no number less than a majority could legally be counted a quorum of the Assembly because it had been so fixed by the charter. He upheld the dignity of the Assembly as a law-making body and utterly repudiated the doctrine that its highest function was to register the will of the Crown. He maintained that no power on earth could constitutionally levy taxes on the people of North Carolina except their representatives in the General Assembly and rejected the theory that they were represented in the British Parliament. The sincerity of his convictions, the fearlessness and ability with which he maintained them, gradually won for him the foremost place in the councils of his party and led to his election in 1765 to the speakership of the Assembly. That place of leadership he held, except for one Assembly which ill health prevented his attending, until his death in 1775. During that decade he was the acknowledged leader of that remarkable group of North Carolina statesmen who prevented the triumph of the ministerial policy in North Carolina, swung the colony into line with the other colonies in the continental movement toward union, reduced the royal government to impotency, organized a provincial government independent of the Crown, inaugurated the Revolution and led the way to independence. Throughout these great movements, Harvey's leadership was characterized by clearness of vision that appealed to men's judgment, firmness of purpose that inspired their confidence, and boldness of action that stirred their imagination and aroused their enthusiasm. Such were the qualities that led his associates in one of the ablest assemblages in our history to make him their unanimous choice for their presiding officer.

The Congress remained in session but three days. In a series of spirited and clear-cut resolutions it gave expression to the American views on the questions in dispute with the mother country; denounced the several acts aimed at Massachusetts and Boston; declared that the people of Massachusetts had "distinguished themselves in a manly support of the rights of America in general"; endorsed the proposal for a Continental Congress to which it elected William Hooper, Joseph Hewes, and Richard Caswell delegates; pledged the honor of the province in support of whatever measures the Continental Congress might recommend to the colonies; adopted a non-importation agreement and provided for its execution. John Harvey was authorized to call another Congress whenever he deemed it necessary.

No more significant step had ever been taken in North Carolina than the successful meeting of this Congress. It revealed the people to themselves. Said the freeholders of Pitt County: "As the Constitutional Assembly of this Colony are prevented from exercising their right of providing for the security of the liberties of the people, that right again reverts to the people as the foundation from whence all power and legislation flow." The Congress was a practical demonstration of how the people might exercise this right. They began to understand that there was no peculiar power in the writs and proclamations of a royal governor. They themselves could elect delegates and organize legislatures without the intervention of the king's authority, and this was a long step toward independence.

This Congress and every county meeting held in North Carolina in the summer of 1774, had re-echoed the cry, then ringing throughout America, that Boston was suffering in the common cause, and the people of North Carolina by their generous contributions to the stricken city showed that it was no mere rhetorical expression. From the counties along the coast, and even from as far in the back country as Anson County, provisions poured into New Bern, Wilmington, and Edenton to be shipped free of all freight and other charges to the suffering poor of the New England metropolis. At their meeting on August 18, 1774, the freeholders of Anson County appointed a committee "to open and promote a subscription for contributing toward the relief of those indigent Inhabitants of the Town of Boston" whom the Boston Port Bill had "deprived of the means of subsisting themselves." Pitt County followed the example and loaded a ship with supplies for the relief of "the poor of Boston." From Craven also sailed a vessel bound for Salem with a cargo of corn, peas and pork "for the relief of the distressed inhabitants of Boston." At Wilmington a subscription was opened "for the Relief of the poor Artizans and Labourers" of Boston, and the committee in charge was able to declare with just pride, "we have reason to congratulate ourselves upon the generous contributions of the Inhabitants which has put it in our power to load a vessel with provisions which will sail this week for the port of Salem." From Edenton, too, sailed in September,

1774, the sloop Penelope carrying a cargo of 2,096 bushels of corn, 22 barrels of flour, and 17 barrels of pork, which John Harvey and Joseph Hewes had collected from "the inhabitants of two or three counties in the neighborhood of Edenton." "I hope to be able to send another cargo this winter, for the same charitable purpose," wrote Harvey to the Massachusetts Committee of Correspondence, "as the American inhabitants of this colony entertain a just sense of the suffering of our brethren in Boston, and have yet hopes that when the united determinations of the continent reach the royal ear, they will have redress from the cruel, unjust, illegal and oppressive late acts of the British Parliament."

Foiled in his purpose to hold North Carolina aloof from the Continental Congress, Governor Martin determined to make the best of a bad situation and summoned the Assembly to meet him at New Bern, April 4, 1775. John Harvey immediately called a congress to meet at the same place on April 3d. It was a wise precaution, for the Assembly sat only at the pleasure of the governor who would certainly dissolve it at the first manifestation of disloyalty. The leaders of the popular party intended that the same individuals should compose both bodies and with few exceptions this plan was carefully carried into execution. Martin was furious and denounced Harvey's action in two resounding proclamations. The Congress replied by electing Harvey moderator, the Assembly by electing him speaker. The governor roundly scored both bodies, and both bodies roundly scored the governor. It was indeed a pretty situation. One set of men composed two assemblies—one constitutional, sitting by authority of the royal governor, and in obedience of his writ; the other extra-constitutional, sitting in defiance of his authority, and in direct disobedience of his command. The governor impotently demanded that the Assembly join him in denouncing and dispersing the Congress, composed largely of the same men whose aid he solicited. The two bodies met in the same hall, the Congress at 9 o'clock A. M., the Assembly at 10, and were presided over by the same man. "When the governor's private secretary was announced at the door, in an instant, in the twinkling of an eye, Mr. Moderator Harvey * * * would become Mr. Speaker Harvey * * * and gravely receive his Excellency's message."[6]

Neither body accomplished much. The Congress declared

---

[6] Saunders: Prefatory Notes to *Colonial Records of North Carolina*, Vol. IX, p. xxxiv.

the right of the people themselves, or through their representatives, to assemble and petition the throne for redress of
grievances, and concluded, therefore, that "the Governor's
Proclamation issued to forbid this meeting, and his Proclamation afterwards, commanding this meeting to disperse, are
illegal and an infringement of our just rights, and therefore
ought to be disregarded as wanton and Arbitrary Exertions
of power." The Continental Association adopted by the Continental Congress was approved, signed, and recommended
to the people of the province; Hooper, Hewes, and Caswell
were thanked for their services in the Continental Congress
and re-elected; and John Harvey, or in the event of his death
Samuel Johnston, was authorized to call another congress
whenever he considered it necessary.

The Assembly had time only to organize and exchange
messages with the governor when it, too, came to an end.
Its first offense was the election of Harvey as speaker. His
election was a bitter pill to the governor and he winced at
having to take it, but held his peace. He wrote to Lord
Dartmouth, secretary of state for the colonies, that he had
hoped the Assembly after hearing what he had to say would
secede from the Congress, although he knew many of its members were also members of the Congress, "and this hope,"
he added, "together with my desire to lay no difficulty in
the way of the public business, induced me on the next day
to admit the election of Mr. Harvey, who was chosen speaker
of the Assembly, and presented by the House for my approbation. Indeed to say the truth, my Lord, it was a measure to
which I submitted upon these principles not without repug-
nance even after I found the Council unanimously of opinion
that it would not be expedient to give a new handle of discontent to the Assembly by rejecting its choice if it should
fall as was expected upon Mr. Harvey, for I considered his
guilt of too conspicuous a nature to be passed over with neglect. The manner however of my admitting him I believe
sufficiently testified my disapprobation of his conduct while
it marked my respect to the election of the House." The following day the Assembly again offended by inviting the delegates to the Congress who were not also members of the Assembly to join in the latter's deliberations. The governor
promptly issued his proclamation forbidding this unhallowed
union, which was read to the Assembly by the sheriff of
Craven County. "Well, you have read it," exclaimed James
Coor, member from Craven, "and now you can take it back
to the governor"; and except for this contemptuous exclama-

tion no notice was taken of it. "Not a man obeyed it," wrote Martin, who thus far had succeeded in keeping his temper admirably. But on the fourth day of the session the Assembly adopted resolutions approving the Continental Association, thanking the delegates to the Continental Congress for their services, and endorsing their re-election. This was more than Martin had bargained for; his wrath boiled over, and on April 8, 1774, he issued his proclamation putting an end to the last Assembly that ever met in North Carolina at the call of a royal governor.

In a letter to Lord Dartmouth describing these events, Martin wrote: "I am bound in conscience and duty to add, My Lord, that Government is here as absolutely prostrate as impotent, and that nothing but the shadow of it is left. * * * I must further say, too, my Lord, that it is my serious opinion which I communicate with the last degree of concern that unless effectual measures such as British Spirit may dictate are speedily taken there will not long remain a trace of Britain's dominion over these Colonies." Before this dispatch had found its way to its pigeon hole in the Colonial Office, Martin was a fugitive from the Governor's Palace seeking protection from the guns of Fort Johnston, revolutionary conventions and committees were in full control throughout the province, in every community companies of rebels were organizing, arming, and drilling for war, and British rule was at an end forever in North Carolina.

CHAPTER XX

COMMITTEES OF SAFETY

In order to provide an executive authority to enforce its policy, the Provincial Congress of August, 1774, recommended that "a committee of five persons be chosen in each county" for that purpose. The Continental Congress in October recommended a similar system throughout the thirteen colonies. In North Carolina the plan as finally worked out contemplated one committee in each of the towns, one in each of the counties, one in each of the six military districts, and one for the province at large. In all our history there has been nothing else like these committees. Born of necessity, originating in the political and economic confusion of the time, they touched the lives of the people in their most intimate affairs, and gradually extended their jurisdiction until they assumed to themselves all the functions of government. They enforced with vigor the resolves of the Continental and Provincial Congresses, some of which were most exacting in their demands and burdensome in their effects. They conducted inquiries into the actions and opinions of individuals, and not only "determined what acts and opinions constituted a man an enemy of his country, but passed upon his guilt or innocence, and fixed his punishment." They raised money by voluntary subscriptions, fines and assessments for the purchase of gunpowder, arms, and all the other implements of war. The militia had to be enlisted, organized, equipped and drilled. In short, a revolution had to be inaugurated and it fell to these committees to do it. "Usurping some new authority every day, executive, judicial or legislative, as the case might be, their powers soon became practically unlimited." Governor Martin characterized them as "extraordinary tribunals." In every respect they were extraordinary, insurrectionary, revolutionary. Illegally constituted, they assumed such authority as would not have been tolerated in the royal government and received such obedience as the king with all his armies could not have exacted. Yet not only did they not abuse their power, they voluntarily

354

resigned it when the public welfare no longer needed their services. They were the offspring of misrule and rose and fell with their parent.

Records are extant, in some cases complete, in others very meager, of the organization of committees in eighteen counties and four towns. Especially active and effective were the committees of New Hanover, Rowan, Tryon, Pitt, Craven and Surry counties. The people were thoroughly alive to the importance of the step they took in organizing these committees. The men whom they selected represented the wealth, the intelligence, and the culture of their communities. Some of them achieved eminence in the history of North Carolina. The chairman of the Wilmington-New Hanover committee was Cornelius Harnett. Among his colleagues was William Hooper. Joseph Hewes, like Hooper, a signer of the Declaration of Independence, was a member of the Edenton committee. The dominant spirit of the Halifax committee was Willie Jones, for many years the most distinguished of the radical leaders in the colony. Among the members of the Craven committee was Abner Nash, afterwards governor. Robert Howe, afterwards a major-general in Washington's army, served on the Brunswick committee. Benjamin Cleaveland, famous as one of the "heroes of King's Mountain," was chairman of the Surry committee. Many others scarcely less distinguished served on these "extraordinary tribunals." They were men of approved character and ability. Entrusted with despotic power, they fulfilled their trust with fidelity, exercising tyranny over individuals that they might preserve the liberty of the community. They uniformly discharged their duties with firmness and patience, with prudence and wisdom, and in the interest of the public welfare.

The policy of both the Continental Congress and the Provincial Congress aimed to promote economy and industry, to encourage and stimulate manufactures, to discourage extravagance and luxury, and to enforce the non-importation and non-exportation associations. Upon the committees of safety fell the task of making this policy effective. It was neither an easy nor an agreeable task, for some features of the policy were extremely irritating in their operations and at times produced restlessness among the people. It required as much tact as determination for the committees to execute their orders with vigor without at the same time losing the support of their constituents. In this double task they met with a remarkable degree of success. "Agreeable to the Resolves of the Continental Congress," Surry County undertook to "suppress all

Immorality and Vice, and all kinds of sporting, Gaming, Betting or Wagering whatsoever." Although the New Hanover committee strictly enforced the resolves against "expensive diversions and entertainments," forbidding horse-races, billiards, dancing and other amusements, the people submitted without complaint. "Nothing," declared the committee, "will so effectually tend to convince the British Parliament that we are in earnest in our opposition to their measures, as a voluntary relinquishment of our favorite amusements. * * * Many will cheerfully part with part of their property to secure the remainder. He only is the determined patriot who willingly sacrifices his pleasures on the altar of freedom." An interesting experiment was initiated by the committee of Chowan County which undertook to raise a fund to be used "for the encouragement of Manufactures," securing £80 sterling "for that laudable purpose." Premiums were accordingly offered for the first output in the province within eighteen months of 500 pairs of wool cards and a like number of cotton cards and for the first 2,000 pounds of steel "fit for edged tools," all of which the committee obligated itself to purchase at a good profit. These premiums, said the committee, were "too inconsiderable" in themselves to induce any person to establish such manufactories but it offered them in the hope that other counties, "stimulated by the same laudable motives to promote industry," would increase them by offering similar rewards. Many of the committees found it necessary to take a determined stand to prevent profiteering in such essential articles as salt, steel, and gunpowder, not only by fixing prices, but also by seizing for public use such supplies as were found within their jurisdictions.

One of the most important phases of the work of the committees of safety was the enforcement of the Non-Importation Association. Large quantities of goods were imported in violation either of the spirit or of the letter of the prohibition—some by merchants who had ordered them before the prohibition became effective, some were brought in only in technical violation of the resolve, while others were imported by disloyal merchants purposely to test the determination of the patriots. All alike was seized and sold at public auction for the benefit of the public fund. "The safety of the people is, or ought to be, the supreme law," wrote a Wilmington merchant whose goods were thus seized; "the gentlemen of the committee will judge whether this law, or any act of Parliament, should, at this particular time, operate in North Carolina." Some Cape Fear planters who thought upon one pretext or another to get around the resolve forbidding the importation of slaves, were promptly summoned before the New Hanover committee to "give a particular account" of their conduct, and as promptly required to re-ship their negroes out of the province by the first opportunity. When Parliament, in an effort to break up the Continental Association, passed an act "to restrain the trade and commerce" of certain colonies, from which North Carolina and some others were exempted, the Wilmington-New Hanover joint-committees at a largely attended meeting "resolved, unanimously, that the exception of this colony, and some others, out of the said act, is a mean and base artifice, to seduce them into a desertion of the common cause of America"; and therefore determined "that we will not accept of the advantages insidiously thrown out by the said act, but will strictly adhere to such plans as have been, and shall be, entered into by the Honorable Continental Congress, so as to keep up a perfect unanimity with our sister colonies."

In their work the committees met with just enough opposition to enable them to make a display of firmness and energy. Neither wealth nor position could purchase immunity from their inquisition, neither poverty nor obscurity was accepted as an excuse for disobedience. Social and commercial ostracism was the favorite weapon, and few there were with spirit and courage determined enough to withstand it. Andrew Miller, a prominent merchant of Halifax, refusing to sign the Association, the committee though composed of his neighbors and former friends resolved to have "no commerce or dealing" with him and to "recommend it to the people of this County in particular and to all who wish well of their Country to adopt the same measure." Governor Martin cited this incident to the ministry as evidence "of the spirit of these extraordinary Tribunals." Three merchants of Edenton, who had imported goods contrary to the Association, were summoned before the Chowan County committee, required publicly to acknowledge their fault and to promise obedience in the future. Craven County committee ordered that all persons who refused to sign the Association be disarmed. The sanctity of the church itself failed to serve as a cloak to cover disaffection and disloyalty. Rev. James Reed, missionary of the Society for the Propagation of the Gospel and rector at New Bern, refusing to conduct service on the Fast Day set apart by the Continental Congress, the Craven committee severely censured him for "deserting his congregation," and requested the vestry to suspend him "from his ministerial function"; while the Rowan County committee compelled a Baptist preacher named Cook who had signed a "protest against the cause of Liberty," to appear and express his regret "in the most explicit and humiliating Terms." When the Wilmington committee submitted to the people of Wilmington a test pledging the signers to "observe strictly" the Continental Association, eleven of the most prominent men in the community refused to sign. They were promptly ostracized as "unworthy the rights of freemen and as inimical to the liberties of their country"; and held up before the public that they might be "treated with the contempt they deserve." There were no braver men than some of those thus cut off from their fellows, but they could not stand out against the open scorn of their neighbors; within less than a week eight of their number gave way and subscribed the test. The committee justified their course as being "a cement of allegiance" to the Crown and as "having a tendency to promote a constitutional attachment for the mother country."

But in May, 1775, the last bond of such allegiance was snapped, and the last sentiment of such attachment destroyed, by news that came from Massachusetts. American blood had been shed at Lexington and through the colonies expresses rode day and night, carrying the news of the battle, of the rising of the minute-men, and of the retreat from Concord. In no other way did the committees of safety give a better illustration of their usefulness than in the transmission of this news. From colony to colony, from town to town, from committee to committee, they hurried it along. New York received the dispatches at midday, New Brunswick at midnight. They aroused Princeton at 3 o'clock in the morning. Trenton read them at daybreak, Philadelphia at noon. They reached Baltimore at bed-time, Alexandria at the breakfast hour. Three days and nights the express rode on, down the Potomac, across the Rappahannock, the York and the James, through scenes since made famous, and on to Edenton. Edenton received the dispatches at 9 a. m., May 4th, and hurried them on to Bath with the injunction to "disperse the material passages through all your parts." Bath hastened them on to New Bern with a message to send them forward "with the utmost dispatch." "Send them on as soon as possible to the Wilmington Committee," directed New Bern to Onslow. "Disperse them to your adjoining counties," echoed Onslow to Wilmington. At 3 o'clock P. M., May 8th, the messenger delivered his dispatches to

Cornelius Harnett, chairman of the Wilmington committee. Delaying just long enough to make copies, Harnett urged him on to Brunswick. "If you should be at a loss for a man and horse," he wrote to the Brunswick committee, "the bearer will proceed as far as the Boundary House. You will please direct Mr. Marion or any other gentleman to forward the packet immediately to the Southward with the greatest possible dispatch. * * * For God's sake send the man on without the least delay and write to Mr. Marion to forward it by night and day." Brunswick received the papers six hours later and although it was then "9 o'clock in the evening" the chairman of the committee urged the bearer onward to Isaac Marion at Boundary House to whom he wrote: "I must entreat you to forward them to your community [committee] at Georgetown to be conveyed to Charlestown from yours with all speed." Thus the news was sped to the southward, inspiring the forward, stirring the backward, and arousing the continent. The committees made the most of their opportunity. Governor Martin complained that the rebel leaders received the news more than a month before he did, and that he received it "too late to operate against the infamous and false reports of that transaction which were circulated to this distance from Boston in the space of 12 or 13 days." The first impression took "deep root in the minds of the vulgar here universally and wrought a great change in the face of things, confirming the seditious in their evil purposes, and bringing over vast numbers of the fickle, wavering and unsteady multitude to their party."

The battle of Lexington was the beginning of war. For this result the patriots of North Carolina were not wholly unprepared, for the committees had made efforts to be ready for "the worst contingencies." The Rowan committee seized all the gunpowder in Salisbury. Tryon County raised money to purchase powder for the public use. Surry ordered that if any members of the committee "should find out any Ammunition in this county they shall be justifiable in securing the same for the Public Service." Other committees were no less active in this essential work. The most effective work was done by the Wilmington-New Hanover committees which foresaw that the first armed conflict in North Carolina would probably come on the Cape Fear, and determined to be prepared for it. They required the merchants to sell their gunpowder to the committees for the public use, they bought it from other committees, imported it from other colonies, and employed agents to manufacture it. They hired men to

mould bullets. They seized the public arms, and they compelled every person who owned more than one gun to surrender all but one for the public service. They smuggled
arms and ammunition from other colonies and the West
Indies in such quantities that Governor Martin "lamented
that effectual steps have not been taken to intercept the supplies of warlike stores that * * * are frequently brought
into this colony", and asked for three or four cruisers to
guard the coast, for the sloop stationed at Fort Johnston "is
not sufficient to attend to the smugglers in this [Cape Fear]
river alone." The committees also undertook to re-organize
the militia. Rowan called for 1,000 volunteers to "be ready
at the shortest Notice to march out to Action." The Pitt
County committee required the militia companies to choose
new officers to be approved by the committee. The Wilmington committee required "every white man capable of bearing arms" to enlist in one of the companies that had been
organized; and early in July, 1775, gave as one reason for a
provincial congress which Harnett, Ashe and Howe urged
Johnston to call, "that a number of men should be raised
and kept in pay for the defense of the country." So active
and successful were the committees in organizing military
companies that Governor Martin issued a proclamation denouncing the "evil minded persons" who were "endeavouring
to engage the People to subscribe papers obliging themselves
to be prepared with Arms, to array themselves in companies,
and to submit to the illegal and usurped authorities of Committees."

Nor were the committees unmindful of the necessity of
preparing the minds of the people for war. In this respect, too, success crowned their efforts. Even historians
who think North Carolina did not give "general and heroic
support to the cause of independence," declare that at the
outbreak of the Revolution the people were "aroused to an
extraordinary degree of enthusiasm." [1] This enthusiasm Governor Martin charged particularly to the committees of
safety. To Lord Dartmouth he wrote on June 30, 1775, that
the people "freely talk of Hostility toward Britain in the
language of Aliens and avowed Enemies," and later he attributed this spirit to "the influence of Committees" which,
he said, "hath been so extended over the Inhabitants of the
Lower part [Cape Fear section] of this Country, * * *

---

[1] Dodd, W. E.: "North Carolina in the Revolution," in *The
South Atlantic Quarterly,* Vol. I, p. 156.

and they are at this day to the distance of an hundred miles from the Sea Coast, so generally possessed with the spirit of revolt" that the "spirits of the loyal and well effective to Government droop and decline daily" while "the authority, the edicts and ordinances of Congresses, Conventions and Committees are established supreme and omnipotent by general acquiescence or forced submission, and lawful Government is completely annihilated."

Martin wrote these dispatches from Fort Johnston at the mouth of Cape Fear River where, frightened from the Palace at New Bern by the New Bern committee, he had taken refuge. His flight was one of the turning points in the revolutionary movement in North Carolina; it closed the last door against reconciliation. To trace the events which induced him to take this extraordinary step, we must turn back to the beginning of the year 1775. It must not be supposed that the people of North Carolina were a unit in support of the revolutionary movement. The movement received its chief strength from the eastern counties where men of English descent, trained in English institutions and imbued with English ideals of government, predominated, and from the counties which had been largely settled by Scotch-Irish immigrants whose religious principles and church organizations had given them training in democratic ideals and institutions. But from the Scotch-Highlanders and the Germans, neither of whom understood what the quarrel was about, it received scant sympathy, while the old Regulators naturally distrusted a cause which counted among its most conspicuous advocates the author of the "Riot Act" and those who, acting under its authority, had but recently so completely crushed their own revolt against oppression. By the opening of the year 1775 these elements of the population began to make themselves heard. Addresses signed by 1,500 inhabitants of Rowan, Surry, Guilford, Anson and other inland counties, expressing the utmost loyalty to the king and utter detestation of all revolutionary proceedings, were sent in to the governor, who received similar assurances from the Scotch-Highlanders along the Upper Cape Fear.

Encouraged by these evidences of loyalty, Martin began to contemplate a more aggressive policy. On March 16th, therefore, he wrote to General Thomas Gage, at Boston, "if your Excellency shall assist me with two or three Stands of arms and good store of ammunition, * * * I will be answerable to maintain the Sovereignty of this Country to his Majesty if the present spirit of resistance * * * shall urge mat-

ters to the extremity that the people of New England seem
to be meditating.'' While Martin was anxiously awaiting
Gage's reply, events in North Carolina hastened to a climax.
In April met the last royal Assembly and the second Provincial Congress, and in May came news of the battle of
Lexington. Rumors were afloat that the governor contemplated armed action against the people, and it
was whispered here and there that he was even planning to arm the slaves against their masters. Everywhere the people were arming, organizing companies and
drilling for war. ''The Inhabitants of this Country on the
Sea Coast,'' wrote Martin, from New Bern, May 18th, ''are
* * * arming men, electing officers and so forth. In this
little Town they are now actually endeavouring to form what
they call independent Companies under my nose, and Civil
Government becomes more and more prostrate every day.''
While everybody's nerves were on an edge from these events
and rumors, Martin's action in dismantling some cannon at
the Palace in New Bern so alarmed the New Bern committee that it set a watch over him to report his every movement.
In the latter part of May a messenger from the governor of
New York arrived at the Palace and sought an interview
with Martin. From him Martin learned that Gage had complied with his request and ordered arms and ammunition to
be sent to him from New York. Whether they would be sent
by a man-of-war or by a merchant ship Martin's informant
could not say, but thought probably by the latter as the people of the northern colonies had a mistaken idea of the loyalty of the people of the South. This information was extremely disconcerting. Martin felt certain that the supplies,
unless brought by a war vessel, would be seized by the committees as he himself ''had not a man to protect them.'' He
was also greatly perturbed by rumors that the committees
in all the colonies were planning to seize the persons of the
royal governors. Prompt action, therefore, was necessary
to save his military supplies and to assure his personal safety.
His decision was perhaps wise from a personal point of view,
but disastrous to his cause. Sending his family in haste to
New York, and dispatching his secretary to Ocracoke Inlet,
the entrance to the port of New Bern, to prevent the supply
ship from entering there, he himself fled in secret to the protection of the guns of Fort Johnston.

Martin reached Fort Johnston on June 2d, and began at
once to concoct new schemes for reducing the province to
obedience. His activity took the form of a thundering procla-

mation, in which he denounced the committees of safety and warned the people against their illegal proceedings; of an application to General Gage for a royal standard around which the loyal and faithful might rally; and of an elaborate plan for the organization of the Highlanders and Regulators of the interior for military service. His plans were approved by the king who promised such assistance as might be necessary. They gave great alarm to the Whigs. "Our situation here is truly alarming," wrote the Wilmington committee; "the Governor [is] collecting men, provisions, warlike stores of every kind, spiriting up the back country, and perhaps the Slaves; finally strengthening the fort with new works in such a manner as may make the Capture of it extremely difficult." "Nothing," declared Harnett, "shall be wanting on our part to disconcert such diabolical schemes." The committees kept such close watch over his movements that Martin declared no messenger or letter could escape them. They intercepted his dispatches, frustrated his plans, and in general made life so miserable for him that he bemoaned his situation as "most despicable and mortifying to any man of greater feelings than a Stoic." "I daily see indignantly, the Sacred Majesty of my Royal Master insulted, the Rights of His Crown denied and violated, His Government set at naught and trampled upon, his servants of highest dignity reviled, traduced, abused, the Rights of His Subjects destroyed by the most arbitrary usurpations, and the whole Constitution unhinged and prostrate, and I live, alas! ingloriously only to deplore it."

On June 20th, the committees of New Hanover, Brunswick, Bladen, Duplin, and Onslow counties, in session at Wilmington, declared that the governor had "by the whole tenor of his conduct, since the unhappy disputes between Great Britain and the colonies, discovered himself to be an enemy to the happiness of this colony in particular, and to the freedom, rights and privileges of America in general." Determined, therefore, to treat him as an enemy, the Wilmington committee passed an order forbidding any communications with him. Expulsion from the province was the logical result of this order, and the leaders were soon ready to take this step also. In a letter to Samuel Johnston, July 13th, urging him to call a provincial convention, the Wilmington committee said: "We have a number of Enterprising young fellows that would attempt to take the fort [Fort Johnston], but are much afraid of having their Conduct disavowed by the Convention." But what these "enterprising young fellows" were afraid to attempt, Cornelius Harnett, John Ashe and Robert Howe made up their minds to do. Captain John Collet, the commander of the fort, who felt all the professional soldier's contempt for the militia and all the Britisher's contempt for the provincials, took no pains to conceal his feelings. A long series of studied insults had exasperated the people of the Cape Fear against him, but they had borne them all patiently. But now news came that at Governor Martin's command, he was preparing the fort "for the reception of a promised reinforcement," the arrival of which would be the signal for the erection of the king's standard. The committee regarded this as a declaration of war, and "having taken these things into consideration, judged it might be of the most pernicious consequences to the people at large, if the said John Collet should be suffered to remain in the Fort, as he might thereby have an opportunity of carrying his iniquitous schemes into execution." They accordingly called for volunteers to take the fort, and in response "a great many volunteers were immediately collected."

The committee's preparations alarmed Governor Martin. Nobody realized better than he that the fort could not be held against a determined attack. Yet its defense was a matter of honor and its surrender would have a bad effect in the province. Besides it held artillery "considerable in value," with a quantity of movable stores and ammunition. "Its Artillery which is heavy," wrote Martin, "might in the hands of the Mob be turned against the King's Ship, and so annoy her as to oblige her to quit her present station which is most convenient in all respects." Then, too, an unsuccessful defense meant the capture of the governor himself. In this perplexing situation, Martin decided to remove the stores to a transport, to withdraw the garrison, dismantle the fortifications, and seek refuge on board the Cruizer. These plans he successfully carried into effect on July 16th. Almost at the very hour of his flight, Lord Dartmouth was writing to him: "I hope His Majesty's Government in North Carolina may be preserved, and His Governor and other officers not reduced to the disgraceful necessity of seeking protection on Board the King's Ships."

Smarting keenly under his disgrace, Martin hastened to put on record the punishment he desired to inflict on those most responsible for it. From the cabin of the "Cruizer, Sloop of War, in Cape Fear River," July 16th, he wrote to Lord Dartmouth:

"Hearing of a Proclamation of the King, proscribing John Hancock and Sam[ue]l Adams of the Massachusetts Bay, and seeing clearly that further proscriptions will be necessary before Government can be settled again upon sure Founda-

tions in America, I hold it my indispensable duty to mention
to your Lordship Cornelius Harnett, John Ashe, Robert
Howes [2] and Abner Nash, as persons who have marked themselves out as proper objects for such distinction in this Colony
by their unremitted labours to promote sedition and rebellion
here from the beginning of the discontents in America to this
time, that they stand foremost among the patrons of revolt and
anarchy.''

Rumors of Martin's plans at Fort Johnston having reached
the committees of New Hanover and Brunswick, they determined to take steps to prevent their execution. A call for
volunteers was promptly answered by 500 minute-men. Before setting out for the fort, Col. John Ashe, who commanded
the New Hanover contingent, dispatched to Governor Martin
a declaration of their purpose. The fort, he said, had been
built and maintained by the people of the province to protect
them in time of war and to aid their trade and navigation in
time of peace, but these ends had been defeated by Captain
Collet. He had illegally invaded the rights and property of
private persons by wantonly detaining vessels applying for
bills of health; by threatening vengeance against magistrates
whose actions in the execution of the duties of their offices he
happened to disapprove; by setting at defiance the high sheriff
of the county in the execution of his office; by treating the
king's writs served on him for just debts with shameful contempt and insult; by unparalled injustice in detaining and em-
bezzling a large quantity of goods which having been unfortunately wrecked near the fort, had from every principle of
humanity the highest claims to his attention and care for the
benefit of the unhappy sufferers; by his base encouragement of
slaves to elope from their masters and his atrocious and horrid
declaration that he would incite them to insurrection. These
things, and many others of like character, had excited the indignation and resentment of the people but they had submitted to them for a time in the hopes that the Assembly
would grant relief; but now they learned that Captain Collet
was dismantling the fort and they proposed to prevent it.
Replying to this communication, Martin declared that Captain
Collet was acting at his command and he hoped, therefore, the
people would not proceed with their design of attacking the
fort.

[2] "Robert Howes," wrote Martin, "is commonly called Howe, he
having impudently assumed that name for some years past in affecta-
tion of the noble family that bears it, whose least eminent virtues have
ever been far beyond his imitation." Col. Rec., Vol. X, p. 98.

John Ashe's answer was an order to all the masters and commanders of ships in the Cape Fear to furnish their boats to convey his men and arms down the river to Fort Johnston. On July 18th, 500 minute-men under his command rendezvoused at Brunswick and during the night marched on the fort and applied the torch. Early in the morning of July 19th, Martin was aroused from his quarters on the Cruizer by the announcement that Fort Johnston was on fire. Hurrying to the deck he watched the rapid spread of the flames as they reduced the fort to ashes. The "rabble," he wrote, burned several houses that had been erected by Captain Collet, and thus, in the words of the Wilmington committee, "effectually dislodged that atrocious Freebooter." "Mr. John Ashe and Mr. Cornelius Harnett," wrote the enraged governor, "were ringleaders of this savage and audacious mob."

CHAPTER XXI

THE PROVINCIAL COUNCIL

Upon the adjournment of the second Provincial Congress, April 7, 1775, authority was given to John Harvey, or in the event of his death to Samuel Johnston, to call another Congress whenever it became necessary. Harvey dying in May, the leadership of the revolutionary party devolved upon Johnston. Although a native of Scotland, Johnston had passed his life since early infancy in North Carolina, and felt for the colony all the affection and loyalty that men usually feel only for the land of their nativity. His public career, which began in 1759 with his election to represent Chowan County in the General Assembly, covered a period of forty-four years and embraced every branch of the public service. He was legislator, delegate to four provincial congresses, president of two constitutional conventions, member of the Continental Congress, judge, governor, United States senator. By inheritance, by training and by conviction he was a conservative in politics. He clung tenaciously to the things that were and viewed with apprehension, if not with distrust, any departure from the beaten path of experience. Holding the principles of the British Constitution in great reverence, he regarded the policies of the British ministry toward America as revolutionary in their tendency, and therefore threw the whole weight of his influence against them.

In the great crises of our history, immediately preceding and immediately following the Revolution, Johnston saw perhaps more clearly than any of his colleagues the true nature of the problem confronting them. This problem was, on the one hand, to preserve in America the fundamental principles of English liberty against the encroachments of the British Parliament, and on the other, to secure the guarantees of law and order against the well-meant but ill-considered schemes of honest but ignorant reformers. For a full quarter of a century he pursued both of these ends so patiently and persistently that neither the wrath of a royal governor, threaten-

SAMUEL JOHNSTON
From a portrait in the Governor's office, Raleigh

ing withdrawal of royal favor and deprivation of office, nor the fierce and passionate denunciations of party leaders, menacing him with loss of popular support and defeat at the polls, could swerve him a hair's breadth from the path of what he considered the public good. He had in the fullest degree that rarest of all virtues in men who serve the public, courage—courage to fight the battles of the people, if need be, against the people themselves. While he never questioned the right of the people to decide public questions as they chose, he frequently doubted the wisdom of their decisions; and when such doubt arose in his mind he spoke his sentiments without fear or favor, maintaining his positions with a relentlessness in reasoning that generally carried conviction and out of defeat wrung ultimate victory. More than once in his public career the people, when confronted by his immovable will, in fits of party passion, discarded his leadership for that of more compliant leaders, but only in their calmer moments to turn to him again to point the way out of the mazes into which their inexperience had led them. An ample fortune made him independent of public office. He possessed a vigorous and penetrating intellect, seasoned with sound and varied learning. "His powerful frame," says McRee, "was a fit engine for the vigorous intellect that gave it animation. Strength was his characteristic. In his relations to the public an inflexible sense of duty and justice dominated. There was a remarkable degree of self-reliance and majesty about the man. His erect carriage and his intolerance of indolence, meanness, vice and wrong gave him an air of sternness. He commanded the respect and admiration, but not the love of the people." [1]

Such was the man upon whose shoulders now fell the mantle of John Harvey. It became necessary for him to exercise the authority with which he was clothed sooner than was expected. The flight of the governor left the province without a government or a constitutional method of calling an Assembly. The battle of Lexington, followed by the destruction of Fort Johnston, produced a state of war. Both sides, recognizing this fact, were straining every nerve to get ready for the conflict. The situation, therefore, called for a larger authority than had been granted to the committees of safety. A new government had to be formed, a currency devised, an army organized, munitions of war collected, and a system of defense planned; and all these preparations had to be made

---

[1] Life and Correspondence of James Iredell, Vol. 1, p. 37.

with a view to continental as well as provincial affairs. The leaders of the Whig party on the Cape Fear were required daily to exercise authority and accept responsibilities that exceeded the powers granted them; and they realized earlier than their friends elsewhere the necessity for organizing a government that could act independently of the royal authority. Only a general congress could provide this government. Accordingly on May 31, 1775, Howe, Harnett and Ashe joined in a letter to Samuel Johnston—Harvey having died a few days before—suggesting that he call a congress "as soon as possible." Johnston, however, thought the suggestion premature, and was reluctant to take a step that would widen still further the breach with the royal government. Besides the Assembly had been summoned to meet July 12, and he thought it wise not to call a convention until then, as "many members of the Assembly would probably be chosen to serve in convention." But at his quiet home on the Albemarle, Johnston failed to appreciate the situation on the Cape Fear, where a state of war practically existed, and he hesitated. "I expect my Conduct in not immediately calling a Provincial Congress," he wrote, "will be much censured by many, but being conscious of having discharged my duty according to my best Judgment I shall be the better able to bear it." The Cape Fear leaders became impatient. On June 29, Howe, Harnett and Ashe wrote again to Johnston, taking him to task for his delay. "The circumstances of the times," and "the expectations of the people," they thought, ought to determine his conduct. The people, wrote the Wilmington committee, were "Continually clamouring for a Provincial Convention. They hope everything from its Immediate Session, fear everything from its delay." In the meantime Governor Martin prorogued the Assembly. Thereupon other committees joined in the request for a convention. Thus pressed, Johnston yielded and issued his call for a Congress to meet at Hillsboro, August 20th.

Nothing shows the progress that had been made toward revolution during the year more clearly than the full attendance at this Congress. Just a year, lacking but five days, had passed since the first Congress met at New Bern. At that Congress seventy-one delegates were present, while five counties and three towns sent no representatives. But in the Hillsboro Congress of August, 1775, every county and every borough town were represented, and 184 delegates were present. No abler body of men ever sat in North Carolina. More than half of them had served in the Assembly or in the first two Congresses. Among them were Johnston, Caswell, Howe, Hooper, Hewes, Burke, Harnett, John Ashe, Abner Nash and Willie Jones. Appearing for the first time in a revolutionary assemblage were Samuel Ashe, afterwards governor; Joseph Winston and Frederick Hambright, distinguished among the heroes of King's Mountain; Francis Nash, who fell gloriously leading his brigade at Germantown; Thomas Polk, Waightstill Avery, John McNitt Alexander, and their Mecklenburg colleagues, fresh from setting up a county government "independent of the Crown of Great Britain and former constitution of this Province"; John Penn, a recent arrival from Virginia, whose name is indissolubly associated with those of Hooper and Hewes as signers of the Declaration of Independence; Jethro Sumner and James Hogun, soldiers whose services on the battlefield helped to make that Declaration good. The Congress organized by the election of Samuel Johnston "president"—a significant change in the title of its presiding officer.

The delegates brought to their deliberations a spirit and a point of view almost national. No such thing as a truly national sentiment existed in America at that time, but the Hillsboro Congress approached it as nearly as any body that had yet assembled in the colonies. Among their first acts was to approve anew the Continental Association which the first Continental Congress had recommended, and to adopt and subscribe a test denying the right of Parliament "to impose Taxes upon these Colonies to regulate the internal police thereof"; declaring that "the people of this province, singly and collectively, are bound by the Acts and resolutions of the Continental and Provincial Congresses, because in both they are freely represented by persons chosen by themselves;" and solemnly binding themselves to support and maintain the policies and plans of the Continental Congress. Since the Continental Congress had resolved to raise an army and to emit $3,000,000 for its support, the Provincial Congress resolved unanimously that North Carolina would bear her proportionate share of the burden and made provision for the redemption of the sum allotted to her by the Continental Congress, and also authorized the raising and organization of two regiments of Continental troops. Throughout its proceedings, in its appeals to the people, in the organization of an army, and in the formation of a provisional government,

the one clear note sounding above all others was "the common cause of America."

Although the delegates were unanimous in expressing this
sentiment, there was no such unanimity among the people,
and Governor Martin had been alarmingly successful in his
efforts to arouse and organize the disaffected elements. His
agents were especially active among the former Regulators
and Highlanders. Hillsboro and Cross Creek, therefore, were
the chief centers of disaffection to the American cause. The
Whig leaders, of course, recognized the importance of coun-
teracting Governor Martin's influence in these sections. This
was the chief reason for changing the meeting place of Congress from New Bern to Hillsboro. Immediately after organizing, therefore, Congress turned its attention to these problems. Consideration was given to the Regulators first, for
Governor Martin had succeeded in persuading them that they
were still subject to punishment for their late insurrection,
and that their only chance of securing pardon was to aid the
government in the present crisis. Congress adopted a resolution declaring all such representations false and promising
to protect the Regulators "from every attempt to punish them
by any Means whatever." A committee was appointed, of
which Thomas Person, who had been a leader among the Regulators, was a member, to confer with such persons as entertained "any religious or political Scruples" against "associating in the common Cause of America, to remove any ill
impressions that have been made upon them by the artful
devices of the enemies of America, and to induce them by
Argument and Persuasion" to unite with the Whig party in
defense of their liberties. Another committee, numbering
among its members Archibald Maclaine, Alexander McAlis-
ter, Alexander McKay, and Farquard Campbell, good Highlanders, all, was appointed to explain to the Highlanders who
had lately arrived in North Carolina "the Nature of our Unhappy Controversy with Great Britain, and to advise and
urge them to unite with the other Inhabitants of America in
defence of those rights which they derive from God and the
Constitution." Nor were the people at large to be neglected.
Maurice Moore, Hooper, Howe, Caswell and Hewes were directed to prepare an address to the people of North Carolina,
"stating the present Controversy in an easy, familiar stile
and manner obvious to the very Meanest Capacity;" vindicat-
ing the taking up of arms by showing the necessity which had
been forced upon the colonies by the British ministry, and

ascribing the silence of the legislative powers to the governor's "refusing to exercise the Functions of office." Unhappily these plans to unite the people were better conceived than they were executed; North Carolina remained divided throughout the Revolution and that strength and vigor which she should have contributed to the support of the general cause was largely consumed in civil strife at home.

The two most important matters before the Congress were the organization of an army and the formation of a provisional government. "Our principal debates," wrote Johnston, "will be about raising troops." As a preliminary to this step, the Congress first issued what may not inaptly be called a declaration of war. It declared that whereas "hostilities being actually commenced in the Massachusetts Bay by the British troops under the command of General Gage; * * * And whereas His Excellency Governor Martin hath taken a very active and instrumental share in opposition to the means which have been adopted by this and the other United Colonies for the common safety, * * * therefore [resolved that] this colony be immediately put into a state of defense." Two regiments of 500 men each were ordered "as part of and on the same establishment with the Continental army." Col. James Moore was assigned to the command of the first, Col. Robert Howe to the second. Both won military fame in the war that followed. Six regiments of 500 minute-men each, were ordered to be raised in the six military districts, in which the province was divided. These districts with their colonels were: Edenton District, Edward Vail, colonel; Halifax District, Nicholas Long, colonel; Salisbury District, Thomas Wade, colonel; Hillsboro District, James Thackston, colonel; New Bern District, Richard Caswell, colonel; Wilmington District, Alexander Lillington, colonel. Of these officers only Caswell and Lillington attained distinction. The minute-men were to be enlisted for six months, and when called into active service were to be under the same discipline as the continental troops. In addition to these 4,000 troops, provision was made for a more effective organization of the militia, and for raising and organizing independent companies.

The problem of financing these military organizations early occupied the attention of the Congress. A committee appointed to make a statement of the public funds reported that the province owed large sums to individuals, but how much it had on hand with which to meet these claims the

committee could not say, as the accounts of the provincial
treasurers were not accessible. It also found that there were
"divers large sums of money due from sundry sheriffs,"
and urged that steps be taken to compel speedy settlements.
Congress, however, had little confidence in ever receiving any
considerable sums from this source and accordingly to meet
the expenses necessary for defense of the province resorted
to the old familiar policy of issuing paper money. The amount
determined upon was $125,000 in bills of credit, for the re-
demption of which the faith of the province was pledged.
Significant of the drift of sentiment was the change from the
English pound to the Spanish milled dollar as the standard
of value. The new bills were to pass at the rate of eight
shillings to the dollar, and for their redemption a tax of two
shillings was to be levied annually on each taxable from 1777
to 1786, "unless the money should be sooner sunk." Any
person who should refuse to receive the bills in payment of
any debt, or "speak disrespectfully" of them, or offer them
at a greater rate than eight shillings for a dollar should "be
treated as an enemy to his country." Persons convicted of
counterfeiting, altering, or erasing them, or of knowingly
passing such counterfeited, or altered bills, were to "suffer
Death, without Benefit of Clergy."

To agree upon a plan of civil government was a more difficult task than the organization of the army. Most men will
frankly confess their ignorance of military matters, and willingly submit to the opinions of experts, but no American
would consider himself loyal to the teachings of the fathers
were he to admit himself incapable of manufacturing offhand
a perfect plan of civil government. Congress, therefore,
found no lack of plans and ideas. On August 24th a strong
committee was appointed to prepare a plan of government
made necessary by the "absence" of Governor Martin. The
committee reported September 9th. The plan proposed and
adopted continued the Congress as the supreme branch of
the government with a few changes that will be noticed. The
executive and judicial authority was vested in a Provincial
Council, six district committees of safety, and the local committees of safety.

Congress was to be the supreme power in the province.
Henceforth it was to meet annually at such time and place
as should be designated by the Provincial Council. Delegates
were to be elected annually in October. Each county was
to be entitled to five delegates, and each borough town to one.

The privilege of suffrage was limited to freeholders. The members of Congress were to qualify by taking an oath in the presence of three members of the Provincial Council, acknowledging allegiance to the Crown, denying the right of Parliament to levy internal taxes on the colonies, and agreeing to abide by the acts and resolutions of the Provincial and Continental Congresses. Each county and each town was to have one vote in Congress. No constitutional limitation was placed on the authority of Congress, and as the supreme power in the province it could review the acts of the executive branches of the government.

The executive powers of the government were vested in the committees. The committees of the counties and towns were continued practically as they were. Some limitation was placed on their power by making their acts reviewable by the district committees with the right of appeal to the Provincial Council. They were empowered to make such rules and regulations as they saw fit for the enforcement of their authority, but they could not inflict corporal punishment except by imprisonment. Within their own jurisdictions, they were to execute the orders of the district committees and the Provincial Council. They were to enforce the Continental Association and the ordinances of the Provincial and Continental Congresses. Each committee was required to organize a sub-committee of secrecy, intelligence and observation to correspond with other committees and with the Council. They were vested with the power to arrest and examine suspected persons and if deemed necessary to hold them for trial by a higher tribunal. Members of the committees were to be elected annually by the freeholders.

Above these local committees was placed a system of district committees, one in each of the military districts, composed of a president and twelve members. The members were to be elected by the delegates in Congress from the counties which composed the several districts. They were to sit at least once in every three months. Power was given to them, subject to the authority of the Provincial Council, to direct the movements of the militia and other troops within their districts. They were to sit as courts for the trial of civil causes, for investigations into charges of disaffection to the American cause, and as appellate courts over the town and county committees. They shared with the Council authority to compel debtors suspected of intention to leave the province to give security to their creditors. Finally, they were to superintend the collection of the public revenue.

The Provincial Council was the chief executive authority of the new government. It was to be composed of thirteen members, one elected by the Congress for the province at at large, and two from each of the military districts. Vacancies occurring during the recess of Congress were to be filled by the committee of safety for the district in which the vacancy fell. Military officers, except officers of the militia, were ineligible for membership. The members were to qualify by subscribing the oath prescribed for members of Congress. The Council was to meet once every three months, and a majority of the members was to constitute a quorum. Authority was given to them to direct the military operations of the province, to call out the militia when needed, and to execute the acts of the Assembly that were still in force with respect to the militia. They could issue commissions, suspend officers, order courts-martial, reject officers of the militia chosen by the people, and fill vacancies. But their real power lay in a sort of "general welfare" clause which empowered them "to do and Transact all such matters and things as they may judge expedient to strengthen, secure and defend the Colony." To carry out their powers, they were authorized to draw on the public treasury for such sums of money as they needed, for which they were accountable to Congress. In all matters they were given an appellate jurisdiction over the district committees, and in turn were subject to the authority of Congress. Their authority continued only during the recess of Congress, and Congress at each session was to review and pass upon their proceedings.

Such was the government that was to organize, equip and direct the military forces raised by Congress and to inaugurate the great war about to burst upon the colony. As Saunders says, the die was now cast and North Carolina was at last a self-governing commonwealth. The people had so declared through representatives whom they had chosen after a campaign of forty days. Nobody was taken by surprise, for all knew that the Congress elected in that campaign would formulate a provisional government. This action was taken fully eight months before the Continental Congress advised the colonies to adopt new constitutions. "The more the action of this great Hillsborough Congress is studied, and the events immediately preceding," writes Saunders, "the more wonderful seems the deliberate, well-considered, resolute boldness of our ancestors." [2]

The efficiency of the new government depended, of course, upon the men chosen to administer it. The members of the Provincial Council were elected Saturday, September 9th. Samuel Johnston was chosen by the Congress for the province at large. The other members were: Cornelius Harnett and Samuel Ashe, for the Wilmington District; Thomas Jones and Whitmill Hill, for the Edenton District; Abner Nash and James Coor, for the New Bern District; Thomas Person and John Kinchen, for the Hillsboro District; Willie Jones and Thomas Eaton, for the Halifax District; Samuel Spencer and Waightstill Avery, for the Salisbury District. On October 18th the Council held their first session at Johnston Court House and elected Cornelius Harnett president.

Cornelius Harnett thus became the first chief executive of North Carolina independent of the British Crown. Governor in all but name, he exercised greater authority than the people have since conferred on their governor, and occupied a position of honor and power, but also of great responsibility and peril. He had long been in the public service. Entering the Assembly in 1754 as the representative of the borough of Wilmington, he had represented that town in every Assembly since that date. His legislative career covered a period of twenty-seven years, embracing service in the Assembly, in the Provincial Congress, and in the Continental Congress. From 1765 he was conspicuous in every movement in opposition to the colonial policy of the British ministry. He led the resistance to the Stamp Act on the Cape Fear; was chairman of the Sons of Liberty and their leader in enforcing the Non-Importation Association; and was among the foremost in organizing and directing the activities of the Committee of Correspondence. Perhaps his chief service was rendered as chairman of the Wilmington-New Hanover committees of safety. Of these he was the acknowledged master spirit. By his activity in "warning and watching the disaffected, encouraging the timid, collecting the means of defence, and communicating its enthusiasm to all orders," he made this local committee the most effective agency, except the Provincial Congress itself, in getting the Revolution under way in North Carolina. Governor Martin recognized in him the chief source

---

[2] Prefatory Notes to *Colonial Records of North Carolina*, Vol. X, p. viii-ix.

of opposition to the royal government, marked him out for special punishment, and induced Sir Henry Clinton to except him, together with Robert Howe, from his offer of general amnesty to all who would return to their allegiance. As president of the Provincial Council, he fully sustained his reputation for executive skill, energy and foresight. From the outbreak of the Revolution Harnett had taken a broad and liberal view of the relations of the colonies to each other, and he inspired his colleagues on the Council with the same continental spirit that was the chief characteristic of his own statesmanship. He was foremost among the advocates of a united Declaration of Independence, and wrote the first resolution adopted by any of the colonies favoring such a step by the Continental Congress. As a delegate to the Continental Congress he bore an important part in framing the Articles of Confederation, which he regarded as "the best confederacy that could be formed, especially when we consider the number of states, their different interests [and] customs."

Harnett was not politically ambitious. He loved ease and pleasure, and had sufficient fortune to enjoy both. Public office, therefore, as such, made no appeal to him. He did not need its emoluments. He cared little for its distinctions. Indeed, the offices which he held brought more of sacrifice than of gain, more of drudgery than of glory. Desire to serve his country, regardless of the cost to himself, alone held him to the duties, burdens and dangers of the public service. With a profound faith in popular government, he had in his nature none of the elements of the demagogue. He appealed neither to the prejudices nor to the passions of mankind. His work lay not on the hustings, nor in the legislative hall, but rather in the council chamber. His chief service was executive in its nature. In the performance of his duties, we are told, "he could be wary and circumspect, or decided and daring, as exigency dictated or emergency required." Such work as he did was the backbone of the Revolution, without which the eloquence of the orator, the wisdom of the legislator, and the daring of the soldier would have been barren of results. Yet it was work that offered but little opportunity for display, and brought but little fame. For Cornelius Harnett its only opportunity was for service, its only reward a wasted body and a martyr's grave.

The Provincial Council were forced to work under the most unfavorable conditions. To begin with there was not a place in the province, except possibly the Palace at New Bern, suitable for their sessions. From necessity, as well as from policy, they became a migratory body. The members were subjected to almost every personal inconvenience and discomfort. But these were among the least of their difficulties. Almost without any of the means with which governments usually administer public affairs, they were compelled to struggle against political and economic conditions that might well have daunted the most determined. They had to rely for success on a public sentiment which they themselves, to a large extent, had to create, and at the same time to enforce measures that were at once burdensome and irritating. They had no powerful press to uphold their hands. The people were scattered over an immense area, with means of communication crudely primitive. There were no public highways except a few rough and dangerous forest paths frequently impassable. Their principal river was held at the mouth by hostile ships of war, and at the head of navigation by an enemy bold, hardy, and enthusiastic in the king's cause. The East was dominated by an oligarchy of wealthy planters and merchants, living in an almost feudal state, supported by slave labor; the West was a pure democracy, composed of small farmers, living on isolated farms, tilled by their own hands. Both East and West, aristocracy and democracy, were equally determined in their opposition to the British government, but between the two, right through the heart of the province, were projected the Scotch Highlanders and the former Regulators—the one eager to prove their loyalty to the throne against which they were but recently in rebellion, the other equally as eager to wreak vengeance upon the men who had but lately crushed and humiliated them at Alamance. The province was a rural community without a single center of population. There were no mills or factories. The only port of any consequence was in the hands of the enemy. Thus the Council's task was to organize an army among a people divided in sentiment and unused to war; to equip it without factories for the manufacture of clothes, arms or ammunition; to train it without officers of experience; to maintain it without money; and to direct its movements in the face of an enemy superior in numbers, in equipment, and in military experience.

The Council was created as a war measure, and its principal work related to military affairs. The province was threatened in front and in the rear. In front Governor Martin was organizing the Highlanders and Regulators for a descent on the lower Cape Fear, and Governor Dunmore of Virginia was encouraging an insurrection of slaves on the Albemarle. In the rear bands of Tories were overrunning Western South Carolina and threatening the frontier of North Carolina, while the Indians, instigated by British agents, were showing signs of restlessness. Foreseeing that the province would "soon be invaded by British troops," the Council issued orders to Colonel Moore and Colonel Howe of the continental regiments to resist "to the utmost of their power" any attempt to invade the province; directed the committees of Wilmington and Brunswick to stop all communications, "on any pretense whatever," between the people and the governor, and "to cut off all supplies of provisions to any of the ships of war lying in Cape Fear River;" and commanded Colonel Griffith Rutherford and Colonel Thomas Polk of the Salisbury District to raise two regiments for defense of the frontier. Had they been less than tragical, these high-sounding orders, in comparison with the Council's means for enforcing them, would have been ludicrous. The Council found the minute-men and continental troops practically without clothes, arms, ammunition, or any of the necessary equipment of war, the people "destitute of sufficient arms for defense of their lives and property," and the outlook for supplying them unpromising enough. They drew upon every conceivable source. They bought and borrowed, made and mended, begged and confiscated, and though their efforts fell far short of what the emergency required, yet they were sufficient to enable the western militia to march to the aid of South Carolina on the famous "Snow Campaign", to enable Colonel Howe to drive Lord Dunmore out of Norfolk, and to enable Colonel Moore to win a brilliant campaign against the Highlanders at Moore's Creek Bridge. South Carolina and Virginia were profuse in their thanks to President Harnett for important assistance in their hour of need, while Governor Martin expressed great "mortification," and declared it was a matter "greatly to be lamented."

With war impending, both sides began to give anxious thought to the attitude of the Indian tribes along the frontier. The British expected their active aid, the Americans knew they could hope for nothing better than their neutrality. Unfortunately, in the competition which immediately arose the Americans were at every disadvantage. It was they who, coming in daily contact with the red man, had driven him from his hunting grounds, destroyed his property, burned his towns, reduced his women and children to slavery, and slain his warriors. Eternal enmity seemed to be decreed between them. On the other hand, since the expulsion of the French in 1763, the Indians had been trained to look to British officials and agents as the sole representatives of authority standing between them and the encroachments of the American borderer. Licensed British traders dwelt in almost every Indian village, married Indian women, adopted Indian customs, and made the Indians' interests their own. The British government, too, had been especially fortunate in its agents among the Indians. In the Northern Department Sir William Johnson and in the Southern Department Captain John Stuart were known to the Indians as generous, sympathetic friends, ever watchful over their interests. From the Americans, therefore, ever steadily encroaching upon their possessions, the Indians knew they could expect nothing but rivalry and oppression; from the British they had been taught to expect assistance and protection.

Accordingly when the severance came the Indians, almost to a tribe, threw their power into the scale with the Crown. As early as June, 1775, the British government decided to call them into active service. Presents and clothing were distributed among all the tribes from the Great Lakes to the Gulf; hatchets, arms and ammunition were issued to the warriors, and liberal bounties were offered for American scalps. All along the border the Indians awaited the command to begin their work of fire and slaughter. In August, 1775, the Cherokee sent to Alexander Cameron, the deputy agent resident among them, a "talk," assuring him that they were ready at a signal to fall upon the frontier settlements of Georgia and the Carolinas. Circulars were distributed among the border Tories, apprising them of the plans and directing them to repair to Cameron's headquarters to join in the assault. Fortunately, the Cherokee "talk" fell into the hands of the Americans and warned them of the impending danger.

The Americans themselves had not been inactive. Indian affairs had received the attention of both the Continental Congress and the Provincial Congress. The former divided the colonies into three Indian departments and appointed agents in each. In the Southern Department the agents were John Walker of Virginia, Willie Jones of North Carolina, Robert Rae, Edward Wilkinson and George Galphin of South Carolina. The Provincial Congress at Hillsboro directed that all persons who had any information about Indian affairs should submit it to Willie Jones. Accordingly Thomas Wade, Thomas Polk and John Walker laid before him information relative to the "hostile intentions" of Governor Martin and the Indians which was of "so serious and important a Nature" that it was referred to the Congress for consideration. The necessity for placating the Indians was urgent. Congress, therefore, appropriated £1,000 to be used by Willie Jones in the purchase of presents for them. The southern agents also were active. Galphin and Rae held a "talk" with the Creek Indians at Augusta, and in November, 1775, all five agents met a delegation of Creek warriors at Salisbury. The burden of their "talks" was neutrality; "you have been repeatedly told the nature of the disputes between the father and his children," they said, "and we desire you to have no concern in it."

One of the results of these efforts to placate the Indians was the "Snow Campaign" to which allusion has just been made. In October, 1775, the Council of Safety of South Carolina, in accordance with their agreement with the Cherokee, dispatched a large supply of powder and lead to the Lower Towns of that nation. The Loyalists of Western South Carolina, who were led to believe that the Whigs were planning to bring the Indians down upon them, embodied in force under Major Joseph Robinson and Captain Patrick Cunningham, intercepted the supply wagons, seized the powder and lead, compelled a Whig force under Major Andrew Williamson, who had been sent to disperse them, to seek refuge in the fort at Ninety-Six, and after a vigorous siege forced him to capitulate. Their success spread alarm among the Whigs of both the Carolinas. The South Carolina Congress immediately dispatched a force of 2,500 men under Colonel Richard Richardson to the scene, while 700 men from Western North Carolina hastened into South Carolina to co-operate with him. This force was composed of 220 Continentals under Lieutenant-Colonel Alexander Martin, 200 militia of Rowan County under Colonel Griffith Rutherford, and 300 Mecklenburg militia under Colonel Thomas Polk. Thus reinforced, in spite of the inclement weather and the indifferent equipment of his men, Colonel Richardson pushed forward vigorously against the enemy, breaking up such parties as ventured to oppose him and capturing several of their leaders. The campaign came to an end with a battle at Cane Brake on Reedy River, about four miles within the Cherokee reservation, in which Colonel William Thomson surprised and destroyed a Loyalist force under Cunningham. Colonel Richardson, considering the campaign now at an end and its object accomplished, dismissed the North Carolina troops and marched his own men back to their homes. In his campaign he had captured most of the Loyalist leaders and about 400 of their followers. Governor Martin in a letter to Lord Dartmouth wrote that the reinforcements from North Carolina "put the Rebels of the Country in sufficient force to disarm the loyal people who had made so noble a stand and who were collecting strength so fast that they must have carried everything before them if it had been possible to afford them the least support. This check of the friends of Government in that Province is greatly to be lamented." In local tradition the campaign became known as the "Snow Campaign" because of the heavy fall of snow in which it was waged.

In the meantime another force of North Carolinians had gone to the aid of the Virginians in their campaign against their royal governor, Lord Dunmore. Like Martin of North Carolina and Campbell of South Carolina, Dunmore had fled from the province and sought refuge on board a man-of-war. During the summer he assembled in Chesapeake Bay a flotilla which enabled him to capture Norfolk, the chief town of the province with a population of 6,000. On November 7th, from his cabin on the Fowney, he issued a proclamation in which he declared war on the people of Virginia, denounced as traitors all persons capable of bearing arms who did not repair at once to his standard, and offered freedom to "all indentured servants, negroes, or others appertaining to rebels." His emissaries were also busy trying to incite the slaves of the Albemarle section of North Carolina to insurrection. To prevent the success of his schemes a force of Virginia militia under Colonel William Woodford fortified Great Bridge near Norfolk, where they were joined by 150 minute-men from North Carolina under Colonel Nicholas Long and Major Jethro Sumner. On December 8th a force of British regulars attempted to drive them away, but were repulsed with loss and forced to retreat into Norfolk. Three days later Colonel Robert Howe, with the Second North Carolina Continentals, arrived at Great Bridge and took command. Howe pushed forward immediately, compelled the British to evacuate Norfolk, and entered the town December 14th. "Lord Dunmore had abandoned the town," wrote an officer, describing these events, "and several of the Tories had fled on board their vessels, with all their effects; others of them are applying for forgiveness to their injured countrymen." For this service Colonel Howe received the thanks of the Virginia Convention. Dunmore could not afford to leave the rebels in possession of Norfolk. On New Year's day, 1776, therefore, he began a bombardment of the town. "About four o'clock in the afternoon," wrote an officer on His Majesty's ship Otter, "the signal was given from the Liverpool, when a dreadful cannonading began from the three ships, which lasted till it was too hot for the Rebels to stand on their wharves. Our boats now landed and set fire to the town in several places. It burnt fiercely all night and the next day; nor are the flames yet extinguished; but no more of Norfolk remains than about twelve houses, which have escaped the flames." The destruction of Norfolk served no military purpose but it inflamed the people of Virginia and North Carolina and hastened the development of sentiment for independence.

Following hard upon the "Snow Campaign" and the destruction of Norfolk, came the defeat of the Highlanders at Moore's Creek Bridge, February 27, 1776. The victory of Moore's Creek Bridge was an event of much greater significance than is generally accorded it in the histories of the Revolution, and Frothingham is guilty of no exaggeration when he calls it "the Lexington and Concord" of the South. So far from being an isolated event, it was part of an extensive campaign planned by the king and ministry for the subjugation of all the southern colonies which but for the victory, at Moore's Creek Bridge would probably have succeeded.

Governor Martin in his cabin on the Cruizer had never once relaxed his efforts to restore the king's authority in North Carolina. Some Loyalists, who in spite of the vigilance of the committees found means of communicating with him, assured him that the people were tired of the rule of "the little tyrannies" called committees which they had set up and were eager for him "to relieve them from the self-made yoke which they now found intolerable." Encouraged by such reports, Martin submitted to the ministry a well-conceived plan for the reduction not of North Carolina only, but also of Virginia, South Carolina and Georgia. According to this plan, he was to raise 10,000 Tories, Regulators and Highlanders in the interior of North Carolina; Lord Cornwallis was to sail from Cork, Ireland, with seven regiments of British regulars escorted by a fleet of seventy-two sail under command of Sir Peter Parker, and Sir Henry Clinton was to sail from Boston with 2,000 regulars and take command of the combined forces, which were to effect a junction at Wilmington about the middle of February. On January 3, 1776, Martin received dispatches from Lord Dartmouth informing him that his plan had been heartily approved; that Clinton and Cornwallis had received their orders accordingly, and that he might proceed with his part of the program. Accordingly he promptly issued commissions to Donald Mac-Donald, a veteran of Culloden whom Clinton had sent from Boston to take command of the North Carolina Highlanders; to Allan MacDonald, husband of the Scottish heroine, Flora MacDonald, and to twenty-four others in Cumberland, Anson, Chatham, Guilford, Orange, Mecklenburg, Rowan, Surry and Bute counties, empowering them to raise and organize troops and ordering them to press down on Brunswick by February 15th. A few days later he received word that the Loyalists were in high spirits, were fast collecting, and were well equipped with wagons and horses. They planned to leave 1,000 men at Cross Creek and with the remainder to march at once upon Wilmington; the governor might feel assured that they would place that rebellious town in his possession by February 25th at the latest. On February 18th, 1,600 Highlanders, led by Donald MacDonald, encouraged by the presence and the stirring words of Flora MacDonald herself, with bagpipes playing and the royal standard flying in their midst, marched gaily out of Cross Creek and took the Brunswick road for Wilmington. Upon receiving information of this movement, Governor Martin with the men-of-war which were stationed at the mouth of the Cape Fear moved up the river and dropped anchor opposite Wilmington to be ready to support his friends.

In the meantime the Whig leaders had not been inactive. Colonel James Moore of the First Regiment of Continentals had been closely watching the movements of the Highlanders and was fully informed of their plans. On February 15th he took a position on the southern bank of Rockfish Creek, where he was soon joined by enough minute-men under James Kenan, Alexander Lillington and John Ashe to raise his little army to 1,100 men. Colonel Alexander Martin was approaching with a small force from Guilford County; Colonel James Thackston with another small force was hastening from the southwest, and Colonel Richard Caswell was on the march with 800 militia from the New Bern District. Moore was in

Vol. I—25

supreme command and directed the movements of all these detachments.

On February 19th MacDonald approached to within four miles of Moore's encampment on Rockfish Creek. Now began a series of movements in which Moore out-generaled Mac-Donald, displayed military capacity of a high order and clearly won the honors of the campaign. Some years later a dispute arose among the friends of Alexander Lillington and Richard Caswell as to which of the two was due the credit of the victory over the Highlanders. It has since taken its place along with Alamance and Mecklenburg among the historic controversies in our annals. The truth is that the real hero of Moore's Creek Bridge was neither Lillington nor Caswell, but Moore. This is said without any purpose to detract from the just fame of either of those eminent patriots. Their work was plain and could be seen of all men; Moore's part in the campaign, owing to his absence from the scene of the actual fighting, was not so evident and can not be understood without a careful study of the events of the week preceding the battle. It was he who directed the movements which on the morning of February 27th brought Caswell, Lillington and Ashe with 1,100 minute-men face to face with MacDonald's 1,600 Highlanders at Moore's Creek Bridge, eighteen miles above Wilmington.

On the afternoon of February 26th, in obedience to Moore's directions, Caswell took up a position at the west end of Moore's Creek Bridge, toward which MacDonald was approaching, while Ashe and Lillington held the east end. About daybreak the following morning MacDonald reached within striking distance of Caswell's camp, expecting to find him with the creek in his rear between his forces and those of Lillington and Ashe. But in the night Caswell, leaving his campfires burning, as Washington afterwards did at Trenton, (a fact which Caswell's friends commented on at the time), crossed the bridge and joined Lillington and Ashe. He then had the planks of the bridge removed, leaving only the sills in place. The Highlanders having formed for the attack on the west bank of the stream were greatly surprised when they marched into a deserted camp and immediately concluded that the enemy had fled. Leading his troops, Donald McLeod, who commanded, MacDonald being too ill to take the field, reached the bridge while it was still dark. "Who goes there?" challenged Caswell's sentinel. "A friend," replied McLeod. "A friend to whom?" answered the voice in the darkness. "To the king," replied the Highlander. Receiving no further reply and thinking the challenge might have come from one of his friends, McLeod called out in Gaelic. Still no answer. Raising his gun, he fired toward the spot whence the voice came and made a dash across the bridge. The Whigs fired and McLeod fell. Those who attempted to follow him were cut down and fell into the creek below. More than thirty of the bravest were shot down. The others losing heart, shamefully abandoned their sick general and fled. The victory could not have been more complete. Of the Whigs only one man was killed and one wounded. The total loss of the Highlanders in killed and wounded was estimated at fifty. Their army was completely scattered. Moore arriving on the field shortly after the battle pressed the pursuit so vigorously that 350 guns, 150 swords and dirks, 1,500 excellent rifles, a box containing £15,000 sterling, 13 wagons, 850 soldiers and many officers, including their commanding general, fell into his hands. Two days after the victory Caswell reported it to President Harnett of the Provincial Council and on March 2d Colonel Moore sent to him a more detailed account of the campaign. Both these reports were widely published throughout the colonies and everywhere encouraged the advocates of independence.

Martin's plan for the subjugation of the province was excellent, but it failed because the Loyalists were too eager and the regulars were not eager enough. During the month of February, while the ill-fated Highlanders were marching to their doom at Moore's Creek Bridge, Sir Henry Clinton, with the two thousand regulars he was to bring from Boston, was leisurely coasting southward, now calling at New York for a talk with former Governor Tryon, now peeping in at Chesapeake Bay to pass the time of day with Governor Dunmore; while Sir Peter Parker, whose fleet was to bear Lord Cornwallis' seven regiments to the Cape Fear, was still lingering at Cork. Consequently when Clinton finally arrived at Cape Fear in April and Cornwallis in May, they found that they were too late. The Highlanders rising prematurely had been crushed, and the Americans forewarned were under arms in large numbers. Clinton therefore dared not attempt a landing, and after wasting more than a month plundering the plantations of prominent Whig leaders along the Cape Fear, weighed anchor and set sail for Charleston. With him sailed Josiah Martin, the last royal governor of North Carolina.

The victory at Moore's Creek Bridge was the crowning achievement of the Provincial Council. But for the sleepless vigilance and resourceful energy of President Harnett and his colleagues in organizing, arming and equipping the troops, MacDonald's march down the Cape Fear would have been but a holiday excursion. As it was, the royal governor had again measured strength with the people and again was beaten. High ran the enthusiasm of the Whigs, and high their confidence. Ten thousand men sprang to arms and hurried to Wilmington. "Since I was born," wrote an eye witness, "I never heard of so universal an ardor for fighting and so perfect a union among all degrees of men." Clinton and Cornwallis came with their powerful armaments, but finding no Loyalist force to welcome them at Cape Fear, they sailed away to beat in vain at the doors of Charleston. The victory at Moore's Creek Bridge saved North Carolina from conquest, and in all probability postponed the conquest of Georgia and South Carolina for three more years. Of this victory Bancroft wrote: "In less than a fortnight, more than nine thousand four hundred men of North Carolina rose against the enemy; and the coming of Clinton inspired no terror. * * * Almost every man was ready to turn out at an hour's warning. * * * Virginia offered assistance, and South Carolina would gladly have contributed relief; but North Carolina had men enough of her own to crush insurrection and guard against invasion; and as they marched in triumph through their piney forests, they were persuaded that in their own woods they could win an easy victory over British regulars. The terrors of a fate like that of Norfolk could not dismay the patriots of Wilmington; the people spoke more and more of independence; and the Provincial Congress, at its impending session, was expected to give an authoritative form to the prevailing desire." [3]

---

[3] History of the United States, ed. 1860, Vol. VIII, p. 289.

CHAPTER XXII

INDEPENDENCE

"Moore's Creek was the Rubicon over which North Carolina passed to independence and constitutional self-government." Before that event the Whig leaders had rather dreaded than sought independence. They met with indignant denial the assertions of their enemies that they had aimed at it from the beginning of their dispute with the mother country. Perhaps they did not foresee as clearly as the Tories did the logical result of their contentions. At any rate, they approached independence slowly, through a long process of development, and finally adopted it, as emancipation was afterwards adopted, as a war measure. Officially North Carolina led the way with the first resolution adopted by any of the colonies authorizing their delegates in the Continental Congress to vote for independence. It seems proper, therefore, to trace briefly the rise and development of the sentiment for independence in North Carolina, and to point out what influence the action of the North Carolina Congress had in other colonies.

It cannot be said that the sentiment for independence "originated" in any particular place. It was a growth and was present, perhaps unconsciously, in the minds of political thinkers and leaders long before England's policy crystallized it into conscious thought. Academic discussions of the possibility of an independent American nation were not uncommon, either in Europe or America, for many years before the Revolution; but it is safe to say that the idea took no definite shape even in the minds of the most advanced thinkers until after the struggle over the Stamp Act. The principles upon which the Americans opposed the Stamp Act had been regarded in the colonies as so firmly fixed, both by the British Constitution and by the colonial charters, that they were astonished to find them seriously questioned. Adherence to their charters and resistance to their perversion were cardinal principles with North Carolinians throughout their colonial history, and their records for a hundred years before the passage of the Stamp Act are full of the assertions of the principles upon which the American Revolution was fought.

The ministry, therefore, no sooner asserted the constitutional authority of Parliament to levy internal taxes in the colonies than the people of North Carolina denied it. Their contest, however, before the outbreak of hostilities was for constitutional government within the British Empire, though a few far-sighted leaders soon began to think of independence as possibly the ultimate solution of their political troubles with the mother country. Among the leaders of North Carolina who foresaw it, first place must be assigned to William Hooper. On April 26, 1774, in a letter to James Iredell, Hooper made this remarkable forecast of the political tendencies of the time:

"With you I anticipate the important share which the Colonies must soon have in regulating the political balance. They are striding fast to independence, and ere long will build an empire upon the ruins of Great Britain, will adopt its constitution purged of its impurities, and from an experience of its defects will guard against those evils which have wasted its vigor and brought it to an untimely end."

In the same prophetic vein, Samuel Johnston, writing September 23, 1774, with reference particularly to the Declaratory Act and the Boston Port Bill, said: "It is useless, in disputes between different Countries, to talk about the right which one has to give Laws to the other, as that generally attends the power, tho' where that power is wantonly or cruelly exercised, there are Instances where the weaker state has resisted with Success; for when once the Sword is drawn all nice distinctions fall to the Ground; the difference between internal and external taxation will be little attended to, and it will hereafter be considered of no consequence whether the Act be to regulate Trade or raise a fund to support a majority in the House of Commons. By this desperate push the Ministry will either confirm their power of making Laws to bind the Colonies in all cases whatsoever, or give up the right of making Laws to bind them in any Case."

These utterances, however, expressed political judgment rather than sentiment, for neither Hooper nor Johnston at that time desired independence. Nor did their judgment express the general sentiment of the colony. This sentiment found more accurate expression in the proceedings of the local meetings which were held in the various counties during the summer of 1774 to elect delegates to the Provincial Congress, and to adopt instructions to them. They invariably required the delegates to take a firm stand for the constitutional rights of the colonists, but at the same time professed the utmost loyalty to the king; while in August the Provincial Congress spoke for the province as a whole when it resolved to "maintain and defend the succession of the House of Hanover as by law established," and avowed "inviolable and unshaken Fidelity" to George III. But while these expressions undoubtedly represent the general sentiment of the colony at that time, they are less significant than other utterances which point to the change unconsciously working in the minds of men. Significant were the instructions of Pitt County, whose delegates were directed to make "a declaration of American rights," and, while acknowledging "due subjection to the Crown of England," to make it equally clear that in submitting to the authority of the king, the Americans did so "by their own voluntary act," and were entitled to enjoy "all their free chartered rights and libertys as British free subjects." But surpassing all other resolutions in the clearness and accuracy with which they stated the American idea, and reaching the most advanced ground attained in North Carolina during the year 1774, were the instructions of Granville County, adopted August 15th. They declared "that those absolute rights we are entitled to as men, by the immutable Laws of Nature, are antecedent to all social and relative duties whatsoever; that by the civil compact subsisting between our King and His People, Allegiance is right of the first Magistrate, and protection the right of the People; that a violation of this Compact would rescind the civil Institution binding both King and People together."

Political sentiment in North Carolina, therefore, during the year 1774 reached this point: The people owe and acknowledge allegiance to the king, but in return for this allegiance the king owes protection to the people; if either violates the "civil compact" subsisting between them, the other is released from all obligations to maintain it; however, the acts of which the people now complain are not the acts of the king, but of a corrupt Parliament and a venal and tyrannical ministry; the people are convinced that the king, if only they could reach his royal ears with their grievances, would throw the mantle of his protection around them; and therefore they determined, in the words of the Granville resolutions: "Although we are oppressed, we will still adhere to the civil Obligation exacting our allegiance to the best of Kings, as we entertain a most cordial affection to His Majesty's Person.''

A severe blow was dealt this position with the opening of the year 1775. In February the two houses of Parliament presented an address to the king declaring the colonies in rebellion, and assuring his majesty of their determination to support him in his efforts to suppress it; and the king returning his thanks for their loyal address, called for an increase of both the land and naval forces to be used in America. A few months later those who held that the king was not responsible for the acts of Parliament were still further shaken in their position by the announcement that he was hiring Hessians for service against the Americans; and in October they were driven completely from their ground by his proclamation declaring the colonists out of his protection.

The effect of these measures on the development of sentiment for independence is marked, first in the opinion of individual leaders, afterwards in the utterances of public assemblies. On April 7th, just after the adjournment of the second Provincial Congress and the dissolution of the last Assembly held under royal authority, Governor Martin, in a letter to Lord Dartmouth declared that the royal government in North Carolina was absolutely prostrate and impotent; that ''nothing but the shadow of it is left,'' and that unless strong measures were taken at once ''there will not long remain a trace of Britain's dominion over these colonies.'' Three months later Joseph Hewes urged Samuel Johnston to use his influence and example to ''drive every principle of Toryism'' out of every part of the province; he considered himself ''over head and ears in what the ministry call Rebellion,'' but felt ''no compunction'' for the part he had taken, or for the number of ''our enemies lately slain in the battle at Bunkers Hill.'' Another North Carolina Whig, writing July 31st to a business house in Edinburgh, declared that ''every American, to a man, is determined to die or be free,'' and closed his letter with the warning: ''This Country, without some step is taken, and that soon, will be inevitably lost to the Mother Country.'' Thomas McKnight, a Tory, believed there had been ''from the beginning of the dispute, a fixed design in some peoples breasts to throw off every connection with G[reat] B[ritain] and to act for the future as totally independent.'' After the king's proclamation in October, Hewes at Philadelphia entertained ''but little expectation of a reconciliation" and saw "scarcely a dawn of hope that it will take place"; and thought that independence would come soon "if the British ministry pursue their present diabolical scheme." The year 1775 closed in North Carolina with the publication of a remarkable open letter to "The Inhabitants of the United Colonies" by one who called himself "A British American." He declared that the salvation of the colonies lay in "declaring an immediate independency," in "holding forth, to all the Powers of Europe, a general neutrality," and in "immediately opening all our ports, and declaring them free to every European Power, except Great Britain." "We must separate," he concluded, "or become the laboring slaves of Britain, which we disdain to be."

Men of course are more radical in expressing their opinions in private than in public assemblies and official documents. It will be found, therefore, that during the year 1775 the sentiment of public assemblies, though much in advance of the sentiment of 1774, was more conservatively expressed than the private opinions of the leaders might lead us to expect. On April 6, 1775, the Assembly of the province, in reply to a message from the governor reminding them of their duty to the king, declared that "the Assembly of North Carolina have the highest sense of the allegiance due to the King; the Oath so repeatedly taken by them to that purpose made it unnecessary for them to be reminded of it"; at the same time, however, they called the governor's attention to the fact that the king "was by the same Constitution which established that allegiance and enjoined that oath, happily for his Subjects, solemnly bound to protect them in all their just rights and privileges by which a reciprocal duty became incumbent upon both."

This declaration was made before the people had heard of the address of Parliament in February and the king's reply declaring them in rebellion. How quickly they assumed that the withdrawal of protection by the sovereign released the subject from the obligations of allegiance is made manifest by the Mecklenburg Resolutions of May 31. "Whereas," so runs this striking document, "by an address presented to his majesty by both Houses of Parliament in February last, the American colonies are declared to be in a state of actual rebellion, we conceive that all laws and commissions confirmed by or derived from the authority of the King and Parliament are annulled and vacated and the former civil constitution of these colonies for the present wholly suspended;" therefore, it was resolved that "the Provincial Congress of each Province under the direction of the great Continental Congress is invested with all legislative and executive powers within their respective Provinces and that no other legislative or executive power does or can exist at this time in any of these colonies." Under these circumstances it was thought necessary to inaugurate a new county government, to organize the militia, and to elect officials "who shall hold and exercise their several powers by virtue of this choice and independent of the Crown of Great Britain and former constitution of this Province." These resolves and this organization were declared to be "in full force and virtue until instructions from the Provincial Congress regulating the jurisprudence of the Province shall provide otherwise or the legislative body of Great Britain resign its unjust and arbitrary pretensions with respect to America." [1]

The day after the meeting at Charlotte, the Rowan committee, which had declared a year before that they were ready to die in defense of the king's title to his American dominions, resolved "that by the Constitution of our Government we are a free People"; that the constitution "limits both Sovereignty and Allegiance," and "that it is our Duty to Surrender our lives, before our Constitutional privileges to any set of Men upon earth;" and referred any who might be of

---

[1] An attempt twenty-five years later to reproduce these resolves from memory resulted in the document famous in the controversial literature of the Revolution as the "Mecklenburg Declaration of Independence" of May 20, 1775. It is not necessary to refer to this controversy here further than to vindicate the statesmanship of the Mecklenburg patriots from the suspicion of having promulgated so absurd a declaration. For what, indeed, could be more absurd than a declaration of independence and assertion of sovereignty by a single county while in the same breath acknowledging its subordination to a Continental Congress which at that very moment was sincerely protesting the utmost loyalty to the Crown and .earnestly exerting itself to restore the colonies to their former relations to the mother country? When the time came to act, even the Provincial Congress did not venture to declare the province itself independent but referred the question to the Continental Congress where it properly belonged. It is no credit to either the patriotism or the statesmanship of the Mecklenburg patriots, representing a mere artificial administrative unit dependent for its very existence upon the provincial authority, to suppose that in such a grave matter they would assume to do what the Provincial Congress did not consider itself competent to do. On the other hand the course which they actually pursued, viz., the setting up of a county government to take the place of that which had been annulled until the proper authority, the Provincial Congress, should provide otherwise, was a wise and statesmanlike procedure which reflects credit upon their wisdom and patriotism alike.

a different opinion to "the Compact on which the Constitution is founded." And, finally, in August, just before the meeting of the Provincial Congress, Tryon County resolved to bear true allegiance to the king, but only "so long as he secures to us those Rights and Liberties which the principles of Our Constitution require."

Thus it seems clear that when the Provincial Congress met in August, 1775, the entire province had reached the advanced ground on which Granville County stood in August of 1774. But just as these local assemblies were more conservative in expressing their sentiments than individuals, so the Provincial Congress was more conservative than the local assemblies, though both were controlled largely by the same men. This Congress, September 8, unanimously adopted an address to "The Inhabitants of the British Empire," in which they said:

"To enjoy the Fruits of our own honest Industry; to call that our own which we earn with the labour of our hands and the sweat of our Brows; to regulate that internal policy by which we and not they [Parliament] are to be affected; these are the mighty Boons we ask. And Traitors, Rebels, and every harsh appellation that Malice can dictate or the Virulence of language express, are the returns which we receive to the most humble Petitions and earnest supplications. We have been told that Independance is our object; that we seek to shake off all connection with the parent State. Cruel Suggestion! Do not all our professions, all our actions, uniformly contradict this?

"We again declare, and we invoke that Almighty Being who searches the Recesses of the human heart and knows our most secret Intentions, that it is our most earnest wish and prayer to be restored with the other United Colonies to the State in which we and they were placed before the year 1763."

Soon after the adjournment of this Congress came news of the king's proclamation in October declaring the Americans out of his protection and commanding his armies and navy to levy war against them. After this nothing more is heard from public assemblies and conventions of loyalty to the Crown. Sentiment hastened rapidly toward independence. "My first wish is to be free," declared Hooper, a delegate in the Continental Congress; " my second to be reconciled to Great Britain." Eight days later, February 14, 1776, John Penn, also a delegate in the Continental Congress, urged the necessity of forming alliances with foreign countries although he foresaw that "the consequences of making alliances is perhaps a total separation with Britain." And Hewes, writing from Congress to Samuel Johnston, March 20, declared: "I see no prospect of a reconciliation. Nothing is left now but to fight it out. * * * Some among us urge strongly for Independency and eternal separation."

Thus spoke the three delegates in the Continental Congress; but in no respect were they in advance of their constituents. Samuel Johnston in March, 1776, thought it "highly probable * * * that the Colonies will be under the necessity of throwing off their Allegiance to the K[ing] and P[arliament] of G[reat] B[ritain] this Summer," and replying to Hewes' letter of March 20th, said: "I have apprehensions that no foreign power will treat with us till we disclaim our dependancy on Great Britain and I would wish to have assurances that they would afford us effectual Service before we take that step. I have, I assure you, no other Scruples on this head; the repeated Insults and Injuries we have received from the people of my Native Island has [sic] done away all my partiality for a Connection with them." On April 12, 1776, eight days after the fourth Provincial Congress convened at Halifax, in a letter written from Petersburg, Virginia, the writer says: "From several letters I have received from North Carolina since that convention met, I find they are for independence. * * * Mr. ———— was some little time at Halifax. He says they are quite spirited and unanimous; indeed, I hear nothing praised but 'Common Sense' and Independence."

On April 14, Hooper and Penn arrived at Halifax from Philadelphia to attend the Provincial Congress. Three days later Hooper wrote to Hewes, who had remained at Philadelphia, and Penn wrote to John Adams, describing the situation as they found it in Virginia and North Carolina. "The Language of Virginia," wrote Hooper, "is uniformly for Independence. If there is a single man in the province who preaches a different doctrine I had not the fortune to fall in his Company. But rapid as the change has been in Virginia, North Carolina has the honour of going far before them. Our late Instructions afford you some specimen of the temper of the present Congress and of the people at large. It would be more than unpopular, it would be Toryism, to hint the possibility of future reconciliation." Likewise wrote Penn: "As I came through Virginia I found the inhabitants desirous to be independent from Britain.

However, they were willing to submit their opinion on the subject to whatever the General Congress should determine. North Carolina by far exceeds them occasioned by the great fatigue, trouble and danger the people here have undergone for some time past. Gentlemen of the first fortune in the province have marched as common soldiers; and to encourage and give spirit to the men have footed it the whole time. Lord Cornwallis with seven regiments is expected to visit us every day. Clinton is now in Cape Fear with Governor Martin, who has about forty sail of vessels, armed and unarmed, waiting his arrival. The Highlanders and Regulators are not to be trusted. Governor Martin has coaxed a number of slaves to leave their masters in the lower parts; everything base and wicked is practiced by him. These things have wholly changed the temper and disposition of the inhabitants that are friends to liberty; all regard or fondness for the king or nation of Britain is gone; a total separation is what they want. Independence is the word most used. They ask if it is possible that any colony after what has passed can wish for a reconciliation? The convention have tried to get the opinion of the people at large. I am told that in many counties there was not one dissenting voice."

Thus in letters, in conversations by the fireside and at the cross-roads, in newspapers, and in public assemblies, the Whig leaders worked steadily to mould public sentiment in favor of a Declaration of Independence. But the crowning arguments that converted thousands to this view were the guns of Caswell and Lillington at Moore's Creek Bridge in the early morning hours of February 27, and the black hulks of Sir Henry Clinton's men-of-war as they rode at anchor below Brunswick. Moore's Creek Bridge, says Frothingham, "was the Lexington and Concord of that region. The newspapers circulated the details of this brilliant result. The spirits of the Whigs ran high. 'You never,' one wrote, 'knew the like in your life for true patriotism.' "[2] In the midst of this excitement the Provincial Congress met, April 4, at Halifax. The next day Samuel Johnston wrote: "All our people here are up for independence," and added a few days later: "We are going to the Devil   *   *   *   without knowing how to help ourselves, and though many are sensible of this, yet they would rather go that way than to submit to the British Ministry.   *   *   *   Our people are full of the idea of inde-

---

[2] Rise of the Republic, p. 503.

pendance." "Independence seems to be the word," wrote General Robert Howe; "I know not one dissenting voice."

To this position, then, within a year, the king had driven his faithful subjects of North Carolina and they now expected their Congress to give formal and public expression to their sentiments. When Hooper and Penn arrived at Halifax they found that the Congress had already spoken. On April 8, a committee was appointed, composed of Cornelius Harnett, Allen Jones, Thomas Burke, Abner Nash, John Kinchen, Thomas Person, and Thomas Jones, "to take into consideration the usurpations and violences attempted and committed by the King and Parliament of Britain against America, and the further measures to be taken for frustrating the same, and for the better defense of this Province." After deliberating four days, on April 12th, this committee, through its chairman, Cornelius Harnett, submitted the following report which the Congress unanimously adopted:

"It appears to your committee, that pursuant to the plan concerted by the British Ministry for subjugating America, the King and Parliament of Great Britain have usurped a power over the persons and properties of the people unlimited and uncontrouled; and disregarding their humble petitions for peace, liberty and safety, have made divers legislative acts, denouncing war, famine, and every species of calamity, against the Continent in general. That British fleets and armies have been, and still are daily employed in destroying the people, and committing the most horrid devastations on the country. That Governors in different Colonies have declared protection to slaves who should imbrue their hands in the blood of their masters. That ships belonging to America are declared prizes of war, and many of them have been violently seized and confiscated. In consequence of all which multitudes of the people have been destroyed, or from easy circumstances reduced to the most lamentable distress.

"And whereas the moderation hitherto manifested by the United Colonies and their sincere desire to be reconciled to the mother country on constitutional principles, have procured no mitigation of the aforesaid wrongs and usurpations, and no hopes remain of obtaining redress by those means alone which have been hitherto tried, your committee are of opinion that the House should enter into the following resolve, to wit:

"Resolved, That the delegates for this Colony in the Continental Congress be impowered to concur with the delegates of the other Colonies in declaring Independency, and forming

foreign alliances, reserving to this Colony the sole and exclusive right of forming a Constitution and laws for this
Colony, and of appointing delegates from time to time (under
the direction of a general representation thereof,) to meet
the delegates of the other Colonies for such purposes as shall
be hereafter pointed out.''

"Thus,'' declares Frothingham, "the popular party carried North Carolina as a unit in favor of independence, when
the colonies from New England to Virginia were in solid
array against it.'' [3] Comment is unnecessary. The actors,
the place, the occasion, the time, the action itself, tell their own
story.   "The   American   Congress,''   declared   Bancroft,
"needed an impulse from the resolute spirit of some colonial
convention, and the example of a government springing wholly
from the people.   * * *   The word which South Carolina
hesitated to pronounce was given by North Carolina. That
colony, proud of its victory over domestic enemies, and roused
to defiance by the presence of Clinton, the British general,
in one of their rivers, * * * unanimously'' voted for separation. "North Carolina was the first colony to vote explicit
sanction to independence.'' [4]

A copy of the resolution was immediately dispatched to
Joseph Hewes at Philadelphia to be laid before the Continental Congress. Its effect on the movement for independence
was immediate and wide-spread. The newspapers gave it
wide publicity. Leaders in the Continental Congress hastened to lay it before their constituents. "I hope it will be
forthwith communicated to your honorable Assembly,'' wrote
Elbridge Gerry, "and hope to see my native colony follow
this laudable example.'' To a like effect wrote Samuel Adams,
John Adams, and Caesar Rodney. On May 15th, Virginia
followed North Carolina's lead, and on the 27th of the same
month, just after Joseph Hewes had presented to the Continental Congress the resolution of the North Carolina Congress, the Virginia delegates presented their instructions.
Virginia had gone one step further than North Carolina, for
while the latter "impowered'' her delegates to "concur''
with the other colonies in declaring independence, the former
"instructed'' her representatives to "propose'' it. Hence it
was that Richard Henry Lee, of Virginia, and not Joseph
Hewes, of North Carolina, won the distinction of moving

---

[3] Rise of the Republic, p. 504.
[4] History of the United States, ed. 1860, Vol. VIII, p. 345-352.

"that these United Colonies are and of right ought to be free and independent States."

Lee's motion was made June 7th, but no vote was taken on it until July 1st. On June 28th, John Penn who had recently returned to Philadelphia from Halifax wrote to Samuel Johnston: "The first of July will be made remarkable. Then the question relative to independence will be agitated, and there is no doubt but a total separation from Britain will take place." Accordingly on July 1st, the Congress, meeting in committee of the whole, took a vote with New Hampshire, Connecticut, Massachusetts, Rhode Island, New Jersey, Maryland, Virginia, North Carolina, and Georgia voting in the affirmative. The New York delegates personally favored the Declaration and believed that their constituents also favored it, but they were bound by an old instruction of the previous year against independence; accordingly they withdrew from Congress, declining to vote at all. Delaware's two delegates were divided and the vote of that colony was lost. Only South Carolina and Pennsylvania voted against it. It was known, however, that the New York Convention which was to meet soon would repeal the old instruction and declare for independence; and that certain delegates from Delaware and Pennsylvania who favored it but were absent when the vote was taken would attend next day and carry their colonies for it. Thus South Carolina was alone in opposition. Therefore when the committee of the whole arose and reported the resolution to Congress, Edward Rutledge, the senior delegate from South Carolina, "requested the determination might be put off to the next day, as he believed his colleagues, though they disapproved of the resolution, would then join in it for the sake of unanimity."[5] The request was granted. The next day a third member from Delaware and members from Pennsylvania who favored the Declaration attended. New York still declined to vote. When Congress met on July 2, therefore, South Carolina "for the sake of unanimity" changed her vote and joined with her sister colonies in declaring the United Colonies "free and independent States." The final draft of the Declaration was laid before Congress on July 4th and formally adopted. It was signed in behalf of the State of North Carolina by William Hooper, Joseph Hewes, and John Penn.

After adopting the Resolution of April 12th, the Congress

---

[5] Jefferson's Notes in *Works*, Memorial Edition, Vol. XV, p. 199.

WILLIAM HOOPER   JOSEPH HEWES

North Carolina Signers of the Declaration of Independence

(There is no authentic portrait of John Pern, the other signer from North Carolina)

of North Carolina, proceeding as if independence were an accomplished fact, immediately took up the task of reorganizing the government. On April 13th a committee was appointed "to prepare a temporary Civil Constitution." Prominent among the members of this committee were Johnston, Nash, Harnett, Burke, and Person. Hooper was afterwards added. They were men of political sagacity and ability, but their ideas of the kind of constitution that ought to be adopted were woefully inharmonious. Heretofore in the measures of resistance to the British ministry remarkable unanimity had prevailed in the councils of the Whigs. But when they undertook to frame a constitution faction at once raised its head. In after years historians designated these factions as "Conservatives" and "Radicals." These terms carry their own meaning, and need no further explanation, but perhaps it may not be out of place to say that while both were equally devoted to constitutional liberty, the Radicals seem to have laid the greater emphasis upon "liberty," the Conservatives upon the modifier "constitutional." Of the members of the committee, Thomas Person was the leader of the former, Samuel Johnston of the latter. As the lines between the two factions at that time were not sharply drawn, it is not always possible to assign prominent politicians to either; indeed, many of them would not have admitted that they belonged to any faction, or party, for agreeing with some of the views of both, they agreed with the extreme views of neither.

The committee worked hard at its task. Its discussions were not always tempered with good feeling. "I must confess," wrote Johnston, April 17, "our prospects are at this time very gloomy. Our people are about forming a constitution. From what I can at present collect of their plan, it will be impossible for me to take any part in the execution of it." In fact, the next day he withdrew from the committee in disgust, though later he was persuaded to reconsider his action. It should be remembered that many political policies which we now regard as elementary were then in their experimental stage. Should suffrage be universal, or should a property qualification be required? Should there be one, or two houses of legislation? Should the representatives of the people be chosen annually, and what check should be imposed upon their power over the rights of the people? How should the executive branch of the government be constituted? How should the governor and other "great officers" be chosen and for what terms? Should the judges be elected by the people? Or chosen by the legislature? Or appointed by the executive? And what should be their tenure? Such were the questions that puzzled and divided our first constitution-makers.

The more they discussed them, the more hopeless became their divisions. Congress finally found that no agreement could be reached, while continued debate on the constitution would consume time that ought to be given to more urgent matters. Accordingly on April 30th, the committee was discharged and a second committee appointed to frame "a temporary form of government until the end of the next Congress." This committee brought in a report on May 11th, which the Congress promptly adopted. But few changes were made in the plan already in operation, but these changes were not without significance. The district committees of safety were abolished. The term "Provincial" was thought to be no longer appropriate and "Council of Safety" was accordingly substituted for "Provincial Council." No change was made in its organization. The Provincial Council had been required to sit once in every three months; the Council of Safety was to sit continuously, and its authority was considerably extended. All the powers of its predecessor were bequeathed to it, while among its additional powers was the authority to grant letters of marque and reprisal; to establish courts and appoint judges of admiralty; and to appoint commissioners of navigation to enforce the trade regulations of the Continental and Provincial Congresses.

The election of the members of the Council of Safety revealed the growth of factions. Willie Jones, chief of the Radicals, defeated Samuel Johnston for member at large. Other changes in the membership were as follows: in the New Bern District, John Simpson in place of Abner Nash; in the Halifax District, Joseph John Williams in place of Willie Jones; in the Hillsboro District, John Rand in place of John Kinchen; in the Salisbury District, Hezekiah Alexander and William Sharpe, both new members. Two only of the six districts retained their same members, Edenton District reelected Jones and Hill; Wilmington District, Harnett and Ashe. The other members who retained their seats were Coor, Eaton and Person.

Such was the personnel of the Council that was to put into execution the measures of the Congress for the defense of the province. This was the most important business that came before Congress. Clinton with a large force of British regulars was at Cape Fear awaiting the arrival of Sir Peter Parker's fleet with Cornwallis' army. "Our whole time," wrote Thomas Jones, May 7, "has been taken up here in raising and arming men, and making every necessary military arrangement. The word is war, or as Virgil expresses it, *bella, horrida bella.* Two thousand ministerial troops are in Cape Fear, 5,000 more hourly expected; to oppose the whole will require a large force." The Congress, accordingly, in addition to the troops already in the field, ordered the levying of four continental regiments, the enlistment of three companies of light-horse, the drafting of 1,500 militia, and the organization into five companies of 415 independent volunteers. The light-horse were offered to the Continental Congress and accepted; the militia were ordered to Wilmington "for the protection of this province;" and the independent companies were directed to patrol the coast against the ravages of small armed vessels which were accustomed in this way to secure fresh supplies for the troops below Wilmington.

It was comparatively an easy matter to raise these troops; to clothe, feed and equip them was another problem. It is of course, unnecessary to say that this was a problem that was not solved at all during the Revolution, either by the United Colonies or by any of them; but perhaps North Carolina came as near to it as the former, or as any of the latter. This was the work which, during the year 1776, was entrusted to the Council of Safety. The Council held its first session at Wilmington, June 5, and unanimously elected Cornelius Harnett president. Harnett served until August 21st when he resigned and was succeeded by his colleague, Samuel Ashe who resigned in September and was succeeded by Willie Jones. Jones served until the meeting of the Constitutional Convention in December which superseded the provisional government with a permanent government.

An attempt to follow in detail the numerous problems presented for the consideration of President Harnett and his colleagues would doubtless make but a dull and lifeless narrative. Yet upon the proper disposition of these matters depended the execution of laws, the administration of justice, the preservation of order, and the success of armies; and when we consider these facts, we may well doubt whether in subordinating such details to more dramatic and striking events, the narrative does not lose in instructiveness what it may gain in interest. The fidelity with which the members of the Council attended to the details of these problems is a good index to their characters and patriotism. Nothing less than boundless faith in the justice of their cause and in its ultimate success could have sustained them in the discharge of their delicate and exacting duties. There was nothing in the character of their labor, such as the soldier finds in the excitement of the campaign, to lighten fatigue or banish anxiety. Nor were they, like the soldier, inspired by the hope of glory and renown; on the contrary their duties were of such a nature that to discharge them with fidelity and impartiality, would more likely invite criticism and denunciation than applause and popularity. There was no popular applause to be gained by even the strictest attention to the commonplace details incident to the detection, apprehension and punishment of rioters, counterfeiters, traitors and other malefactors. Little popularity was to be expected from efforts, however successful, to adjust disputes among army officers over their relative ranks; to pass impartially upon applications for military and civil commissions; to hear and determine justly appeals for pardon and prayers for mercy; to enforce rigid discipline among a mutinous soldiery; to execute martial law against former friends and neighbors whose only crime was refusal to join in rebellion and revolution; to enforce without an adequate police obedience to a confessedly revolutionary government among those who denied its moral or legal right to rule. Whatever glory was to be won by successful military achievements all knew well enough would go to the soldiers in the field, not to the councilors in the cabinet who, by grinding out their spirits and lives over the details of organizing and equipping armies, made such success possible. Nevertheless day and night, week in and week out, President Harnett and his associates with unfailing tact, patience and energy, and with remarkable success, gave conscientious and efficient attention to a thousand and one details as uninspiring as they were necessary.

The chief problems of the Council related to defense. The Indians on the frontier, the Tories of the interior, and Clinton on the coast threatened the province with attack from three directions. A few days before the Council met, Clinton withdrew from the Cape Fear River, but nobody knew where he had gone nor what his plans were, and all apprehended that his movement was but a change of base for an attack on North Carolina. Clinton did contemplate such a movement, but was frustrated by the activity of the committees and the Council. The Council's problem was to organize and equip the troops ordered to be raised by the Congress. The or-

ganization was more tedious than difficult, but it required
much time and labor. A harder task was to equip them.
Even the utmost exertions of the Council could not keep the
several arsenals sufficiently supplied to meet the constant
calls on them for arms and ammunition. The Council continued to press into public service arms found in private
hands; they appointed commissioners to purchase warlike
supplies; they imported them from other states; they manufactured them; they purchased them in the North through
the delegates in the Continental Congress; and they chartered
vessels which they loaded with cargoes of staves and shingles
to be exchanged for military supplies. The Polly, the Heart
of Oak, the King Fisher, the Lilly, the Little Thomas, the
Johnston, and other fast sailing vessels slipped through
the inlets of Eastern Carolina, ran down to the West Indies,
sold their cargoes of lumber, and eluding the British cruisers
which patrolled those waters returned safely to Ocracoke,
Edenton, and New Bern with cargoes of small arms, cannon,
gunpowder, salt, clothes and shoes. Their enterprising crews,
the prototypes of the more famous blockade-runners of later
days, continued this work throughout the Revolution, and
made no inconsiderable contributions to the cause of American independence. The Council issued letters of marque and
reprisal to the Pennsylvania Farmer, the King Tammany,
the General Washington, the Heart of Oak, and the Johnston;
and they organized courts of admiralty and appointed judges.
They set up iron works for casting cannon and shot, and
salt works for supplying that necessary article. In one way
or another they managed to put into the field equipped for
service 1,400 troops to aid in the defense of Charleston, 300
militia to aid Virginia against the Indians, and an army of
2,400 riflemen for a campaign against the Creeks and the
Cherokee beyond the Alleghanies.

The efforts to secure the neutrality of the Indians had
failed. In the spring of 1776, while Clinton was on the coast,
Cameron determined to stir up the Cherokee on the frontier.
Under his leadership, the warriors of the Upper and Middle
towns, with some Creeks and Tories of the vicinity, took up
arms and laid waste the border far and wide. Aroused by
their common danger, Virginia, North Carolina, South Carolina, and Georgia determined to strike a blow at the Cherokee
that would compel them to remain passive during the struggle
with England. Accordingly, during the summer of 1776 four
expeditions were simultaneously launched against them from

four different quarters. The North Carolina expedition of 2,400 men was under command of General Griffith Rutherford. Crossing the Blue Ridge at Swannanoa Gap in August he struck the first Indian town, Stikayi, on the Tuckasegee, and acting with vigor destroyed in rapid succession every town on the Tuckasegee, Oconaluftee, the upper part of the Little Tennessee, and on the Hiwassee to below the junction of Valley River. The Indians attempted resistance but were everywhere defeated. Their most determined opposition was offered while Rutherford was passing through Waya Gap of the Nantahala Mountains. The invaders lost more than forty men, killed and wounded, before they put the red men to flight. Unable to offer further resistance the Cherokee fled to the fastnesses of the Great Smoky Mountains, leaving their crops and towns at the mercy of the enemy. All told Rutherford destroyed thirty-six towns and laid waste a vast stretch of the surrounding country. In the meantime Coloned Andrew Williamson with an army of 1,800 men from South Carolina was pushing up from the south through the Lower Towns, and on September 26, reached Hiwassee River, near the present town of Murphy, where he effected a junction with Rutherford; while Colonel William Christian, of Virginia, with a force of about 1,700 Virginians and 300 North Carolinians, was advancing from the north.

The effect upon the Cherokee of this irruption of more than 6,000 armed men into their territory was paralyzing. More than fifty of their towns were destroyed, their fields laid waste, their cattle and horses driven off, hundreds of their warriors killed, captured and sold into slavery, and their women and children driven to seek refuge in the recesses of the mountains. From the Virginia line to the Chattahoochee the destruction was complete, and the red men were compelled to sue for peace. Accordingly, at De Witts Corners in South Carolina, May 20, 1777, was concluded the first treaty ever made by the Cherokee with the new states. By its terms the Lower Cherokee surrendered all of their remaining territory in South Carolina except a small strip along the western border. Two months later, July 20, at the Long Island in the Holston, Christian concluded a treaty with the Middle and Upper Cherokee by which they ceded everything east of the Blue Ridge, together with all the disputed territory on the Watauga, Nolichucky, upper Holston and New rivers.

While Rutherford was engaged with the red men on the frontier, the Council of Safety were wrestling with a strong and energetic domestic enemy in the very heart of the State. The Tories of North Carolina, as the Council declared, were "a numerous body of people * * * who, although lately subdued, are only waiting a more favorable opportunity to wreak their vengeance upon us." The Tories hoped and the Whigs feared that this opportunity would come through a British success either at Wilmington or at Charleston. Moore's Creek Bridge had warned the former of the folly of an uprising without the co-operation of the British army, and the result at Charleston dashed their hopes of an immediate insurrection. Nevertheless they regarded this as only a temporary setback which necessitated a postponement but not a surrender of their plans. Though forced to work more quietly, they seized every opportunity to undermine and counteract the work of the Council. The Council, therefore, were compelled to devote a large part of their time to the detection and punishment of these domestic enemies. Their active leaders were arrested and brought before the Council on such general charges as denouncing the Council and the committees for exercising arbitrary and tyrannical powers; as uttering "words inimical to the cause of liberty"; as endeavoring "to inflame the minds of the people against the present American measures"; as using their influence to prevent the people from "associating in the common cause." More specific charges were correspondence with the enemy; refusal to receive the continental currency; and efforts to depreciate both the continental and provincial bills of credit. The Council dealt with each case upon its individual merits. In a general way, however, they permitted those who were willing to subscribe the test and submit to the revolutionary government to remain at home unmolested. They "naturalized" prisoners captured in battle who expressed a willingness to take the oath of allegiance, and admitted them to the privileges of free citizens. Persons suspected of disaffection, but who had committed no overt act, were required to give bond for their good behavior. Those whose presence among their neighbors was regarded as dangerous were taken from their homes and paroled within prescribed limits; while the most active leaders were imprisoned, some in North Carolina, some in Virginia and some in Philadelphia. The last two methods of punishment in some cases worked real hardships and moving appeals were made to President Harnett for relaxations of the restrictions.

While a majority of the cases that came before the Council involved the conduct of individuals only, a few instances were reported in which something like general disaffection appeared in a community. In such cases the Council acted with determination and vigor. Those whom they believed to have been led into disaffection through ignorance they undertook to instruct in "their duty to Almighty God," and to "the United States of America." But to those "who had been nursed up in the very bosom of the country," and yet "by their pretended neutrality declare themselves enemies to the American Union,'" the Council offered but one course,—the pledge either of their property or their persons for their good behavior. On July 4, 1776, they directed the county committees to require under oath from all suspected persons inventories of their estates, and ordered the commanding officers of the militia to arrest all who refused and bring them before the Council for trial. This order going forth simultaneously with the news of Clinton's defeat at Charleston, carried dismay into the ranks of the Loyalists. "This glorious news [Clinton's defeat], with the Resolve of Council against the Tories," wrote James Davis, the public printer, "has caused a very great Commotion among them. They are flocking in to sign the Test and Association." By these vigorous measures the Council dealt Toryism in North Carolina a serious blow, and saved the province during the summer of 1776 from the horrors of civil war. It must of course be confessed that these measures, though taken in the name of liberty, smacked themselves of tyranny; their justification lies in the fact that they were in behalf of peace and the rights of mankind.

On July 22d, while the Council were in session at Halifax, came the welcome news that the Continental Congress had adopted a Declaration of Independence. The Council received the news with great joy. No longer rebellious subjects in arms against their sovereign, they were now the leaders of a free people in their struggle for constitutional self-government. The Council, therefore, immediately resolved that by the Declaration of Independence the people "were absolved from all Allegiance to the British Crown," and therefore "the Test as directed to be subscribed by the Congress at Halifax [was] improper and Nugatory." The first clause of this test —"We the Subscribers professing our Allegiance to the King, and Acknowledging the constitutional executive power of Government"—was accordingly stricken out, and the amended test, which contained no allusion to the king, was signed. The Council also directed that members of courts martial should be required to take an oath to try well and truly all matters before them "between the Independant State of North Carolina and the prisoner to be tried."

At Halifax the people of North Carolina gave the first official utterance in favor of a national declaration of independence. Cornelius Harnett was their mouthpiece. At Halifax the Declaration of Independence was first officially proclaimed to the people of North Carolina. Again, Cornelius Harnett was their mouthpiece. One incident was the logical outcome of the other, and the two together enriched our annals with a dramatic story. The first entry in the Council's journal for July 22, is a resolution requiring the committees throughout the State upon receiving the Declaration of Independence to "cause the same to be proclaimed in the most public Manner, in Order that the good people of this Colony may be fully informed thereof." The Council set the example, and set apart Thursday, August 1, "for proclaiming the said Declaration at the Court House in the Town of Halifax; the freeholders and Inhabitants of the County of Halifax are requested to give their Attendance at the time and place aforesaid." The people were profoundly interested. On the first day of August an "immense concourse of people" gathered in the county town to hear President Harnett make official proclamation of their independence. The ceremony was simple enough. At noon the militia proudly paraded in such uniforms as they could boast, and with beating drums and flying flags escorted the Council to the court-house. The crowd cheered heartily as President Harnett ascended the platform. When the cheers had died away he arose and midst a profound silence read to the people the "Unanimous Declaration of the Thirteen United States of America." As he closed with the ringing words pledging to the support of that Declaration their lives, their fortunes, and their sacred honor, the people with shouts of joy gave popular ratification to the solemn pledge their representatives had made for them. In the exuberance of their enthusiasm the soldiers seized President Harnett and, forgetful of his staid dignity, bore him on their shoulders through the crowded streets, applauding him as their champion and swearing allegiance to American Independence.

CHAPTER XXIII

THE INDEPENDENT STATE

Since the State was now independent it was desirable that a permanent form of government should displace the provisional government as soon as possible. Accordingly on the 9th of August, 1776, the Council of Safety, in session at Halifax, resolved "that it be recommended to the good people of this now Independant State of North Carolina to pay the greatest attention to the Election to be held on the fifteenth day of October next, of delegates to represent them in Congress, and to have particularly in view this important Consideration, that it will be the Business of the Delegates then Chosen not only to make Laws for the good Government of, but also to form a Constitution for this State, that this last, as it is the Corner Stone of all Law, so it ought to be fixed and Permanent, and that according as it is well or ill Ordered, it must tend in the first degree to promote the happiness or Misery of the State."

This resolution was the signal for the opening of a campaign famous in our history for its violence. Feeling ran high. Riots were numerous. Everywhere democracy exulting in a freedom too newly acquired for it to have learned the virtue of self-restraint expressed itself in irregularities, tumults, and carousings. In Guilford County many voters were intimidated by threats of personal abuse; at one voting place a candidate, "with a whip clubbed in his hand," took possession of the polls and drove his opponents away. In Orange County the election was held in such "a tumultuous and disorderly manner," that the Convention afterwards declared it null and void. Drunkenness and unbridled abuse characterized the campaign in Chowan. Throughout the State the campaign opened wider than ever the cleaveage in the Whig party. The Radicals were determined to wrench control of public affairs from the Conservatives. Abner Nash in New Bern and Thomas Jones in Chowan, both Conservatives, won seats only by narrow margins from constituencies in which they had rarely had serious opposition. In New Hanover so strong was the opposition to William Hooper that, to assure his having a seat in the Convention, Cornelius Harnett relinquished his hold on the borough of Wilmington in Hooper's favor, himself standing for election in Brunswick County. Samuel Spencer was defeated in Anson, and John Campbell, for many years a representative in the Assembly as well as in the four Provincial Congresses, was left out of the Bertie delegation. The climax of the campaign was the fight in Chowan County against Samuel Johnston. Johnston was recognized as chief of the Conservatives, and the Radicals determined that he should not have a seat in the Convention. "No means," says McRee, "were spared to poison the minds of the people; to inflame their prejudices; excite alarm; and sow in them, by indirect charges and whispers, the seeds of distrust. * * * It were bootless now to inquire what base arts prevailed, or what calumnies were propagated. Mr. Johnston was defeated. The triumph was celebrated with riot and debauchery; and the orgies were concluded by burning Mr. Johnston in effigy." [1] While the chief of the Conservatives was thus defeated, Willie Jones, his great radical rival, was elected. The Radicals as a rule were successful in those counties in which the influence of the former Regulators was most potent.

When the Convention assembled at Halifax, November 12th, the violence of the campaign had been followed by a reaction. Richard Caswell, a moderate if not a conservative, was unanimously elected president. The committee appointed to frame a "Bill of Rights and Form of a Constitution for the Government of this State," embraced among its members Willie Jones, Thomas Person, and Griffith Rutherford, radical leaders; Allen Jones, Thomas Jones, Samuel Ashe, and Archibald Maclaine, conservative leaders; Richard Caswell and Cornelius Harnett, who may be classed as moderates. Since the adjournment of the preceding Congress the Americans had progressed considerably in the science of constitution-making, and the North Carolina Convention in December had before it several precedents which had been lacking in April. Among them were the constitutions of Delaware, New Jersey, Virginia, and South Carolina. John Adams, too, apparently upon the invitation of Caswell, had submitted

---

[1] Life and Correspondence of James Iredell, Vol. I, p. 334.

some interesting "Thoughts on Government." Better still were the views of the people of North Carolina, some of whom had reduced their ideas to writing in "instructions" to their delegates. Thus the Scotch-Irish of Mecklenburg and Orange counties, putting into practice the principle of the responsibility of representatives to their constituents, which the Regulators had tried in vain to establish, had adopted elaborate instructions in which they stated the fundamental principles on which the new government should be founded and outlined some of its details. Many of these details found their way into the new Constitution, but the Convention did not establish, as Mecklenburg desired, "a simple democracy," nor did it accede to Mecklenburg's demand that the Constitution be submitted "to the people at large for their approbation and consent if they should choose to give it, to the end that it may derive its force from the principal supreme power."

With these precedents before them, the men who could not agree on a form of government in April found no such difficulty in December. The committee on the Constitution was appointed on November 13th; on December 6th it reported a Constitution, and on December 12th a Bill of Rights, to the Convention. Both documents received from the Convention the serious consideration their importance demanded. After being debated paragraph by paragraph, the Bill of Rights was adopted December 17th, and the Constitution the following day. These results were not attained without much sharp debate, acrimonious interchange of views, and the acceptance by both factions of numerous compromises. "God knows when there will be an end of this trifling here," wrote Samuel Johnston who, as public treasurer, was at Halifax in attendance on the Convention. "A draft of the constitution was presented to the House yesterday and lies over for consideration. * * * As well as I can judge from a cursory view of it, it may do as well as that adopted by any other Colony. Nothing of the kind can be good." Two days later he was "in great pain for the honor of the Province," and much alarmed at the tendency to turn affairs over to "a set of men without reading, experience or principle to govern them." But Johnston's pessimistic views were scarcely justified. Discussion and a spirit of compromise eliminated most of the "absurdities" which so excited his disgust, and the instrument which finally emerged was in many ways admirably adapted to the needs of the people for whom it was designed. After passing it upon its final reading the Convention directed that a copy be sent to the state printer "with directions that he do immediately print and distribute a number of copies to each county in the State."

The new Constitution was short and simple. It contained merely the framework of government and the great fundamental principles upon which it was founded. The Convention left the details of administration to be worked out by the legislature. Since 1776 there has been a radical change in the popular conception of what is proper to be included in a constitution. What that change has produced in constitution-making may be seen by contrasting the Constitution of 1776 with its seventy-one sections and general statements of political principles with the Constitution of 1919 with its 198 sections and innumerable details of legislation. Between the new state government and the old colonial government there was no violent break; the members of the Convention were practical statesmen intent only on establishing a working government, not philosophers testing out political theories, and they thought it wise to follow as far as possible the forms with which the people had long been familiar. Following the form of the colonial government, therefore, they provided for a legislative department to consist of two houses, a senate and a house of commons; a judiciary department to embrace a supreme court of law and equity, an admiralty court, and county courts; and an executive department, to be composed of a governor, a council, and such administrative officers as might be needed.

One radical change was introduced, not so much in the form as in the working of the government, viz., the shifting of the center of political power from the executive to the legislative branch. Under the royal government neither the people nor the Assembly exercised any constitutional control over the governor. They had no voice in his selection, no control over his conduct, and no means of removing him from office. His authority was neither fixed nor definite. He acted under instructions from the Crown, whose representative he was, and those instructions he could not make public unless especially authorized by the Crown to do so. As the personal representative of the sovereign he was apt to entertain extravagant ideas of his prerogatives and to seek to extend his power to the utmost extreme. The Assembly struggled hard to hedge him about with restrictions, and the result was a perpetual conflict between the executive and the legislative branches of the government with every advantage in favor of

the former. Through his right of veto the governor had
power to negative acts of the Assembly, while the right of
prorogation and dissolution placed the very life of the Assembly in his hands. In consequence of this system the people
felt hampered in the only branch of the government in which
they had a direct share, and chafed impatiently under the restriction. Accordingly when the Convention of 1776 came to
define the powers of the chief executive in the new state government, its members were in a decidedly reactionary frame
of mind. "What powers, sir," inquired one of Hooper's constituents, "were conferred upon the governor?" "Power,"
replied Hooper, "to sign a receipt for his salary." In truth
the legislative branch now had the upper hand; the pendulum
had swung to the other extreme. The governor was to be the
creature of the Assembly, elected by it and removable by it.
Not only was he shorn of his most important powers; with
every power was coupled a restriction. He could take no important step without the advice and consent of the Council of
State, and in the selection and removal of his councilors he
had no voice. But the Council exercised a restraining authority only; to the governor belonged the right of initiative and
this fact, added to the moral influence of the office, gave the
incumbent opportunity for service and usefulness.

The Constitution was not the work of any one man, or
group of men, though tradition and an occasional reference
in contemporaneous documents attribute a few features to the
influence of certain individuals. Tradition credits Cornelius
Harnett with the authorship of the thirty-fourth article which
declares, "That there shall be no Establishment of any one
religious Church or Denomination in this State in Preference
to any other, * * * but all persons shall be at Liberty to
exercise their own mode of Worship;" while Governor Caswell attributed to Harnett's influence the refusal of the Convention to clothe the governor with adequate powers. In the
Convention of 1835, John D. Toomer quotes tradition to the
effect that Richard Caswell "dictated the principles, if not
the terms," of the Constitution; and while the word "dictated" is surely too strong a term to be used in this connection, it is certain that Caswell's influence was very great.
Samuel Johnston, in a letter written in 1777, describes the
plan of organization of the legislature as Thomas Burke's
plan, of which he heartily disapproved. Johnston himself,
although not a member of the Convention, was able to secure
the incorporation of many of his views in the Constitution,

especially those relating to the qualifications for suffrage and the method of selection and the tenure of judicial officers. It is interesting to note that Johnston, the great Conservative and, according to his enemies, the stern foe of democracy, advocated annual elections. Writing while a constitution was under discussion in April, he said: ''The great difficulty in our way is, how to establish a check on the representatives of the people, to prevent their assuming more power than would be consistent with the liberties of the people. * * * After all, it appears to me that there can be no check on the representatives of the people in a democracy but the people themselves; and in order that the check may be more eficent I would have annual elections.'' To Johnston's great rival, Willie Jones, has been ascribed the determining influence in the final shaping of the Constitution. The Constitution, declared a delegate in the Convention of 1835, ''is thought to have been as much or more the work (the 32d section excepted) of Willie Jones than any other one individual.'' Upon which Ashe quite pertinently comments that if this is so, Willie Jones was not the radical democrat he is popularly supposed to have been.[2]

Indeed, the student can make no graver mistake than to suppose that North Carolina, or any other American State, began its independent existence in 1776 as a pure democracy. ''America in 1776 was not a democracy. It was not even a democracy on paper. It was at best a shadow-democracy.''[3] To say this neither impeaches the wisdom nor decries the work of the framers of our first State Constitution. The truth is they did not intend to establish a democracy. The men who led and dominated the political thought in North Carolina in 1776 were English landowners whose political ideals were found in the British Constitution. This Constitution in its full vigor, as has been pointed out before, the early English settlers in North Carolina had demanded should follow them to the New World; and they had insisted that their charters should guarantee to them ''all liberties, franchises and privileges'' enjoyed by their fellow subjects in England. In 1776 they were in rebellion against the mother country because they believed her rulers had a purpose, in order to carry out their imperialistic policies, to ride roughshod over these same ''liberties, franchises and privileges:'' Accordingly when they came to write their own constitution in 1776 they were much

---

[2] History of North Carolina, Vol. I, p. 565.
[3] Weyl: The New Democracy, p. 12.

more determined to write into it those safeguards of political liberty which they considered had been guaranteed by the British Constitution, i. e., representative government, the principle that taxation without representation is tyranny, the right of trial by jury, the privilege of the writ of *habeas corpus,* the prohibition against the passage of *ex post facto* laws, the guarantee that no man should be deprived of his life, liberty, or property, "but by the law of the land," and all those other great constitutional principles that characterized the British Constitution—they were much more anxious to secure these principles to themselves and their posterity than they were to establish a democracy.

Consequently the government established by the Constitution of 1776 was a representative democracy in form, but in form only. In fixing the basis of representation in the legislature the Convention paid no attention to population, but gave to every county the same number of representatives in both houses of the General Assembly, and to certain towns one representative each in the House of Commons, without regard to population. Nor were the qualifications for suffrage and office-holding fixed upon a democratic basis. To English statesmen of 1776—and such were the framers of our first State Constitution—manhood suffrage was a Utopian dream, interesting, doubtless, as a subject for philosophical speculation, but an impossibility in practical politics; and, although they conferred the right to vote for members of the House of Commons upon all freemen who had paid their taxes, they were careful to offset this concession to democracy by restricting the right to vote for senators to those who possessed a freehold of fifty acres. Even less democratic were the qualifications for office holding. No person could be a member of the House of Commons unless he possessed in the county which he represented "not less than one hundred acres of land in fee, or for the term of his own life;" no person could be a senator unless he possessed in the county which he represented "not less than three hundred acres of land in fee;" and no person was eligible for the office of governor unless he was possessed of a "freehold in lands and tenements, above the value of one thousand pounds"—an amount comparable to a fortune in our own day of at least ten times that sum. Other undemocratic features forbade any clergyman, while in the exercise of his pastoral functions, to sit in the General Assembly and imposed a sectarian test for office holding designed to exclude Roman Catholics, Jews, and Atheists. The people had no voice in the selection of their public servants other than members of the General Assembly, for the governor and other executive officers, the councilors of state, and the judges were all elected by the General Assembly; and the judges held office for life. No provision was made for calling a constitutional convention, or for amending the Constitution in any other way, and the Constitution itself, as has been pointed out, was never submitted to the people for ratification. As undemocratic as this Constitution was in form, it was even less so in spirit. Inasmuch as all officials were elected by the General Assembly, and membership in the General Assembly was based upon a property qualification, property not men controlled the government. The theory of property was then, as it always has been, that the best government is that which governs least. It teaches that government has fulfilled its mission when it has preserved order, protected life and property, punished crime, and kept down the rate of taxation. Such was the theory of government which prevailed in North Carolina in 1776 and which, under the Constitution adopted in that year, continued to prevail in North Carolina for more than half a century.

After adopting the Constitution the Convention passed a series of ordinances providing for the government of the State until the close of the first session of the General Assembly under the new Constitution. All those parts of the common law and such statutes in force under the royal government which were "not destructive of, repugnant to or inconsistent with the freedom and Independence of this State, or of the United States of America," were declared to be still in force; and a commission including among its members such eminent lawyers as Samuel Johnston, Archibald Maclaine, James Iredell, Samuel Ashe, Waightstill Avery, and Samuel Spencer, was appointed to revive, and present to the General Assembly bills for re-enacting, such former statutes as were "consistent with the Genius of a Free People" and their new form of government. The Convention performed a long delayed act of justice in adopting an ordinance empowering all regularly ordained ministers of the Gospel of every denomination to perform the marriage ceremony according to the rites of their respective churches. Another ordinance defined treason against the new-born State and prescribed its punishment. The State was divided into judicial districts, courts of oyer and terminer and general gaol delivery were erected, and the governor was authorized upon the recommendation of the Council of State to appoint judges to hold them. William Hooper, Joseph Hewes, and Thomas Burke were appointed a commission to procure a Great Seal, but in the meantime the governor for the time being was authorized to use his own "private Seal at Arms" on all public documents. Other ordinances named officials who should put the new government into operation. Collectors were appointed for the ports of Currituck, Roanoke, Bath, Beaufort, and Brunswick; and justices, sheriffs, and constables in the several counties; while Richard Caswell was named as governor; James Glasgow as secretary of state; and Cornelius Harnett, Thomas Person, William Dry, William Haywood, Edward Starkey, Joseph Leech, and Thomas Eaton as councilors of state, until their successors could be chosen by the General Assembly.

Richard Caswell, the first governor of the independent State, was perhaps the most versatile man of his generation in North Carolina. He was distinguished among his contemporaries as surveyor, lawyer, orator, soldier, and statesman. A native of Maryland he had come to North Carolina in 1746 as a youth of seventeen seeking his fortune. He was a surveyor by profession in which he was so skilful and energetic that within three years after his arrival he was appointed deputy-surveyor for the province. North Carolina at that time was an attractive field for surveyors. So rapidly were the vacant spaces in the colony filling up that at almost every sitting of the Council thousands of acres were granted to new settlers, and upon the skill, activity, and integrity of the surveyors depended not only the interests of the Crown but the security of the thousands of pioneers who had braved all the hardships and dangers of the wilderness in their search for homes. A surveyor on the frontier must needs have steady nerves, keen eyes, and trained muscles, combined with indefatigable industry and determination, a cool head, and sound judgment. He must be skilled in woodcraft, and able to circumvent the cunning of the savage and the craft of the land-grabber. His work brought him in close touch with the people, and made him familiar with their conditions of life, problems, and habits of thought. No better school for the training of the man who was to become the civil and military leader of a pioneer people in a great revolution could have been found. It is interesting to note that while Richard Caswell was attending this school in North Carolina, another young surveyor, a few years his junior,

SOUTH OF THIS TABLET, 166 YARDS, IS THE GRAVE
OF RICHARD CASWELL, THE FIRST GOVERNOR OF
NORTH CAROLINA, AS AN INDEPENDENT STATE.

"I WILL MOST CHEERFULLY JOIN ANY OF MY
COUNTRYMEN, EVEN AS A RANK AND FILE MAN,
AND WHILST I HAVE BLOOD IN MY VEINS FREELY
OFFER IT IN SUPPORT OF THE LIBERTIES
OF MY COUNTRY."
(CASWELL TO HIS SON IN 1776)

ERECTED 1919 BY
THE NORTH CAROLINA HISTORICAL COMMISSION,
CITIZENS OF LENOIR COUNTY AND CASWELL-NASH CHAPTER, D.A.R.

BRONZE TABLET ON STATE HIGHWAY NEAR KINSTON

was attending a similar school on the vast estates of Lord Fairfax in the wilds of Western Virginia. The same training that fitted George Washington for his career as commander-in-chief of the armies and the first chief executive of the United States, fitted Richard Caswell for similar duties in his more contracted field.

Caswell rose to his position of leadership through the regular gradations of service as assemblyman, speaker of the House of Commons, colonial treasurer, member of the Provincial Congress, delegate to the Continental Congress, and president of the first Constitutional Convention. In the various contests between the Assembly and the governor which led up to the Revolution, he stood among the foremost in support of popular government. He was ambitious for military fame, and entered with zest into the two campaigns conducted by Governor Tryon against the Regulators. These campaigns were excellent training for him and served to prepare him for his subsequent military career in the same way that the campaigns of the French and Indian War prepared a much greater American soldier for his career. Caswell was one of the first to see that the contest with the mother country would probably lead to war, and was urgent in his appeals to the Provincial Congress to make military preparations for the emergency. Writing to his son from Philadelphia in 1774, he tells him to urge upon his neighbors that "it is indispensably necessary for them to arm and form into a company or companies of independents," adding: "If I live to return I shall most cheerfully join any of my countrymen even as a rank and file man." When the Congress of August, 1775, provided for raising an army, he entered into the plans with zeal, and upon his election as colonel of the New Bern District, resigned his seat in the Continental Congress to take steps to raise, organize, equip and drill his regiment. His energy enabled him to meet the Scotch Highlanders at Moore's Creek Bridge and win the initial victory of the Revolution in the South. His reward for this victory was his election as the first governor of the independent State. As governor he displayed the same zeal and foresight, but for reasons over which he had no control not the same success which had previously characterized his public actions. His patriotism though deep, fervent, and sincere, was stimulated by ambition for personal fame and power. Aggressive and domineering in overcoming opposition, he showed consummate address and skill in winning the confidence of the people which he possessed to a remarkable degree. He was elected governor of North Carolina seven times.

The executive branch of the new government went into operation January 16, 1777, when Caswell and the other state officials met at New Bern, took the oath of office, and entered upon the discharge of their duties. On April 7th, the legislative branch went into operation when the first Assembly under the Constitution met at New Bern and organized by the election of Samuel Ashe as speaker of the Senate and Abner Nash as speaker of the House of Commons. Since all the ordinances of the Convention were to expire at the close of this session, it fell to the lot of the Assembly to enact such legislation as was necessary to put the new government into complete operation. The Assembly accordingly re-enacted the ordinance declaring what parts of the common law and former statutes were still in force. It amplified the ordinance defining treason so as to check active opposition from the Loyalists and prevent "the Dangers which may arise from the Persons disaffected to the State." The counterfeiting of the bills of the State and of the Continental Congress was made a felony punishable by death. Other acts provided for the better regulation of the militia, the establishment of criminal courts, the collection of import duties, and the erection of admiralty courts. A radical but timely innovation in the fiscal policy of the State was introduced by an act which provided for the general assessment of property and the levying of an *ad valorem* tax on land, negroes, and other property. The Assembly also made provision for the administration of county affairs by the erection of county courts and the appointment of justices, sheriffs and registers in the several counties. On April 18th, it re-elected Caswell governor, Glasgow secretary of state, and all of the former councilors except Dry and Person whose places it filled with William Cray and William Taylor. The work of this Assembly fairly launched the new State upon her stormy voyage of independence and sovereignty.

A situation full of difficulties, dangers, and pitfalls confronted Caswell and his advisers. The remarkable fervor that had swept the colony into revolution and created an independent government had been followed by reaction. Enthusiasm had given way to apathy, and henceforth, as far as the people generally were concerned, support of the common cause was spasmodic and forced. This situation may be traced to four causes: first, the weakness of the executive under the new Constitution; second, the cleavage in the patriot party; third, the presence of a large and active Loyalist element in the population; and fourth, the utter breakdown of the financial systems of both State and United States.

The successful conduct of war requires concentration of responsibility and power. It was unfortunate, therefore, that North Carolina, especially at a time when there was no national executive, should have entered upon a long and exhausting war with an executive to which all real power had been denied. An active, aggressive and resourceful governor, seeing things that ought to be done and lacking authority to do them, was apt to chafe greatly under the restrictions. Caswell had not been in office a year before the mistake of the Convention in this respect became apparent. Urged to pursue more "spirited measures" for filling up the State's battalions, he replied that his hands were tied because "by the Constitution of this State, nothing can be done by the Executive power itself, towards this most desirable purpose" and complained of the Constitution "for cramping so much the powers of the executive." The longer the war continued, the more apparent became the mistake of the Convention in withholding power from the governor. In 1781, Governor Nash wrote, "The Constitutional power of a Government [governor] in this State, is at best but very small, and in time of War, insufficient for purposes of Government and Defence." In the military crisis of 1780-81 the executive broke down completely, and to meet the emergency the Assembly created first a board of war which it later superseded with a council extraordinary of three persons upon whom it conferred extra-constitutional powers, authorizing them not only to exercise all the powers "which the council of state might have exercised in a state of war," but also "to do and execute every other act and thing which may conduce to the security, defence and preservation of this State." But this expedient did not solve the difficulty since it merely divided the executive functions among three men instead of concentrating and unifying them under a single head. As Governor Nash declared in a letter to Burke, the executive power was so divided and sub-divided that it had lost its force and "men, not knowing whom to obey, obeyed nobody."

The constitutional deficiencies of the chief executive would have been greatly minimized if the several governors had

had the support of a united constituency, determined to subordinate all lesser objects to the winning of independence.
Unfortunately the cleavage in the patriot party rendered such
united support impossible. During the session of the first
Assembly under the Constitution, Abner Nash writing from
New Bern thought "we are all harmony" and expected to see
"a perfect good agreement" prevail in the two houses. But
Nash having just been elected speaker of the House of Commons saw things through too rosy a medium. At the very
moment that he was predicting an era of good feeling, the
Radicals were laying plans to elect John Penn to the Continental Congress in place of Joseph Hewes. "A warm struggle" ensued, in which Hewes was defeated. The result and
the manner in which it was accomplished drove the iron into
the souls of the Conservatives. Bitterly Johnston denounced
the "fools and knaves" who were in control of the Assembly.
"When I tell you," he wrote to Thomas Burke, a delegate in
the Continental Congress, "that I saw with indignation such
men as G—th R—d [Griffith Rutherford], T—s P-s-n
[Thomas Person], and your Collegue J. Penn, with a few
others of the same stamp, principal leaders in both houses,
you will not expect that anything good or great should proceed from the counsels of men of such narrow, contracted
principle, supported by the most contemptible abilities.
Hewes was supplanted of his seat in Congress by the most
insidious arts and glaring falsehood, and Hooper, though no
competitor appeared to oppose him, lost a great number of
votes. Quince for no crime alleged against him, but that he
was a man of fortune, was turned out of his appointment of
Naval Officer of Port Brunswick." Johnston resigned as
treasurer, and Hooper, piqued at his loss of popularity, declined to accept the seat in Congress to which he had been
elected. Other Conservatives following the example of these
leaders withdrew from public life.

Their retirement of course left the Radicals in control.
Since Caswell was acceptable to them, as long as he was eligible for the office, they made no contest over the election of
governor. In 1777, 1778, and 1779, therefore, Caswell was
unanimously elected. But in 1780 he was no longer eligible,
and for the first time a contest in the election of governor ensued. Abner Nash, who is generally reckoned as a Conservative, was elected, but before his term was half gone the
radical Assembly seem to have repented of their choice, and
by an act creating a board of war deprived the governor of

most of the few powers which the Constitution had conferred on him. Nash denounced the act as an unconstitutional change in the form of government. "When you elected me Governor of the State," he wrote, " you presented me the Bill of Rights and the Constitution, at the same time you presented me with the Sword of State as an emblem of the power I was invested with for the protection of the Constitution and the rights of the people, and in a solemn manner you bound me by an oath to preserve the Constitution inviolate; and yet four months after my election the very same Assembly deprived me of almost every power, privilege and authority belonging to my office. * * * I have no doubt that the secret Enemies of our Free Constitution exult at the introduction of such innovation and rejoice at seeing the first office in the State rendered useless and contemptible." Declaring that the creation of the Board of War left the governor nothing "but an empty title," he declined to permit himself to be considered for re-election. To succeed him, therefore, the Conservatives nominated Samuel Johnston, the Radicals, Thomas Burke. Burke was elected, but during his term, he was captured by a band of Tories and sent to Charleston, then held by the British, as a political prisoner. Unfortunately for his fame he broke his parole, made his escape and returning to North Carolina reassumed the duties of his office. Although he insisted that the cruelties and the illegal treatment to which he had been subjected justified his action, nevertheless it ruined his political career and compelled him to retire to private life.

In the election of 1782, at which Burke's successor was to be chosen, party spirit rose to a height greater than it had yet attained in the State. Five candidates were in nomination, but the real contest was between Samuel Johnston and Alexander Martin. The Conservatives had good grounds for anticipating victory when their hopes were dashed to pieces by the course of Richard Caswell who threw all of his great influence in the scale with Martin. His action was decisive and Martin was elected. Johnston and his friends brought out of the contest a bitter grudge against Caswell, and eagerly awaited an opportunity for retaliation. It came sooner than they could have expected. In 1783, Caswell, again eligible under the Constitution, appeared "with all his interest and address" in the field against Martin. The Conservatives in the Assembly, now under the aggressive leadership of the able but vitriolic Maclaine, threw themselves into the

GOVERNOR ABNER NASH
From a portrait in the Governor's office, Raleigh

contest for Martin with all the eagerness of avengers of imaginary wrongs. "Among others," wrote Maclaine, "I interested myself warmly for the present Governor, not only from principle, but in opposition to a man who had basely abandoned his important trusts, and deserted his colors in the hour of distress."[4] Caswell himself describing the contest in a letter to his son, William Caswell, wrote: "Ten days ago Governor Martin was re-elected by 66 Votes against 49 who voted for me. Mr. Johnston and General Rutherford were in nomination, but neither was Voted for. The Edenton and Halifax men with a very few exceptions Voted for Governor Martin, saying I had crammed him down their throats last year and they were now determined to keep him there." In this election there appeared for the first time in our history the tendency, which so long prevailed in North Carolina, to divide in political matters along sectional lines. The West supported Martin, while the East, with the exception of the men of the Edenton and Halifax districts, who were moved by the motive mentioned by Caswell, and a few Cape Fear men, who wanted the help of the West in making Cross Creek the capital of the new State, supported Caswell. The contests, which have been described, show clearly that by 1783, the unanimity and harmony that had prevailed among the patriots in 1774 and 1775 had disappeared, that the factions of 1776 had become stronger and more clearly defined, and that they needed only the struggle that was yet to come over the Federal Constitution to turn them into full fledged political parties. Never again was North Carolina to enjoy that political unity and harmony that marked the opening days of the Revolution.

At the very time that the factions in the patriot party were becoming more and more irreconcilable, the Loyalists, recovering somewhat from their crushing defeat at Moore's Creek Bridge, were beginning to show signs of activity. In the summer of 1776, disaffection openly manifested itself in Guilford County; to General Rutherford's request for troops from the Hillsboro brigade for his expedition against the Cherokee, the Council of Safety returned a refusal because of "the many disaffected persons in that district and neighborhood;" while in Surry County the Tories were ac-

---

[4] Probably referring to Caswell's action in resigning his commission after the battle of Camden in resentment at the appointment of General Smallwood of Maryland to the command of the North Carolina militia.

tually in arms against the provisional government. The in-
auguration of the new state government in April, 1777, was
the signal for renewed activity on the part of the Loyalists.
A Loyalist conspiracy in the Albemarle region was discovered just in time to prevent an uprising. About the same
time "many evil persons" in Edgecombe and neighboring
counties "joined in a most wicked conspiracy" against the
new government. Disaffection was suppressed at the time,
but continued to smoulder and two years later broke out
again in a still more violent form. A large number of persons in Edgecombe, Nash, Johnston, and Dobbs counties entered into an association by which they "obligated themselves to prevent the Militia from being drafted," to aid and
protect deserters from the American army, and to resist the
civil officers in the discharge of their duties. In the Cape
Fear section, too, a militia officer reported to the governor
that he "was alarmed by these dam rascals, the Tories," and
Colonel John Ashe felt it advisable to take extraordinary
precautions to prevent a descent upon Wilmington by the
"Scotch Tories and others from Cross Creek and Bladen."
In September, 1777, Governor Caswell wrote to Cornelius
Harnett: "We have been alarmed with the rising of Tories
and forming of conspiracies: the former among the Highlanders and Regulators and in the county [Chowan] in which
you had the honor to draw your first breath, and in Bertie
and Martin." In the West the situation was quite as bad,
perhaps worse than in the East. Officers of Anson reported
"many disaffected persons in our County." Tryon County
was a hotbed of Tories. In the spring of 1779 a noted Tory
leader, named John Moore, embodied 300 men in Tryon,
forcibly prevented the execution of the draft, and spread
terror throughout that region. Farther west, the conditions
in Burke County might easily have been duplicated in Surry,
Rowan, Guilford, and other western counties. In July, 1779,
General Rutherford reported that bands of Tories were organized in Burke "who publicly Rob all the Friends of America;" that "British Officers were actually recruiting in that
County;" and that the Tories openly boasted that "immediately after harvest they were to take up Arms and put to
death the principal Friends to the Cause and March off to the
Enemy." Indeed, in every section, in every county, in almost every neighborhood large numbers of the people were
disaffected and only wanted a favorable opportunity to raise
their hands against the new government.

The presence of the Tories not only menaced the peace

of the State and the stability of the government, but also weakened the financial and military resources of the State. They refused to pay taxes or to contribute in any other way to the support of the government, and the civil authorities were compelled to use the militia for collecting the revenues of the State. An even more insidious and effective form of Loyalist propaganda was directed at the credit of the State. In 1779 Samuel Ashe, one of the judges of the Superior Court called the General Assembly's attention to the steady depreciation in the value of the State's bills of credit, adding, "nor can they without the immediate effectual interposition of the legislature continue at their present stand against the constant endeavours of the mongrel Tory Traders and others among us to destroy their Credit." The Tories offered an equally effective opposition to recruiting, and at times actually took up arms to prevent the enforcement of the draft. The State, therefore, was compelled to hold in reserve a considerable force for any emergency that might arise. The presence of these inveterate domestic enemies, therefore, not only cost the State considerable sums of money sorely needed by both state and continental treasuries, but retained at home many regiments of fighting men who should have been with Washington and Greene.

The policy of the State with respect to the Loyalists was one of the first questions that came up for consideration. The Whigs at first were inclined to be conciliatory. Although many Tories had but recently been "in actual Arms against the liberties of the United States of America," and in numerous other ways had given aid and comfort to the enemy, yet the Convention of 1776, hoping "that such Persons are now become sensible of the Wickedness and Folly" of their conduct, and eager to win for the new state government as much support as possible, determined to throw wide open the door of reconciliation. It therefore directed the governor to issue a proclamation offering free pardon to all who would take the oath of allegiance within ninety days. This generous offer the Loyalists seem to have interpreted as evidence of weakness in the new government and but few took advantage of it. Accordingly the Assembly at its first session entered upon a sterner policy. It adopted a test which held out to all the alternative of allegiance to the State or banishment. True to their principles most of those who were Loyalists from conviction accepted the latter choice and however much we may deprecate their mistaken judgment we cannot withhold our admiration from men who pre-

ferred exile to apostasy. Many of these exiles were people
of wealth, intelligence and character. In July, 1777, a large
vessel sailed from New Bern carrying "a great number of
Tories," with their families, "mostly Gentlemen of Considerable Property." Among them was Martin Howard, last
chief justice of North Carolina under the Crown. Many
others departed from Bertie, Chowan, and Halifax counties. Samuel Johnston testified that those who went from
Chowan were "men of fair character and inoffensive in their
conduct." The Scotch Highlanders departed in large numbers. "Two-thirds of Cumberland County intend leaving this
State," reported the colonel of the militia of that county in
July, 1777. "Great Numbers of these infatuated and over-
loyal People," said the *North Carolina Gazette,* in October,
1777, "returned from America to their own Country," among
whom was Flora MacDonald. Others found new homes in
Nova Scotia. Among the prominent Highlanders who left
North Carolina in 1777 was John Hamilton, "a merchant of
considerable note," who sailed from New Bern on a "Scotch
transport, having on Board a Number of Gentlemen of that
Nation." Hamilton afterwards organized these Highlanders into a Loyalist regiment which on numerous battlefields
in the South worthily maintained the high reputation of their
race for its fighting qualities. This exodus of the Highlanders from North Carolina in 1777 was comparable to their
exodus from Scotland after Culloden. The policy which was
responsible for it was perhaps the only course open to the
new State; nevertheless one may be permitted to regret that
circumstances compelled North Carolina to drive from her
borders so many men and women of this strong, virile race.

As the war progressed feeling against the Tories grew
more bitter. Trials for treason became frequent and the Assembly entered upon more vigorous measures. In November, 1777, it determined upon a policy of confiscation, and in
January, 1779, passed the first of a long series of confiscation acts. A still more sweeping act was passed in October
of that year. This act not only confiscated the property of
Loyalists generally, but mentioned by name a long list of the
more prominent members of that party among whom were
William Tryon, Josiah Martin, Edward Brice Dobbs, Edmund Fanning, Henry Eustace McCulloh, and John Hamilton. Its provisions excited such strong opposition that fifteen members of the House of Commons, under the lead of
Willie Jones, entered a vigorous protest against it declaring that it involved "such a Complication of Blunders and

betrays such ignorance in Legislation as would disgrace a Set of Drovers.'' Their objections were, first, that it violated the conditions of the Treason Act of 1777 under which many Loyalists had left the State, and, second, that it repealed the provisions made in the Confiscation Act of January, 1779, for ''such unfortunate and Innocent Wives and Children resident in the State, who had been abandoned by their Fathers and Husbands, and also for aged parents in particular Cases.'' The harshness of the act, and the vigor with which it was enforced, reveal the intensity of the feeling which the Tories had aroused against themselves. North Carolina, therefore, was not prepared to accept gracefully the clause in the Treaty of 1783 which stipulated that Congress should recommend to the several states the restitution of this confiscated property to its original owners. The State had not only received large sums from this source, but had guaranteed the title to the property sold under the confiscation acts upon which many of the purchasers had spent considerable sums. The treaty, therefore, was alarming both to the State which had sold the property and to the hundreds of individuals who had bought it. However the delegates from North Carolina in the Continental Congress took pains to call the governor's attention to the fact that the provision was ''but a promise of a recommendation,'' which the Assembly could comply with or not, and the Assembly thus re-assured treated it with silent contempt.

To the weakness of the executive, the intensity of party spirit, and the menace of the Tories, must be added a fourth cause of the failure of North Carolina to throw her full strength into the war for independence, i.e., the breakdown of her finances. The State entered upon its independent career with an empty treasury, without credit, and with no intercolonial or foreign commerce as a basis of credit. The necessities of the new government and the demands of war imposed upon the people financial burdens and responsibilities beyond anything they had ever experienced. If they did not solve their financial problems with the same wisdom and success with which they solved their political problems, they were not alone in their failure. No other state, nor the United States, obtained any better results.

The principal sources from which North Carolina derived her means for support of the war were issues of paper money, taxes, loans, and the proceeds of the sale of confiscated property. Paper money the people of North Carolina had been familiar with from long experience and the Provincial Congress naturally resorted to it as the means for financing the war. In September, 1775, Congress issued $125,000, and in May, 1776, $1,000,000, in bills of credit. To maintain their value and provide for their redemption the faith of the province was pledged and a poll tax levied to begin, for the redemption of the first issue, in 1777 and to run for nine years, for the redemption of the second, in 1780 and to run for twenty years. The delay in the levy and collection of these taxes and the uncertainty as to the sums they would ultimately yield had a bad effect on the credit of the province. This fact coupled with the sudden expansion of the currency, the counterfeits with which the colony was immediately flooded, and the effect of the unfavorable comparisons which the Tories were at pains to make between the bills of the Provincial Congress and those issued under authority of the British government, resulted in rapid depreciation. The General Assembly, therefore, thought it advisable to retire both these issues, and in August, 1778, passed an act issuing $2,125,000 of new bills, making them a legal tender, and directing that $1,575,000 be used to redeem the old bills. But this mandate was not carried into effect because as the demands upon the treasury increased from year to year, the Assembly postponed the date at which the old bills were to be redeemed. The old bills, therefore, remained in circulation, but the failure of the Assembly to keep faith with their holders by refusing either to redeem them or to levy and collect the taxes promised for their redemption, had an unfortunate effect upon their value, as also upon the credit of the State. As the war progressed other issues of paper currency became necessary. In 1779 $1,250,000, in 1780, $3,100,000, and in 1783, $250,000 were emitted. All of these bills were made a legal tender, but except in case of the last no tax was levied for their redemption.

In spite of every effort to sustain the value of the currency depreciation set in early and progressed rapidly. In December, 1778, the decline in value was about 5 per cent; a year later it was 30 per cent. In January, 1779, Samuel Ashe declared in a communication to the General Assembly, "that the great depreciation of our Bills of Credit and the rapid and extravagant rise in price of every necessary article," made it impossible for him to live on his salary. "The Depreciation of our Bills," he said, "is a matter of such notoriety that every one knows and feels it. Their value at this time bears not the proportion of twelve to one of their original value." The rapidity with which depreciation progressed may be seen by comparing Ashe's statement with the prices quoted by Richard Cogdell of New Bern in August, 1780. "Corn," he wrote, "[is] £100 per Bble., Meal £20 per bushel, Beef £48 per pound, Mutton £4 per lb., and every thing in proportion. A String of Fish which used to cost 12d is now 1920d, or 20 Dollars. What a horrible prospect this exhibits!" But the worst was not yet. By the close of the year the Assembly itself was compelled by law to recognize a depreciation in its currency of 800 per cent.

As early as 1777, the General Assembly began to realize that it could not carry on the government indefinitely on a paper currency and that it must sooner or later resort to taxation. Although convinced of its necessity, the legislature approached this policy reluctantly and entered upon it timidly. No *ad valorem* tax had ever been levied in North Carolina, and what the effect of such a tax would be, no man could tell. But it had to come, and at the April session, 1777, the Assembly directed that a general assessment be made of all property in the State, levied upon it a tax of half-penny in the pound, and provided machinery for its collection. This act fixed the future policy of the State. As the expenses of the war increased and the currency depreciated, the Assembly gradually increased the rate of taxation, but the yield from this source was never very large. In 1786 after eleven years of trial the estimated receipts from taxation were less than £65,000. Loose methods of assessment, inefficiency of administration, and corruption among officials consumed a large per cent of the revenues. In 1781 Governor Burke discussed these matters at length in his annual message, urged the Assembly "to provide effectually for calling to speedy account and payment all public collectors and other accountants," and declared that "the numberless hands at present employed in the collecting of the public revenues exhaust much of the product and create perplexities and difficulties without and in the public accounts."

In 1780 the tide of war rolled back once more upon the South. Georgia and South Carolina were quickly overrun by the enemy, who then threatened North Carolina with immediate invasion. An army of defense had to be immediately raised, equipped and supplied. But Governor Nash informed the General Assembly that the treasury was empty and the financial resources of the State exhausted. How to obtain means of supplying the army was accordingly an urgent problem. The Assembly had found that the continued emission of paper money had a "tendency to increase the prices of necessaries" which was "greatly injurious to the public." No relief could be expected from taxation. "The public money is unaccounted for," Governor Burke told the Assembly, "the taxes uncollected or unproductive, * * * and the Treasury totally unable to make payment." Even had the State had the money, the high prices of all necessities would have been practically prohibitory. In this emergency, therefore, the Assembly hit upon two new methods of supplying the public needs, i. e., a specific tax and loans. The former payable in Indian corn, wheat, flour, oats, rye, rice, pork and beef, was continued through 1782. Warehouses were established and stored with supplies which were distributed to the army. The system was primitive, cumbersome and wasteful, yet it is difficult to see how the army could have been supplied without it. But some money was absolutely necessary. In September, 1780, therefore, the Assembly determined upon a system of loans. The treasurers were authorized to issue loan certificates bearing interest at 5 per cent and exempt from all taxation, and to appeal to the people to lend the State money on them. The same act levied a tax "equal to double the amount of the public tax," i. e., 12 pence in the pound, for the redemption of these certificates when due. Another source of revenue was the confiscated property of the Loyalists which in 1783 was pledged to redeem the issue of $250,000 of bills of credit, authorized for the payment of the dues to soldiers.

North Carolina's failure to meet her financial obligations to the Confederacy was even more conspicuous than her failure to meet her own obligations. In this respect, however, the State was not peculiar since the same statement may be made of all the states. At the beginning of the struggle the rule was adopted that the states should meet all expenses incurred for purely state purposes, but those incurred in the common cause should be met out of a common or continental treasury. The chief sources from which the continental treasury drew its revenues were bills of credit, domestic loans, foreign loans, and requisitions on the states. During the war the Continental Congress issued bills of credit to the amount of $242,000,000, which it apportioned among the states for redemption on a basis of population. The several states pledged their faith to redeem this currency, but none kept its pledge, and the continental currency having no other basis of value depreciated even more rapidly than the state currency. To say that anything was "not worth a continental" became a common expression for describing its utter worthlessness.

In 1776 Congress decided to supplement its bills of credit with loan certificates and accordingly established loan offices for soliciting loans for which it issued certificates bearing at first 4 per cent interest, later 6 per cent. By 1783, $65,000,000 had been raised in this way of which North Carolina had contributed but $1,200,000, an amount below the State's proportion whether estimated on a basis of wealth or of population. After the consummation of the alliance with France in 1778 foreign loans became the principal item in continental finances, and from 1779 to the close of the war interest on these loans constituted one of the most pressing demands upon the Continental Treasury. Congress having no power of taxation was compelled to look to the states to supply the funds to meet these demands, and it looked in vain.

The case of North Carolina was but typical; from 1781 to 1784 the State was too exhausted financially to make any contribution toward the payment of the interest on the public debt. For the same reason the State fell badly behind in its general contributions to the support of the war. Congress had adopted population as the basis for its requisitions on the states both for men and money, and while this was not quite fair for the southern states with their large negro population, yet they had readily accepted it. The North Carolina Congress of August, 1775, had unanimously pledged the full support of the colony to the continental cause on this basis, but as the war progressed and its burdens increased, the State found itself increasingly unable to redeem this pledge. In August, 1781, it was indebted to the Continental Treasury $18,230,000; while at the beginning of 1784 three other requisitions had been made on which the State had paid nothing. But here again North Carolina's case was not peculiar, for none of the states had met their quotas. From November 22, 1777, to October 6, 1779, for instance, there were four requisitions on the states calling for $95,000,-000 in paper money, on which the payments amounted to less than $55,000,000; while three specie requisitions from August 26, 1780, to March 16, 1781, amounting to more than $10,000,-000, yielded but little more than $1,500,000. The basis of assessment was obviously inequitable, and each state was so afraid that it would contribute more than its just share that it took pains to contribute less.

With all these obstacles and difficulties, and numerous others scarcely less serious, how was it possible for the "men of '76" to carry their cause through to its final triumph?

The answer to this question is certainly to be found in the reality of the existence of those intangible and spiritual forces which so many modern historians, recognizing only material forces in shaping the affairs of mankind, refuse to consider as proper subjects for historical notice. Devotion and loyalty to their ideals, confidence in the justice of their cause, and faith in its ultimate triumph were quite as real to the Revolutionary patriots as were the material obstacles with which they had to deal, and it was the reality of these spiritual forces that enabled them to overcome difficulties, to endure sacrifices and hardships, to rise superior to disaster, and to wring victory out of defeat. No man not a professional cynic can read the public or private correspondence of the public men of that time without feeling the truth and justice of these observations. Had North Carolina been able to set up an efficient government, had all her people been in "a perfect good agreement," had there been no vigilant domestic foe nestling in her bosom, had she enjoyed a substantial financial credit, the task of her leaders would have been far easier and simpler, but it would not have called forth that daring in action, that constancy in good and in ill fortune, that fortitude in suffering, that faith which shown brightest in the darkness of defeat which entitles them to the admiration and gratitude of all succeeding generations. "While every community and section of the State was more or less divided in sentiment, it is to the honor of the public men of that period that no representative of the people, no man who had been honored with their confidence flinched when the test came or failed to move steadily forward through the gloom and obscurity of the doubtful and hazardous issue." [5]

---

[5] Clark, Walter: Prefatory Notes to *State Records of North Carolina,* Vol. XI, p. xvii.

CHAPTER XXIV

MILITARY AFFAIRS

From 1775 to the close of the Revolution military affairs were of course the most urgent concern of the government and people of North Carolina. The Indians on the frontier, ever ready to take up the hatchet; the Tories in the interior, always lying in wait for favorable opportunities for revolt; the British on the coast, constantly threatening invasion from the sea, menaced the State from three directions. Besides providing for her own defence against these dangers, North Carolina was expected to contribute her proportionate part to the common defence. The chief problems of the new State, therefore, during the first seven years of its existence were those which concerned the raising, organizing and equipping of troops, their maintenance in camps, and their operations in the field.

For home defence North Carolina depended chiefly upon her minute men and militia. Organizations of these classes of troops were first authorized by the Congress of August, 1775, which provided that the colony should be divided into six military districts in each of which should be raised one battalion of minute men. Their field officers were to be elected by the Congress, their company officers by the companies. The minute men were placed under the orders of the Provincial Council and when in active service were to be subject to the same discipline as soldiers on the continental establishment. They were enlisted for six months only and at the expiration of their term were disbanded by order of the Provincial Congress. In that brief time, however, they fought and won the battle of Moore's Creek Bridge. The Provincial Congress also authorized the organization of companies of independent volunteers, light horse troops, rangers, and artillery. All these organizations, however, like the minute men, were temporary, existing only during the period of the provisional government.

North Carolina's first line of defence was her militia. The right to bear arms in defence of the State is one of the

437

fundamental rights secured to the people of North Carolina by their Bill of Rights, adopted in 1776. Accordingly Chapter I, Laws of 1777, passed by the first Assembly held under the new Constitution, is "An Act to Establish a Militia in this State." Several other acts relating to the militia were subsequently passed during the Revolution but they did not materially change the main features of the first act which was based largely upon the militia law of the colonial government. Under its terms all effective men in the State from sixteen to fifty years of age, inclusive, were embraced in the militia, and subject to draft. When called into service each man was to be "furnished with a good Gun, shot bag and powder horn, [and] a Cutlass or Tomahawk."

The basis of the organization of the militia was the county. Every county was required to enroll its militia into companies of not less than fifty men each, exclusive of commissioned officers. The men of each company were divided by lot into four classes, each of which was to be called in its turn into active service. Company musters were required to be held at least once a month. All the companies of each county were organized into one or more regiments, or battalions which were required to hold two general musters a year. In each of the six military districts the battalions formed a brigade under the command of a brigadier-general. All general and field officers were elected by the General Assembly. Under the Constitution the governor was the commander-in-chief of the militia with power, during the recess of the Assembly, to call them into active service. No accurate muster rolls of the militia during the Revolution were kept, and the records of their services are very meager. In 1782, Governor Alexander Martin reported the total militia of the State at 26,822, but how many of these saw active service it is impossible to say. As a rule during the Revolution the militia justified the contempt which professional soldiers have always felt for militia; yet justice requires that it be said that when well led the militia often displayed fighting qualities which might well excite the envy of veteran regulars. No troops ever fought better than Dixon's North Carolina militia at Camden, while it must not be forgotten that it was the militia of Virginia and the Carolinas that struck the blow at King's Mountain that turned the tide of the Revolution and assured the ultimate triumph at Yorktown.

In 1775 the Continental Congress determined to raise a Continental Army to which it asked the several states to contribute in proportion to their populations. At first the men were to be enlisted for one year only although Washington repeatedly pointed out the folly of such a policy, warning Congress that "no dependence could be put in a militia," or other short-term troops and expressing his earnest conviction "that our liberties must, of necessity, be greatly hazarded, if not entirely lost, if their defence be left to any but a permanent army." His warnings made but little impression until reinforced by the military disasters of the summer of 1776, which culminated in his defeat on Long Island, on August 27th. Alarmed by these events, in September, Congress resolved to raise a regular army enlisted "for the war," to be composed of eighty-eight battalions.

North Carolina's quota was nine battalions. Six of these had already been organized by authority of the Provincial Congress. As we have already seen the Congress of August, 1775, raised two battalions of 500 men each on the continental establishment, and placed them under command of Colonel James Moore and Colonel Robert Howe. They became the first and second North Carolina Continentals. Four additional battalions were provided for by the Congress of April, 1776. The third was placed under command of Colonel Jethro Sumner, the fourth under Colonel Thomas Polk, the fifth under Colonel Edward Buncombe, and the sixth under Colonel Alexander Lillington. To complete the State's quota, the Congress of November, 1776, authorized the raising of three more battalions to be commanded by Colonel James Hogun, Colonel James Armstrong, and Colonel John Williams. These three completed the quota on paper. Nevertheless, in April, 1777, the General Assembly directed the raising of a tenth battalion to be commanded by Colonel Abraham Sheppard and requested the Continental Congress to place it on the continental establishment. The request was granted and Sheppard's became the tenth battalion of the North Carolina Continental Line.

North Carolina Continentals saw their first service outside their own province in the defence of Charleston in the summer of 1776. As soon as Sir Henry Clinton's purpose to strike a blow at the South became known the Continental Congress created the Southern Department consisting of Virginia, North Carolina, South Carolina, and Georgia, and assigned the command to General Charles Lee. Lee, who was at New York when notified of his assignment, set out immediately, March 7, 1776, for his department, arriving at Charleston almost simultaneously with Clinton. He was accompanied by Howe who, together with Moore, had been promoted to the rank of brigadier-general and ordered to report to Lee. Moore himself remained at Wilmington to keep watch over a small British fleet which still lingered in the Cape Fear, but. he dispatched four of his continental battalions to the defence of Charleston. An account of the brilliant defence of that city, and the disastrous repulse sustained by the British fleet and army on June 28th, forms no appropriate part of this narrative. Of the 6,522 troops which Lee gathered there under his command, 1,400 were North Carolina Continentals. These troops bore a conspicuous part in the battle winning high praise from their commanding officer. "I know not which corps I have the greatest reason to be pleased with," wrote Lee to the president of the Virginia Council, "Muhlenberg's Virginians, or the North Carolina troops; they are both equally alert, zealous, and spirited." To Washington he reported that Thompson's South Carolina rangers, "in conjunction with a body of North Carolina Regulars," twice repulsed determined attempts by the enemy to land on Sullivan's Island, adding: "Upon the whole, the South and North Carolina troops, and the Virginia Rifle Battalion we have here, are admirable soldiers."

Upon their promotion, Moore and Howe were succeeded in command of their battalions by Francis Nash and Alexander Martin. Lee having been recalled, Howe succeeded him in command of the Southern Department. He retained under his command the third and some companies of the first and second North Carolina continental battalions; the others rejoined Moore at Wilmington. The troops under Moore were organized into a brigade and in January, 1777, ordered to join Washington's army in Pennsylvania. While preparing for this movement, Moore died and Nash, who had recently been promoted to the rank of brigadier-general, was assigned to the command of the brigade. Nash immediately marched northward and joined Washington on July 1st. His brigade took part in the maneuvres which led up to the battle of Brandywine, September 11, 1777. Only a small part of the brigade took part in that battle. The first battle in which the brigade participated as a unit was the battle at Germantown, October 4, 1777. Its heavy losses bear witness to its gallantry on that field. Nash himself while leading his men into action fell mortally wounded. He died three days later universally lamented as an officer of ability and a sincere patriot. The brigade passed the winter at Valley Forge and in the summer of 1778 formed part of the army with which Washington pursued Clinton across New Jersey into New York. On June 29 it participated with credit in the battle of Monmouth.

Nash had been succeeded by Gen. Lachlan McIntosh of Georgia under whose command the brigade passed the winter at Valley Forge. By the spring of 1778 losses in battle, from disease, and by desertion had so decreased the enrolment in the brigade that Congress resolved to reduce the six battalions to three by consolidating the sixth, fourth, and fifth with the first, second, and third. A little later Colonel Sheppard arrived with the tenth thus adding a fourth battalion to the brigade. The appointment of General McIntosh had wounded the state pride of the troops and hurt their morale, because they felt that the appointment of any one other than a North Carolinian was a reflection on the State. "They imagine," declared Harnett, "that they appear contemptible in the eyes of the Army, not having one General Officer from our State." "Our troops are uneasy," he wrote at another time, "at not having a General Officer of our State to command them. * * * Our Officers are exceedingly anxious about it. Colonel Sumner writes to me that it is absolutely necessary." Nevertheless more than a year passed before the Assembly acted. Finally on January 9, 1779, upon the nomination of the Assembly, Congress promoted Colonel Sumner to the rank of brigadier-general, assigned him to the command of the North Carolina brigade, and ordered him south to the defence of Georgia and South Carolina.

In the meantime some of the officers who had lost their commands by the consolidation of the battalions in May, had been at work in North Carolina raising and organizing four new battalions of nine months' Continentals which the Assembly, in April, 1778, had directed to be enlisted. The first of these new battalions, numbering 600 men, was placed under command of Colonel Hogun who in the fall of 1778 marched it to join Washington at White Plains. The others were sent south to reinforce Sumner. On January 9, 1779, Congress promoted Hogun to the rank of brigadier-general and placed him in command of a new brigade composed of all the North Carolina Continentals then in Washington's army. On July 19th 200 volunteers from the brigade, under command of Major Hardy Murfree, took part in the storming of Stony Point. In this assault, one of the most brilliant episodes of the war, they won high praise from their commanding general, "Mad Anthony" Wayne, for their "good conduct and intrepidity" in action. As the summer of 1779 advanced the situation in the South became so critical that on September 20th the Continental Congress requested Washington to send Hogun's brigade, numbering about 700 effectives, to the aid of General Benjamin Lincoln at Charleston. Hogun reached Charleston on March 3, 1780, and shared the fate of that unhappy city. Its surrender carried with it North Carolina's entire Continental Line except a few officers, including General Sumner, who happened to be absent at the time on other duties.

North Carolina was never able to recruit her Continental Line up to its full strength. Some of the reasons for this failure—viz., the weakness of the executive authority, the divided counsels of the Whigs, the presence of the Tories, and the financial breakdown of both State and United States —have already been pointed out. Another cause was the generosity with which the State permitted South Carolina and Georgia to recruit their battalions in North Carolina. As early as December, 1776, the North Carolina Council declared that the State was greatly handicapped "in making up her quota of men in the continental service" because so many of the militia she had sent to the defence of Charleston were enlisting, with the consent of their officers, in the service of South Carolina and Georgia; and the Council found it necessary to forbid such enlistments from the organized militia of the State except by express consent either of the executive or the legislative authority. A fifth cause was the influence of politics in determining military appointments. Governor Caswell, writing in April, 1777, says: "The recruiting service goes slowly, owing in a great measure to the negligence, want of abilities, or want of influence in the officers." But the chief cause of the thin ranks of North Carolina's continental battalions was the failure of the General Assembly to pass an effective draft law. In 1775, Moore and Howe had no difficulty in raising their battalions because they had the full advantage of the wave of enthusiasm which swept the colony into rebellion; but by 1777 that wave had spent its force. Recruiting officers, therefore, found it difficult to induce men to volunteer "for the war" when they could satisfy both the law and their consciences by an occasional brief service in the militia. Nor were men eager to enlist in units that would take them away from their homes to service in distant states. The North Carolina continental battalions, therefore, never went into battle with anything like their full complement of men. This fact occasioned great mortification to both the political and military representatives of the State.

The delegates in the Continental Congress were urgent in their appeals to the General Assembly to adopt "spirited measures" to fill up the State's battalions. In December, 1777, Harnett begged his colleague, Burke, then at home attending the session of the legislature, to inform him "of the temper you find our Assembly in. Are they inclined to pursue spirited measures? For God's sake, fill up your Battalions," he exclaimed, "lay taxes, put a stop to the sordid and avaricious spirit which [has] affected all ranks and conditions of men. * * * All our foreign intelligence indicates that Europe will soon be in a flame. Let us not depend upon this. If we have virtue, we certainly have power to work out our own salvation, I hope without fear or trembling."

But the Assembly, though aware of the necessity, lacked either the wisdom or the courage to adopt and enforce the "spirited measures" required. It never gave the State a consistent, effective military policy. When it met in April, 1778, the returns submitted to it by the governor showed the North Carolina brigade short of its quota by 2,648 men. The Assembly declaring that since it was "absolutely necessary" to complete the battalions and experience had demonstrated that it was "impracticable to obtain that End in the common Mode of recruiting," made its first effort at a draft law. It provided that the men were to be drafted by lot from the militia, placed on the continental establishment, and enlisted for nine months. The act failed to accomplish its purpose because the machinery for enforcing it was defective. Accordingly when the Assembly met a year later, the State's continental battalions were still short 2,000 men, and the Assembly could think of no better way of filling the gaps than by offering to every ten militiamen who should furnish one continental recruit for eighteen months exemption from military service for that period except in case of actual invasion or insurrection. It is difficult to imagine a more vicious piece of legislation. It not only failed to raise the men needed, but it also thoroughly disorganized the militia. In order to secure the 600 continental recruits which it produced, it was necessary to exempt 6,000 other men from military service for eighteen months. Accordingly when it became necessary for the governor in the summer of 1780 to call out 2,000 militia, the organizations which had been built up with so much care and labor were found to be completely undermined by the operations of the act of 1779.

In 1780, the Assembly, again faced with the same problem, decided to try the effect of more liberal bounties. To volun-

teers in the continental service it offered $500 at the time of
enlistment; $500 at the end of each year's service; 200 acres
of land and one prime slave, or his value in currency, at the
end of three years, or of the war; and it solemnly set aside
and dedicated to this purpose immense tracts of the State's
western lands. But the promise of liberal bounties brought
no better results than the promise of exemption from service, and in 1781, the Assembly finding it impossible to fill up
its continental battalions, adopted the advice of the Continental Congress, reduced their number to four, and again resorted to an ineffective draft to fill their ranks. But none of
these expedients succeeded; the State's continental battalions
were never full. At Germantown, Nash led to battle a brigade
of less than 800 men. On December 23, 1777, the brigade,
which should have numbered 6,552 officers and men, numbered only 881, of whom but 434 were present and fit for duty.
The published roster of North Carolina's ten continental battalions contains a total of 5,454 names, and this number includes all those who had died, all who had been made prisoners, all who had been discharged, and all who had deserted;
and this last class numbered not less than 10 per cent of the
whole.

Throughout the Revolution the State retained immediate
control over its militia and ultimate control over its Continentals. The militia were raised, organized, armed, paid and
maintained solely by the State; their field officers were elected
by the General Assembly; their commander-in-chief was the
governor. The authority of the State over its militia was
complete whether in or beyond its borders. Over its Continentals it was only less complete. The State raised and organized them and appointed their battalion officers, but their
general officers were appointed by the Continental Congress
upon the recommendation of the legislature. When actually
forming a part of the Continental Army under command of
Washington, or other Continental generals, the State's continental troops were subject to the orders of the commanding general, but even then the commanding general exercised
only a delegated authority. The State never surrendered its
ultimate authority over them. It not only raised and organized them in the first instance, but recruited their ranks, created new units or consolidated old units as it saw fit, censured,
suspended or removed officers and appointed new ones, punished deserters, and exercised all these and other powers
over them even when they were under the immediate command of Washington himself. In 1777, the General Assembly

conferred upon the governor authority "to give such orders as he may think necessary for the removal, marching or disposition of the Continental Troops in this State or any of them."

This assertion and exercise by the several states of the right of control over their continental troops was one of the most serious defects of the continental government. It possessed not that centralization of authority and power so necessary to secure military efficiency. The Continental Congress could suggest, advise, and request the use of the continental troops for continental purposes, but it could not command them. The ultimate authority lay with thirteen different states, each claiming and exercising the powers of sovereignty, jealous of their rights, and quick to resent any act of the general government that suggested encroachments upon them.

Throughout the Revolution, North Carolina troops, both Continentals and militia, in common with the troops of the other states, endured cruel suffering, hunger and sickness, and loss of physical vitality which diminished their fighting capacity by reason of the failure of State and United States to equip and maintain them properly. On January 31, 1778, out of a total of 992 men and officers enrolled in the North Carolina brigade at Valley Forge, 249 were reported unfit for duty for lack of clothes and shoes, and 323 were sick. This condition continued all the winter, reaching its climax on March 30th when the returns showed 360 on the sick list and only 352 present and fit for duty. "I am very sorry to have to report to you," wrote their commanding general to Governor Caswell, in March, "that the men of my Brigade here have suffered severely this winter for want of clothing and other necessaries. Fifty of them died in and about Camp since the beginning of January last, and near two hundred sick here now besides as many more reported sick absent in different Hospitals of this State and Jersey, a most distressing situation!"

Valley Forge is, of course, the synonym for suffering and heroic endurance, and its story is known to all the world; but Valley Forge was not the only place at which men suffered and endured every extreme of cold and hunger and disease for the cause of American independence. When General Greene took command of the American army at Charlotte in December, 1780, he at once reported to Washington the condition of his army, "if," he adds, "it deserves the name of one. Nothing can be more wretched and distressing," he continued, "than the condition of the troops, starving with cold and hunger, without tents and camp equipage." The Virginia troops were "literally naked and a great part totally unfit for any kind of duty." "A tattered remnant of some garment," wrote Greene evidently depressed at the condition of his men, "clumsily stuck together with the thorns of the locust tree form the sole covering of hundreds, * * * and more than 1,000 are so naked that they can be put on duty only in case of desperate necessity." Moreover he found 300 of them without arms or ammunition. Nor were these conditions confined to the enlisted men. In 1779, General Hogun wrote that his officers were "in great want," it being out of their power to purchase clothes and other necessities "at the exhorbitant prices" prevailing. On account of the depreciation of the currency in which their salaries were paid, the condition of the officers of the Continental Line became so desperate that they threatened to resign in a body unless the General Assembly came to their relief.

In general these distressing conditions were due less to official indifference or incapacity than to the inability of the government to mobilize the resources of the State. Before 1775 there were no manufactures in North Carolina, and when war broke out the provincial government of course found the source of supply of manufactured articles suddenly cut off. To encourage industrial enterprises in the colony, the Provincial Congress in September, 1775, offered premiums ranging from £25 to £750 to persons who would establish factories for making saltpeter, gunpowder, cotton, woolen and linen goods, and other needed articles. But in North Carolina the Revolution was a civil war which produced such internal conditions as made it impossible for such enterprises to be developed with any great success. As in the great Civil War of 1861-1865, therefore, the State was compelled to look abroad for most of her supplies. But during the Revolution, North Carolina had no credit, and no such universally needed product as cotton on which to base a credit. In 1780, Benjamin Hawkins, the State's agent for purchasing military stores, bought at St. Eustatia several hundred stand of arms for the State for which he was obliged to pledge his personal credit. "I could procure nothing," he reported, "on the faith of the State." When these and other difficulties, some of which have already been discussed, are duly weighed and considered the thing which impresses one is not so much the failure as the astonishing success which attended the efforts of the State to equip and supply her troops in the Revolution.

As the war progressed the State established factories for making arms an1 ammunition, set up salt works, and employed large numbers of non-combatants to make shoes and clothes for the soldiers. Other means for raising supplies were purchases from private persons, impressments, and the levying of specific taxes. In every section of the State the government constantly had agents laying in supplies of pork, beef, flour, and other provisions for the army. In letters to Burke and Washington, both written February 15, 1778, Caswell gives us some idea of his activities in this work. To Burke he wrote: "I am to buy leather and skins, shoes and other clothing, procure manufactures, set them to work, purchase salt and provisions, and procure boats and wagons for sending those articles on. All this I am really constantly, almost busily [daily?] employed about myself." "The distresses of the Soldiery for want of clothing," he wrote to Washington, "are truly alarming, and the feelings of every man of the least sensibility must be wounded on receiving the information of their unhappy circumstances. Since I was favored with your Excellency's account of their sufferings, I have been happy in purchasing for our Troops about 4,000 yards of woolen Cloth, 300 Blankets, 1,500 yards of Osnaburgs, some Shoes and Stockings. I have also purchased a considerable quantity of Tanned leather and Deerskins, all which will be sent on to the Clothier General as soon as I can procure wagons. A considerable quantity of salt and salted provisions have been also purchased under my directions."

Unfortunately many of the agents employed in this business were inefficient and corrupt. Money entrusted to them was squandered on their personal wants or lost at gambling tables; while large quantities of supplies which they purchased never reached the commissaries. In 1780, the General Assembly declared that "many persons have been intrusted with large sums of public money for the use of the State, and also public property, for which they have never accounted, but have abused the trust reposed in them by misapplying the same, to the great injury of the public credit," and created a board of auditors to investigate the accounts of all such agents and require them to settle with the State. Another species of corruption was practiced by "sundry persons who have lately," according to the Assembly of 1782, "stiled themselves State Commissaries, Quarter-masters, [and] Superintendents," and by such misrepresentations "committed great abuses and waste, by making unlawful impressments and misapplication of public stores.'' A special act was therefore passed to reach and punish this class of grafters and robbers.

The chief sources from which North Carolina, like many of the other states, received military supplies were the French, Spanish and Dutch West Indies. No sooner had war begun than the harbors of Ocracoke, Edenton, Beaufort, New Bern and Wilmington became white with the sails of merchantmen and privateers. ''The contemptible Port of Ocracoke,'' wrote former Governor Martin, in January, 1778, ''* * * has become a great channel of supply to the Rebels. * * * They have received through it and continued to receive at that inlet * * * as lately as the beginning of this month very considerable importations of the necessaries they most want for the purpose of carrying on their Warfare from the Ports of France and the French West Indian Islands.'' This trade though hazardous held out prospects of large profits. Enterprising merchants invested their fortunes in it. To seamen they offered ''such exhorbitant pay,'' that the State found it difficult to find crews for the public ships. The State itself engaged in this business on a large scale. It carried on its negotiations both through French agents and agents of its own. In 1779 the Assembly appointed Benjamin Hawkins agent to purchase military supplies both at home and abroad. The next year, in order to introduce more system in the business, it appointed Richard Caswell, Robert Bignall and Benjamin Hawkins commissioners ''for the express purpose of carrying on a trade for the benefit of this State,'' empowered them to hire, purchase, and build ships, to load them with naval stores, tobacco and other North Carolina products, ''for the purpose of importing or procuring arms and other military stores for the army, as well as for the importation of salt and all kinds of merchandize'' for general use.

This trade was a great stimulus to ship building. Shipyards sprang up at Edenton, Beaufort, New Bern and Wilmington and were busy throughout the war building and launching almost every kind of river craft and seagoing vessel. Some of the noted ships built at these yards were the armed brigs, King Tammany and Pennsylvania Farmer, which were built at Edenton for the State, and the Governor Burke, ''a fine, fast sailing Brig,'' also built at Edenton; the Eclipse, a 14-gun brig built at Beaufort; the armed brigantine, General Washington, built and fitted out at Wilmington; and the Betsey, the Heart of Oak, the General Caswell, the General Nash, and the Sturdy Beggar, "allowed to be the handsomest vessel ever built in America," all built at New Bern. These and many other fast sailing vessels slipped through the inlets of Eastern North Carolina, ran down to the West Indies, or crossed the Atlantic to France and Spain, sold their cargoes, and successfully eluding the British cruisers that patrolled our waters, returned to our ports laden with all manner of articles from heavy artillery and West Indian rum to French laces, silk stockings, and night caps. In June, 1776, the Polly and the Heart of Oak arrived at New Bern with "2,000 weight of gunpowder and 20 stand of small Arms, Compleate with Iron ramrods [and] bayonets," which their owner offered to the province at "a reasonable profit." In March, 1778, several vessels arrived at New Bern from the Bermudas with cargoes of salt, "which 'tis hoped," said *The North Carolina Gazette,* "will bring down the extravagant price of that article." The next year the Holy Heart of Jesus imported from France twenty-three cannon for which the State paid 140 hogshead of tobacco. The Ferdinand, also from a French port, brought into Lookout Bay a large cargo including silk stockings, woolen and thread night caps, silk gown patterns, silk and thread handkerchiefs, "plumes for ladies and officers," and numerous other articles of equal military value.

Most of the vessels engaged in this trade were privateers sailing under letters of marque and reprisal. Although those who engaged in it were liable if captured to be hanged as pirates, the profits were so enormous, the life so stimulating and the results so invaluable to the country that many an adventurous youth, who preferred the excitement of the quarter-deck to the dull drudgery of the army camp, eagerly enlisted in this service. When the General Gates was lost in 1778 great anxiety was expressed at Edenton for the fate of "six young gentlemen of the first families and best expectations in this part of the country, who went [on her] volunteers to try their fortunes." The service was important not only for the supplies obtained, but also for the damage inflicted on British commerce. In the fall of 1777, the Lydia, 12 guns and 50 men, took a large British slaver with a cargo of negroes just from Africa "worth between Twenty and Thirty Thousand Pounds." At about the same time the Nancy captured the Invermay bound from Jamaica to Pensacola "with Rum and Slaves, said to be worth £35,000 Proclamation," and the Severn, bound from Jamaica to Bristol, with a cargo valued at £40,000. In September, 1778, the Bellona, 16 guns,

CANNON PURCHASED BY GOVERNOR CASWELL DURING THE REVOLUTION
(Now in Capitol Square at Raleigh flanking Houdon's
Statue of Washington)

Inscription on the Tablets

Bought in France by Richard Caswell
Mounted at Edenton, 1778.
Re-mounted 1861. Captured by U. S. Force
1862. Trunnion broken off.
Presented by Edenton to the
State of North Carolina, 1903.

returned to New Bern "from a short cruize" with four prizes containing among other valuable commodities "a considerable sum in specie." The enormous losses of provisions and military stores occasioned by Gates' defeat at Camden, in August, 1780, was nearly made good in September by the arrival at Wilmington of the General Nash with two prizes containing almost everything needed by the army, one valued at £10,800 sterling, the other at £40,000. This latter prize was declared to be "the most valuable Cargo ever imported into this State." "The enemy," wrote Governor Nash, in December, 1780, "have not been entirely free of trouble off Charleston and on the coast in that quarter during this summer. They have suffered very considerably by our privateers, particularly by open row boats. These boats, with 40 or 50 men aboard, take in almost everything that comes their way. Two that went out in company returned here [New Bern] this week, after a leave of about 20 days, in which time they took and sent in 12 valuable prizes, besides burning, I think, four."

All the victories, however, were not won, nor were all the prizes taken by the Americans. Early in the war British cruisers and privateers began to patrol our coast and keep vigilant watch over our inlets. They frequently crossed the bars, cut out merchantmen which had taken refuge behind them, landed raiding parties, and plundered the country almost with impunity. "The coast," so runs a report to Governor Caswell, in 1778, "is much infested at this time with the enemy which are constantly landing men and plundering." In April, 1778, a British privateer captured two French vessels which were loading behind Ocracoke Bar "with a considerable quantity of Tobacco." "Thus has a small sloop with 4 guns and 30 men," commented *The North Carolina Gazette,* lamenting the lack of protection to the inlets, "robbed this State of two fine vessels with more than 100 hogshead of tobacco and a considerable quantity of salt." In 1780 a vessel carrying 3,000 stand of arms to the American army in the South "was chased ashore in Virginia by one of the Enemy's privateers." The climax came in 1781 when Major James H. Craige with an insignificant force sailed up the Cape Fear River and occupied Wilmington without opposition.

Most of these disasters could have been prevented had the Assembly provided adequate coast defences. In 1777, after a visit of "some men of war" to the Cape Fear, during which they did "what mischief they transiently could," Samuel Ashe wrote to Burke: "These visits might be ren ered disagreeable, if not altogether prevented, would your Western members lay aside their local prejudices, and consider the True interest of the whole State, and suffer us to have a fort here." "God send our Assembly may have wisdom enough to fortify their seaports," wrote Cornelius Harnett from the Continental Congress. "I am distressed beyond measure," he declared in a letter to Caswell, "to find our seacoast so much neglected." "Mr. Maclaine writes me," he wrote at another time, "he had hopes of getting our river [Cape Fear] fortified, but I have despaired of it long ago; if the Assembly should agree to it, I shall believe that miracles have not yet ceased." But so far as the Assembly gave evidence to the contrary miracles had ceased. As so often happens, the people's representatives saved their constituents' money, and the people paid the price in blood and suffering.

One reason why North Carolina's battalions were always short of men and equipment was the liberality with which the State stripped herself in aid of her sister states. Whatever may be said of the public men of North Carolina of the Revolution, it cannot be denied that in their public conduct they were inspired by a spirit that knew no boundaries between colonies struggling in the common cause. And so we find that in the summer of 1779, at the very time North Carolina militia were fighting among the palmettoes on the Stono, North Carolina Continentals were storming the rocky promontory of Stony Point on the Hudson.

It was to her immediate neighbors that North Carolina rendered the greatest service in the Revolution. When Virginia threatened by the Indians in the West appealed to her for aid, she promptly sent 300 of her western militia to Virginia's assistance. In the East, too, as we have seen, North Carolina Continentals under Howe assisted the Virginia troops in expelling the British from Norfolk. In 1777, a British fleet of one hundred sails entered Chesapeake Bay and Lieutenant-Governor John Page, anticipating an immediate invasion, appealed to Governor Caswell for help saying, "we hope to receive considerable assistance from you, having on a former occasion experienced the readiness with which North Carolina furnished it." Caswell promptly ordered the commanding officers of the first and second brigades "to hold themselves in readiness to march at the shortest notice." In other chapters of this history something has been said of the bad feeling which existed between North Carolina and Virginia in early colonial times; it is a pleasure, therefore, to be able to record now the incidents that obliterated the last traces of such feelings between the two commonwealths and laid the foundation for that mutual esteem and respect in which they have now for nearly a century and a half held each other. Acknowledging Governor Caswell's prompt action, Governor Page wrote: "I cannot refrain from acknowledging the obligations I think the State is under to you, Sir, for the orders you issued for one third of your Militia to hold themselves in readiness to march to our assistance on the late alarming occasion, and to the good people of North Carolina for the readiness they have always shown to assist us. May an affectionate mutual attachment between Carolina and Virginia ever increase, to the Honor and security of the United States in general, and of these contiguous sister States in particular."

From the beginning of the war both South Carolina and Georgia drew largely upon the superior resources of North Carolina. In 1776, President Harnett of the North Carolina Council of Safety assured President John Rutledge of South Carolina that North Carolina would "upon all occasions afford South Carolina every possible assistance." This promise was made good. During the invasion of 1776, North Carolina poured troops, arms, ammunition and supplies into South Carolina with a liberality that "left this colony almost in a defenceless state, defenceless and very, very alarming," declared the Council, "as we have every reason to expect General Clinton's return here should he fail in his Expedition against South Carolina." Early in the war both South Carolina and Georgia sought permission to recruit their battalions in North Carolina. The Convention of 1776, considering that "the Defence of South Carolina is of the last Importance to the Well being of the United States," not only granted the request, but also offered to raise two additional brigades of volunteers to be sent to her assistance. A similar response was given to Georgia's request. "We have given every facility and assistance to the recruiting officers from the State of Georgia," wrote the Council of Safety to the North Carolina delegates in the Continental Congress, "and have the pleasure to acquaint you that they have met with great success." Indeed, so great was their success that John Penn thought it would "be prudent to stop the officers of the neighboring States from inlisting any more men in North Carolina untill we have compleated our Quota."

But such prudence did not appeal sympathetically to the men then directing the affairs of North Carolina. They cared little whether the men were enlisted in the service of North Carolina, South Carolina, or Georgia, provided only they were in the service of the United States. Consequently North Carolina became the "recruiting ground for the entire South," and many a soldier who followed the flag of another State thought, as he struck down his country's enemies, of his little cabin nestling among the pines of North Carolina. It was the manifestation of this spirit that led Charles Pinckney of South Carolina, during the invasion of that colony in 1779, to write with pardonable exaggeration: "As to further aid from North Carolina they have agreed to send us 2,000 more troops immediately. We have now upwards of 3,000 of their men with us, and I esteem this last augmentation as the highest possible mark of their affection for us and as the most convincing proof of their zeal for the glorious cause in which they are engaged. They have been so willing and ready on all occasions to afford us all the assistance in their power, that I shall ever love a North Carolinian, and join with General Moultrie in confessing that they have been the salvation of this country."

But North Carolina's policy toward her sister states was not altogether altruistic. Her statesmen of course realized that her fate was involved in the fate of all and recognized the wisdom of the policy of defending North Carolina on the soil of Georgia and South Carolina. Harnett gave expression to the general feeling when, urging that the utmost exertions be made to aid Georgia and South Carolina, he said: "I am one of those old Politicians who had much rather see my neighbour's house on fire than my own, but at the same time would lend every assistance in my power to quench the flame." The progress of events proved the wisdom of this policy. When it finally came North Carolina's turn to suffer invasion the enemy was so exhausted by his efforts to conquer Georgia and South Carolina that after his Pyrrhic victory at Guilford Court House he was unable to maintain the struggle and soon departed from the State. Thus was North Carolina saved from the unhappy fate which had befallen her two neighbors.

CHAPTER XXV

THE WAR IN THE SOUTH

North Carolina was able to send generous military assistance to her sister states because from 1776 to 1780, except for the Tories in her midst, her own soil was free from the enemy. A similar immunity was enjoyed by the other southern states for more than two years after Clinton's repulse at Charleston, but in the winter of 1778 this happy situation came to an end. The royal governors of North Carolina, South Carolina, and Georgia had never ceased to represent the people of those states as Loyalists at heart, eagerly awaiting the arrival of a British force which would enable them to overthrow the rebel governments and restore the royal authority. Accordingly having failed in the North, in the summer of 1778, Sir Henry Clinton determined to transfer the seat of war once more to the South. "If the rebellion could not be broken at the center, it was hoped that it might at least be frayed away at the edges; and should fortune so far smile upon the royal armies as to give them Virginia also, perhaps the campaign against the wearied North might be renewed at some later time and under better auspices." [1]

The first blow fell on Georgia. In December, 1778, a British force of 3,500 men, under Colonel Archibald Campbell, convoyed by a British squadron, landed near Savannah, routed General Robert Howe's army of 1,200 Americans who attempted to resist their movement, and entered the city in triumph. In January, 1779, General Augustine Prevost with 2,000 regulars from Florida reached Savannah, took command of the united forces, and dispatched Campbell into the interior of the State. Campbell drove the militia before him, occupied Augusta without opposition, and established posts in various parts of Western Georgia. Within six weeks from the time of Campbell's arrival at Savannah, the conquest of Georgia was so complete that the royal governor was invited to return from England to resume his government.

---

[1] Fiske: The American Revolution, Vol. II, p. 163.

The Americans, however, were not ready to acknowledge defeat. General Benjamin Lincoln, who had superseded Howe in command of the Southern Department, arrived at Howe's camp on January 2d, and took command, Howe going north to join Washington's army. Lincoln had collected at Charleston about 7,000 men, of whom a third were North Carolina militia under command of General John Ashe and North Carolina Continentals under General Sumner. Feeling strong enough to assume the offensive, Lincoln dispatched Ashe with 1,500 men against Augusta, but on March 3d, at Briar Creek, Ashe permitted his army to be surprised and routed. His men were so badly scattered that only 450 of them rejoined Lincoln's army. Ashe's defeat destroyed all hope of recovering Georgia at that time. Indeed a movement of Prevost compelled Lincoln to retire from Georgia and hasten to the defence of Charleston. Movements in and about that city culminated on June 20th in the battle of Stono Ferry in which Lincoln made a determined but unsuccessful attack on the enemy. North Carolina troops under Sumner formed the right and the Continentals under General Isaac Huger the left of the attacking force, while Hamilton's North Carolina and South Carolina Loyalists were in the front of the British line. The Americans lost heavily in killed and wounded. Among the wounded was a brilliant young cavalry officer, Major William R. Davie, twenty-three years of age that day, who was destined to win renown as a soldier and statesman. Although able to parry this blow, Prevost deemed it wise to abandon his attempt against Charleston and withdraw to Savannah. The intense heat and sickly season of July and August put a stop to further operations during that summer.

In this interval Lincoln planned an attempt to recapture Savannah and recover Georgia in co-operation with the French fleet under Count d'Estaing who was then cruising among the West Indies. Accordingly on September 1st, D'Estaing with an army of 6,000 men convoyed by a fleet of thirty-seven ships appeared off Savannah while Lincoln with 6,000 troops invested the town from the land side. Prevost defended the city with about 3,000 men. Prompt action and intelligent leadership would probably have forced him to surrender, but the allies displayed neither. Failing to reduce the place after a three weeks' seige, on October 9th they undertook to carry it by storm. Again North Carolina Continentals led by Colonel Gideon Lamb and North Carolina Loyalists under Hamilton fought gallantly on opposing sides. The assault failed, D'Estaing weighed anchor and sailed away, and Lincoln was forced to fall back on Charleston leaving Georgia in the hands of the enemy.

The British had struck their first blow against Georgia because it was the weakest of the thirteen states, and its conquest would give them the necessary base for operations against the Carolinas. "Georgia should be taken first," Germain had written to Clinton, "and the passage into South Carolina will then be comparatively easy." Clinton, now commander-in-chief of the British armies in America, had never ceased to cherish hopes of taking Charleston and recovering the prestige which his repulse there in 1776 had cost him; and keeping an observant eye on the operations in the South he saw in the conquest of Georgia the opportunity for which he had been waiting. With Savannah as its base an army could easily march overland and attack Charleston in the rear while a fleet assailed the city in front. Clinton resolved, therefore, upon operations against Charleston under his own command, and on the day after Christmas, 1779, sailed from New York with an army of 8,500 men, convoyed by a fleet of five ships of the line and nine frigates manned by crews numbering about 5,000. Later he was joined at Charleston by 2,500 men under Lord Rawdon whom he had ordered to follow him from New York. These together with the troops ordered up from Savannah raised Clinton's army to about 13,000 men. Not only were these troops the flower of the British army in America, but they were led by a group of extraordinarily able officers. Conspicuous among them were Lord Cornwallis, Lord Rawdon, Colonel James Webster, Colonel Patrick Ferguson and Colonel Banastre Tarleton. Confident of the outcome, Clinton approached his task with the utmost deliberation, planning every operation carefully before he finally opened the seige on March 29, 1780. In the meantime Lincoln had been making the utmost exertions to defend the city, throwing up works and gathering behind them all the troops he could summon to his aid. On March 3d, he was joined by 700 North Carolina Continentals under Hogun whom Washington had dispatched from his own army. He had also 1,000 North Carolina militia under Lillington, but about 800 of these departed during the seige; later, however, this loss was partially made good by the arrival of 300 other North Carolina militia. Altogether Lincoln gathered in the doomed city about 6,000 men. Military policy dictated the abandonment of the city and the preservation of the army; but the civil authorities of both State and city would not listen to such a proposal. The result was that after withstanding a seige of over a month, on May 12th both city and army were forced to capitulate. Seven generals, 290 other officers, and more than 5,000 rank and file laid down their arms. The surrender carried with it the entire North Carolina Continental Line, numbering 815 officers and men, including General Hogun, and about 600 North Carolina militia.

The fall of Charleston stripped South Carolina of her organized defenders and opened the way for the conquest of the State. All the strategic points on the coast—Georgetown, Charleston, Beaufort and Savannah—were already in the hands of the enemy, and nothing prevented their occupying those in the interior at will. Of these the most important were Augusta, "the gateway to Georgia;" Ninety-Six which dominated the line of communication between Augusta and the backwoods settlements of North Carolina; and Camden, "the key between the North and the South," in which centered the principal inland roads by which South Carolina could be entered from the north. The line of communication between Camden and Ninety-Six, a distance of eighty miles, was commanded by the smaller post of Rocky Mount. Northeast of Camden was Cheraw, controlling the northeastern section of South Carolina and overlooking the settlements of the loyal Highlanders in North Carolina. Immediately after the surrender of Charleston, Lord Cornwallis advanced inland and seized all of these points. No resistance was offered; the several posts were easily "possessed, fortified and garrisoned; all the immediate country was submissive, and protestations of loyalty resounded in every quarter." The interior secured, Cornwallis returned to Charleston to complete the restoration of the civil authority in South Carolina and to prepare for the invasion of North Carolina.

Confident that Georgia and South Carolina were subjugated beyond recovery, on June 5th Clinton sailed for New York leaving Cornwallis with 8,345 men to hold those states and complete the work in the South by the conquest of North Carolina and Virginia. Clinton had no doubt of Cornwallis' ability to accomplish these tasks. The surrender of Charleston, he thought, "insures the reduction of this and the next province." He had ample grounds for his confidence. British troops held all the strategic points in South Carolina and Georgia. The way into North Carolina was open, and that State was helpless to prevent invasion. Her resources were exhausted. Her organized forces had been sacrificed in the defence of Charleston. Her people were dispirited and alarmed, her enemies jubilant, arrogant, and confident.

Whigs and Tories alike anticipated the immediate invasion of the State, the former with dread and apprehension, the latter with enthusiasm and hope. Had Cornwallis advanced promptly, he would certainly have laid North Carolina at his feet, but pleading the intensity of the heat, the necessity of giving his men rest, and the lack of provisions and stores, he decided to spend the summer at Charleston and enter North Carolina at his leisure in the fall.

The chief reason for his decision was the confidence which he placed in the representations of former Governor Martin and other fugitive Loyalists as to the general loyalty of the people of North Carolina. "Our hopes of success in offensive operations," he wrote, "were not founded only upon the efforts of the corps under my immediate command, which did not much exceed three thousand men; but principally upon the most positive assurances given by apparently creditable deputies and emissaries that, upon the appearance of a British army in North Carolina, a great body of the inhabitants were ready to join and co-operate with it, in endeavoring to restore his Majesty's Government." Accordingly from Charleston he established communications with the Tories of North Carolina to whom he sent emissaries to bid them attend to their harvests, collect provisions, and remain quiet until the king's army was ready to enter the State in August or September.

The very completeness of the British victory proved Cornwallis' ruin. It conspired with the exaggerated representations of the loyalty of the Carolinas which the exiled Loyalists unceasingly poured into his ears to produce a feeling of over-confidence which the real situation did not warrant. After the surrender of Charleston, Clinton had issued a proclamation offering pardon to all persons, except those guilty of crime, who would return to their allegiance to the king; and many of the people, looking upon the cause of independence as hopeless, tired of war and eager for peace, hastened to take advantage of his offer. Clinton reported to Lord Germain, secretary of state for the colonies, that "the inhabitants from every quarter repair to the detachments of the army, and to this garrison [Charleston] to declare their allegiance to the King." "A general revolution of sentiment seemed to take place, and the cause of Great Britain appeared to triumph over that of the American Congress." [2] But Clinton was not satisfied with passive obedience, and just before departing for

---

[2] Tarleton: Campaigns, p. 25.

New York, issued a second proclamation discharging all
paroles, except prisoners captured in battle, and commanding all persons to take an active part in the restoration of
the royal government upon pain of being treated as rebels
and enemies. The folly of this action became immediately
apparent. It "produced a counter-revolution in the minds and
inclinations of the people," says Stedman, the British historian, "as complete and as universal as that which succeeded
the fall of Charlestown." [3] The people of South Carolina refused to become the instruments of their own subjugation;
they rose again in rebellion, organized themselves into bands
of partisans under the leadership of James Williams, Andrew
Pickens, Thomas Sumter, and Francis Marion, and opened a
form of fierce guerrilla warfare upon the enemy's outposts
which made it impossible for Cornwallis to advance with
safety into North Carolina.

North Carolina took advantage of the British general's
procrastination to reorganize her scattered forces and prepare
for resistance. Caswell, who had been appointed to the command of the militia with the rank of major-general, concentrated the eastern militia at Cross Creek to overawe the Highlanders. In the West, Rutherford, Davie, Davidson, Francis
Locke and other bold and aggressive partisan leaders aroused
the Scotch-Irish of Mecklenburg, Rowan, and surrounding
counties, and by the middle of June, had assembled 900 men
under Rutherford near Charlotte, and 400 under Locke and
other officers near Ramsaur's Mill. Though short of ammunition and "obliged to turn their implements of husbandry
into those of war by hammering up their scythes and sickles
and forming them into swords and spears," [4] they more than
made good their deficiency in equipment by the fierce and
warlike zeal with which they rallied to the defense of their
homes.

These partisan bands were too weak in numbers, too loose
in discipline, and too short of equipment for extended campaigns, but for the sudden gatherings and hasty dispersions,
the quick advances and the rapid retreats of guerrilla warfare
they were unsurpassed. For this kind of service no troops
ever had more skillful leaders. Rutherford, Davie, Davidson
and Locke of North Carolina worked in complete harmony and
co-operation with Williams, Pickens, Sumter and Marion of

---

[3] History of the American War, Vol. 2, p. 198.
[4] Moultrie, William: Memoirs of the American Revolution, Vol.
II, p. 213.

South Carolina. No foraging party escaped their vigilance. No Tory gathering was safe from their sudden onsets. No British post was immune from their attacks. Though not always successful, they were a source of constant annoyance and apprehension to the British, while their activity and daring kept alive the spirit of resistance among the patriots during the dark days of the summer of 1780.

The story of their exploits resembles rather the romances of knight errantry than the sober facts of history. At sunrise in the morning of June 20th, Locke with a band of 400 men surprised and routed 1,300 Tories whom emissaries of Cornwallis, contrary to his lordship's orders, had embodied at Ramsaur's Mill in Lincoln County preparatory to joining the British at Camden. Davie's cavalry arriving after the battle had begun, pursued the fugitives, killing and capturing many of them and completely dispersing the rest. On July 2d, Davie surprised and captured a convoy of provisions and clothing on its way to the British garrison at Hanging Rock. A few days later, July 21st, Davidson with 160 light horse from Rutherford's brigade attacked 250 Tories under Colonel Samuel Bryan, one of the most active of the Tory leaders, at Colston's Mill on Pee Dee River, killed and captured about fifty, "and put the rest to flight," reported Major Thomas Blount to Governor Nash, "with more precipitation than we fled from Bryar Creek." Ten days later, under the very eyes of the British garrison at Hanging Rock, Davie fell upon three companies of Bryan's Loyalists returning from an excursion, cut them to pieces, captured 100 muskets and 60 horses without the loss of a man, and before the British garrison recovered from their consternation sufficiently to beat to arms was safely beyond their reach. Emboldened by the success of these and many other similar exploits, on August 6th Davie and Sumter united forces for an attack on Hanging Rock itself. Its garrison numbered 500 men of whom 160 were of Tarleton's famous legion. The attacking party consisted of about 500 North Carolinians under Davie and Colonel Irwin of Mecklenburg County, and 300 South Carolinians under Sumter. Taking the enemy by surprise, they drove through the British camp and were on the point of winning a brilliant victory when some of Sumter's men stopping to plunder the camp threw the American lines into confusion. The British rallied and Sumter and Davie were compelled to draw off their forces having, however, inflicted a heavier loss upon the enemy than they themselves sustained. These exploits are cited here not because they were more important than others.

but because they were typical of many such enterprises too numerous to mention.

Such an outburst of activity among a people whom he had thought completely subjugated astounded Cornwallis, while the boldness and success of the Americans thoroughly cowed the great mass of Loyalists and neutrals in the two Carolinas. Cornwallis declared that he had not expected any hostile demonstrations in North Carolina and having "much business to do at Charlestown," was arranging his affairs in that city quite satisfactorily "when our tranquility was first disturbed by the accounts of a premature rising of our friends [at Ramsaur's Mill] in Tryon County, North Carolina, in the latter end of June, who having assembled without concert, plan or proper leaders, were two days after surprised and totally routed. * * * Many of them fled into this Province, where their reports tended much to terrify our friends and encourage our enemies." So too Bryan's men fleeing from Colston's Mill did not halt "until they reached the Enemy's next Post at the Waxhaws, where they threw the whole into the utmost confusion and Consternation." The British soon found their grip on South Carolina slipping. In August the whole country between the Pee Dee and the Santee rivers was "in an absolute State of Rebellion." Hostilities were constantly breaking out "in different parts of the frontier" where, wrote Cornwallis, "General Sumpter [sic], an active and daring man, * * * was constantly Menacing our small posts." Then, too, "reports industriously propagated in this Province of a large Army coming from the Northward had very much intimidated our friends, encouraged our enemies, and determined the wavering against us." Before the summer was over Cornwallis became convinced that if he did not advance into North Carolina and subjugate that State he "must give up both South Carolina and Georgia, and retire within the Walls of Charlestown."

In the meantime the critical situation of the Carolinas had aroused both Washington and Congress to action. Early in the summer Washington had dispatched from his own army 2,000 excellent Delaware and Maryland troops under Baron de Kalb to reinforce Lincoln at Charleston. Kalb arrived at Hillsboro on June 20th. Everywhere he found an utter lack of preparation to meet the crisis, and complained bitterly that he was compelled to subsist his army by his own efforts. He could obtain supplies from the people only by military force and in his efforts received "no assistance from the legislative or executive power" of the State. Governor Nash defended himself by pointing out his lack of power under the Constitution which he declared to be totally "inadequate to the public exigencies." However, Kalb's presence greatly encouraged the Whig leaders. Caswell in command of Gregory's and Butler's brigades of North Carolina militia and General Edward Stevens in command of the Virginia militia hastened to put themselves under the baron's command. Rutherford, too, with his command and Colonel William Porterfield then near the South Carolina border with 400 Virginia Continentals, prepared to join the main army. Kalb was planning an advance into South Carolina when on July 25th, he was superseded in command by General Horatio Gates. After the surrender of Charleston, Congress had unanimously chosen Gates, still masquerading as the conqueror of Burgoyne, to succeed Lincoln in command of the Southern Department. Notifying Gates of his appointment, Richard Peters, secretary of the Board of War, wrote: "Our affairs to the Southward look blue; so they did when you took Command before the Burgoynade. I can only now say 'Go and do likewise.' " But Gates' friend Charles Lee, who had formed a juster estimate of Gates' military capacity, cynically warned him to beware lest his northern laurels should change to southern willows. However, there were few who then doubted Gates' title to his northern laurels, and his appointment was, therefore, hailed with joy by the Americans and with apprehension by the British and Tories.

Gates began with a blunder and ended with a disaster. He took command at Hillsboro, July 25th. His objective was Camden, the chief British post, held by Lord Rawdon. Two roads led to Camden. Kalb, who had studied the situation carefully, advised the route through Salisbury and Charlotte which though the longer of the two ran through a region inhabited by friends and abounding in provisions. The shorter and more direct route ran through a barren region, thinly settled and generally hostile. Every consideration urged the choice of the former, yet Gates rejecting the advice of all his generals and pleading his eagerness to meet the enemy, chose the latter and on July 27th put his army in motion. On the march he was joined by Porterfield with 400 Virginia Continentals, Stevens with 700 Virginia militia, and Caswell with 1,200 North Carolina militia. When he encamped ten miles from Camden on the afternoon of August 15th, Gates had under his command 3,052 men of whom more than half were untrained militia. On their long march green corn and unripe fruit had been their principal diet, and dysentery and

cholera morbus had wrought such havoc with their health
that they were in no condition for a battle. Nevertheless
Gates on the evening of August 16th, moved out of his camp
to attack Lord Rawdon at daybreak.

Gates had scorned the use of cavalry and consequently was
entirely ignorant of the situation in the enemy's camp. Lord
Rawdon who knew every movement made by his adversary
had called in the garrisons from the smaller posts scattered
throughout the interior and concentrated his forces at Augusta, Ninety-Six and Camden. Moreover at his request Cornwallis had come with reinforcements from Charleston arriving at Camden unknown to Gates on August 14th. The combined forces under his command were but little more than
2,000 but they were seasoned troops. Among them were two
regiments of North Carolina Loyalists. Although aware of
his numerical inferiority to Gates, Cornwallis, relying upon
the superior discipline and greater experience of his troops,
determined to take the offensive.

Unknown to each other Gates and Cornwallis both
planned a night attack. About 2 o'clock in the morning of
August 16th, their advance guards came in contact about five
miles from Camden. In the skirmish that followed the
Americans were routed. From prisoners Gates now learned
for the first time that Cornwallis had arrived at Camden with
regulars and was himself in command. In a panic he thought
only of retreat. He had in the first instance stubbornly taken
the wrong road that he might hasten to meet the enemy, now
in the presence of the foe both his eagerness and his courage
vanished. Calling a council of war, he asked what should be
done. Silence greeted his query until General Stevens exclaimed, "Well, gentlemen, is it not now too late to do anything but fight?" Each side having now lost the advantage of
a surprise, both drew up their forces for battle, about 200
yards from each other. Gates placed the Delaware regiment
and the second Maryland brigade on his right under Kalb,
the North Carolina militia under Caswell in the center, and
Stevens with the Virginia militia on his left. The first Maryland brigade, under General William Smallwood, was held in
reserve. The British left opposed to Kalb was under command of Rawdon, their right opposed to Caswell and Stevens
was led by Colonel James Webster. Tarleton's cavalry
hovered in the rear, ready to give aid where needed.

At daylight Cornwallis opened the battle with a vigorous
attack on the Carolina and Virginia militia. As Webster's
regulars in perfect formation swept down upon them, the un-

trained militia were seized with a panic. The Virginians without firing a shot threw down their arms and fled. Caswell's militia immediately followed suit. Breaking through the first Maryland brigade, they threw it into confusion and catching Gates up in the fleeing mass swept him along with them. As they fled, Tarleton's horse fell upon them like an avalanche cutting them down in large numbers. One regiment of North Carolina militia, under command of Major Hal Dixon, attaching itself to the brave Marylanders on its right, refused to join in the shameful rout. "None, without violence to the claims of honor and. justice," wrote "Light Horse Harry" Lee in his "Memoirs," [5] "can withhold applause from Colonel [sic] Dixon and his North Carolina regiment of militia. Having their flank exposed by the flight of the other militia, they turn with disdain from the ignoble example; and fixing their eyes on the Marylanders, whose left they became, determined to vie in deeds of courage with their veteran comrades. Nor did they shrink from this daring resolve. In every vicissitude of the battle, this regiment maintained its ground, and when the reserve under Smallwood, covering our left, relieved its naked flank, forced the enemy to fall back." Gregory's North Carolina militia also acquitted themselves well. Formed immediately on the left of the Continentals, they kept the field while they had a bullet to fire; and many of those who were captured had no wounds except from bayonets. On the American right the Delaware and Maryland troops under the gallant Kalb fought like veterans for nearly an hour, and did not break until Kalb was killed, and Webster's regulars had attacked them in the rear. The whole line then gave way and the rout became general.

The American army was destroyed. Its colors, artillery, ammunition wagons, military stores, baggage and camp equipage, and 2,000 muskets fell into the hands of the enemy. More than 800 Americans were killed, including a third of the Continentals, and 1,000 were captured. Among the killed were Porterfield, Gregory and Kalb; among the captured Rutherford. "The taking of that violent and cruel incendiary, General Rutherford," wrote Cornwallis, "has been a lucky circumstance." "None were saved," wrote Lee, "but those who penetrated swamps which had been deemed impassable." All along the line of retreat evidences of the completeness of the British victory were abundant. "The road was heaped with the dead and the wounded. Arms, artillery, horses, and bag-

[5] P. 186.

gage were strewed in every direction; and the whole adjacent country presented evidences of the signal defeat.'' The laurels of Saratoga had indeed changed to the willows of Camden.

Four hundred of North Carolina's militia had been killed, wounded and captured, the rest completely dispersed. Again the State lay open to invasion; again Cornwallis had but to advance to reap the fruits of his victory; again he let the opportunity slip from his grasp. His delay gave the Americans a breathing spell in which to rally their broken forces. Undismayed at their misfortune they set themselves to the task with determination. Gates at Hillsboro was all activity but being "execrated by the officers, unrevered by the men and hated by the people,'' he could accomplish but little. Caswell was more successful. On the retreat from Camden, he stopped long enough at Charlotte to order out the militia of Mecklenburg, Rowan and Lincoln counties; while from Hillsboro he directed three regiments of the eastern militia which fortunately had not reached him in time for the battle to rendezvous at Ramsay's Mill in Chatham County, organized them into a brigade under General Jethro Sumner, and led them to the camp which General Smallwood had established at Salisbury. Smallwood had under his command ''the shattered remains of the Maryland Division,'' numbering about 270 cavalry and infantry. He also was active in getting out the militia. ''I have used every exertion,'' he wrote, ''to encourage and induce the militia to assemble at Charlotte and am happy to acquaint you that they have turned out in great numbers, seem spirited and desirous of being commanded by some Continental officer.'' Governor Nash called out the second draft of militia and directed them to embody at Hillsboro, Salisbury and Charlotte. On September 6th Gates reported to Washington that ''1,400 of the Second Draught of the Militia of this State are marched to cover Salisbury and the country from thence to Charlotte, where Colonel Sumpter has a command. * * * Three hundred Virginia Riflemen under Colonel Campbell and Militia from the back Counties are marching to the East Bank of the Yadkin at the ford, and General Stevens, with what have not run home of the other Virginia Militia is at Guilford Court House. The Maryland division and the Artillery are here to be refitted. The former will be put into one strong Regiment, with a good Light Infantry Company under Colonel Williams. * * * General Muhlenburg acquaints me that near Five Hundred Regulars are upon their march from Petersburgh to this place;

these with the Marylanders above mentioned will make us stronger in Continental troops than I was before the action.''

There were men enough under arms in North Carolina to repel an invasion could they but be organized, equipped, and properly led. At Salisbury Smallwood's men were ''in a most wretched situation for want of cloaths of all kinds.'' When Sumner took command of his new brigade at Ramsay's Mill he found the arms in bad order, a shortage of ammunition, no organized commissary, and one-third of his soldiers scattered about at various farm houses threshing out wheat. The Continentals at Hillsboro were ''in want of everything except arms,'' many ''almost naked,'' and large numbers unable to take the field for want of shoes. The General Assembly which met at Hillsboro August 23d undertook to relieve this situation. Governor Nash had so strongly represented his lack of authority without the Council, and complained so bitterly of his councilors' neglect of their duties, that the Assembly determined to confer all the war powers of the governor and Council upon a board of war composed of Alexander Martin, John Penn and Oroondates Davis. To this board was given extra-constitutional powers for raising, organizing and equipping troops. Most important of all was the finding of a competent commanding officer. Gates' reputation was irrevocably lost but the Assembly had no control over him. Caswell's reputation had suffered only less than Gates', and over Caswell who commanded the state militia the Assembly exercised complete authority. The only general officer who survived the rout at Camden with an increased reputation for courage and military talent was Smallwood, and although he was a Marylander, the necessity was so urgent that the Assembly, sinking all state pride, offered him the command of the North Carolina militia, with the rank of major-general. Thereupon Caswell indignantly withdrew from the service, resigned his place on the Board of Trade, and retired to the privacy of his home at Kingston.

After Camden Cornwallis, strangely enough, repeated the blunder he had committed after the fall of Charleston. Tarleton and other officers urged upon him the advantages of an ''immediate advance of the King's troops into North Carolina,''[6] but Cornwallis was less impressed by these advantages than he was by ''the number of sick in the hospital, the late addition of the wounded, the want of troops,'' ''the deficiency of the stores, the heat of the climate, the scarcity of provisions

---

[6] Tarleton's Campaigns, p. 155.

in North Carolina," and the other hardships incident to war
which he seems to have expected to avoid. But again his
chief reason for delay was over-confidence. He believed that
at Camden he had struck the American cause its death blow.
Former Governor Josiah Martin, who was with Cornwallis, reflected his views in a letter to Lord Germain in which he declared the victory was so "glorious, compleat and critical,"
that "it could receive no additional splendour.   *   *   *   It
is consequential to the Nation, my Lord, in proportion to the
importance of America to Great Britain, for her cause and
Interests on this continent depending, as I conceive, absolutely
on the issue of this action, may be fairly said to be rescued,
saved, redeemed and restored." In England the impression
was created that "North Carolina was only considered as the
road to Virginia." [7] Cornwallis was confirmed in his view of
the situation not only by the confusion and disorganization of
the American army, but also by the protestations of loyalty
and assurances of support which again poured in upon him
from the North Carolina Tories. Unwittingly these men did
the cause of independence a great service for their professions, together with other reasons, confirmed Cornwallis in his
determination to delay his march into North Carolina until
his plans were perfected to the last detail.

Consequently it was not until September 8th that he broke
camp at Camden and set out on his invasion of North Carolina. His advance was far from being the triumphant pro-
cession his friends had led him to expect. Partisan bands
hung upon his flanks and so harassed his movements that he
did not reach Charlotte until September 25th. On September 20th, Davie, who had recently been appointed to the command of the cavalry with the rank of colonel, with 150 men
surprised an enemy detachment of 300 men at Wahab's plantation, killed and wounded 60 of their number, routed the
rest, and brought off 120 stand of arms and 96 horses. On the
morning of September 26th, Davie posted a small force behind the courthouse in Charlotte, which stood in the center
of the village where its two streets intersected, and when
the head of the British column appeared, composed of Tarleton's famous legion of dragoons, greeted it with so effective a fire that it recoiled three times and Cornwallis was
obliged to ride up and rally the troops himself. "The whole
of the British army," says its historian Stedman, himself an
officer under Cornwallis, "was actually kept at bay for some

---

[7] Annual Register, Vol. 24, p. 54.

minutes by a few mounted Americans, not exceeding twenty in number."

Thus the British army entered Charlotte, where on October 3d Josiah Martin, who accompanied Cornwallis, issued his proclamation announcing the triumph of the king's arms, the suppression of the rebellion, and the restoration of the royal government, and calling upon all faithful subjects to rally to the defence of the royal standard. Seriously as Martin took this proclamation, Cornwallis must have known that it was the merest bombast. It had not taken him a whole week to realize that he was in the "Hornets' Nest" of the Revolution. "It is evident" * * * he wrote, "that Mecklenburg and Rowan Counties are more hostile to England than any [others] in America." The situation of the British at Charlotte, wrote the Board of War, "hath been rendered very troublesome by the close attention paid them by Davidson and Davie." These active young officers with their sleepless bands patrolled the surrounding country day and night, watching every movement of the enemy, breaking up his foraging parties, capturing his scouts, and cutting off his messengers so effectively that nearly a week passed after the event before Cornwallis, who was anxiously awaiting intelligence of "Colonel Ferguson's movements to the westward," heard of his defeat and death at King's Mountain.

When Cornwallis began his movement from Camden into North Carolina he sent Colonel Patrick Ferguson, one of his best and most trusted officers, into the Ninety-Six District to arouse the Tories to action and to secure his left flank from attack by some bands of over-mountain men who, under Charles McDowell, Isaac Shelby and John Sevier, were showing signs of activity in that region. On July 30th they captured Thicketty Fort, a Tory stronghold on a tributary of Broad River. A few days later they were themselves defeated at Cedar Springs on the Pacolet River. On August 19th, they had just won a particularly brilliant action at Musgrove's Mill on the Enoree when they received intelligence of the defeat of Gates at Camden, which compelled them to retire into North Carolina. It was primarily to protect his flank against these men that Cornwallis dispatched Ferguson to the borders of Tryon County, with a force of 200 regulars and 900 Tory militia who, according to Cornwallis, had been "got into very tolerable order." Ferguson boldly pursued the mountain-men as far as Gilbert Town in Rutherford County, whence he sent them a contemptuous message declaring that unless they speedily

Isaac Shelby

dispersed and desisted from further resistance to the king's troops, he would cross the mountains, hang their leaders, and lay waste their settlements with fire and sword.

Shelby and Sevier answered this challenge by calling the mountain men to arms. In its suddenness and its numerical strength the response to their call resembled a rising of the Scottish clans when the "fiery cross" was dispatched through the Highlands. To the rendezvous at Sycamore Shoals on Watauga River, September 25th, came Shelby with 240 men from Sullivan County, Sevier with 240 from Washington, McDowell with 160 from Burke and Rutherford, and William Campbell with 400 Virginians. Without delay, they set out in search of their enemy, and on the march were joined by 350 men from Wilkes and Surry under Benjamin Cleaveland and Joseph Winston. As there was some rivalry among the North Carolina colonels, Campbell was asked to assume the leadership of the expedition. During their long and arduous march over the mountains many of the men dropped out and only about 700 finally reached Cowpens where they camped on October 6th. There, however, they were joined by Frederick Hambright with 50 men from Lincoln County and Edward Lacey and James Williams with 400 South Carolinians.

Although Ferguson affected to despise his enemies as "a set of mongrels," still upon learning of their approach he dispatched a messenger to Cornwallis calling for aid and himself sought refuge on the southern extremity of King's Mountain, a ridge about sixteen miles long, running from a point in what is now Cleveland County, North Carolina, southwest into York County, South Carolina. The spur reached by Ferguson is in York County, one and a half miles from the North Carolina line, and six miles from the highest elevation of the mountain. About 600 yards in length, it rises from a base of 250 yards to a top of from 60 to 220 yards wide, and commands a wide view of the surrounding country. The crest can be approached from three sides only; on the north it is an unbroken precipice. On the summit of this ridge Ferguson sought safety from his enemies. To his mind, trained in European methods of warfare, the steep ascent, together with the thick shrubbery and underbrush which covered the rugged mountain sides, seemed to make his position impregnable, and he boasted that all the rebels out of hell could not drive him from it. But he forgot that he was dealing with men who were used to climbing mountains and followed other rules of warfare than those laid down by European text-writers.

On October 6th, while at Cowpens, the American officers selected from their several bands 920 picked men, confirmed the choice of Campbell as their leader; and set out for King's Mountain. Reaching the foot of the ridge about 3 o'clock in the afternoon of October 7th, they organized in three columns, and prepared for an immediate assault. On the north side of the mountain were the bands of Shelby, Hill and Lacey, under Shelby's command; on the south, those of Campbell, Sevier, and Joseph McDowell, led by Campbell; while across the northeast end were the men of Cleaveland, Hambright, and Winston, commanded by Cleaveland. So quickly were these dispositions made that Ferguson first learned of them by the fire of the attacking parties. His own force consisted of nearly 1,000 men, of whom 200 were regulars of his old corps, 430 were North Carolina Loyalists, and 320 were South Carolina Loyalists. He arranged his men in two lines along the height, one to resist attack by volleys of musketry, the other under his immediate command to charge the enemy with bayonets.

The attack was opened by Campbell whose men ascended the most difficult part of the ridge. Near the summit, Ferguson repulsed them with a bayonet charge, but before he could regain his position, he was assailed in the rear by Shelby's men advancing up the opposite side of the mountain. Turning upon these new assailants, he drove them back in their turn, but while he was thus engaged, not only did Campbell's men rally and return to the attack, but Cleaveland's men also came into action. The Americans were unerring marksmen and advancing with the utmost deliberation from tree to tree and from rock to rock, firing with great precision, they made easy marks of Ferguson's men whom they picked off by the score. The British on the other hand from their elevated position fired wildly over the heads of their elusive foes, while their bayonet charges were broken up by the thick underbrush, trees, and rocks which covered the mountain. Though assailed first from one side and then from another; though repulsing Campbell only to be attacked in the rear by Shelby; though turning on Shelby only to have his flank fiercely assaulted by Cleaveland, nevertheless Ferguson sustained his high reputation as a gallant and skillful officer. Mounted on his white charger, making his presence known by a silver whistle, he fearlessly exposed himself in order to animate the drooping spirits of his men. Twice they raised the white flag, twice he struck it down with an oath that he would never surrender to such a damned set of banditti. Finally a bullet

COLONEL JOSEPH McDOWELL, OF "QUAKER MEADOWS"

pierced his heart and saved him from the disgrace of having to hoist the white flag. His second in command, Captain Abraham De Peyster, seeing the hopelessness of further resistance, thereupon raised the symbol of surrender.

The battle had lasted about an hour. No victory could be more complete. Ferguson's corps was entirely wiped out. Himself and 119 of his men were killed, 123 wounded, and 664 captured. This signal achievement had cost the Americans 28 killed, 62 wounded. It was the first ray of light to pierce the general gloom which had enveloped the country since the fall of Charleston. Washington saw in it "a proof of the spirit and resources of the country;" Clinton lamented it as a "fatal catastrophe." Everywhere patriots hailed it as the turning point in the struggle. "The victory at King's Mountain," says Bancroft, "which in the spirit of the American soldiers was like the rising at Concord, in its effects like the successes at Bennington, changed the aspect of the war. The Loyalists of North Carolina no longer dared rise. It fired the patriots of the two Carolinas with fresh zeal. It encouraged the fragments of the defeated and scattered American army to seek each other and organize themselves anew. It quickened the North Carolina legislature to earnest efforts. It inspirited Virginia to devote her resources to the country south of her border." [8] It "Threw South Carolina (wrote Clinton) into a state of confusion and rebellion." It "totally disheartened" the Tories, disconcerted Cornwallis' plans, and made his position at Charlotte untenable. Deserted by his "friends" and threatened by fresh swarms of enemies, Cornwallis thought no longer of conquest, but of flight, and on October 12th hastily abandoning Charlotte, fled "with great precipitation" to Winnsboro, South Carolina. The fugitives, reported the Board of War to the governor, were closely pursued "by Davidson and Davie, who, with Colonel Morgan, are now hanging on and greatly distress them." Thus was the soil of North Carolina once more freed from the invader.

---

[8] History of the United States, (ed. 1888), Vol. V, p. 400.

CHAPTER XXVI

THE INVASION OF 1780-1781

The rapidity with which the patriots of the two Carolinas rallied from the disaster at Camden was proof enough that they possessed both the physical force and the spirit to defend their country if only they could have competent leadership. Congress had tried its favorites—Howe, Lincoln, Gates, —and had lost two states by the experiment. In a chastened mood, therefore, it now turned to Washington and requested him to select a commander for the Southern Department. Both Congress and the army knew well enough who Washington's choice would be for he had urged the appointment of Nathanael Greene when Congress selected Gates. "In every campaign since the beginning of the war," says John Fiske, "Greene had been Washington's right arm; and for indefatigable industry, for strength and breadth of intelligence, and for unselfish devotion to the public service, he was scarcely inferior to the commander-in-chief."[1] Congress promptly ratified Washington's choice and conferred upon Greene every power, subject to the control of the commander-in-chief, necessary to carry on the war in the South and recover the conquered states.

Greene arrived at Charlotte and took command December 2d. He found there "only the shadow of an army." On paper it numbered 2,000 men, but fully half of them were untrained militia, 300 were without arms, 1,000 too naked to take the field, and only 800 sufficiently armed and equipped for active service. Upon reviewing the situation, Greene's heart sank, but he did not despair. His message to Washington— "I will recover the country or die in the attempt"--truly expressed his indomitable purpose. His quick intelligence discerned in his men, beneath their tattered clothes, a spirit like his own, and in the unorganized mass before him he saw the raw material of a great army. To organize, train, and equip it, and to inspire it with his own unconquerable spirit, was

---

[1] The American Revolution, Vol. II, p. 250.

his first task. In this task he had the help of as brilliant
a group of subordinates as ever surrounded a general,—Kosciusko, the able Polish engineer; Smallwood of Maryland;
Daniel Morgan, "always a host in himself," William Washington and "Light Horse Harry" Lee of Virginia; Sumner,
Davidson and Davie of North Carolina; Isaac Huger, Pickens,
Sumter and Marion of South Carolina. The services of most
of these men had been available to Gates, but he did not know
how to use them and looked with contempt upon their irregular methods of warfare. Greene, on the contrary, fully
appreciated their value, while they recognized in him their
master genuis.

From the beginning general and subordinates felt for
each other complete confidence and gave each other unstinted
support. Greene's most pressing need was supplies. His
quick eye had already discerned the merits of Davie whom
he induced reluctantly to become his commissary-general.
Colonel Edward Carrington, of South Carolina, was appointed quartermaster-general. To the tireless energy and
patriotic sacrifices of these two officers, who cheerfully gave
up their commands in the field with their opportunities for
military renown to accept the drudgery of less conspicuous
but more important positions, Greene owed much of the success of his southern campaign, which he acknowledged with
generous appreciation. Gates rejecting the advice of those
who knew the country had plunged headlong down the wrong
road to destruction at Camden, but Greene followed an entirely different course. Trusting nothing to chance, he studied
carefully every detail of the topography of the probable field
of his operations. He sent Carrington to map the Dan, Stevens the Yadkin, and Kosciusko the Catawba, and so completely did he master their maps that afterwards in a discussion of the fords of the Catawba during the retreat across
North Carolina, Davidson exclaimed in admiration, "Greene
never saw the Catawba before, but he knows more about it
than those who have been raised on its banks."

Greene determined upon a daring plan of operations. Since
his army was too small to take the field against Cornwallis,
he resolved to divide it into two strong partisan bands to
operate against the smaller posts held by the British in the
interior. One consisting of 1,100 troops, under Huger, which
he himself accompanied, he ordered to Cheraw on the Pee
Dee River to support Marion's movements in Eastern South
Carolina and to threaten Rawdon at Camden. The other,

consisting of about 1,000 men under Morgan he ordered to cross the Catawba, join Sumter and other partisans operating in that region, and threaten the British hold on Ninety-Six and Augusta. Morgan's command was made up of 320 Maryland Continentals, 200 Virginia militia, 60 Virginia dragoons under Washington, 300 North Carolina militia under Joseph McDowell, and enough militia of South Carolina and Georgia to bring his force up to 1,000 men. To cover as much territory as possible, he pitched his camp on the Pacolet River. Thus the two detachments of the American army were 140 miles apart with Cornwallis at Winnsboro between them. Greene was playing a hazardous game for Cornwallis, whose force was superior to both the American detachments combined, might easily have crushed either of them before the other could come to its aid. But such a movement required a quickness of comprehension and aggressiveness of character which Greene believed his lordship did not possess, and events proved that he had correctly forecast what Cornwallis would do. Reinforced by the arrival of General Alexander Leslie with 2,500 men, Cornwallis had in South Carolina a total of more than 11,000 men, but they were so scattered among the garrisons of the several posts throughout the State that he had not more than 4,000 under his own command. Upon learning of Greene's movements, he still further weakened his force, as Greene had foreseen, by dividing it. Ordering Leslie to Camden to protect that post against Huger, he sent Tarleton with 1,100 men to pursue Morgan, while he himself kept his main army idle at Winnsboro.

When Morgan learned of Tarleton's movements, he fell back upon Cowpens on Broad River, and there prepared for battle. He threw out first a skirmish line of 150 picked Georgia and North Carolina militia under Major John Cunningham and Colonel Joseph McDowell. These men were to fire two volleys "at killing distance" and then retire. Behind them was the main body of militia, 270 in number, under Pickens. The third line, 150 yards farther back, was composed of 290 Maryland Continentals and 140 experienced Virginia and Georgia militia. Still farther in the rear, 125 dragoons under Washington formed the reserve. Behind the whole flowed the Broad River. Except for his legion of New York Loyalists, who were veterans of several years' experience, Tarleton's command was composed entirely of regulars from the British line. Tarleton reached Cowpens at about 8 o'clock in the morning of January 17th, and rushed precipitately into battle, expecting to drive Morgan's untrained militia into the Broad River, which flowed behind his lines, and to capture or destroy the rest of his force. But the militia met the enemy's assault with several volleys at close range, and after doing terrible execution, retired in good order to make way for the Continentals. Mistaking their movement for the retreat which they had expected, the **British charged impetuously** only to be met by an unexpected fire from the Continentals at a range of thirty yards. As the enemy recoiled, the Continentals dashed forward in a bayonet charge. Thrown into confusion by this unexpected onset, the British troops became panic stricken when Washington's dragoons, appearing suddenly from behind the Continentals, swept down upon their flank. Most of them threw down their arms and surrendered at discretion, the rest fled, pursued by Washington's dragoons. Tarleton himself after a desperate hand-to-hand fight with Washington escaped capture only by the fleetness of his horse. But 270 of his men found their way back to Cornwallis's camp; 230 were killed or wounded, 600 captured. The loss of this corps, following hard upon the loss of Ferguson's corps at King's Mountain, was a blow from which Cornwallis never recovered. "Had Lord Cornwallis had with him at the action at Guildford Courthouse, those troops that were lost by Colonel Tarleton at the Cowpens, on the fifteenth of March, 1781," says Stedman, "it is not extravagant to suppose that the American colonies might have been reunited to the empire of Great Britain." [2]

Morgan lost no time in rejoicing over his victory. With Cornwallis only twenty-five miles away, his situation was too dangerous for delay, and his first thought was to secure his prisoners, save his own army, and unite with Greene and Huger before Cornwallis could overtake him. Before his cavalry returned from the pursuit, therefore, he started for the fords of the Catawba to put that stream between himself and the enemy. Cornwallis, stung to unwonted celerity by the great disaster which had befallen the British arms, set out in hot pursuit. On January 25th, he reached Ramsaur's Mill. but in the meantime Morgan had crossed the Catawba at Sherrill's Ford about twenty-five miles away.

On the same day that Cornwallis reached Ramsaur's

---

[2] American War, Vol. II, p. 346.

Mill, Greene at Cheraw learned of Morgan's victory and retreat. His quick mind took in the situation at once and he prepared his plans accordingly. Directing Huger to move rapidly up the Yadkin to the vicinity of Salisbury, he himself struck out across the country to lay his plans before Morgan. Traversing the intervening distance of 125 miles in three days, he joined Morgan at Sherrill's Ford on January 30th, and there these two consummate leaders completed the details of their campaign. They would draw Cornwallis as far as possible from his base of supplies and uniting their two armies turn upon the enemy and destroy him. On January 31st, accordingly, they took up their retreat from Sherrill's Ford with Cornwallis following twenty-five miles in the rear. Greene's management of this retreat entitles him to a place among the first soldiers of his age. No detail of routes, marches, supplies, or camps; no means of facilitating his own movements or of obstructing those of the enemy escaped his active and restless mind. From the maps of his engineers he had acquired accurate knowledge of the country, its roads, streams and fords, and had sent out parties to scour the streams and collect at designated fords all the boats that could be found, while he posted guards at every ford to delay the passage of the enemy. His personal participation in the dangers and hardships of the retreat was a constant inspiration to his men whose suffering and heroic endurance equalled if it did not surpass that of Washington's men in the Trenton campaign. In was the depth of winter. The weather was wet and cold. The roads were knee-deep in mud and ice. Drenched with constant rain and sleet; often compelled to wade waist-deep through foaming rivers; without tents, without blankets; pinched with hunger; half naked; marking the line of their march with the blood which flowed from their bare feet; constantly fighting rear-guard actions, Greene's men outmarched, outmaneuvered, and outfought their better-equipped adversaries, and when, after a continuous retreat of twenty-two days, they finally united forces with Huger at Guilford Court House, the British at Salem twenty-five miles distance were no nearer to them than they were on the day of Morgan's victory at Cowpens.

Cornwallis of course realized the importance of overtaking Morgan before he could unite with Huger. Accordingly at Ramsaur's Mill he stripped his army of its heavy baggage, wagons, and all other material that might encumber the move-

ment of his troops. He fully appreciated the danger of the
course he was pursuing, but he also realized that it was
too late to turn back. The prize he sought was great enough
to justify the hazard he took. From the time he left Ramsaur's Mill, he put aside all hesitation and on January 28th
his army, stated by Clinton to be "considerably above three
thousand, exclusive of cavalry and militia," moved forward
with most soldier-like precision and swiftness. On January
31st, he reached Beattie's Ford of the Catawba and feinting
there with his main force, sent General O'Hara to force a
crossing at Cowan's Ford four miles below, which Davidson
guarded with a small body of militia. At daybreak on February 1st, O'Hara's men forced the passage, killing the gallant Davidson, and dispersing his men. Taking up the pursuit again, on February 3d, the British reached Trading Ford
on the Yadkin, seven miles from Salisbury, just in time to
see the last of Morgan's men safely over. After their passage
a sudden rise in the river made it impassable and again Cornwallis was baffled. Realizing that he could not now prevent
the union of Morgan and Huger, Cornwallis endeavored by
a rapid march to prevent Greene's crossing the Dan by taking possession of the upper fords; but again he was defeated
in his object by Greene's forethought in collecting enough
boats to enable him to transfer his army at Irwin's Ferry
seventy miles from Guilford Court House which Cornwallis
had dismissed from consideration since it could only be
crossed by ferry.

Greene had now placed an impassable river between himself and his enemy. He had not only saved his own army,
he had led his enemy into a trap from which he could extricate himself only at great sacrifice. For Cornwallis was 230
miles from his base; in the enemy's country in dead of winter; without supplies; among timid friends, and with an
ever increasing hostile militia swarming in his rear. Greene's
campaign elicited the highest praise from both enemy and
friends. "Every movement of the Americans during their
march from the Catawba to Virginia," wrote Tarleton, "was
judiciously designed and vigorously executed." "The rebels
conduct their enterprises in Carolina," declared Lord Germain, "with more spirit and skill than they have shown in
any other part of America." But assuredly the praise that
Greene and his ragged heroes valued most were the judicious
words that came from their great commander-in-chief. "Your

retreat before Cornwallis," wrote Washington, "is highly applauded by all ranks."

Balked of his prey, Cornwallis abandoned the pursuit and retired to Hillsboro to rest his army and rally the Tories to his support. His men were exhausted and badly in need of supplies. During the march he had lost 250 men and he now hoped to make the loss good by recruits from the Loyalists. On February 20th, therefore, he issued a proclamation declaring his purpose to rescue the king's loyal subjects in North Carolina "from the cruel tyranny under which they have groaned for several years," and inviting "all such faithful and loyal subjects to repair, without loss of time, with their arms and ten days provisions, to the Royal Standard now erected at Hillsborough." Five days later a band of 300 Tories, under Colonel John Pyle of Chatham County, attempting to reach Hillsboro in response to Cornwallis's proclamation, were surprised by "Light Horse Harry" Lee's battalion of dragoons and utterly cut to pieces. Nearly 100 were killed, most of the others wounded, and but few escaped. Lee did not lose a man. News of this disaster, together with the startling news that on February 23d the defeated Greene had actually re-crossed the Dan and was moving on Guilford Court House, decidedly dampened the enthusiasm of the Tories for rallying to "the Royal Standard." "Our situation," wrote Cornwallis, [was] "amongst timid friends, and adjoining to inveterate Rebels." Accordingly when, on February 26th, he moved out of Hillsboro to meet Greene, his army was numerically weaker than it was when he set out from Ramsaur's Mill in pursuit of Morgan.

Greene had been more fortunate. The skill with which he had conducted his retreat had inspired confidence in his leadership, and the Whigs now rallied to him. From Virginia Steuben sent him 400 Continentals and a force of militia. Pickens was busy rallying the militia which had been dispersed by Cornwallis's passage of the Catawba. The General Assembly recalled Caswell to the command of the North Carolina militia and placed him at the head of the Council Extraordinary which, having superseded the Board of War, was bestirring itself to furnish Greene with men and supplies. Governor Nash was exerting himself to get out the militia. From all these sources reinforcements poured into Greene's camp. When he crossed the Dan on February 13, in his retreat, his army consisted of 1,430 exhausted troops; three weeks later it had been increased to more than 5,000

NATHANAEL GREENE

troops of whom 1,715 were Continentals. Even before all
these reinforcements had reached him, Greene felt strong
enough to recross the Dan, and challenge Cornwallis to battle.

Both generals were eager for the contest. With Cornwallis, 230 miles from his base and in the enemy's country,
nothing less than an out-and-out victory would suffice. Greene
on the contrary could afford to fight a drawn battle; even a
defeat, which inflicted serious damage on the enemy and left
his own army intact, might have beneficial results. During
his retreat he had selected the battleground, near Guilford
Court House, and now having decided to fight, by a series of
skillful maneuvers he succeeded in drawing the enemy thither.
His force numbered 4,404 men, most of whom had never seen
a battle. Exclusive of officers, Cornwallis had 2,253 men, at
least 2,000 of whom were seasoned veterans. When to
Greene's numerical superiority is added the advantage of his
position, which he had selected with great care, the odds
were about even.

Greene posted his North Carolina militia in front, flanking them on the right with Virginia militia and on the left
with Virginia and Delaware troops. About 300 yards behind
them was a line of Virginia militia whose flanks were protected on the right by Washington's cavalry, on the left by
Lee's. The third line, 550 yards in the rear of the second,
was composed of the Continentals. Cornwallis opened the
battle with a slight cannonade a little after noon on March
15th, after which the whole British line advanced with admirable precision, their bayonets glittering in the bright sun
of a cloudless day. The North Carolina militia, who were
to receive the first shock, had no bayonets; they were armed
only with hunting rifles which took three minutes to load.
They had never before been under fire, but as they were expert marksmen they were expected to fire two volleys with
telling effect and then to retire. These orders they carried
out effectively. Their first fire was delivered at 150 yards;
their second at forty, and wrought, according to the British historian, Lamb, who was there, "dreadful havoc" in
the British ranks, but failed to check their advance. Thereupon, while attempting to retire according to orders, the
untrained militia broke and retreated in confusion. The second line in turn was attacked with great vigor and after a
gallant defence forced to retreat. Then the British regulars
came in contact with the Continentals, and the fighting was
stubborn and bloody. Twice the British were repulsed with

heavy losses, and Cornwallis was compelled to rally them
in person. Having restored his lines and brought up fresh
troops, he prepared for a final assault with the seven battalions which he still had. But Greene, determined not to
risk the destruction of his own army, and satisfied with the
damage inflicted upon the enemy, withdrew from the field
leaving Cornwallis in possession. Greene had lost 78 killed,
183 wounded, and 1,046 militia who were missing; but he had
inflicted upon Cornwallis a loss of 93 killed, 413 wounded,
and 26 missing, which was more than 25 per cent of his total
strength.

Retiring to a strong defensive position about ten miles
from Guilford, Greene awaited his opponent's next move with
confidence. In spite of their victory, no such feeling of confidence prevailed in the camp of the British, or among their
friends. Cornwallis announced his victory in a proclamation,
called upon "all loyal subjects to stand forth and take an
active part in restoring good order and government," and offered pardon and restoration "as soon as possible to all the
privileges of constitutional government" to all rebels who
would surrender themselves to the royal authorities. But
Cornwallis was whistling to keep up his courage and none
knew it better than the Tories, who were not minded to risk
their necks on the strength of a victory by proclamation.
"Many of the Inhabitants rode into Camp," wrote Cornwallis,
"shook me by the hand, said they were glad to see us, and to
hear that we had beat Greene, and then rode home again." He
was in a dilemma. Though victorious, his losses had been too
heavy to justify his resuming the offensive, while his position was too precarious to admit of his doing nothing. He
must move, but whither? A march to Wilmington seemed
to be the most feasible step. Wilmington was already in possession of a British force under Major James H. Craige. It
was in close touch with the Highlanders upon whom Cornwallis placed his chief dependence. Moreover at Wilmington he would have the aid of the British fleet. If he could
draw Greene after him, with his army refitted he might again
turn upon the Americans, defeat them, and re-establish the
prestige of British arms. To Wilmington, therefore, Cornwallis determined to go, and on March 18th, abandoning his
wounded, the victorious general broke camp and beat a hasty
retreat to the Cape Fear.

Greene followed his retreating foe as far as Ramsay's
Mill, stopping there to watch his further movements and to

reorganize his own army. When assured that Cornwallis really intended to go to Wilmington, Greene resolved to dismiss him from further consideration and to turn his own attention to the recovery of South Carolina and Georgia. He discharged his militia, whose time was up, and with his army thus reduced to about 1,500 Continentals of the Maryland and Virginia lines, and the cavalry of Washington and Lee, he broke camp and again turned his face southward. On his march he was joined by about 500 North Carolina Continentals, composed of the militia whom the Council Extraordinary, by a curious order, had "sentenced to twelve months' duty as Continentals," because of their precipitate flight at Guilford Court House. Disciplined, trained, equipped, and skillfully led, these men on many a hard-fought field in South Carolina demonstrated that their conduct at Guilford was chargeable to other causes than cowardice. Thus reinforced, and further strengthened with occasional additions of militia, Greene began that remarkable series of movements in which, losing every battle, but winning every campaign, he succeeded in wrenching Camden, Augusta, Ninety-Six, and all other posts in the interior, and Georgetown on the coast, from the grasp of the enemy.

North Carolina troops took part in all of these campaigns. There were 248 North Carolina militia at Hobkirk's Hill, and more than 200 of the new North Carolina Continentals at the seige of Augusta. At Eutaw Springs, September 8, about half of Greene's army of 2,300 men were North Carolinians. A few were militia, the rest, brigaded under General Jethro Sumner, were the "Guilford runaways," now serving on the continental establishment. Discipline and training had turned them into excellent soldiers and at Eutaw Springs they completely recovered the prestige which they had lost at Guilford Court House. The North Carolina militia forming the center of Greene's front line, after fighting gallantly fell back before the charge of the British regulars. As they retired Sumner's Continentals rushed forward in a charge which Greene himself declared "would have graced the veterans of the great King of Prussia," and restored the line. "I was at a loss which to admire most," said Greene, "the gallantry of the officers or the good conduct of the men." The battle of Eutaw was practically won when the hungry Americans, having captured the British camp, stopped to regale themselves with delicacies with which they had long been strangers, and thus gave the retreating foe a chance to rally and return to the attack. Though finally forced to relinquish the field, thus giving his enemy the right to claim the victory, Greene brought off his army in good order saving his wounded and prisoners. Again he had inflicted a greater loss upon his enemy than he himself sustained, and as a result forced him to abandon his last stronghold in the interior of South Carolina and seek safety within the British fortifications at Charleston.

After Eutaw there was no further serious fighting in either South Carolina or Georgia. The British then held only Charleston and Savannah from which without sea power the Americans could not hope to drive them, but elsewhere throughout those two states the American governments were firmly re-established.

It had not occurred to Cornwallis that Greene would altogether disregard his movements and dismiss him from further consideration. Consequently when he reached Wilmington, April 7th, and found that Greene had gone to South Carolina, his situation was extremely humiliating. "My situation here is very distressing," he wrote; "Greene took the advantage of my being obliged to come to this place, and has Marched to South Carolina." "My present undertaking," he confessed to Clinton, "sits heavy on my mind." What should he do next? He could not remain idle at Wilmington. To transport his army to Charleston, and begin his work all over again, he declared, "would be as ruinous and disgraceful to Britain as most events could be." The only alternative seemed to be to march into Virginia, unite his forces with those of General Phillips, whom Clinton had recently sent thither, and overrun that State. Accordingly again proclaiming the conquest of North Carolina, he left Josiah Martin at Wilmington to administer the royal government, and on April 25th set out on his march to Virginia.

The Whigs had no force with which to oppose Cornwallis' movements had they desired to do so; indeed, those were fortunate who could save themselves by abandoning their property and hiding in the woods and swamps until the British columns had passed. Cornwallis, himself a kindly, humane man, waged war only with the armed forces of his enemy, and kept his soldiers under strict discipline, severely punishing those found guilty of pillage and abuse of the inhabitants; but he could exercise no such control over the Tories and camp followers in the wake of his army. They plundered with impunity every plantation along their route. "The whole

country was struck with terror," wrote William Dickson
of Duplin County, an eye witness to the scenes he describes,
"almost every man quit his habitation and fled." "Not a
man of any rank or distinction or scarcely any man of property has lain in his house," wrote Benjamin Seawell on
May 13th, "since the British passed through Nash County.
We are distressed with all the rogues and vagabonds that
Cornwallis can raise to pester us with." However there was
no disposition on the part of Cornwallis, or of his subordinates, to condone abuses and crimes. Near Halifax, records
Stedman, "some enormities were committed that were a disgrace to the name of man;" while "Bloody" Tarleton ordered
that a sergeant and a private, "accused of rape and robbery,"
be arrested and "conducted to Halifax, where they were condemned to death by Martial law," and immediately executed.[3]

The departure of the main armies left North Carolina
in the grip of numerous loosely organized, undisciplined
bands of armed men, both Whigs and Tories, who during the
next year carried on in every county, in almost every neighborhood, a relentless civil war. During this period North
Carolina was the victim of a carnival of pillage, rapine and
murder that surpasses that of the Era of Reconstruction.
Each side having no authority to restrain its excesses committed abuses and crimes against its enemy which served
only to give the other excuse for retaliations. Bands of
robbers, masquerading under the guise of patriots or of
Loyalists as suited their purpose, took advantage of the situation to inaugurate a reign of terror in many communities.
Plantations were plundered, houses were burned, men were
murdered, women were outraged. The Tories were primarily
responsible for these conditions. They were probably guilty
of no greater crimes as individuals than the Whigs, but as
a party they kept up the strife long after it could serve any
useful purpose, either military or political, and obviously
could have no other result than to desolate the country and
impoverish or destroy its inhabitants.

Their course was due chiefly to the presence at Wilmington of Major James H. Craige who with 450 British regulars
had occupied that town in January, 1781. Craige was a bold
and aggressive soldier. His appearance on the Cape Fear
animated the spirits of the Tories and greatly discouraged

[3] Campaigns, p. 290.

the Whigs. For four years the latter had slept in fancied security as if they expected the victories of 1776 to be a perpetual safe-guard against attack. Craige gave them a rude awakening, forcing them to abandon their homes and seek refuge in obscure retreats in the backwoods. But flight could not save them from the restless energy of the British troopers and their Tory sympathizers. The Tories especially scoured the country day and night in search of the men who had so long lorded it over them. Typical of the situation in all the eastern counties was that described by William Dickson in Duplin. Immediately after the departure of Cornwallis ''came on our greatest troubles,'' he wrote; ''for the Loyalists, or as we term them Tories, began to assemble and hold councils in every part of the State, and thinking the country already conquered, because the enemy had gone through without being checked, they were audacious enough to apprehend and take several of our principal leading men prisoners and carry them down to Wilmington and deliver them to the guards. There were numbers of our good citizens thus betrayed, perished on board prison-ships and in their power. This so alarmed the inhabitants that none of us dared to sleep in our houses or beds at night for fear of being surprised by those blood-suckers and carried off to certain destruction.'' Chief among those who were thus betrayed by their old-time friends and neighbors were John Ashe and Cornelius Harnett. Both were captured and imprisoned at Wilmington; both were later paroled only to die within a few days of their release, victims of the severity of their inhuman treatment.

In numerous raids conducted out of Wilmington, Craige laid waste wide stretches of country and spread terror among the inhabitants. His most extensive raid was in August, 1781. Leaving Wilmington, August 1st, with 400 regulars and eighty Tories he swept through Duplin, Dobbs, Jones, and Craven counties, captured and plundered New Bern, and returned without serious opposition to his base at Wilmington. On their march, reported General William Caswell to Governor Burke, the British ''plundered every Plantation that was in their way of all that they could find. It is impossible for me to inform Your Excellency of the ruin, ravage and Distress committed on the Inhabitants of this Country.'' The raid was effective for, except for a few small bands of militia, it thoroughly subdued the people throughout the invaded region. Craige required all men over fifty to take the oath of allegiance to the king; and enrolled in his force, or imprisoned all others, who did not make their escape. Almost all the people between Kingston and New Bern, wrote Caswell, "will be exceeding fond of becoming British Subjects, and most of the Inhabitants of Beaufort and Hyde Counties to the North of Newbern will join them. * * * Dobbs has part of it fallen into the Hands of the British, and Three Companies out of Seven have to a Man joined them." Between Wilmington and New Bern more than 400 Tories enrolled themselves under Craige.

These disasters, however, did not dismay the leaders of the patriots. "I am determined to do every Thing that a Distressed Officer can do," wrote William Caswell, brigadier-general of the New Bern District, "and as long as Life lasts defend the District." A similar spirit animated Alexander Lillington, brigadier-general of the Wilmington District, while James Kenan and Thomas Brown, colonels of Duplin and Bladen counties, never relaxed their vigilance. To these four men more than to any others is due the fact that the patriots of Eastern North Carolina did not give up in despair during the gloomy days of the summer of 1781. Their chief difficulty was not to raise men, but to equip them. "Arms cannot be had," reported Caswell, "to Arm as many men as may be raised." Governor Burke, who rendered every assistance in his power, which however was not much, thought it wise to order Lillington and Caswell to avoid a general engagement with Craige's force.

There were, however, many skirmishes, too numerous to mention in detail, some of which rise almost to the dignity of battles. In February, Craige with about 400 regulars attempted unsuccessfully to dislodge 700 militia whom Lillington had posted at Great Bridge on the North East River, twelve miles above Wilmington, to prevent incursions of the enemy. He was more successful at Rockfish Creek Bridge, which Kenan had seized with 330 militia. Craige had to cross this bridge on his march to New Bern; on August 2d, therefore, with a force numbering nearly 500 regulars and Tories he attacked and dispersed Kenan's force. Although but a trifling skirmish, this success so excited the ardor of the Duplin Tories that they rose in numbers, "gathered together very fast," and "were more cruel to the distressed inhabitants than Cornwallis's army had been before." Their triumph however was brief for as Dickson writes, "Craige having again returned to Wilmington the Whigs again re-

sumed their courage and determined to be revenged on the
Loyalists, our neighbors, or hazard all; accordingly we collected about eighty light-horsemen and equipped them as well
as we could; marched straight into the neighborhood where
the Tories were embodied, surprised them; they fled; our
men pursued them, cut many of them to pieces, took several
and put them to instant death. This action struck such terror on the Tories in our county that they never attempted
to embody again." A similar result in Bladen County followed the battle of Elizabethtown in which, on August 29th,
400 Tories under Colonel John Slingsby were surprised in
a night attack, totally routed, and their commanding officer
killed, by 150 Whigs under Colonel Thomas Brown. "This
put an end to the disturbances in Bladen," wrote Dickson;
"the Tories never embodied there any more, so by this time
our two distressed counties of Duplin and Bladen began
to get the upper hand of their enemies."

Long after the other Tory leaders, recognizing the hope
lessness of their cause, had either submitted to the State or
gone into exile, and even after the last British soldier had
left the State, civil strife in North Carolina was kept alive
by the notorious David Fanning. As a partisan leader Fanning had no superior on either side in the Carolinas. He
had all the dash and daring of Sumter, the fertility and dispatch of Marion, and the resourcefulness of Davie, without
possessing, however, those qualities of moral character which
made these men so much his superiors. Crafty and treacherous, cruel and vindictive, sparing neither age nor sex, he
openly boasts in his published "Narrative" of the brutality
with which he destroyed his enemies and desolated their
country. It is but fair, however, to say that many of his
crimes were committed in retaliation for similar crimes committed by Whigs against his followers; but in every case
wherein Fanning undertook to cancel such debts of vengeance,
he repaid them with usury. Ashe thinks that had Fanning
been on the Whig side "his fame would have been more en-
during than that of any other partisan officer whose memory
is now so dear to all patriots." [4] But something more than
a mere shifting of sides would be necessary to justify one
in ranking Fanning as the equal of the great Whig partisans.
Not only was his character far inferior to theirs, even his

---

[4] David Fanning in *Biographical History of North Carolina*, Vol.
V, p. 93.

work was of much less historical significance. The Whig partisans directed their activities chiefly against the organized forces of the enemy with the purpose of loosening his grip on the country, always keeping in view their effects on the movements of the main armies; Fanning, on the contrary, although performing his work with equal ability, never aimed at the destruction of the enemy's organized forces, exercised no influence upon the ultimate outcome of the war, and produced no other result than to increase the undying hatred which thousands of Americans never ceased to feel for the mother country.

Craige regarded Fanning as his ablest and most trustworthy lieutenant, and on July 5, 1781, commissioned him colonel of the loyal militia of Chatham and Randolph counties. With his headquarters at Coxe's Mill on Deep River in Chatham County, he harried the country far and wide. In July with 150 men he swooped down on Pittsboro, broke up a general muster of the Whig militia, and captured fifty-three prisoners, including all the militia officers of the county present and three members of the General Assembly. A few weeks later, learning that Colonel Thomas Wade of Anson County, had collected a band of Whigs for an attack on some Tories on Drowning Creek, Fanning made a rapid and unexpected movement, fell upon Wade's force, and routed it, killing twenty-three and capturing fifty-three of his men. He continued his hostilities for six months after the surrender of Cornwallis, breaking up Whig gatherings, dispersing militia musters, destroying his enemies individually and in bands, and terrorizing all the region from Guilford to Cape Fear.

The most famous of his exploits occurred on September 12, 1781. Gathering at Coxe's Mill a band of 1,100 Tories, he set out for an attack on a force of Whigs which General Butler had assembled on Haw River; but Governor Burke who was then at Hillsboro learned of Fanning's movement in time to warn Butler who made his escape. Thereupon Fanning determined to put into execution a project he had been turning over in his mind for some time, and turning suddenly eastward, he dashed into Hillsboro early in the morning, put to rout the Whig force guarding the town, killed 15 of their number, and captured 200 among whom was the governor himself. Lingering just long enough for his men to sack the town, Fanning put out for Wilmington. The Whigs gathering in haste under General Butler attacked him vigorously at Lindsay's Mill on Cane Creek, but were repulsed. Both sides suffered heavy losses. Fanning himself, was among the wounded and unable to continue his retreat, but his next in command conveyed the governor and other prisoners safely to Wilmington and turned them over to Craige.

This exploit was the climax but not the conclusion of Fanning's career. He continued his activities well into the year 1782 when he made overtures of peace to the state government. But the State rejected his advances, refusing to regard him in any other light than as an outlaw and compelled him to seek safety in flight. He never returned to North Carolina for when the General Assembly in 1783 came to pass "An Act of Pardon and Oblivion," offering amnesty to Loyalists generally, it excepted from its benefits three notorious Tory leaders, and one of the three was David Fanning.

From Wilmington Governor Burke was sent to Sullivan's Island. He regarded himself as a prisoner of war, but his view was not shared by his captors, to whom he was a political prisoner. They denied him the right of exchange, kept him in close confinement, and declared that they held him as a hostage for the safety of Fanning. Burke protested so vigorously against this treatment that his captors finally paroled him on James' Island. But he soon found that he had gained nothing by this change. On the island were many North Carolina Tory refugees who had been driven from their homes by the rebel government, and they regarded Burke, as the head of that government, with an intense and bitter hatred. They daily subjected him to unsparing indignities, gross insults, and threats of personal injury, and on one occasion fired into his quarters, wounding one man and killing another at his side. His appeals to General Leslie, commanding at Charleston, for protection were treated with such studied indifference, that he became convinced that he had been parolled among these venomous enemies as part of a scheme to destroy him in such a way as to relieve the British authorities of the responsibility and odium of his death while their prisoner. Brooding over his unhappy situation, he finally convinced himself that having given his parole in exchange for protection, the refusal to grant him protection released him from his moral if not from his legal obligation to keep his part of the contract and on January 16, 1782, made his escape, returned to North Carolina, and resumed his duties as governor. Afterwards he offered through General Greene to secure the release of any officer in the hands

of the Americans whom the British general might designate
in exchange for himself; but the British general refused to
consider any proposal that did not involve the return to them
of their prisoner. This Burke refused to consider, and learning that many of the American officers, including General
Greene, condemned his course in violating his parole, he
finally withdrew all negotiations with the British. At the
expiration of his term as governor he retired to private life,
gave himself over to dissipation, and died within less than
two years.

During Burke's captivity, Alexander Martin, who, as
speaker of the Senate discharged the duties of the governor,
carried into execution plans which Burke had made for the
relief of the Cape Fear patriots, sending to their aid a force
of 1,100 men under Rutherford, who had been exchanged,
and Butler. Rutherford entered upon his work with that
vigor for which he was justly distinguished. He distressed
the Tories in every possible way, rivalling in this respect
the activities of Fanning, "with a view of drawing the troops
out of Wilmington to an engagement." In numerous skirmishes, scarcely deserving the name of battles, at Rockfish
Creek, at Moore's Plantation, at North East Bridge above
Wilmington, at Seven Creeks below Wilmington, he broke up
Tory gatherings, destroyed Craige's foraging parties, cut
off his supplies, and practically cleared the Cape Fear section, outside of Wilmington, of the enemy.

While Rutherford was thus recovering Eastern Carolina,
and preparing an effort to drive the enemy out of Wilmington, came news that aroused the Americans to a frenzy of
delight and sent Craige flying from North Carolina with all
the speed his crowded sails could bear him. Cornwallis had
surrendered! Swift express riders spread the glad tidings
throughout the country. Everywhere the war-wearied patriots heard the news with unbounded joy and enthusiasm.
Correspondents hastened to exchange congratulations "on
this happy occasion." One good patriot rejoiced because the
good folk of Hillsboro could now "enjoy peace in their beds
without a dread of Mr. Fanning or his adherents." In many
places business was suspended in a riot of celebrations. The
judges could not attend their Edenton court because "upon
the confirmation of the news of the capture of Cornwallis,
we were all so elated, that the time elapsed in frolicking."
Rutherford paraded his men, proclaimed the glorious news
to them, and ordered suitable salutes. To the Cape Fear

patriots not the least glorious result was the evacuation of their chief town by their hated enemy. On November 18th, Craige embarked his troops and taking with him the last representative of the British Crown who ever claimed political authority in North Carolina, Josiah Martin, and the last British soldier within her limits, sailed for Charleston.

CHAPTER XXVII

PEACE

Except for the activities of Fanning, who did not leave the State until May, 1782, the departure of Craige brought the war to a close in North Carolina, although a year was to elapse before peace was declared and the independence of the colonies acknowledged. Six years of war had wrought ruin and disaster in many sections of the State. Conditions in North Carolina at the close of the struggle have nowhere been better described than by Ashe.[1] "The contest had been doubtful," he says. "It brought many vicissitudes and much suffering. The state as well as the continental currency had ceased to have value. Many families had been utterly impoverished. Misery and desolation were diffused through innumerable households. Civil war and carnage had raged from Surry to Brunswick. Murder and pillage had stalked through a large section of the State, and families expelled from their homes had sought asylums in distant parts, and were too impoverished to return. Many mothers and children were bereft of their last support, their sacrifices in the cause of independence being irreparable. In the desolated region of the Cape Fear even the wealthiest of the patriots were ruined by the ravages of the war. They had cheerfully laid their all on the altar of their country. Hard had been the conflict, but in the darkest hours the brave hearts of the North Carolina patriots became still more courageous, and in their adversity they bore their sufferings with resolution and fortitude. At length the storm-clouds passed away, the sky was no longer obscured, and hope gave place to assurance. The ardent longing became a joyful realization."

The people of North Carolina, however, lost no time in mourning over their losses or rejoicing over their victories. The tasks of repairing the wastes of war, of providing for the wants of the soldiers, and of solving the problems of

---

[1] History of North Carolina. Vol. I, p. 722.

independence were too immediate and pressing to be postponed. The General Assembly met at Hillsboro, April 15,
1782. In an able address Governor Burke reviewed conditions in the State and pointed out some of the problems which
called for immediate solution. He reminded the Assembly
that the war was not over, that British garrisons still held
Charleston and Savannah, and that "the Enemy have still
larger forces in our Country" than the Americans themselves, and urged therefore the importance of keeping up
the military establishment. "Though we have gained great
advantages," he said, "that is not enough, those advantages
are to be secured and ought to be improved into compleat
and indisputable success. Victory gives strength and energy.
Defeat imposes weakness and dismay. While our Arms are
prevailing is therefore the precise season for such actions
as remain to put us in possession of peace and prosperity."
He strongly emphasized the State's "indispensable duty to
support her Quota of force, of expense and of Council" in
continental affairs. Her military laws needed strengthening.
Penalties should be imposed upon officers for failure to make
proper returns of drafts for recruiting the Continental Line,
the number of causes for exemption from militia service
ought to be reduced, and provisions made for better discipline of both militia officers and soldiers. Point was given
to this last recommendation by the conduct of Rutherford's
men upon their entering Wilmington after Craige's retirement, which was still fresh in everybody's recollection; "they
seemed to regard the place as one carried by storm, a fair
theatre for plunder and the display of the worst passions of
our nature." [2]

Among the important matters which Burke urged upon the
attention of the Assembly was that it should support not only
the State's quota of force and expense, but also "of Council"
in continental affairs. It was a timely recommendation. Following the Declaration of Independence Congress had taken
up the problem of a closer and more permanent union of the
thirteen states. Its discussion resulted in the Articles of Confederation. When the final vote was taken on this plan of
union North Carolina was represented in Congress by Thomas
Burke, John Penn, and Cornelius Harnett. Burke who was
absent in North Carolina at the time was opposed to the plan

---

[2] McRee, G. J.: Life and Correspondence of James Iredell, Vol. I,
p. 562.

which he laughed at "as a Chimerical Project." Penn and Harnett favored it. "I think," wrote the latter, "that unless the States confederate a door will be left open for Continental Contention and Bloodshed, and that very soon after we are at peace with Europe." The Articles were adopted by Congress on November 15, 1777, and sent to the states for ratification. "The child Congress has been big with these two years past," wrote Harnett to Burke, "is at last brought forth—(Confederation). I fear it will by several Legislatures be thought a little deformed;—you will think it a Monster." He thought it "the most difficult piece of Business that ever was undertaken by any public Body," and regarded it as "the best Confederacy that could be formed especially when we consider the number of states, their different Interests, [and] Customs." Harnett of course was solicitous as to the fate of the Articles in North Carolina, but apparently without cause. They were laid before the Assembly April 24, 1778, and promptly ratified.

The Articles of Confederation required each State to be represented in the Continental Congress by not more than seven nor less than two delegates. But this obligation the states failed to meet. After 1776 the Continental Congress rapidly lost its early prestige. Most of the eminent leaders who had given it distinction and influence had retired from its halls to the councils of their own states, to foreign courts, and to the battlefields. These now offered greater opportunities for fame and service than Congress. Still there was important work for Congress to do. The army was to be maintained. The navy was to be created, organized and manned. Congress alone represented the United States in foreign affairs. In its name American ministers were received at foreign courts. By its authority they negotiated treaties. Upon its credit they borrowed money. It alone could ratify the treaty which acknowledged the independence of the thirteen states. Yet at home its authority had become merely nominal. The states no longer treated its decrees with respect, or its requisitions with obedience; and they became increasingly more and more indifferent to maintaining their delegations in it.

North Carolina had been among the worst offenders in this matter. Her delegation had generally been composed of her ablest and most distinguished leaders—among them Caswell, Hooper, Hewes, Penn, Harnett, Burke, Johnston, Hugh Williamson, and Benjamin Hawkins. One of them, Samuel Johnston, had been elected president of the Congress, but had declined to serve. After 1780, however, the State was seldom represented in Congress by a full delegation and at times even was not represented at all. From July 21 to September 21, 1781, William Sharpe alone represented the State. Then followed an interval when no delegate from the State was present. On October 4, 1781, Benjamin Hawkins took his seat and alone represented the State until March 19, 1782, when he departed, leaving the State again unrepresented until July 19 when Hugh Williamson appeared and took his seat. Accordingly when the Assembly next met Governor Burke pointed out its duty of "the appointing of Delegates to represent the State in Congress and providing for their decent support while employed in that high and important service." His recommendation, however, seems to have had but little effect. The State's delegates continued to attend only spasmodically. Nor did the other states show any greater interest. In a Congress entitled to ninety-one members, only twenty-three were present, January 14, 1784, to vote for the ratification of the treaty of peace which acknowledged their independence. Representing North Carolina on that occasion were Hugh Williamson and Richard Dobbs Spaight.

In his message Governor Burke pointed out the necessity for important reforms in the civil affairs of the State. He called attention to the negligence and corruption that prevailed among the specific tax collectors, commissaries and quartermasters; the "disorder of the public accounts;" the "insufficiency of the provisions for the Judges and Attorney-General" which "has much embarrassed the Judiciary Department of the Government and threatens to leave the State altogether without Courts of Justice." One of the most forcible passages in his address deals with the evils of arbitrary impressments for public purposes, which he had set himself "absolutely to restrain and hoped finally to render them unnecessary." Perceiving "that rendering the merchant's property precarious, and depriving him of the means of carrying on his trade by seizing without payment his stock, must infallibly ruin our Importations and exportations, and leave us without foreign supplies," he recommended "to the patronage of the General Assembly this important source of wealth, strength and population." The message itself, in style, in spirit and in content was a strong document; the circumstances under which it was delivered made it all the more impressive. All realized that it was the last act of a distinguished public career, which had begun with brilliance and was closing under a dark cloud of adversity.

The Assembly hastened to carry many of the governor's recommendations into effect. It passed an act to complete the State's continental battalions and imposed a penalty of £50 upon any officer who failed to make proper returns. Another act required specific tax collectors, commissaries, and quartermasters to make settlements of their accounts. The war had produced unsettled business conditions. Titles to property had become insecure because many persons in the State "through the confusion of the times," had not been able to prove and register deeds and other conveyances as required by law, and because others had not completed buildings on town lots "within the time limited by law" on account of the "impossibility of procuring necessary materials for building * * * occasioned by the present war with Great Britain." The Assembly accordingly passed several acts designed to give necessary relief from such conditions, and to stabilize business. With the same purpose in view it established a scale of depreciation for paper currency. An important reform was made in the judiciary by granting equity jurisdiction to the superior court judges. Several acts were passed granting relief to towns from conditions produced by the war. Illustrative of this kind of legislation is an act relating to the election of commissioners for the town of Edenton. By an act of 1745 the General Assembly named the commissioners and conferred upon them the power of self-perpetuation; this act was now declared to be "inconsistent with the spirit of our present Constitution," and the commissioners were made elective by the freeholders of the town. Other acts resulting from the war provided for the re-opening of the land office; for the sale of confiscated property; and for the relief of the officers and soldiers of the Continental Line.

One of the first problems to which the Assembly turned its attention was to provide for the men whose sacrifices, endurance and courage had brought the struggle to its triumphant close. An act was passed to make good to the officers and soldiers of the Continental Line the losses they had sustained by reason of the depreciation of the currency, and a commission consisting of John Hawks, James Coor, and William Blount was appointed to carry it into effect. In 1780, it will be recalled, the Assembly reserved an immense tract of the State's western lands to be used as bounties for her soldiers. At the April session, 1782, therefore, declaring that it was "proper that some effectual and permanent reward should be rendered for the signal bravery and persevering zeal of the Continental officers and soldiers in the service of the State," the Assembly passed an act providing for the distribution of this land, allotting to each private soldier, 640 acres; to each non-commissioned officer, 1,000 acres; to each subaltern, 2,560 acres; to each captain 3,840 acres; to each major, 4,800 acres; to each lieutenant-colonel, 5,760 acres; to each colonel, 7,200 acres; to each brigadier-general, 12,000 acres; to each chaplain, 7,200 acres; to each surgeon, 4,800 acres; and to each surgeon's mate, 2,560 acres. Similar allotments were made to the heirs of those who had been killed in the service. To General Greene, "as a mark of the high sense this State entertains of the extraordinary services of that brave and gallant officer," the General Assembly granted 25,000 acres. Absalom Tatom, Isaac Shelby, and Anthony Bledsoe were appointed commissioners to lay off these claims.

The Assembly also turned its attention to those citizens of the State who were prisoners in the hands of the British. Every war has its stories of prison brutalities and horrors, and the war of the American Revolution was no exception. Each side freely charged the other with intentional mistreatment of its prisoners, and unfortunately each was able to cite incidents which seem to sustain its charges. But even if we dismiss from consideration all accusations of intentional mistreatment by either side, there remains a story of terrible privations and sufferings. The British perhaps were more blameable than the Americans since their resources and means of alleviating suffering were greater. Stories of British prison-ships of the American Revolution find their parallel in the stories of Andersonville and Fort Delaware during the Civil War. After the fall of Charleston the soldiers of the North Carolina Continental Line who became prisoners of war were placed on prison-ships in Charleston harbor; many others were sent thither after Camden. Close confinement, improper food, and ill-usage proved fatal to scores of them. Others were sent to the West Indies where under heavy pressure, amounting practically to compulsion, they entered the British service against Spain. But many were still in captivity when the Assembly met in 1782. The General Assembly accordingly adopted a resolution requesting the governor to open negotiations with General Leslie, the British commander at Charleston, for an exchange of these captives for "such of our disaffected Inhabitants [who were] guilty of Military offences only." Governor Martin complied with this resolution with such success, through the mediation of General Greene, that when the Assembly met April 18, 1783, he was able to report that the exchanges had been effected "and our late suffering people restored to their friends and families."

Having provided rewards for its soldiers, and secured the release of those in prison, the Assembly next sought to adopt a policy that would tend to allay the bitterness which the war had aroused. When the Assembly met, April 18, 1783, Governor Martin announced that the king had acknowledged the independence of the United States, adding that to the General Assembly "belongs the Task, that in sheathing the Sword, you soften the horrors [of war] and repair those ravages which war has made with a skillful hand, and thereby heal the wounds of your bleeding Country. Our late revolted Citizens who, through ignorance and delusion, have forfeited their lives but are endeavouring to expiate their crimes by new proofs of fidelity, have fresh claims to your Clemency on this happy occasion." Following this advice and declaring it to be the policy, "of all wise states on the termination of civil wars, to grant an act of pardon and oblivion for past offenses," the Assembly passed an act providing that all treasons, misprision of treason, felonies, and misdemeanors, committed since July 4, 1776, by any person or persons, should be "pardoned, released, and put in total oblivion," but from the benefits of this amnesty it excepted five classes of persons. They were: (1), citizens of the State who had accepted commissions as officers and acted as such under the king; (2), those who were named in the confiscation acts; (3), those who had left the State with the British armies and should fail to return within twelve months after the passage of this law; (4), Peter Mallette, Samuel Andrews, and David Fanning; and (5), persons guilty of deliberate and wilful house-burning, murder, and rape. But in spite of legislative leniency, the people of North Carolina never really pardoned or forgave the men whose voices and hands had been raised against them in their struggle for independence. Many of the Loyalists returned expecting to resume their old places in their communities, only to find themselves under a ban socially and politically, and unable to bear the frowns and contempt of their former friends and neighbors, finally abandoned North Carolina to seek new homes in Canada, Florida, or in the new regions to the south and west. A few went to England where they spent the remaining years of their lives in begging from an ungrateful government compensation for the losses which they had sustained in its behalf in America.

Its "Act of Pardon and Oblivion" the Assembly wished to be accepted as evidence of its "earnest desire to observe the articles of peace." These articles, containing the acknowledgment of the independence of the United States, the governor laid before "the representatives of this free, Sovereign and Independent State" on April 19, 1783,—the eighth anniversary of the battle of Lexington,—saying: "With impatience I hasten to communicate the most important intelligence that has yet arrived in the American Continent. His Britannic Majesty having acknowledged the United States of America free, Sovereign and Independent, * * * for this most happy and auspicious event, which involves in it a most precious inheritance for ages and all the blessings that can flow from Independent Empire, with the most lively, fervent and heart-felt joy, I congratulate you and through you all my fellow-citizens of the State of North Carolina. * * * Nothing now remains but to enjoy the fruits of uninterrupted Constitutional Freedom, the more sweet and precious as the tree was planted by [the] virtue, raised by the Toil, and nurtured by the blood of Heroes."

BIBLIOGRAPHY

The following list of references makes no pretense to completeness; only a few titles are given which for their accessibility may be easily consulted, or for other reasons are of especial interest or importance. They are intended to be but little more than a list for parallel reading.

SOURCES.

Carr, James O. (ed.): *The Dickson Letters*. 1911.

Clark, Walter (ed.): *State Records of North Carolina*. Vols. XI-XXVI. 1895-1906. (Continuation of Saunders: Colonial Records.)

Collections of the Georgia Historical Society. 2 V. 1840.

Grimes, J. Bryan: *Abstract of North Carolina Wills*. 1910.

Grimes, J. Bryan: *North Carolina Wills and Inventories*. 1912.

Hakluyt, Richard: *Navigations, Voyages, Traffiques and Discoveries of the English Nation*. 5 V. Edition of 1809.

Hathaway, J. R. B. (ed.): *The North Carolina Historical and Genealogical Register*. Vols. I and II, and Nos. 1, 2, 3, of Vol. III. 1900-1903.

MacDonald, William: *Select Charters and other Documents illustrative of American History, 1606-1775*. 1899.

Salley, Alexander S.: *Narratives of Early Carolina, 1650-1708*. (Original Narratives of Early American History, J. F. Jameson, editor.) 1911.

Saunders, William L. (ed.): *The Colonial Records of North Carolina*, Vols. I-X. 1886-1890.

Stevens, Benjamin Franklin (ed.): *The Clinton-Cornwallis Controversy*. 2 V. 1888.

AUTOBIOGRAPHIES, TRAVELS, AND MEMOIRS.

Bartram, William: *Travels Through North and South Carolina, Georgia, East and West Florida*. 1791.

Bassett, John S. (ed.) : *The Writings of Colonel William Byrd of Westover in Virginia Esqr.* 1901.

Brickell, John: *The Natural History of North Carolina.* 1737. (J. Bryan Grimes, ed., 1910.)

Catesby, Mark: *Natural History of Carolina, Florida, and the Bahama Islands.* 1731.

Fanning, David: *Narrative of His Adventures in North Carolina.* Written by himself. 1861.

Lawson, John: *The History of North Carolina.* 1718 edition.

Lee, Henry: *Memoirs of the War in the Southern Department.* 1820.

Smyth, J. F. D.: *A Tour of the United States of America,* 2 V. 1784.

Stedman, C.: *The History of the American War.* 2 V. 1794.

Tarleton, Sir B.: *History of the Campaign of 1780-81.* 1787.

Watson, Elkanah: *Men and Times of the Revolution.* 1856.

BIOGRAPHIES.

Al erman, E. A.: *William Hooper.*

Ashe, Samuel A'Court (ed.) : *Biographical History of North Carolina from Colonial Times to the Present.* 8 V. 1905-1917.

Caruthers, E. W.: *Life and Character of Rev. David Caldwell.* 1842.

Connor, R. D. W.: *Cornelius Harnett: An Essay in North Carolina History.* 1909.

Connor, R. D. W.: *Revolutionary Leaders of North Carolina.* (John Harvey, Cornelius Harnett, Richard Caswell, Samuel Johnston.) (North Carolina State Normal and Industrial College Historical Publications, Number 2.) 1916.

Graham, William A.: *General Joseph Graham and His Papers on North Carolina Revolutionary History.* 1904.

Haywood, Marshall DeLancey: *Governor William Tryon and His Administration in the Province of North Carolina, 1765-1771.* 1903.

Henderson, Archibald: *Richard Henderson: the Authorship of the Cumberland Compact and the Founding of Nashville.* (Tennessee Historical Magazine, Sept. 1916.)

MacLean, J. P.: *Flora MacDonald in America.* 1909.

McRee, Griffith J.: *Life and Correspondence of James Iredell.* 2 V. 1857.

Moore, M. H.: *Sketches of the Pioneers of Methodism in North Carolina and Virginia.* 1884.

Sabine, Lorenzo: *Loyalists of the American Revolution.* 2 V. 1864.

Stebbing, William: *Sir Walter Raleuh.* 1899.

Stevens, Henry: *Thomas Hariot and His Associates.* 1900.

Waddell, Alfred Moore: *A Colonial Officer and His Times: A Biographical Sketch of Gen. Hugh Waddell.* 1890.

North Carolina Booklet: Appearing in the North Carolina Booklet are a number of interesting biographies of this perio l, the following of men whose biographies do not appear in Ashe's "Biographical History of North Carolina": Bellamy, John D.: *General Robert Howe* (VII-3); Connor, R. D. W.: *Joseph Hewes and the Declaration of Independence* (X-3); Connor, R. D. W.: *Sir Walter Raleigh and His Associates* (XI-3); Henderson, Archibald: *The Creative Forces in Westward Expansion: Henderson and Boone* (XIV-3); Henderson, Archibald: *Elizabeth Maxwell Steele* (XII-2); Henderson, Archibald: *Isaac Shelby* (XVI-3); Hill, D. H.: *Edward Moseley: Character Sketch* (V-3); Weeks, Stephen B.: *Thomas Person* (IX-1).

COUNTY AND LOCAL HISTORY.

Albertson, Catherine: *In Ancient Albemarle.* 1914.

Allen, W. C.: *History of Halifax County.* 1918.

Arthur, John Preston: *Western North Carolina: A History from 1730 to 1913.* 1914.

Arthur, John Preston: *A History of Watauga County.* 1915.

Cooper, Francis Hodges: *Some Colonial History of Beaufort County.* (James Sprunt Historical Publications, 14-2.)

King, Henry T.: *Sketches of Pitt County, 1740-1910.* 1911.

Nash, Francis: *Hillsboro, Colonial and Revolutionary.* 1903.

Rumple, Jethro: *A History of Rowan County.* 1881. (Reprinted 1916.)

Tompkins, D. A.: *History of Mecklenburg County.* 2 V. 1903.

Waddell, Alfred Moore: *A History of New Hanover County.* Vol. I. 1909.

Winborne, Benjamin Brodie: *The Colonial and State Political History of Hertford County.* 1906.

Sprunt, James: *Tales and Traditions of the Lower Cape Fear.* 1896.

Sprunt, James: *Chronicles of the Cape Fear River,* 1660-1916. 1916.

Bassett, John S.: *The County of Clarendon.* (North Carolina Booklet, II-9.)

Brinson, S. M.: *The Early History of Craven County.* (North Carolina Booklet, X-4.)

McNeely, Robert Ney: *Union County and the Old Waxhaw Settlement.* (North Carolina Booklet, XII-1.)

Nash, Francis: *The History of Orange County.* (North Carolina Booklet, X-2.)

Nixon, Alfred: *The History of Lincoln County.* (North Carolina Booklet, IX-3.)

GENERAL HISTORIES.

Ashe, Samuel A'Court: *History of North Carolina,* Vol. I. 1908.

Bancroft, George: *History of the United States.* 6 V.

Hawks, Francis L.: *History of North Carolina.* 2 V. 1857.

Haywood, John: *Civil and Political History of Tennessee.* 1823.

Hill, Daniel Harvey: *Young People's History of North Carolina.* 1907.

McCrady, Edward: *The History of South Carolina under the Proprietary Government.* 1897.

McCrady, Edward: *The History of South Carolina under the Royal Government,* 1719-1776. 1899.

McCrady, Edward: *The History of South Carolina in the Revolution,* 1775-1780. 1902.

McCrady, Edward: *The History of South Carolina in the Revolution,* 1780-1783. 1902.

Martin, Francis Xavier: *The History of North Carolina.* 2 V. 1829.

Moore, John W.: *History of North Carolina.* 2 V. 1880.

Phelan, James: *History of Tennessee.* 1888.

Ramsay, J. G.: *Annals of Tennessee.* 1860.

Wheeler, John H.: *Historical Sketches of North Carolina from 1584 to 1851.* 1851.

Williamson, Hugh: *A History of North Carolina.* 2 V. 1812.

Winsor, Justin: *Narrative and Critical History of America.* 8 V. 1889.

Histories of Special Topics and Periods.

Bassett, J. S.: *The Constitutional Beginnings of North Carolina,* 1663-1729. (Johns Hopkins University Studies. 12th Series, No. III.) 1894.

Bassett, John S.: *Landholding in Colonial North Carolina.* (Trinity College Historical Papers, Series II.) 1898.

Bassett, John S.: *The Regulators of North Carolina,* 1765-1771. (Report of the American Historical Association, 1894.)

Bassett, John S.: *Slavery and Servitude in the Colony of North Carolina.* (Johns Hopkins University Studies, 14th Series, Nos. IV-V.) 1896.

Bernheim, G. D.: *History of the German Settlements and of the Lutheran Church in North and South Carolina.* 1872.

Bernheim, G. D. and Cox, George A.: *History of the Evangelical Lutheran Synod and Ministerium of North Carolina.* 1902.

Biggs, Joseph: *History of the Kehukee Baptist Association.* 1830.

Bond, Beverly W., Jr.: *The Quit Rent System in the American Colonies.* 1919.

Branson, E. C. (ed.): *County Government and County Affairs in North Carolina.* 1919.

Cheshire, Joseph B.: *How Our Church Came to North Carolina.* (The Spirit of Missions, LXXXIII-5.)

Clewell, John Henry: *History of Wachovia in North Carolina.* 1902.

Connor, Henry G.: *The Granville Estate and North Carolina.* (University of Pennsylvania Law Review, 62-9.)

Connor, Henry G., and Cheshire, Joseph B., Jr.: *The Constitution of North Carolina Annotated.* 1911.

Cooke, William D. (ed.): *Revolutionary History of North Carolina.* 1853.

Draper, Lyman C.: *King's Mountain and Its Heroes.* 1881.

Faust, Albert Bernhardt: *The German Element in the United States.* 2 V. 1909.

Fiske, John: *Old Virginia and Her Neighbours.* 2 V. 1897.

Fiske, John: *New France and New England.* 1902.

Fiske, John: *The American Revolution.* 2 V. 1896.

Fitch, William Edward: *Some Neglected History of North Carolina.* 1914.

Foote, William Henry: *Sketches of North Carolina: Historical and Biographical.* 1846; 1912.

Frothingham, Richard: *The Rise of the Republic of the United States.* 1872.

Graham, George W.: *The Mecklenburg Declaration of Independence, May 20, 1775, and Lives of Its Signers.* 1905.

Greene, Francis Vinson: *The Revolutionary War and the Military Policy of the United States.* 1911.

Grimes, J. Bryan: *The Great Seal of North Carolina, 1666-1909.* (Publications of the North Carolina Historical Commission, Bulletin No. 5.)

Grissom, W. L.: *History of Methodism in North Carolina from 1772 to the Present Time.* 2 V. 1905.

Hanna, Charles A.: *The Scotch-Irish.* 2 V. 1902.

Historic Sketch of the Reformed Church in North Carolina. 1908.

Hoyt, William Henry: *The Mecklenburg Declaration of Independence.* 1907.

Hughson, S. C.: *The Carolina Pirates and Colonial Commerce.* (Johns Hopkins University Studies. Series XII. Nos. 2 to 7.)

Jones, Jo. Seawell: *A Defense of the Revolutionary History of the State of North Carolina.* 1834.

Knight, Edgar W.: *Public School Education in North Carolina.* 1916.

Lossing, Benson J.: *Pictorial Field Book of the Revolution.* 2 V. 1851.

MacLean, J. P.: *Scotch-Highlanders in America.* 1900.

McPherson, O. M. (Compiler): *Indians of North Carolina.* (Senate Document No. 677, 63d Congress, 3rd Session.) 1915.

Mooney, James: *Myths of the Cherokee.* (Nineteenth Annual Report of the Bureau of Ethnology, Part I, pp. 11-576.) 1898.

Moore, James H.: *Defence of the Mecklenburg Declaration of Independence.* 1908.

Parkman, Francis: *Montcalm and Wolfe.* 2 V. 1903.

Raper, Charles Lee: *North Carolina: A Study in English Colonial Government.* 1904.

Raper, Charles Lee: *Church and Private Schools in North Carolina.* 1898.

Roosevelt, Theodore: *The Winning of the West.* 6 V. 1903.

Royce, Charles C.: *The Cherokee Nation of Indians.* (Fifth Report of the Bureau of Ethnology, pp. 129-378.) 1883-84.

Schenck, David: *North Carolina, 1780-81.* 1889.

Sikes, Enoch Walter: *The Transition of North Carolina from Colony to Commonwealth.* 1898.

Smith, Charles Lee: *The History of Education in North Carolina.* 1888.

Stewart, S. A.: *Court System of North Carolina Before the Revolution.* (Trinity College Historical Papers, Series IV.) 1900.

Weeks, Stephen B: *The Religious Development in the Province of North Carolina.* (Johns Hopkins University Studies, Tenth Series, Nos. V-VI.) 1892.

Weeks, Stephen B.: *Church and State in North Carolina.* (Johns Hopkins University Studies, Eleventh Series, Nos. V-VI.) 1893.

Weeks, Stephen B.: *The Press of North Carolina in the Eighteenth Century.* 1891.

Weeks, Stephen B.: *Southern Quakers and Slavery.* 1896.

Williams, C. B.: *History of the Baptists in North Carolina.* 1901.

North Carolina Booklet: MacRae, James C.: *The Highland-Scotch Settlement in North Carolina* (IV-10); McKelway, A. J.: *The Scotch-Irish of North Carolina* (IV-11); Cheshire, Joseph B.: *First Settlers in North Carolina, Not Religious Refugees* (V-4); Dillard, Richard: *St. Paul's Church, Edenton, and Its Associations* (V-1); Nash, Frank: *The Continental Line of North Carolina* (XVII-3); Ashe, S. A.: *Our Own Pirates* (II-2); McCorkle, Mrs. L. A.: *Was Alamance the First Battle of the Revolution* (III-7); Haywood, Marshall DeLancey: *Number of North Carolinians in the Revolutionary War* (XIV-5); Clark, Walter: *North Caro-*

lina in South America (The Cartagena Expedition) (IV-6); Graham, William A.: *Battle of Ramsaur's Mill* (IV-2); Hill, D. H.: *Greene's Retreat* (I-7); Clark, Walter: *Indian Massacre and Tuscarora War, 1711-13* (II-3); Noble, M. C. S.: *The Battle of Moore's Creek Bridge* (III-11); Ashe, S. A.: *Rutherford's Expedition Against the Indians, 1776* (IV-8); Waddell, Alfred M.: *North Carolina in the French and Indian War* (VII-1); Boyd, William K.: *The Battle of King's Mountain* (VIII-4); King, Clyde L.: *Military Organizations of North Carolina During the American Revolution* (VIII-1); Carr, J. O.: *The Battle of Rockfish Creek* (VI-3); Raper, Charles Lee: *The Finances of the North Carolina Colonists* (VII-2); Raper, Charles Lee: *Social Life in Colonial North Carolina* (III-5); Pittman, Thomas M.: *Industrial Life in Colonial Carolina* (VII-1); Poe, Clarence: *Indians, Slaves, and Tories: Our 18th Century Legislation Regarding Them* (IX-1); Holladay, Alexander Q.: *Social Conditions in Colonial North Carolina* (III-10); Grimes, J. Bryan: *Some Notes on Colonial North Carolina, 1700-1750* (V-2); Smith, Charles Lee: *Schools in Colonial Times,* (VII-4); Haywood, Marshall DeLancey: *The Story of Queen's College, or Liberty Hall in the Province of North Carolina* (XI-3); Weeks, Stephen B.: *Pre-Revolutionary Printers of North Carolina: Davis, Steuart, and Boyd* (XV-2); Davis, Junius: *Locke's Fundamental Constitution* (VII-1); Battle, Kemp P.: *The Lords Proprietors of Carolina* (IV-1); Sikes, E. W.: *Our First Constitution, 1776* (VII-2); Dillard, Richard: *The Historic Tea Party of Edenton* (I-4); Waddell, A. M.: *The Stamp Act on the Cape Fear* (I-3); Pittman, Thomas M.: *The Revolutionary Congresses of North Carolina* (II-6); McKoy, W. B.: *Incidents of the Early and Permanent Settlement of the Cape Fear* (VII-3); Boyd, William K.: *Early Relations of North Carolina and the West* (VII-3); Clark, Walter: *The Colony of Transylvania* (III-9); Nash, Francis: *The Borough Towns of North Carolina* (VI-2).

James Sprunt Historical Publications: Rand, James Hall: *North Carolina Indians* (XII-2); Oliver, David D.: *The Society for the Propagation of the Gospel in the Province of North Carolina* (IX-1); Nash, Frank: *The North Carolina Constitution of 1776 and Its Mak-*

ers (II-2); Guess, William Conrad: *County Government in Colonial North Carolina* (II-1); Whitaker, Bessie Lewis: *The Provincial Council and Committees of Safety in North Carolina* (No. 8); Alderman, Ernest H.: *The North Carolina Colonial Bar* (XIII-1); Cooke, C. S.: *The Governor, Council and Assembly in Royal North Carolina* (XII-1); Coulter, E. Merton: *The Granville District* (13-1); Morgan, L. N.: *Land Tenure in Proprietary North Carolina* (12-1); Nixon, Joseph R.: *German Settlers in Lincoln County and Western North Carolina* (11-2).

INDEX